Fig. VI   Size C Sheet (17.00″ × 22.00″)

Fig. VII   Form 4. Title Block

Fig. VIII   Form 5. Title Block

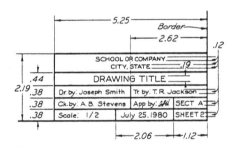

Fig. IX   Form 6. Title Block

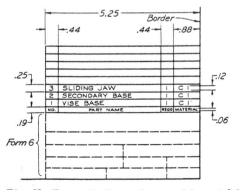

Fig. X   Form 7. Parts List or Material List

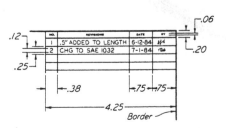

Fig. XI   Form 8. Revision Block

TECHNICAL
DRAWING

Eleventh Edition

TECHNICAL DRAWING

FREDERICK E. GIESECKE

Late Professor Emeritus of Drawing
Texas A & M University

ALVA MITCHELL

Late Professor Emeritus of Engineering Drawing
Texas A & M University

HENRY CECIL SPENCER

Late Professor Emeritus of Technical Drawing;
Formerly Director of Department
Illinois Institute of Technology

IVAN LEROY HILL

Professor Emeritus of Engineering Graphics;
Formerly Chairman of Department
Illinois Institute of Technology

JOHN THOMAS DYGDON

Professor of Engineering Graphics,
Chairman of the Department,
and Director of the Division of Academic Services
and Office of Educational Services
Illinois Institute of Technology

JAMES E. NOVAK

Associate Director/Executive Officer of Educational Services
Illinois Institute of Technology

PRENTICE HALL
Upper Saddle River, NJ 07458

Library of Congress Cataloging-in-Publication Data

Technical drawing / Frederick E. Giesecke . . . [et al.]. -- 11th ed.
    p.   cm.
    Includes bibliographical references and index.
    ISBN 0–13–022569–X
    1. Mechanical drawing.   I. Giesecke, Frederick E.
  T353.T28 1999
  604.2—dc21   99–40466
                           CIP

Developmental editor: *Rose Kernan*
Acquisitions editor: *Eric Svendsen*
Editorial / production supervisor: *Rose Kernan*
Editor in chief: *Marcia Horton*
Executive managing editor: *Vince O'Brien*
Managing editor: *Eileen Clark*
Assistant vice president of production and manufacturing: *David W. Riccardi*
Copyeditor: *Rose Kernan*
Manufacturing buyer: *Pat Brown*
Interior designer: *Amy Rosen*
Cover design: *Bruce Kenselaar*
Editorial assistant: *Griffin Cable*
Art director: *Amy Rosen*
Insert designer: *Joe Sengotta*
Art manager: *Gus Vibal*
Art editor: *Michele Giusti*
Cover photo: *Onne vander Wal / Young America*
Marketing manager: *Danny Hoyt*
Composition: *Preparé / Emilcomp*

© 2000 by **PRENTICE-HALL, Inc.**
Upper Saddle River, NJ 07458

Printed in the United States of America
10 9 8 7 6 5 4 3 2 1

ISBN 0-13-022569-X

Prentice-Hall International (UK) Limited, *London*
Prentice-Hall of Australia Pty. Limited, *Sydney*
Prentice-Hall Canada, Inc., *Toronto*
Prentice-Hall Hispanoamericana, S.A., *Mexico*
Prentice-Hall of India Private Limited, *New Delhi*
Prentice-Hall of Japan, Inc., *Tokyo*
Prentice-Hall (Singapore) Pte. Ltd., *Singapore*
Editora Prentice-Hall do Brasil, Ltda., *Rio de Janeiro*
Prentice-Hall, Inc., *Upper Saddle River, New Jersey*

P R E F A C E

■ ABOUT THIS BOOK

Over the last sixty years, *Technical Drawing* has taught well over a million students the practices and techniques of graphical communication. Both instructors and their students have come to depend on this text as the authority on the subject, and most students have used this book as a professional reference long after they have finished taking this course. Why has this book been so successful? First, the main goal of the text has always been to explain each principle so clearly that the student is certain to understand it, and to make the text interesting enough to encourage all students to read and study on their own. Second, this book has also had what are unquestionably the best, most detailed, and accurate set of drawings on the market. A student skilled with this book's drawings will have a full repertoire of graphical skills in his or her hands. Lastly, *Technical Drawing* continually has sought to address the new technologies and the skills that constantly change this field. By doing so, this text prepares students to enter the marketplace and face the challenges of a rapidly changing playing field.

■ THE ELEVENTH EDITION

The Eleventh Edition of *Technical Drawing* continues to offer the best coverage of basic graphics principles available. Edition after edition, this text serves as the authoritative source on the subject. With this new version, we have acted upon the requests of over 30 reviewers to improve certain aspects of the book while preserving its core presentation. In particular, this new volume features:

- Greatly increased coverage of the design process in Chapter 14. This chapter now includes coverage of 3D solid modeling, and parametric or constraint-based modeling.
- Thoroughly revised chapter on manufacturing processes. We especially thank Professor Serope Kalpakjian of the Illinois Institute of Technology and the author *of Manufacturing Engineering and Technology* for his assistance with this chapter.
- Over 50 brand new questions/problems. These problems feature parts that come from a variety of industries.
- Material on Instrumental Drawing and Lettering condensed to one chapter.
- New coverage of Geometric Dimensioning and Tolerancing.
- Extensive updating of text graphics to comply to most recent ANSI standards.
- New "Graphics Spotlights" feature that highlights a particular use of graphics in industry.
- A decrease in the overall size of the book. Instructors have told us that students are finding books too large. However, they want their students to have access to important reference material. To achieve both these goals, we have eliminated the chapters on Graphs and Diagrams and Alignment Charts included in the last edition, and included them in Adobe pdf format on a free CD. This CD also contains over 30 animations of graphics concepts.
- Updated web site **http://www.prenhall.com/giesecke** now includes even more questions for review, as well as a new feature available for January of 2000 that lets professors create their own

on-line syllabus. Using a simple interface, instructors build a graphic assignment list and use it to interact with their class over the web. This site also features links to other graphics related areas, a selection of animations available for class instruction or student review, an exploration of VRML technology, a case studies exploring how graphics communication is handled at an engineering company, and more. This site will be a constant resource to help instructors and students remain as current as possible.

- Eight-Page Color Insert. To give students a feel for how color is often used in CAD software and other technological processes, but without overloading and obscuring the book's core content, we have included an eight-page color insert.

■ SUPPLEMENTS

INSTRUCTOR'S MANUAL WITH SOLUTIONS/RESOURCE CD

This new manual prepared by Tom Kane of Pueblo Community College includes outlines, teaching tips, extra quiz questions, and other tools designed to aid in class preparation. In addition, this manual comes with **a new CD-ROM containing answer files for over 450 Giesecke drawing problems**. The problems are in both dwg and dwf form for easy electronic access and display. This CD also includes pdf files of all art in the text for quick integration in course web pages. Instructors have long asked for this supplement and we are happy to provide it with the new edition.

WORKBOOKS

Three workbooks with additional problems are available. These workbooks are fully class tested for effectiveness and relevance to the course. They range from having more traditional problems to more modern approaches.

- **Engineering Drawing, Problem Series 1** (ISBN — 0-13-658536-1): Contains traditional, mechanical workbook problems.
- **Engineering Drawing, Problem Series 2** (ISBN — 0-13-658881-6): Contains traditional problems with an emphasis on engineering concepts.
- **Engineering Drawing, Problem Series 3, New 2nd Edition** (ISBN — 0-13-025954-3): The new edition of a workbook by Paige Davis and Karen Juneau of the Louisiana State University. This book contains modern problems, as well as an extensive CAD based project, and comes with its own disk of starter CAD files.

WORLDWIDE WEB SITE— http://www.prenhall.com/giesecke - AVAILABLE WITH SYLLABUS BUILDER FOR JANUARY 2000

In order to provide instructors and their students with the most exciting information available, Prentice Hall has created the Giesecke Web Site. This site now includes even more questions for review, as well as a new feature available for January of 2000 that lets professors create their own on-line syllabus. Using a simple interface, instructors build a graphic assignment list and use it to interact with their class over the web. This site features links to other graphics related areas, a selection of animations available for class instruction or student review, an exploration of VRML technology, a case study exploring how graphics communication is handled at an engineering company, and more. We hope it will be a constant resource to help instructors and students remain as current as possible.

PRENTICE HALL NEW YORK TIMES SUPPLEMENT

A bi-annual, free collection of articles excerpted from *The New York Times* covers areas of interest to freshman engineers and drafting students. Contact your Prentice Hall sales rep for a free supply of these supplements.

BUNDLES

To make the cost of purchasing several books for one course more manageable for students, Prentice Hall offers discounts when you purchase this book with several other Prentice Hall textbooks. Discounts range from up to 20% off the price of the two books purchased separately. At press time, you may bundle this text for discounts with several of our CAD books, including our new AutoCAD 2000 titles *Discovering AutoCAD 2000* by Dix/Riley, and *AutoCAD 2000 — One Step at a Time* (either the *Basics* or *Advanced* version) by Timothy Sean Sykes. You may also bundle this book with several books based on older releases of AutoCAD. Users of Pro/ENGINEER, I-DEAS, or SolidWorks may choose to bundle with books by Robert Rizza, Sheryl Sorby, or Robert Lueptow. To request more specific and up-to-date pricing information, get ISBN's for ordering bundles, and learn more about Prentice Hall's offerings in graphics and CAD, either contact your Prentice Hall Sales Rep, or go to http://www.pren-hall.com/cadgraphics/. For the name and number of your sales rep, please contact Prentice Hall Faculty Services at 1-800-526-0485.

■ ACKNOWLEDGMENTS

This edition underwent extensive reviewing. We would like to thank those who helped with their comments and suggestions:

Thomas Bledsaw, *ITT Educational Services-Indianapolis*
Jeff Cope, *Macon Technical Institute*
Sherwood Davis, *Salt Lake Community College*
Debra C. Edwards, *Appalachian State University*
Catherine M. Ferman, *Schoolcraft College*
Wallace J. Franklin, *U.S. Merchant Marine Academy*
Bill Gordon, *Louisville Technical Institute*
Michael Hayden, *Indiana State University*
Tim Hogue, *Oklahoma State University*
Jane Hook, *Salt Lake Community College*
Dean R. Kerste, *Monroe County Community College*
J.C. Malitzke, *Moraine Valley Community College*
William McCullough, *Triangle Tech*
Cliff Monroe, *Mission College*
Manuel Villalpando, *Texas State Technical College*
David L. Webb, *Salt Lake Community College*

The publisher wishes to thank all of the members of the "Giesecke" team for their efforts in bringing this Eleventh Edition to fruition, but especially would like to thank Rose Kernan and the staff at Prepare/Emilcomp for their hard work, dedication, and professionalism in seeing the project through from manuscript to press.

C O N T E N T S

C H A P T E R 1

THE GRAPHIC LANGUAGE AND DESIGN

OBJECTIVES

After studying the material in this chapter, you should be able to:

1. Describe the role of the engineer on a design team.
2. List two types of drawings.
3. Explain why standards are important.
4. Draw examples of parallel and perspective projection.
5. Define *plane of projection* and *projectors*.
6. Identify uses of the graphic language.
7. Describe the differences between mechanical drawing and sketching.

OVERVIEW

A new machine, structure, or system must exist in the mind of the engineer or designer before it can become a reality. This original concept or idea is usually placed on paper or as an image on a computer screen and communicated to others by way of the *graphic language* in the form of freehand sketches. These first sketches are followed by other, more exact, sketches as the idea is developed more fully.

The engineer and drafter for the twenty-first century century must understand how to read and write in the graphic language. Everyone on the engineering and design team must be able to communicate quickly and accurately in order to compete in the world market. Like carpenters learning to use the tools of their trade, engineers, designers, and drafters must learn the tools of technical drawing. While CAD has replaced traditional drafting tools for many design teams, the basic concepts of the graphic language remain the same. Those students who can become proficient in graphic communication will succeed and add value to the employer who hires them.

Engineers and designers must be able to create idea sketches, calculate stresses, analyze motions, size parts, specify materials and production methods, make design layouts, and supervise the preparation of drawings and specifications that will control the numerous details of product manufacture, assembly, and maintenance. To perform or supervise these many tasks, engineers make liberal use of freehand sketches. They must be able to record and communicate ideas quickly to associate and support personnel. Both facility in freehand sketching (Chapter 3) and the ability to work with computer-controlled drawing techniques require a thorough knowledge of the graphic language. Engineers and designers who use a computer for drawing and design work must be proficient in drafting, designing, and conceptualizing.

Typical engineering and design departments are shown in Figs. 1.2 and 1.3. Such staffs include people who have considerable training and experience as well as recent graduates who are gaining experience. There is much to be learned on the job, and inexperienced people must to start at a low level and then advance to more responsible positions as they gain experience.

■ INTRODUCTION

The old saying that "necessity is the mother of invention" is still true, and a new machine, structure, system, or device is the result of that need. If the new object is really needed or desired, people will buy it or use it as long as they can afford it.

Before a new object of any kind goes into production, certain questions must be answered: What is the potential market for this object? Can the object (device or system) be sold at a price that people are willing to pay? If the potential market is large enough and the estimated selling price seems reasonable, then the inventor, designer, or company officials may choose to proceed with development, production, and marketing plans for the new project.

A new machine, structure, or system, or even an improvement of an existing system, must exist in the mind of the inventor, engineer, or designer before it can become a reality. This original concept is usually placed on paper or as an image of a computer screen. It is then communicated to others by way of the *graphic language* in the form of freehand *idea sketches*, or *design sketches* (Figs. 1.1 and 5.1). As the idea is developed more fully, these original sketches are followed by other sketches, such as *computation sketches*.

■ 1.1 THE GRAPHIC LANGUAGE

Although people around the world speak different languages, a universal graphic language has existed since the earliest of times. The earliest forms of writing were through picture forms, such as the Egyptian hieroglyphics (Fig. 1.4). Later these forms were simplified and became the abstract symbols used in our writing today.

A drawing is a *graphic representation* of a real thing, an idea, or a proposed design for later manufacture or construction. Drawings may take many forms, but the graphic method of representation is a basic natural form of communication of ideas that is universal and timeless.

■ 1.2 ARTISTIC AND TECHNICAL DRAWINGS

Graphic representation has been developed along two distinct lines, according to purpose: (1) artistic and (2) technical.

From the beginning of time, artists have used drawings to express aesthetic, philosophic, or other abstract ideas. People learned by conversing with their elders and by looking at sculptures, pictures, or drawings

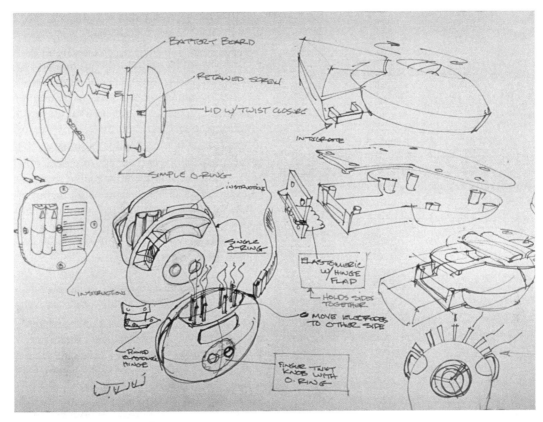

FIGURE 1.1   **An Initial Idea Sketch.** *Courtesy of Ratio Design Lab, Inc.*

FIGURE 1.2   **Engineers Work To Have an In-depth Understanding of a Product's Design.** *Courtesy of AC Engineering, Inc.*

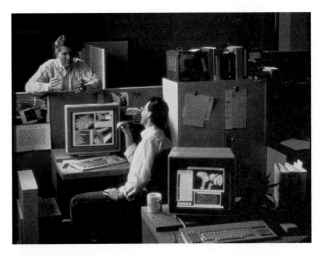

FIGURE 1.3   **Part of a Typical Engineering Design Department.** *Courtesy of Hewlett-Packard Company.*

FIGURE 1.4   **Egyptian Hieroglyphics.**

in public places. Everybody could understand pictures, and they were a principal source of information.

The other line along which drawing has developed has been the technical. From the beginning of recorded history, people have used drawings to represent the design of objects to be built or constructed. No trace remains of these earliest drawings, but we know that drawings were used, for people could not have designed and built as they did without using fairly accurate drawings.

■ 1.3 EARLY TECHNICAL DRAWING

Perhaps the earliest known technical drawing in existence is the plan view for a design of a fortress drawn by the Chaldean engineer Gudea and engraved on a stone tablet (Fig. 1.5). It is remarkable how similar this plan is to those made by modern architects, although it was "drawn" thousands of years before paper was invented.

FIGURE 1.5   **Plan of a Fortress. This stone tablet is part of a statue now in the Louvre, in Paris, and is classified in the earliest period of Chaldean art, about 4000 B.C.** *From Transactions ASCE, May 1891.*

In museums we can see actual specimens of early drawing instruments. Compasses were made of bronze and were about the same size as those in current use. As shown in Fig. 1.6, the old compass resembled the dividers of today. Pens were cut from reeds.

The scriber-type compass gave way to the compass with a graphite lead shortly after graphic pencils were developed. At Mount Vernon we can see the drawing instruments used by the great civil engineer George Washington, bearing the date 1749. This set is very similar to the conventional drawing instruments used today. It consists of a divider and compass with pencil and pen attachments plus a ruling pen with parallel blades similar to the modern pens (Fig. 1.7).

The theory of projections of objects on imaginary planes of projection (to obtain *views*; see Chapter 6) apparently was not developed until the early part of the fifteenth century by the Italian architects Alberti, Brunelleschi, and others. It is well known that Leonardo da Vinci used drawings to record and transmit to others his ideas and designs for mechanical constructions, and many of these drawings are still in existence (Fig. 1.8). It is not clear whether Leonardo ever made mechanical drawings showing orthographic views as we now know them, but it is probable that he did. Leonardo's treatise on painting, published in 1651, is regarded as the first book ever printed on the theory of projection drawing; however, its subject was perspective and not orthographic projection.

■ 1.4 EARLY DESCRIPTIVE GEOMETRY

Descriptive geometry is the science of graphic representation and solution of spatial problems. The beginnings of descriptive geometry are associated with the problems encountered in designs for building construction and military fortifications of France in the eighteenth century. Gaspard Monge (1746–1818) is considered the "inventor" of descriptive geometry, although his efforts were preceded by publications on

FIGURE 1.6   **Roman Stylus, Pen, and Compass.** *From Historical Note on Drawing Instruments, published by V & E Manufacturing Co.*

FIGURE 1.7   George Washington's Drawing Instruments. *From Historical Note on Drawing Instruments, published by V & E Manufacturing Co.*

FIGURE 1.8   An Arsenal, by Leonardo da Vinci. *Courtesy of the Bettmann Archive.*

stereotomy (the art or science of cutting solid bodies, especially stone, into desired shapes), architecture, and perspective, in which many of the principles were used. It was while he was a professor at the Polytechnic School in France near the close of the eighteenth century that Monge developed the principles of projection that are now the basis of our technical drawing. [A view of a part for a design is technically known as a **projection** (see §6.9; Chapter 6)]. These principles of descriptive geometry were soon recognized to be of such military importance that Monge was compelled to keep his principles secret until 1795, after which they became an important part of technical education in France and Germany and later in the United States. His book, *La Géométrie Descriptive*, is still regarded as the first text to expound the basic principles of projection drawing.

Monge's principles were brought to the United States from France in 1816 by Claude Crozet, an alumnus of the Polytechnic School and a professor at the United States Military Academy at West Point. He published the first text on the subject of descriptive geometry in the English language in 1821. In the years immediately following, these principles became a regular part of early engineering curricula at Rensselaer Polytechnic Institute, Harvard University, Yale University, and others. During the same period, the idea of manufacturing interchangeable parts in the early arms industries was being developed, and the principles of projection drawing were applied to these problems.

■ 1.5 MODERN TECHNICAL DRAWING

Perhaps the first text on technical drawing in this country was *Geometrical Drawing*, published in 1849 by William Minifie, a high school teacher in Baltimore. In 1850 the Alteneder family organized the first drawing instrument manufacturing company in the United States (Theo. Alteneder & Sons, Philadelphia). In 1876 the blueprint process was introduced at the Philadelphia Centennial Exposition. Up to this time the graphic language was more or less an art, characterized by fine-line drawings made to resemble copper-plate engraving, by the use of shade lines, and by the use of watercolor "washes." These techniques became unnecessary after the introduction of blueprinting, and drawings gradually were made less ornate to obtain the best results from this method of reproduction. This was the beginning of modern technical drawing. The graphic language now became a relatively exact method of representation, and the building of a work-

ing model as a regular preliminary to construction became unnecessary.

Up to about 1900, drawings everywhere were generally made in what is called *first-angle projection*, in which the top view was placed under the front view, the left-side view was placed at the right of the front view, and so on (§6.38). At this time in the United States, after a considerable period of argument pro and con, practice gradually settled on the present *third-angle projection*, in which the views are situated in what we regard as their more logical or natural positions. Today, third-angle projection is standard in the United States, but first-angle projection is still used throughout much of the world.

During the early part of the twentieth century, many books were published in which the graphic language was analyzed and explained in connection with its rapidly changing engineering design and industrial applications. Many of these writers were not satisfied with the term because they recognized that technical drawing was really a graphic language. Anthony's *An Introduction to the Graphic Language*, French's *Engineering Drawing*, and Giesecke et al., *Technical Drawing*, were all written with this point of view.

■ 1.6 DESIGN PROCESS

Design is the ability to combine ideas, scientific principles, resources, and often existing products into a solution for a problem. This ability to solve problems in design is the result of an organized and orderly approach to the problem known as the **design process**. The design process is not the haphazard operation of an inventor working in a garage or basement, although it might well begin in that manner. Nearly all successful companies support a well-organized design effort, and the vitality of the company depends to a large extent on the planned output of its designers.

The design process leads to manufacturing, assembly, marketing, service, and the many activities necessary for a successful product, and it is composed of several phases. Although many industrial groups may identify them in their own particular way, one procedure for the design of a new or improved product follows these five stages:

1. Problem identification
2. Concepts and ideas
3. Compromise solutions
4. *Models* and/or *prototypes*
5. Production and/or working drawings

Ideally, the design moves through these stages, but as new information becomes available, it may be necessary to return to a previous stage and repeat a procedure. The design process will be discussed in detail in Chapter 14.

■ 1.7 DRAFTING STANDARDS

Modern technical drawing books tended to standardize the characters of the graphic language, to eliminate its provincialisms and dialects, and to give industry, engineering, and science a uniform, effective graphic language. Of prime importance in this movement in the United States has been the work of the American National Standards Institute (ANSI) with the American Society for Engineering Education, the Society of Automotive Engineers, and the American Society of Mechanical Engineers. As sponsors, they have prepared the *American National Standard Drafting Manual— Y14*, which is comprised of a number of separate sections that were published as approved standards as they were completed over a period of years (see Appendix 1).

These sections outline the most important idioms and usages in a form that is acceptable to the majority. They are considered the most authoritative guide to uniform drafting practices in this country today. The Y14 Standard gives the characters of the graphic language, and it remains for the textbooks to explain the grammar and the penmanship (see §1.9 for a definition of penmanship as it applies to technical drawing).

■ 1.8 DEFINITIONS

After this brief survey of the historical development of the graphic language, and before we begin a serious study of theory and applications, a few terms need to be defined.

DESCRIPTIVE GEOMETRY This is the three-dimensional geometry forming the background for the practical applications of the graphic language and through which many of its problems may be solved graphically.

INSTRUMENTAL DRAWING OR MECHANICAL DRAWING These terms properly apply only to a drawing made with drawing instruments. The use of "mechanical drawing" to denote all industrial drawings is unfortunate not only because such drawings are not always mechanically drawn, but also because that usage tends to belittle the broad scope of the graphic language by naming it superficially for its principal mode of execution.

COMPUTER GRAPHICS This is the application of conventional computer techniques (with the aid of one of many graphic data processing systems available) to the analysis, modification, and finalizing of a graphical solution. The use of computers to produce technical drawings is called computer-aided design or computer-aided drafting (CAD) and also computer-aided design and drafting (CADD). (See Fig. 1.9.)

You can use CAD to create a useful database that accurately describes the three-dimensional geometry of the machine part, structure, or system you are designing. This database can be used to perform analysis, directly machine parts, or create illustrations for catalogs and service manuals.

ENGINEERING DRAWING AND ENGINEERING DRAFTING These are broad terms widely used to denote the graphic language. However, since the graphic language is also used by a much larger group of people in diverse fields who are concerned with technical work or industrial production, these terms are not broad enough.

TECHNICAL DRAWING This is a broad term that adequately suggests the scope of the graphic language. It is rightly applied to any drawing used to express technical ideas. This term has been used by various writers since Monge's time at least and is still widely used, mostly in Europe.

ENGINEERING GRAPHICS OR ENGINEERING DESIGN GRAPHICS These terms are generally applied to drawings for technical use and have come to

FIGURE 1.9 **A CAD workstation.** *Courtesy of Digital Equipment Corporation.*

GRAPHICS SPOTLIGHT

From Art to Part

SINGLE DATABASE

You can use a single CAD database to design, document, analyze, create prototypes, and directly manufacture finished parts for your design. The term *art to part* is sometimes used to describe a CAD database being utilized for many or all of these purposes.

SKETCHING FREEDOM

Initial ideas for the design are frequently sketched freehand, as shown in Fig. A. While generating ideas for the design, it is important to be able to quickly generate creative ideas without the confines of using the computer. Sketching is still generally the best tool to help in this process.

INTELLIGENT MODELS

After generating the initial ideas, the best alternatives for the design are developed further. At this point, the engineer may create rough 3D drawing geometry like you see in Fig. B, perhaps using a parametric modeling software. *Parametric modeling* uses variables to constrain the shape of the geometry. Using parametric modeling the designer roughly sketches initial shapes and applies drawing dimensions and constraints to create models that have "intelligence." Later the de-

(B)

signer can change the dimensions and constraints as the design is refined so that new models do not have to be created for each design change. Realistic renderings of the model help you visualize the design.

OPTIMIZING THE DESIGN

You can export the refined model directly into a Finite Element Analysis (FEA) program to perform structural, thermal, and modal analysis as shown in Fig. C. The parametric model can easily be changed if the

(A)

(C)

(D)

(E)

analysis shows that the initial design will not meet requirements. Simulation programs may even animate the performance and function of the system before a prototype is ever constructed. The tolerances and fits between mating parts can be checked within the parametric modeling and design software. Fig. D shows a shaded 3D model that closely resembles the final part.

RAPID PROTOTYPING

While refining the design ideas, engineers often work concurrently with manufacturing to determine the best ways to make and assemble the necessary parts. After several cycles of refining, analyzing, and synthesizing the best ideas, the final design is ready to go into production. Rapid prototyping systems allow parts to quickly be generated directly from the 3D models for mockup and testing. Fig. E shows the prototyped part.

When the design is approved the finished parts can be created using numerical controlled machines which get their tool paths directly from the 3D models.

GET NEW PRODUCTS TO MARKET QUICKLY

The necessary documentation for the design, manuals, brochures and other literature can be created directly from the same geometry used for design and manufacturing. Shortened design cycle time, improved communication, better opportunity to analyze and make design changes, are all advantages for companies using integrated CAD software for the design, documentation, and manufacture of their products.

Photographic material reprinted with the permission from and under the copyright of Autodesk, Inc.

mean that part of technical drawing that is concerned with the graphical representation of designs and specifications for physical objects and data relationships as used in engineering and science.

TECHNICAL SKETCHING This is the freehand expression of the graphic language. Technical sketching is a valuable tool for engineers and others engaged in technical work because through it most technical ideas can be expressed quickly and effectively without the use of special equipment.

BLUEPRINT READING This is the term applied to the "reading" of the language from drawings made by others. Actually, the blueprint process has now been replaced by other more efficient processes, but the term "blueprint reading" has been accepted through usage to mean the interpretation of all ideas expressed on technical drawings, whether or not the drawings are blueprints.

■ 1.9 WHAT ENGINEERING, SCIENCE, AND TECHNOLOGY STUDENTS SHOULD KNOW

From the dawn of history, the development of technical knowledge has been accompanied, and to a large extent made possible, by a corresponding graphic language. Today the intimate connection between engineering and science and the universal graphic language is more vital than ever before, and engineers, scientists, and technicians ignorant of or deficient in their field's principal mode of expression in technical field are professionally illiterate. Thus, training in the application of technical drawing is required in virtually every engineering school in the world.

The old days of fine-line drawings and of shading and "washes" are gone forever; artistic talent is no longer a prerequisite to learning the fundamentals of the graphic language. Instead, today's graphics student needs the same aptitudes, abilities, and computer skills that are needed in science and engineering courses.

The well-trained engineer, scientist, or technician must be able to make and read correct graphical representations of engineering structures, designs, and data relationships. This means that the individual must understand the fundamental principles, or the *grammar*, of the language and be able to execute the work with reasonable skill (which is *penmanship*).

Graphics students often try to excuse themselves for inferior results (usually caused by lack of application) by arguing that after graduation they do not expect to do any drafting at all. Such students presumptuously expect, immediately after graduation, to be accomplished engineers concerned with bigger things. They forget that first assignments may involve working with drawings and possibly revising drawings, either on a board or on a computer, under the direction of an experienced engineer. Entering the engineering profession via graphics provides an excellent opportunity to learn about the product, the company operations, and the supervision of others.

Even a young engineer who has not been successful in developing a skillful penmanship in the graphic language will have use for its grammar, since the ability to *read* a drawing will be of utmost importance. Furthermore, the engineering student is apt to overlook that, in practically all the subsequent courses taken in college, technical drawings will be encountered in most textbooks. The student is often called on by instructors to supplement calculations with mechanical drawings or sketches. Thus, a mastery of a course in technical drawing utilizing both traditional methods and computer systems (CAD) will aid materially, not only in professional practice after graduation but more immediately in other technical courses.

Besides the direct advantages of a serious study of the graphic language, many students learn the meaning of neatness, speed, and accuracy for the first time in a drawing course. These are basic and necessary habits for every successful engineer, scientist, and technician.

The ability to *think in three dimensions* is one of the most important requisites of successful scientists, designers, and engineers. Learning to visualize objects in space, to use the constructive imagination, is one of the principal values to be obtained from a study of the graphic language. Persons of extraordinary creative ability possess the ability to *visualize* to an outstanding degree. It is difficult to think of Edison, De Forest, or Einstein as being deficient in constructive imagination.

■ 1.10 PROJECTIONS

Behind every drawing of an object is a space relationship involving four imaginary things:

1. The observer's eye, or the *station point*
2. The object
3. The *plane of projection*
4. The *projectors*, also called *visual rays* or *lines of sight*.

For example, in Fig. 1.10a the drawing EFGH is the projection, on the plane of projection A, of the square

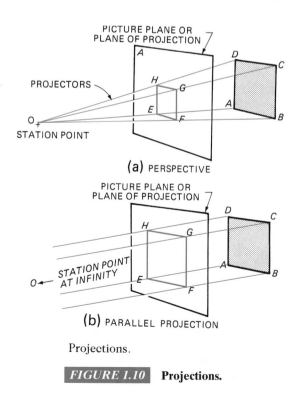

(a) PERSPECTIVE

(b) PARALLEL PROJECTION

Projections.

FIGURE 1.10   Projections.

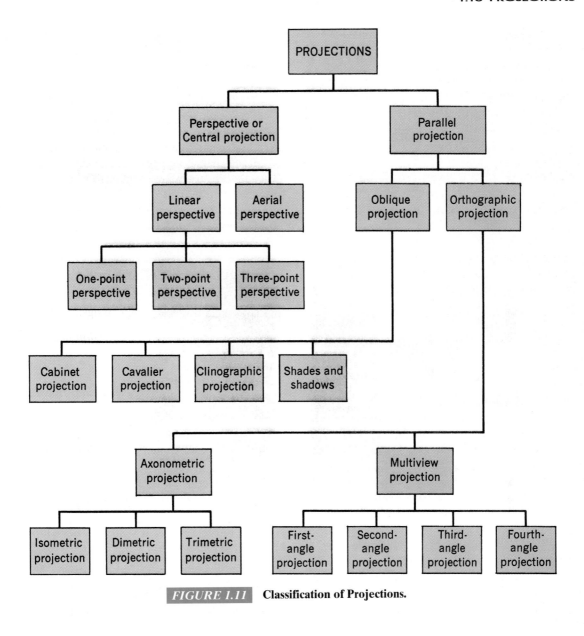

FIGURE 1.11   Classification of Projections.

ABCD as viewed by an observer whose eye is at the point O. The projection or drawing on the plane is produced by the points at which the projectors pierce the plane of projection (*piercing points*). In this case, where the observer is relatively close to the object and the projectors form a "cone" of projectors, the resulting projection is known as a *perspective*.

If the observer's eye is imagined as infinitely distant from the object and the plane of projection, the projectors will be parallel, as shown in Fig. 1.10b; hence, this type of projection is known as a *parallel projection*. If the projectors, in addition to being paral-

lel to each other, are perpendicular (normal) to the plane of projection, the result is an *orthographic*, or right-angle, *projection*. If they are parallel to each other but oblique to the plane of projection, the result is an *oblique projection*.

These two main types of projection—perspective or central projection, and parallel, or central, projection—are further broken down into many subtypes, as shown in Fig. 1.11, and will be treated at length in the various chapters that follow.

A classification of the main types of projection according to their projectors is shown in Table 1.1.

Classes of Projection	Distance from Observer to Plane of Projection	Direction of Projectors
Perspective	Finite	Radiating from station point
Parallel	Infinite	Parallel to each other
Oblique	Infinite	Parallel to each other and oblique to plane of projection
Orthographic	Infinite	Perpendicular to plane of projection
Axonometric	Infinite	Perpendicular to plane of projection
Multiview	Infinite	Perpendicular to planes of projection

TABLE 1.1   **Classification by Projectors.**

■ KEY WORDS

GRAPHIC LANGUAGE

TECHNICAL DRAWING

DRAWING INSTRUMENTS

COMPUTER GRAPHICS

PERSPECTIVE

DESIGN PROCESS

DESIGN TEAM

DESCRIPTIVE GEOMETRY

STANDARDS

PROJECTION

PLANE OF PROJECTION

■ CHAPTER SUMMARY

- The members of the engineering design project team must be able to communicate among themselves and with the rest of the project team in order to contribute to the team's success.
- The graphic language is the universal language used by every engineering team designing and developing products throughout the world.
- There are two basic types of drawings: artistic and technical.
- Technical drawing is based on the universal principles of descriptive geometry, developed in the late eighteenth century in France.
- The design process is the ability to combine ideas, scientific principles, resources, and existing products into a solution for a problem. It consists of five specific stages.

- Every technical drawing is based on standards that prescribe what each symbol, line, and arc means.
- Computer running CAD software are the current tools used by drafters. However, the basic drawing principles are the same ones used for hundreds of years.
- Drawings are based on the projection of an image onto a plane of projection. There are two types of projection: parallel and perspective.
- Successful companies hire skilled people who can add value to their design team. The proper use of equipment and a thorough understanding of the graphic language are two essential skills employers require.

■ REVIEW QUESTIONS

1. What is the role of the engineer on the design team?
2. What is the difference between mechanical drawing and sketching?
3. Describe the main difference between parallel projection and perspective projection.
4. When is sketching an appropriate form of graphic communication?
5. Why are standards so important for members of the engineering design team?

6. What is the most important new tool used by drafters?
7. What is a plane of projection?
8. What are projectors and how are they drawn?
9. What is the design process?
10. What are the five phases of the design process?

C H A P T E R 2

INTRODUCTION TO CAD

OBJECTIVES

After studying the material in this chapter, you should be able to:

1. List the basic components of a computer-aided drawing workstation.
2. Describe the relationship between computer-aided drawing (CAD) and computer-aided manufacturing (CAM).
3. List the major parts of a computer and describe their function.
4. Describe the purpose of a computer operating system.
5. List several input and output devices.
6. Describe ways in which a computer stores information.
7. Explain the differences between ROM and RAM.
8. Explain the differences between a bit and a byte.
9. Understand issues that affect the choice and the use of a CAD system.
10. Explain features common to most CAD software.

OVERVIEW

The use of electronic computers today in nearly every phase of engineering, science, business, and industry is well known. The computer has altered accounting and manufacturing procedures, as well as engineering concepts. The integration of computers into the manufacturing process from design to prototyping, manufacture, and marketing, is changing the methods used in the education and training of technicians, drafters, designers, and engineers.

Engineering, in particular, is a constantly changing field. As new theories and practices evolve, more powerful tools are developed and perfected to allow the engineer and designer to keep pace with the expanding body of technical knowledge. The computer has become an indispensable and effective tool for design and practical problem solving. New methods for analysis and design, the creation of technical drawings, and the solving of engineering problems, as well as the development of new concepts in automation and robotics, are the result of the influence of the computer on current engineering and industrial practice.

Computers are not new. Charles Babbage, an English mathematician, developed the idea of a mechanical digital computer in the 1830s, and many of the principles used in Babbage's design (Fig. 2.1) are the basis of today's computers. The computer has appeared in literature and science fiction to be a mysterious, uncompromising, often sinister, machine, but it is nothing more than a tool. It is capable of data storage, basic logical functions, and mathematical calculations. Computer applications have expanded human capabilities to such an extent that virtually every type of business and industry utilizes a computer directly or indirectly.

FIGURE 2.1   **A Working Model of Charles Babbage's "Difference Engine" Originally Designed in 1833.** *From the New York Public Library Picture Collection.*

■ 2.1 COMPUTER SYSTEMS AND COMPONENTS

Engineers and drafters have used computers for many years to perform the mathematical calculations required in their work. Only recently, however, has the computer been accepted as a valuable tool in the preparation of technical drawings. Traditionally, drawings were made by using drafting instruments and applying ink, or graphite, to paper or film. Revisions and reproductions of these drawings were time consuming and often costly. Now the computer is used to produce, revise, store, and transmit original drawings. This method of producing drawings is called *computer-aided design* or *computer-aided drafting* (CAD) and *computer-aided design and drafting* (CADD). Since these and other comparable terms are used synonymously, and since industry and software creators are beginning to standardize, they will be referred to throughout this book simply as CAD.

Other terms, such as *computer-aided manufacturing* (CAM), *computer-integrated manufacturing* (CIM), and *computer-assisted engineering* (CAE), are often used in conjunction with the term "CAD." The term "CAD/CAM" refers to the integration of computers into the design and production process (see Fig. 2.2). The term "CAD/CAE/CAM/CIM" describes the use of computers in the total design and manufacturing process, from design to production, publishing of technical material, marketing, and cost accounting. The single concept that these terms refer to is the use of a computer and software to aid the designer or drafter in the preparation and completion of a task. (See Chapter 10 for a further discussion on CAD and manufacturing processes.)

Computer graphics is a very broad field. It covers the creation and manipulation of computer-generated images and may include areas in photography, busi-

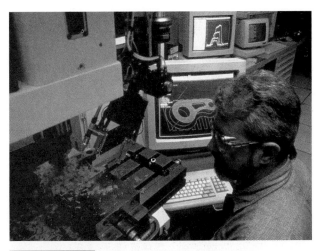

FIGURE 2.2 **CAD/CAM Driven Machine Tool Cutting.** *Courtesy of David Sailors.*

ness, cartography, animation, publication, as well as drafting and design.

A complete computer system consists of *hardware* and *software*. The various pieces of physical equipment that comprise a computer system are known as hardware. The programs and instructions that permit the computer system to operate are classified as software. Computer programs are categorized as either *application programs* or *operating systems*. Operating systems, such as DOS, Windows (Fig. 2.3), and UNIX, are sets of instructions that control the operation of the computer and peripheral devices as well as the execution of specific programs. This type of program may also provide support for activities and programs (such as input/output [I/O] control, editing, storage assignment, data management, and diagnostics), assign drives for I/O devices, and provide

FIGURE 2.3 **Screenshot of the Windows 98 Operating System.** *Courtesy of Microsoft Corporation.*

FIGURE 2.4   **AutoCAD is a Widely Used Drafting Application Program.** *This material has been reprinted with the permission from and under the copyright of Autodesk, Inc.*

FIGURE 2.5   **Advanced CAM Technology Used in High-Resolution Color Picture Tube Production.** *Courtesy of Zenith Electronics Corporation and Charlie Westerman.*

support for standard system commands and networking. Application programs are the link between specific system use and its related tasks—design, drafting, desktop publishing, etc.—and the general operating system program (Fig. 2.4).

■ 2.2 COMPUTER TYPES

Computers may be classified as one of two distinct types: *analog* or *digital*. An analog computer measures continuously without steps, whereas the digital computer counts by digits, going from one to two, three, and so on, in distinct steps. An electric wall clock with minute and hour hands and the radial speedometer on a car are examples of analog devices. An abacus and a digital watch are examples of digital devices. Digital computers are more widely used than analog computers because they are more flexible and can do a greater variety of jobs.

Analog computers are generally used for mathematical problem solving. This type of computer, which measures continuous physical properties, is often used to monitor and control electronic, hydraulic, or mechanical equipment. Digital computers have extensive applications in business and finance, engineering, numerical control, and computer graphics (Fig. 2.5).

Both types of computers have undergone great changes in appearance and in operation. Equipment that once filled the greater part of a large room has now been replaced by machines that occupy small

desktop areas. The single most important advancement in computer technology has been the development of the *integrated circuit* (IC). The IC chip has replaced thousands of components on the *printed circuit* (PC) board and made possible the development of microprocessors. The microprocessor is the processing unit of a computer. The difference in size between a PC board with individual components and an IC chip is shown in Fig. 2.6. The term "microminiaturization" is applied to advanced integrated circuit chip technology. The evolution of IC chip technology has led to the increased production of low-cost microcomputers. Microcomputers are largely responsible for the increase in use of computer-aided drafting systems in industry. Low-cost microcomputer CAD systems can now be cost justified by industrial users

FIGURE 2.6   **Size Comparison of a PC Board and an IC Chip.**

(a)   (b)   (c)

FIGURE 2.7   **(a) Computer with Intel Pentium III.** *Courtesy of Dell Corporation.* **(b) Think pad.** *Courtesy of IBM Corporation.* **(c) Intel Pentium III chip.** *Courtesy of Intel Corporation.*

(Figs. 2.7a-c). With the recent release of the Pentium III processor, CAD applications can run faster and more efficiently than ever before (See Figs. 2.7a and c). Thinkpad computers make mobile reference to CAD files not only possible, but commonplace (See Fig. 2.7b).

Since CAD systems utilize digital computers, we will restrict our discussion of computer types to digital computers.

■ 2.3 COMPUTER-AIDED DRAFTING

The first demonstration of the computer as a design and drafting tool was given at the Massachusetts Institute of Technology in 1963 by Dr. Ivan Sutherland. His system, called "Sketchpad," used a cathode ray tube and a light pen for graphic input to a computer. An earlier system, called SAGE, was developed in the 1950s for the Air Defense Command and used the light pen for data input. The first commercial computer-aided drafting system was introduced in 1964 by International Business Machines (IBM).

Many changes have taken place since the introduction of the first CAD system. The changes are due to the advent of the microprocessor, more sophisticated software (programs), and new industrial applications. In most cases, the drafter/engineer can create, revise, obtain prints (hard copy), and store drawings with relative ease, utilizing less space. CAD was originally used to aid in creating production drawings. The advent of three-dimensional CAD software made it apparent that a 3D computer model (Fig. 2.8) could assist not only in the manufacture of the part but also,

FIGURE 2.8   **A CAD Solid Model of the Ball Bracket from a Trailor Hitch Assembly.** *From* **Machine Design: An Integrated Approach** *by Robert Norton, © 1996. Reprinted by permission of Prentice-Hall, Inc., Upper Saddle River, NJ.*

along with its three-dimensional database, in testing the design with finite element analysis programs (Fig. 2.9), in developing technical manuals and other documentation that combine illustrations of the design with text from word processing programs, and in marketing (for which the 3D solid models can be used with a rendering and animation program). Increases in productivity and cost effectiveness are two advantages constantly stressed by CAD advocates. In addition, CAD stations can be linked either directly or through a *local area network* (LAN) to the manufacturing or production equipment, or they can be linked with *numerical control* (NC) equipment to program NC machines automatically in manufacturing operations or in robotics (Fig. 2.10).

FIGURE 2.9 **An FEM Mesh Applied to the Solid Model of the Ball Bracket.** *From* **Machine Design: An Integrated Approach** *by Robert Norton, © 1996. Reprinted by permission of Prentice-Hall, Inc., Upper Saddle River, NJ.*

The primary users of CAD are in mechanical engineering and electronic design, civil engineering, and cartography. The design and layout of printed circuits are a principal application of CAD in the electronics industry, which, prior to 1976, was the largest CAD user. Mechanical engineering has since overtaken electronics and continues to expand its CAD applications and use. Continued expansion in mechanical design applications is expected because the design, analysis, and numerical control capabilities of CAD can be applied to a varied range of products and processes. Cartography, seismic data display, demographic analysis, urban planning, piping layouts, and especially architectural design also show growth in CAD use. A relatively new area in computer graphics is *image processing*,

FIGURE 2.10 **Computers Work with NC Machines in Modern Industry. This is an Example of a Computer Numerical Control (CNC) Four-Axis Turning Center.**

which includes animation, 35-mm slide preparation, photocolor enhancement, and font and character generation (used in television broadcasting and the graphic arts industry).

■ 2.4 CAD SYSTEM CONFIGURATIONS

All computer-aided drafting systems consist of similar hardware components (Fig. 2.11), such as input devices, a central processing unit, data storage devices, and output devices. For input devices, the system will have one or more of the following: a keyboard, mouse, trackball, digitizer/graphics tablet, and light pen. For output, The CAD system will include devices such as plotters, printers, and some type of monitor. The system must also have a data storage device, such as a tape drive, a hard (fixed) or soft (floppy) disk drive, or an optical disk drive. Finally, a computer or central processing unit (CPU) is needed to do all the numerical manipulations and to control all the other devices connected to the system.

Frequently, some devices are combined. For example, a terminal or workstation can contain the keyboard, monitor, disk drives, and a CPU all in the same cabinet. Such a combined device is often called a *workstation* (Fig. 2.12).

■ 2.5 CENTRAL PROCESSING UNIT

The CPU (Fig. 2.13), or computer, receives all data and manages, manipulates, and controls all functions of the CAD system. CAD systems use digital computers. All data must be converted into a binary form or

FIGURE 2.11 **Complete CAD Systems Need Input Devices, Output Devices, Storage Devices, and a Central Processing Unit.** *Courtesy of Hewlett-Packard Company.*

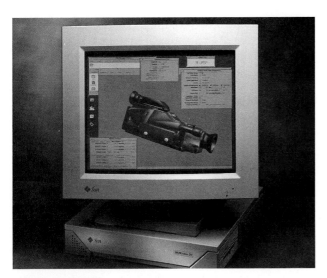

FIGURE 2.12 **A Powerful Computer Workstation.**
Courtesy of Sun Microsystems.

code for the computer to understand and accept. This code is called *binary coded decimal instructions* (BC-DI). This binary code uses a two-digit system, 1 and 0, to transmit all data through the circuits. The number 1 is the "on" signal; the 0 is the "off" signal. A *bit* is a binary digit. Bits are grouped, or organized, into larger instructions. Word length, which is expressed as bits, differs with various computers. The most common word lengths are 8, 16, and 32 bits. The word length in-

dicates the maximum word size that can be processed, as a unit, during an instruction cycle. Often, computers are categorized by their word length, such as 16-bit or 32-bit computers. The number of bits in the word length indicates the processing power of the computer (the larger the word length, the greater the processing power). A sequential group of adjacent bits in a computer is called a *byte*. The current industry standard is that 8 bits equal 1 byte. A byte represents a character that is operated on as a unit by the CPU. The length of a word on a majority of computer system is currently 4 bytes. This means that each word in any of these storage systems occupies a 32-bit storage location. The memory capacity of a computer is therefore expressed as a number of bytes rather than bits.

Inside the CPU is the brain of the computer—the microprocessor chip (Fig. 2.13). IBM-compatible computers have used the 386, 486, Pentium (P5), P6, II, and III chips. MacIntosh computers use the Motorola chips or PowerPC chip. Intel's Pentium III processor along with Apple's PowerPC G3 processor have kept pace with industries' every expanding need for speed and memory. Silicon Graphics and Sun computers use their own chips. The job of the microprocessor is to execute the instructions of the software programs.

The microprocessor chip's speed is rated in *megahertz* (MHz), and its power is rated in *millions of instructions per second* (MIPS). It is the largest chip in the CPU and is mounted on the main circuit board,

FIGURE 2.13 **Inside a CPU Box.**
Courtesy of Apple Computer.

called the *motherboard*. Attached to the motherboard are all the devices inside the CPU: the memory chips, power supply, connection ports (where the external cables are attached), internal modems, video cards, network interface cards, sound cards, and special hard drive controller cards.

Computer memory is stored on small circuit boards called *single inline memory modules* (SIMMs). Most of the SIMMs are for the main memory, called the *random access memory* (RAM). This memory is temporary. When you turn off the computer, the information in the memory is erased. The software programs and user files are stored in RAM when the program is actively running. The more RAM in a computer, the more programs you can run at one time. If you do not have enough memory, you may have a hard time running even one large program.

There is also permanent memory on the motherboard, which is called *read only memory* (ROM). When the computer is turned off, the ROM chips do not forget what is stored in them. The ROM chips contain basic operating system programs, like simple diagnostic programs that check the computer system to make sure all circuits and devices are operational when the computer is turned on. One type of ROM is called *flash* ROM, and it can be reprogrammed. Normal ROM cannot be reprogrammed.

FIGURE 2.14   **A Mother Board with 10 Bus Slots for Adding Capabilities Such as Video Display Cards.** *Courtesy of International Business Machines.*

The motherboard contains slots for peripheral devices. (See Fig. 2.14.) Internal modems, video display cards, and network interface cards are typical cards that can be plugged into the motherboard. These cards talk to the microprocessor via an electrical pathway called the *bus*. The bus is like an expressway that allows electrical information to be shared between all the devices connected to the motherboard. Just like an expressway, computer busses have speed limits. They are rated in megahertz like the CPU. The faster the bus, the more quickly information can be transported into the computer.

The rear panel of the CPU contains a series of connector ports (plug receptacles). Different types of ports transfer data differently. Each corresponds to a matching cable that connects the CPU to an external peripheral device. Most printers, for example, use a 25-pin D connector to connect to the parallel port. The keyboard and mouse each have their own connection port (usually a small round port). Many of the cards inside the CPU have connection ports attached to the card that protrude through the back of the CPU. For example, the monitor connects to the port on the video display card. The modem telephone line connects to a port on the back of the internal modem. The LAN cable connects to the port on the back of the network interface card.

■ 2.6 DISPLAY DEVICES

Another major reason for the rapid growth in CAD systems is improvements in display devices. These display devices, commonly referred to as monitors (Fig. 2.15), utilize a wide variety of imaging principles. Each device has definite characteristics with regard to brightness, clarity, resolution, response time, and color. The purpose of any graphics display is to project an image on a screen. The image that is displayed may be alphanumeric (text symbols, letters, and/or numerals) or graphical (pictorial symbols and/or lines). Users of interactive CAD systems communicate directly or indirectly through graphics terminals. The information requested by the user may be displayed as animated figures, graphs, color-coded diagrams, or simply a series of lines.

Most interactive CAD systems use a raster scan monitor. *Raster scan* devices are similar to conventional television screens. These devices produce an image with a matrix of picture-element dots, called *pixels*, within a grid. Each pixel is either a light or dark image that appears on the screen as a dot. As in conventional

FIGURE 2.15   **21″ Monitor for CAD Hi-Res Images.**
Courtesy of NEC Technologies, Inc.

television, an electron beam is swept across the entire screen, line by line, top to bottom. This process is called raster scanning. A signal turns on or illuminates a pixel according to a pattern stored in memory. The screen is scanned around 60 times a second to update the image before the phosphor dims.

Most CAD computers use a 17-inch or 21-inch display. These sizes are measured diagonally across the front of the screen. The image on the monitor is generated by the video display card. These cards determine the resolution of the display and the number of colors. Standard *video graphics array* (VGA) resolution is 640 × 480 pixels. The more pixels per inch, the greater the resolution and the easier it is to read details on the monitor. Large-screen monitors can support up to 1600 pixels horizontally and 1200 pixels vertically.

In addition to resolution, video display cards can generate a range of colors. Normal color density is 256 colors. Photographic quality requires a color density of 16.7 million colors. When a monitor has a lot of pixels and many colors on the screen, it takes a lot of processing power and video memory to draw the image on the monitor. The microprocessor chip of the CPU cannot handle this load so the video display card often provides its own processor, called a video accelerator, and its own memory. Professional CAD computers usually have a very fast video accelerator that provides high resolution and a large number of colors. With a fast video accelerator, even the largest, high-resolution monitor can redraw in the blink of an eye. Slower video display cards can take up to a minute to redraw the screen. Most video display cards use a standard 15-pin VGA connector. However, larger monitors may require four separate cables.

Video monitors are rated by the speed with which they can refresh the screen. There are two ratings: horizontal refresh rate and vertical refresh rate. The faster the refresh rate, the easier the monitor is on the eyes. For example, if you are using a monitor with only a 60-Hz vertical refresh rate, you will begin to see a flicker on the screen after using it for several hours. Higher refresh rates reduce this annoying flicker. Quality large-screen monitors can cost as much as the CPU, but they are part of the user interface and can affect the long-term productivity of the operator.

■ 2.7 INPUT DEVICES

A CAD system may use one or a combination of input devices to create images on the display screen. Graphic input devices may be grouped into three categories: (1) *keyboard* and *touch sensitive*, (2) *time-dependent* devices, and (3) *coordinate-dependent* devices.

The keyboard is the universal input device by which data and commands are entered. A typical keyboard consists of alphanumeric character keys for keying in letters, numbers, and common symbols, such as #, &, and %; cursor control keys with words or arrows, printed on them, indicating directional movement of the screen cursor, and special function keys, which are used by some software programs for entering commands with a single keystroke. Many large mainframe-based CAD systems have used a special function keypad, or menu pad, that allows access to a command with a single keystroke (Fig. 2.16). Single-stroke command selection was considered so essential for cost effectiveness and ease of use that developers of mini- and microcomputer-based CAD systems included this feature of single and double keystroke command access into their program utilizing the CTRL, ALT, SHIFT, and function keys. Typically, a CAD system will use a keyboard for inputting commands and text, and another input device for cursor control.

A popular input device in use with both large and small CAD systems is a *mouse* (Fig. 2.17a-c). A mouse may be of the mechanical type or the optical type. A mechanical mouse uses a roller, or ball, on the underside of the device to detect movement. An optical mouse senses movement and position by bouncing a light off a special reflective surface. These optical mice track most reliably on a mousepad, but also can function on other surfaces, with the exception of glass. Most mice will have from one to three buttons on top

FIGURE 2.16   **An AutoCAD Menu Pad.** *This material has been reprinted with the permission from and under the copyright of Autodesk, Inc.*

(a) Standard Mouse

(b) Cordless Mouse

(c) Microsoft IntelliEye Optical Mouse

FIGURE 2.17   **Mice (a–c).** *Courtesy of Logitech, Inc. and Microsoft, Inc.*

of them to select positions or commands. Microsoft's new IntelliEye optical mouse comes with two extra buttons. The advantages of a mouse include ease of use, small required working area, and is relatively low cost. A mouse cannot, however, be used to digitize existing drawings into a CAD format.

Digitizing tablets (Fig. 2.18) are another commonly used input device. They can be used to create an original CAD drawing or to convert an existing pen or pencil and paper drawing into a CAD drawing. Digitizing tables range in size from 80 × 110 to 360 × 480. Tablets larger than 360 × 480, called digitizing tables, are used primarily for converting existing drawings to a CAD system format. The *resolution* of digitizing tablets is important. This determines how small a movement the input device can detect (usually expressed in thousandths of an inch) and depends on the number of wires per inch in the tablet's grid system. The working area on a tablet can have areas that are used as menus to pick commands from the CAD system. Attached to the tablet will be either a puck or stylus. A *puck* is a small, hand-held device with a clear plastic extension (or window containing crosshairs) that transfers the location of the puck on the tablet-grid to the relative location on the screen. Single or multiple buttons on top of the puck are used to select points and/or commands. A *stylus* appears to be a ball-point pen with an electronic cable attached to it. The tip of the stylus senses the position on the tablet grid and relays these coordinates to the computer. When the stylus is moved across the tablet, the screen cursor

FIGURE 2.18 **Tablets with Picking Devices—Puck and Stylus—Wired and Wireless.** *Courtesy of CalComp Digitizer Division.*

FIGURE 2.19 **Large Format Scanners for Capturing Documents Electronically.** *Courtesy of CalComp Digitizer Division.*

moves correspondingly across the screen. The stylus also contains a pressure-sensitive tip that enables the user to select points or commands by pressing down on the stylus.

Existing paper drawings can also be converted to CAD drawings using a scanner (Fig. 2.19) to read the existing drawing. Scanners create raster or bitmapped files, so the scanned images need to be converted to vector (line drawing) formats before they are useful for CAD. There are a number of raster-to-vector conversion programs on the market that help automate this process.

One of the oldest input devices used on CAD systems is the *trackball* (Fig. 2.20a). Trackballs were used on many large mainframe-based CAD systems and were often incorporated into the keyboard. Now they are a popular input device on portable computer systems. A trackball consists of a ball nested in a holder or cup, much like the underside of a mechanical mouse, and from one to three buttons for entering coordinate data into the system. Within the holder are

sensors that pick up the movement of the ball. The ball is moved in any direction with the fingers or hand to control cursor movement on the CRT screen. Cursor speed and button functions can be set by the user. Figure 2.20b shows a thumb mouse, similar to a trackball, which is actually a 3-D controller. These controllers allow the user to manipulate objects on x, y, and z axes, as well as control pitch, roll and yaw movements. These 3-D controllers allow the user complete control of graphic objects in six degrees of freedom and are readily used in CAD applications.

A *joystick* (Fig. 2.21) is an input device more commonly used with video games today than with CAD systems. This device looks like a small rectangular box with a lever extending vertically form the top surface. This hand-controlled lever is used to manipulate the screen cursor and manually enter coordinate data. Buttons of the device can be used to enter coordinate location or specific commands. This device is inexpensive and requires a very small working area, but it sometimes presents a problem when precise cursor positioning is important.

The *light pen* is the oldest type of CAD input device currently in use (Fig. 2.22). It looks much like a ballpoint pen or the stylus on a digitized tablet. A light pen is a hand-held photosensitive device that works only with raster scan or vector refresh monitors and is used to identify displayed elements of a design or to specify a location on the screen where an action is to take place. The pen senses light created by the electron beam as it scans the surface of the CRT. When the

(a)   (b)

FIGURE 2.20   (a) A Trackball. *Photo Courtesy of Logitech, Inc.* (b) This Magellan 3-D Controller Allows the User to Manipulate Graphic Objects with *x, y, z*, Pitch, Roll and Yaw Movement. *Courtesy of Logitech, Inc.*

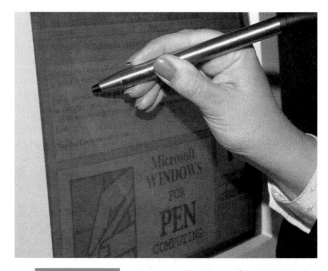

FIGURE 2.21   Joystick. *Courtesy of Logitech, Inc.*   **FIGURE 2.22**   Lightpen. *Courtesy of HEI, Inc.*

pen is held close to or touches the CRT screen, the computer can determine its location and position the cursor under the pen. Because this input device more closely emulates the traditional drafter's pencil or pen than other devices, it quickly gained popularity in the technical drawing field. It is popular for uses in which the user selects buttons or areas from the screen, because it is quick and easy to use.

Touch-panel displays, although not widely used with CAD systems, are another type of input device. These devices allow the user to touch an area on the

screen with a finger to activate commands or functions. This area on the screen contains a pressure-sensitive mesh that picks up the location of the finger and transfers it to the computer, which activates the command associated with that specific location. These devices work well with function or command entry but are inaccurate for CAD coordinate entry.

Bar code readers, although not often used with CAD programs, can offer users a way of labeling, tracking, and storing data and diagrams fro future use. (See Fig. 2.23.)

FIGURE 2.23 **Bar code reader** *Courtesy of Worthington Data Solutions.*

A relatively recent development in data input is *voice recognition* technology. This technology utilizes a combination of specialized integrated circuits and software to recognize spoken words. The system itself must first be "trained" by repeating commands into a microphone. The computer converts the operator's oral commands to digital form and then stores the characteristics of the operator's voice. When the operator gives an oral command, the system will check the sound against the words stored in its memory and then execute the command. A disadvantage of voice recognition systems is that the vocabulary supported by the system is limited. In addition, the memory required for storing complex sound or voice patterns can be extremely large. Access time, or time between the spoken word and command activation, may be several seconds. Finally, if the operator's voice changes in some manner or words have similar voice patterns, the system may not recognize the oral input.

■ 2.8 OUTPUT DEVICES

In most instances, the user of a CAD system will need a record of images that are stored on database files or displayed on the CRT. When an image is placed on paper, film, or other media, it is then referred to as *hard copy*. This hard copy can be produced by one of several types of output devices.

A commonly used device for the reproduction of computerized drawings is the *pen plotter*. Pen plotters may be classified as drum, flatbed, or microgrip. The *drum plotter* utilizes a long, narrow cylinder in combination with a movable pen carriage. The medium to be

drawn on (paper, vellum, or film) is mounted curved rather than flat and conforms to the shape of the cylinder drum. The drum rotates, moving the drawing surface, and provides one axis of movement, while the pen carriage moves the pen parallel to the axis of the cylinder and provides the other axis of movement. The combined movement of drum and pen allows circles, curves, and inclined lines to be drawn. The pen carriage on a drum plotter typically holds more than one pen, so varied line weights or multicolor plots can be drawn. These plotters accept up to E size paper in single sheets or in a roll, which is cut after the drawing is plotted.

Flatbed plotters (Fig. 2.24) differ from drum plotters in that the medium to be drawn on is mounted flat and held stationary by electrostatic or vacuum attraction while the pen carriage controls movement in box axes. The area of these plotters may be as small as A size (80 × 110) or larger than E size (340 × 440), and from one to eight pens may be used for varied line weights and multicolor plots.

Microgrip plotters (Fig. 2.25) have become one of the most widely used types of output devices. Their popularity is due to their adaptability to all types of computers, their size ranges, their low maintenance requirements, and their relatively inexpensive pricing. Microgrip plotters are similar to drum plotters in that the medium to be drawn on is moved in one axis while the pen moves along the other axis. These plotters get their name from the small rollers that grip the edges of the medium and move it back and forth under the pen carriage. These plotters range from A to E size, with single or multiple pen carriages, and may accept cut sheets or rolls.

FIGURE 2.24 **Flatbed Plotter.** *Courtesy of Houston Instruments, a division of CalComp Canada, Inc., Downsview, Canada.*

FIGURE 2.25   Microgrip Plotter. *Courtesy of Houston Instruments, a division of CalComp, Canada Inc., Downsview, Canada.*

All pen plotters are rated according to specified standards for accuracy, acceleration, repeatability, and speed. Accuracy is the amount of deviation in the geometry the pen plotter is supposed to draw (usually ranging from .0010 to .0050 in.). Acceleration is the rate at which the pen attains plotting speed and is expressed in *G*s (for gravitational force). Pen speed is important because slower speeds usually produce darker lines. The faster the pen attains a constant speed, the more consistent the line work will be. The ability of a plotter to retrace the same drawing over and over again is called repeatability. The deviation of the pen in redrawing the same line is the measure of repeatability and usually varies from .0010 to .0050. Plotter pen speed determines how fast the pen moves across the drawing medium. Most CAD software also allows the operator to adjust the pen speed to achieve maximum line quality and consistency. Slow pen speeds normally produce better quality plots than high pen speeds.

Other factors help determine the quality of a pen-plotted drawing. The variety of pens, inks, and drawing media available allows the operator to coordinate pen, ink, and paper to produce the most desirable hard copy.

Dot matrix or raster plotting is another method by which hard copy can be produced. These devices use a process called rasterization to convert images to a series of dots. The image is transferred optically (or sometimes by a laser) to the surface of the medium on a selenium drum that is electrostatically charged. Sometimes the image may be created by an array of nibs that electrically charge small dots on the medium.

A high-quality raster scan plotter can produce an image so fine and of such quality that it is not obvious how the image was produced unless examined under a magnifying glass.

Electrostatic plotters (Fig. 2.26) produce hard copy by placing an electrostatic charge on specially coated paper and having a toner, or ink, adhere to the charged area. Drawing geometry is converted through rasterization into a series of dots. These dots represent the charged area. Resolution of these plotters is determined by the number of dots per inch (dpi), usually ranging from 300 to 600 dpi. This type of plotter produces hard-copy drawings in single color or multicolors much faster than pen plotters, but the cost, power, and environmental requirements are also much greater.

An *ink jet printer/plotter* (Fig. 2.27) produces images by depositing droplets of ink on paper. These droplets correspond to the dots created by the rasterization process. This device places a charge on the ink rather than the paper, as in the electrostatic process. Ink jet plotters can produce good quality color-rendered images in addition to standard technical drawings.

Laser technology represents the newest evolution in plotter technology. A *laser printer/plotter* (Fig. 2.28 and 2.29) uses a beam of light to create images. This

FIGURE 2.26   Electrostatic Printer. *Courtesy of Houston Instruments, a division of CalComp, Canada Inc., Downsview, Canada.*

FIGURE 2.27   **Inkjet Printer.** *Photo courtesy of CalComp, Downsview, Ontario.*

FIGURE 2.29   **Full Size Laserjet Printer.** *Photo courtesy of CalComp.*

device utilizes electrostatic charging and raster scanning to produce a plotted image that is of very high quality.

Dot matrix printers (Fig. 2.30) produce images by one of two processes. They can produce images through impact on carbon or ink ribbon, or they may use a heat (thermal) process. Each method uses a number of pins in a specific configuration, such as 5×7, 7×9, or 9×9, set in the printer head. Machine commands control the sequence in which the pins strike the medium to produce an image. Dot matrix printers are normally less expensive than other types, but they are also associated with lower-quality printing.

FIGURE 2.28   **Laserjet Printer.** *Courtesy of Hewlett-Packard Company.*

FIGURE 2.30   **Dot Matrix Printer Character Formation—Each Character is Formed in a Matrix as the Print Head Moves Across the Paper.** *Photo from Computers, 4/E by Long/Long. © 1996. Reprinted by permission of Prentice-Hall, Inc., Upper Saddle River, NJ.*

■ 2.9 DATA STORAGE DEVICES

Since all data kept in RAM will be lost when the computer is turned off, they must be saved, or stored, before the power is off. Data storage devices provide a place to save information permanently for later use. CAD programs, for example, are stored on a disk; when loaded (or activated), portions of the program go into RAM, which is temporary memory. While a drawing is being worked on, all data associated with that drawing are kept in the same temporary memory. Periodically the operator must save that drawing and all the associated data to a storage device before the program is exited or the power is shut off. Otherwise, all accumulated data from that work session will be lost. These storage devices can be considered electronic file cabinets.

Disk drives, optical drives, and magnetic tape are distinct categories of storage devices. Disk storage devices are the most commonly used method of data storage. *Disk drives* may be of the fixed (hard disk) variety, flexible (floppy) variety, or optical type. Disk drives file and read data in random order. This means that the device writes data to any portion of the disk that is empty, and it is able to locate data almost instantly because it has access to the whole disk at once. Disk drives are rated according to their type, access time, capacity, and transfer rate.

The *fixed disk drive*, or hard disk (Fig. 2.31) is the most common method of data storage. This type of drive uses an aluminum disk as the medium for storage. These drives may be internal, attached inside the computer case, or external, in a separate case of cabinet. A disk controller or controller card must be installed in the computer to allow the computer and drive to communicate or interface with each other. The storage capacity of these drives will range from 200 MB to several gigabytes. Access time is expressed in milliseconds (ms) and will range from 6 to 80 ms. The lower the number in milliseconds, the faster the access time.

FIGURE 2.32   3.5 Inch Floppy Disk and Drive. *Photo from* Computers, 4/E by Long/Long. © 1996. *Reprinted by permission of Prentice-Hall, Inc., Upper Saddle River, NJ.*

Floppy disk drives (Fig. 2.32) derive their name from the removable flexible plastic disks used in this device. The disks used in this drive are typically $3\frac{1}{2}''$ in diameter. The density of a disk refers to the amount of data the disk will hold. Typically, a $3\frac{1}{2}''$ disk, called microdiskette, will hold 1.44 MB of data in double-sided, high-density format. The floppy disk is inexpensive and convenient to use but holds less data and is slower than fixed disk drives.

Zip drives (Fig. 2.33) are high-capacity magnetic disk drives, similar to floppy drives, that can store up to 100 MB on a $3\frac{1}{2}''$ disk. The disks used in zip drives are a special high-capacity medium and are not the same as a standard floppy disk. Zip drives are popular because there are external parallel and SCSI transfer models available which can be used to transport large amounts of data from one machine to another. They

FIGURE 2.31   Fixed or Hard Disk Drive Interior. *Courtesy of Western Digital Corporation.*

FIGURE 2.33   Zip Disk and Drive. *Courtesy of Iomega, Inc.*

FIGURE 2.34   **Jaz Drive and Disk.** *Courtesy of Iomega Corporation.*

can also be used for effective short-term backup (disks have a shelf life of 10 years).

Jaz drives are similar to Zip drives but their disks can hold up to 2 GB of data (Fig. 2.34).

Similarly, *superdisks* can hold up to 120 MB of data while $\frac{1}{4}''$ *data cartridges* can hold up to 20 GB of information.

The ever-increasing need for larger storage capacity has spurred the development of new technologies. The newest technology in data storage uses lasers to read and write data and is generally termed optical storage. Optical storage media are capable of holding many gigabytes of data.

CD-ROM drives are a type of optical drive. Previously, CD-ROM disks were usually created from a master, so when you purchased a CD it already had the digital information written to it. Now you can store information on recordable CD-ROM systems, which produce a *write once read many* (WORM) disk. WORM devices allow data to be written to them, but the data become permanent on the disk and cannot be erased. This storage device is especially suited for archival purposes. CD-ROM drives use a laser to read and write data to a chemically coated aluminum disk (Fig. 2.35). The data is "burned" into the disk surface by a laser so the information becomes permanent (unlike magnetic storage) and the disk is removable. Recordable CD-ROM systems can store about 650 MB of information on a single disk.

FIGURE 2.35   **CD-Rom and Disk.** *Courtesy of NEC Technologies, Inc.*

FIGURE 2.36 **Optical Disk Cartridge and Optical Disk Drive.** *Courtesy of SyQuest Technology.*

Optical disk drives (Fig. 2.36) allow data to be erased and written over. These drives use a laser to change the state of optical magnetic media. These optical magnetic media can be changed again and again (write many read many). Because optical magnetic media are not sensitive to dust, like hard drives, optical disks can be removed from the drive and replaced with a new disk when additional storage capacity is needed.

Magnetic tape storage (Fig. 2.37) uses plastic tape coated with magnetic particles. A read/write head in the tape drive charges magnetic particles to store information on the tape. The data being sent are recorded as a series of charges along the tape. Once these particles are charged, they will remain charged until

FIGURE 2.37 **Tape Back-up System.** *Courtesy of Iomega, Inc.*

the head writes over them or they are demagnetized. Tape drives file and read data in sequential order. This means they must look through data in the order that the tape is wound or unwound. (This is similar to forwarding or rewinding a videotape to look for a specific scene, or an audiotape to play a particular song.) Gigabytes of data may be stored on some tape systems. These cassettes resemble audiocassettes in both size and appearance. Tape storage is essentially used for backing up data from a hard drive, or for archival purposes (since the tapes can be removed and stored for later use).

■ 2.10 CAD SOFTWARE

CAD software tells the computer how to interact with the flow of data entered by the user through an input device. For example, it lets the computer "use" formulas to solve complictaed questions requiring detailed analysis of large amounts of data, such as finding the center of gravity for a truncated cone. It also handles drawing processes, like creating many different models or views of the same object automatically (Fig. 2.38). Software helps organize data; it will find previously stored drawing symbols, and it will help create and archive new ones. Software can be used to count, measure, and direct devices to print or plot drawings, create a bill of materials, or exchange files with other programs. CAD software is extremely powerful and has been designed to serve all major branches of engineering. It will be an important tool in most engineering careers.

■ 2.11 COMMON CORE

CAD SOFTWARE All CAD software generates familiar geometric terminology for creating drawings. But even though the geometry is common and the procedures for construction are similar, every CAD software program will vary in operational procedures typically involving the basic hierarchy of command structure.

Three features are found in all CAD software. You can access these features interactively through basic commands and menu options.

1. Commands for geometry generators (basic geometric construction)
2. Functions to control viewing of drawing geometry
3. Modifiers for changing the drawing or editing variations in the drawing (rotate, mirror, delete, group, etc.).

FIGURE 2.38   **CAD Software Easily Creates Different Outputs of the Same Object.** *Courtesy of SDRC, Milford, OH.*

The commands and menu options may often be selected in two basic ways: by typing or by picking using a tablet (digitizer) or mouse. The Cartesian coordinates may be accessed with the keyboard or the mouse. You may switch between these two input methods at any time to issue commands and select options. The sequence of selection is called the hierarchy of command structure and provides an ease of operation that is the basis for selecting one software program over another.

■ 2.12 CAD CAPABILITY CHECKLIST

CAD software can offer the following characteristics required for creating technical documents (Fig. 2.39):

1. Draw construction lines at any convenient spacing through any points, at any angles, and create tangent lines to one or more arcs.
2. Draw any type of line, such as visible, center, hidden, or section.
3. Draw circles and arcs of any size with given data.
4. Perform cross-hatching within specified boundaries.
5. Establish a scale or set a new scale within a drawing for various drawings within a document.
6. Calculate or list pertinent data of graphic construction, such as actual distances or angles.
7. Create a group of geometric figures for editing or copying.

8. Relocate drawing elements to any new position. Correct or change additions in stored documents.
9. Edit all or erase (delete) any part of a line, arc, or any geometric form on a drawing. Correct dimensions.
10. Make a mirrored image or create symmetrical forms.
11. Perform associative or datum unit dimensioning.

FIGURE 2.39   **CAD Assembly Drawing.** *Courtesy of Sputnik Equipment Corporation, Inc.*

FIGURE 2.40   **Desktop PCs Running the Windows Operating System Can Now Provide Capabilities to Create Parametric Solid Models.**

12. Label drawings with notes and create title blocks and bills of material.
13. Save the entire drawing or any part for use on other documents and in other formats.
14. Create pictorials from three-view drawings.
15. Create orthographic views from a 3D model.
16. Retrieve and use stored drawings.

However, software programmers are constantly adding new capabilities and options to CAD software. For instance, many new programs offer very sophisticated 3D capabilities, often in a Windows environment (Fig. 2.40).

■ 2.13 DRAWING WITH CAD SOFTWARE

The geometry that is created, drawn, or generated with CAD programs is generally referred to as objects, entities, or elements. These geometric entities are individually constructed figures or groups of elements that consist of points, lines, arcs, circles, rectangles, polygons, splines, solids, surfaces, symbols or blocks, cross-hatching, dimensions, and notes. These basic building units are selected from the menu and constructed at specific graphic locations of the monitor screen by the CAD user. Many CAD systems can store standard drawing symbols (called blocks) and use overlays on the digitizer for retrieval.

■ 2.14 USING A CAD SYSTEM

After a CAD system has been installed, the beginning user must become thoroughly familiar with it and learn how to use it effectively. This will require learning some new skills as well as a different vocabulary. The CAD operator will need to learn to create accurate drawings and construct them to various scales. In addition, the operator will need to learn to interact effectively with the operating system to store and copy drawings and to routinely perform backups so that no data are lost. Most CAD manufacturers offer training programs and tutorials that will make the learning process much easier (Fig. 2.41). They will provide instruction and training manuals that give information and details about the operation of the system. These manuals can be used not only during the initial training period but also for reference purposes during later operation of the system.

Most experienced drafters have developed shorter or simpler methods for creating a drawing, such as using overlays or templates. CAD systems also have simplified methods for drawing. Some systems have symbol libraries that contain many of the frequently used symbols, such as electrical relays, switches, transformers, resistors, bolts, nuts, keys, piping, and architectural symbols. These symbols may be in a symbol library, or the symbol may be located on one of the templates in the library of templates. Most CAD systems allow users to customize their symbol libraries. The desired symbols must first be drawn by the user

FIGURE 2.41   **CAD Training Helps the User Learn the Software Quickly. *Courtesy of Jeff Kaufman and FPG International.***

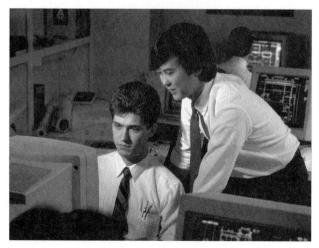

on the CAD system the same as they would appear on a drawing board. This process may initially take as much time as it would manually, but once the image has been entered in the computer database, it need never be drawn again. The symbol can easily be retrieved from the symbol library whenever required.

■ 2.15 SELECTING A CAD SYSTEM

As the number of manufacturers of computer system equipment has increased, there has been a corresponding decrease in the cost of these systems. Some CAD systems may contain only those features necessary to produce simple two-dimensional entities, while others have the capability to create true three-dimensional drawing objects. The manufacturers of some of these systems are eager to promote new or improved functions that may not be found on other systems. Almost daily the computer industry announces amazing advances.

Since the newer CAD systems are generally easier to operate, the words "user friendly" are frequently used by manufacturers to promote their systems. However, there has been a tendency to exaggerate what particular systems can do. A prospective user should therefore view all claims with some skepticism until proved, for they can be misleading and often lead to disappointment. Unfortunately, many firms have purchased a system only to discover that it did not perform as well as expected.

Before purchasing a CAD system, a careful, well-thought-out plan for selecting a system should be developed and followed. This plan can be divided into five phases:

1. Establish the need for a CAD system.
2. Survey and select system features.
3. Request CAD system demonstrations.
4. Review selected systems.
5. Select, purchase, and install a CAD system.

Let us now discuss each of these phases in greater detail.

ESTABLISH THE NEED FOR A CAD SYSTEM   The first consideration in the selection process is to determine whether a CAD system is needed. All potential users of the CAD system should be consulted regarding how, when, and where a system would be used and whether it would be cost effective in their particular operations (see Fig. 2.42). Never purchase a system

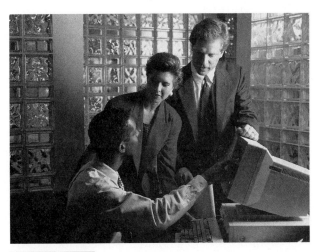

FIGURE 2.42   CAD Systems Can Be Expensive, So it is Important to Make Informed Decisions. *Courtesy of Ron Chapple and FPG International.*

simply because it may be considered a first step into the future and your firm wants to project a progressive image. It is important to investigate and evaluate the time- and cost-saving claims of manufacturers by contacting firms that have CAD systems in operation. Contact as many firms as possible, especially those with a wide range of experience. Prepare a brief questionnaire to survey these firms, asking questions regarding costs, training periods, system operation, and so on. Also ask at what point after installation the system became cost effective. Evaluate the responses to these questions and compare them with your specific requirements. This information will assist you in deciding if a CAD system can be beneficial to your firm at present.

Undoubtedly, you will hear many spectacular claims about the productivity of CAD systems. The productivity, however, will depend on the type of engineering operation. For example, among the first companies to introduce and use CAD systems were the electronic industry manufacturers. They found that drafters were constantly redrawing many symbols (resistor, transistor, etc.) and standard hardware parts (nuts, screws, etc.). Although they used plastic templates, common in all drafting departments, a considerable amount of time was spent doing tedious, repetitive drawing tasks. Since much of the time was devoted to tracing or redrawing something that was previously drawn, it was determined that a CAD system would save as much as 50% of the drafting time compared to using traditional methods. It is important to remember that with CAD it is only necessary to draw something once, even though initially it may take as long, or perhaps longer, to create it on the system as on the drawing board. From that point on, however, you need only recall this information from data storage, which a CAD system can do with amazing speed. In this example the benefits of CAD are obvious.

It is difficult to place a direct monetary value on many benefits of using CAD. These benefits include things like shorter design cycle time, improved ability to visualize complex fits between parts, links to direct manufacturing, better ability to reuse existing drawing and designs, and improved analysis early in the design phase.

The process of determining the need for a CAD system can be time consuming and frustrating. Nevertheless, speed should be sacrificed to careful deliberation in this phase.

SURVEY AND SELECT SYSTEM FEATURES   It is generally agreed that software should be selected before hardware. However, some CAD systems are *turnkey* system—that is, a total system with software and hardware combined and inseparable. Therefore, you should examine all the features of any given system very carefully before being attracted by spectacular hardware. For example, some systems use dual monitors. The chance of being impressed by this feature may overshadow the question of whether one really needs the two displays.

Consider whether the system will be multipurpose or used strictly for CAD. Will other office operations, such as word processing or accounting, be done on this machine? The answer to this question may add or eliminate CAD programs based on their operating system software.

Investigate how well a system will exchange information or interface with other CAD or CAM systems. Many systems do not have this capability. One important consideration is the CAD system's ability to exchange information with other CAD systems and other engineering applications. One standard for such exchange is the initial graphics exchange specification (IGES). There are also a number of other common formats. Make sure that the system you select can export common file formats, particularly to other applications you are planning to use.

It is suggested that you survey the people who will use the system to determine what they think is desirable in a CAD system. From this survey, develop a checklist of hardware and software features that your future system should have.

REQUEST CAD SYSTEM DEMONSTRATIONS   After the checklist has been created and approved by all parties concerned, make arrangements to see the various CAD systems in operation. A list of vendors can be compiled from advertisements in trade journals, magazines, and so on, or from the various directories of computer graphics manufacturers that are published. Contact the vendors to arrange demonstrations. Explain to them exactly what you expect the system to do. If the vendors are completely aware of your requirements, they will be able to give a more realistic presentation. Most of all, be prepared to ask questions. With each succeeding demonstration, your questions will be more effective. Moreover, the answers that you receive will be more meaningful. It is a good idea to select your own project which you would like to have demonstrated. Some CAD systems run their own canned example well but may not be flexible enough to meet your needs. Having your own project also helps you to contrast the systems fairly. Some systems may have a fancy demonstration, while others will not look as good initially. You want to select a system that will perform well for your needs, not look good running a canned demonstration.

Some of the questions that you should ask are as follows:

1. What are the brand names of the equipment used?
2. Are service contracts available? If so, what are the details and the cost of the contract? In most instances, service contracts are very expensive. Are you required to buy the service contract? Doing so may not be cost effective compared to having repairs done as you need them. Can you afford to have some downtime if something goes wrong with your system? If not, you may want a service contract. It is also possible in some situations to obtain service contracts from third parties that specialize in this type of business. The service provided by these firms for preventive and downtime maintenance may be less costly than that offered by the original manufacturer.
3. What is the warranty period, or periods, if parts of the system are furnished by different vendors? Also, is the warranty paid for by the original vendor or is the cost shard by the user and vendor?

4. What types of CAD software are provided, and what operations can be performed?

5. What kind and length of training will be provided to the user staff? How long after installation will it take for the staff to be proficient enough for the system to be cost effective?

6. Does the vendor issue software updates? If so, how often is this done and what is the cost?

7. What is the reputation of the vendor for providing user support in the form of toll-free telephone assistance or other methods of communication? Is the vendor readily available when the user encounters software and/or hardware problems and requires assistance?

8. Who currently uses the particular system? Will the vendor provide a list of current users? Users that have several months' experience with a CAD system are best qualified to answer question 7.

A CAD system analysis worksheet can be helpful when demonstrations are presented. Items to be included on the worksheet may be arranged according to hardware and software specifications. The hardware features that should be listed will generally be included in the following five categories: (1) central processor, (2) input devices, (3) monitors, (4) data storage, and (5) output devices. You may want to create a worksheet similar to the one shown in Fig. 2.43 that you can use to track CAD system features during demonstrations. The worksheet may be expanded or modified to reflect particular requirements. You should also develop a similar worksheet listing CAD system software feature requirements.

With the completion of this phase, you will have achieved several important goals. Your knowledge and understanding of CAD systems will have increased, and you will be in a position to identify those system features that you require and can afford. In addition, you will have assembled a list of current users of CAD systems for future reference or exchange of information.

REVIEW SELECTED SYSTEMS   It is important at this stage that all of the collected information be organized and carefully reviewed. A list should be made of only those systems that merit further serious consideration. You may wish to request another demonstration of the particular systems that are on your revised list and to request additional information from current users regarding equipment performance, staff training, vendor

support, and so on. Remember, if you select a system made by a reputable and financially stable manufacturer, and purchase it from a dependable retailer, you will sacrifice nothing in terms of service and support. Throughout this chapter we have made every effort to feature or illustrate systems and equipment made by such firms.

FINAL SELECTION, PURCHASE, AND INSTALLATION OF A CAD SYSTEM   This last phase occurs when the final decision will be made regarding whether or not to purchase a CAD system. The decision invariably will depend on how you plan to use the system and how much you can afford to pay for it. You may want to consider a leasing arrangement, or lease-purchase arrangement. This can be effective for keeping the technology up to date. New technology is available constantly, and the lifetime of computer equipment is generally considered to be about three years. If your system cannot pay for itself in three years, perhaps it is not a good investment. You should plan to upgrade or purchase new equipment and software on a regular cycle. If the decision is made to acquire a system, determine costs, choose a delivery date, and arrange for installation and training.

■ 2.16 SUMMARY

The information presented in this chapter is intended to familiarize the student with the basic concepts, hardware, peripherals, and systems in CAD. It is not possible (nor was it intended) to present a comparison of CAD programs or all the commands used on CAD systems.

When possible, the instructor should arrange for students to visit nearby engineering and drafting departments that have CAD systems in operation. Those students who wish to obtain additional information on this subject should consult their school or local library.

The CAD system on the personal computer is replacing many drafting instruments, drafting tables, and drafting files. However, like no other drafting tool before, it raises engineering productivity without replacing the basic functions of the designer, engineer, and drafting technician. CAD developers, in their quest to harness computer technologies, have had a profound impact on the high-tech teams as they resolve problems in research, development, design, production, and operation (the five basic engineering functions).

The skills learned "on the board" are related and complementary to those needed by the CAD user.

FIGURE 2.43   **Worksheet for Evaluating CAD System Hardware.**

Item	Y/N	Size/Type	Comments	Cost
Central Processor				
memory (MB)				
word size (16/32 bit)				
cache				
speed (MHz/Mips)				
bus type (eisa, vesa, pci)				
expansion/upgrade				
Operating System				
32 bit				
multitasking				
software availability				
Data Input Devices				
mouse				
trackball				
digitizer				
light pen				
thumb wheel				
Display				
monochrome				
color				
screen size				
resolution				
Video Card				
memory				
software support				
dual display support				
Storage, Hard Drive				
type				
access time				
capacity				
expansion				
removable				
Storage, Floppy				
type				
access time				
capacity				
removable				
CD-ROM				
type				
speed				
capacity				
read/write				

FIGURE 2.43   (cont.)

Item	Y/N	Size/Type	Comments	Cost
Backup System				
type				
capacity				
speed				
automation				
Output Devices				
type				
provided with system?				
medium				
cost per sheet				
speed				
resolution/accuracy				
color				
Maintenance				

Learning the performance skills needed for creating drawings with CAD tools is time consuming and requires practice and manual dexterity. Both methods of drafting use simple and familiar geometric terminology for structuring the graphic production of technical documents, and both have the same goal—drawings that will meet industry standards.

The basic principles of drafting are common to traditional drafting and computer-aided drafting. The American National Standards Institute (ANSI) has well-established standards for shaping engineering drawings. Knowledge of drafting principles from the alphabet of lines to dimensioning and sectioning procedures, continues to be essential in shaping CAD documents. CAD can help you produce consistent lettering and regulate line work to improve the production of working drawings better than any other tool.

The CAD user is responsible for preparing engineering documents that are an integral part of the total manufacturing process (Fig. 2.44). The ability to interact with all forms of technical information increases the significant role of the drafting technician.

■ KEY WORDS

CAD

CAM

SOFTWARE

OPERATING SYSTEMS

HARDWARE

CPU

MICROPROCESSOR

MIPS

MEGAHERTZ (MHZ)

MOTHERBOARD

SIMM

RAM

WORM DISK

PORT

VIDEO DISPLAY MONITOR

MOUSE

DIGITIZING TABLET

PRINTER

PLOTTER

FLOPPY DISK

HARD DISK DRIVE

MODEM

MENU

WIRE FRAME

CD-ROM

ZIP DISK

JAZ DISK

SUPERDISKS

DATA CARTRIDGES

GRAPHICS SPOTLIGHT

Unlocking the Power of Solid Modeling

Successful use of solid modeling should increase the size of a company's market, increase its market share, and increase its profit margin. Early CAD systems basically only automated the drafting process, but solid modeling has the potential to affect the entire production process, from preliminary design through engineering and manufacturing. Ancillary functions, such as purchasing and marketing, can also be affected.

Solid modeling can create all the critical information for a product, and a company needs to take advantage of all the information contained in these models. Good implementation of solid modeling is marked by the wide-ranging use of the solid models in downstream applications. This maximizes return because it permits many operations to work from the original solid model rather than re-creating the design for each operation. Solid models should be the basis for virtual prototypes, engineering analyses, machine tool paths, purchase orders, marketing images, etc. Anywhere a design is re-created or its related data is retyped into another computer is a sign that solid modeling may be underutilized.

Although downstream use is an important consideration, there is nothing to be gained by insisting that all design be done with solid-modeling when various operations are just as well served by 2D processes. Another consideration in introducing a new technology is whether it affects existing bottlenecks in the production process. Unless the use of solid modeling (or any other technological innovation) helps to eliminate or decrease the bottlenecks, or constraints, in the overall process, it will not improve productivity or profits.

Introduction of solid modeling into company operations requires careful planning. First, there are many solid modeling systems on the market, and choice of the correct one is of paramount importance. Second, it will probably be necessary to undertake an expensive hardware upgrade because solid modeling requires larger workstations, better graphics, more memory, etc. than simpler programs. Third, everyone who will use the solid model should be given extensive training. Introducing solid modeling in a pilot project is also widely recommended. The gradual implementation of solid modeling on a project-by-project basis has been found to be more successful than a one-step installation throughout the company.

Small and medium-sized companies have an advantage over large companies in using solid modeling for maximum return. Large companies may have the resources and dedication to make it work, but the smaller companies have the most flexibility in terms of organizational structure.

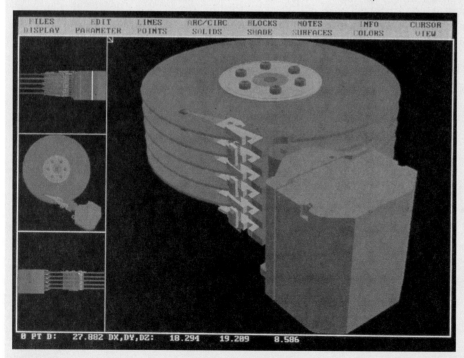

Multiview CAD Solid Model. *Courtesy of CADKEY.*

Adapted from "Unlocking the Power of Solid Modeling" by Caren D. Potter, *Computer Graphics World*, Nov. 1995, Vol. 18, No. 11, p. S3(4). ©PennWell Publishing Company 1995.

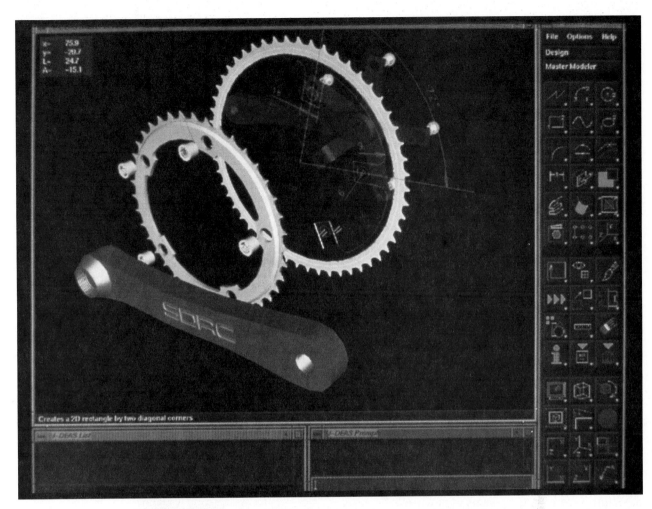

FIGURE 2.44   **CAD Documents Supply a Multitude of Information which Engineers and Technicians Must Understand and Use.** *Courtesy of SDRC, Milford, OH.*

■ CHAPTER SUMMARY

- Computers have revolutionized the drawing process. New technologies are constantly invented which make this process quicker, more versatile, and more powerful.

- CAD is the tool of choice for engineering design companies. The effective user of this tool requires an understanding of technical drawing fundamentals as well as training on the CAD software program.

- The microprocessor, RAM, and hard disk drive of the computer are essential components of a computer system. The keyboard and mouse are typical input devices. Printers and plotters output the drawing to paper for review and approval. The display monitor shows the drafter what is being drawn and offers command choices.

- CAD software can draw in three dimensions (width, height, and depth), unlike paper drawing which only consists of two dimensions in a single view.

- Different CAD packages have different operational procedures, and different strengths and weaknesses. Three features found in all CAD software are commands for geometry generators, functions to control the viewing of drawing geometry, and modifiers for changing the drawing or editing variations.

- Operating a CAD system typically has required extensive training. Newer CAD systems are becoming more user friendly, but one should not overestimate the claims CAD packages make. It is important to evaluate each package thoroughly and make an informed decision.

■ REVIEW QUESTIONS

1. What are the basic components of a computer-aided drawing (CAD) system?

2. Discuss the relationship between CAD and CAM in modern design and manufacturing facilities?

3. List the similarities and differences between a mouse and a digitizing pad with puck?

4. What are the main advantages of CAD over traditional drawing methods?

5. What is faster, a computer with a 100 Mhz microprocessor and a 500 MB hard disk, or a 500 Mhz computer with a 100 MB hard disk? Which will store more information?

6. What is the difference between RAM storage and hard disk storage? What computer parts are typically found on the motherboard?

7. What is the difference between plotting and printing?

8. What are the hardware and software specifications of your school's CAD system?

9. What are questions you should ask about any CAD system you consider buying?

■ CAD PROBLEMS

When necessary, refer to the appropriate sections of the chapter to check your answers.

Prob. 2.1 Define the following terms: computer system, hardware, software, analog, digital, computer graphics, CAD, CADD, and CAM.

Prob. 2.2 What are the principal components of a computer system? A CAD system? Draw a systems flowchart that illustrates the sequence of operations for each of the systems.

Prob. 2.3 Prepare a list of CAD system hardware components and give examples of each.

Prob. 2.4 Call a hardware company and compare the prices for three graphics monitors of different resolutions and sizes. Which purchase do you recommend? Give your reasoning.

Prob. 2.5 Prepare a list of possible data storage devices and determine total storage capabilities for each.

Prob. 2.6 Determine what would be your best storage device, in terms of value, if your average CAD drawing file size is 1500k and you store 10–20 drawings per week.

Prob. 2.7 Arrange a visit to the computer center at your school, or to a local engineering design office, and prepare a written report on the use of computers in design and drafting at these facilities.

The following problems ask you to use CAD software to solve some typical geometric construction that is similar from one software program to another. All the problems have been prepared on a CAD system. Prepare the required CAD drawing problems, as shown with your CAD system, and produce a hard copy with a printer or plotter for approval.

Prob. 2.8 Prepare a list of modifying (or editing) commands available on the CAD system you will be using.

Prob. 2.9 The unknown distance KA in Fig. 2.45 has been determined and the angle measured using CAD. Re-create this problem with your CAD system, changing the 908 angle at H to 758; then determine the angles at K and A and the length of line KA.

Prob. 2.10 Prepare a revised version of the CAD drawing (Fig. 2.46) by increasing the radius 0.40 to 0.4375 and changing the slot dimension 1.60 to 1.70.

Prob. 2.11 Prepare a detailed CAD drawing of the Safety Key (Fig. 2.47) with the following changes: Correct the right-side view and add the missing dimension 0.40. Examine the placement of dimensions and relocate where necessary. Change 1.12 to 1.25 and add the difference to dimension 4.70.

Prob. 2.12 Using a CAD system, determine the true length of lines AD and CD (Fig. 2.48) when the horizontal projection of point A is relocated to a new coordinate reading of (0, 3.125) and the horizontal projection of point D is relocated to a Cartesian coordinate of (1.75, 1.625). Revise the drawing using the "F" notation for the frontal projections instead of the V notation, as shown. What is the new slope of line CD?

FIGURE 2.45

FIGURE 2.46

FIGURE 2.47

FIGURE 2.48

C H A P T E R 3

INSTRUMENT DRAWING, FREEHAND SKETCHING, AND LETTERING TECHNIQUES

OBJECTIVES

After studying the material in this chapter, you should be able to:

1. Identify the basic tools used by the drafter.
2. List the four objectives of drafting.
3. Describe the difference between the T-square, parallel rule, and drawing machine.
4. Identify various types of lines and how they are used.
5. Draw lines, arcs, and circles of specific size using drawing instruments.
6. Draw lines at specific angles.
7. Read and measure with the architect's scale, engineer's scale, and metric scale.
8. Draw irregular curves.
9. Identify several drawing media and standard sheet sizes.
10. Create freehand sketches using the correct sketching techniques.
11. Sketch parallel, perpendicular, and evenly spaced lines.
12. Sketch a circle and an arc of a given diameter.
13. Use techniques to keep your sketch proportionate.
14. Enlarge an object using grid paper.
15. Sketch various line types.
16. Add lettering to a sketch.

OVERVIEW

The traditional method of creating technical drawings is with drawing instruments. Since the eighteenth century, precision instruments have been the tools of drafters. Today, CAD software is another tool used by many drafters. The basic concepts of drawing and measuring lines and circles is the same for traditional and CAD drawing. The alphabet of lines and the meaning of line types is the same for traditional and CAD drawings. By understanding the basic principles of drawing, the properly trained drafter can create and modify any type of drawing. While some students may think that CAD software can replace the knowledge required to construct a drawing, this is not so. While CAD makes drawing easier, it does not replace the basic knowledge that enables a skilled drafter to manipulate either a pencil or CAD software.

Sketching technique is one of the most important skills for engineering visualization. Sketching is a quick way to communicate ideas with other members of the design team. A picture is often worth a thousand words (or 1K words, as it were). Sketching is a time-efficient way to plan out the drawing processes needed to create a complex object. Sketches act like a road map for the completion of a final paper or CAD drawing. When you sketch basic ideas ahead of time, you can often complete a drawing sooner and with fewer errors. Legible hand lettering is used on the sketch to specify important information.

INSTRUMENT DRAWING

■ 3.1   TYPICAL DRAWING EQUIPMENT

For many years the essential equipment for students in technical schools and for engineers and designers in professional practice remained unchanged. This equipment included a drawing board, T-square, triangles, an architects' or engineers' scale, and a professional-quality set of drawing instruments. Now, however, other equipment has come into general use, including the drafting machine, parallel-ruling straightedge, technical fountain pen, and, of course, the computer.

The basic items of drawing equipment are shown in Fig. 3.1. For best results, the drawing equipment you use should be of high grade. When you are ready to buy drawing instruments (item 3), you should talk to an experienced drafter or designer, or reliable dealer,

about your purchase because it is difficult for beginners to distinguish high-grade instruments from inferior instruments.

1. Drawing board (approximately 20″ × 24″), drafting table, or desk.
2. T-square (24″, transparent edge), drafting machine, or parallel-ruling edge (§§3.4, 3.51, and 3.52)
3. Set of instruments (§§3.28 and 3.29)
4. 45° triangle (8″ sides) (§3.11)
5. 30° × 60° triangle (10″ long side) (§3.11)
6. Ames Lettering Guide or lettering triangle
7. Architects' triangular scale (§3.24)
8. Engineers' triangular scale (§3.22)
9. Metric triangular scale (§3.20)
10. Irregular curve (§3.48)
11. Protractor (§3.13)
12. Mechanical pencils and/or thin-lead mechanical pencils and HB, F, 2H, and 4H to 6H leads, or drawing pencils (§3.7)
13. Drawing paper, tracing paper, tracing cloth, or films as required; backing sheet (drawing paper white, cream, or light green) to be used under drawings and tracings
14. Drafting tape (§3.6)
15. Templates
16. Calculator
17. Cleansing tissue or dust cloth
18. Eraser

■ 3.2   OBJECTIVES IN DRAWING

The following pages explain the correct methods for instrumental drawing. Students who practice and learn correct manipulation of their drawing instruments will eventually be able to draw correctly by habit and will be able to give their full attention to the problems at hand.

The following are the important objectives students should strive to attain:

1. *Accuracy.* No drawing is of maximum usefulness if it is not accurate. The engineer or designer cannot achieve success in professional employment if the habit of accuracy is not acquired.
2. *Speed.* Time is money in industry, and there is no demand for a slow drafter, technician, or engineer.

FIGURE 3.1   **Principal Items of Equipment.**

However, speed is not attained by hurrying; it is an unsought byproduct of *intelligent and continuous work*. It comes with study and practice

3. *Legibility*. Drafters, technicians, and engineers must remember that a drawing is a means of communication to others, and that it must be clear and legible to serve its purpose well. Care should be given to details, especially to lettering (discussed further at the end of this chapter).

4. *Neatness*. If a drawing is to be accurate and legible, it must also be clean. Untidy drawings are the result of sloppy and careless methods and will be unacceptable to an instructor or employer.

■ 3.3 DRAWING BOARDS

If the left edge of the drawing table top has a true straightedge and if the surface is hard and smooth (such as Masonite™), a drawing board is unnecessary,

provided that drafting tape is used to fasten the drawings. It is recommended that a backing sheet of heavy drawing paper be placed between the drawing and the table top.

In most cases a drawing board will be needed. Boards vary from 9″ × 12″ (for sketching and field work) up to 48″ × 72″ or larger. The recommended size for students is 20″ × 24″, which will accommodate the largest sheet likely to be used.

Drafters using drafting tape to hold paper in place, which in turn permits surfaces such as hardwood or other materials to be used for drawing boards.

For right-handed people, the left-hand edge of the board is the *working edge* because the T-square head slides against it (Fig. 3.2). (*Left-handers*: Place the head of the T-square on the right.) This edge must be straight, and you should test the edge with a T-square blade that has been tested and found straight (Fig. 3.3). If the edge of the board is not true, it should be replaced.

FIGURE 3.2 **The T-square.**

FIGURE 3.3 **Testing the Working Edge of the Drawing Board.**

■ 3.4 T-SQUARES

The T-square is made of a long strip, called the *blade*, fastened rigidly at right angles to a shorter piece called the *head* (Fig. 3.2). The upper edge of the blade and the inner edge of the head are *working edges* and must be straight. The working edge of the head must not be convex, or the T-square will rock when the head is placed against the board. The blade should have transparent plastic edges and should be free of nicks along the working edge. Transparent edges are recommended, because they allow the drafter to see the drawing in the vicinity of the lines being drawn.

Do not use the T-square for any rough purpose. Never cut paper along its working edge, as the plastic is easily cut and even a slight nick will ruin the T-square.

■ 3.5 TESTING AND CORRECTING T-SQUARES

To test the working edge of the head, see if the T-square rocks when the head is placed against a

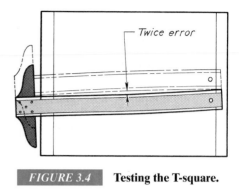

FIGURE 3.4 **Testing the T-square.**

straightedge, such as a drawing board working edge that has already been tested and found true. If the working edge of the head is not straight, the T-square should be replaced.

To test the working edge of the blade, draw a sharp line very carefully with a hard pencil along the entire length of the working edge; then turn the T-square over and draw the line again along the same edge (Fig. 3.4). If the edge is straight, the two lines will coincide; otherwise, the space between the lines will be twice the error of the blade.

It is difficult to correct a crooked T-square blade, and if the error is considerable, it may be necessary to discard the T-square and obtain another.

■ 3.6 FASTENING PAPER TO THE BOARD

The drawing paper should be placed close enough to the working edge of the board to reduce to a minimum any error resulting from a slight "give," or bending, of the blade of the T-square. The paper should also be close enough to the upper edge of the board to permit space at the bottom of the sheet for using the T-square and supporting the arm while drawing (Fig. 3.5).

FIGURE 3.5 **Placing Paper on Drawing Board.**

FIGURE 3.6 Positions of Drafting Tape.

Drafting tape is preferred for fastening the drawing to the board because it does not damage the board and it will not damage the paper if it is removed by *pulling it off slowly toward the edge of the paper.*

To fasten the paper in place, press the T-square head firmly against the working edge of the drawing board with the left hand, while the paper is adjusted with the right hand until the top edge coincides with the upper edge of the T-square. Then move the T-square to the position shown and fasten the upper left corner, then the lower right corner, and finally the remaining corners (Fig. 3.6). Large sheets may require additional fastening, whereas small sheets may require fastening only at the two upper corners.

Tracing paper should not be fastened directly to the board because small imperfections in the surface of the board will interfere with the line work. Always fasten a larger backing sheet of heavy drawing paper on the board first; then fasten the tracing paper over this sheet.

■ 3.7 DRAWING PENCILS

High-quality drawing pencils should be used in technical drawing never ordinary writing pencils (Fig. 3.7a).

Many makes of mechanical pencils are also available, together with refill leads of conventional size in all grades (Fig. 3.7b). Choose a holder that feels comfortable in your hand and that grips the lead firmly without slipping. Mechanical pencils have the advantages of maintaining a constant length of lead while permitting the use of a lead practically to the end, of being easily refilled with new leads, of affording a ready source for compass leads, of having no wood to be sharpened, and of easy sharpening of the lead by various mechanical pencil pointers.

Thin-lead mechanical pencils are available with 0.3-, 0.5-, 0.7-, or 0.9-mm-diameter drafting leads in several grades (Fig. 3.7c). These thin leads produce uniform width lines without sharpening, providing both a time savings and a cost benefit. Mechanical pencils are recommended as they are less expensive in the long run.

Drawing pencils are made of graphite with the addition of either a polymer binder or kaolin (clay) in varying amounts to make 18 grades from 9H, the hardest, to 7B, the softest. The uses of these different grades are described in Fig. 3.8. Note that small-diameter leads are used for the harder grades, whereas large-diameter leads are used to give more strength to the softer grades. Therefore, the degree of hardness in a wood pencil can be roughly judged by a comparison of diameters.

FIGURE 3.7 Drawing Pencils.

SHARP CONICAL POINT
For general line work and lettering
(a)
DRAWING PENCIL
GRADE MARK
2H
Do not sharpen this end!

DRAFTING PENCIL LEADS
Available in all grades
(b)
MECHANICAL PENCIL

Thin leads require no sharpening
0.5mm
(c)
THIN-LEAD MECHANICAL PENCIL

Hard	Medium	Soft
9H 8H 7H 6H 5H 4H	3H 2H H F HB B	2B 3B 4B 5B 6B 7B

Hard

The hard leads in this group (left) are used where extreme accuracy is required, as on graphical computations and charts and diagrams. The softer leads in this group (right) are sometimes used for line work on engineering drawings, but their use is restricted because the lines are apt to be too light.

Medium

These grades are for general purpose work in technical drawing. The softer grades (right) are used for technical sketching, for lettering, arrowheads, and other freehand work on mechanical drawings. The harder leads (left) are used for line work on machine drawings and architectural drawings. The H and 2H leads are widely used on pencil tracings for reproduction.

Soft

These leads are too soft to be useful in mechanical drafting. Their use for such work results in smudged, rough lines that are hard to erase, and the lead must be sharpened continually. These grades are used for art work of various kinds, and for full-size details in architectural drawing.

FIGURE 3.8   **Lead Grade Chart.**

Specifically formulated leads of carbon black particles in a polymer binder are also available in several grades for use on the polyester films now used quite extensively in industry (see §3.56).

In the selection of a grade of lead, the first consideration is the type of line work required. For light construction lines, guide lines for lettering, and accurate geometrical constructions or work in which accuracy is of prime importance, use a hard lead, such as 4H to 6H.

For mechanical drawings on drawing paper or tracing paper, the lines should be **black**, particularly for drawings to be reproduced. The lead chosen must be soft enough to produce jet black lines, but hard enough not to smudge too easily or permit the point to crumble under normal pressure. The same comparatively soft lead is preferred for lettering and arrowheads.

This lead will vary from F to 2H, depending on the paper and weather conditions. If the paper is hard, it will generally be necessary to use harder leads. For softer surfaces, softer leads can be used. On humid days, paper absorbs moisture from the atmosphere and becomes soft. This can be recognized because the paper expands and becomes wrinkled. It is necessary to select softer leads to offset the softening of the paper. If you have been using a 2H lead, for example, change to an F until the weather becomes drier.

■ 3.8 ALPHABET OF LINES

Each line on a technical drawing has a definite meaning and is drawn in a certain way. The line conventions endorsed by the American National Standards Insti-

tute, ANSI Y14.2M–1992, are presented in Fig. 3.9, together with illustrations of various applications.

Two widths of lines are recommended for use on drawings. The ratio of line widths should be approximately two-to-one. It is recommended the thin line width be 0.3 mm minimum, and the thick line width be 0.6 mm minimum. All required lines should be clean-cut, dark, uniform throughout the drawing, and properly spaced for legible reproduction by all commonly used methods. Spacing between parallel lines may be exaggerated to a maximum of 3 mm .120 so there is no fill-in when the drawing is reproduced. The size and style of the drawing and the smallest size to which it is to be reduced govern the actual width of each line. The contrast between the two widths of lines should be distinct. Pencil leads should be hard enough to prevent smudging, but soft enough to produce the dense black lines necessary for quality reproduction.

When photoreduction and blowback are not necessary, as is the case for most drafting laboratory assignments, three weights of lines may improve the appearance and legibility of the drawing. The "thin lines" may be made in two widths regular thin lines for hidden lines, and stitch lines, and a somewhat thinner version for the other secondary lines (such as center lines, extension lines, dimension lines, leaders, section lines, phantom lines, and long-break lines).

For the "thick lines" visible, cutting plane, and short break use a relatively soft lead, such as F or H. All thin lines should be made with a sharp medium-grade lead, such as H or 2H. All lines (except construction lines) must be *sharp* and *dark*. Make construction

Visible line — THICK — Approx. width 0.6 mm (.024")

Hidden line — 0.8 mm(.03") — THIN — 3.2 mm (.12") — Approx. width 0.3 mm (0.12")

Section line — THIN

Center line — 19 – 38 mm (.75 – 1.50") — 3.2 mm(.12") — 1.6 mm(.06") — THIN

Dimension line, Extension line, Leaders — 90.5 THIN — Extension Line — Dimension Line — 86

Cutting-plane or Viewing-plane lines — 1.6 mm(.06") — THICK — 6.4 mm(.25") — 3.2 mm(.12") — 1.6 mm(.06") — THICK — 19 – 38 mm (.75 – 1.50")

Short-break line — THICK — Freehand

Long-break line — THIN — 19 – 38 mm (.75 – 1.50") — Freehand

Phantom line — 3.2 mm(.12") — 1.6 mm(.06") — THIN — 19 – 38 mm (.75 – 1.50")

Stitch lines — THIN — 1.6 mm(.06") — 1.6 mm(.06") — Width 0.38 - 0.55 mm (.015 - .022") — THIN — 1.6 mm (.06")

Chain line — THICK — 10 – 20mm (.38 - .75") — 1.6mm (.06") — 1.6mm (.06")

FIGURE 3.9 **Alphabet of Lines (Full Size).**

lines with a sharp 4H or 6H lead so thin that they can barely be seen at arm's length and need not be erased.

In Fig. 3.9, the ideal lengths of all dashes are indicated. You would do well to measure the first few hidden dashes and center-line dashes you make and thereafter to estimate the lengths carefully by eye. The line gage (Fig. 3.10) is a convenient reference for lines of various widths.

.005 in.	.007 in.	.010 in.	.012 in.	.014 in.	.020 in.	.024 in.	.028 in.	.031 in.	.039 in.	.047 in.	.055 in.	.079 in.
.13 mm	.18 mm	.25 mm	.30 mm	.35 mm	.50 mm	.60 mm	.70 mm	.80 mm	1.00 mm	1.20 mm	1.40 mm	2.00 mm

FIGURE 3.10 **Line Gage.** *Courtesy of Koh-I-Noor Rapidograph, Inc.*

■ 3.9 DRAWING HORIZONTAL LINES

To draw a horizontal line, press the head of the T-square firmly against the working edge of the board with your left hand; then slide your hand to the position shown in Fig. 3.11a so that the blade is pressed tightly against the paper. Lean the pencil in the direction of the line at an angle of approximately 60° with the paper, and draw the line from left to right (Fig. 3.11b). Keep the pencil in a vertical plane; otherwise, the line may not be straight (Fig. 3.11c). While drawing the line, let the little finger of the hand holding the pencil glide lightly on the blade of the T-square, and rotate the pencil slowly, except for the thin-lead pencils, between your thumb and forefinger to distribute the wear uniformly on the lead and maintain a symmetrical point. Thin-lead pencils should be held nearly vertical to the paper and not rotated. Also, pushing the thin-lead pencil from left to right, rather than pulling it, tends to minimize lead breakage.

When great accuracy is required, the pencil may be "toed in" to produce a perfectly straight line (Fig. 3.11d). *Left-handers*: In general, reverse the procedure just outlined. Place the T-square head against the right

edge of the board, and with the pencil in the left hand, draw the line from right to left.

■ 3.10 DRAWING VERTICAL LINES

Use either the 45° triangle or the 30° × 60° triangle to draw vertical lines. Place the triangle on the T-square with the *vertical edge on the left*, as shown in Fig. 3.12a. With the left hand, press the head of the T-square against the board; then slide the hand to the position shown where it holds both the T-square and the triangle firmly in position. Draw the line upward, rotating the pencil slowly between the thumb and forefinger. (The only time it is advisable for right-handers to turn the triangle so that the vertical edge is on the right is when drawing a vertical line near the right end of the T-square. In this case, the line would be drawn downward.)

Lean the pencil in the direction of the line at an angle of approximately 608 with the paper and in a vertical plane (Fig. 3.12b). Meanwhile, the upper part of the body should be twisted to the right (Fig. 3.12c). (*Left-handers*: In general, reverse the foregoing procedure. Place the T-square head on the right and the ver-

FIGURE 3.11   **Drawing a Horizontal Line.**

Pencil approx
60° to paper

Rotate pencil
slowly

(a)

Pencil

60°

(b)

HORIZONTAL LINES

90°

NORMAL
POSITION

Small space

(c)

POSITION
FOR
MORE
ACCURACY

No space

(d)

FIGURE 3.12   **Drawing a Vertical Line.**

tical edge of the triangle on the right; then, with the right hand, hold the T-square and triangle firmly together, and with the left hand draw the line upward.)

■3.11 TRIANGLES

Most inclined lines in mechanical drawing are drawn at standard angles with the *45° triangle* and the *30° × 60° triangle* (Fig. 3.13). The triangles are made of transparent plastic so that lines of the drawing can be seen through them. A good combination of triangles is the 30° × 60° triangle with a long side of 10″ and a 45° triangle with each side 8″ long.

FIGURE 3.13   **Triangles.**

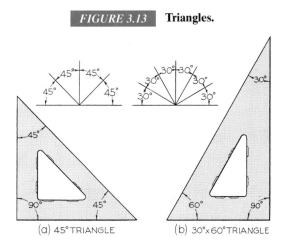

(a) 45°TRIANGLE   (b) 30°x60°TRIANGLE

■3.12 DRAWING INCLINED LINES

The positions of the triangles for drawing lines at all of the possible angles are shown in Fig. 3.14. In the figure it is understood that the triangles in each case are resting on the blade of the T-square. Thus, it is possible to divide 360° into twenty-four 15° sectors with the triangles used singly or in combination. Note carefully the directions for drawing the lines, as indicated by the arrows, and that all lines in the left half are drawn *toward the center*, while those in the right half are drawn *away from the center*.

■3.13 PROTRACTORS

For measuring or setting off angles other than those obtainable with the triangles, the *protractor* is used. The best protractors, which produce the most accurate measurements, are made of nickel silver (Fig. 3.15a). For ordinary work, a plastic protractor is satisfactory and much cheaper (Fig. 3.15b). To set off angles with greater accuracy, use one of the methods presented in §4.19.

■3.14 DRAFTING ANGLES

There are a variety of devices that combine the protractor with triangles to produce great versatility of use. One such device is shown in Fig. 3.16.

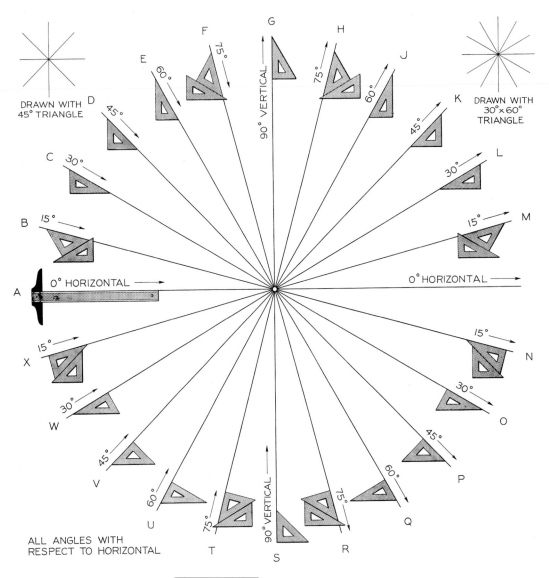

DRAWN WITH
45° TRIANGLE

DRAWN WITH
30° × 60°
TRIANGLE

90° VERTICAL

0° HORIZONTAL

0° HORIZONTAL

90° VERTICAL

ALL ANGLES WITH
RESPECT TO HORIZONTAL

FIGURE 3.14   The Triangle Wheel.

Vernier

25°6'

(a)

33°

(b)

FIGURE 3.15   Protractors.

FIGURE 3.16 Adjustable Triangle.

FIGURE 3.17 To Draw a Pencil Line Through Two Points.

■3.15 DRAWING A LINE THROUGH TWO POINTS

To draw a line through two points, place the pencil vertically at one of the points (Fig. 3.17), and move the straightedge about the pencil point as a pivot until it lines up with the other point; then draw the line along the edge.

■3.16 DRAWING PARALLEL LINES

To draw a line parallel to a given line, move the triangle and T-square as a unit until the hypotenuse of the triangle lines up with the given line (Fig. 3.18a); then,

holding the T-square firmly in position, slide the triangle away from the line, and draw the required line along the hypotenuse (Figs. 3.18b and 3.18c).

Obviously, any straightedge, such as one of the triangles, may be substituted for the T-square in this operation, as shown in Fig. 3.18a.

■3.17 DRAWING PERPENDICULAR LINES

To draw a line perpendicular to a given line, move the T-square and triangle as a unit until one edge of the triangle lines up with the given line (Fig. 3.19a); then slide the triangle across the line and draws the required line (Figs. 3.19b and 3.19c).

FIGURE 3.18 To Draw a Line Parallel to a Given Line.

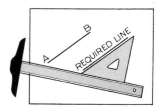

(a) MOVE T-SQUARE AND TRIANGLE TO LINE UP WITH AB

(b) SLIDE TRIANGLE ALONG T-SQUARE

(c) DRAW REQUIRED LINE PARALLEL TO AB

FIGURE 3.19 To Draw a Line Perpendicular to a Given Line.

(a) MOVE T-SQUARE AND TRIANGLE TO LINE UP WITH AB

(b) SLIDE TRIANGLE ALONG T-SQUARE

(c) DRAW REQUIRED LINE PERPENDICULAR TO AB

FIGURE 3.20   **Perpendicular Lines.**

To draw perpendicular lines when one of the lines makes 15° with horizontal, arrange the triangles as shown in Fig. 3.20.

■ 3.18 DRAWING LINES AT 30°, 60°, OR 45° WITH A GIVEN LINE

To draw a line making 30° with a given line, arrange the triangle as shown in Fig. 3.21. Angles of 60° and 45° may be drawn in a similar manner.

■ 3.19 SCALES

A drawing of an object may be the same size as the object (full size), or it may be larger or smaller than the object. The ratio of reduction or enlargement depends on the relative sizes of the object and of the sheet of paper on which the drawing is to be made. For example, a machine part may be half size; a building may be drawn size; a map may be drawn size; or a printed circuit board, may be drawn four times its size (Fig. 3.22).

Scales are instruments used in making technical drawings full size at a given enlargement or reduction. Figure 3.23 shows various types of scales, including (a) the *metric scale*, (b) the *engineers' scale*, (c) the *decimal scale*, (d) the *mechanical engineers' scale*, and (e) the *architects' scale*. A full-divided scale is one in which

FIGURE 3.21   **Line at 30° with Given Line.**

FIGURE 3.22   **Printed Circuit Board.** *United Nations/Guthrie.*

the basic units are subdivided throughout the length of the scale. The architects' scale is an open divided scale, one in which only the end unit is subdivided.

Scales are usually made of plastic or boxwood. The better wood scales have white plastic edges. Scales are either triangular or flat. The triangular scales have the advantage of combining many scales on one stick, but the user will waste much time looking for the required scale if a *scale guard* (Fig. 3.24) is not used. The scale guard marks the scale that is being used. Flat scales are almost universally used by professional drafters because of their convenience, but several flat scales are necessary to replace one triangular scale, and the total cost is greater.

■ 3.20 METRIC SYSTEM AND METRIC SCALES

The metric system is an international standard of measurement that, despite modifications over the past 200 years, has been the foundation of science and industry and is clearly defined. The modern form of the metric system is the International System of Units, commonly referred to as SI (from the French name, Le Système International d'Unités). The SI system was established in 1960 by international agreement and is now the international standard of measurement.

The metric scale is used when the meter is the standard for linear measurement. The meter was

(a) Metric Scale

(b) Engineers' Scale

(c) Decimal Scale

(d) Mechanical Engineers' Scale

(e) Architects' Scale

FIGURE 3.23   **Types of Scales.**

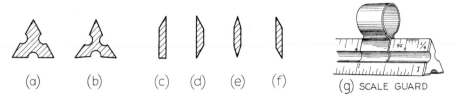

(a)   (b)   (c) (d) (e)   (f)   (g) SCALE GUARD

FIGURE 3.24   **Scale Guard.**

established by the French in 1791 with a length of one ten-millionth of the distance from the Earth's equator to the pole. The meter is equal to 39.37 inches or approximately 1.1 yards.

The metric system for linear measurement is a decimal system similar to our system of counting money. For example,

$$
\begin{aligned}
1 \text{ mm} &= 1 \text{ millimeter} \left(\tfrac{1}{1000} \text{ of a meter}\right) \\
1 \text{ cm} &= 1 \text{ centimeter} \left(\tfrac{1}{100} \text{ of a meter}\right) \\
&= 10 \text{ mm} \\
1 \text{ dm} &= 1 \text{ decimeter} \left(\tfrac{1}{10} \text{ of a meter}\right) \\
&= 10 \text{ cm} = 100 \text{ mm} \\
1 \text{ m} &= 1 \text{ meter} \\
&= 100 \text{ cm} = 1000 \text{ mm} \\
1 \text{ km} &= 1 \text{ kilometer} = 1000 \text{ m} \\
&= 100{,}000 \text{ cm} = 1{,}000{,}000 \text{ mm}
\end{aligned}
$$

The primary unit of measurement for engineering drawings and design in the mechanical industries is the millimeter (mm). Secondary units of measure are the meter (m) and the kilometer (km). The centimeter (cm) and the decimeter (dm) are rarely used.

In recent years, automotive and other industries have used a dual dimensioning system of millimeters and inches. Manufacturers of large agricultural machinery use all metric dimensions with the inch equivalents given in a table on the drawing.

Many of the dimensions in the illustrations and the problems in this text are given in metric units. Dimensions that are given in the customary units (inches and feet, either decimal or fractional) may be converted easily to metric values. In accordance with standard practice, the ratio 1 in. = 25.4 mm is used. Decimal equivalents tables can be found inside the front cover, and conversion tables are given in Appendix 31.

Metric scales are available in flat and triangular styles with a variety of scale graduations. The triangular scale illustrated in Fig. 3.35 has one full-size scale and five reduced-size scales, all full divided. By means of these scales a drawing can be made full size, enlarged sized, or reduced sized. To specify the scale on a drawing see §3.26.

FULL SIZE   The 1:1 scale (Fig. 3.25a) is full size, and each division is actually 1 mm in width with the numbering of the calibrations at 10-mm intervals. The same scale is also convenient for ratios of 1:10, 1:100, 1:1000, and so on.

HALF SIZE   The 1:2 scale (Fig. 3.25a) is one-half size, and each division equals 2 mm with the calibration numbering at 20-unit intervals. This scale is also convenient for ratios of 1:20, 1:200, 1:2000, and so on.

The remaining four scales on this triangular metric scale include the typical scale ratios of 1:5, 1:25, 1:33⅓, and 1:75 (Figs. 3.25a and 3.25b). These ratios may also be enlarged or reduced as desired by multiplying or dividing by a factor of 10. Metric scales are

FIGURE 3.25   **Decimal Dimensions.**

(a) FULL SIZE

(b) HALF SIZE

(c) FULL SIZE

also available with other scale ratios for specific drawing purposes.

The metric scale is used in map drawing and in drawing force diagrams or other graphical constructions that involve such scales as 1 mm = 1 kg and 1 mm = 500 kg.

■ 3.21 INCH-FOOT SCALES

Several scales that are based on the inch-foot system of measurement continue in domestic use today along with the metric system of measurement, which is accepted worldwide for science, technology, and international trade.

■ 3.22 ENGINEERS' SCALES

The *engineers' scale* is graduated in the decimal system. It is also frequently called the *civil engineers' scale* because it was originally used mainly in civil engineering. The name *chain scale* also persists because it was derived from the surveyors' chain composed of 100 links, used for land measurements.

The engineers' scale is graduated in units of 1 in. divided into 10, 20, 30, 40, 50, and 60 parts. Thus, the engineers' scale is convenient in machine drawing to set off dimensions expressed in decimals. For example, to set off 1.650″ full size, use the 10-scale and simply set off one main division plus $6\frac{1}{2}$ subdivisions (Fig. 3.26a).

FIGURE 3.26   **Metric Scales.**

To set off the same dimension half size, use the 20-scale, since the 20-scale is exactly half the size of the 10-scale (Fig. 3.26b). Similarly, to set off a dimension quarter size, use the 40-scale.

The engineers' scale is also used in drawing maps to scales of $1'' = 50'$, $1'' = 500'$, $1'' = 5$ miles, and so on and in drawing stress diagrams or other graphical constructions to such scales as $1'' = 20$ lb and $1'' = 4000$ lb.

■ 3.23 DECIMAL SCALES

The increasing use of decimal dimensions has brought about the development of a scale specifically for that use. On the full-size scale, each inch is divided into fiftieths of an inch, or $.02''$ (Fig. 3.26c), and on the half- and quarter-size scales, the inches are compressed to half size or quarter size and then are divided into 10 parts, so that each subdivision stands for $.1''$.

The complete decimal system of dimensioning in which this scale is used is described in §12.10.

■ 3.24 ARCHITECTS' SCALES

The *architects' scale* is intended primarily for drawings of buildings, piping systems, and other large structures that must be drawn to a reduced scale to fit on a sheet of paper. The full-size scale is also useful in drawing relatively small objects, and for that reason the architects' scale has rather general usage.

The architects' scale has one full-size scale and ten overlapping reduced-sized scales. By means of these scales a drawing may be made to various sizes from full size to $\frac{1}{128}$ size. Note that, in all the reduced scales the major divisions represent feet, and their subdivisions represent inches and fractions thereof. Thus, the scale marked $\frac{3}{4}$ means $\frac{3}{4}$ inch = 1 foot, not $\frac{3}{4}$ inch = 1 inch; that is, one-sixteenth size, not three-fourths size. And the scale marked $\frac{1}{2}$ means $\frac{1}{2}$ inch + 1 foot, not $\frac{1}{2}$ inch = 1 inch, (that is, one twenty-fourth-size, not half size).

All the scales, from full size to $\frac{1}{128}$ size, are shown in Fig. 3.27. Some are upside down, just as they may occur in use. These scales are described as follows.

FULL SIZE Each division in the full-size scale is 0 (Fig. 3.27a). Each inch is divided first into halves, then quarters, eighths, and finally sixteenths, the dividing lines diminishing in length with each subdivision. To set off $\frac{1}{32}''$, estimate visually one half of $\frac{1}{16}''$; to set off $\frac{1}{64}''$, estimate one fourth of $\frac{1}{16}''$.

HALF SIZE Use the full-size scale, and divide every dimension mentally by two. (Do not use the $\frac{1}{2}''$ scale, which is intended for drawing to a scale of $\frac{1}{2}'' = 1'$, or one-twenty-fourth size.) To set off $1''$, measure $\frac{1}{4}''$; to set off $2''$, measure $1''$; to set off $\frac{6.5}{16}''$, measure $1\frac{1}{2}$ (half of $30''$), then $\frac{1}{8}''$ (half of $\frac{1}{4}''$); to set off $2\text{-}\frac{13}{16}''$ (see Fig. 3.27), measure $1''$ then $\frac{13}{32}''$ ($\frac{6.5}{16}''$ or half of $\frac{13}{16}''$).

QUARTER SIZE Use the $3''$ scale in which $3'' = 1'$ (Fig. 3.27b). The subdivided portion to the left of zero, which represents 1 foot, is divided into inches, half inches, quarter inches, and eighth inches. The entire portion representing 1 foot actually measures 3 inches; therefore, $3'' = 1'$. To set off anything less than $12''$, start at zero and measure to the left.

To set off $10\frac{1}{8}''$, read off $9''$ from zero to the left and add $1\frac{1}{8}''$ and set off the total $10\frac{1}{8}''$, as shown. To set off more than $12''$ for example, $1'\text{-}\frac{9}{38}''$ (see your scale) find the $1'$ mark to the right of zero and the $9\frac{3}{8}''$ mark to the left of zero; the required distance is the distance between these marks and represents $1'\text{-}9\frac{3}{8}''$.

EIGHT SIZE Use the $1\frac{1}{2}''$ scale in which $1\frac{1}{2}'' = 1'$ (Fig. 3.27b). The subdivided portion of the right of zero represents $1'$ and is divided into inches, then half inches, and finally quarter inches. The entire portion, representing $1'$, actually is $1\frac{1}{2}''$; therefore, $1\frac{1}{2}'' = 1'$. To set off anything less than $12''$, start at zero and measure to the right.

DOUBLE SIZE Use the full-size scale, and multiply every dimension mentally by 2. To set off $1''$, measure $2''$; to set off $3\frac{1}{4}''$, measure $6\frac{1}{2}''$; and so on. The double-size scale is occasionally used to represent small objects. In such cases, a small actual-size outline view may be shown near the bottom of the sheet to help the shop worker visualized the actual size of the object.

OTHER SIZE The scales besides those just described are used chiefly by architects. Machine drawings are customarily made only double size, full size, half size, one-fourth size, or one-eighth size.

■ 3.25 MECHANICAL ENGINEERS' SCALES

The objects represented in machine drawing vary in size from small parts, an inch or smaller in size, to equipment or parts of large dimensions. By drawing these objects full size, half size, quarter size, or eighth size, the drawings will readily come within the limits of

FIGURE 3.27   **Architects' Scales.**

the standard-size sheets. For this reason the mechanical engineers' scales are divided into units representing inches to full size, half size, quarter size, or eighth size (Fig. 3.27c). To make a drawing of an object to a scale of one-half size, for example, use the mechanical engineer's scale marked half size, which is graduated so that every $\frac{1}{2}''$ represents $1''$. Thus, the half-size scale is simply a full-size scale compressed to one-half size.

These scales are also very useful in dividing dimensions. For example, to draw a $3\frac{11}{16}''$ diameter circle full size, we need half of $3\frac{11}{16}''$ to use as radius. Instead of using arithmetic to find half of $3\frac{11}{16}''$, it is easier to set off $3\frac{11}{16}''$ on the half-size scale.

Triangular combination scales are available that include the full- and half-size mechanical engineers' scales, several architects' scales, and an engineer's scale.

■ 3.26 SPECIFYING THE SCALE ON A DRAWING

For machine drawings, the scale indicates the ratio of the size of the drawn object to its actual size, irrespective of the unit of measurement used. The recommended practice is to letter FULL SIZE or 1:1; HALF SIZE or 1:2; and similarly for other reductions. Expansion or enlargement scales are given as 2:1 or 2:3; 3:1 or 3:3; 5:1 or 5:3; 10:1 or 10 3; and so on.

The various scale calibrations available on the metric scale and the engineers' scale provide almost unlimited scale ratios. The preferred metric scale ratios appear to be 1:1; 1:2; 1:5, 1:10, 1:20, 1:50, 1:100, and 1:200.

Map scales are indicated in terms of fractions, such as Scale $\frac{1}{62500}$, or graphically, such as

400   0   400   800 Ft

■ 3.27 ACCURATE MEASUREMENTS

Accurate drafting depends considerably on the correct use of the scale in setting off distances. Do not take measurements directly off the scale with the dividers or compass, as damage will result to the scale. Place the scale on the drawing with the edge parallel to the line on which the measurement is to be made and, with a sharp pencil having a conical point, make a short dash at right angles to the scale and opposite the correct graduation mark, as shown in Fig. 3.28a. If extreme accuracy is required, a tiny prick mark may be made at the required point with the needle point or stylus, (Fig. 3.28b),or with one leg of the dividers.

Avoid cumulative errors in the use of the scale. If a number of distances are to be set off end-to-end, all should be set off at one setting of the scale by adding each successive measurement to the preceding one, if possible. Avoid setting off the distances individually by moving the scale to a new position each time, since slight errors in the measurements may accumulate and give rise to a large error.

■ 3.28 DRAWING INSTRUMENTS

In technical drawing, accuracy, neatness, and speed are essential, §3.2. These objectives are not likely to be obtained with cheap or inferior drawing instruments. For the student or the professional drafter, it is advisable, and in the end more economical, to purchase the best instruments that can be afforded. Good instruments will satisfy the most rigid requirements, and the satisfaction, saving in time, and improved quality of work that good instruments can produce will more than justify the higher price.

Unfortunately, the qualities of high-grade instruments are not likely to be recognized by the beginner, who is not familiar with the performance characteristics required and who is apt to be attracted by elaborate sets containing a large number of shiny, low-quality instruments. Therefore, the student should obtain the advice of the drafting instructor, an experienced drafter, or a reliable dealer.

■ 3.29 GIANT BOW SETS

Giant bow sets contain various combinations of instruments, but all feature a large bow compass in place of the traditional large compass (Fig. 3.29). Most of the large bows are of the center-wheel type (Fig. 3.30a). Several manufacturers now offer different varieties of quick-acting bows. The large bow compass shown at (b) can be adjusted to the approximate setting by sim-

FIGURE 3.28   **Accurate Measurements.**

(a)   (b)

FIGURE 3.29 **Giant Bow Set.** *Courtesy of Frank Oppenheimer.*

ply opening or closing the legs in the same manner as for the other bow-style compass.

3.30 COMPASSES

The compass, with pencil and inking attachments, is used for drawing circles of approximately 25 mm (10) radius or larger.

The giant bow compass (Figs. 3.29–3.31) has a socket joint in one leg that permits the insertion of either pencil or pen attachments. A *lengthening bar* or a *beam attachment* is often provided to increase the radius. Most of the large bows are of the center-wheel type (Fig. 3.30a). Several manufacturers now offer different varieties of quick-acting bows. The large bow compass shown in Fig. 3.30b can be adjusted to the approximate setting by simply opening or closing the legs in the same manner as for the other bow-style compass. For production drafting, in which it is necessary to make dense black lines to secure clear legible reproductions, the giant bow or an appropriate template is preferred. The large bow instrument is much sturdier than the traditional compass and is capable of taking the heavy pressure necessary to produce dense black lines without losing the setting.

3.31 USING COMPASSES

The following instructions apply generally both to old style and giant bow compasses.

FIGURE 3.31 **Using the Giant Bow Compass.**

Most compass needle points have a plain end for use when the compass is converted into dividers and a shoulder end for use as a compass. Adjust the needle point with the shoulder end out and so that the small point extends *slightly* farther than the pencil lead or pen nib (Fig. 3.33d).

To draw a penciled circle, (1) set off the required radius on one of the center lines, (2) place the needle point at the exact intersection of the center lines, (3) adjust the compass to the required radius (25 mm or more), and (4) lean the compass forward and draw the circle clockwise while rotating the handle between the thumb and forefinger. To obtain sufficient weight of line, it may be necessary to repeat the movement several times.

Any error in radius will result in a doubled error in diameter; so it is best to draw a trial circle first on scrap paper or on the backing sheet and then check the diameter with the scale.

FIGURE 3.30 **Giant Bow Compass.** *Courtesy of Frank Oppenheimer.*

(a) CENTER-WHEEL

(b) QUICK ACTING

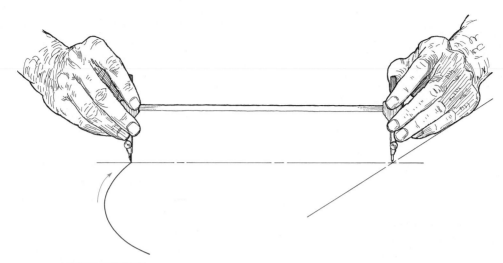

FIGURE 3.32   **Drawing a Circle of Large Radius with the Beam Compass.**

On drawings that have circular arcs and tangent straight lines, draw the acrs first, whether in pencil or in ink, as it is much easier to connect a straight line to an arc than the reverse.

For very large circles, a beam compass (discussed later in this section) is preferred, or use the lengthening bar to increase the compass radius. Use both hands, as shown in Fig. 3.32, but be careful not to jar the instrument and thus change the adjustment.

When using the compass to draw construction lines, use a 4H to 6H lead so that the lines will be very dim. For required lines, the arcs and circles must be black, and softer leads must be used. However, since heavy pressure cannot be exerted on the compass as it can on a pencil, it is usually necessary to use a compass lead that is one or two grades softer than the pencil used for the corresponding line work. For example, if an H lead is used for visible lines drawn with a pencil, then an F lead might be found suitable for the com-

pass work. The hard leads supplied with the compass are usually unsatisfactory for most line work except construction lines. In summary, use leads in the compass that will produce arcs and circles that *match* the straight pencil lines.

It is necessary to exert pressure on the compass to produce heavy "reproducible" circles, and this tends to enlarge the compass center hole in the paper, especially if there are a number of concentric circles. In such cases, use a horn center, or center tack, in the hole, and place the needle point of the compass in the center of the tack.

■ 3.32 SHARPENING THE COMPASS LEAD

Various forms of compass lead points are illustrated in Fig. 3.33. In Fig. 3.33a, a single elliptical face has been formed by rubbing on the sandpaper pad, as shown in Fig. 3.34. In Fig. 3.33b, the point is narrowed by small

FIGURE 3.33   **Compass Lead Points.**

(a)   (b)   (c)   (d)

FIGURE 3.34   **Sharpening Compass Lead.**

side cuts. In Fig. 3.33c, two long cuts and two small side cuts have been made to produce a point similar to that on a screwdriver. In Fig. 3.33d, the cone point is prepared by chucking the lead in a mechanical pencil and shaping it in a pencil pointer. Avoid using leads that are too short to be exposed as shown.

In using the compass, *never use the plain end of the needle point.* Instead, use the shoulder end, as shown in Fig. 3.33d, adjusted so that the tiny needlepoint extends about halfway into the paper when the compass lead just touches the paper.

■ 3.33 BEAM COMPASSES

The beam compass, or trammel (Fig. 3.35), is used for drawing arcs or circles larger than can be drawn with the regular compass and for transferring distances too great for the regular dividers. Besides steel points, pencil and pen attachments are provided. The beams may be made of nickel silver, steel, aluminum, or wood and are procurable in various lengths. A square nickel silver beam compass set is shown in Fig. 3.35a, and a set with the beam graduated in millimeters and inches is shown in Fig. 3.35b.

■ 3.34 DIVIDERS

Dividers, as the name implies, are used for *dividing* distances into a number of equal parts. They are also used for *transferring distances* or for *setting off* a series of equal distances. Dividers are similar to compasses in construction and are made in square, flat, and round forms.

The friction adjustment for the pivot joint should be loose enough to permit easy manipulation with one hand, as shown in Fig. 3.36. If the pivot joint is too tight, the legs of the divider tend to spring back instead of stopping at the desired point when the pressure of the fingers is released. To adjust tension, use a small screwdriver.

Many dividers are made with a spring and thumbscrew in one leg so that minute adjustments in the setting can be made by turning the small thumbscrew.

■ 3.35 USING DIVIDERS

Dividers are used for spaces of approximately 25 mm (10) or more. For spaces less than 25 mm, use the bow dividers (Fig. 3.40a). *Never use the large dividers for small spaces when the bow dividers can be used; the latter are more accurate.*

(a)

(b)

FIGURE 3.35   **Beam Compass Sets.** *(a) Courtesy of Frank Oppenheimer; (b) Courtesy of Tacro, Div. of A&T Importers, Inc.*

FIGURE 3.36　**Adjusting the Dividers.**

Dividing a given distance into a number of equal parts is a matter of trial and error (Fig. 3.36). Adjust the dividers with the fingers of the hand that holds them, to the approximate unit of division, estimated by eye. Rotate the dividers counterclockwise through 180°, and so on, until the desired number of units has been stepped off. If the last prick of the dividers falls short of the end of the line to be divided, increase the distance between the divider points proportionately. For example, to divide the line AB into three equal parts, the dividers are set by eye to approximately one-third the length AB. When it is found that the trial radius is too small, the distance between the divider points is increased by one-third the remaining distance. If the last prick of the dividers is beyond the end of the line, a similar decreasing adjustment is made.

Cumulative errors may result when dividers are used to set off a series of distances end to end. To set off a large number of equal divisions say, 15 first set off three equal large divisions and then divide each of these into five equal parts. Wherever possible in such cases, use the scale instead of the dividers (§3.27), or set off the total and then divide into the parts by means of the parallel-line method (§4.13).

■ 3.36　PROPORTIONAL DIVIDERS

For enlarging or reducing a drawing, proportional dividers are convenient (Fig. 3.38). They may also be

FIGURE 3.37　**Using the Dividers.**

used for dividing distances into a number of equal parts, or for obtaining a percentage reduction of a distance. For this purpose, points of division are marked on the instrument to secure the required subdivisions readily. Some instruments are calibrated to obtain special ratios, such as 1:square root of 2, the diameter of a circle to the side of an equal square, and feet to meters.

■ 3.37　BOW INSTRUMENTS

The bow instruments are classified as the *bow dividers*, *bow pen*, and *bow pencil*. A combination pen and pencil bow, usually with center-wheel adjustment, and separate instruments, with either side-wheel or center-wheel adjustment, are available (Figs. 3.39 and 3.40). The choice is a matter of personal preference.

■ 3.38　USING BOW INSTRUMENTS

Bow pencils and bow pens are used for drawing circles of approximately 25 mm (10) radius or smaller. Bow dividers are used for the same purpose as the large dividers, but they are used for smaller (approximately 25 mm or less) spaces and more accurate work.

Whether a center-wheel or side-wheel instrument is used, the adjustment should be made with the

FIGURE 3.38　**Proportional Dividers.**

FIGURE 3.39 **Combination Pen and Pencil Bow.**
Courtesy of Frank Oppenheimer.

(a)   (b)

FIGURE 3.41 **Using the Bow Instruments.**

BOW DIVIDERS   BOW PEN   BOW PENCIL
(a)   (b)   (c)

FIGURE 3.40 **Bow Instruments with Side Wheel.**

COMPASS LEAD SHARPENED
ON INSIDE
(a)

COMPASS LEAD SHARPENED
ON OUTSIDE
(b)

FIGURE 3.42 **Compass-Lead Points.**

thumb and finger of the hand that holds the instrument (Fig. 3.41a). The instrument is manipulated by twirling the head between the thumb and fingers (Fig. 3.41b).

The lead is sharpened in the same manner as for the large compass except that for small radii, the inclined cut may be turned *inside* if preferred (Fig. 3.42a). For general use, the lead should be turned on to the outside, as shown in Fig. 3.42b. In either case, always keep the compass lead sharpened. *Avoid stubby compass leads*, which cannot be properly sharpened. At least 6 mm (0) of lead should extend from the compass at all times.

In adjusting the needle point of the bow pencil or bow pen, be sure to have the needle extending slightly longer than the pen or the lead (Fig. 3.42b), the same as for the large compass.

In drawing small circles, greater care is necessary in sharpening and adjusting the lead and the needle point, and especially in accurately setting the desired radius. If a 6.35 mm (0) diameter circle is to be drawn, and if the radius is "off" only 0.8 mm (0), the total error on diameter is approximately 25%, which is far too much.

Appropriate templates may also be used for drawing small circles.

■ 3.39 DROP SPRING BOW PENCILS AND PENS

Drop spring bow pencils and pens (Fig. 3.43) are designed for drawing multiple identical small circles, such as drill holes or rivet heads. A central pin is made to move easily up and down through a tube to which the pen or pencil unit is attached. To use the instrument, hold the knurled head of the tube between your thumb and second finger, placing your first finger on top of the knurled head of the pin. Place the point of the pin at the desired center, lower the pen or pencil until it touches the paper, and twirl the instrument clockwise with your thumb and second finger. Then lift the tube independently of the pin, and finally lift the entire instrument.

■ 3.40 TO LAY OUT A SHEET

After the sheet has been attached to the board, as explained in §3.6, proceed as shown in Fig. 3.44 (see also Layout A-2, inside back cover).

1. Using the T-square, draw a horizontal *trim line* near the lower edge of the paper and then, using the triangle, draw a vertical trim line near the left edge of the paper. Both should be *light construction lines*.

2. Place the scale along the lower trim line with the full-size scale up. Draw short and light dashes *perpendicular* to the scale at the required distances (see Fig. 3.28a).

FIGURE 3.43   **Drop Spring Bow Instruments.**

(a) DROP SPRING BOW PENCIL   (b) DROP SPRING BOW PEN

FIGURE 3.44   **To Lay Out a Sheet. Layout A–2; see inside front cover.**

3. Place the scale along the left trim line with the full-size scale to the left, and mark the required distances with short and light dashes perpendicular to the scale.

4. Draw horizontal construction lines with the aid of the T-square through the marks at the left of the sheet.

5. Draw vertical construction lines *from the bottom upward* along the edge of the triangle through the marks at the bottom of the sheet.

6. Retrace the border and the title strip to make them heavier. Notice that the layout is made independently of the edges of the paper.*

■ 3.41 TECHNIQUE OF PENCIL DRAWING

Most commercial drafting is executed in pencil. Most prints or photocopies are made from pencil tracings, and all ink tracings must be preceded by pencil drawings. It should therefore be evident that skill in drafting chiefly implies skill in pencil drawing.

Technique is a style or quality of drawing imparted by the individual drafter to the work. It is characterized by crisp black line work and lettering. Technique in lettering is discussed later in this chapter.

---

*In industrial drafting rooms the sheets are available, cut to standard sizes, with border and title strips already printed. Drafting supply houses can supply such papers, printed to order, to schools for little extra cost.

DARK ACCENTED LINES   The pencil lines of a finished pencil drawing or tracing should be very dark (Fig. 3.45). Dark crisp lines are necessary to give punch or snap to the drawing. (a) The ends of lines should be accented by a little extra pressure on the pencil. (b) Curves should be as dark as other lines. (c) and (d) Hidden-line dashes and center-line dashes should be carefully estimated as to length and spacing and should be of uniform width throughout their length.

Dimension lines, extension lines, section lines, and center lines also should be dark. The difference between these lines and visible lines is mostly in width there is very little difference, if any, in blackness.

A simple way to determine whether your lines on tracing paper or cloth are dense black is to hold the tracing up to the light. Lines that are not opaque black will not print clearly by most reproduction processes.

Construction lines should be made with a sharp, hard lead and *should be so light that need not be erased* when drawing is completed.

CONTRAST IN LINES   Contrast in pencil lines, like that in ink lines, should be mostly in *widths* of the lines, with little if any difference in the degree of darkness (Fig. 3.46). The visible lines should contrast strongly with the thin lines of the drawing. If necessary, draw over a visible line several times to get the desired thickness and darkness. A short retracing stroke backward (to the left), producing a jabbing action, results in a darker line.

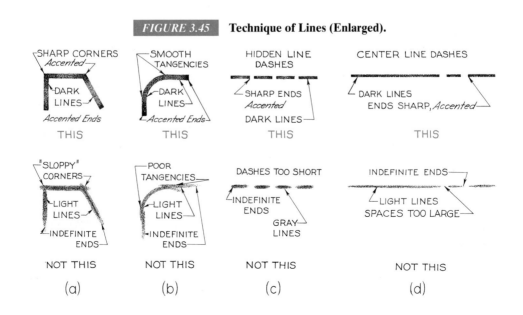

FIGURE 3.45   Technique of Lines (Enlarged).

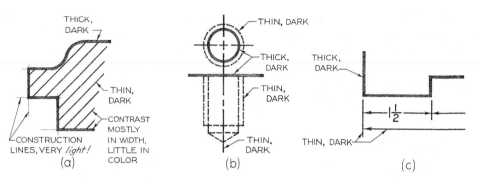

FIGURE 3.46   Contrast of Lines (Enlarged).

■ 3.42 PENCIL TRACING

While some pencil tracings are made of a drawing placed underneath the tracing paper (usually when a great deal of erasing and changing is necessary on the original drawing), most drawings today are made directly in pencil on tracing paper, pencil tracing cloth, films, or vellum. These are not tracings but pencil drawings, and the methods and technique are the same as previously described for pencil drawing.

In making a drawing directly on a tracing medium, a smooth sheet of heavy white drawing paper, a backing sheet, should be placed underneath. The whiteness of the backing sheet improves the visibility of the lines, and the hardness of the surface makes it possible to exert pressure on the pencil and produce dense black lines without excessive grooving of the paper.

All lines must be dark and cleanly drawn when drawings are to be reproduced.

■ 3.43 TECHNICAL FOUNTAIN PENS

Technical fountain pens (Fig. 3.47), with tube and needle point are available in several line widths. Many people prefer this type of pen because the line widths are fixed and it is suitable for freehand or mechanical lettering and line work. The pen requires an occasional filling and a minimum of skill to use. For uniform line work, the pen should be used perpendicular to the paper (Fig. 3.48). For best results, follow the manufacturer's recommendations for operation and cleaning.

FIGURE 3.47   Technical Fountain Pen and Pen Set. *Courtesy of Koh-I-Nor Rapidograph, Inc.*

■3.44 RULING PENS

The ruling pen (Fig. 3.49), is used to ink lines drawn with instruments, never to ink freehand lines or freehand lettering.

Ruling pens should be of the highest quality, with blades of high-grade tempered steel sharpened properly at the factory. The nibs should be sharp, but not sharp enough to cut the paper.

The *detail pen*, capable of holding a considerable quantity of ink, is extremely useful for drawing long heavy lines (Fig. 3.49b). This type of pen is preferred for small amounts of ink work because the pen is easily adjusted for the desired line width and is readily cleaned after use.

■3.45 USING RULING PENS

The ruling pen should lean at an angle of about 60° with the paper in the direction in which the line is being drawn and in a vertical plane containing the line (Fig. 3.50).

(a) FRONT VIEW

FIGURE 3.50   **Position of Hand in Using the Ruling Pen.**

The ruling pen is used in inking irregular curves, as well as straight lines. The pen should be held more nearly vertical when used with an irregular curve than when used with the T-square or a triangle. The ruling pen should lean only slightly in the direction in which the line is being drawn. The proper method for filling ruling pens is shown in Fig. 3.50.

■3.46 DRAWING INK

Drawing ink is composed chiefly of carbon in colloidal suspension and gum. The fine particles of carbon give the deep, black luster to the ink, and the gum makes it waterproof and quick to dry. The ink bottle should not be left uncovered, as evaporation will cause the ink to thicken.

Special drawing ink is available for use on acetate and polyester films. Such inks should not be used in technical fountain pens unless the pens are specifically made for acetate-based inks.

For removing dried waterproof drawing ink from pens or instruments, pen-cleaning fluids are available at dealers.

FIGURE 3.48   **Using the Technical Fountain Pen.**

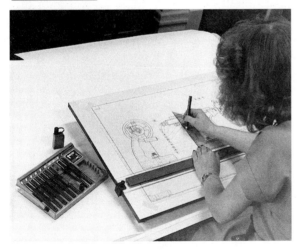

■3.47 TECHNIQUE OF INKING

The various widths of lines used for inked drawings or tracings are shown in Fig. 3.51. In inking a drawing or tracing (Fig. 3.52), proceed in the following order:

1. (a) Mark all tangent points in pencil directly on the drawing or tracing.
   (b) Indent all compass centers (with pricker or divider point).
   (c) Ink visible circles and arcs.
   (d) Ink hidden circles and arcs.
   (e) Ink irregular curves, if any.

FIGURE 3.49   **Ruling Pens.**

(a)

(b)

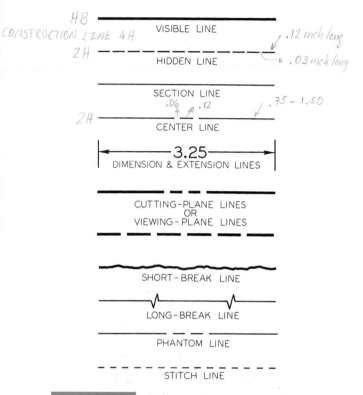

FIGURE 3.51 **Alphabet of Ink Lines (Full Size).**

2. In (a) through (c), ink horizontal lines first, vertical lines second, and inclined lines last:
   (a) Ink invisible straight lines.
   (b) Ink hidden straight lines.
   (c) Ink center lines, extension lines, dimension lines, leader lines, and section lines (if any).

3. (a) Ink arrowheads and dimension figures
   (b) Ink notes titles, etc. (Pencil guide lines directly on the drawing or tracing.)

Some drafters prefer to ink center lines before indenting the compass centers because ink can go through the holes and cause blots on the back of the sheet.

When an ink blot is made, the excess ink should be taken up with a blotter, paper towel or tissue, and not allowed to soak into the paper. When the spot is thoroughly dry, the remaining ink can be erased easily.

For cleaning untidy drawings or for removing the original pencil lines from an inked drawing, a Pink Pearl or the Mars-Plastic eraser is suitable if used lightly.

When a gap in a thick ink line is made by erasing, the gap should be filled in with a series of fine lines

FIGURE 3.52 **Order of Inking.**

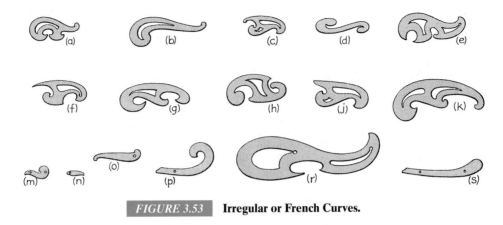

FIGURE 3.53   **Irregular or French Curves.**

that are allowed to run together. A single heavy line is difficult to match and is more likely to run and cause a blot.

■ 3.48 IRREGULAR CURVES

Drawing mechanical curves other than circles or circular arcs generally requires the use of an irregular or French curve. An irregular curve is a device for the *mechanical drawing of curved lines and should not be applied directly to the points* or used for purposes of producing an initial curve. Many different forms and sizes of curves are manufactured (Fig. 3.53).

The curves are composed largely of successive segments of the geometric curves, such as the ellipse, parabola, hyperbola, and involute. The best curves are made of transparent plastic. Among the many special types of curves available are hyperbolas, parabolas, ellipses, logarithmic spirals, ship curves, and railroad curves.

Adjustable curves are also available. Figure 3.54a consists of a core of lead, enclosed by a coil spring attached to a flexible strip. Figure 3.54b consists of a spline to which "ducks" (weights) are attached. The

spline can be bent to form any desired curve, limited only by the elasticity of the material. An ordinary piece of solder wire can be used very successfully by bending the wire to the desired curve.

■ 3.49 USING IRREGULAR CURVES

The proper use of the irregular curve requires skill, especially when the lines are to be drawn in ink (Fig. 3.55). After points have been plotted through which the curve is to pass, a light pencil line should be sketched freehand smoothly through the points.

To draw a mechanical line over the freehand line with an irregular curve, you match the various segments of the irregular curve with successive portions of the freehand curve and draw the line with pencil or ruling pen along the edge of the curve (Fig. 3.56). The irregular curve must match the sketched curve for some distance at each end beyond the segment to be drawn for any one setting of the curve so that successive sections of the curve will be tangent to each other, without any abrupt change in the curvature of the line (Fig. 3.56). In placing the irregular curve, the short-radius end of the curve should be turned toward

FIGURE 3.54   **Adjustable Curves.**

(a)

(b)

FIGURE 3.55   **Using the Irregular Curves.**

FIGURE 3.56   **Settings of Irregular Curve.**

the short-radius part of the curve to be drawn; that is, the portion of the irregular curve used should have the same curvilinear tendency as the portion of the curve to be drawn. This will prevent abrupt changes in direction.

The drafter should change the position of the drawing when necessary to avoid working on the lower side of the curve.

When plotting points to establish the path of a curve, it is desirable to plot more points, and closer together, where sharp turns in the curve occur.

Free curves may also be drawn with the compass, as shown in Fig. 4.42.

For symmetrical curves, such as an ellipse, use the same segment of the irregular curve in two or more opposite places (Fig. 3.57). For example, in Fig. 3.57a the irregular curve is matched to the curve and the line drawn from 1 to 2. Light pencil dashes are then drawn directly on the irregular curve at these points. (The curve will take pencil marks well if it is lightly "frosted" by rubbing with a hard pencil eraser.) In Fig. 3.57b the irregular curve is turned over and matched so that the line may be drawn from 2 to 1. In similar manner, the same segment is used again in Figs. 3.57c and 3.57d. The ellipse is completed by filling in the gaps at the ends by using the irregular curve, or if desired, a compass.

■ **3.50 TEMPLATES**

Templates are available for a great variety of specialized needs (Fig. 3.58). A template may be found for drawing almost any ordinary drafting symbols or repetitive features. The engineers' triangle (Fig. 3.58a) is useful for drawing hexagons or for bolt heads and nuts; the draftsquare (Fig. 3.58b) is convenient for drawing the curves on bolt heads and nuts, for drawing circles, thread forms, and so forth; and the chemistry stencil (Fig. 3.58c) is useful for drawing chemical apparatus in schematic form.

FIGURE 3.57   **Symmetrical Figures.**

FIGURE 3.58   **Templates.**

Ellipse templates (§4.53), are perhaps more widely used than any other type. Circle templates are useful for drawing small circles quickly and for drawing fillets and rounds: such templates are used extensively in tool and die drawings.

■ 3.51 DRAFTING MACHINES

The drafting machine is an ingenious device that replaces the T-square, triangles, scales, and protractor (Figs. 3.59 and 3.60). The links, or bands, are arranged so that the controlling head is always in any desired fixed position regardless of where it is placed on the board; thus, the horizontal straightedge will remain horizontal if so set. The controlling head is graduated in degrees (including a vernier on certain machines), which allows the straightedges, or scales, to be set and locked at any angle. There are automatic stops at the more frequently used angles, such as 15°, 30°, 45°, 60°, 75°, and 90°.

The chief advantage of the drafting machine is that it speeds up drafting. Since its parts are made of metal, their accurate relationships are not subject to change, whereas T-squares, triangles, and working edges of drawing boards must be checked and corrected frequently. Drafting machines for left-handers are available from the manufacturers.

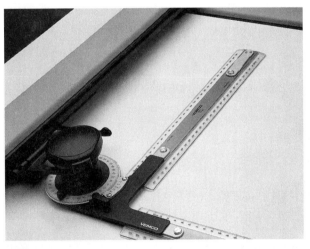

FIGURE 3.59   **Drafting Machine.** *Courtesy of VEMCO Corporation.*

■ 3.52 PARALLEL-RULING STRAIGHTEDGE

For large drawings, the long T-square becomes unwieldy, and considerable inaccuracy may result from the "give" or swing of the blade. In such a case the parallel-ruling straightedge is recommended (Fig. 3.61). The ends of the straightedge are controlled by a system of cords and pulleys that permit the straightedge to be moved up or down on the board while maintaining a horizontal position.

FIGURE 3.60   **Adjustable Drafting Table with Track Drafting Machine.** *Courtesy of Keuffel & Esser Co.*

FIGURE 3.61   **Parallel-Ruling Straightedge.**

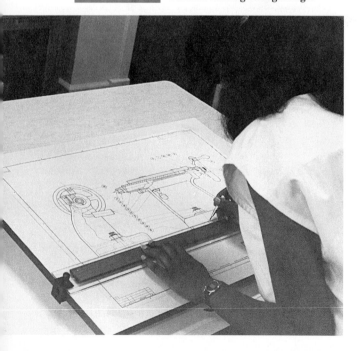

■ 3.53 DRAWING PAPERS

Drawing paper, or *detail paper*, is used whenever a drawing is to be made in pencil but not for reproduction. From working drawings and for general use, the preferred paper is light cream or buff in color, and it is available in rolls of widths 24″ and 36″ and in cut sheets of standard sizes, such as 8.5″ × 11″, 11″ × 17″, 17″ × 22″, and so on. Most industrial drafting rooms use standard sheets with printed borders and title strips (§3.57). Since the cost for printing adds so little to the price per sheet, many schools have also adopted printed sheets.

The best drawing papers have up to 100% pure rag stock; they have strong fibers that afford superior erasing qualities, folding strength, and toughness; and they will not discolor or grow brittle with age. The paper should have a fine grain or tooth that will pick up the graphite and produce clean, dense black lines. However, if the paper is too rough, it will wear down the pencil excessively and will produce ragged, grainy lines. The paper should have a hard surface so that it will not groove too easily when pressure is applied to the pencil.

For ink work, as for catalog and book illustrations, white papers are used. The better papers, such as Bristol Board and Strathmore, come in several thicknesses, such as 2-ply, 3-ply, and 4-ply.

■ 3.54 TRACING PAPERS

Tracing paper is a thin transparent paper on which drawings are made for the purpose of reproducing by blueprinting or by other similar processes. Tracings are usually made in pencil but may also be made in ink. Most tracing papers will take pencil or ink, but some are especially suited to one or to the other.

Tracing papers called *vellums* have been treaded with oils, waxes, or similar substances to render them more transparent; other tracing papers are not so treated, but may be quite transparent due to the high quality of the raw materials and the methods of manufacture. Some treated papers deteriorate rapidly with age, becoming brittle within a few months, but some excellent vellums are available. Untreated papers made entirely of good rag stock will last indefinitely and will remain tough.

■ 3.55 TRACING CLOTH

Tracing cloth is a thin transparent muslin fabric (cotton, not linen as commonly supposed) sizes with a starch compound or plastic to provide a good working surface for pencil or ink. It is much more expensive than tracing paper. Tracing cloth is available in rolls of standard widths, such as 30″, 36″, and 42″, and also in sheets of standard sizes, with or without printed borders and title forms.

For pencil tracings, special pencil tracing cloths are available. Many concerns make their drawings in pencil directly on this cloth, dispensing entirely with the preliminary pencil drawing on detail paper, thus saving a great deal of time. These cloths generally have a surface that will produce dense black lines when hard pencils are used. Hence, these drawings do not easily smudge and will stand up well to handling.

■ 3.56 POLYESTER FILMS AND COATED SHEETS

Polyester film is a superior drafting material available in rolls and sheets of standard size. It is made by bonding a matte surface to one or both sides of a clear polyester sheet. The transparency and printing qualities are very good, the matte drawing surface is excellent for pencil or ink, erasures leave no ghost marks, and the film has high dimensional stability. Its resistance to cracking, bending, and tearing makes it virtually indestructible, if given reasonable care. The film has rapidly replaced cloth and is competing with vellum in some applications. Some companies have found it more economical to make their drawings directly in ink on the film.

Large coated sheets of aluminum (which provides a good dimensional stability) are often used in the aircraft and auto industry for full-scale layouts that are scribed into the coating with a steel point rather than a pencil. The layouts are reproduced from the sheets photographically.

■ 3.57 STANDARD SHEETS

Two systems of sheet sizes, together with length, width, and letter designations, are listed by ANSI, as shown in the accompanying table.

The use of the basic sheet size, 8.5″ × 11.0″ or 210 mm × 297 mm, and multiples thereof permits filing of small tracings and of folded prints in standard files with or without correspondence. These sizes can be cut without waste from the standard rolls of paper, cloth, or film.

For layout designations, title blocks, revision blocks, and a list of materials blocks (see inside the front cover of this book).

Nearest International Size[a] (millimeter)	Standard U.S. Size[a] (inch)
A4 210 × 297	A 8.5 × 11.0
A3 297 × 420	B 11.0 × 17.0
A2 420 × 594	C 17.0 × 22.0
A1 594 × 841	D 22.0 × 34.0
A0 841 × 1189	E 34.0 × 44.0

[a] ANSI Y14.1m-1992.

■ 3.58 THE COMPUTER AS A DRAFTING TOOL

Many of you will be using a CAD system as your drafting tool. Drawings created using a computer are basically the same as drawings created by hand. Accuracy, speed, and the ability to understand spatial and visual information, are equally important in instrumental drawing and in using a CAD system. Drawings created using a CAD system should follow the proper drafting standards so that they can be easily interpreted. Most CAD drawings are plotted on standard sheet sizes and to similar scales as hand prepared instrumental drawings. You still need to master the concepts and standards for orthographic and pictorial projections in order to use a CAD system effectively to create models and drawings.

An advantage of using CAD is that the system contains commands for easily drawing perfectly straight uniform lines and other geometric elements. Also the various styles of lines can be quickly represented by the CAD system (Fig. 3.62). Though it will take you some time to learn the command structure of your CAD system, you would take as long to learn instrumental drawing techniques for preparing neat accurate drawings. Keeping your drawing files organized and following conventions for naming the drawings so that you can find them on the CAD system is also an important consideration. Even when using a CAD system, skill in freehand sketching is still necessary to quickly get your ideas down on paper.

FIGURE 3.62   **A Drawing Created Using CAD.** *Courtesy of Zura Sports, Inc.*

FREEHAND SKETCHING*

■ 3.59 TECHNICAL SKETCHING

Freehand sketches are a helpful way to organize your thoughts and record ideas. They provide a quick, low-cost way to explore various solutions to a problem so that the best choice can be made. Investing too much time in doing a scaled layout before exploring your options through sketches can be a costly mistake. Sketches are also used to clarify information about changes in design or provide information on repairing existing equipment.

The degree of precision needed in a given sketch depends on its use. Quick sketches to supplement verbal descriptions may be rough and incomplete. Sketches that are supposed to convey important and precise information should be drawn as carefully and accurately as possible.

The term freehand sketch does not mean a sloppy drawing. As shown in Figure 3.63, a freehand sketch shows attention to proportion, clarity, and correct line widths.

■ 3.60 SKETCHING MATERIALS

One advantage of freehand sketching is that it requires only pencil, paper, and eraser. Small notebooks or sketch pads are useful in the field (when working at a site) or when an accurate record is needed. Graph paper can be helpful in making neat sketches like the one in Figure 3.64. Paper with 4, 5, 8, or 10 squares per inch is convenient for maintaining correct proportions.

Find a style of pencil that suits your use. Figure 3.7 (see page 47) shows three styles which are all good for preparing sketches. Automatic mechanical pencils (shown as C in the illustration) come in .3-mm, .5-mm, .7-mm, and .9-mm leads that advance automatically and are easy to use. The .5-mm lead is a good general size, or you can use a .7-mm lead for thick lines and .3-mm for thin lines. The lead holder shown as part B requires a special sharpener, so it is not usually suit-

---

* Freehand sketching is discussed again, at length, in detail in Chapter 5 within the discussion on "Technical Sketching Shape Description."

FIGURE 3.63   Great Ideas Often Start as Freehand Sketches Made on Scratch Paper. *Courtesy of ANATech, Inc.*

FIGURE 3.64   **Sketch on Graph Paper.**

able for work in the field. Plain wooden pencils work great. They are inexpensive and make it easy to produce thick or thin lines by the amount you sharpen them.

A sketch pad of plain paper with a master grid sheet showing through underneath works well as a substitute for grid paper. You can create your own master grid sheets for different sketching purposes using CAD. Specially ruled isometric paper is available for isometric sketching.

Figure 3.8 (see page 48) shows the grades of lead and their uses. Use soft pencils, such as HB or F, for freehand sketching. Soft vinyl erasers are recommended.

■3.61 TYPES OF SKETCHES

Technical sketches of 3-D objects are usually one of four standard types of projection, shown in Figure 3.65:

- Multiview projection
- Axonometric (isometric) projection
- Oblique projection
- Perspective sketches

FIGURE 3.65   **Types of Projection.**

(a) MULTI-VIEW   (b) AXONOMETRIC

(c) OBLIQUE   (d) PERSPECTIVE

Multiview projection shows one or more necessary views. You will learn multiview projection in Chapter 6. Axonometric, oblique, and perspective sketches are methods of showing the object pictorially in a single view. They will be discussed in Chapters 16, 17, 18.

■ 3.62 SCALE

Sketches are not usually made to a specific scale. Sketch objects in their correct proportions as accurately as possible by eye. Grid paper helps you sketch the correct proportions by providing a ready-made scale (by counting squares). The size of the sketch is up to you, depending on the complexity of the object and the size of the paper available. Sketch small objects oversize to show the details clearly.

■ 3.63 TECHNIQUE OF LINES

The main difference between an instrument drawing and a freehand sketch is in the style or technique of the lines. A good freehand line is not expected to be precisely straight or exactly uniform, as is a CAD or instrument-drawn line. Freehand lines show freedom and variety. Freehand construction lines are very light, rough lines. All other lines should be dark and clean.

■ 3.64 STYLES OF LINES

Each line on a technical drawing has a definite meaning. Drawings use two different line widths thick and thin and different line styles indicate the meaning of the line. Aperson reading a drawing depends on line styles to communicate whether a line is visible or hidden, if it represents a center axis, or if its purpose is to convey dimension information. Without making these distinctions, drawings would become a confusing jumble of lines. To make your drawings clear and easy to read, make the contrast between the two widths of lines distinct. Thick lines such as visible lines and cutting plane lines should be twice as thick as thin lines. Thin lines are used for construction lines, hidden lines, dimension lines, extension lines, center lines, and phantom lines. Figure 3.9 (see page 49) shows the different styles of lines that you will be using. All lines except for construction lines should be sharp and dark. Construction lines should be very light so that they are not visible (or are barely visible) in the completed drawing. Figures 3.66 and 3.67 show examples of technique for sketching using different line patterns.

■ 3.65 SKETCHING CIRCLES, ARCS, AND ELLIPSES

Small circles and arcs can be sketched in one or two strokes without any preliminary blocking in. Sketching arcs is similar to sketching circles. In general, it is easier to sketch arcs by holding your pencil on the inside of the curve. In sketching arcs, look closely at the actual geometric constructions and carefully approximate all points of tangency so that the arc touches a line or other entity at the right point. Circle templates also make it easy to sketch accurate circles of various sizes.

If a circle is tipped away from your view, it appears as an ellipse. Figure 3.68 shows a coin viewed so

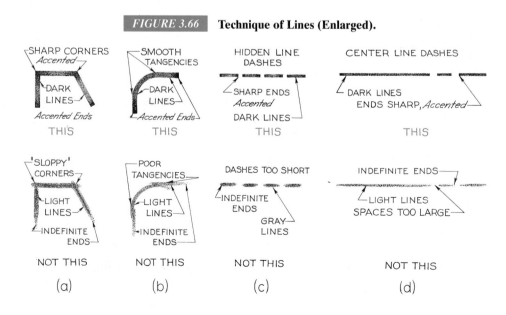

FIGURE 3.66   **Technique of Lines (Enlarged).**

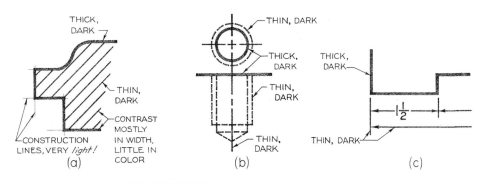

FIGURE 3.67   **Contrast of Lines (Enlarged).**

FIGURE 3.68   **Circle Viewed as an Ellipse.**

that it appears as an ellipse. You can learn to sketch small ellipses with a free arm movement similar to the way you sketch circles, or you can use ellipse templates to help you easily sketch ellipses. These templates are usually grouped according to the amount a circular shape the would be rotated to form the ellipse. They provide a number of sizes of ellipses on each template, but usually only one or a couple typical rotations.

■ 3.66 MAINTAINING PROPORTIONS

The most important rule in freehand sketching is to keep the sketch in proportion. No matter how brilliant the technique or how well-drawn the small details, if the proportions are bad, the sketch will be of little use. To keep your sketch in proportion, first determine the relative proportions of the height to the width and lightly block them in. Then lightly block in the medium-size areas and the small details.

Compare each new estimated distance with already-established distances. One way to estimate dis-

tances is to mark an arbitrary unit on the edge of a card or strip of paper. Then see how many units wide and how many units high the object is.

To sketch an object with many curves to a different scale, use the squares method. On the original picture, rule accurate grid lines to form squares of any convenient size. It is best to use a scale and some convenient spacing, such as $\frac{1}{2}$ inch or 10 mm. On the new sheet, rule a similar grid, marking the spacing of the lines proportional to the original, but reduced or enlarged as needed. Draw the object's contours in and across the new grid lines to match the original as closely as you can by eye.

LETTERING

Lettered text is often necessary to completely describe an object or to provide detailed specifications. Lettering should be legible, be easy to create, and use styles acceptable for traditional drawing and CAD drawing.

■ 3.67 FREEHAND LETTERING

Most engineering lettering is single-stroke Gothic font. A font is the name for a particular shape of letters. Figure 3.69 shows some common fonts. Most hand-drawn notes are lettered $\frac{1}{8}''$ high and are drawn within light horizontal guidelines. CAD notes are typed from the keyboard and sized according to the plotted size of the drawing.

■ 3.68 LETTERING STANDARDS

The modern styles of letters were derived from the design of Roman capital letters, whose origins date all the way back to Egyptian hieroglyphics. The term

ABCDEFGH
abcdefghij

ABCDEFGHI
abcdefghijklm

Roman *All letters having elementary strokes "accented" or consisting of heavy and light lines, are classified as Roman.*

Italic- All slanting letters are classified as Italics~ These may be further designated as Roman-Italics, Gothic Italics or Text Italic.

FIGURE 3.69   Serif and Sans-Serif Lettering.

Roman refers to any letter that has wide downward strokes, thin connecting strokes, and ends terminating in spurs called serifs. In the late 19th century, the development of technical drawing created a need for a simplified, legible alphabet that could be drawn quickly with an ordinary pen. Single-stroke Gothic sans-serif (meaning without serifs or spurs) letters are used today because they are very legible.

3.69 COMPUTER LETTERING

Lettering is a standard feature available in computer graphics programs. Using CAD software, you can add titles, notes, and dimensioning information to a drawing. Several fonts and a variety of sizes may be selected. When modifications are required, it is easy to make appropriate lettering changes on the drawing by editing existing text.

CAD drawings typically use a Gothic style of lettering, but often use a Roman style of lettering for titles. When adding lettering to a CAD drawing, a good rule of thumb is not to use more than two fonts within the same drawing. You may want to use one font for the titles and a different one for notes and other text. However, you may have a couple different sizes of lettering in the drawing and perhaps some slanted lettering all using the same font. It is sometimes tempting to use many different fonts in a drawing because of the wide variety available on CAD systems, but drawings that use too many different fonts have been jokingly referred to as having a ransom note style of lettering.

3.70 LETTERING TECHNIQUE

Lettering is more similar to freehand drawing than it is to writing, so the six fundamental drawing strokes and their directions are basic to lettering. Horizontal strokes are drawn left to right. Vertical, inclined, and curved strokes are drawn downward. If you are left-handed, you can use a system of strokes similar to the sketching strokes that work for you.

Lettering ability has little relationship to writing ability. You can learn to letter neatly even if you have

terrible handwriting. There are three necessary aspects of learning to letter:

• Proportions and forms of the letters (to make good letters, you need to have a clear mental image of their correct shape)

• Composition the spacing of letters and words

• Practice

3.71 VERTICAL LETTERS AND NUMERALS

The proportions of vertical capital letters and numerals are shown in Figure 3.70 in a grid six units high. Numbered arrows indicate the order and direction of strokes. The widths of the letters can be easily remembered: The letter l and the numeral 1 are only a pencil width. The W is eight grid units wide ($1\frac{1}{3}$ times its height) and is the widest letter in the alphabet. All the other letters or numerals are either five or six grid units wide, and it is easy to remember the six-unit letters because when assembled they spell TOM Q. VAXY. This means that most letters are as wide as they are tall, which is probably wider than your usual writing. All numerals except the 1 are five units wide.

Lowercase letters are rarely used in engineering sketches except for lettering large volumes of notes. Vertical lowercase letters are used on map drawings, but very seldom on machine drawings. Lowercase letters are shown in Figure 3.71. The lower part of the letter is usually two-thirds the height of the capital letter.

3.72 INCLINED LETTERS AND NUMERALS

Inclined capital letters and numerals, shown in Figure 3.72, are similar to vertical characters, except for the slope. The slope of the letters is about 68° from the horizontal. While you may practice drawing slanted hand-lettering at approximately this angle, it is important in CAD drawings to always set the amount of incline for the letters at the same value within a drawing so that the lettering is consistent. Inclined lowercase letters, shown in Figure 3.73, are similar to vertical lowercase letters.

STRAIGHT-LINE LETTERS

"W" is only letter over 6 units wide. Letters in "TOM Q. VAXY" are 6 units wide – all others are 5, except "I" and "W."

CURVED-LINE LETTERS

The letters O, Q, C, G, and D are based on a true circle. The lower portion of the J and U is elliptical.

CURVED-LINE LETTERS AND NUMERALS

The 8 is composed of two ellipses. The 3, S, and 2 are based on the 8.

The 0, 6, and 9 are elliptical.

FIGURE 3.70   **Vertical Capital Letters and Numerals.**

FIGURE 3.71   **Vertical Lowercase Letters.**

FIGURE 3.72   Inclined Capital Letters and Numerals.

FIGURE 3.73   Inclined Lowercase Letters.

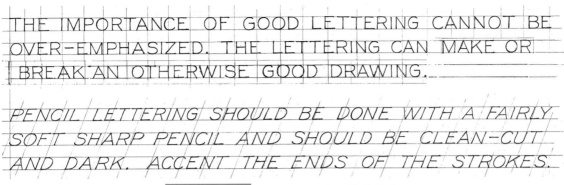

FIGURE 3.74   Pencil Lettering (Full Size).

■ 3.73 GUIDELINES

Use extremely light horizontal guidelines to keep letter height uniform, as is shown in Figure 3.74. Capital letters are commonly made $\frac{1}{8}''$ (3.2 mm) high, with the space between lines of lettering being from three-fifths to full height of the letters. Lettering size may vary depending on the size of the sheet. Do not use vertical guidelines to space the letters this should be done by eye while lettering. Use a vertical guideline at the beginning of a row of text to help you line up the left edges of the following rows, or use randomly spaced vertical guidelines to help you maintain the correct slant.

A simple method of spacing horizontal guidelines is to use a scale and set off a series of $\frac{1}{8}''$ spaces, making both the letters and the spaces between lines of letters

$\frac{1}{8}''$ high. Another quick method of creating guidelines is to use a guideline template like the Berol Rapidesign 925 shown in Figure 3.75.

When large and small capitals are used in combination, the small capitals should be three-fifths to two-thirds as high as the large capitals.

■ 3.74 GUIDELINES FOR WHOLE NUMBERS AND FRACTIONS

Beginners should use guidelines for whole numbers and fractions. Draw five equally spaced guidelines for whole numbers and fractions, as shown in Figure 3.76. Fractions are twice the height of the corresponding whole numbers. Make the numerator and the denominator each about three-fourths as high as the whole number to allow enough space between them and the

FIGURE 3.75   The Berol Rapidesign 925 template is used to quickly create guidelines for lettering.

FIGURE 3.76   Guide Lines for Dimension Figures.

$$\underbrace{\frac{5}{8}}_{Spaces} \quad \xrightarrow{RIGHT} \quad \frac{5}{8} \atop Wrong!$$

(a)

$$\frac{1}{4} \quad \xrightarrow{RIGHT} \quad \frac{1}{4} \atop Wrong!$$

(b)

$$\frac{1}{2} \quad \xrightarrow{RIGHT} \quad \frac{1}{2} \atop Wrong!$$

(c)

$$\frac{25}{32} \quad \xrightarrow{RIGHT} \quad \frac{25}{32} \atop Wrong! \quad \frac{25}{32} \atop Wrong!$$

(d)

FIGURE 3.77   **Common Errors.**

fraction bar. For dimensioning, the most commonly used height for whole numbers is $\frac{1}{8}''$ (3.2 mm), and for fractions $\frac{1}{4}''$ (6.4 mm), as shown in the figure.

Some of the most common errors in lettering fractions are shown in Figure 3.77. To make fractions appear correctly:

- Never let numerals touch the fraction bar.
- Center the denominator under the numerator.
- Never use an inclined fraction bar, except when lettering in a narrow space, as in a parts list.
- Make the fraction bar slightly longer than the widest part of the fraction.

■ 3.75 SPACING OF LETTERS AND WORDS

Uniform spacing of letters is a matter of equalizing spaces by eye. The background areas between letters, not the distances between them, should be approximately equal. Equal distances from letter to letter causes the letters to appear unequally spaced. Equal background areas between letters results in an even and pleasing spacing.

Some combinations, such as LT and VA, may even have to be slightly overlapped to secure good spacing. In some cases the width of a letter may be decreased. For example, the lower stroke of the L may be shortened when followed by A. These pairs of letters that need to be spaced extra closely to appear correctly are called kerned pairs in typesetting.

Space words well apart, but space letters closely within words. Make each word a compact unit well separated from adjacent words. For either uppercase or lowercase lettering, make the spaces between words approximately equal to a capital O. Be sure to have space between rows of letters, usually equal to the letter height. Rows spaced too closely are hard to read. Rows that are too far apart do not appear related.

■ 3.76 TITLES

In most cases, the title and related information are lettered in title boxes or title strips, which may be printed directly on the drawing paper or polyester film, as shown in Figure 3.78. The main drawing title is usually centered in a rectangular space, which is easy to do in CAD. When lettering by hand, arrange the title symmetrically about an imaginary centerline, as shown in Figure 3.79. In any kind of title, the most important words are given most prominence by making the lettering larger, heavier, or both. Other data, such as scale and date, can be smaller.

■ 3.77 WEB SITES FOR FURTHER INFORMATION

Check the sites below for engineering graphics supplies and equipment:

- http://www.reprint-draphix.com/
- http://www.eclipse.net/~essco/draft/draft.htm
- http://www.seventen.com/art_eng/index.html

These sites feature typography information:

- http://www.graphic-design.com/type/
- http://www.webcom.com/cadware/letease2.html

To find other sites like these, use keywords like reprographic supplies or engineering type fonts.

FIGURE 3.78   **Centering Title in Title Box.**

Equal

DRAWING TITLE

Scrap of paper underneath

FIGURE 3.79   **Balanced Machine-Drawing Title.**

TOOL GRINDING MACHINE
TOOL REST SLIDE
SCALE : FULL SIZE
AMERICAN MACHINE COMPANY
NEW YORK CITY

DRAWN BY ____ CHECKED BY ____

■ KEY WORDS

CAD	**CONSTRUCTION LINES**
SCALE	OBLIQUE
ALPHABET OF LINES	GRID PAPER
PARALLEL	HIDDEN LINES
VERTICAL	CENTERLINES
RADIUS	SHADING
DRAWING MEDIA	SKETCH
PROTRACTOR	PROPORTIONS
TRIANGLE	LETTERING
T-SQUARE	GOTHIC
IRREGULAR CURVE	ROMAN
LINE TYPE	SERIF
HORIZONTAL	INCLINED
DIAMETER	STABILITY
TEMPLATE	SPACING
COMPASS	GUIDELINES
DIVIDERS	TITLE BLOCK
PERPENDICULAR	KERNED PAIRS
FREEHAND SKETCH	

■ CHAPTER SUMMARY

- An understanding of the basic principles of drawing is required to draw with either a pencil or with CAD software.
- The line weight (thickness) and type (dashed or solid) has specific meaning in all technical drawings. This is called the alphabet of lines and is essential knowledge for every drafter.
- Both CAD and traditional drawing have specific methods for drawing lines, arcs, and circles. Proper understanding of the elements of this basic geometry is essential for both mechanical and CAD drawing.
- Every drawing tool, including every CAD software program, requires careful study of the tools and procedures for using the tools. Proper use of each tool facilitates the creation of neat, accurate drawings. Improper use of a tool creates sloppy, inaccurate drawings.
- The proper sizing of a drawing requires complete understanding of the use of scales. Paper drawings are scaled before they are drawn. CAD drawings are scaled when they are printed.
- Complex circles and arcs are difficult to draw using either CAD software or a mechanical compass. The prescribed techniques for either tool require understanding of the proper technique and practice with the appropriate tool.

- There are many drawing and printing media used in the creation of traditional drawings and the printing of CAD drawings. Each media type has specific advantages. Drawing and printing media are chosen based on the cost, durability, image quality, and reproduction capability.
- Sketching is a quick way of visualizing and solving a drawing problem. It is an effective way of communicating with all members of the design team.
- There are special techniques for sketching lines, circles, and arcs. These techniques should be practiced so they become second nature.
- Moving your thumb up or down the length of a pencil at arms length is an easy method for estimating proportional size.
- Using a grid makes sketching in proportion an easy task. Grid paper comes in a variety of types, including square grid and isometric grid.
- You can sketch circles by constructing a square and locating the four tangent points where the circle touches the square.
- A sketched line does not need to look like a mechanical line. The main distinction between instrumental drawing and freehand sketching is the character or technique of the line work.

- Freehand sketches are made to proportion, but not necessarily to a particular scale.
- Notes and dimensions are added to sketches using uppercase letters drawn by hand.

- The standard shapes of letters used in engineering drawing have been developed to be legible and quick to produce.

■ REVIEW QUESTIONS

1. What tools are used to draw straight lines?
2. What tools are used to draw arcs and circles?
3. Draw the alphabet of lines and label each line.
4. Describe the proper technique for erasing a line using an erasing shield.
5. Why is the pencil pulled and never pushed when drawing lines?
6. Which architect's scale represents a size ratio of 1 : 24? Which metric scale represents a half size? Which engineering scale would be used for full size?
7. Which scale type is the only one to use fractions of an inch?
8. Is the bevel of a compass lead sharpened on the inside or outside surface?
9. What are the minimum number of points that you should connect when using an irregular curve?
10. What are the main advantages of polyester film as a drawing media?

11. What are the four standard types of projections?
12. What are the advantages of using grid paper for sketching?
13. What is the correct technique for sketching a cricle or an arc?
14. Sketch the alphabet of lines. Which lines are thick? Which are thin? Which are very light and should not reproduce when copied?
15. What is the advantage of sketching an object first before drawing it using CAD?
16. What is the difference between proportion and scale?
17. What font provides the shape of standard engineering lettering?
18. Describe the characteristics of good freehand lettering.
19. Why must guidelines always be used for lettering?
20. How are sketches used in the design process?

■ DRAWING PROBLEMS

The constructions in Figs. 3.80 to 3.90 are to be drawn in pencil on Layout A–2 (see the inside front cover of this book). The steps in drawing this layout are shown in Fig. 3.44. Draw all construction lines *lightly*, using a hard lead (4H to 6H), and all required lines dense black with a softer lead (F to H). If construction lines are drawn properly—that is, *lightly*—they need not be erased in the final drawing.

If the layout is to be made on the A4 size sheet, width dimensions for title-strip forms will need to be adjusted to fit the available space.

The pencil drawings of Figs. 3.85 to 3.90 should be done on tracing paper or vellum; then prints should be made to show the effectiveness of the student's technique. If ink tracings are required, the originals may be drawn on film or on detail paper and then traced on vellum or tracing cloth. For any assigned problem, the instructor may require that all dimensions and notes be lettered to afford further lettering practice.

Since many of the problems in this chapter are of a general nature, they can also be solved on most computer graphic systems. If a system if available, the instructor may choose to assign specific problems to be completed by this method.

Prob. 3.1 Using Layout A–2 or A4–2 (adjusted), divide working space into six equal rectangles and draw visible lines, as shown in Fig. 3.80. Draw construction lines AB through centers C at right angles to required lines; then along each construction line, set off 0.50″ spaces and draw required visible lines. Omit dimensions and instructional notes.

Problems in convenient form for solution may be found in *Technical Drawing Problems*, Series 1, by Giesecke, Mitchell, Spencer, Hill, Dygdon, and Novak; *Technical Drawing Problems*, Series 2, by Spencer, Hill, Dygdon, and Novak; and *Technical Drawing Problems*, Series 3, by Spencer, Hill, Dygdon, and Novak; all designed to accompany this text and published by Prentice Hall.

FIGURE 3.80   Using Layout A-2 or A4-2 (adjusted), divide working space into six equal rectangles and draw visible lines as shown. Draw construction lines AB through centers C at right angles to required lines; then along each construction line, set off 0.50″ spaces and draw required visible lines. Omit dimensions and instructional notes.

Prob. 3.2   Using Layout A–2 or A4–2 (adjusted), divide working space into six equal rectangles and draw lines as shown in Fig. 3.81. In the first two spaces, draw conventional lines to match those in Fig. 3.9. In remaining spaces, locate centers C by diagonals, and then work constructions out from them. Omit the metric dimensions and instructional notes.

Prob. 3.3   Using Layout A–2 or A4–2 (adjusted), draw views in pencil, as shown in Fig. 3.82. Omit all dimensions.

Prob. 3.4   Using Layout A–2 or A4–2 (adjusted), draw figures in pencil, as shown in Fig. 3.83. Use bow pencil for all arcs and circles within it radius range. Omit all dimensions.

Prob. 3.5   Using Layout A–2 or A4–2 (adjusted), draw views in pencil, as shown in Fig. 3.84. Use bow pencil for all arcs and circles within its radius range. Omit all dimensions.

Prob. 3.6   Using Layout A–2 or A4–2 (adjusted), draw in pencil the friction plate in Fig. 3.85. Omit dimensions and notes.

FIGURE 3.81   Using Layout A–2 or A4–3 (adjusted), divide working space into six equal rectangles, and draw lines as shown. In first two spaces, draw conventional lines to match those in Fig. 3.9. In remaining spaces, locate centers C by diagonals, and then work constructions out from them. Omit the metric dimensions and instructional notes.

FIGURE 3.82   Using Layout A–2 or A4–2 (adjusted), draw views in pencil as shown. Omit all dimensions.

FIGURE 3.83   Using Layout A–2 or A4–3 (adjusted), draw figures in pencil as shown. Use bow pencil for all arcs and circles within its radius range. Omit all dimensions.

Prob. 3.7   Using Layout A–2 or A4–2 (adjusted), draw views in pencil of the seal cover in Fig. 3.86. Omit dimensions and notes.

Prob. 3.8   Using Layout A–2 or A4–2 (adjusted), draw in pencil the Geneva cam in Fig. 3.87. Omit dimensions and notes.

Prob. 3.9   Using Layout A–2 or A4–2 (adjusted), draw accurately in pencil the shear plate in Fig. 3.88. Give length of KA. Omit other dimensions and notes.

Prob. 3.10   Using Layout A–2 or A4–2 (adjusted), draw in pencil the ratchet wheel in Fig. 3.89. Omit dimensions and notes.

Prob. 3.11   Using Layout A–2 or A4–2 (adjusted), draw in pencil the latch plate in Fig. 3.90. Omit dimensions and notes.

| OIL PUMP BODY | VAXY, TOM Q. | 1"=1" | 9-24-85 | A-5 | 5 |

FIGURE 3.84 Using Layout A–2 or A4–2 (adjusted), draw views in pencil as shown. Use bow pencil for all arcs and circles within its radius range. Omit all dimensions.

FIGURE 3.85 Friction Plate. Using Layout A–2 or A4–2 (adjusted), draw in pencil. Omit dimensions and notes.

FIGURE 3.86 Seal Cover. Using Layout A–2 or A4–2 (adjusted), draw in pencil. Omit dimensions and notes.

FIGURE 3.87   Geneva Cam. Using Layout A–2 or A4–2 (adjusted), draw in pencil. Omit dimensions and notes.

FIGURE 3.88   Ratchet Wheel. Using Layout A–2 or A4–2 (adjusted), draw in pencil. Omit dimensions and notes.

FIGURE 3.89   Shear Plate. Using Layout A–2 or A4–2 (adjusted), draw accurately in pencil. Give length of KA. Omit other dimensions and notes.

FIGURE 3.90   Latch Plate. Using Layout A–2 or A4–2 (adjusted), draw in pencil. Omit dimensions and notes.

■ LETTERING PROBLEMS

Layouts for lettering problems are given in Figs. 3.91 through 3.94. Draw complete horizontal and vertical or inclined guide lines *very lightly*. Draw the vertical or inclined guide lines through the full height of the lettered area of the sheet. For practice in ink lettering, the last two lines and the title strip on each sheet may be lettered in ink, if assigned by the instructor. Omit all dimensions.

Prob. 3.12 As shown in Fig. 3.91, lay out sheet, add vertical or inclined guide lines, and fill in vertical or inclined capital letters as assigned. For decimal-inch and millimeter equivalents of given dimensions, see table inside of back cover.

Prob. 3.13 As shown in Fig. 3.92, lay out sheet, add vertical or inclined guide lines, and fill in vertical or inclined capital letters as assigned. For decimal-inch and millimeter equivalents of given dimensions, see table inside of back cover.

Prob. 3.14 As shown in Fig. 3.93, lay out sheet, add vertical or inclined guide lines, and fill in vertical or inclined capital letters as assigned. For decimal-inch and millimeter equivalents of given dimensions, see table inside of back cover.

Prob. 3.15 As shown in Fig. 3.94, lay out sheet, add vertical or inclined guide lines, and fill in vertical or inclined capital letters as assigned. For decimal-inch and millimeter equivalents of given dimensions, see table inside of back cover.

Lettering sheets in convenient form for lettering practice may be found in *Engineering Drawing Problems*, Series 1, by Giesecke, Mitchell, Spencer, Hill, Dygdon, and Novak; *Engineering Drawing Problems*, Series 2, by Spencer, Hill, Dygdon, and Novak; and *Engineering Drawing Problems*, Series 3 by Davis and Juneau; all designed to accompany this text and published by Prentice Hall.

FIGURE 3.91 **Prob. 3.12.**

FIGURE 3.92 **Prob. 3.13.**

FIGURE 3.93   **Prob. 3.14.**

FIGURE 3.94   **Prob. 3.15.**

C H A P T E R 4

GEOMETRIC CONSTRUCTIONS

OBJECTIVES

After studying the material in this chapter, you should be able to:

1. Identify and draw four different types of lines.
2. Identify and draw any size angle.
3. Identify and draw four different types of triangles and five types of parallelograms.
4. Identify and draw a regular triangle, square, hexagon, and octagon.
5. Divide a space into equal parts; divide an angle in half; divide a line into equal parts.
6. Draw lines and arcs tangent to each other.
7. Identify and draw several conic sections.
8. Define the meaning of a tangent point and construct its location on any tangent construction.

OVERVIEW

All traditional drawing and CAD drawing techniques are based on the construction of basic geometric elements. A point, line, arc, and circle are the basic elements used to create the most complex drawings. The geometry of drawing is the same for traditional drawing and CAD drawing. The drafting student must understand basic geometric construction techniques in order to draw on paper or with CAD, or to apply these geometric techniques to solving problems.

Pure geometry problems may be solved with only the compass and a straightedge, and in some cases these methods may be used to advantage in technical drawing. However, drafters and designers have available the T-square, triangles, dividers, and other equipment, that can often yield accurate results more quickly by what we may term "preferred methods." Therefore, many of the solutions in this chapter are practical adaptations of the principles of pure geometry.

This chapter is designed to present definitions of terms and geometric constructions of importance in technical drawing, suggest simplified methods of construction, point out practical applications, and afford opportunity for practice in accurate instrumental drawing.

■4.1 POINTS AND LINES

A *point* represents a location in space or on a drawing and has no width, height, or depth (Fig. 4.1). A point is represented by the intersection of two lines (Fig. 4.1a), by a short crossbar on a line (Fig. 4.1b), or by a small cross (Fig. 4.1c). Never represent a point by a simple dot on the paper.

A **line** is defined by Euclid as "that which has length without breadth." A *straight line* is the shortest distance between two points and is commonly referred to simply as a "line." If the line is indefinite in extent, the length is a matter of convenience, and the endpoints are not fixed (Fig. 4.1d). If the endpoints of the line are significant, they must be marked by means of small mechanically drawn crossbars (Fig. 4.1e). Other common terms are illustrated in Figs. 4.1f to 4.1h. Either straight lines or curved lines are parallel if the shortest distance between them remains constant. The common symbol for parallel lines is ||, and for perpen-

dicular lines it is ⊥ (singular) or ⊥s (plural). Two perpendicular lines may be marked with a "box" to indicate perpendicularity, as shown in Fig. 4.1k. Such symbols may be used on sketches, but not on production drawings.

■4.2 ANGLES

An angle is formed by two intersecting lines. A common symbol for angle is / (singular) or / s (plural) (Fig. 4.2).

There are 360 degrees (360°) in a full circle, as shown in Fig. 4.2a. A degree is divided into 60 minutes (60′), and a minute is divided into 60 seconds (60″). Thus, 37° 26′ 10″ is read 37 degrees, 26 minutes, and 10 seconds. When minutes alone are indicated, the number of minutes should be preceded by 0°, as in 0° 20′.

The different kinds of angles are illustrated in Fig. 4.2b to 4.2e. Two angles are *complementary* (Fig. 4.2f) if they total 90°, and are *supplementary* (Fig. 4.2g) if they total 180°. Most angles used in technical drawing can be drawn easily with the T-square or straightedge and triangles. To draw odd angles, use a protractor. For considerable accuracy, use a *vernier protractor*, or the tangent, sine, or chord methods (§4.19).

■4.3 TRIANGLES

A triangle is a plane figure bounded by three straight sides, and the sum of the interior angles is always 180° (Fig. 4.3). A right triangle (Fig. 4.3d) has one 90° angle, and the square of the hypotenuse is equal to the sum of the squares of the two sides (Fig. 4.3c). As shown in Fig. 4.3f, any triangle inscribed in a semicircle is a right triangle if the hypotenuse coincides with the diameter.

■4.4 QUADRILATERALS

A *quadrilateral* is a plane figure bounded by four straight sides (Fig. 4.4). If the opposite sides are parallel, the quadrilateral is also a *parallelogram*.

■4.5 POLYGONS

A *polygon* is any plane figure bounded by straight lines (Fig. 4.5). If the polygon has equal angles and equal sides, it can be inscribed in or circumscribed around a circle and is called a *regular polygon*.

FIGURE 4.1   Points and Lines.

FIGURE 4.2   Angles.

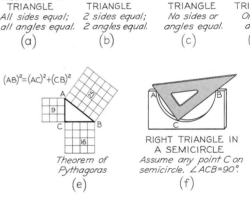

FIGURE 4.3   Triangles.

■ 4.6 CIRCLES AND ARCS

A *circle* is a closed curve, all points of which are the same distance from a point called the center (Fig. 4.6a). *Circumference* refers to the circle or to the distance around the circle. This distance equals the diameter multiplied by π (called pi) or 3.1416. Other definitions are illustrated in Figs. 4.6b through 4.6e.

■ 4.7 SOLIDS

Solids bounded by plane surfaces are called ***polyhedra*** (Fig. 4.7). The surfaces are called *faces*, and if the faces are equal regular polygons, the solids are called *regular polyhedra*.

A ***prism*** has two bases, which are parallel equal polygons, and three or more lateral faces, which are parallelograms. A triangular prism has a triangular base; a rectangular prism has rectangular bases; and so on. If the bases are parallelograms, the prism is a parallelpiped. A right prism has faces and lateral edges perpendicular to the bases; an oblique prism has faces and laterals edge oblique to the bases. If one end is cut off to form an end and not parallel to the bases, the prism is said to be truncated.

A ***pyramid*** has a polygon for a base and triangular lateral faces intersecting at a common point called the *vertex*. The center line from the center of the base to the vertex is the *axis*. If the axis is perpendicular to the base, the pyramid is a right pyramid; otherwise it is an oblique pyramid. A triangular pyramid has a triangular base; a square pyramid has a square base; and so

FIGURE 4.4 Quadrilaterals.

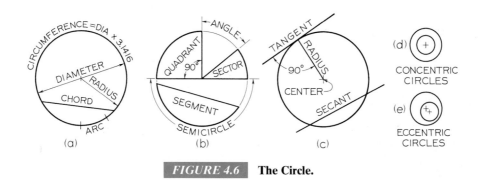

FIGURE 4.5 Regular Polygons.

FIGURE 4.6 The Circle.

on. If a portion near the vertex has been cut off, the pyramid is *truncated*, or it is referred to as a *frustum*.

A **cylinder** is generated by a straight line, called the *generatrix*, moving in contact with a curved line and always remaining parallel to its previous position or to the axis. Each position of the generatrix is called an element of the cylinder.

A **cone** is generated by a straight line moving in contact with a curved line and passing through a fixed point, the *vertex* of the cone. Each position of the generatrix is an element of the cone.

A **sphere** is generated by a circle revolving about one of its diameters. This diameter becomes the axis of the sphere, and the ends of the axis are *poles* of the sphere.

A **torus**, which is shaped like a doughnut, is generated by a circle (or other curve) revolving about an axis that is eccentric to the curve.

FIGURE 4.7 Solids.

Examples of Solids Created with CAD. *Courtesy of American Small Business Computers.*

An oblate or prolate **ellipsoid** is generated by revolving an ellipse about its minor or major axis, respectively. For more information on working with solids, see Chapter 14 for an in-depth discussion on solid modeling.

■ 4.8 BISECTING A LINE OR CIRCULAR ARC

Figure 4.8a shows the given line or arc AB to be bisected.

I. From A and B draw equal arcs with radius greater than half AB.

II. and III. Join intersections D and E with a straight line to locate center C.

■ 4.9 BISECTING A LINE WITH TRIANGLE AND T-SQUARE

As shown in Fig. 4.9, from endpoints A and B, draw construction lines at 30°, 45°, or 60° with the given line; then through their intersection, C, draw a line perpendicular to the given line to locate the center D, as shown.

■ 4.10 BISECTING AN ANGLE

Figure 4.10a shows the given angle BAC to be bisected.

FIGURE 4.8   **Bisecting a Line or a Circular Arc (§4.8).**

FIGURE 4.10   **Bisecting an Angle (§4.10).**

FIGURE 4.9   **Bisecting a Line with Triangle and T-square (§4.9).**

I. Strike large arc R.

II. Strike equal arcs r with radius slightly larger than half BC, to intersect at D.

III. Draw line AD, which bisects the angle.

■4.11 TRANSFERRING AN ANGLE

Figure 4.11a shows the given angle BAC to be transferred to the new position at A′B′.

I. Use any convenient radius R, and strike arcs from centers A and A′.

II. Strike equal arcs r, and draw side A′C′.

■4.12 DRAWING A LINE THROUGH A POINT AND PARALLEL TO A LINE

With given point P as center, and any convenient radius R, strike arc CD to intersect the given line AB at E (Fig. 4.12a). With E as center and the same radius, strike arc R′ to intersect the given line at G. With PG as radius and E as center, strike arc r to locate point H. The line PH is the required line.

FIGURE 4.11   **Transferring an Angle (§4.11).**

FIGURE 4.12 Drawing a Line Through a Point Parallel to a Line (§4.12).

PREFERRED METHOD As shown in Fig. 4.12b, move the triangle and T-square as a unit until the triangle lines up with given line AB; then slide the triangle until its edge passes through the given point P. Draw CD, the required parallel line.

■4.13 DRAWING A LINE PARALLEL TO A LINE AND AT A GIVEN DISTANCE

Let AB be the line and CD the given distance. As shown in Fig. 4.13a, draw two arcs with points E and F near A and B, respectively, as centers, and CD as radius. The line GH, tangent to the arcs, is the required line.

PREFERRED METHOD With any point E of the line as center and CD as radius, strike an arc JK (Fig. 4.13b). Move the triangle and T-square as a unit until the triangle lines up with the given line AB; then slide the triangle until its edge is tangent to the arc JK, and draw the required line GH.

As shown in Fig. 4.13c, with centers selected at random on the curved line AB and with CD as radius, draw a series of arcs; then draw the required line tangent to these arcs.

■4.14 DIVIDING A LINE INTO EQUAL PARTS

There are two methods for dividing a line into equal parts. The first method is shown in Fig. 4.14:

I. Draw a light construction line at any convenient angle from one end of line.

II. With dividers or scale, set off from intersection of lines as many equal divisions as needed (in this case, three).

III. Connect last division point to the other end of line, using triangle and T-square, as shown.

IV. Slide triangle along T-square and draw parallel lines through other division points, as shown.

The second method for dividing a line into equal parts is shown in Fig. 4.15:

I. Draw vertical construction line at one end of given line.

II. Set zero of scale at other end of line.

III. Swing scale up until third unit falls on vertical line, and make tiny dots at each point, or prick points with dividers.

FIGURE 4.13 Drawing a Line Parallel to a Line at a Given Distance (§4.13).

FIGURE 4.14   **Dividing a Line into Equal Parts (§4.14).**

FIGURE 4.15   **Dividing a Line into Equal Parts (§4.14).**

IV. Draw vertical construction lines through each point.

Some practical applications of this method are shown in Fig. 4.16.

4.15 DIVIDING A LINE INTO PROPORTIONAL PARTS

Let it be required to divide the line AB into three parts proportional, to 2, 3, and 4.

PREFERRED METHOD   Draw a vertical line from point B (Fig. 4.17a). Select a scale of convenient size for a total of nine units and set the zero of the scale at A. Swing the scale up until the ninth unit falls on the vertical line. Along the scale, set off points for 2, 3, and 4 units, as shown. Draw vertical lines through these points.

Draw a line CD parallel to AB and at any convenient distance (Fig. 4.17b). On this line, set off 2, 3, and 4 units, as shown. Draw lines through the ends of the two lines to intersect at the point O. Draw lines through O and the points 2 and 5 to divide AB into the required proportional parts.

Given AB, divide into proportional parts, in this case proportional to the square of x, where $x = 1$, 2, 3, ... (Fig. 4.17c). Set zero of scale at end of line and set off divisions 4, 9, 16, ... Join the last division to the other end of the line, and draw parallel lines as shown. This method may be used for any power of x.

FIGURE 4.16   **Practical Applications of Dividing a Line into Equal Parts (§4.14).**

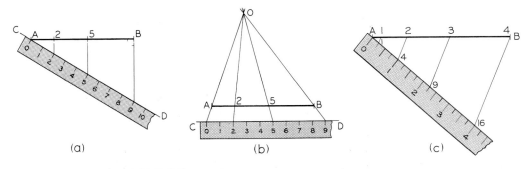

FIGURE 4.17 **FIGURE 4.17**   **Dividing a Line into Proportional Parts (§4.15).**

■ 4.16 DRAWING A LINE THROUGH A POINT AND PERPENDICULAR TO A LINE

The line AB and a point P (Fig. 4.18) are given.

WHEN THE POINT IS NOT ON THE LINE   From P, draw any convenient inclined line, as PD (Fig. 4.18a). Find center C of line PD, and draw arc with radius CP. The line EP is the required perpendicular.

With P as center, strike an arc to intersect AB at C and D (Fig. 4.18b). With C and D as centers and radius slightly greater than half CD, strike arcs to intersect at E. The line PE is the required perpendicular.

WHEN THE POINT IS ON THE LINE   With P as center and any radius, strike arcs to intersect AB at D and G (Fig. 4.18c). With D and G as centers and radius slightly greater than half DG, strike equal arcs to intersect at F. The line PF is the required perpendicular.

As shown in Fig. 4.18d, select any convenient unit of length (for example, 6 mm or $\frac{1}{4}''$). With P as center and 3 units as radius, strike an arc to intersect the given line at C. With P as center and 4 units as radius, strike arc DE. With C as center and 5 units as radius,

strike an arc to intersect DE at F. The line PF is the required perpendicular.

This method makes use of the 3–4–5 right triangle and is frequently used in laying off rectangular foundations of large machines, buildings, or other structures. For this purpose a steel tape may be used and distances of 30′, 40′, and 50′ measured as the three sides of the right triangle.

PREFERRED METHOD   Move the triangle and T-square as a unit until the triangle lines up with AB (Fig. 4.18e); then slide the triangle until its edge passes through the point P (whether P is on or off the line), and draw the required perpendicular.

■ 4.17 DRAWING A TRIANGLE WITH SIDES GIVEN

Given the sides A , B, and C, as shown in Fig. 4.19a:

I.   Draw one side, as C, in desired position, and strike arc with radius equal to side A.

II.   Strike arc with radius equal to side B.

III.   Draw sides A and B from intersection of arcs, as shown.

FIGURE 4.18   **Drawing a Line Through a Point and Perpendicular to a Line (§4.16).**

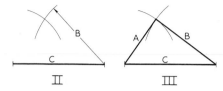

FIGURE 4.19   **Drawing a Tringle with Sides Given (§4.17).**

■4.18   DRAWING A RIGHT TRIANGLE WITH HYPOTENUSE AND ONE SIDE GIVEN

Given sides S and R (Fig. 4.20), with AB as a diameter equal to S, draw a semicircle. With A as center and R as radius, draw an arc intersecting the semicircle at C. Draw AC and CB to complete the right triangle.

■4.19   LAYING OUT AN ANGLE

Many angles can be laid out directly with the triangle, or they may be laid out with the protractor. Other methods, for which considerable accuracy is required, are discussed next (Fig. 4.21).

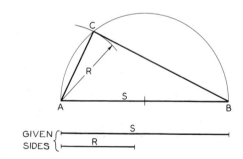

FIGURE 4.20   **Drawing a Right Triangle (§4.18).**

TANGENT METHOD   The tangent of angle θ is y/x and $y = x \tan \theta$. To construct the angle, assume a convenient value for x, preferably 10 units of convenient length (Fig. 4.21a). (The larger the unit, the more accurate will be the construction.) Find the tangent of angle θ in a table of natural tangents, multiply by 10, and set off $y = 10 \tan \theta$.

> **EXAMPLE**   To set off $31\frac{1}{2}°$, find the natural tangent of $31\frac{1}{2}°$, which is 0.6128. Then
>
> $$y = 10 \text{ units} \times 0.6128 = 6.128 \text{ units.}$$

SINE METHOD   Draw line x to any convenient length, preferably 10 units (Fig. 4.21b). Find the sine of angle θ in a table of natural sines, multiply by 10, and strike arc $R = 10 \sin \theta$. Draw the other side of the angle tangent to the arc, as shown.

> **EXAMPLE**   To set off $25\frac{1}{2}°$, find the natural sine of $25\frac{1}{2}°$, which is 0.4304. Then
>
> $$R = 10 \text{ units} \times 0.4305 = 4.305 \text{ units.}$$

CHORD METHOD   Draw line x to any convenient length, and draw arc with any convenient radius R—say 10 units (Fig. 4.21c). Find the chordal length C in a table of chords (see a machinists' handbook), and multiply the value by 10 since the table is made for a radius of 1 unit.

FIGURE 4.21   **Laying Out Angles (§4.19).**

EXAMPLE To set off 43° 20′, the chordal length *C* for 1 unit radius, as given in a table of chords equals 0.7384; and if *R* = 10 units, then *C* = 7.384 units.

If a table is not available, the chord *C* may be calculated by the formula $C = 2 \sin \theta/2$.

EXAMPLE Half of 43° 20′ = 21° 40′. The sine of 21° 40′ = 0.3692. $C = 2 \times 0.3692 = 0.7384$ for a 1 unit radius. For a 10 unit radius, $C = 7.384$ units.

■ 4.20 DRAWING AN EQUILATERAL TRIANGLE

Side AB is given. With A and B as centers and AB as radius, strike arcs to intersect at C (Fig. 4.22a). Draw lines AC and BC to complete the triangle.

PREFERRED METHOD Draw lines through points A and B, making angles of 60° with the given line and intersecting C (Fig. 4.22b).

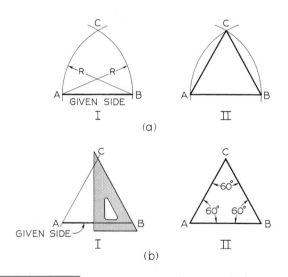

FIGURE 4.22   **Drawing an Equilateral Triangle (§4.20).**

■ 4.21 DRAWING A SQUARE

One side AB (Fig. 4.23a) is given. Through point A, draw a perpendicular (see Fig. 4.18c). With A as center and AB as radius, draw the arc to intersect the perpendicular at C. With B and C as centers and AB as radius, strike arcs to intersect at D. Draw lines CD and BD.

PREFERRED METHOD One side AB (Fig. 4.23b) is given. Using the T-square or parallel straightedge and 45° triangle, draw lines AC and BD perpendicular to AB and the lines AD and BC at 45° with AB. Draw line CD.

PREFERRED METHOD Given the circumscribed circle (distance "across corners"), draw two diameters at right angles to each other (Fig. 4.23c). The intersections of these diameters with the circle are vertexes of an inscribed square.

PREFERRED METHOD Given the inscribed circle (Fig. 4.23d) (distance "across flats," as in drawing bolt heads), use the T-square (or parallel straightedge) and 45° triangle and draw the four sides tangent to the circle.

■ 4.22 DRAWING A REGULAR PENTAGON

Given the circumscribed circle, do the following:

PREFERRED METHOD Divide the circumference of the circle into five equal parts with the dividers, and join the points with straight lines (Fig. 4.24a).

GEOMETRICAL METHOD
As shown in Fig. 4.24b:

I.   Bisect radius OD at C.
II. With C as center and CA as radius, strike arc AE. With A as center and AE as radius, strike arc EB.

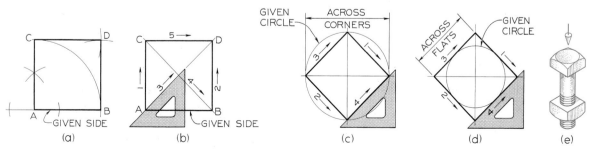

FIGURE 4.23   **Drawing a Square (§4.21).**

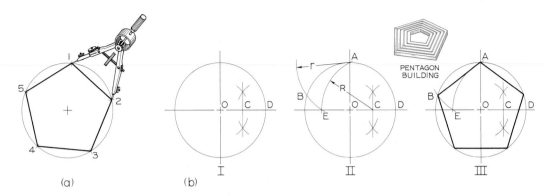

FIGURE 4.24 **Drawing a Pentagon (§4.22).**

III. Draw line AB; then set off distances AB around the circumference of the circle, and draw the sides through these points.

■ 4.23 DRAWING A HEXAGON

The circumscribed circle (Fig. 4.25) as given. Each side of a hexagon is equal to the radius of the circumscribed circle (Fig. 4.25a). Therefore, using the compass or dividers and the radius of the circle, set off the six sides of the hexagon around the circle, and connect the points with straight lines. As a check on the accura-

cy of the construction, make sure that opposite sides of the hexagon are parallel.

PREFERRED METHOD This construction (Fig. 4.25b) is a variation of the one shown in Fig. 4.25a. Draw vertical and horizontal center lines. With A and B as centers and radius equal to that of the circle, draw arcs to intersect the circle at C, D, E, and F, and complete the hexagon as shown.

Given the circumscribed circle (distance "across corners") (Figs. 4.26a and 4.26b), draw vertical and horizontal center lines, and then diagonals AB and CD

FIGURE 4.25 **Drawing a Hexagon (§4.23).**

FIGURE 4.26 **Drawing a Hexagon (§4.23).**

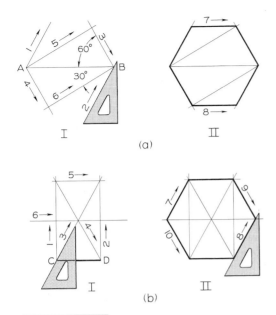

FIGURE 4.27   **Drawing a Hexagon (§4.23).**

at 30° or 60° with horizontal; finally, with the 30° × 60° triangle and the T-square, draw the six sides as shown.

Given the inscribed circle (distance "across flats") (Figs. 4.26c and 4.26d), draw vertical and horizontal center lines; then with the 30° × 60° triangle and the T-square or straightedge, draw the six sides tangent to the circle. This method is used in drawing bolt heads and nuts. For maximum accuracy, diagonals may be added, as in Figs. 4.26a and 4.26b.

As shown in Fig. 4.27, use the 30° × 60° triangle and the T-square or straightedge; draw lines in the order shown in Fig. 4.27a, where the distance AB ("across corners") is given or, as shown in Fig. 4.27b, where a side CD is given.

■ 4.24 DRAWING AN OCTAGON

Given an inscribed circle, or distance "across flats" (Fig. 4.28a), use a T-square or straightedge and a 45° triangle to draw the eight sides tangent to the circle, as shown.

Given a circumscribed square, or distance "across flats" (Fig. 4.28b), draw diagonals of square; then with the corners of the given square as centers and with half the diagonal as radius, draw arcs cutting the sides as shown in I. Using a T-square and 45° triangle, draw the eight sides, as shown in II.

■ 4.25 TRANSFERRING PLANE FIGURES BY GEOMETRIC METHODS

TRANSFERRING A TRIANGLE TO A NEW LOCATION   Set off any side of the given triangle (Fig. 4.29a), such as AB, in the new location (Fig. 4.29b). With the ends of the line as centers and the lengths of the other sides of the given triangle as radii, strike two arcs to intersect at C. Join C to A and B to complete the triangle.

TRANSFERRING A POLYGON BY THE TRIANGLE METHOD   Divide the polygon into triangles as shown, and transfer each triangle as explained previously (Fig. 4.29c).

TRANSFERRING A POLYGON BY THE RECTANGLE METHOD   Circumscribe a rectangle abut the given polygon (Fig. 4.29d). Draw a congruent rectangle in the new location and locate the vertexes of the polygon by transferring location measurements a, b, c, and so on along the sides of the rectangle to the new rectangle. Join the points thus found to complete the figure.

TRANSFERRING IRREGULAR FIGURES   Figures composed of rectangular and circular forms are readily transferred by enclosing the elementary features in rectangles and determining centers of arcs and circles (Fig. 4.29e). These may then be transferred to the new location.

TRANSFERRING FIGURES BY OFFSET MEASUREMENTS   *Offset location measurements* are frequently useful in transferring figures composed of free curves (Fig. 4.29f). When the figure has been enclosed by a rectangle, the sides of the rectangle are used as reference lines for the location of points along the curve.

FIGURE 4.28   **Drawing an Octagon (§4.24).** *Photo by Laima Druskis.*

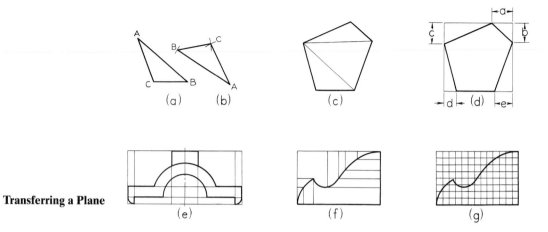

FIGURE 4.29   **Transferring a Plane Figure (§4.25).**

TRANSFERRING FIGURES BY A SYSTEM OF SQUARES   Figures involving free curves are easily copied, enlarged, or reduced by the use of a system of squares (Fig. 4.29g). For example, to enlarge a figure to double size, draw the containing rectangle and all small squares double their original size. Then draw the lines through the corresponding points in the new set of squares.

■ 4.26 TRANSFERRING DRAWINGS BY TRACING-PAPER METHODS

To transfer a drawing to an opaque sheet, the following procedures may be used.

PRICKED-POINT METHOD   Lay tracing paper over the drawing to be transferred. With a sharp pencil, make a small dot directly over each important point of the drawing. Encircle each dot so it is not lost. Remove the tracing paper, place it over the paper to receive the transferred drawing, and maneuver the tracing paper into the desired position. With a needle point (such as a point of the dividers), prick through each dot. Remove the tracing paper and connect the pricked points to reproduce the lines of the original drawing.

To reproduce arcs or circles, it is only necessary to transfer the center and one point on the circumference. To duplicate a free curve, transfer as many pricked points on the curve as desired.

TRACING METHOD   Lay tracing paper over the drawing to be transferred, and make a pencil tracing of it. Turn the tracing paper over and mark over the lines with short strokes of a soft pencil to provide a coating of graphite over every line. Turn tracing face up and fasten in position where drawing is to be transferred. Trace over all lines of the tracing, using a hard pencil. The graphite on the back acts as a carbon paper and will produce dim but definite lines. Heavy in the dim lines to complete the transfer.

If one half of a symmetrical object has been drawn (Fig. 4.30), such as the ink bottle in I, the other half may be drawn with the aid of tracing paper, as follows:

I.   Trace the half already drawn.

II.   Turn tracing paper over and maneuver to the position for the right half. Then trace over the lines freehand or mark over the lines with short strokes, as shown.

III.   Remove the tracing paper, revealing the dim imprinted lines for the right half. Heavy in these lines to complete the drawing.

■ 4.27 ENLARGING OR REDUCING A DRAWING

The construction shown in Fig. 4.31a is an adaptation of the parallel-line method (Figs. 4.12 and 4.13); it may

FIGURE 4.30   Transferring a Symmetrical Half (§4.26).

FIGURE 4.31   Enlarging or Reducing (§4.27).

be used to enlarge or reduce any group of dimensions to the same ratio. Thus, if full-size dimensions are laid off along the vertical line, the enlarged dimensions will appear along the horizontal line, as shown.

To enlarge or reduce a rectangle (say, a photograph), a simple method is to use the diagonal, as shown in Fig. 4.31b. A simple method of enlarging or reducing a drawing is to make use of radial lines (Fig. 4.31c). The original drawing is placed underneath a sheet of tracing paper, and the enlarged or reduced drawing is made directly on the tracing paper.

■ 4.28 DRAWING A CIRCLE THROUGH THREE POINTS

I. Let A, B, and C be the three given points not in a straight line (Fig. 4.32a). Draw lines AB and BC,

FIGURE 4.32   Finding Center of Circle (§§4.28 and 4.29).

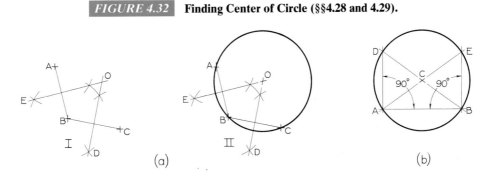

which will be chords of the circle. Draw perpendicular bisectors EO and DO intersecting at O (see Fig. 4.8).

II. With center at O, draw required circle through the points.

■ 4.29 FINDING THE CENTER OF A CIRCLE

Draw any chord AB, preferably horizontal as shown (Fig. 4.32b). Draw perpendiculars from A and B, cutting the circle at D and E. Draw diagonals DB and EA whose intersection C will be the center of the circle. This method uses the principle that any right triangle inscribed in a circle cuts off a semicircle (see Fig. 4.3f).

Another method, slightly longer, is to reverse the procedure of Fig. 4.32a. Draw any two nonparallel chords and draw perpendicular bisectors. The intersection of the bisectors will be the center of the circle.

■ 4.30 DRAWING A CIRCLE TANGENT TO A LINE AT A GIVEN POINT

Given a line AB and a point P on the line (Fig. 4.33a):

I. At P, erect a perpendicular to the line.

II. Set off the radius of the required circle on the perpendicular.

III. Draw a circle with radius CP.

■ 4.31 DRAWING A TANGENT TO A CIRCLE THROUGH A POINT

PREFERRED METHOD Given point P on the circle (Fig. 4.34a), move the T-square and triangle as a unit until one side of the triangle passes through the point P and the center of the circle; then slide the triangle until the other side passes through point P, and draw the required tangent.

Given point P outside the circle (Fig. 4.34b), move the T-square and triangle as a unit until one side of the triangle passes through point P and, by inspection, is tangent to the circle; then slide the triangle until the other side passes through the center of the circle, and lightly mark the point of tangency T. Finally, move the triangle back to its starting position, and draw the required tangent.

In both constructions either triangle may be used. Also, a second triangle may be used in place of the T-square.

FIGURE 4.33 **Drawing a Circle Tangent to a Line (§4.30).**

FIGURE 4.34 **Drawing a Tangent to a Circle Through a Point (§4.31).**

■ 4.32 DRAWING TANGENTS TO TWO CIRCLES

Move the triangle and T-square as a unit until one side of the triangle is tangent, by inspection, to the two circles (Figs. 4.35a and 4.35b); then slide the triangle until the other side passes through the center of one circle, and lightly mark the point of tangency. Then slide the triangle until the slide passes through the center of the other circle, and mark the point of tangency. Finally, slide the triangle back to the tangent position, and draw the tangent lines between the two points of tangency. Draw the second tangent line in a similar manner.

■ 4.33 DRAWING AN ARC TANGENT TO A LINE OR ARC AND THROUGH A POINT

Given line AB, point P, and radius R (Fig. 4.36a), draw line DE parallel to the given line and distance R from it. From P draw arc with radius R, cutting line DE at C, the center of the required tangent arc.

Given line AB, with tangent point Q on the line and point P (Fig. 4.36b), draw PQ, which will be a chord of the required arc. Draw perpendicular bisector DE, and at Q erect a perpendicular to the line to intersect DE at C, the center of the required tangent arc.

Given arc with center Q, point P, and radius R (Fig. 4.36c), from P, strike arc with radius R. From Q,

FIGURE 4.35   **Drawing Tangents to Two Circles (§4.32).**

(a)   (b)

FIGURE 4.36   **Tangents (§4.33).**

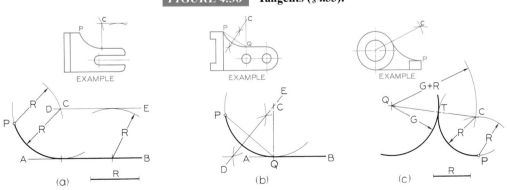

(a)   (b)   (c)

strike arc with radius equal to that of the given arc plus R. The intersection C of the arcs is the center of the required tangent arc.

■ 4.34 DRAWING AN ARC TANGENT TO TWO LINES AT RIGHT ANGLES

I. Two lines are given at right angles to each other (Fig. 4.37a).

II. With given radius R, strike arc intersecting given lines at tangent points T.

III. With given radius R again, and with points T as centers, strike arcs intersecting at C.

IV. With C as center and given radius R, draw the required tangent arc.

For small radii, such as $\frac{1}{8}R$ for fillets and rounds, it is not practicable to draw complete tangency constructions. Instead, draw a 45° bisector of the angle and locate the center of the arc by trial along this line (Fig. 4.37b).

Note that the center C can be located by intersecting lines parallel to the given lines, as shown in Fig. 4.13b. The circle template can also be used to draw the arcs R for the parallel line method of Fig. 4.13b. While the circle template is convenient to use for small radii up to about $\frac{5}{8}''$ or 16 mm, the diameter of the template circle is precisely equal twice the required radius.

■ 4.35 DRAWING AN ARC TANGENT TO TWO LINES AT ACUTE OR OBTUSE ANGLES

I. Two lines intersecting not making 90° with each other (Fig. 4.38a and 4.38b) are given.

II. Draw lines parallel to given lines, at distance R from them, to intersect at C, the required center.

III. From C, drop perpendiculars to the given lines, respectively, to locate tangent points T.

IV. With C as center and with given radius R, draw the required tangent arc between the points of tangency.

FIGURE 4.37   **Drawing a Tangent Arc in a Right Angle (§4.34).**

FIGURE 4.38   **Drawing Tangent Arcs (§4.35).**

■ 4.36 DRAWING AN ARC TANGENT TO AN ARC AND A STRAIGHT LINE

I. An arc with radius G and a straight line AB (Figs. 4.39a and 4.39b) are given.

II. Draw a straight line and an arc parallel, respectively, to the given straight line and arc at the required radius distance R from them, to intersect at C, the required center.

III. From C, drop a perpendicular to the given straight line to obtain one point of tangency T. Join the centers C and O with a straight line to locate the other point of tangency T.

IV. With center C and given radius R, draw the required tangent arc between the points of tangency.

■ 4.37 DRAWING AN ARC TANGENT TO TWO ARCS

I. Arcs with centers A and B and required radius R (Figs. 4.40a and 4.40b) are given.

II. With A and B as centers, draws arcs parallel to the

FIGURE 4.39 Drawing an Arc Tangent to an Arc and a Straight Line (§4.36).

FIGURE 4.40 Drawing an Arc Tangent to Two Arcs (§4.37).

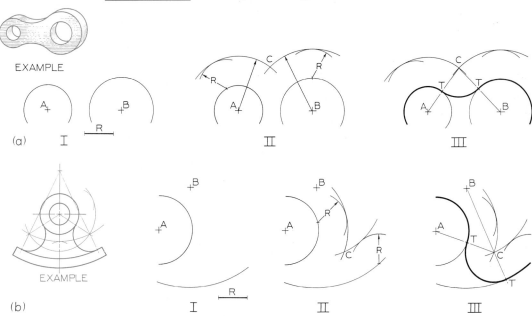

given arcs and at a distance R from them; their intersection C is the center of the required tangent arc.

III. Draw lines of centers AC and AC to locate points of tangency T, and draw the required tangent arc between the points of tangency, as shown.

■ 4.38 DRAWING AN ARC TANGENT TO TWO ARCS AND ENCLOSING ONE OR BOTH

REQUIRED ARC ENCLOSES BOTH GIVEN ARCS
With A and B as centers, strike arcs HK − r (given radius minus radius of small circle) and HK − R (given radius minus radius of large circle) intersecting at G, the center of the required tangent arc. Lines of centers GA and GB (extended) determine points of tangency T (Fig. 4.41a).

REQUIRED ARC ENCLOSES ONE GIVEN ARC
With C and D as centers, strike arcs HK + r (given radius plus radius of small circle) and HK − R (given radius minus radius of large circle) intersecting at G, the center of the required tangent arc. Lines of centers GC and GD (extended) determine points of tangency T (Fig. 4.41b).

■ 4.39 DRAWING A SERIES OF TANGENT ARCS CONFORMING TO A CURVE

First sketch lightly a smooth curve as desired (Fig. 4.42). By trial, find a radius R and a center C, produc-

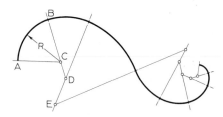

FIGURE 4.42   Drawing a Series of Tangent Arcs Conforming to a Curve (§4.39).

ing an arc AB that closely follows that portion of the curve. The successive centers D, E, and so on will be on lines joining the centers with the points of tangency, as shown.

■ 4.40 DRAWING AN OGEE CURVE

CONNECTING TWO PARALLEL LINES   Let NA and BM be the two parallel lines. Draw AB, and assume inflection point T (at midpoint if two equal arcs are desired) (Fig. 4.43a). At A and B, erect perpendiculars AF and BC. Draw perpendicular bisectors of AT and BT. The intersections F and C of these bisectors and the perpendiculars, respectively, are the centers of the required tangent arcs.

Let AB and CD be the two parallel lines, with point B as one end of the curve and R the given radii (Fig. 4.43b). At B, erect perpendicular to AB, make BG = R, and draw the arc as shown. Draw line SP parallel to CD at distance R from CD. With center G, draw the arc of radius 2R, intersecting line SP at O. Draw perpendicular OJ to locate tangent point J, and

FIGURE 4.41   Drawing an Arc Tangent to Two Arcs and Enclosing One or Both (§4.38).

(a)

(b)

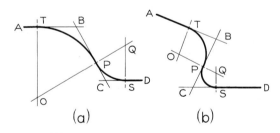

FIGURE 4.43   Drawing an Ogee Curve (§4.40).

join centers G and O to locate point of tangency T. Using centers G and O and radius R, draws the two tangent arcs as shown.

CONNECTING TWO NONPARALLEL LINES Let AB and CD be the two nonparallel lines (Fig. 4.43c). Erect perpendicular to AB at B. Select point G on the perpendicular so that BG equals any desired radius, and draw the arc as shown. Erect perpendicular to CD at C and make CE = BG. Join G to E and bisect it. The intersection F of the bisector and the perpendicular CE, extended, is the center of the second arc. Join centers of the two arcs to locate tangent point T, the inflection point of the curve.

■ 4.41 DRAWING A CURVE TANGENT TO THREE INTERSECTING LINES

Let AB, BC, and CD be the given lines (Fig. 4.44a and 4.44b). Select point of tangency P at any point on line

FIGURE 4.44   Drawing Two Curves Tangent to Three Intersecting Lines (§4.41).

BC. Make BT equal to BP, and CS equal to CP, and erect perpendiculars at the points P, T, and S. Their intersections O and Q are the centers of the required tangent arcs.

■ 4.42 RECTIFYING A CIRCULAR ARC

To *rectify* an arc is to lay out its true length along a straight line. The constructions are approximate, but well within the range of accuracy of drawing instruments.

TO RECTIFY A QUADRANT OF A CIRCLE, AB Draw AC tangent to the circle BC at 60° to AC, as shown (Fig. 4.45a). The line AC is almost equal to the arc AB; the difference in length is about 1 in 240.

TO RECTIFY ARC, AB Draw tangent at B (Fig. 4.45b). Draw chord AB and extend it to C, making BC equal to half AB. With C as center and radius CA, strike the arc AD. The tangent BD is slightly shorter than the given arc AB. For an angle of 45° the difference in length is about 1 in 2866.

Use the bow dividers and, beginning at A, set off equal distances until the division point nearest B is reached (Fig. 4.45c). At this point, reverse the direction and set off an equal number of distances along the tangent to determine point C. The tangent BC is slightly shorter than the given arc AB. If the angle subtended

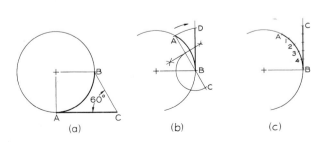

FIGURE 4.45   Rectifying Circular Arcs (§§4.42 and 4.43).

by each division is 10°, the error is approximately 1 in 830. *

■ 4.43 SETING OFF A GIVEN LENGTH ALONG A GIVEN ARC

To transfer distances from the tangent line to the arc, reverse the preceding method (Fig. 4.45c).

To set off the length BC along the arc BA, draw BC tangent to the arc at B (Fig. 4.45d). Divide BC into four equal parts. With center at 1, the first division point, and radius 1–C, draw the arc CA. The arc BA is practically equal to BC for angles less than 30°. For 45° the difference is approximately 1 in 3232, and for 60° it is about 1 in 835.

■ 4.44 THE CONIC SECTIONS

The conic sections are curves produced by planes intersecting a right circular cone (Fig. 4.46). Four types of curves are produced: the *circle*, *ellipse*, *parabola*, and *hyperbola*, according to the position of the planes, as shown. (Also see §19.7.) These curves were studied in detail by the ancient Greeks and are of great interest in mathematics, as well as in technical drawing. For equations, see any text on analytic geometry.

---

* If the angle θ subtending an arc of radius R is known, the length of the arc is

$$2\pi R \frac{\theta}{360°} = 0.01745R\theta.$$

■ 4.45 ELLIPSE CONSTRUCTION

The long axis of an ellipse is the major axis and the short axis is the minor axis (Fig. 4.47a). The foci E and F are found by striking arcs with radius equal to half the major axis and with center at the end of the minor axis. Another method is to draw a semicircle with the major axis as diameter, and then to draw GH parallel to the major axis and GE and HF parallel to the minor axis as shown.

An *ellipse* is generated by a point moving so that the sum of its distances from two points (the foci) is constant and equal to the major axis. As shown in Fig. 4.47b, an ellipse may be constructed by placing a looped string around the foci E and F and around C, one end of the minor axis, and moving the pencil point P along its maximum orbit while the string is kept taut.

■ 4.46 DRAWING A FOCI ELLIPSE

Let AB be the major axis and CD the minor axis (Fig. 4.48). This method is the geometrical counterpart of the pin-and-string method. Keep the construction very light, as follows:

I.   To find foci E and F, strike arcs R with radius equal to half the major axis and with centers at the ends of the minor axis.

II. Between E and O on the major axis, mark at random a number of points (spacing those on the left more closely), equal to the number of points de-

FIGURE 4.46   Conic Sections (§4.44).

FIGURE 4.47   Ellipse Constructions (§4.45).

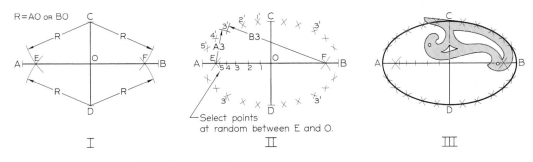

FIGURE 4.48 Drawing a Foci Ellipse (§4.46).

sired in each quadrant of the ellipse. In this figure, five points were deemed sufficient. For large ellipses, more points should be used—enough to ensure a smooth, accurate curve. Begin construction with any one of these points, such as 3. With E and F as centers and radii A–3 and B–3, respectively (from the ends of the major axis to point 3), strike arcs to intersect at four points 3′, as shown. Using the remaining points 1, 2, 4, and 5, for each find four additional points on the ellipse in the same manner.

III. Sketch the ellipse lightly through the points; then heavy in the final ellipse with the aid of an irregular curve.

A "long trammel" or a "short trammel" may be prepared from a small strip of stiff paper or thin cardboard (Fig. 4.49). In both cases, set off on the edge of the trammel distances equal to the semimajor (AC or BC) and semiminor (DC or EC) axes. With the short trammel, these distances overlap; with the long trammel they are end to end. To use either method, place the trammel so that two of the points are on the respective axes, as shown; the third point will then be on the curve and can be marked with a small dot. Find additional points by moving the trammel to other positions, always keeping the two points exactly on the respective axes. Extend the axes to use the long trammel. Find enough points to ensure a smooth and symmetrical ellipse. Sketch the ellipse lightly through the

points; then heavy in the ellipse with the aid of an irregular curve.

4.48 DRAWING A CONCENTRIC-CIRCLE ELLIPSE

If a circle is viewed so that the line of sight is perpendicular to the plane of the circle, as shown for the silver dollar in Fig. 4.50a, the circle will appear as a circle, in true size and shape. If the circle is viewed at an angle, as shown in Fig. 4.50b, it will appear as an ellipse. If the circle is viewed edgewise, it appears as a straight line, as shown in Fig. 4.50c. The case shown in Fig. 4.50b is the basis for the construction of an ellipse by the concentric-circle method, which follows. (Keep the construction very light.)

I. Draw circles on the major and minor axes, using them as diameters; draw any diagonal XX through center O. From the points X, where the diagonal intersects the large circle, draw lines XE parallel to the minor axis, and from the points H, where the diagonal intersects the small circle, draw lines HE parallel to the major axis. The intersections E are points on the ellipse. Two additional points, S and R, can be found by extending lines XE and HE, giving a total of four points from the one diagonal XX.

II. Draw as many additional diagonals as needed to provide a sufficient number of points for a smooth and symmetrical ellipse, each diagonal accounting for four points on the ellipse. Notice that where the curve is sharpest (near the ends of the ellipse),

GRAPHICS SPOTLIGHT

Virtual Reality on the World Wide Web

You can access 3D virtual reality sites on the World Wide Web (WWW) using special add-on software. One of the popular formats for showing virtual reality models on the web is VRML, which stands for Virtual Reality Modeling Language.

THE BEGINNINGS OF THE WEB

When the Internet was first started, its main use was to allow text and data to be stored on various hosts in a consistent format so that the information could be shared effectively. Originally it was difficult to use as you had to keep track of how to get to where the data was stored. A pioneer, Tim Berners-Lee, working at CERN, developed the World Wide Web creating the Universal Resource Locators (URLs) which are used to tell someone where to go and how to access your data on the Web, although you still have to remember the URL.

VRML STANDARD

By 1994 several groups were already working on building 3D visualization tools for the WWW. There was the possibility that there would be no clear standard for how 3D information would be stored and accessed. Tim Berners-Lee and Dave Raggett organized a session to discuss virtual reality interfaces to the World Wide Web and from this session VRML was conceived. The need for virtual reality tools to have a common language to describe 3D scenes and WWW links similar to HTML (hypertext markup language) was a common goal. In 1995 VRML 1.0 was developed. It allows you to move around static scenes, examine objects, and jump to links within the scene. The VRML 2.0 standard allows dynamic object behaviors, multi-user interaction, as well as animation, sound, and video. Using a VRML browser you can interact with VRML web sites in a way that is fun and visual. This is especially important for 3D information, like engineering designs. Software packages like *ANSYS/AutoFEA—Validation* include ways to export your models for VRML browsers so that you can use them on the WWW to interact with other members of your engineering team.

LIVE3D BROWSER FOR NETSCAPE

There are a number of different virtual reality browsers that you can use in order to view and interact with 3D worlds on the WWW. Live3D is a browser provided by Netscape. You may want to look for others such as Black Sun's Cybergate, Vream's WIRL, Superscape's Viscape, among many others. Live3D may not be quite as easy to control movement as some of the others, however it is a good starting point to view virtual reality worlds.

DYNOJET RESEARCH'S SITE USES VRML

One site you may find interesting to visit is Dynojet Research Incorporated's web site. It contains VRML models showing Dynojet Dynamometers which are used to diagnose motorcycle and car performance (see Fig. A). The dynamometer uses computerized technology to simulate road testing in the shop. In the VRML car dynamometer model, you can use Live3D to even walk into the pit and see the equipment under the dyno. In the VRML model shown below, you can walk all around the dyno and even view the calendars on the wall. Bruce Olson, CAD Engineer at Dynojet says, "Notice that the back wheel of the motorcycle is actually turning." It is animated, and as you are walking around the motorcycle dynamometer, you can see that the wheel turns just as it would on the real thing.

Another site that uses VRML that you may find interesting is Worlds, Inc.'s Alpha World, where you can interact with other uses, if you enroll as a citizen. In Alpha World you can have an *avatar*, a name from Hindu mythology meaning an incarnation of a god, as your 3D presence on the WWW. You can recreate yourself in almost any shape you wish. Your avatar can chat with other avatars, and you can even create your own buildings, grass, and other structures. (Hurry, real estate is hard to find!) Alpha World is only one of many such 3D interactive worlds.

INTRANET

Many companies are using VRML on their Intranet, a version of Internet that can only be accessed from inside the company's firewall. This can be a useful way for engineering groups to share and access up to date information, which may be sensitive or not ready for publication on the WWW.

(A) Copyright Dynojet Research.
Rendering by Bruce A. Olson.

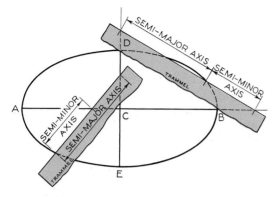

FIGURE 4.49   Drawing a Trammel Ellipse (§4.47).

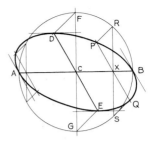

FIGURE 4.51   Oblique-Circle Ellipse (§4.49).

the points are constructed closer together to determine the curve better.

III. Sketch the ellipse lightly through the points, and then heavy in the final ellipse with the aid of an irregular curve.[†]

■ 4.49 DRAWING AN ELLIPSE ON CONJUGATE DIAMETERS: THE OBLIQUE-CIRCLE METHOD

Let AB and DE be the given conjugate diameters (Fig. 4.51). *Two diameters are conjugate when each is parallel to the tangents at the extremities of the other.* With center at C and radius CA, draw a circle; draw the diameter GF perpendicular to AB, and draw lines joining points D and F and points G and E.

Assume that the required ellipse is an oblique projection of the circle just drawn; the points D and E of the ellipse are the oblique projections of the points F and G of the circle, respectively; similarly, the points P

and Q are the oblique projections of the points R and S, respectively. The points P and Q are determined by assuming point X at any point on AB and drawing the lines RS and PQ, and RP and SQ, parallel, respectively, to GF and DE and FD and GE.

Determine at least five points in each quadrant (more for larger ellipses) by assuming additional points on the major axis and proceeding as explained for point X. Sketch the ellipse lightly through the points; then heavy in the final ellipse with the aid of an irregular curve.

■ 4.50 DRAWING A PARALLELOGRAM ELLIPSE

Given the major and minor axes, or the conjugate diameters AB and CD, draw a rectangle or parallelogram with sides parallel to the axes, respectively (Fig. 4.52a and 4.52b). Divide AO and AJ into the same number of equal parts, and draw *light* lines through these points from the ends of the minor axis, as shown. The intersection of like-numbered lines will be points on the ellipse. Locate points in the remaining three quadrants in a similar manner. Sketch the ellipse lightly through the points; then heavy in the final ellipse with the aid of an irregular curve.

[†] In Fig. 4.50, part I, the ordinate EZ of the ellipse is to the corresponding ordinate XZ of the circle as b is to a, where b represents the semiminor axis and a the semimajor axis. Thus, the area of the ellipse is equal to the area of the circumscribed circle multiplied by b/a; hence, it is equal to πab.

FIGURE 4.50   Drawing a Concentric-Circle Ellipse (§4.48).

FIGURE 4.52   **Parallelogram Ellipse (§4.50).**

■ 4.51 FINDING THE AXES OF AN ELLIPSE WITH CONJUGATE DIAMETERS GIVEN

Conjugate diameters AB and CD and the ellipse are given (Fig. 4.53a). With intersection O of the conjugate diameters (center of ellipse) as center, and any convenient radius, draw a circle to intersect the ellipse in four points. Join these points with straight lines, as shown; the resulting quadrilateral will be a rectangle whose sides are parallel, respectively, to the required major and minor axes. Draw the axes EF and GH parallel to the sides of the rectangle.

An ellipse only is given (Fig. 4.53b). To find the center of the ellipse, draw a circumscribing rectangle or parallelogram about the ellipse; then draw diagonals to intersect at center O as shown. The axes are then found as shown in Fig. 4.53a.

Conjugate diameters AB and CD only are given (Fig. 4.53c). With O as center and CD as diameter, draw a circle. Through center O and perpendicular to CD, draw line EF. From points E and F, where this perpendicular intersects the circle, draw lines FA and EA to form angle FAE. Draw the bisector AG of this angle. The major axis JK will be parallel to this bisector, and the minor axis LM will be perpendicular to it. The length AH will be one half the major axis, and HF one half the minor axis. The resulting major and minor axes are JK and LM, respectively.

■ 4.52 DRAWING A TANGENT TO AN ELLIPSE

CONCENTRIC-CIRCLE CONSTRUCTION   To draw a tangent at any point on an ellipse, such as E, draw the ordinate at E to intersect the circle at V (Fig. 4.54a). Draw a tangent to the circumscribed circle at V (§4.31), and extend it to intersect the major axis extended at G. The line GE is the required tangent.

To draw a tangent from a point outside the ellipse, such as P, draw the ordinate PY and extend it. Draw DP, intersecting the major axis at X. Draw FX and extend it to intersect the ordinate through P at Q. Then, from similar triangles QY:PY = OF:OD. Draw a tangent to the circle from Q, (§4.31), find the point of tangency R, and draw the ordinate at R to intersect the ellipse at Z. The line ZP is the required tangent. As a check on the drawing, the tangents RQ and ZP should intersect at a point on the major axis extended. Two tangents to the ellipse can be drawn from point P.

FOCI CONSTRUCTION   To draw a tangent at any point on the ellipse, such as point 3, draw the focal radii E–3 and F–3, extend one, and bisect the exterior angle, as shown in Fig. 4.54b. The bisector is the required tangent.

To draw a tangent from any point outside the ellipse, such as point P, with center at P and radius PF,

FIGURE 4.53   **Finding the Axes of an Ellipse (§4.51).**

(a) CONJUGATE DIAMETERS AND ELLIPSE ARE GIVEN

(b) FINDING CENTER

(c) CONJUGATE DIAMETERS GIVEN

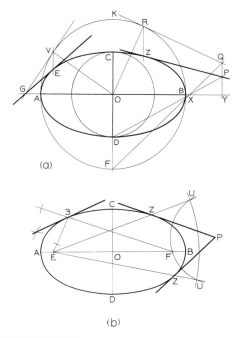

(a)

(b)

FIGURE 4.54 **Tangents to an Ellipse (§4.52).**

strike an arc as shown. With center at E and radius AB, strike an arc to intersect the first arc at points U. Draw the lines EU to intersect the ellipse at the points Z. The lines PZ are the required tangents.

4.53 ELLIPSE TEMPLATES

To save time in drawing ellipses and to ensure uniform results, ellipse templates are often used (Fig. 4.55a). These are plastic sheets with elliptical openings in a wide variety of sizes, and they usually come in sets of six or more sheets.

Ellipse guides are usually designated by the ellipse angle, the angle at which a circle is viewed to appear as an ellipse. In Fig. 4.55b, the angle between the line of sight and the edge view of the plane of the circle is found to be about 49°; hence the 50° ellipse template is indicated. Ellipse templates are generally available in ellipse angles at 5° intervals, such as 15°, 20°, and 25°. The 50° template provides a variety of sizes of 50° ellipses, and it is only necessary to select the one that fits. If the ellipse angle is not easily determined, you can always look for the ellipse that is approximately as long and as "fat" as the ellipse to be drawn.

A simple construction for finding the ellipse angle when the views are not available is shown in Fig. 4.55c. Using center O, strike arc BF; then draw CE parallel to the major axis. Draw diagonal OE, and measure angle EOB with a protractor. Use the ellipse template nearest to this angle; in this case a 35° template is selected.

Since it is not feasible to have ellipse openings for every exact size that may be required, it is often necessary to use the template somewhat in the manner of an irregular curve. For example, if the opening is too long and too "fat" for the required ellipse, one end may be drawn and then the template may be shifted slightly to draw the other end. Similarly, one long side may be drawn and then the template may be shifted slightly to draw the opposite side. In such cases, leave gaps between the four segments, to be filled in freehand or with the aid of an irregular curve. When the differences between the ellipse openings and the required ellipse are small, it is only necessary to lean the pencil slightly outward or inward from the guiding edge to offset the differences.

For inking the ellipses, a technical fountain pen is recommended (Fig. 4.55d).

FIGURE 4.55 **Using the Ellipse Template (§4.53).**

(a) ELLIPSE TEMPLATE   (b) ELLIPSE ANGLE   (c) FINDING ELLIPSE ANGLE   (d) USING ELLIPSE TEMPLATE

■ 4.54 DRAWING AN APPROXIMATE ELLIPSE

For many purposes, particularly where a small ellipse is required, the approximate circular-arc method is perfectly satisfactory (Fig. 4.56). Such an ellipse is sure to be symmetrical and may be quickly drawn.

Given axes AB and CD,

I. Draw line AC. With O as center and OA as radius, strike the arc AE. With C as center and CE as radius, strike the arc EF.

II. Draw perpendicular bisector GH of the line AF; the points K and J, where it intersects the axes, are centers of the required arcs.

III. Find centers M and L by setting off OL = OK and OM = OJ. Using centers K, L, M, and J, draw circular arcs as shown. The points of tangency T are at the junctures of the arcs on the lines joining the centers.

■ 4.55 DRAWING A PARABOLA

The curve of intersection between a right circular cone and a plane parallel to one of its elements, is a parabola (see Fig. 4.46d). The parabola is used to reflect surfaces for light and sound, for vertical curves in highways, for forms of arches, and approximately for forms of the curves of cables for suspension bridges. It is also used to show the bending moment at any point on a uniformly loaded beam or girder.

A *parabola* is generated by a point moving so that its distances from a fixed point, the focus, and from a fixed line, the directrix, remain equal.

Focus F and directrix AB are given. A parabola may be generated by a pencil guided by a string (Fig. 4.57a). Fasten the string at F and C; its length is GC. The point C is selected at random; its distance from G depends on the desired extent of the curve. Keep the

FIGURE 4.57   **Drawing a Parabola (§4.55).**

string taut and the pencil against the T-square, as shown.

Given focus F and directrix AB, draw a line DE parallel to the directrix and at any distance CZ from it (Fig. 4.57b). With center at F and radius CZ, strike arcs to intersect the line DE in the points Q and R, which are points on the parabola. Determine as many additional points as are necessary to draw the parabola ac-

FIGURE 4.56   **Drawing an Approximate Ellipse (§4.54).**

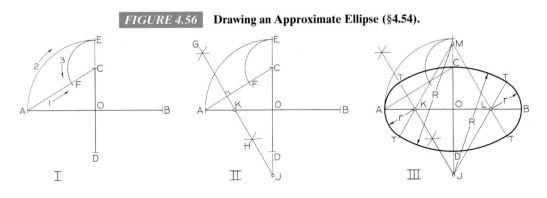

curately, by drawing additional lines parallel to line AB and proceeding in the same manner.

A tangent to the parabola at any point G bisects the angle formed by the focal line FG and the line SG perpendicular to the directrix.

Given the rise and span of the parabola (Fig. 4.57c), divide AO into any number of equal parts, and divide AD into a number of equal parts amounting to the square of that number. From line AB, each point on the parabola is offset by a number of units equal to the square of the number of units from point O. For example, point 3 projects 9 units (the square of 3). This method is generally used for drawing parabolic arches.

To find the focus, F, given points P, R, and V of a parabola (Fig. 4.57d), draw a tangent at P, making a = b. Draw perpendicular bisector of AP, which intersects the axis at F, the focus of the parabola.

Draw a parabola given rectangle or parallelogram ABCD (Figs. 4.58a and 4.58b). Divide BC into any even number of equal parts, divide the sides AB and DC each into half as many parts, and draw lines as shown. The intersections of like-numbered lines are points on the parabola.

■ 4.56 JOINING TWO POINTS BY A PARABOLIC CURVE

Let X and Y be the given points (Fig. 4.59). Assume any point O, and draw tangents XO and YO. Divide

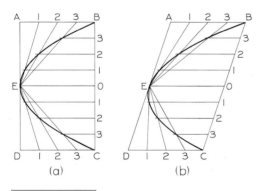

FIGURE 4.58   Drawing a Parabola (§4.55).

XO and YO into the same number of equal parts, number the division points as shown, and connect corresponding points. These lines are tangents of the required parabola and form its envelope. Sketch a light smooth curve, and then heavy in the curve with the aid of an irregular curve.

These parabolic curves are more pleasing in appearance than circular arcs and are useful in machine design. If the tangents OX and OY are equal, the axis of the parabola will bisect the angle between them.

■ 4.57 DRAWING A HYPERBOLA

The curve of intersection between a right circular cone and a plane making an angle with the axis smaller than that made by the elements is a hyperbola (see Fig. 4.46e). A *hyperbola* is generated by a point moving so that the difference of its distances from two fixed points, the foci is constant and equal to the transverse axis of the hyperbola.

Let F and F′ be the foci and AB the transverse axis (Fig. 4.60a). The curve may be generated by a pencil guided by a string, as shown. Fasten a string at F′ and C; its length is FC minus AB. The point C is chosen at random; its distance from F depends on the desired extent of the curve.

Fasten the straightedge at F. If it is revolved about F, with the pencil point moving against it and with the string taut, the hyperbola may be drawn as shown.

To construct the curve geometrically, select any point X on the transverse axis produced (Fig. 4.60b). With centers at F and F′ and BX as radius, strike the arcs DE. With the same centers, F and F′, and AX as radius, strike arcs to intersect the arcs first drawn in the points Q, R, S, and T, which are points of the required hyperbola. Find as many additional points as are necessary to draw the curves accurately by selecting other points similar to point X along the transverse axis and proceeding as described for point X.

To draw the tangent to a hyperbola at a given point P, bisect the angle between the focal radii FP and F′P. The bisector is the required tangent.

FIGURE 4.59   Parabolic Curves (§4.56).

(a)

(b)

(c)

FIGURE 4.60   **Drawing a Hyperbola (§4.57).**

To draw the asymptotes HCH of the hyperbola, draw a circle with the diameter FF′ and erect perpendiculars to the transverse axis at the points A and B to intersect the circle in the points H. The lines HCH are the required asymptotes.

■4.58 DRAWING AN EQUILATERAL HYPERBOLA

Let the asymptotes OB and OA, at right angles to each other, and the point P on the curve be given (Fig. 4.61).

In an equilateral hyperbola, the asymptotes, which are at right angles to each other, may be used as the axes to which the curve is referred. If a chord of the hyperbola is extended to intersect the axes, the intercepts between the curve and the axes are equal (Fig. 4.61a). For example, a chord through given point P intersects the axes at points 1 and 2, intercepts P–1 and 2–3 are equal, and point 3 is a point on the hyperbola. Likewise, another chord through P provides equal intercepts P–1′ and 3′–2′, and point 3′ is a point on the curve. Not all chords need be drawn through given point P, but as new points are established on the curve, chords may be drawn through them to obtain more

FIGURE 4.61   **Equilateral Hyperbola (§4.58).**

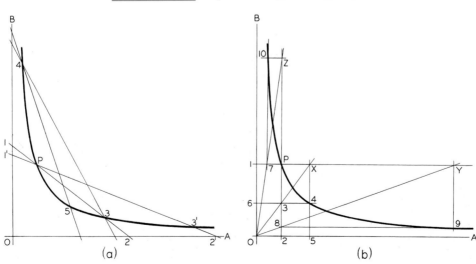

points. After enough points are found to ensure an accurate curve, the hyperbola is drawn with the aid of an irregular curve.

In an equilateral hyperbola, the coordinates are related so their products remain constant. Through given point P, draw lines 1–P–Y and 2–P–Z parallel, respectively, to the axes (Fig. 4.61b). From the origin of coordinates O, draw any diagonal intersecting these two lines at points 3 and X. At these points draw lines parallel to the axes, intersecting at point 4, a point on the curve. Likewise, another diagonal from O intersects the two lines through P at points 8 and Y, and lines through these points parallel to the axes intersect at point 9, another point on the curve. A third diagonal similarly produces point 10 on the curve, and so on. Find as many points as necessary for a smooth curve, and draw the parabola with the aid of an irregular curve. It is evident from the similar triangles O–X–5 and O–3–2 that lines P–1 × P–2 = 4–5 × 4–6.

The equilateral hyperbola can be used to represent varying pressure of a gas as the volume varies,

since the pressure varies inversely with the volume; that is, pressure × volume is constant.

■ 4.59 DRAWING A SPIRAL OF ARCHIMEDES

To find points on the curve, draw lines through the pole C, making equal angles with each other, such as 30° angles (Fig. 4.62). Beginning with any one line, set off any distance, such as 2 mm or $\frac{1}{16}''$; set off twice that distance on the next line, three times on the third, and so on. Through the points thus determined, draw a smooth curve, using irregular curve.

■ 4.60 DRAWING A HELIX

A *helix* is generated by a point moving around and along the surface of a cylinder or cone with a uniform angular velocity about the axis, and with a uniform linear velocity about the axis, and with a uniform velocity in the direction of the axis (Fig. 4.63). A cylindrical helix is generally known simply as a helix. The distance measure parallel to the axis traversed by the point in one revolution is called the lead.

If the cylindrical surface on which a helix is generated is rolled out onto a plane, the helix becomes a straight line (Fig. 4.63a). The portion below the helix becomes a right triangle, the altitude of which is equal to the lead of the helix; the length of the base is equal to the circumference of the cylinder. Such a helix, therefore, can be defined as the shortest line that can be drawn on the surface of a cylinder connecting two points not on the same element.

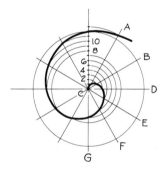

FIGURE 4.62   **Spiral of Archimedes (§4.59).**

FIGURE 4.63   **Helix (§4.60).**

(a)

(b)

(c) A LEFT-HAND HELIX

(d)

To draw the helix, draw two views of the cylinder on which the helix is generated (Fig. 4.63b). Divide the circle of the base into any number of equal parts. On the rectangular view of the cylinder, set off the lead and divide it into the same number of equal parts as the base. Number the divisions as shown (in this case 16). When the generating point has moved one sixteenth of the distance around the cylinder, it will have risen one sixteenth of the lead; when it has moved halfway around the cylinder, it will have risen half the lead; and so on. Points on the helix are found by projecting up from point 1 in the circular view to line 1 in the rectangular view, from point 2 in the circular view to line 2 in the rectangular view, and so on.

Figure 4.63b is a right-hand helix. In a left-hand helix (Fig. 4.63c), the visible portions of the curve are inclined in the opposite direction—that is, downward to the right. The helix shown in Fig. 4.63b can be converted into a left-hand helix by interchanging the visible and hidden lines.

The helix finds many applications in industry, as in screw threads, worm gears, conveyors, spiral stairways, and so on. The stripes of a barber pole are helical in form.

The construction for a right-hand conical helix is shown in Fig. 4.63d.

■4.61 DRAWING AN INVOLUTE

An *involute* is the path of a point on a string as the string unwinds from a line, polygon, or circle.

TO DRAW AN INVOLUTE OF A LINE   Let AB be the given line. With AB as radius and B as center, draw the semicircle AC (Fig. 4.64a). With AC as radius and A as center, draw the semicircle CD. With BD as radius and B as center, draw the semicircle DE. Continue similarly, alternating centers between A and B, until a figure of the required size is completed.

TO DRAW AN INVOLUTE OF A TRIANGLE   Let ABC be the given triangle. With CA as radius and C as center, strike the arc AD (Fig. 4.64b). With BD as radius and B as center, strike the arc DE. With AE as radius and A as center, strike the arc EF. Continue similarly until a figure of the required size is completed.

TO DRAW AN INVOLUTE OF A SQUARE   Let ABCD be the given square. With DA as radius and D as center, draw the 90° arc AE (Fig. 4.64c). Proceed as for the involute of a triangle until a figure of the required size is completed.

TO DRAW AN INVOLUTE OF A CIRCLE   A circle may be regarded as a polygon with an infinite number of sides (Fig. 4.64d). The involute is constructed by dividing the circumference into a number of equal parts, drawing a tangent at each division point, setting off along each tangent the length of the corresponding circular arc (see Fig. 4.45c), and drawing the required curve through the points set off on the several tangents.

An involute can be generated by a point on a straight line that is rolled on a fixed circle (Fig. 4.64e). Points on the required curve may be determined by setting off equal distances 0–1, 1–2, 2–3, and so on, along the circumference, drawing a tangent at each division point, and proceeding as explained for Fig. 4.64d.

The involute of a circle is used in the construction of involute gear teeth. In this system, the involute forms the face and a part of the flank of the teeth of gear wheels; the outlines of the teeth of racks are straight lines.

■4.62 DRAWING A CYCLOID

A *cycloid* generated by a point P in the circumference of a circle that rolls along a straight line (Fig. 4.65).

FIGURE 4.64   Involutes (§4.61).

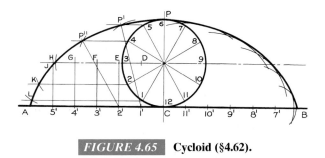

FIGURE 4.65 Cycloid (§4.62).

Either method may be used; however, the second is the shorter one and is preferred. It is evident, from the tangent arcs drawn in the manner just described, that the line joining the generating point and the point of contact for the generating circle is a normal of the cycloid. The lines 1′–P″ and 2′–P′, for instance, are normals; this property makes the cycloid suitable for the outlines of gear teeth.

Given the generating circle and the straight line AB tangent to it, make the distances CA and CB each equal to the semicircumference of the circle (see Fig. 4.45e). Divide these distances and the semicircumference into the same number of equal parts (six, for instance) and number them consecutively, as shown. Suppose the circle rolls to the left; when point 1 of the circle reaches point 1′ of the line, the center of the circle will be at D, point 7 will be the highest point of the circle, and the generating point 6 will be at the same distance from the line AB as point 5 is when the circle is in its central position. Hence, to find the point P′, draw a line through point 5 parallel to AB and intersect it with an arc drawn from the center D with a radius equal to that of the circle. To find point P″, draw a line through point 4 parallel to AB, and intersect it with an arc drawn from the center E, with a radius equal to that of the circle. Points J, K, and L are found in a similar manner.

Another method that may be employed is shown in the right half of Fig. 4.64. With center at 11′ and the chord 11–6 as radius, strike an arc. With 10′ as center and the chord 10–6 as radius, strike an arc. Continue similarly with centers 9′, 8′, and 7′. Draw the required cycloid tangent to these arcs.

■ **4.63 DRAWING AN EPICYCLOID OR A HYPOCYCLOID**

If the generating point P is on the circumference of a circle that rolls along the convex side of a larger circle, the curve generated is an epicycloid (Fig. 4.66a). If the circle rolls along the concave side of a larger circle, the curve generated is a hypocycloid (Fig. 4.66b). These curves are drawn in a manner similar to the cycloid (Fig. 4.65). Like the cycloid, these curves are used to form the outlines of certain gear teeth and are, therefore, of practical importance in machine design.

■ **4.64 COMPUTER GRAPHICS**

Through the use of various application programs and routines available in computer graphics, it is possible to establish accurately the various geometric constructions shown in this chapter. CAD programs are particularly well suited for repetitive operations, such as dividing a line into a number of equal parts, and for generating lines representing mathematical curves, such as the hyperbola and parabola. Examples of CAD-produced geometric shapes and surfaces are shown in Fig. 4.67.

FIGURE 4.66 Epicycloid and Hypocycloid (§4.63).

(a) EPICYCLOID

(b) HYPOCYCLOID

SURFACE OF REVOLUTION　　　　SWEPT SURFACE　　　　MESH SURFACE

RULED SURFACE　　　PLANE/SURFACE INTERSECTION　　　SPHERE

FIGURE 4.67 **Geometric Shapes and Surfaces Produced with TRI-CAD System.** *Courtesy of Lodgrafix, Inc.* **(§4.64).**

■ KEY WORDS

POINT	**LINE**
ARC	**CIRCLE**
TANGENT	**TANGENT POINT**
PARALLEL	**PERPENDICULAR**
POLYGON	**REGULAR POLYGON**
BISECT	**CONIC SECTION**
CONSTRUCTION LINES	**CENTER**
RADIUS	**DIAMETER**
CONCENTRIC	**RIGHT ANGLE**

■ CHAPTER SUMMARY

- Understanding basic geometric construction techniques is fundamental to the success of both traditional drawing and CAD drawing.
- All drawings are made up of points, lines, arcs, and circles drawn at various sizes and constructed in specific location to each other. Geometric construction cannot be approximated.
- Every point, line, arc and circle must be precisely located. CAD cannot draw correctly if you cannot tell the program where you want an element drawn.
- The advantage that CAD provides in geometric construction is drawing precision. Only the drafter knows where a point, line, arc, or circle needs to be drawn, and more importantly, *how* to draw it. A poor paper drafter will most likely be a poor CAD drafter.
- One of the more difficult types of geometric construction are tangencies. There are many different types of tangencies and each requires a special drawing technique.
- Knowing when to draw a line parallel or perpendicular to another line is an important part of geometric construction.
- Unless the drafter knows the basics of geometric construction, it will be difficult to create a drawing using either instruments or CAD.

■ REVIEW QUESTIONS

1. What are the four basic conic sections and how are they cut from a cone?
2. How can you divide a line into equal parts? A space into equal parts?
3. How many ways can an arc be tangent to one line? To two lines? To a line and an arc? To two arcs? Draw an example of each.
4. Draw an equilateral triangle, a right triangle, and an isosceles triangle.
5. Given a line, draw another line (1) parallel to the first, (2) perpendicular to the first. Then draw a horizontal line through the intersection of the lines. Finally, draw a vertical line through the intersection.
6. Draw a regular square, hexagon, and octagon so that the distance from flat to flat is 2 inches.
7. List the different methods for drawing an approximation of an ellipse. Pick one and draw an ellipse with a major diameter of 6 inches and a minor diameter of 3 inches.
8. Demonstrate the technique for drawing a line parallel to a given line using only a pencil, triangle, and straight edge.
9. Demonstrate the technique for drawing a line perpendicular to a given line using only a pencil, triangle, and straight edge.

■ GEOMETRIC CONSTRUCTION PROBLEMS

Geometric constructions should be done very accurately, using a hard pencil (2H to 4H) with a long, sharp, conical point. Draw given and required lines dark and medium in thickness, and draw construction lines *very light*. Do not erase construction lines. Indicate points and lines as described in §4.1.

In your assignments from the following problems, use Layout A–2 (see inside of front cover) divided into four parts, as shown in Fig. 4.68, or Layout A4–2 (adjusted). Additional sheets with other problems selected from Figs. 4.69–4.80 and drawn on the same sheet layout may be assigned.

Many problems are dimensioned in the metric system. Your instructor may ask you to convert these remaining problems to metric measure. (See the inside front cover for decimal and millimeter equivalents.)

Set up each problem so as to make the best use of the space available, to present the problem to best advantage, and to produce a pleasing appearance. Letter the principal points of all constructions in a manner similar to the various illustrations in this chapter.

Since many of the problems in this chapter are of a general nature, they can also be solved on most computer graphics systems. If a system is available, your instructor may choose to assign specific problems to be completed by this method.

The first four problems are shown in Fig. 4.68.

Prob. 4.1 Draw an inclined line AB 65 mm long and bisect it (see Fig. 4.8).

Prob. 4.2 Draw any angle with vertex at C. Bisect it (see Fig. 4.10), and transfer one half to a new position at D (see Fig. 4.11).

Prob. 4.3 Draw in inclined line EF and assume distance GH = 42 mm. Draw a line parallel to EF and at the distance GH from it (see Fig. 4.13a).

Prob. 4.4 Draw the line JK 95 mm long and divide it into five equal parts using dividers. Draw a line LM 58 mm long and divide it into three equal parts by the parallel-line method (see Fig. 4.15).

FIGURE 4.68   (Probs. 4.1–4.4) Geometric Constructions. Layout A–2 or A4–2 (adjusted).

Prob. 4.5 Draw a line OP 92 mm long and divide it into three proportional parts to in the ratio of 3:5:9 (see Fig. 4.17a).

Prob. 4.6 Draw a line 87 mm long and divide it into parts proportional to the square of x, where $x = 1, 2, 3$, and 4 (see Fig. 4.17c).

Prob. 4.7 Draw a triangle with sides of 76 mm, 85 mm, and 65 mm (see Fig. 4.19). Bisect the three interior angles (see Fig. 4.10). The bisectors should meet at a point. Draw the inscribed circle with the point as center.

Prob. 4.8 Draw a right triangle having a hypotenuse 65 mm and one leg 40 mm (see Figs. 4.3 and 4.20), and draw a circle through the three vertexes (see Fig. 4.32).

Prob. 4.9 Draw an inclined line QR 84 mm long. Select a point P on the line 32 mm form Q, and erect a perpendicular (see Fig. 4.18c). Assume a point S 45.5 mm from the line, and erect a perpendicular from S to the line (see Fig. 4.18b).

Prob. 4.10 Draw two lines making an angle of $35\frac{1}{2}°$ with each other using the tangent method (see Fig. 4.21a). Check with a protractor.

Prob. 4.11 Draw two lines making an angle of 33° 16′ with each other using the sine method (see Fig. 4.21b). Check with a protractor.

Prob. 4.12 Draw an equilateral triangle having 63.5-mm sides (see Fig. 4.22a). Bisect the interior angles (see Fig. 4.10). Draw the inscribed circle using the intersection of the bisectors as center.

Prob. 4.13 Draw inclined line TU 55 mm long, and then draw a square on TU as a given side (see Fig. 4.23a).

Prob. 4.14 Draw a 54-mm diameter-circle (lightly); inscribe a square in the circle and circumscribe a square on the circle (see Figs. 4.23c and 4.23d).

Prob. 4.15 Draw a 65-mm-diameter circle (lightly). Find the vertexes of a regular inscribed pentagon (see Fig. 4.24a), and join the vertexes to form a five-pointed star.

Prob. 4.16 Draw a 65-mm-diameter circle (lightly). Inscribe a hexagon (see Fig. 4.25b), and circumscribe a hexagon (see Fig. 4.26d).

Prob. 4.17 Draw a square (lightly) with 63.5-mm sides (see Fig. 4.23b), and inscribe an octagon (see Fig. 4.28b).

Prob. 4.18 Draw a triangle similar to that in Fig. 4.29a, with sides 50 mm, 38 mm, and 73 mm long. Transfer the triangle to a new location and turned 180° similar to that in Fig. 4.29b. Check by the pricked-point method (§4.29).

Prob. 4.19 In the center of your space, draw a rectangle 88 mm wide and 61 mm high. Show construction for reducing this rectangle first to 70 mm wide and then to 58 mm wide (see Fig. 4.31b).

Prob. 4.20 Draw three points arranged approximately as those in Fig. 4.32a), and draw a circle through the three points.

Prob. 4.21 Draw a 58-mm-diameter circle. Assume a point S on the left side of the circle and draw a tangent at that point (see Fig. 4.34a). Assume a point T to the right of the circle 50 mm from its center. Draw two tangents to the circle through the point (see Fig. 4.34b).

Prob. 4.22 Draw a horizontal center line through your space. Then draw two circles with 50-mm-diameter and 38-mm-diameter, respectively, with centers 54 mm apart. Locate the circles so that the construction will be centered in the space. Draw "open-belt" tangents to the circles (see Fig. 4.35a).

Prob. 4.23 Do the same as for Prob. 4.21 except draw "crossed-belt" tangents to the circle (see Fig. 4.35b).

Prob. 4.24 Draw a vertical line VW 33 mm from the left side of your space. Assume point P 44 mm farther to the right and 25 mm down from top of space. Draw a 56-mm-diameter circle through P, tangent to VW (see Fig. 4.36a).

Prob. 4.25 Draw a vertical line XY 35 mm from the left side of your space. Assume point P 44 mm farther to the right and 25 mm down from the top of the space. Assume point Q on line XY and 50 mm from P. Draw a circle through P and tangent to XY at Q (see Fig. 4.36b).

Prob. 4.26 Draw a 64-mm-diameter circle with center C 16 mm directly to left of center of space. Assume point P at the lower right and 60 mm from C. Draw an arc with 25-mm-radius through P and tangent to the circle (see Fig. 4.36c).

Prob. 4.27 Draw a vertical line and a horizontal line, each 65 mm long (see Fig. 4.37, part I). Draw an arc with a 38 mm radius, tangent to the lines.

Prob. 4.28 Draw a horizontal line 20 mm up from the bottom of your space. Select a point on the line 50 mm from the left side of space, and through it draw a line upward to the right at 60° to horizontal. Draw arcs with a 35 mm radius within an obtuse angle and acute angle, respectively, tangent to the two lines (see Fig. 4.38).

Prob. 4.29 Draw two intersecting lines making an angle of 60° with each other similar to Fig. 4.38a. Assume a point P on one line at a distance of 45 mm from the intersection. Draw an arc tangent to both lines with one point of tangency at P (see Fig. 4.33).

Prob. 4.30 Draw vertical line AB 32 mm from the left side of your space. Draw an arc of 42 mm radius with its center 75 mm to the right of the line and in the lower right portion of your space. Draw an arc of 25 mm radius tangent to AB and to the first arc (see Fig. 4.39).

Prob. 4.31 With centers 20 mm up from the bottom of your space and 86 mm apart, draw arcs of radii 44 mm and 24 mm, respectively. Draw an arc of 32 mm radius tangent to the two arcs (see Fig. 4.40).

Prob. 4.32 Draw two circles as in Prob. 4.22. Draw an arc of 70 mm radius tangent to the upper sides of, and enclosing, the circles (see Fig. 4.41a). Draw an arc of 50 mm radius tangent to the circles but enclosing only the smaller circle (see Fig. 4.41b).

Prob. 4.33 Draw two parallel inclined lines 45 mm apart. Choose a point on each line and connect them with an ogee curve tangent to the two parallel lines (see Fig. 4.43a).

Prob. 4.34 Draw an arc of 54 mm radius that subtends an angle of 90°. Find the length of the arc by two methods (see Figs. 4.45a and 4.45c). Calculate the length of the arc and compare with the lengths determined graphically. (See first-note in §4.42).

Prob. 4.35 Draw a major axis 102 mm long (horizontally) and a minor axis 64 mm long, with their intersection at the enter of the space. Draw an ellipse by the foci method with at least five points in each quadrant (see Fig. 4.48).

Prob. 4.36 Draw axes as in Prob. 4.35, and draw an ellipse by the trammel method (see Fig. 4.49).

Prob. 4.37 Draw axes as in Prob. 4.35, and draws an ellipse by the concentric-circle method (see Fig. 4.50).

Prob. 4.38 Draw axes as in Prob. 4.35, and draw an ellipse by the parallelogram method (see Fig. 4.52a).

Prob. 4.39 Draw conjugate diameters intersecting at the center of your space. Draw 88-mm-diameter horizontally, and 70-mm-diameter at 60° with horizontal. Draw an oblique-circle ellipse (see Fig. 4.51). Find at least five points in each quadrant.

Prob. 4.40 Draw conjugate diameters as in Prob. 4.39, and draw the ellipse by the parallelogram method (see Fig. 4.52b).

Prob. 4.41 Draw axes as in Prob. 4.35, and draw an approximate ellipse (see Fig. 4.56).

Prob. 4.42 Draw a parabola with a vertical axis and the focus 12 mm from the directrix (see Fig. 4.57b). Find at least nine points on the curve.

Prob. 4.43 Draw a hyperbola with a horizontal transverse axis 25 mm long and the foci 38 mm apart (see Fig. 4.60b). Draw the asymptotes.

Prob. 4.44 Draw a horizontal line near the bottom of the space, and a vertical line near the left side of the space. Assume point P 16 mm to the right of the vertical line and 38 mm above the horizontal line. Draw an equilateral hyperbola through P and with reference to the two lines as asymptotes. Use either method shown in Fig. 4.61.

Prob. 4.45 Using the center of the space as the pole, draw a spiral of Archimedes with the generating point moving in a counterclockwise direction and away from the pole at the rate of 25 mm in each convolution (see Fig. 4.62).

Prob. 4.46 Through center of your space, draw a horizontal center line, and on it construct a right-hand helix 50 mm diameter, 64 mm long, and with a lead of 25 mm (see Fig. 4.63). Draw only a half-circular end view.

Prob. 4.47 Draw the involute of an equilateral triangle with 15-mm sides (see Fig. 4.64b).

Prob. 4.48 Draw the involute of a 20-mm-diameter circle (see Fig. 4.64d).

Prob. 4.49 Draw a cycloid generated by a 30-mm-diameter circle rolling along a horizontal straight line (see Fig. 4.65).

Prob. 4.50 Draw and epicycloid generated by a 38-mm-diameter circle rolling along a circular arc with a radius of 64 mm (see Fig. 4.66a).

Prob. 4.51 Draw a hypocycloid generated by a 38-mm-diameter circle rolling along a circular arc with a radius of 64 mm (see Fig. 4.66b).

FIGURE 4.69   **(Prob. 4.52) Spanner.**

FIGURE 4.70   **(Prob. 4.53) Rocker Arm.**

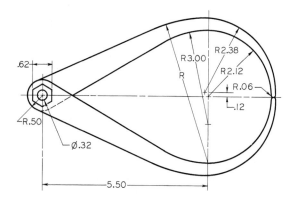

FIGURE 4.71   **(Prob.4.54) Outside Caliper.**

FIGURE 4.72   **(Prob. 4.55) Special Cam.**

FIGURE 4.73   **(Prob. 4.56) Boiler Stay.**

Prob. 4.52 Using Layout A–2 or A4–2 (adjusted), draw the spanner in Fig. 4.69. Omit dimensions and notes unless assigned.

Prob. 4.53 Using Layout A–2 or A4–2 (adjusted), draw the rocker arm in Fig. 4.70. Omit dimensions and notes unless assigned.

Prob. 4.54 Using Layout A–2 or A4–2 (adjusted), draw the outside caliper in Fig. 4.71. Omit dimensions and notes unless assigned.

Prob. 4.55 Using Layout A–2 or A4–2 (adjusted), draw the special cam in Fig. 4.72. Omit dimensions and notes unless assigned.

Prob. 4.56 Using Layout A–2 or A4–2 (adjusted), draw the boiler stay in Fig. 4.73. Omit dimensions and notes unless assigned.

Prob. 4.57 Using Layout A–2 or A4–2 (adjusted), draw the shaft hanger casting in Fig. 4.74. Omit dimensions and notes unless assigned.

Prob. 4.58 Using Layout A–2 or A4–2 (adjusted), draw the shift lever in Fig. 4.75. Omit dimensions and notes unless assigned.

Prob. 4.59 Using Layout A–2 or A4–2 (adjusted), draw the gear arm in Fig. 4.76. Omit dimensions and notes unless assigned.

FIGURE 4.74   (Prob. 4.57) Shaft Hanger Casting.

FIGURE 4.76   (Prob. 4.59) Gear Arm.

FIGURE 4.75   (Prob. 4.58) Shift Lever.

FIGURE 4.77   (Prob. 4.60) Form Roll Lever.

Prob. 4.60   Using Layout A–2 or A4–2 (adjusted), draw the form roll lever in Fig. 4.77. Omit dimensions and notes unless assigned.

Prob. 4.61   Using Layout A–2 or A4–2 (adjusted), draw the press base in Fig. 4.78. Omit dimensions and notes unless assigned.

Prob. 4.62   Using Layout A–2 or A4–2 (adjusted), draw the special S-wrench in Fig. 4.79. Omit dimensions and notes unless assigned.

Prob. 4.63   Using Layout A–2 or A4–2 (adjusted), draw the photo floodlight reflector in Fig. 4.80. Omit dimensions and notes unless assigned.

FIGURE 4.78   (Prob. 4.61) Press Base.

FIGURE 4.79   (Prob. 4.62) Special S-Wrench.

FIGURE 4.80   (Prob. 4.63) Photo Floodlight Reflector.

C H A P T E R 5

TECHNICAL SKETCHING AND SHAPE DESCRIPTION

OBJECTIVES

After studying the material in this chapter, you should be able to:

1. Read any type of sketch and understand the object depicted in the sketch.
2. Create sketches of both two- and three-dimensional objects using the correct sketching methods.
3. Demonstrate how to sketch parallel, perpendicular, and evenly spaced lines.
4. Demonstrate how to sketch a circle and arc of a given diameter.
5. Demonstrate how to estimate and compare dimensions of an object using a pencil at arms length.
6. Sketch an object to scale using grid drawing media.
7. Prepare a sketch of an object to be drawn using CAD showing all tangents, centers, and sizes.
8. Sketch an object on isometric grid paper.
9. Sketch the primary views of an orthographic drawing in proper orientation and alignment.
10. Show examples of the correct use of the alphabet of sketch lines.
11. Describe the difference between a sketch and a drawing.

OVERVIEW

Proper sketching technique is one of the most important skills that a traditional or CAD drafter must master. Sketching is a formal process of visualizing three-dimensional objects in preparation for drawing on paper or with CAD. Sketching is a quick way to communicate ideas with other members of the design team. (The old Chinese saying that "one picture is worth a thousand words" is not without foundation.) Sketching is an excellent way of planning out the drawing process necessary to effectively create a complex object. A properly drawn sketch will act like a road map for the completion of the final paper or CAD drawing. Drafters who sketch solutions before placing lines on paper or the CAD screen can often complete a drawing sooner and with fewer errors than those who cannot sketch effectively. Sketching is an excellent way of learning how to represent three-dimensional objects on a two-dimensional surface.

■ 5.1 TECHNICAL SKETCHING

Freehand sketches are of great value to designers in organizing their thoughts and recording their ideas. Sketching is an effective and economical means of formulating various solutions to a given problem so that a choice can be made between them. Time can be lost if the designer starts to do a scaled layout before adequate preliminary study with the aid of sketches. Information about changes in design or covering replacement of broken parts or lost drawings is usually conveyed through sketches.

The degree of perfection required in a given sketch depends on its intended use. Quick sketches done to supplement oral descriptions may be rough and incomplete. On the other hand, sketches that are supposed to convey important and precise information to engineers, technicians, or skilled workers should be executed as carefully and exactly as possible.

The term "freehand sketch" does not mean a crude or sloppy freehand drawing in which no particular effort has been made. On the contrary, as shown in Fig. 5.1, a freehand sketch should be made with care and with attention to proportion, clarity, and correct line widths.

■ 5.2 SKETCHING MATERIALS

One advantage of freehand sketching is that it requires only pencil, paper, and eraser. When sketches are made in the field and an accurate record is required, small notebooks or sketching pads are frequently used. Graph paper can be helpful, especially to someone who cannot sketch reasonably well without guide lines. Paper with 4, 5, 8, or 10 squares per inch is recommended. Such paper is convenient for maintaining correct proportions (Fig. 5.2).

Sketching pads of plain tracing paper may be accompanied by a master cross-section sheet, which shows clearly through a transparent sheet placed on top of it. (A master cross-section sheet can also be drawn with instruments.) A specially ruled isometric paper is available for isometric sketching (see Fig. 5.26).

Soft pencils, such as HB or F, should be used for freehand sketching. Use a mechanical pencil, and sharpen it to a conical point. Use this sharp point for center lines, dimension lines, and extension lines. For visible lines, hidden lines, and cutting-plane lines, round off the point slightly to produce the desired thickness of line (Fig. 5.3). For carefully made sketches, two soft erasers are recommended—Pink Pearl and a Mars-Plastic.

■ 5.3 TYPES OF SKETCHES

Since technical sketches are made of three-dimensional objects, the form of the sketch conforms approximately to one of the four standard types of projection. In multiview projection (Fig. 5.4a), the object is described by its necessary views (§§5.14–5.16). As shown in Figs. 5.4b through 5.4d, the object may also be shown pictorially in a single view, by *axonometric (isometric)*, *oblique*, or *perspective sketches*, respectively (see §§5.9–5.13).

■ 5.4 SCALE

Sketches usually are *not made to any scale*. Objects should be sketched in their correct proportions as accurately as possible, by eye. However, cross-section paper provides a ready scale (by counting squares) that may be used to assist in sketching to correct proportions. The size of the sketch is purely optional, depending on the complexity of the object and the size of paper available. Small objects are often sketched oversize to show the necessary details clearly.

■ 5.5 TECHNIQUE OF LINES

The chief difference between an instrument drawing and a freehand sketch lies in the character or *tech-*

FIGURE 5.1   **Great Ideas Often Start as Freehand Sketches Made on Scratch Paper.** *Courtesy of ANATech, Inc.*

FIGURE 5.2   **Sketch on Graph Paper.**

FIGURE 5.3   **Pencil Points.**

nique of the lines. A good freehand line is not expected to be as rigidly straight or exactly uniform as an instrument line. While the effectiveness of an instrument line lies in exacting uniformity, the quality of a freehand line lies in its *freedom* and *variety* (Figs. 5.5 and 5.7).

Conventional lines drawn instrumentally and freehand are shown in Fig. 5.6. The freehand construction line is a very light, rough line in which some strokes may overlap. All other lines should be dark and clean-cut. Accent the ends of all dashes, and maintain a sharp contrast between the line thicknesses. In particular, make visible lines **heavy** so the outline will stand out clearly, and make hidden lines, center lines, dimension lines, and extension lines *thin*.

5.6 SKETCHING STRAIGHT LINES

Since most lines on an average sketch are straight lines, you should learn to make them correctly. Hold your pencil naturally, about $1\frac{1}{2}''$ back from the point, and approximately at right angles to the line to be drawn. Draw horizontal lines from left to right with a

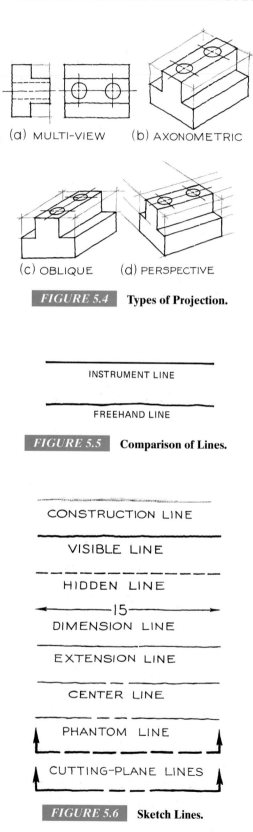

(a) MULTI-VIEW   (b) AXONOMETRIC

(c) OBLIQUE   (d) PERSPECTIVE

FIGURE 5.4   **Types of Projection.**

INSTRUMENT LINE

FREEHAND LINE

FIGURE 5.5   **Comparison of Lines.**

CONSTRUCTION LINE

VISIBLE LINE

HIDDEN LINE

—15—
DIMENSION LINE

EXTENSION LINE

CENTER LINE

PHANTOM LINE

CUTTING-PLANE LINES

FIGURE 5.6   **Sketch Lines.**

Keep eye on
end point

(a) POOR–SHOWS TIGHT GRIP
ON PENCIL–DOES NOT CONTINUE ALONG
STRAIGHT PATH– IS AN ATTEMPT TO
IMITATE MECHANICAL LINES.

(b) BETTER–SHOWS FREE HANDLING OF
PENCIL–CONTINUES ALONG STRAIGHT PATH–
SLIGHT WIGGLES DO NOT DETRACT.

(c) BEST–HAS EFFECTIVENESS OF (b), PLUS
SNAP ADDED BY OCCASIONAL GAPS –
EASIER TO DRAW STRAIGHT.

FIGURE 5.7   **Drawing Horizontal Lines.**

Keep eye on
end point

FIGURE 5.8   **Drawing Vertical Lines.**

free and easy wrist-and-arm movement (Fig. 5.7). Draw vertical lines downward with finger and wrist movements (Fig. 5.8).

Inclined lines may be made to conform in direction to horizontal or vertical lines by shifting position with respect to the paper or by turning the paper slightly; hence, they may be drawn with the same general movements (Fig. 5.9).

In sketching long lines, mark the ends of the line with light dots. Then move the pencil back and forth between the dots in long sweeps, always keeping your eye on the dot toward which the pencil is moving. The point of the pencil should touch the paper lightly, with each successive stroke correcting the defects of the preceding strokes. When the path of the line has been established sufficiently, apply a little more pressure, replacing the trial series with a distinct line. Then dim the line with a soft eraser and draw the final line clean-

FIGURE 5.9   **Drawing Inclined Lines.**

cut and dark, now keeping your eye on the point of the pencil.

An easy method for blocking in horizontal or vertical lines is to hold your hand and pencil rigidly and glide your fingertips along the edge of the pad or board, as shown in Fig. 5.10a. Another method is to mark the distance on the edge of a card or a strip of paper and transfer this distance at intervals (Fig. 5.10b); then draw the final line through these points. A third method is to hold your pencil as shown in the lower part of Fig. 5.10b and to make distance marks on the paper at intervals by tilting the lead down to the paper. All of these methods of transferring distances are substitutes for dividers and have many uses in sketching.

To find the midpoint of a line AB (Fig. 5.10c), hold the pencil in your left hand with your thumb gauging the estimated half-distance. Try this distance on the left and then on the right until you locate the center by trial and mark it C. Another method is to mark the total distance AB on the edge of a strip of paper and then to fold the paper to bring points A and B together, thus locating center C at the crease. To find quarter points, the folded strip can be folded once more.

■5.7 SKETCHING CIRCLES AND ARCS

Small circles and arcs can be easily sketched in one or two strokes without any preliminary blocking in.

One method of sketching a larger circle (Fig. 5.11) is to first sketch lightly the enclosing square, mark the midpoints of the sides, draw light arcs tangent to the sides of the square, and then heavy in the final circle. Another method (Fig. 5.12) is to sketch the two center lines, add light 45° radial lines, sketch light arcs across the lines at the estimated radius distance from the center, and finally sketch the required circle heavily. Dim all construction lines with a soft eraser before heavying in the final circle.

An excellent method, particularly for large circles (Fig. 5.13a), is to mark the estimated radius on the edge of a card or scrap of paper, to set off from the center as many points as desired, and to sketch the final heavy circle through these points.

Clever drafters will prefer the method shown in Fig. 5.13b and 5.13c, in which the hand is used as a compass. You place the tip of your little finger or the knuckle joint of your little finger at the center, "feed" the pencil out to the desired radius, hold this position rigidly, and carefully revolve the paper with the other hand, as shown. If you are using a sketching pad, place the pad on your knee and revolve the entire pad.

In Fig. 5.13d, two pencils are held rigidly like a compass and the paper is slowly revolved.

Methods of sketching arcs (Fig. 5.14) are adaptations of those used for sketching circles. In general, it is easier to sketch arcs with your hand and pencil on the concave side of the curve. In sketching tangent arcs,

FIGURE 5.10   **Blocking in Horizontal and Vertical Lines.**

(a)   FINGER RIGID — SLIDE ALONG EDGE   (b)   (c)

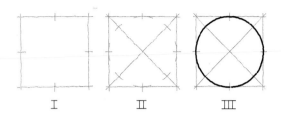

FIGURE 5.11   **Sketching a Circle.**

FIGURE 5.12   **Sketching a Circle.**

always keep in mind the actual geometric constructions, carefully approximating all points of tangency.

■ 5.8 SKETCHING ELLIPSES

If a circle is viewed obliquely, it appears as an ellipse (see Fig. 5.50b). With a little practice, you can learn to sketch small ellipses with a free arm movement (Fig. 5.15a). Hold the pencil naturally, rest the weight on the upper part of the forearm, and move the pencil rapidly above the paper in the elliptical path desired; then lower the pencil to describe several light overlapping ellipses, as shown in Fig. 5.15a, part I. Lighten all lines with a soft eraser and heavy in the final ellipse (Fig. 5.15a, part II).

Another method (Fig. 5.15b) is to sketch lightly the enclosing rectangle (Fig. 5.15b, part I), mark the midpoints of the sides, and sketch light tangent arcs, as shown. Then complete the ellipse lightly (Fig. 5.15b,

FIGURE 5.13   **Sketching Circles.**

FIGURE 5.14   **Sketching Arcs.**

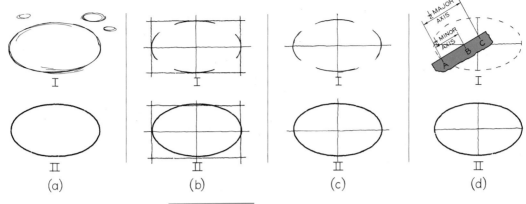

FIGURE 5.15 Sketching Ellipses.

part II), lighten all lines with a soft eraser, and heavy in the final ellipse. The same general procedure shown in Fig. 5.15b may be used in sketching the ellipse on the given axes (Fig. 5.15c).

The trammel method (Fig. 5.15d), is excellent for sketching large ellipses. Prepare a trammel on the edge of a card or strip of paper, move it to different positions, and mark points on the ellipse at A. (The trammel method is explained in §5.50.) Sketch the final ellipse through the points, as shown. For sketching isometric ellipses, see §5.12.

■5.9 MAINTAINING PROPORTIONS

The most important rule in freehand sketching is *keep the sketch in proportion*. No matter how brilliant the technique or how well the small details are drawn, if the proportions—especially the large overall proportions—are bad, the sketch will be bad. First, the relative proportions of the height to the width must be

carefully established; then as you proceed to the medium-sized areas and the small details, constantly compare each new estimated distance with already established distances.

If you are working from a given picture, such as the utility cabinet in Fig. 5.16a, you must first establish the relative width compared to the height. One way is to use the pencil as a measuring stick, as shown. In this case, the height is about $1\frac{3}{4}$ times the width. Then

1. Sketch the enclosing rectangle in the correct proportion (Fig. 5.16I). In this case, the sketch is to be slightly larger than the given picture.

2. Divide the available drawer space into three parts with the pencil by trial (Fig. 5.16II). Sketch light diagonals to locate centers of drawers, and block in drawer handles. Sketch all remaining details.

3. Dim all construction with a soft eraser, and heavy in all final lines (Fig. 5.16III).

FIGURE 5.16 Sketching a Utility Cabinet.

FIGURE 5.17   Sketching a Desk.

Another method of estimating distances is illustrated in Fig. 5.17. On the edge of a card or strip of paper, mark an arbitrary unit. Then see how many units wide and how many units high the desk is. If you are working from the actual object, you can use a scale, a piece of paper, or the pencil itself as a unit to determine the proportions.

To sketch an object composed of many curves to the same scale or to a larger or smaller scale, the method of "squares" is recommended (Fig. 5.18). On the given picture, rule accurate grid lines to form squares of any convenient size. It is best to use a scale and some convenient spacing, such as either .50″ or 10 mm. On the new sheet rule a similar grid, marking the spacing of the lines proportional to the original, but reduced or enlarged as desired. Make the final sketch by drawing the lines in and across the grid lines as in the original, as near as you can estimate by eye.

In sketching from an actual object, you can easily compare various distances on the object by using the pencil to compare measurements, as shown in Fig. 5.19. While doing this, do not change your position, and always hold your pencil at arm's length. The length sighted can then be compared in a similar manner with any other dimension of the object. If the object is small, such as a machine part, you can compare distances in the manner of Fig. 5.16, by actually placing the pencil against the object itself.

In establishing proportions, the blocking-in method is recommended, especially for irregular shapes. The steps for blocking in and completing the sketch of a shaft hanger are shown in Fig. 5.20. As always, first give attention to the main proportions, next to the general sizes and direction of flow of curved shapes, and finally to the snappy lines of the completed sketch.

In making sketches from actual machine parts, it is necessary to use the measuring tools used in the

FIGURE 5.18   Squares Method.

FIGURE 5.19   **Estimating Dimensions.**

I   II

III   IV

FIGURE 5.20   **Blocking in an Irregular Object (Shaft Hanger).**

shop, especially those needed to determine dimensions that must be relatively accurate. For a discussion of these methods, see Chapter 10.

■ 5.10 PICTORIAL SKETCHING

We will now examine several simple methods of preparing pictorial sketches that will be of great assistance in learning the principles of multiview projection. A detailed and more technical treatment of pictorial drawing is given in Chapters 16 through 18.

■ 5.11 ISOMETRIC SKETCHING

Isometric sketching is one of several simple methods of preparing pictorial sketches that will be of great assistance in learning the principles of multiview projection. A detailed and more technical treatment of pictorial drawing is given in Chapters 16 through 18.

To make an ***isometric sketch*** from an actual object, hold the object in your hand and tilt it toward you, as shown in Fig. 5.21a. In this position, the front

FIGURE 5.21   **Isometric Sketching.**

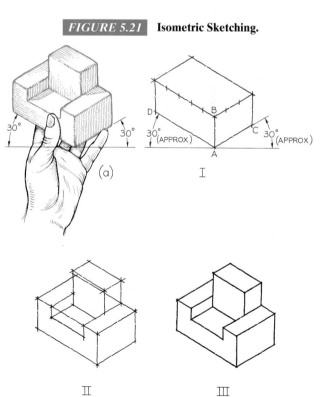

(a)

I

II   III

corner will appear vertical, and the two receding bottom edges and those parallel to them, respectively, will appear at about 30° with horizontal, as shown. The steps in sketching are as follows:[*]

1. Sketch the enclosing box lightly, making AB vertical and AC and AD approximately 30° with horizontal (Fig. 5.21I). These three lines are the *isometric axes*. Make AB, AC, and AD approximately proportional in length to the actual corresponding edges on the object. Sketch the remaining lines parallel, respectively, to these three lines.
2. Block in the recess and the projecting block (Fig. 5.21II).
3. Lighten all construction lines with a soft eraser, and heavy in all final lines (Fig. 5.21III).

■ 5.12 ISOMETRIC ELLIPSES

When objects with cylindrical or conical shapes are placed in isometric or other oblique positions, the circles are seen at an angle and appear as ellipses (Fig. 5.22a).

---

[*] The angle of the receding lines may be less than 30° (say, 20° or 15°). Although the result will not be an isometric sketch, the sketch may be more pleasing and effective in some cases.

The most important consideration in sketching isometric ellipses is as follows: *The major axis of the ellipse is always at right angles to the center line of the cylinder, and the minor axis is at right angles to the major axis and coincides with the center line.*

Two views of a block with a large cylindrical hole are shown in Fig. 5.23a. The steps in sketching the object are as follows:

1. Sketch the block and the enclosing parallelogram for the ellipse, making the sides of the parallelogram parallel to the edges of the block and equal in length to the diameter of the hole (Fig. 5.23I). Draw diagonals to locate the center of the hole, and then draw center lines AB and CD. Points A, B, C, and D will be midpoints of the sides of the parallelogram, and the ellipse will be tangent to the sides at those points. The major axis will be on the diagonal EF, which is at right angles to the center line of the hole, and the minor axis will fall along the short diagonal. Sketch long, flat elliptical sides CA and BD, as shown.
2. Sketch short, small-radius arcs CB and AD to complete the ellipse (Fig. 5.23II). Avoid making the ends of the ellipse "squared off" or pointed like a football.
3. Sketch lightly the parallelogram for the ellipse

FIGURE 5.22 **Isometric Ellipses.**

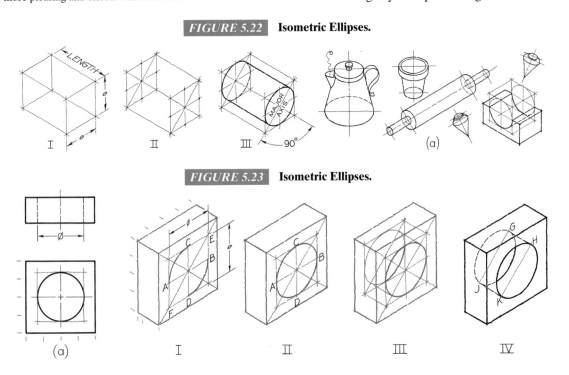

FIGURE 5.23 **Isometric Ellipses.**

that lies in the back plane of the object, and sketch the ellipse in the same manner as the front ellipse (Fig. 5.23III).

4. Draw lines GH and JK tangent to the two ellipses (Fig. 5.23IV). Dim all construction with a soft eraser, and heavy in all final lines.

Another method for determining the back ellipse is shown in Fig. 5.24.

1. Select points at random on the front ellipse and sketch "depth lines" equal in length to the depth of the block (Fig. 5.24I).

2. Sketch the ellipse through the ends of the lines (Fig. 5.24II).

Two views of a bearing with a semicylindrical opening are shown in Fig. 5.25a. The steps in sketching are as follows:

1. Block in the object, including the rectangular space for the semicylinder (Fig. 5.25I).

2. Block in the box enclosing the complete cylinder (Fig. 5.25II). Sketch the entire cylinder lightly.

3. Dim all construction lines, and heavy in all final lines, showing only the lower half of the cylinder (Fig. 5.25III).

FIGURE 5.25   Sketching Semiellipses.

■ 5.13 SKETCHING ON ISOMETRIC PAPER

Two views of a guide block are shown in Fig. 5.26a. The steps in sketching illustrate not only the use of isometric paper, but also the sketching of individual planes or faces to build up a pictorial visualization from the given views.

1. Sketch the isometric of the enclosing box, counting off the isometric grid spaces to equal the cor-

FIGURE 5.24   Isometric Ellipses.

FIGURE 5.26   Sketching on Isometric Paper.

(a) GUIDE BLOCK

I

II

III

responding squares on the given views (Fig. 5.26I). Sketch surface A, as shown.

2. Sketch additional surfaces B and C and the small ellipse (Fig. 5.26II).

3. Sketch additional surfaces E, F, G, and H to complete the sketch (Fig. 5.26III).

■ 5.14 OBLIQUE SKETCHING

Another simple method for sketching pictorially is oblique sketching. Hold the object in your hand (Fig. 5.27a).

1. Block in the front face of the bearing, as if you were sketching a front view (Fig. 5.27I).

2. Sketch receding lines parallel to each other and at any convenient angle (say, 30° or 45°) with the horizontal (Fig. 5.27II). Cut off the receding lines at the correct depth. These lines may be full length, but three quarters or one half size produces a more natural appearance. If the lines are full length, the sketch is a ***cavalier sketch***. If half size, the sketch is a ***cabinet sketch*** (see §18.4).

3. Lighten all construction lines with a soft eraser and heavy in the final lines (Fig. 5.27III).

Oblique sketching is not a very desirable method for sketching an object that has circular shapes in or parallel to more than one plane of the object because ellipses result when circular shapes are viewed obliquely. Therefore, place the object with most or all of the circular shapes toward you so that they will appear as true circles and arcs in oblique sketching, as shown in Fig. 5.27a.

■ 5.15 OBLIQUE SKETCHING ON GRAPH PAPER

Ordinary graph paper is convenient for oblique sketching. Two views of a bearing bracket are shown in Fig. 5.28a. The dimensions are determined simply by counting the squares.

1. Sketch lightly the enclosing box construction (Fig. 5.28I). Sketch the receding lines at 45° diagonally through the squares. To establish the depth at a reduced scale, sketch the receding lines diagonally

FIGURE 5.27   **Sketching in Oblique.**

FIGURE 5.28   **Oblique Sketching on Cross-section Paper.**

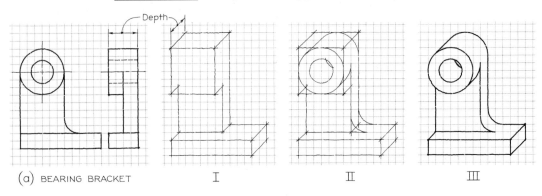

(a) BEARING BRACKET   I   II   III through half as many squares as the given number shown in Fig. 5.28a.

2. Sketch all arcs and circles (Fig. 5.28II).

3. Heavy in all final lines (Fig. 5.28III).

■ 5.16 PERSPECTIVE SKETCHING

The bearing sketched in oblique in Fig. 5.27 can easily be sketched in *one-point perspective*—that is, with one vanishing point (Fig. 5.29).

1. Sketch the true front face of the object just as in oblique sketching (Fig. 5.29I). Select the vanishing point (VP) for the receding lines. In most cases, it is desirable to place VP above and to the right of the picture, as shown, although it can be placed anywhere in the vicinity of the picture. However, if the vanishing point is placed too close to the center, the lines will converge too sharply, and the picture will be distorted.

2. Sketch the receding lines toward VP (Fig. 5.29II).

3. Estimate the depth to look good, and sketch in the back portion of the object (Fig. 5.29III). Note that the back circle and arc will be slightly smaller than the front circle and arc.

4. Lighten all construction lines with a soft eraser, and heavy in all final lines (Fig. 5.27IV). Note the similarity between the perspective sketch and the oblique sketch in Fig. 5.27.

Two-point perspective (two vanishing points) is the most true to life of all pictorial methods, but it requires some natural sketching ability or considerable practice for best results. The simple method shown in Fig. 5.30 can be used successfully by the nonartistic student.

1. Sketch the front corner of the desk in true height, and locate two vanishing points (VPL and VPR) on a horizon line (eye level) (Fig. 5.30I). The distance CA may vary—the greater it is, the higher the eye

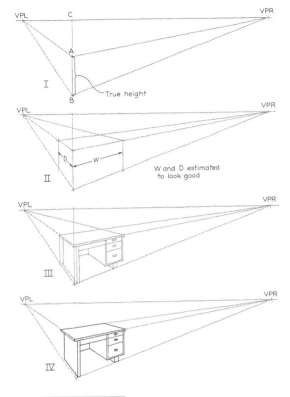

FIGURE 5.30   Two-Point Perspective.

level will be and the more we will be looking down on top of the object. A good rule of thumb is to make C-VPL one third to one fourth of C-VPR.

2. Estimate depth and width, and sketch the enclosing box (Fig. 5.30II).

3. Block in all details (Fig. 5.30III). Note that all parallel lines converge toward the same vanishing point.

4. Lighten the construction lines with a soft eraser as necessary, and heavy in all final lines (Fig. 5.30IV). Make the outlines thicker and the inside lines thinner, especially where they are close together.

FIGURE 5.29   Sketching in One-Point Perspective.

■ 5.17   VIEWS OF OBJECTS

A pictorial drawing or a photograph shows an object as it *appears* to the observer, but not as it *is*. Such a picture cannot describe the object fully, no matter which direction it is viewed from, because it does not show the exact shapes and sizes of the several parts.

In industry, a complete and clear description of the shape and size of an object to be made is necessary to make certain that the object is manufactured exactly as intended by the designer. To provide this information, a number of *views*, systematically arranged, are used. This system of views is called ***multiview projection***. Each view provides certain definite information if the view is from a direction perpendicular to a principal face or side of the object. For example, an observer looking perpendicularly toward one face of an object obtains a true view of the shape and size of that side (Fig. 5.31a). The view as seen by the observer is shown in Fig. 5.31b. (The observer is theoretically at an infinite distance from the object.)

The three principal dimensions of an object are *width*, *height*, and *depth* (Fig. 5.31a). In technical drawing, these fixed terms are used for dimensions taken in these directions, regardless of the shape of the object. The terms "length" and "thickness" are not used because they cannot be applied in all cases. Note that the front view in Fig. 5.31b shows only the height and width of the object and not the depth. In fact, *any one view of a three-dimensional object shows only two dimensions; the third dimension is found in an adjacent view.*

■ 5.18   REVOLVING THE OBJECT

In addition to the three views just described, other views can be obtained by revolving the object, as shown in Fig. 5.32. First, hold the object in the front-view position (Fig. 5.32a). To get the *top view* (Fig. 5.32b), revolve the object to bring the *top of the object up and toward you*. To get the *right-side view* (Fig. 5.32c), revolve the object to bring the *right side toward you*. To obtain views of any of the other sides, merely turn the object to bring those sides toward you.

The top, front, and right-side views, arranged closer together, are shown in Fig. 5.32d. These are called the ***three regular views*** because they are the views most frequently used.

At this stage we can consider spacing between views as purely a matter of appearance. The views should be spaced well apart, yet close enough to appear related to each other. The space between the front and top views may or may not be equal to the space between the front and side views. If dimensions (Chapter 11) are to be added to the sketch, adequate space for them will have to be left between views.

An important advantage of a view over a photograph of an object is that hidden features can be clearly shown by means of hidden lines. In Fig. 5.32d, surface 7–8–9–10 in the front view appears as a visible line 5–6 in the top view and as a hidden line 15–16 in the side view. Also, hole A, which appears as a circle in the front view, shows as hidden lines 1–4 and 2–3 in the top view, and 11–12 and 13–14 in the side view. For a complete discussion of hidden lines, see §5.24. Also note the use of center lines for the hole (see §5.25).

■ 5.19   THE SIX VIEWS

Any object can be viewed from six mutually perpendicular directions, as shown in Fig. 5.33a. These six views may be drawn if necessary, as shown in Fig. 5.33b. Except as explained in §6.8, the six views are always arranged as shown, which is the American National Standard arrangement. The *top*, *front*, and *bottom views* align vertically, while the *rear*, *left-side*, *front*, and *right-side views* align horizontally. To draw a view out of place is a serious error and is generally regarded as one of the worst possible mistakes in drawing.

Note that height is shown in the rear, left-side, front, and right-side views; width is shown in the rear, top, front, and bottom views; and depth is shown in the four views that surround the front view—namely, the left-side, top, right-side, and bottom views. Each view shows two of the principal dimensions. Note also that in the four views that surround the front view, the front of the object faces toward the front view.

Adjacent views are reciprocal. If the front view in Fig. 5.33 is imagined to be the object itself, the right-side view is obtained by looking toward the right side of the front view, as shown by the arrow RS. Likewise, if the right-side view is imagined to be the object, the front view is obtained by looking toward the left side of the right-side view, as shown by the arrow F. The same relation exists between any two adjacent views.

Obviously, the six views may be obtained either by shifting the object with respect to the observer (Fig. 5.32) or by shifting the observer with respect to the object (Fig. 5.33). Another illustration of the second

FIGURE 5.31   **Front View of an Object.**

(d) THE 3 REGULAR VIEWS

FIGURE 5.32   **The Three Regular Views.**

FIGURE 5.33   The Six Views.

FIGURE 5.34   Six Views of a House.

method is given in Fig. 5.34, which show six views of a house. The observer can walk around the house and view its front, sides, and rear and can imagine the top view as seen from an airplane and the bottom or "worm's-eye view" as seen from underneath. Notice the use of the terms "plan," for the top view, and "elevation," for all views showing the height of the build-

ing. These terms are regularly used in architectural drawing and occasionally with reference to drawings in other fields.[*]

---

[*] Architects frequently draw the views of a building on separate sheets because of the large sizes of the drawings.

■ 5.20 ORIENTATION OF FRONT VIEW

Six views of a compact automobile are shown in Fig. 5.35. The view chosen for the front view in this case is the side, not the front of the automobile. In general, the front view should show the object in its operating position, particularly of familiar objects (such as the house shown and the automobile). A machine part is often drawn in the position it occupies in the assembly. However, in most cases this is not important, and the drafter may assume the object to be in any convenient position. For example, an automobile connecting rod is usually drawn horizontally on the sheet (see Fig. 14.28). Also, it is customary to draw screws, bolts, shafts, tubes, and other elongated parts in a horizontal position.

■ 5.21 NECESSARY VIEWS

A drawing for use in production should contain *only* those views needed for a clear and complete shape description of the object. These minimum required views are referred to as the ***necessary views***. In selecting views, the drafter should choose those that best show essential contours or shapes and have the least number of hidden lines.

As shown in Fig. 5.36a, three distinctive features of this object need to be shown on the drawing: (1) rounded top and hole, seen from the *front*; (2) rectangular notch and rounded corners, seen from the *top*; and (3) right angle with filleted corner, seen from the *side*.

Another way to choose required views is to eliminate unnecessary views. Figure 5.36b shows a thumbnail sketch of the six views. Both the front and rear views show the true shapes of the hole and the rounded top, but the front view is preferred because it has no hidden lines. Therefore, the rear view (which is seldom needed) is crossed out. Both the top and bottom views show the rectangular notch and rounded corners, but the top view is preferred because it has fewer hidden lines. Both the right-side and left-side views show the right angle with the filleted corner. In fact, in this case the side views are identical, except reversed. In such instances, it is customary to choose the right-side view.

The necessary views, then, are the three remaining views: the top, front, and right-side views. These are the three regular views referred to in connection with Fig. 5.32. More complicated objects may require more than three views or special views, such as partial views.

■ 5.22 TWO-VIEW DRAWINGS

Often only two views are needed to clearly describe the shape of an object. In Fig. 5.37a, the right-side view shows no significant contours of the object and is crossed out. In Fig. 5.37b, the top and front views are identical, so the top view is eliminated. In Fig. 5.37c, all necessary information is given in the front and top views so the side view is unnecessary.

The question often arises: What are the absolute minimum views required? For example, in Fig. 5.38,

FIGURE 5.35 **Six Views of a Compact Automobile.**

FIGURE 5.36   **Choice of Views.**

FIGURE 5.37   **Two Necessary Views.**

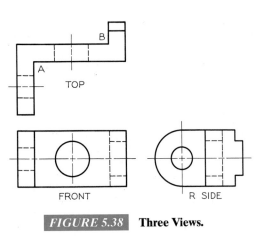

FIGURE 5.38   **Three Views.**

(top view) are square and not filleted. In this example, all three views are necessary.

If an object requires only two views and the left-side and right-side views are equally descriptive, the right-side view is customarily chosen (Fig. 5.39). If contour A were omitted, then the presence of slot B would make it necessary to choose the left-side view in preference to the right-side view.

If an object requires only two views and the top and bottom views are equally descriptive, the top view is customarily chosen (Fig. 5.40).

If only two views are necessary and the top view and right-side view are equally descriptive, the combination chosen is the one that spaces best on the paper (Fig. 5.41).

■ **5.23 ONE-VIEW DRAWINGS**

Frequently, a single view supplemented by a note or lettered symbols is sufficient to describe clearly the shape of a relatively simple object. In Fig. 5.42a, one view of the shim plus a note indicating the thickness

the top view might be omitted, leaving only the front and right-side views. However, it is more difficult to "read" the two views or visualize the object, because the characteristic "Z" shape of the top view is omitted. In addition, one must assume that corners A and B

FIGURE 5.39   **Choice of Right-Side View.**

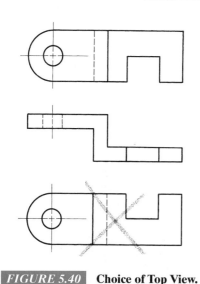

FIGURE 5.40   **Choice of Top View.**

as 0.25 mm is sufficient. In Fig. 5.42b, the left end is 65 mm square, the next portion is 49.22 mm diameter, the next is 31.75 mm diameter, and the portion with the thread is 20 mm diameter, as indicated in the note.

Nearly all shafts, bolts, screws, and similar parts should be represented by single views in this manner.

■ 5.24 HIDDEN LINES

Correct and incorrect practices in drawing hidden lines are illustrated in Fig. 5.43. In general, a hidden line should join a visible line except when it causes the visible line to extend too far, as shown in Fig. 5.43a. In other words, *leave a gap whenever a hidden line is a continuation of a visible line.* Hidden lines should intersect to form ∟ and ⊤ corners (Fig. 5.43b). A hidden line preferably should "jump" a visible line when possible (Fig. 5.43c). Parallel hidden lines should be drawn so that the dashes are staggered, as in bricklaying (Fig. 5.43d). When two or three hidden lines meet at a point, the dashes should join, as shown for the bottom of the drilled hole in Fig. 5.43e and for the top of a countersunk hole in Fig. 5.43f. The example in Fig. 5.43g is similar to that in Fig. 5.43a; hidden lines should not join visible lines when this makes the visible line extend too far. Correct and incorrect methods of drawing hidden arcs are shown in Fig. 5.43h.

FIGURE 5.41   **Choice of Views to Fit Paper.**

(a) PREFERRED   (b) POOR   (c) PREFERRED   (d) POOR

FIGURE 5.42   **One-View Drawings.**

FIGURE 5.43   **Hidden-Line Practices.**

Poorly drawn hidden lines can easily spoil a drawing. Dashes should be about 5 mm long and spaced about 1 mm apart, by eye. Accent the beginning and end of each dash by pressing down on the pencil, whether drawn freehand or mechanically.

As far as possible, views should be chosen that show features with visible lines. Hidden lines should be used where necessary to make the drawing clear. Hidden lines not needed for clarity should be omitted so as not to clutter the drawing and also to save time. The beginner, however, should be cautious about leaving out hidden lines until experience shows when they can be safely omitted.

■ 5.25 CENTER LINES

Center lines (symbol: ₵) are used to indicate axes of symmetrical objects or features, bolt circles, and paths of motion. Typical applications are shown in Fig. 5.44. As shown in Fig. 5.44a, a single center line is drawn in the longitudinal view and crossed center lines in the circular view. The small dashes should cross at the in-

FIGURE 5.44   **Center-Line Applications.**

tersections of center lines. Center lines should extend uniformly about 8 mm outside the feature for which they are drawn.

The long dashes of center lines may vary from 20 to 40 mm or more in length, depending on the size of the drawing. The short dashes should be about 5 mm long, with spaces about 2 mm. Center lines should always start and end with long dashes. Short center lines, especially for small holes, may be made solid (Fig. 5.44e). Always leave a gap when a center line forms a continuation of a visible or hidden line. Center lines should be thin enough to contrast well with the visible and hidden lines, but dark enough to reproduce well.

Center lines are useful mainly in dimensioning and should be omitted from unimportant rounded or filleted corners and other shapes that are self-locating.

■ 5.26 SKETCHING TWO VIEWS

A sketch of the support block in Fig. 5.45a requires only two views. The steps in sketching are as follows:

1. Block in lightly the enclosing rectangles for the two views (Fig. 5.45I). Sketch horizontal lines 1 and 2 to establish the height of the object, while making spaces A approximately equal. Sketch vertical lines 3, 4, 5, and 6 to establish the width and depth in correct proportion to the already

FIGURE 5.45   **Sketching Two Views of a Support Block.**

G R A P H I C S   S P O T L I G H T
Sketching and Parametric Modeling

THE DESIGN PROCESS

Using CAD parametric modeling in many ways mirrors the design process (see Chapter 14). To get the rough ideas down, the designer starts by making hand sketches. Then as the ideas are refined, more accurate drawings are created either with instruments or using CAD. Necessary analysis is performed and in response the design may change. The drawings are revised as needed to meet the new requirements. Eventually the drawings are approved so that the parts may be manufactured.

ROUGH SKETCHES

Using parametric modeling software, initially the designer roughly sketches the basic on the screen. These sketches do not have to have perfectly straight lines or accurate corners. The software interprets the sketch much as you would interpret a rough sketch given to you by a colleague. If the lines are nearly horizontal or vertical, the software assumes that you meant them thus. If the line appears to be perpendicular it is assumed that it is.

CONSTRAINING THE SKETCH

Using a parametric CAD system, you can start by sketching on the computer screen as though you were sketching freehand. Then the two-dimensional sketch is refined by adding geometric constraints, which tell how to interpret the sketch and by adding parametric dimensions, which control the size of sketch geometry. Once the sketch is refined, it can be

(B) Constrained Sketch

created as a 3D feature to which other features can be added. As the design changes the dimensions and constraints that control the sketch geometry can be changed, and the parametric model will update to reflect the new design.

When you are creating sketches by hand or for parametric modeling, think about the implications of the geometry you are drawing. Does the sketch imply that lines are perpendicular? Are the arcs you have drawn intended to be tangent or intersecting? When you are creating a parametric model, the software makes assumptions about how you intend to constrain the geometry based on your sketch. You can remove, change, or add new constraints as you wish.

AutoCAD Mechanical Desktop software contains AutoCAD Designer parametric design software. Using it you can create a rough sketch like the one you see in Fig. A.

You select the Profile command to have the software constrain the sketch automatically. The results of profiling the sketch are shown in Fig. B. The symbols show the constraints that were assumed.

The dialog box shown on the next page in Fig. C lists types of geometric constraints you can use to control the sketch geometry in AutoCAD Designer. The dialog box labeled Fig. D on the left shows the constraints that you can use to control the way parts fit together in an assembly.

(A) Rough Sketch

(C) Assembly Constraints

(D) Sketch Constraints

When you have completed the parametric model, you have an "intelligent" part. When design changes are necessary, you can change a dimension or constraint causing the model to automatically update. Orthographic drawings with correctly shown hidden lines and dimensions can be generated automatically. Or the part can be exported for rapid prototyping or manufacture.

established height, while making spaces B approximately equal and space C equal to or slightly less than space B.

2. Block in smaller details, using diagonals to locate the center (Fig. 5.45II). Sketch lightly the circle and arcs.

3. Lighten all construction lines with a soft eraser, and heavy in all final lines (Fig. 5.45III).

■5.27 SKETCHING THREE VIEWS

A sketch of a lever bracket that requires three views is shown in Fig. 5.46a. The steps in sketching the three views are as follows:

1. Block in the enclosing rectangles for the three views (Fig. 5.46I). Sketch horizontal lines 1, 2, 3, and 4 to establish the height of the front view and the depth of the top view, making spaces A approximately equal and space C equal to or slightly less than one space A. Sketch vertical lines 5, 6, 7, and 8 to establish the width of the top and front views and the depth of the side view. Make sure that this is in correct proportion to the height, while making spaces B approximately equal and space D equal to or slightly less than one space B. Note that spaces C and D are not necessarily equal, but are independent of each other. Similarly, spaces A and B are not necessarily equal. To transfer the depth dimension from the top view to the side view, use the edge of a card or strip of paper, as shown, or transfer the distance by using the pencil as a measuring stick (see Figs. 5.10b and 5.10c). Note that *the depth in the top and side views must always be equal.*

2. Block in all details lightly (Fig. 5.46II).

3. Sketch all arcs and circles lightly (Fig. 5.46III).

4. Lighten all construction lines with a soft eraser (Fig. 5.46IV).

FIGURE 5.46   **Sketching Three Views of a Lever Bracket.**

5. Heavy in all final lines so that the views will stand out clearly (Fig. 5.46V).

■5.28 ALIGNMENT OF VIEWS

Errors in arranging the views are so commonly made by students that it is necessary to repeat this: The views must be drawn in accordance with the American National Standard arrangement shown in Fig. 5.33. Figure 5.47a shows an offset guide that requires three views. These three views, correctly arranged, are shown in Fig. 5.47b. The top view must be directly above the front view, and the right-side view directly to the right of the front view—not out of alignment, as in Fig. 5.47c. Also, never draw the views in reversed positions, with the bottom over the front view or the right-side to the left of the front view (Fig. 5.47d), even though the views do line up with the front view.

■5.29 MEANING OF LINES

A visible line or a hidden line has three possible meanings (Fig. 5.48): (1) intersection of two surfaces, (2) edge view of a surface, and (3) contour view of a curved surface. Since *no shading is used on a working drawing*, it is necessary to examine all the views to determine the meaning of the lines. For example, the line AB at the top of the front view might be regarded as the edge view of a flat surface if we look at only the front and top views and do not observe the curved surface on top of the object, as shown in the right-side view. Similarly, the vertical line CD in the front view might be regarded as the edge view of a plane surface if we look at only the front and side views. However, the top view shows that the line represents the intersection of an inclined surface.

■5.30 PRECEDENCE OF LINES

Visible lines, hidden lines, and center lines often coincide on a drawing, and the drafter must know which line to show. A visible line always takes precedence over (covers up) a center line or a hidden line, as shown at A and B in Fig. 5.49. A hidden line takes precedence over a center line, as shown at C. Note that at A and C the ends of the center line are shown, but are separated from the view by short gaps.

■5.31 COMPUTER GRAPHICS

Preliminary sketches are usually done on paper with a pencil or pen. More detailed CAD drawings usually follow the initial sketches. Finished CAD drawings should apply the same rules for arranging views, clearly depicting the subject of the drawing, using the proper line patterns and line weights, and following all of the necessary standards as manually created drawings (Fig. 5.50).

(a) OFFSET GUIDE   (b) *Correct*   (c) *Never!*   (d) *Never!*

FIGURE 5.47 **Position of Views.**

EDGE VIEW OF SURFACE

CONTOUR

EDGE VIEW OF SURFACE

A   B

C

D

INTERSECTION OF SURFACES

FIGURE 5.48 **Meaning of Lines.**

A

B

C

FIGURE 5.49 **Precedence of Lines.**

FIGURE 5.50 **Multiview CAD Assembly Drawing of a MAXIM Fire Truck.** *Courtesy of CADKEY.*

■ KEY WORDS

CONSTRUCTION LINES	PICTORIAL
ORTHOGRAPHIC PROJECTION	OBLIQUE
ISOMETRIC	GRID PAPER
PRIMARY VIEWS	HIDDEN LINES
VISIBLE LINES	CENTER LINES
PRECEDENCE OF LINES	SHADING
ALIGNMENT OF VIEWS	SKETCH
SHAPE DESCRIPTION	PROPORTIONS

■ CHAPTER SUMMARY

- Sketching is one of the most important skills that a traditional or CAD drafter must learn to become effective.
- Sketching is a quick way of visualizing and solving a drawing problem. It is an effective way of communicating with all members of the design team.
- There are special techniques for sketching lines, circles, and arcs. These techniques should be practiced so they become second nature.
- Moving your thumb up or down the length of a pencil at arms length is an easy method for estimating proportional size.
- Using a sketching grid makes measuring an easy task. Grid paper comes in a variety of types, including square grid and isometric grid.

- You can sketch circles by constructing a square and locating the four tangent points where the circle touches the square. This same technique can be applied to isometric circles by drawing isometric "squares" (parallelograms).
- You can sketch objects using the same view orientation and alignment that traditional drawing conventions demand.
- A sketched line must not look like a mechanical line. The main distinction between instrumental drawing and freehand sketching is the character or technique of the linework.
- Freehand sketches are made to proportion, but not necessarily to a particular scale.

■ REVIEW QUESTIONS

1. What are the four standard types of projections?
2. What are the advantages of using grid paper for sketching?
3. What is the correct technique for sketching a circle or arc?
4. Sketch the alphabet of lines. Which lines are thick? Which are thin? Which are very light and will not reproduce when copied?
5. When is isometric grid paper used? When is square grid paper used?
6. What type of three-dimensional drawing can easily be drawn on square grid paper?
7. What is the advantage of sketching an object first before drawing it using CAD?
8. Why are tangent points so important when sketching, drawing on paper with instruments, or using CAD?
9. What is the difference between proportion and scale?
10. Which view should be sketched directly below the TOP view?
11. Why should center lines, visible lines, and hidden lines line up between views when sketching?

■ SKETCHING PROBLEMS

Figures 5.52 and 5.53 present a variety of objects from which the student is to sketch the necessary views. Using 8.5″ × 11.0″ graph paper, sketch a border and title strip and divide the sheet into two parts (Fig. 5.51). Sketch two assigned problems per sheet. On the problems in Fig. 5.52, "ticks" are given that indicate .50″ or .25″ spaces. Thus, measurements may be easily spaced off on graph paper having .12″ or .25″ grid spacings.

If desired, the "ticks" on the problems in Fig. 5.52 may be used to indicate 10-mm and 5-mm spaces. Thus, metric measurements may be easily utilized on appropriate metric-grid graph paper.

On the problems in Fig. 5.53, no indications of size are given. The student is to sketch the necessary views of assigned problems to fit the spaces comfortably, as shown in Fig. 5.51. It is suggested that the student prepare a small paper scale, making the divisions equal to those on the paper scale in Prob. 5.1. This scale can be used to determine the approximate sizes. Let each division equal either .50″ or 10 mm on your sketch.

Missing-line and missing-view problems are given in Figs. 5.54 and 5.55, respectively. These are to be sketched, two problems per sheet, in the arrangement shown in Fig. 5.51. If the instructor so assigns, the missing lines or views may be sketched with a colored pencil. The problems given in Figs. 5.54 and 5.55 may be sketched in isometric on isometric paper or in oblique on graph paper.

Since many of the problems in this chapter are of a general nature, they can also be solved on most computer graphics systems. If a system is available, the instructor may choose to assign specific problems to be completed by this method.

For all of the following problems, use 8.5″ × 11.0″ graph paper or plain paper. Sketch a border and title strip, and divide the sheet into two parts, as shown in Fig. 5.51. Sketch two assigned problems per sheet.

Prob. 5.1–5.24   (Fig. 5.52) Sketch necessary views using Layout A–1 or A4–1 adjusted (freehand). The "ticks" on the figures indicate .50″ or .25″ spaces. Thus, measurements may be easily spaced off on graph paper having .12″ or .25″ grid spacings. The "ticks" may also be used to indicate 10-mm or 5-mm spaces, so that metric measurements may be easily utilized on appropriate metric-grid graph paper. In these problems, all holes are through holes.

Prob. 5.25–5.48   (Fig. 5.53) Sketch necessary views using Layout A–1 or A4–1 adjusted (freehand). No indication of size is given in these problems. Sketch the necessary views to fit the spaces comfortably. Prepare a small paper scale, making the divisions equal to those on the paper scale in Prob. 5.25, and apply to the problems to obtain approximate sizes. Let each division equal either .50″ or 10 mm on your sketch. For Prob. 5.41–5.48, study §§6.34–6.36.

Prob. 5.49–5.72   (Fig. 5.54) Sketch given views using Layout A–1 or A4–1 adjusted (freehand). Add missing lines. The squares may be either .25″ or 5 mm. The problems may be sketched in isometric on isometric paper or in oblique on graph paper.

Prob. 5.73–5.105   (Fig. 5.55) Using Layout A–1 or A4–1 adjusted (freehand), sketch the two given views and add the missing views, as indicated. The squares may be either .25″ or 5 mm. The given views are either front and right-side views or front and top views. Hidden holes with center lines are drilled holes. Sketch in isometric on isometric paper or in oblique on cross-section paper.

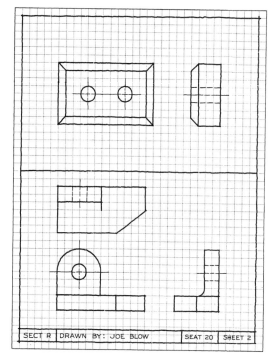

FIGURE 5.51   **Multiview Sketch (Layout A–1).**

FIGURE 5.52 Multiview Sketching Problems. Sketch necessary views, using Layout A–1 (see Fig. 5.51) or A4–1 (see front cover endpapers) adjusted (freehand), on graph paper or plain paper, two problems per sheet as in Fig. 5.51. The units shown may be either .50″ and .25″ or 10 mm and 5 mm. See instructions on page 159. All holes are through holes.

PAPER "SCALE"

FIGURE 5.53 Multiview Sketching Problems. Sketch necessary views, using Layout A–1 or A4–1 adjusted (freehand), on graph paper or plain paper, two problems per sheet as in Fig. 5.51. Prepare paper scale with divisions equal to those in Prob. 1, and apply to problems to obtain approximate sizes. Let each division equal either .50″ or 10 mm on your sketch. See instructions on page 159. For Probs. 17–24, study §§6.34–6.36.

Probs. 1–5: No inclined or oblique surfaces.

FIGURE 5.54   Missing-Line Sketching Problems. (1) Sketch given views, using Layout A–1 or A4–1 adjusted (freehand), on graph paper or plain paper, two problems per sheet as in Fig. 5.51. Add missing lines. The squares may be either .25″ or 5 mm. See instructions on page 159. (2) Sketch in isometric on isometric paper or in oblique on cross-section paper.

1 Add Top
2 Add Top
3 Add Top
4 Add Top
5 Add Top
6 Add Top
7 Add R S

Probs. 1–7: No inclined or oblique surfaces.

8 Add Top
9 Add Top
10 Add Top
11 Add R S
12 Add Top
13 Add Top
14 Add Top
15 Add R S
16 Add R S
17 Add R S
18 Add R S
19 Add R S
20 Add Top
21 Add Top
22 Add Top
23 Add R S
24 Add Top
25 Add Top
26 Add Top
27 Add R S
28 Add R S
29 Add R S
30 Add R S
31 Add R S
32 Add R S
33 Add Top

FIGURE 5.55 **Third-View Sketching Problems. (1) Using Layout A–1 or A4–1 adjusted (freehand), on graph paper or plain paper, two problems per sheet as in Fig. 5.51, sketch the two given views and add the missing views, as indicated. The squares may be either .25″ or 5 mm. See instructions on page 159. The given views are either front and right-side views or front and top views. Hidden holes with center lines are drilled holes. (2) Sketch in isometric on isometric paper or in oblique on cross-section paper.**

C H A P T E R   6

MULTIVIEW PROJECTION

OBJECTIVES

After studying the material in this chapter, you should be able to:

1. Draw the six standard views of an object.
2. Draw any three views using proper conventions, placement, and alignment.
3. Transfer height, width, or depth dimensions between views.
4. Layout a three-view drawing so it is centered on the drawing medium.
5. Apply conventional practices to the revolution of ribs, spokes, and webs.
6. Identify and draw visible and hidden lines in all six standard views.
7. Identify and project surfaces appearing in all views.
8. Identify surface shapes, and determine edge views of surfaces.
9. Draw and project normal, inclined, and oblique surfaces in all views.
10. Draw positive and negative cylinders in all views.
11. Plot conic sections and irregular curves in all views.
12. Understand drawing conventions for hole treatments and machine processes.
13. Describe the concept of first and third angle projections.
14. Understand and use fold lines or miter lines to create new views.

OVERVIEW

A view of an object is known technically as a **projection**. A projection is a view conceived to be drawn or projected onto a plane known as the **plane of projection**. A system of views of an object formed by projectors from the object perpendicular to the desired planes of projection is known as **orthographic**, or **multiview, projection** (see ANSI/ASME Y14.3M–1994). This system of required views provides for the shape description of the object.

Drawing conventions describe the projection process so that all technical drawings can be created and interpreted in the same way. Conventions assure that no ambiguity exists between the drawer's intent and the reader's interpretation. Understanding surface orientations can help students visualize the six standard views of projection. Surfaces are either normal, inclined, or oblique. The endpoints of lines define surface boundaries. Conic sections and irregular curves can be approximated by mapping definable lines from one view to another. Various manufacturing processes for holes, fillets, and rounds are described in specific ways on technical drawings.

■ 6.1 PROJECTION METHOD

The method of viewing an object to obtain a multiview projection is illustrated for a front view in Fig. 6.1a. Between the observer and the object, a transparent plane or pane of glass representing a plane of projection is located parallel to the front surfaces of the object. The outline on the plane of projection shows how the object appears to the observer. Theoretically, the observer is at an infinite distance from the object so that the *lines of sight* are parallel.

In more precise terms, this view is obtained by drawing perpendicular lines, or ***projectors***, from all points on the edges or contours of the object to the plane of projection (Fig. 6.1b). The infinite number of collective piercing points of these projectors form lines on the pane of glass (Fig. 6.1c). As shown, a projector from point 1 on the object pierces the plane of projection at point 7, which is a view or projection of the point. The same procedure applies to point 2, whose projection is point 9. Since 1 and 2 are endpoints of a straight line on the object, the projections 7 and 9 are joined to give the projection of the line 7–9. Similarly, if the projections of the four corners 1, 2, 3, and 4 are

found, the projections 7, 9, 10, and 8 may be joined by straight lines to form the projection of the rectangular surface.

The same procedure can be applied to curved lines—for example, the top curved contour of the object. A point, 5, on the curve is projected to the plane at 6. The projection of an infinite number of such points (a few are shown in Fig. 6.1b) on the plane of projection results in the projection of the curve. If this procedure of projecting points is applied to all edges and contours of the object, a complete view or projection of the object results. This view is necessary in the shape description because it shows the true curvature of the top and the true shape of the hole.

A similar procedure may be used to obtain the top view (Fig. 6.2a). This view is necessary in the shape description because it shows the true angle of the inclined surface. In this view, the hole is invisible and its extreme contours are represented by hidden lines, as shown.

The right-side view (Fig. 6.2b) is necessary because it shows the right-angled characteristic shape of the object and the true shape of the curved intersection. Note how the cylindrical contour at the top of the object appears when viewed from the side. The extreme, or contour, element 1–2 on the object is projected to give the line 3–4 on the view. The hidden hole is also represented by projecting the extreme elements.

The plane of projection on which the front view is projected is called the ***frontal plane;*** that on which the top view is projected, the ***horizontal plane***; and that on which the side view is projected, the ***profile plane***.

■ 6.2 THE GLASS BOX

If planes of projection are placed parallel to the principal faces of the object, they form a "glass box," as shown in Fig. 6.3a. Notice that the observer is always on the outside looking in, so the object is seen through the planes of projection. Since the glass box has six sides, six views of the object can be obtained.

Note that the object has three principal dimensions: *width, height,* and *depth*. These are fixed terms used for dimensions in these directions, regardless of the shape of the object (see §5.17).

To show the views of a solid, or three-dimensional, object on a flat sheet of paper, it is necessary to unfold the planes so that they will all lie in the same plane (Fig. 6.3b). All planes except the rear plane are hinged

FIGURE 6.1 Projection of an Object.

FIGURE 6.2 Top and Right-Side Views.

TOP VIEW
(a)

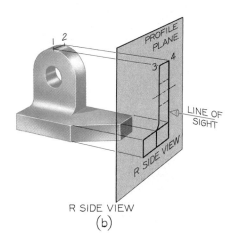

R SIDE VIEW
(b)

to the frontal plane; the rear plane is hinged to the left-side plane, except as explained in §6.8. Each plane revolves outwardly from the original box position until it lies in the frontal plane, which remains stationary. The hinge lines of the glass box are known as *folding lines*.

The positions of these six planes after they have been revolved are shown in Fig. 6.4. Carefully identify each of these planes and corresponding views with its original position in the glass box, and repeat this mental procedure, if necessary, until the revolutions are thoroughly understood.

Observe that in Fig. 6.3b lines extend around the glass box from one view to another on the planes of projection. These are the *projections of the projectors* from points on the object to the views. For example, the projector 1–2 is projected on the horizontal plane at 7–8 and on the profile plane at 16–17. When the top plane is folded up, lines 9–10 and 7–8 will become vertical and line up with 10–6 and 8–2, respectively. Thus, 9–10 and 10–6 form a single straight line 9–6, and 7–8 and 8–2 form a single straight line 7–2, as shown in Fig. 6.4. This explains why the top view is the same width as the front view and why it is placed directly above the front view. The same relation exists between the front and bottom views. Therefore, *the front, top, and bottom views all line up vertically and are the same width.*

In Fig. 6.3b, when the profile plane is folded out, lines 4–13 and 13–15 become a single straight line 4–15, and lines 2–16 and 16–17 become a single straight line 2–17, as shown in Fig. 6.4. The same relation exists between the front, left-side, and rear views. Therefore, *the rear, left-side, front, and right-side views all line up horizontally and are the same height.*

FIGURE 6.3   **The Glass Box.**

FIGURE 6.4   **The Glass Box Unfolded.**

Note that in Fig. 6.3b lines OS and OW and lines ST and WX are respectively equal. These lines of equal length are shown in the unfolded position in Fig. 6.4. Thus, it is seen that the top view must be the same distance from the folding line OZ as the right-side view is from the folding line OY. Similarly, the bottom view and left-side view are the same distance from their respective folding lines as are the right-side view and the top view. Therefore, *the top, right-side, bottom, and left-side views are all equidistant from the respective folding lines and are the same depth*. Note that in these four views that surround the front view, the front surfaces of the object are faced inward or toward the front view. Observe also that the left-side and right-side views and the top and bottom views are the reverse of each other in outline shape. Similarly, the rear and front views are the reverse of each other.

■ 6.3 FOLDING LINES

The front, top, and right views of the object shown in the previous figures are shown in Fig. 6.5a with folding lines between the views. These folding lines correspond to the hinge lines of the glass box, as we have seen. The H/F folding line, between the top and front views, is the intersection of the horizontal and frontal planes. The F/P folding line, between the front and side views, is the intersection of frontal and profile planes (see Figs. 6.3 and 6.4).

The distances X and Y, from the front view to the respective folding lines, are not necessarily equal, since they depend on the relative distances of the object from the horizontal and profile planes. However, as explained in §6.2, distances D_1, from the top and side views to the respective folding lines, must always be

equal. Therefore, the views may be any desired distance apart, and the folding lines may be drawn anywhere between them, as long as distances D_1 are kept equal and the folding lines are at right angles to the projection lines between the views.

It will be seen that distances D_2 and D_3, respectively, are also equal and that the folding lines H/F and F/P are in reality reference lines for making equal *depth* measurements in the top and side views. Thus, any point in the top view is the same distance from H/F as the corresponding point in the side view is from F/P.

While it is necessary to understand the folding lines, particularly because they are useful in solving graphical problems in descriptive geometry, they are as a rule omitted in industrial practice as shown in Fig. 6.5b. Again, the distances between the top and front views and between the side and front views are not necessarily equal. Instead of using the folding lines as reference lines for setting off depth measurements in the top and side views, we may use the front surface A of the object as a reference line. In this way, D_1, D_2, and all other depth measurements are made to correspond in the two views in the same manner as if folding lines were used.

■ 6.4 TWO-VIEW INSTRUMENTAL DRAWING

The complete structure of some objects can be shown with only two views. For example, the necessary views of the operating arm in Fig. 6.6a include only the front and top views, as shown by the arrows.

To draw [full size with instruments in Layout A–2 (inside back cover)] the necessary views of the operating arm in Fig. 6.6, do the following:

FIGURE 6.5   **Folding Lines.**

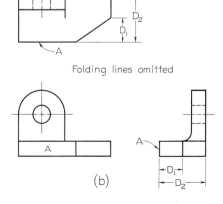

(a)   (b)

Folding lines omitted

FIGURE 6.6   Two-View Instrumental Drawing (dimensions in millimeters).

1. Determine the spacing of the views (Fig. 6.6I). The width of the front and top views is approximately 152 mm (6″; 25.4 mm = 1″), and the width of the working space is approximately 266 mm (10½″). As shown in Fig. 6.6b, subtract 152 mm from 266 mm and divide the result by 2 to get the value of space A. To set off the spaces, place the scale horizontally along the bottom of the sheet and make short vertical marks.

    The depth of the top view is approximately 64 mm (2½″) and the height of the front view is 45 mm (1¾″), while the height of the working space is 194 mm (7⅝″). Assume a space C—say, 25 mm (1″)—between views that will look well and that will provide sufficient space for dimensions, if any.

    Add 64 mm, 25 mm, and 45 mm, subtract the total from 194 mm, and divide the result by 2 to get the value of space B. To set off the spaces, place the scale vertically along the left side of the sheet with the full-size scale on the left, and make short marks perpendicular to the scale.

2. Locate center lines from spacing marks (Fig. 6.6II). Construct arcs and circles lightly.

3. Draw horizontal and then vertical construction lines in the order shown (Fig. 6.6III). Allow construction lines to cross at corners.

4. Add hidden lines and heavy in all final lines, clean-cut and dark (Fig. 6.6IV).

■6.5 TRANSFERRING DEPTH DIMENSIONS

Since all depth dimensions in the top and side views must correspond point for point, accurate methods of transferring these distances must be used.

Professional drafters transfer dimensions between the top and side views either with dividers or a scale (Figs. 6.7a and 6.7b). The scale method is especially convenient when a drafting machine is used because both vertical and horizontal scales are readily available. Beginners may find it convenient to use a 45° miter line to project dimensions between top and side views (Fig. 6.7c). Note that the right-side view may be moved to the right or left, or the top view may be moved upward or downward, by shifting the 45° line accordingly. It is not necessary to draw continuous

(a) DIVIDERS

(b) SCALE

(c) MITER LINE

FIGURE 6.7 **Transferring Depth Dimensions.**

lines between the top and side views via the miter line. Instead, make short dashes across the miter line and project from these.

The 45° miter-line method is also convenient for transferring a large number of points, as when plotting a curve (see Fig. 6.35).

■6.6 PROJECTING A THIRD VIEW

Figure 6.8a is a pictorial drawing of an object that has three necessary views. Each corner of the object is numbered. Figure 6.8I shows the top and front views, with each corner properly numbered. If a point is *visible* in a given view, the number is placed *outside* the corner, but if the point is hidden, the numeral is placed *inside* the corner. For example, in Fig. 6.8I, point 1 is visible in both views and the number is therefore placed outside the corners in both views. However, point 2 is visible in the top view and the number is placed outside, while in the front view it is hidden and is placed inside.

This system, in which points are identified by the same numbers in all views, is useful in projecting known points in two views to unknown positions in a third view. Note that this numbering system assigns the same number to a given point in all views and should not be confused with the system used in Fig. 6.23 and elsewhere, in which a point has different numbers in each view.

Before starting to project the right-side view in Fig. 6.8, try to visualize the view as seen in the direction of the arrow in Fig. 6.8a. Then construct the right-side view point by point, using a hard pencil and very light lines.

As shown in Fig. 6.8I, locate point 1 in the side view by projecting from point 1 in the top view and point 1 in the front view. In Fig. 6.8II, project points 2,

3, and 4 in a similar manner to complete the vertical end surface of the object. In Fig. 6.8III, project points 5 and 6 to complete the side view of the inclined surface 5-6-2-1. This completes the right-side view, since invisible points 9, 10, 8, and 7 are directly behind visible corners 5, 6, 4, and 3, respectively.

As shown in Fig. 6.8IV, the drawing is completed by heavying in the lines in the right-side view.

■6.7 THREE-VIEW INSTRUMENTAL DRAWING

The complete structure of some objects, such as that in Fig. 6.9a, requires three views.

To draw (full size with instruments on Layout A–2), the necessary views of the V-block in Fig. 6.9a, do the following:

1. Determine the spacing of the views (Fig. 6.9I). The width of the front view is 108 mm and the depth of the side view is 58 mm, while the width of the working space is 266 mm. Assume a space C between views (say, 32 mm) that will look well and will allow sufficient space for dimensions, if any.

   As shown in Fig. 6.9b, add 108 mm, 32 mm, and 58 mm, subtract the total from 266 mm, and divide the result by 2 to get the value of space A. To set off these horizontal spacing measurements, place the scale along the bottom of the sheet and make short vertical marks.

   The depth of the top view is 58 mm and the height of the front view is 45 mm, while the height of the working space is 194 mm. Assume a space D between views (say, 25 mm). As explained in §6.3, space D need not be the same as space C. Add 58 mm, 25 mm, and 45 mm, subtract the total from 194 mm, and divide the result by 2 to get the value

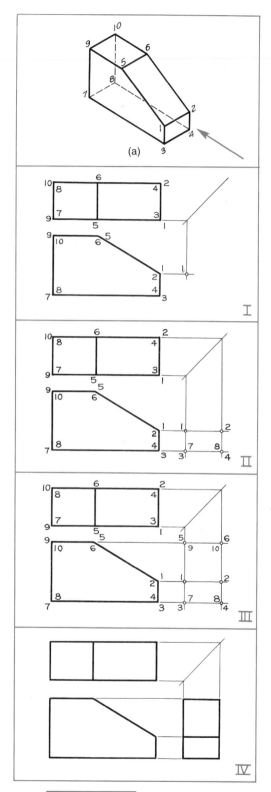

FIGURE 6.8   Use of Numbers.

of space B. To set off these vertical spacing measurements, place the scale along the left side of the sheet with the scale used on the left, and make short marks perpendicular to the scale. Allow space for written dimensions, if required.

2. Locate the center lines from the spacing marks (Fig. 6.9II). Construct lightly the arcs and circles.

3. Draw horizontal, then vertical, then inclined construction lines, in the order shown (Fig. 6.9III). Allow construction lines to cross at the corners. Do not complete one view at a time; construct the views simultaneously. A convenient method for transferring the hole diameter from the top view to the side view is to use the compass with the same setting used for drawing the hole.

4. Add hidden lines and heavy in all final lines, clean-cut and dark (Fig. 6.9IV).

■ 6.8 ALTERNATE POSITIONS OF VIEWS

If three views of a wide, flat object are drawn using the conventional arrangement of views, a large wasted space is left on the paper (Fig. 6.10a). In such cases, the profile plane may be considered hinged to the horizontal plane instead of the frontal plane (Fig. 6.10b). This places the side view beside the top view, which results in better spacing and sometimes makes the use of a reduced scale unnecessary.

It is also permissible in extreme circumstances to place the side view across horizontally from the bottom view. In this case the profile plane is considered hinged to the bottom plane of projection. Similarly, the rear view may be placed directly above the top view or under the bottom view, if necessary. As a result, the rear plane is considered hinged to the horizontal or bottom plane, as the case may be, and then rotated into coincidence with the frontal plane.

■ 6.9 PARTIAL VIEWS

A view may not need to be complete but may show only what is necessary for the clear description of the object (Fig. 6.11). Such a view is a partial view. A break line may be used to limit the partial view (Fig. 6.11a); the contour of the part shown may limit the view (Fig. 6.11b); if symmetrical, a half-view may be drawn on one side of the center line (Fig. 6.11c); or a partial view, "broken out," may be drawn (Fig. 6.11d). The half view shown in Figs. 6.11c and 6.11d should be the

FIGURE 6.9   **Three-View Instrumental Drawing (dimensions in millimeters).**

(a) POOR ARRANGEMENT OF VIEWS

(b) APPROVED ARRANGEMENT OF VIEWS

FIGURE 6.10   **Position of Side View.**

FIGURE 6.11   **Partial Views.**

near side, as shown. For half views in connection with sections, see Fig. 7.33.

Do not place a break line where it will coincide with a visible or hidden line.

Occasionally the distinctive features of an object are on opposite sides. In either complete side view there will be a considerable overlapping of shapes. In such cases two side views are often the best solution (Fig. 6.12). The views are partial views, and in both, certain visible and invisible lines have been omitted for clarity.

■ 6.10 REVOLUTION CONVENTIONS

Regular multiview projections are sometimes awkward, confusing, or actually misleading. For example, Fig. 6.13a shows an object that has three triangular ribs, three holes equally spaced in the base, and a key-

FIGURE 6.12   **Incomplete Side Views.**

FIGURE 6.13   **Revolution Conventions.**

way. The right-side view (Fig. 6.13b) is a regular projection and is not recommended. The lower ribs appear in a foreshortened position, the holes do not appear in their true relation to the rim of the base, and the keyway is projected as a confusion of hidden lines.

The conventional method shown in Fig. 6.13c is preferred, not only because it is simpler to read, but also because it requires less drafting time. Each of the features mentioned has been revolved in the front view to lie along the vertical center line, from where it is projected to the correct side view (Fig. 6.13c).

Figures 6.13d and 6.13e show regular views of a flange with many small holes. The hidden holes in Fig. 6.13e are confusing and take unnecessary time to draw. The preferred representation in Fig. 6.13f shows the holes revolved, and the drawing is clear.

Another example is given in Fig. 6.14. As shown in Fig. 6.14a, a regular projection produces a confusing foreshortening of the inclined arm. To preserve the appearance of symmetry about the common center, the lower arm is revolved to line up vertically in the front view so that it projects true length in the side view (Fig. 6.14b).

Revolutions of the type discussed here are frequently used in connection with sectioning. Such sectional views are called *aligned sections* (see §7.13).

■6.11 REMOVED VIEWS

A removed view is a complete or partial view removed to another place on the sheet so that it no longer is in direct projection with any other view (Fig. 6.15). Such a view may be used to show some feature of the object more clearly, possibly to a larger scale, or to save drawing a complete regular view. A viewing-plane line is used to indicate the part being viewed; the arrows at the corners show the direction of sight (see §7.5). The removed views should be labeled VIEW A–A or VIEW B–B and so on; the letters refer to those placed at the corners of the viewing-plane line.

■6.12 VISUALIZATION

As stated in §1.9, the ability to *visualize* or *think in three dimensions* is one of the most important abilities of successful engineers, designers, and scientists. In practice, this means the ability to study the views of an object and to form a mental picture of it—to *visualize* its three-dimensional shape. To the designer it means the ability to *synthesize*, or form, a mental picture before the object even exists and the ability to express this image in terms of views. The engineer is the master planner in the construction of new equipment, structures, or processes. The ability to visualize and to

FIGURE 6.14   **Revolution Conventions.**

(a)   (b)

No!

TRUE PROJECTION
POOR PRACTICE

CONVENTIONAL METHOD
PREFERRED

FIGURE 6.15   **Removed View.**

use the graphic language as a means of communication or recording of mental images is indispensable.

Even experienced engineers and designers cannot look at a multiview drawing and instantly visualize the object represented (except for the simplest shapes) any more than we can grasp the ideas on a book page merely at a glance. It is necessary to *study* the drawing, to read the lines in a logical way, and to piece together the little things until a clear idea of the whole emerges. How this is done is described in §§6.13–6.32.

■6.13 VISUALIZING THE VIEWS

Figure 6.16 illustrates a method of reading drawings that is essentially the reverse of the mental process used in obtaining the views by projection. The given views of an angle bracket are shown in Fig. 6.16a.

1. The front view (Fig. 6.16I) shows that the object is L-shaped, the height and width of the object, and the thickness of the members. The meaning of the hidden and center lines is not yet clear; nor do we yet know the depth of the object.

2. The top view (Fig. 6.16II) tells us that the horizontal member is rounded at the right end and has a round hole. Some kind of slot is indicated at the left end. The depth and width of the object are shown.

3. The right-side view (Fig. 6.16III) tells us that the left end of the object has rounded corners at the top and has an open-end slot in a vertical position. The height and depth of the object are shown.

Thus, each view provides certain definite information regarding the shape of the object. All views must be considered to visualize the object completely.

■6.14 MODELS

One of the best aids to visualization is an actual model of the object. Such a model need not be made accurately to scale and may be made of any convenient material, such as modeling clay, soap, wood, styrofoam, or any material that can easily be shaped, carved, or cut.

A typical example of the use of soap or clay models is shown in Fig. 6.17. Three views of an object are given in Fig. 6.17a, and the student is to supply a missing line. The model is carved as shown in Figs. 6.17I–6.17III. The "missing" line discovered in the process is added to the drawing (Fig. 6.17b).

FIGURE 6.16   **Visualizing from Given Views.**

GIVEN: 3 VIEWS OF AN
OBJECT, WITH A
MISSING LINE

I CARVE
BLOCK

II SCRATCH LINES
ON SURFACES

III CUT
RECESS

ADD
MISSING LINE

FIGURE 6.17   **Use of Model to Aid Visualization.**

Some typical examples of soap models are shown in Fig. 6.18.

■6.15 SURFACES, EDGES, AND CORNERS

To analyze and synthesize multiview projections, the component elements that make up most solids must be considered. A *surface* (plane) may be bounded by straight lines, curves, or a combination of them. A surface may be *frontal, horizontal,* or *profile,* accord-ing to the plane of projection to which it is parallel (see §6.1).

If a plane surface is perpendicular to a plane of projection, it appears as a line or ***edge view*** (EV) (Fig. 6.19a). If it is parallel, it appears as a *true size* (TS) sur-face (Fig. 6.19b). If it is situated at an angle, it appears as a *foreshortened* (FS) surface (Fig. 6.19c). Thus, *a plane surface always projects as a line or a surface.*

The intersection of two plane surfaces produces an *edge,* or a straight line. Such a line is common to both surfaces and forms a boundary line for each. If an edge

FIGURE 6.18   **Soap Models.**

FIGURE 6.19   **Projections of Surfaces.**

EV = Edge View
TS = True Size
FS = Foreshortened

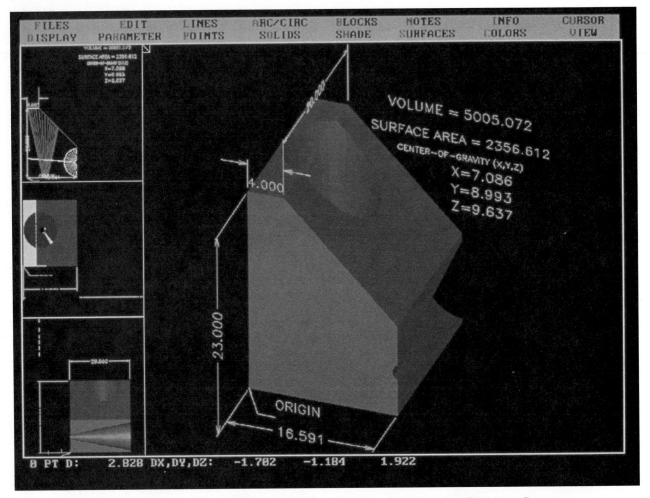

A CAD Solid Model and Several Surface Projections. *Courtesy of American Small Business Computers.*

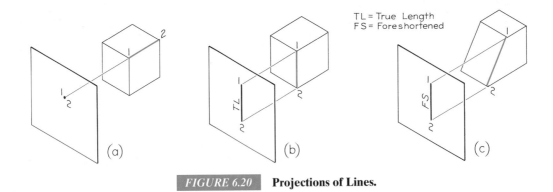

FIGURE 6.20   **Projections of Lines.**

is perpendicular to a plane of projection, it appears as a point (Fig. 6.20a); otherwise it appears as a line, as in Figs.6.20b and 6.20c. If it is parallel to the plane of projection, it shows true length (Fig. 6.20b); if not parallel,

it appears foreshortened (Fig. 6.20c). Thus, a *straight line always projects as a straight line or as a point.* A line may be *frontal, horizontal,* or *profile,* according to the plane of projection to which it is parallel.

A *corner*, or point, is the common intersection of three or more surfaces or edges. A point appears as a point in every view.

■ 6.16 ADJACENT AREAS

Consider the top view in Fig. 6.21a. Lines divide the view into three areas. Each area must represent a surface *at a different level*. Surface A may be high and surfaces B and C lower (Fig. 6.21b). Or B may be lower than C (Fig. 6.21c). Or B may be highest, with C and A each lower (Fig. 6.21d). Or one or more surfaces may be inclined (Fig. 6.21e). Or one or more surfaces may be cylindrical (Fig. 6.21f), and so on. *No two adjacent areas can lie in the same plane.*

The same reasoning can apply, of course, to the adjacent areas in any given view. Since an area (surface) in a view can be interpreted in several different ways, other views must be observed to determine which interpretation is correct.

■ 6.17 SIMILAR SHAPES OF SURFACES

If a surface is viewed from several different positions, it will in each case been seen to have a certain number of sides and to have a certain characteristic shape. An L-shaped surface (Fig. 6.22a) will appear as an L-shaped figure in every view in which it does not appear as a line. A T-shaped surface (Fig. 6.22b), a U-shaped surface (Fig. 6.22c), or a hexagonal surface

(Fig. 6.22d) will in each case have the same number of sides and the same characteristic shape in every view in which it appears as a surface.

This repetition of shapes is one of our best methods for analyzing views.

■ 6.18 READING A DRAWING

Suppose we want to visualize the object shown by three views in Fig. 6.23. Since no lines are curved, we know that the object is made up of plane surfaces.

Surface 2–3–10–9–6–5 in the top view is an L-shaped surface of six sides. It appears in the side view at 16–17–21–20–18–19 and is L-shaped and six-sided. No such shape appears in the front view, but we note that points 2 and 5 line up with 11 in the front view, points 6 and 9 line up with 13, and points 3 and 10 line up with 15. Evidently, line 11–15 in the front view is the edge view of the L-shaped surface.

Surface 11–13–12 in the front view is triangular in shape, but no corresponding triangles appear in either the top or the side view. We note that point 12 lines up with 8 and 4 and that point 13 lines up with 6 and 9. However, surface 11–13–12 of the front view cannot be the same as surface 4–6–9–8 in the top view because the former has three sides and the latter has four. Obviously, the triangular surface appears as line 4–6 in the top view and as line 16–19 in the side view.

Surface 12–13–15–14 in the front view is trapezoidal in shape. But there are no trapezoids in the top

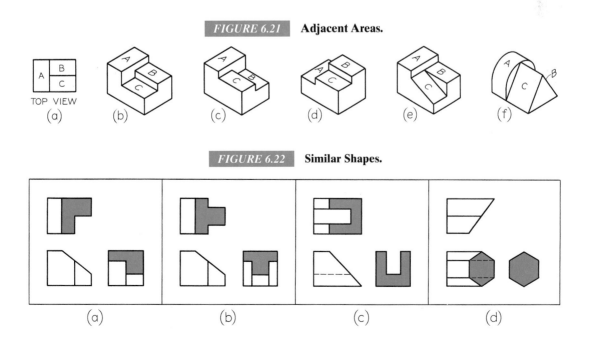

FIGURE 6.21   Adjacent Areas.

FIGURE 6.22   Similar Shapes.

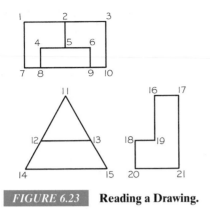

FIGURE 6.23   **Reading a Drawing.**

and side views, so the surface evidently appears in the top view as line 7–10 and in the side view as line 18–20.

The remaining surfaces can be identified in the same manner, where it will be seen that the object is bounded by seven plane surfaces, two of which are rectangular, two triangular, two L-shaped, and one trapezoidal.

Note that the numbering system used in Fig. 6.23 is different from that in Fig. 6.8 in that different numbers are used for all points and there is no significance in a point being inside or outside a corner.

■ 6.19 NORMAL SURFACES

A *normal surface* is a plane surface that is parallel to a plane of projection. It appears in true size and shape on the plane to which it is parallel, and as a vertical or a horizontal line on adjacent planes of projection.

In Fig. 6.24 four stages in machining a block of steel to produce the final tool block in Fig 6.24IV are shown. All surfaces are normal surfaces. In Fig. 6.24I, normal surface A is parallel to the horizontal plane

FIGURE 6.24   **Machining a Tool Block—Normal Surfaces and Edges.**

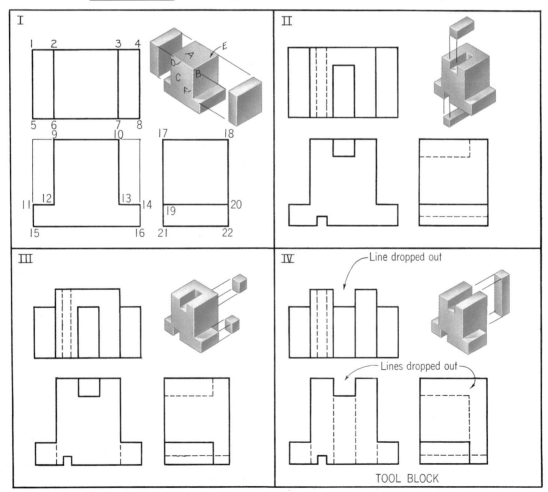

and appears true size in the top view at 2–3–7–6, as line 9–10 in the front view, and as line 17–18 in the side view. Normal surface B is parallel to the profile plane and appears true size in the side view at 17–18–20–19, as line 3–7 in the top view, and as line 10–13 in the front view. Normal surface C, an inverted T-shaped surface, is parallel to the frontal plane and appears true size in the front view at 9–10–13–14–16–15–11–12, as line 5–8 in the top view, and as line 17–21 in the side view.

All other surfaces of the object may be visualized in a similar manner. In the four stages of Fig. 6.24, observe carefully the changes in the views produced by the machining operations, including the introduction of new surfaces, new visible edges, and hidden edges and the dropping out of certain lines as the result of a new cut.

The top view in Fig. 6.24I is cut by lines 2–6 and 3–7, which means that there are three surfaces, 1–2–6–5, 2–3–7–6, and 3–4–8–7. In the front view, surface 9–10 is seen to be the highest, and surfaces 11–12 and 13–14 are at the same lower level. In the side view, both of these latter surfaces appear as one line 19–20. Surface 11–12 might appear as a hidden line in the side view, but surface 13–14 appears as a visible line 19–20, which covers up the hidden line and takes precedence over it (see §5.30).

■6.20 NORMAL EDGES

A *normal edge* is a line that is perpendicular to a plane of projection. It appears as a point on the plane of projection to which it is perpendicular and as a line in true length on adjacent planes of projection. In Fig. 6.24I, edge D is perpendicular to the profile plane of projection and appears as point 17 in the side view. It is parallel to the frontal and horizontal planes of projection and is shown true length at 9–10 in the front view and 6–7 in the top view. Edges E and F are perpendicular, respectively, to the frontal and horizontal planes of projection, and their views may be similarly analyzed.

■6.21 INCLINED SURFACES

An *inclined surface* is a plane surface that is perpendicular to one plane of projection but inclined to adjacent planes. An inclined surface projects as a straight line on the plane to which it is perpendicular; it appears foreshortened (FS) on planes to which it is

inclined, with the degree of foreshortening being proportional to the angle of inclination.

Figure 6.25 shows four stages in machining a locating finger, producing several inclined surfaces. In Fig. 6.25I, inclined surface A is perpendicular to the horizontal plane of projection and appears as line 5–3 in the top view. It is shown as a foreshortened surface in the front view at 7–8–11–10 and in the side view at 12–13–16–15. Note that the surface is more foreshortened in the side view than in the front view because the plane makes a greater angle with the profile plane of projection than with the frontal plane of projection.

In Fig. 6.25III, edge 23–24 in the front view is the edge view of an inclined surface that appears in the top view as 21–2–3–22 and in the side view as 25–14–27–26. Note that 25–14 is equal in length to 21–22 and that the surface has the same number of sides (four) in both views in which it appears as a surface.

In Fig. 6.25IV, edge 29–23 in the front view is the edge view of an inclined surface that appears in the top view as visible surface 1–21–22–5–18 and in the side view as invisible surface 25–14–32–31–30. While the surface does not appear true size in any view, it does have the same characteristic shape and the same number of sides (five) in the views in which it appears as a surface.

To obtain the true size of an inclined surface, it is necessary to construct an auxiliary view (Chapter 8) or to revolve the surface until it is parallel to a plane of projection (Chapter 9).

■6.22 INCLINED EDGES

An *inclined edge* is a line that is parallel to a plane of projection but inclined to adjacent planes. It appears true length on the plane to which it is parallel and foreshortened on adjacent planes, with the degree of foreshortening being proportional to the angle of inclination. The true-length view of an inclined line is always inclined, while the foreshortened views are either vertical or horizontal lines.

In Fig. 6.25I, inclined edge B is parallel to the horizontal plane of projection and appears true length in the top view at 5–3. It is foreshortened in the front view at 7–8 and in the side view at 12–13. Note that plane A produces two normal edges and two inclined edges.

In Figs. 6.25III and 6.25IV, some of the sloping lines are not inclined lines. In Fig. 6.25III, the edge that appears in the top view at 21–22, in the front view at

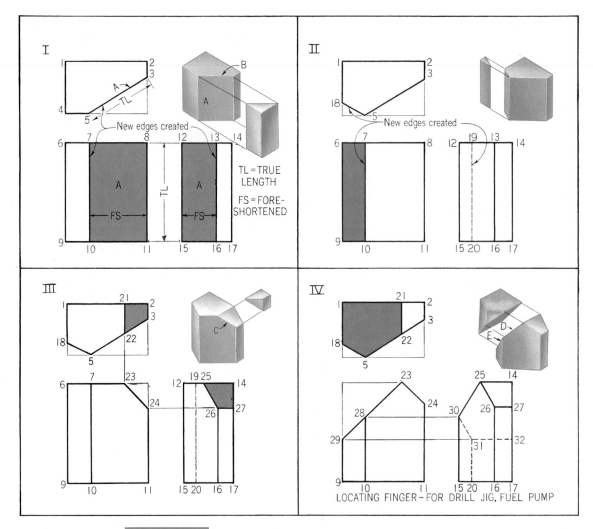

FIGURE 6.25   **Machining a Locating Finger—Inclined Surfaces.**

23–24, and in the side view at 14–27 is an inclined line. However, the edge that appears in the top view at 22–23, in the front view at 23–24, and in the side view at 25–26 is not an inclined line by the definition given here. Actually, it is an oblique line (see §6.24).

■ 6.23 OBLIQUE SURFACES

An *oblique surface* is a plane that is oblique to all planes of projection. Since it is not perpendicular to any plane, it cannot appear as a line in any view. Since it is not parallel to any plane, it cannot appear true size in any view. Thus, an oblique surface always appears as a foreshortened surface in all three views.

In Fig. 6.26II, oblique surface C appears in the top view at 25–3–6–26 and in the front view at

29–8–31–30. What are its numbers in the side view? Note that any surface appearing as a line in any view cannot be an oblique surface. How many inclined surfaces are there? How many normal surfaces?

To obtain the true size of an oblique surface, it is necessary to construct a secondary, auxiliary view (see §§8.21 and 8.22) or to revolve the surface until it is parallel to a plane of projection (see §9.11).

■ 6.24 OBLIQUE EDGES

An *oblique edge* is a line that is oblique to all planes of projection. Since it is not perpendicular to any plane, it cannot appear as a point in any view. Since it is not parallel to any plane, it cannot appear true length in

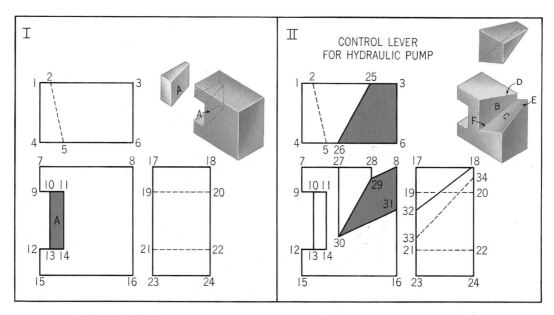

FIGURE 6.26 Machining a Control Lever—Inclined and Oblique Surfaces.

any view. An oblique edge appears foreshortened and in an inclined position in every view.

In Fig. 6.26II, oblique edge F appears in the top view at 26–25, in the front view at 30–29, and in the side view at 33–34.

■ 6.25 PARALLEL EDGES

If a series of parallel planes is intersected by another plane, the resulting lines of intersection are parallel (Fig. 6.27a). In Fig. 6.27b, the top plane of the object intersects the front and rear planes, producing the parallel edges 1–2 and 3–4. If two lines are parallel in space, their projections in any view are parallel. The example in Fig. 6.27b is a special case in which the two lines appear as points in one view and coincide as a single line in another and should not be regarded as an exception to the rule. Note that even in the pictorial drawings the lines are shown parallel. Parallel inclined lines are shown in Fig. 6.27c, and parallel oblique lines in Fig. 6.27d.

Figure 6.28 shows three views of an object after a plane has been passed through the points A, B, and C. As shown in Fig. 6.28b, only points that lie in the same plane are joined. In the front view, join points A and C, which are in the same plane, extending the line to P on the vertical front edge of the block extended. In the side view, join P to B, and in the top view, join B to A.

Parallel planes intersected by another plane
(a)

Lines 1,2 & 3,4 parallel, & parallel to horizontal plane
(b)

Lines 1,2 & 3,4 parallel & parallel to frontal plane
(c)

Lines 1,2 & 3,4 parallel & oblique to all planes
(d)

FIGURE 6.27 Parallel Lines.

Complete the drawing by applying this rule: *Parallel lines in space will be projected as parallel lines in any view.* The remaining lines are thus drawn parallel to lines AP, PB, and BA.

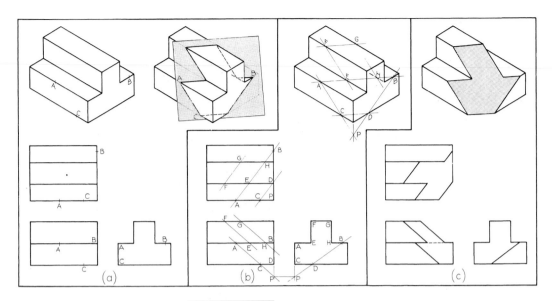

FIGURE 6.28 **Oblique Surface.**

■6.26 ANGLES

If an angle is in a normal plane—that is, parallel to a plane of projection—the angle will be shown true size on the plane of projection to which it is parallel (Fig. 6.29a). If the angle is in an inclined plane, it may be projected either larger or smaller than the true angle, depending on its position (Figs. 6.29b and 6.29c). In Fig. 6.29b, the 45° angle is shown *oversize* in the front view, while in Fig. 6.29c the 60° angle is shown *undersize* in both views.

A 90° angle will be projected true size, even if it is in an inclined plane, provided that one leg of the angle is a normal line (Fig. 6.29d). In this figure, the 60° angle is projected *oversize* and the 30° angle *undersize*. Study these relations, using your own 30° × 60° triangle as a model.

■6.27 CURVED SURFACES

Rounded surfaces are common in engineering practice because they are easily formed on the lathe, the drill press, and other machines using the principle of rotation either of the "work" or of the cutting tool. The most common rounded surfaces are the cylinder, cone, and sphere, a few of whose applications are shown in Fig. 6.30. For other geometric solids, see Fig. 4.7.

■6.28 CYLINDRICAL SURFACES

Three views of a right-circular cylinder, the most common type, are shown in Fig. 6.31a. The single cylindri-

cal surface is intersected by two plane (normal) surfaces, forming two curved lines of intersection or circular edges (the bases of the cylinder). These circular edges are the only actual edges on the cylinder. Figure 6.31b shows a cylindrical hole in a right square prism.

The cylinder is represented on a drawing by its circular edges and the contour elements. An *element* is a straight line on the cylindrical surface, parallel to the axis, as shown in the pictorial view of the cylinder in Fig. 6.31a. In both parts of Fig. 6.31, the circular edges of the cylinder appear in the top views as circles A, in the front views as horizontal lines 5–7 and 8–10, and in the side views as horizontal lines 11–13 and 14–16.

The contour elements 5–8 and 7–10 in the front views appear as points 3 and 1 in the top views. The contour elements 11–14 and 13–16 in the side views appear as points 2 and 4 in the top views.

In Fig. 6.32, four possible stages in machining a cap are shown, producing several cylindrical surfaces. In Fig. 6.32I, the removal of the two upper corners forms cylindrical surface A, which appears in the top view as surface 1–2–4–3, in the front view as arc 5, and in the side view as surface 8–9–Y–X.

In Fig. 6.32II, a large reamed hole shows in the front view as circle 16, in the top view as cylindrical surface 12–13–15–14, and in the side view as cylindrical surface 17–18–20–19.

In Fig. 6.32III, two drilled and counterbored holes are added, producing four more cylindrical surfaces

(a) ANGLE IN NORMAL PLANE

(b) ANGLE IN INCLINED PLANE

(c) ANGLE IN INCLINED PLANE

(d) PROJECTIONS OF THE ANGLES OF THE 30°×60° TRIANGLE.

FIGURE 6.29   **Angles.**

(a) PLUMB BOB

(b) LATHE CENTER

(c) WATER TANK

(d) BAND SHELL

(e) MACHINE HANDLE

FIGURE 6.30   **Curved Surfaces.**

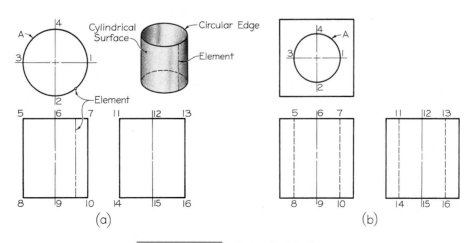

(a)

(b)

FIGURE 6.31   **Cylindrical Surfaces.**

FIGURE 6.32 Machining a Cap—Cylindrical Surfaces.

and two normal surfaces. The two normal surfaces are those at the bottoms of the counterbores.

In Fig. 6.32IV, a cylindrical cut is added, producing two cylindrical surfaces that appear edgewise in the front view as arcs 30 and 33, in the top view as surfaces 21–22–26–25 and 23–24–28–27, and in the side view as surfaces 36–37–40–38 and 41–42–44–43.

■ 6.29 DEFORMITIES OF CYLINDERS

In shop practice, cylinders are usually machined or formed to introduce other, often plane, surfaces. Figure 6.33a shows a cut that introduces two normal surfaces. One surface appears as line 3–4 in the top view, as surface 6–7–10–9 in the front view, and as line 13–16 in the side view. The other appears as line

15–16 in the side view, as line 9–10 in the front view, and as surface 3–4, arc 2 in the top view.

All elements touching arc 2, between 3 and 4 in the top view, become shorter as a result of the cut. For example, element A, which shows as a point in the top view, now becomes CD in the front view and 15–17 in the side view. As a result of the cut, the front half of the cylindrical surface has changed from 5–8–12–11 to 5–6–9–10–7–8–12–11 (front view). The back half remains unchanged.

In Fig. 6.33b, two cuts introduce four normal surfaces. Note that surface 7–8 (top view) is through the center of the cylinder, producing in the side view line 21–24 and in the front view surface 11–14–16–15, which is equal in width to the diameter of the cylinder. Surface 15–16 (front view) is read in the top view as

FIGURE 6.33 **Cylinders and Ellipses.**

7–8–ARC 4. Surface 11–14 (front view) is read in the top view as 5–6–ARC 3–8–7–ARC 2.

In Fig. 6.33c, two cylinders on the same axis are shown, intersected by a normal surface parallel to the axis. Surface 17–20 (front view) is 23–25 in the side view and 2–3–11–9–15–14–8–6 in the top view. A common error is to draw a visible line in the top view between 8 and 9. However, this would produce two surfaces 2–3–11–6 and 8–9–15–14 not in the same plane. In the front view, the larger surface appears as line 17–20 and the smaller as line 18–19. These lines coincide; hence, they are all one surface, and there can be no visible line joining 8 and 9 in the top view.

The vertical surface that appears in the front view at 17–18–ARC 22–19–20–ARC 21 appears as a line in the top view at 5–12, which explains the hidden line 8–9 in the top view.

■ 6.30 CYLINDERS AND ELLIPSES

If a cylinder is cut by an inclined plane, as in Fig. 6.34a, the inclined surface is bounded by an ellipse. The ellipse appears as circle 1 in the top view, as straight line 2–3 in the front view, and as ellipse ADBC in the side view. Note that circle 1 in the top view would remain a circle regardless of the angle of the cut. If the cut is 45° with horizontal, the ellipse will appear as a circle in the side view (see phantom lines) since the major and minor axes in that view would be equal. Finding the true size and shape of the ellipse requires an auxiliary view

FIGURE 6.34 **Deformities of Cylinders.**

with the line of sight perpendicular to surface 2-3 in the front view (see §8.12).

Since the major and minor axes AB and CD are known, the ellipse can be drawn by any of the methods in Figs. 4.48–4.50 and 4.52a (true ellipses) or with the aid of an ellipse template.

If a cylinder is tilted forward its bases or circular edges 1–2 and 3–4 (side view) become ellipses in the front and top views (Fig. 6.34b). Points on the ellipses can be plotted from the semicircular end view of the cylinder, as shown, with distances d being equal. Since the major and minor axes for each ellipse are known, the ellipses can be drawn with the aid of an ellipse template, or by any of the true ellipse methods, or by the approximate method.

If a cylinder is cut by an oblique plane, the elliptical surface appears as an ellipse in two views (Fig. 6.34c). In the top view, points A and B are selected, diametrically opposite, as the high and low points in the ellipse, and CD is drawn perpendicular to AB. These are the projections of the major and minor axes, respectively, of the actual ellipse in space. In the front and side views, points A and B are assumed at the desired altitudes. Since CD appears true length in the top view, it will appear horizontal in the front and side views, as shown. These axes in the front and side views are the conjugate axes of the ellipses. The ellipses may be drawn on these axes by the methods shown in Figs. 4.51 and 4.52b or by trial with the aid of an ellipse template.

The intersection of a plane and a quarter-round molding is shown in Fig. 6.35a, and intersection with a cove molding is shown in Fig. 6.35b. In both figures, assume points 1, 2, 3, … at random in the side views in which the cylindrical surfaces appear as curved lines, and project the points to the front and top views, as shown. A sufficient number of points should be used to ensure smooth curves. Draw the final curves through the points with an irregular curve.

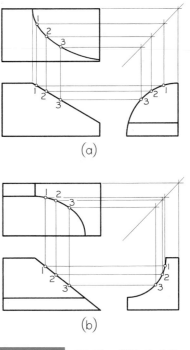

FIGURE 6.35   **Plotting Elliptical Curves.**

FIGURE 6.36   **Space (Irregular) Curve.**

■ 6.31 SPACE CURVES

The views of a space curve (an irregular cuve) are established by the projections of points along the curve (Fig. 6.36). In this figure, any points 1, 2, 3, … are selected along the curve in the top view and then projected to the side view (or the reverse), and points are located in the front view by projecting downward from the top view and across from the side view. The resulting curve in the front view is drawn with an irregular curve.

■ 6.32 INTERSECTIONS AND TANGENCIES

No line should be drawn where a curved surface is tangent to a plane surface (Fig. 6.37a), but when a curved surface *intersects* a plane surface, a definite edge is

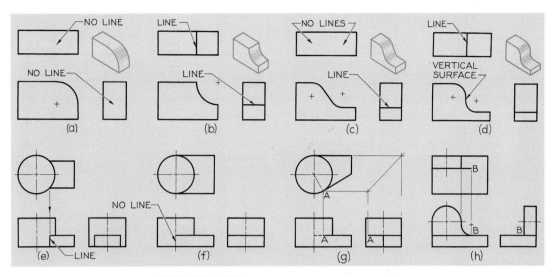

FIGURE 6.37   **Intersections and Tangencies.**

formed (Fig. 6.37b). If curved surfaces are arranged as in Fig. 6.37c, no lines appear in the top view. If the surfaces are arranged as in Fig. 6.37d, a vertical surface in the front view produces a line in the top view. Other typical intersections and tangencies of surfaces are shown in Figs. 6.37e–6.37h. To locate the point of tangency A in Fig. 6.37g, refer to Fig. 4.34b.

The intersection of a small cylinder with a large cylinder is shown in Fig. 6.38a. The intersection is so small that it is not plotted; a straight line is used instead. In Fig. 6.38b, the intersection is larger, but still not large enough to justify plotting the curve. The curve is approximated by drawing an arc whose radius r is the same as radius R of the large cylinder.

The intersection in Fig. 6.38c is significant enough to justify constructing the true curve. Points are selected at random in the circle in the side or top view, and these are then projected to the other two views to locate points on the curve in the front view, as shown. Depending on the size of the intersection, a sufficient number of points should be used to ensure a smooth

and accurate curve. Draw the final curve with the aid of an irregular curve.

In Fig. 6.38d, the cylinders are the same diameter. The figure of intersection consists of two semiellipses that appear as straight lines in the front view.

If the intersecting cylinders are holes, the intersections will be similar to those for the external cylinders in Fig. 6.38 (see also Fig. 7.34d).

In Fig. 6.39a, a narrow prism intersects a cylinder, but the intersection is insignificant and is ignored. In Fig. 6.39b, the prism is larger, and the intersection is noticeable enough to warrant construction, as shown. In Fig. 6.39c and 6.39d, a keyseat and a small drilled hole, respectively, are shown; in both cases the intersection is not important enough to construct.

■ 6.33 HOW TO REPRESENT HOLES

The correct methods of representing most common types of machined holes are shown in Fig. 6.40. Instructions to the machinist are given in the form of

FIGURE 6.38   **Intersections of Cylinders.**

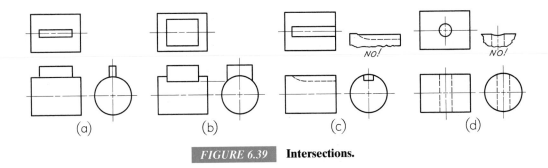

FIGURE 6.39   **Intersections.**

notes, and the drafter represents the holes in conformity with these specifications. In general, the notes tell the machine operator what to do and in which order it is to be done. Hole sizes are always specified by diameter—never by radius. For each operation specified, the diameter is given first, followed by the method—such as drill, ream, and so on—as shown in Figs. 6.40a and 6.40b.

The size of the hole may be specified as a diameter without the specific method (such as drill, ream, and so on) since the selection of the method will depend on available production facilities (Figs. 6.40h–6.40j).

A drilled hole is a *through hole* if it goes through a member. If the hole has a specified depth, as shown in Fig. 6.40a, the hole is called a *blind hole*. The depth includes the cylindrical portion of the hole only. The point of the drill leaves a conical bottom in the hole, drawn approximately with the 30° × 60° triangle, as shown.[*]

A through-drilled or reamed hole is drawn as shown in Fig. 6.40b. The note tells how the hole is to be produced—in this case by reaming. Note that tolerances are ignored in actually laying out the diameter of a hole.

In Fig. 6.40c, a hole is drilled and then the upper part is enlarged cylindrically to a specified diameter and depth. In Fig. 6.40d, a hole is drilled and then the upper part is enlarged conically to a specified angle and diameter. The angle is commonly 82° but is drawn 90° for simplicity. In Fig. 6.40e, a hole is drilled and then the upper part is enlarged cylindrically to a specified diameter. The depth usually is not specified, but is

left to the shop to determine. For average cases, the depth is drawn 1.5 mm ($\frac{1}{16}$″).

6.34 FILLETS AND ROUNDS

A rounded interior corner is called a *fillet*, and a rounded exterior corner is called a *round* (Fig. 6.41a). Sharp corners should be avoided in designing parts to be cast or forged not only because they are difficult to produce but also because, in the case of interior corners, they are a source of weakness and failure (see §10.5 for manufacturing processes involved).

Two intersecting rough surfaces produce a rounded corner (Fig. 6.41b). If one of these surfaces is machined (Fig. 6.41c), or if both surfaces are machined (Fig. 6.41d), the corner becomes sharp. Therefore, in drawings, a rounded corner means that both intersecting surfaces are rough, while a sharp corner means that one or both surfaces are machined. On working drawings, fillets and rounds are never shaded. The presence of the curved surfaces is indicated only where they appear as arcs, except as shown in Fig. 6.45.

Fillets and rounds should be drawn with the filleted corners of a triangle, a special fillets and rounds template, or a circle template.

6.35 RUNOUTS

The correct method of representing fillets in connection with plane surfaces tangent to cylinders is shown in Fig. 6.42. These small curves are called *runouts*. Note that the runouts F have a radius equal to that of the fillet and a curvature of about one eighth of a circle (Fig. 6.42d).

---
[*] For drill sizes, see Appendix 16 ("Twist Drill Sizes"). For abbreviations, see Appendix 4.

FIGURE 6.40 **How to Represent Holes. Dimensions for (a)–(e) in metric.**

Typical filleted intersections are shown in Fig. 6.43. The runouts from Figs. 6.43a–6.43d differ because of the different shapes of the horizontal intersecting members. In Figs. 6.43e and 6.43f, the runouts differ because the top surface of the web in Fig. 6.43e is flat, with only slight rounds along the edge, while the top surface of the web in Fig. 6.43f is considerably rounded. When two different sizes of fillets intersect, as in

FIGURE 6.41   **Rough and Finished Surfaces.**

FIGURE 6.42   **Runouts.**

FIGURE 6.43   **Conventional Fillets, Rounds, and Runouts.**

Figs. 6.43g and 6.43j, the direction of the runout is dictated by the larger fillet, as shown.

■ 6.36 CONVENTIONAL EDGES

Rounded and filleted intersections eliminate sharp edges and sometimes make it difficult to present a clear shape description. In fact, in some cases, true projection may actually be misleading, as in Fig. 6.44a, where the side view of the railroad rail is quite blank. A clearer representation results if lines are added for rounded and filleted edges, as shown in Figs. 6.44b and 6.44c. The added lines are projected from the actual intersections of the surfaces as if the fillets and rounds were not present.

Figure 6.45 shows top views for each given front view. The upper top views are nearly devoid of lines that contribute to the shape descriptions, while the lower top views, in which lines are used to represent the rounded and filleted edges, are quite clear. Note, in the lower top views in Figs. 6.45a and 6.45c, the use of small Ys where rounded or filleted edges meet a

rough surface. If such an edge intersects a finished surface, no Y is shown.

■ 6.37 RIGHT-HAND AND LEFT-HAND PARTS

In industry, many individual parts are located symmetrically so they can function in pairs. These opposite parts are often exactly alike (for example, the wheel covers used on the left and right sides of an automobile). In fact, whenever possible, for economy's sake the designer will design identical parts for use on both the right and left. But opposite parts often cannot be exactly alike, such as a pair of gloves or a pair of shoes. Similarly, the right-front fender of an automobile cannot be the same shape as the left-front fender. Therefore, a left-hand part is not simply a right-hand part turned around; the two parts will be mirror images and not interchangeable.

A left-hand part is referred to as an LH part, and a right-hand part as an RH part. In Fig. 6.46a, the image in the mirror is the "other hand" of the part shown. If

A 3D CAD Representation of Fillets. *Courtesy of SDRC, Milford, OH.*

A 3D CAD Representation of Rounds. *Courtesy of SDRC, Milford, OH.*

FIGURE 6.44   **Conventional Repression of a Rail.**

(a) TRUE PROJECTION
POOR PRACTICE

(b) CONVENTIONAL DRAWING
PREFERRED IN LARGE SIZES

(c) CONVENTIONAL DRAWING
PREFERRED IN SMALL SIZES

FIGURE 6.45   Conventional Edges.

FIGURE 6.46   Right-Hand and Left-Hand Parts.

the part in front of the mirror is an RH part, the image shows the LH part. No matter how the object is turned, the image will show the LH part. Figures 6.46b and 6.46c show LH and RH drawings of the same object; these drawings are also symmetrical with respect to a reference-plane line between them.

If you hold a drawing faced against a windowpane or on a light table so that the lines can be seen through the paper, you can trace the reverse image of the part on the back or on tracing paper. This will be a drawing of the opposite part.

It is customary to draw only one of two opposite parts and to label the one that is drawn with a note, such as LH PART SHOWN, RH OPPOSITE. If the opposite-hand shape is not clear, a separate drawing must be made for it and must be properly identified.

■6.38   FIRST-ANGLE PROJECTION

If the vertical and horizontal planes of projection are considered indefinite in extent and intersecting at 90°

with each other, the four dihedral angles produced are the *first, second, third,* and *fourth* angles (Fig. 6.47a). The profile plane intersects these two planes and may extend into all angles. If the object is placed below the horizontal plane and behind the vertical plane, as in the glass box (see Fig. 6.3), the object is said to be in the third angle. In this case, as we have seen, the observer is always "outside, looking in," so that for all views the lines of sight proceed from the eye *through the planes of projection and to the object.*

If the object is placed above the horizontal plane and in front of the vertical plane, the object is in the first angle. In this case, the observer always looks *through the object and to the planes of projection.* Thus, the right-side view is still obtained by looking toward the right side of the object, the front by looking toward the front, and the top by looking down toward the top; but the views are projected from the object onto a plane in each case. When the planes are unfolded (Fig. 6.47b), the right-side view falls at the left of the front view, and the top view falls below the front view, as

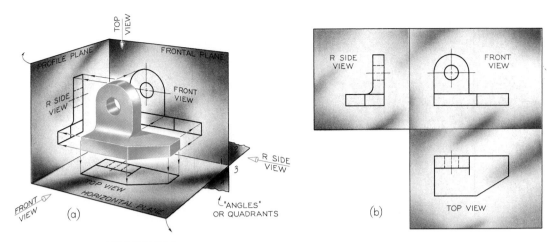

FIGURE 6.47   First-Angle Projection. An object that is above the horizontal plane and in front of the vertical plane is in the first angle. An observer looks through the object to the planes of projection.

(a) FIRST-ANGLE PROJECTION

(b) THIRD-ANGLE PROJECTION

FIGURE 6.48   First-Angle Projection Compared to Third-Angle Projection.

shown. A comparison between first-angle orthographic projection and third-angle orthographic projection is shown in Fig. 6.48. The front, top, and right-side views shown in Fig. 6.47b for first-angle projection are repeated in Fig. 6.48a. The front, top, and right-side views for third-angle projection of Fig. 6.4 are repeated in Fig. 6.48b. Ultimately, the only difference between third-angle and first-angle projection is the arrangement of the views. Still, confusion and possibly manufacturing errors may result when the user reading a first-angle drawing thinks it is a third-angle drawing, or vice versa. To avoid misunderstanding, international projection symbols, shown in Fig. 6.48, have been developed to distinguish between first-an-

gle and third-angle projections on drawings. On drawings where the possibility of confusion is anticipated, these symbols may appear in or near the title box.

In the United States and Canada (and, to some extent, in England), third-angle projection is standard, while in most of the rest of the world, first-angle projection is used. First-angle projection was originally used all over the world, including the United States, but it was abandoned around 1890.

■ 6.39 COMPUTER GRAPHICS

You can use CAD to create 2D multiview projections in a way similar to creating a multiview drawing on

FIGURE 6.49   **Computer-Generated Multiview and Pictorial Drawing.** *Courtesy of SolidWorks*

paper. You can also create 3D models of a part using CAD. From the 3D model, you can create 2D orthographic views automatically. This can save time in creating many drawings because you only have to create the 3D model once to generate as many different views as you want. It is important to develop an understanding of projection in order to use 3D CAD effectively. When you are looking at a 3D wireframe drawing on your computer screen, it can be difficult to tell from which direction you are viewing the model. This is because some objects may look identical on the computer screen even when viewed from different directions. If you do not develop an understanding of orthographic views, it can be very easy to lose yourself in the 3D space of your drawing (Fig. 6.49).

■ KEY WORDS

PROJECTION	THIRD-ANGLE PROJECTION
PROJECTORS	PLANE OF PROJECTION
MITER LINE	ORTHOGRAPHIC
FOLD LINES	THE GLASS BOX
DEPTH	ALIGNMENT OF VIEWS
HEIGHT	INCLINED
WIDTH	OBLIQUE
REVOLUTION	EDGES
NORMAL	HOLE CONVENTIONS
SURFACES	FILLETS AND ROUNDS
CYLINDERS	

CHAPTER SUMMARY

- Orthographic drawings are the result of projecting the image of a three-dimensional object onto one of six standard planes of projection. The planes of projection intersect each other at fold lines. The six standard planes of projection are often thought of as a "glass box."

- Each view in an orthographic projection is aligned with an adjacent view. The principal views most often used are top, front, and right side.

- To help project or verify surfaces you can label them with letters, and the corners of surfaces can be labeled with numbers. There are normal, inclined, and oblique surfaces. Normal surfaces appear true size in one principal view and as an edge in the other two principal views. Inclined surfaces appear as an edge view in one of the three

principal views. Oblique surfaces do not appear in edge view in any of the principal views.

- Conic sections and irregular curves must be plotted by identifying points on the object. The points can be projected to approximate the boundaries of the curved surface.

- Drawing conventions define usual practices for the representation of features such as holes, bosses, ribs, webs, spokes, fillets, and rounds.

- Creating CAD drawings involves applying the same concepts as paper drawing. The main difference is that the paper surface is replaced by the monitor screen, and CAD software can draw a line faster and more accurately than most drafters.

REVIEW QUESTIONS

1. Sketch a representation of third angle projection.
2. List the six principal views of projection.
3. Sketch the top, front, and right side views of an object having normal, inclined, and oblique surfaces.
4. In a drawing that shows the top, front, and right side view, which two views show depth? Which view shows depth vertically? Which view shows depth horizontally?
5. What is the definition of a normal surface? An inclined surface? An oblique surface?
6. Describe the procedure necessary to center a three-view drawing on a sheet of paper.
7. Describe the procedure necessary to center a CAD drawing on a sheet of paper.

8. How is the computer monitor used to view a CAD program similar to a sheet of paper?
9. What dimensions are the same between the top and front view: width, height, or depth? Between the front and right side view? Between the top and right side view?
10. List two ways of transferring depth between the top and right side views.
11. If surface A contained corners 1, 2, 3, 4, and surface B contained corners 3, 4, 5, 6, what is the name of the line where surfaces A and B intersect?
12. If the top view of an object shows a drilled through hole, how many hidden lines would be necessary in the front view to describe the hole?

MULTIVIEW PROJECTION PROBLEMS

The following problems are intended primarily to afford practice in instrumental drawing, but any of them may be sketched freehand on graph paper or plain paper. Sheet layouts such as those in Figs. 6.50 and 6.51 or inside the back cover are suggested, but your instructor may prefer a different sheet size or arrangement. Use metric or decimal-inch as assigned.

   If your instructor requires dimensions, you should

study §§11.1–11.25. In the following problems, often it is not possible for the dimensions to be shown in the preferred places in the standard manner. In doing the problems, you are expected to move dimensions to the preferred locations and to conform to the dimensioning practices recommended in Chapter 11.

   For additional problems, see Fig. 8.29. Draw top views instead of auxiliary views.

| BASE | PUBLICK , JOHN Q. | 1"=1" | 1-1-83 | A-6 | 3 |

FIGURE 6.50 Suggested Layout for Freehand Sketch (Layout A–2 or A4–2 adjusted).

| INSTITUTE OF TECHNOLOGY | | FIXTURE BRACKET | SEAT 25 |
| SCALE: 1/1 | DATE: AUG. 15, 1996 | DRAWN BY : JOSEPH E. BLOUGH, JR. | SHEET 2 |

FIGURE 6.51 Suggested Layout for Mechanical Drawing (Layout A–3 or A4–3 adjusted).

FIGURE 6.52 Missing-View Problems. Using Layout A–2 or 3 or Layout A4–2 or 3 (adjusted), sketch or draw with instruments the given views, and add the missing view, as shown in Figs. 6.50 and 6.51. If dimensions are required, study §§11.1–11.25. Use metric or decimal-inch dimensions as assigned by the instructor. Move dimensions to better locations where possible. In Probs. 1–5, all surfaces are normal surfaces.

1 LOCATER

.76 1.00 2X R
.62
1.06 2.12 1.00 .56
2.50 1.12
1.56 30° 2.26
2.62
4.76
View here

2 V-STOP METRIC

114
16 46 10
2X 6R 2X Ø16 14
66 32 90°
33 16
22 40 27
View here

3 BRACKET METRIC

120
20 30°
54 42
16
22 Ø16-22↓
45
30°
40 42
58
28
10 24 10 6
View here

4 ANGLE BLOCK

Ø.62 VØ1.25 X 90° 1.50
.38
2.18
1.09 45° 1.12
1.00 2.56
2.12 30°
4.56
View here

5 WEDGE BLOCK METRIC

16 72
16
58 26
58 16 Ø12
16
50 56
8
118
View here

6 View here L H FINGER

5.06 1.81
60° 15° 30°
2.62 1.38
45° 1.00
.50
Ø.62 ⊤1.88 45° .62

7 (Surfaces A&B parallel) ADJUSTER

2.75
1.38 .75
A 2.00
B
1.56
Ø.56
A
2.31
1.88 .88
.75 B .25
.75
4.69
View here

8 (Surfaces A&B parallel) ANGLE SLIDE METRIC

121
16
54 B A 6
22 59
16
57 46
46 29
B A
View here
44 33 2 X Ø14

FIGURE 6.53 Missing-View Problems. Using Layout A–2 or 3 or Layout A4–2 or 3 (adjusted), sketch or draw with instruments the given views, and add the missing view, as shown in Figs. 6.50 and 6.51. If dimensions are required, study §§11.1–11.25. Use metric or decimal-inch dimensions as assigned by the instructor. Move dimensions to better locations where possible.

FIGURE 6.54 Missing-View Problems. Using Layout A–2 or 3 or Layout A4–2 or 3 (adjusted), sketch or draw with instruments the given views, and add the missing view, as shown in Figs. 6.50 and 6.51. If dimensions are required, study §§11.1–11.25. Use metric or decimal-inch dimensions as assigned by the instructor. Move dimensions to better locations where possible.

FIGURE 6.55   **Safety Key (Layout A–3).***

FIGURE 6.56   **Finger Guide (Layout A–3).***

FIGURE 6.57   **Rod Support (Layout A–3).***

FIGURE 6.58   **Tool Holder (Layout A–3).***

FIGURE 6.59   **Tailstock Clamp (Layout A–3).***

FIGURE 6.60   **Index Feed (Layout A–3).***

* Draw or sketch necessary views. Layout A4–3 (adjusted) may be used. If dimensions are required, study §§11.1–11.25. Use metric or decimal-inch dimensions as assigned by the instructor.

FIGURE 6.61 Bearing (Layout A–3).*

FIGURE 6.62 Holder Clip (Layout A–3).*

FIGURE 6.63 Cam (Layout A–3).*

FIGURE 6.64 Index Arm (Layout A–3).*

FIGURE 6.65 Roller Lever (Layout A–3).*

FIGURE 6.66 Support (Layout A–3).*

* Draw or sketch necessary views. Layout A4–3 (adjusted) may be used. If dimensions are required, study §§11.1–11.25. Use metric or decimal-inch dimensions as assigned by the instructor.

FIGURE 6.67   **Locating Finger (Layout A–3).**[*]

FIGURE 6.68   **Toggle Lever (Layout A–3).**[*]

FIGURE 6.69   **Cut-off Holder (Layout A–3).**[*]

FIGURE 6.70   **Index Slide (Layout A–3).**[*]

FIGURE 6.71   **Frame Guide (Layout A–3).**[*]

FIGURE 6.72   **Chuck Jaw (Layout A–3).**[*]

[*] Draw or sketch necessary views. Layout A4–3 (adjusted) may be used. If dimensions are required, study §§11.1–11.25. Use metric or decimal-inch dimensions as assigned by the instructor.

Given: Front & Bottom views.
Reqd: Front, Top & RS views.

FIGURE 6.73   Hinge Bracket (Layout A–3). *

Given: Front & LS views.
Reqd: Front, Top, & RS views.

S A E 1315
I REQD

FIGURE 6.74   Tool Holder (Layout A–3). *

Given: Front & LS views.
Reqd: Front, Top, & RS views.

C R S
I REQD

FIGURE 6.75   Shifter Block (Layout A–3). *

C I
I REQD

FILLETS & ROUNDS R3

FIGURE 6.76   Cross-feed Stop (Layout A–3). *

C R S – I REQD

Given: Front & L S views.
Reqd: Front, Top, & R S views.

FIGURE 6.77   Cross Cam (Layout A–3). *

SAE 1315
I REQD

FIGURE 6.78   Roller Stud (Layout A–3). *

* Draw or sketch necessary views. Layout A4–3 (adjusted) may be used. If dimensions are required, study §§11.1–11.25. Use metric or decimal-inch dimensions as assigned by the instructor.

FIGURE 6.79   **Hinge Block (Layout A–3).**[*]

FIGURE 6.80   **Feed Rod Bearing (Layout A–3).**[*]

FIGURE 6.81   **Lever Hub (Layout A–3).**[*]

FIGURE 6.82   **Vibrator Arm (Layout A–3).**[*]

FIGURE 6.83   **Clutch Lever (Layout A–3).**[*]

FIGURE 6.84   **Counter Bearing Bracket (Layout A–3).**[*]

[*] Draw or sketch necessary views. Layout A4–3 (adjusted) may be used. If dimensions are required, study §§11.1–11.25. Use metric or decimal-inch dimensions as assigned by the instructor.

FIGURE 6.85 **Tool Holder (Layout A–3).***

FIGURE 6.88 **Tool Holder (Layout A–3).***

FIGURE 6.86 **Control Block (Layout A–3).***

FIGURE 6.89 **Locating V-Block (Layout A–3).***

FIGURE 6.87 **Socket Bearing (Layout A–3).***

FIGURE 6.90 **Anchor Bracket (Layout A–3).***

* Draw or sketch necessary views. Layout A4–3 (adjusted) may be used. If dimensions are required, study §§11.1–11.25. Use metric or decimal-inch dimensions as assigned by the instructor.

FIGURE 6.91 Door Bearing (Layout B–3).*

FIGURE 6.94 Chuck Jaw (Layout B–3).*

FIGURE 6.92 Vise Base (Layout B–3).*

Given: Front and L Side views.
Reqd: Front, R Side, and Top views.

FIGURE 6.95 Holder (Layout B–3).*

FIGURE 6.93 Dust Cap (Layout B–3).*

FIGURE 6.96 Centering Wedge (Layout B–3).*

*Draw or sketch necessary views. Layout A4–3 (adjusted) may be used. If dimensions are required, study §§11.1–11.25. Use metric or decimal-inch dimensions as assigned by the instructor.

FIGURE 6.97 **Motor Switch Lever. Draw or sketch necessary views (Layout B–3 or A3–3).***

FIGURE 6.98 **Socket Form Roller—LH. Draw or sketch necessary views (Layout B–4 or A3–4 adjusted).***

FIGURE 6.99 **Stop Base. Draw or sketch necessary views (Layout B–3 or A3–3).***

FIGURE 6.100 **Hinge Base. Draw or sketch necessary views (Layout B–3 or A3–3).***

FIGURE 6.101 **Automatic Stop Base. Draw or sketch necessary views (Layout C–3 or A2–3).***

* If dimensions are required, study §§11.1–11.25. Use metric or decimal-inch dimensions as assigned by the instructor.

FIGURE 6.102 Lead Screw Bracket. Draw or sketch necessary views (Layout C–3 or A2–3).*

FIGURE 6.103 Lever Bracket. Draw or sketch necessary views (Layout C–3 or A2–3).*

FIGURE 6.104 Gripper Rode Center. Draw or sketch necessary views (Layout B–3 or A3–3).*

FIGURE 6.105 Bearing Bracket. Draw or sketch necessary views (Layout B–3 or A3–3).*

---

* If dimensions are required, study §§11.1–11.25. Use metric or decimal-inch dimensions as assigned by the instructor.

FIGURE 6.106   Link Arm Connector. Draw or sketch necessary views (Layout B–3 or A3–3).*

FIGURE 6.108   LH Shifter Fork. Draw or sketch necessary views (Layout B–3 or A3–3).*

FIGURE 6.107   Mounting Bracket. Draw or sketch necessary views (Layout B–3 or A3–3).*

FIGURE 6.109   Gear Shift Bracket. Draw or sketch necessary views (Layout C–4).*

* If dimensions are required, study §§11.1–11.25. Use metric or decimal-inch dimensions as assigned by the instructor.

FILLETS &
ROUNDS R3

4X Ø5
THRU
C I
I REQ D

2XØ6
⊔Ø9↧6

METRIC

FIGURE 6.110   **Fixture Base (Layout C–4).**[*]

FILLETS &
ROUNDS R.06

2X Ø.19

C I
I REQ D

FIGURE 6.112   **Tension Bracket (Layout C–4).**[*]

₵ of rib intersects ₵ of hole

VIEW AT A

2X Ø 25.413
       25.387
REAM

Ø 31.762 REAM
   31.737

4XØ13
⊔Ø6↧9

FILLETS
& ROUNDS R6

METRIC

Draw ½ size

R32

VIEW AT B

FIGURE 6.111   **Ejector Base (Layout C–4).**[*]

Ø.998–1.000 REAM

4X Ø.5

Rib is
centered

4XØ1

C I – I REQ D

ALL FILLETS AND
ROUNDS R.125

FIGURE 6.113   **Offset Bearing (Layout C–4 or A2–4).**[*]

[*] Draw or sketch necessary views. Layout A2–4 may be used. If dimensions are required, study §§11.1–11.25. Use metric or decimal-inch dimensions as assigned by the instructor.

FIGURE 6.106   **Link Arm Connector. Draw or sketch necessary views (Layout B–3 or A3–3).**[*]

FIGURE 6.108   **LH Shifter Fork. Draw or sketch necessary views (Layout B–3 or A3–3).**[*]

FIGURE 6.107   **Mounting Bracket. Draw or sketch necessary views (Layout B–3 or A3–3).**[*]

FIGURE 6.109   **Gear Shift Bracket. Draw or sketch necessary views (Layout C–4).**[*]

[*] If dimensions are required, study §§11.1–11.25. Use metric or decimal-inch dimensions as assigned by the instructor.

FILLETS &
ROUNDS R3

FIGURE 6.110   Fixture Base (Layout C–4).*

FILLETS &
ROUNDS R.06

FIGURE 6.112   Tension Bracket (Layout C–4).*

¢ of rib intersects ¢ of hole

VIEW AT A

VIEW AT B

FILLETS
& ROUNDS R6

METRIC

Draw ½ size

FIGURE 6.111   Ejector Base (Layout C–4).*

Ø.998–1.000 REAM

4X Ø.5

Rib is
centered

4X Ø1

C 1–1 REQD

ALL FILLETS AND
ROUNDS R.125

FIGURE 6.113   Offset Bearing (Layout C–4 or A2–4).*

---

* Draw or sketch necessary views. Layout A2–4 may be used. If dimensions are required, study §§11.1–11.25. Use metric or decimal-inch dimensions as assigned by the instructor.

FILLETS &
ROUNDS R3

FIGURE 6.114   Feed Guide (Layout C–4 or A2–4).*

FIGURE 6.115   Feed Shaft Bracket. Given: Front and
top views. Required: Front, top, and right-side views, half
size (Layout B–3 or A3–3).*

FIGURE 6.116   Trip Lever. Given: Front, top, and partial
side views. Required: Front, bottom, and left-side views,
drawn completely (Layout B–3 or A3–3).*

* Draw or sketch necessary views. Layout A2–4 may be used. If dimensions are required, study §§11.1–11.25. Use metric or decimal-inch dimensions as assigned by the instructor.

FIGURE 6.117   Knurl Bracket Bearing. Given: Front and left-side views. Required: Take front as top view on new drawing, and add front and right-side views (Layout B–3 or A3–3).*

FIGURE 6.118   Horizontal Bracket for Broaching Machine. Given: Front and top views. Required: Take top as front view in new drawing; then add top and left-side views (Layout C–4 or A2–4).*

FIGURE 6.119   Boom Swing Bearing for a Power Crane. Given: Front and bottom views. Required: Front, top, and left-side views (Layout C–4 or A2–4).*

* Draw or sketch necessary views. If dimensions are required, study §§11.1–11.25. Use metric or decimal-inch dimensions as assigned by the instructor.

FIGURE 6.120   Sliding Nut for Mortiser. Given: Top and right-side views.
Required: Front, top, and left-side views, full size (Layout C–4 or A2–4).*

FIGURE 6.121   Power Feed Bracket for Universal Grinder. Given: Front
and right-side views. Required: Front, top, and left-side views, full size
(Layout C–4 or A2–4).*

---

* Draw or sketch necessary views. If dimensions are required, study §§11.1–11.25. Use metric or decimal-inch dimensions as assigned by the instructor.

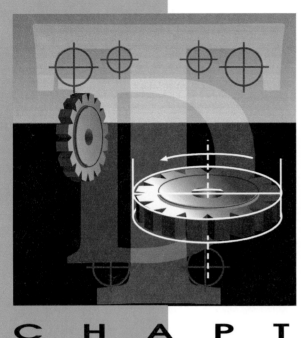

C H A P T E R 7

SECTIONAL VIEWS

OVERVIEW

The basic method of representing objects by views, or projections, has been explained in previous chapters. By means of a limited number of carefully selected views, the external features of the most complicated designs can be fully described. However, we often need to show interiors that cannot be illustrated clearly by hidden lines. We show such interiors by slicing through the object much as we cut through an apple or melon. A cutaway view of the part is then drawn; such views are called **sectional views**, **cross sections**, or simply *sections*.

Drafters use sectional views to improve the clarity of complex objects when internal surfaces result in too many hidden lines. There are many types of sectional views, and a sectional view may replace one of the primary views. The cutting-plane line shows where the object is imagined to be cut. Section lining shows the solid parts of the object that have been in contact with the cutting plane. Hidden lines are not usually found in sectional views. Special conventions are used to make a sectional view easy to understand. Creating a sectional view is one of the more complicated operations for a CAD program. CAD users need to understand thoroughly the concepts of sectional views to create a sectional view with CAD software. See ANSI/ASME Y14.2M–1992 and Y14.3M–1994 for complete standards for multiview and sectional-view drawings.

A Section Created with CAD. *This material has been reprinted with the permission from and under the copyright of Autodesk, Inc.*

tage in clarity of the sectional view. The left-side view would naturally be omitted. In the front view, the cutting plane appears as a line, called a **cutting-plane line** (see §7.5). The arrows at the ends of the cutting-plane line indicate the direction of sight for the sectional view.

To obtain the sectional view, the right half is only *imagined* to be removed and is not actually shown removed anywhere except in the sectional view itself. In the sectional view, the section-lined areas are those portions that have been in actual contact with the cutting plane. Those areas are *cross-hatched* with thin parallel section lines spaced carefully by eye. In addition, the visible parts behind the cutting plane are shown but are not cross-hatched.

As a rule, the location of the cutting plane is obvious from the section itself, and, therefore, the cutting-plane line is omitted. It is shown in Fig. 7.2 for illustration only. Cutting-plane lines should, of course, be used wherever necessary for clarity, as in Figs. 7.21, 7.22, 7.24, and 7.25.

■ 7.1 SECTIONING

To produce a sectional view, a **cutting plane** (§7.5) is assumed to be passed through the part (Fig. 7.1a). The cutting plane is then removed, and the two halves are drawn apart, exposing the interior construction (Fig. 7.1b). In this case, the direction of sight is toward the left half, as shown, and for purposes of the section, the right half is mentally discarded. The sectional view will be in the position of a right-side view.

■ 7.2 FULL SECTIONS

The sectional view obtained by passing the cutting plane fully through the object is called a **full section** (Fig. 7.2c). A comparison of this sectional view with the left-side view (Fig. 7.2a) emphasizes the advan-

■ 7.3 LINES IN SECTIONING

A correct front view and sectional view are shown in Figs. 7.3a and 7.3b. In general, *all visible edges and contours behind the cutting plane should be shown*; otherwise a section will appear to be made up of disconnected and unrelated parts, as shown in Fig. 7.3c.

(a)   (b)

FIGURE 7.1   A Section.

(a)
LEFT-SIDE VIEW

—Hard to visualize.
Compare with right-side
in section for readability.

(b)
FRONT VIEW

(c)
RIGHT-SIDE VIEW
IN FULL SECTION

FIGURE 7.2   Full Section.

Occasionally, however, visible lines behind the cutting plane are not necessary for clarity and should be omitted.

Sections are used primarily to replace hidden-line representation; and, as a rule, *hidden lines should be omitted in sectional views*. As shown in Fig. 7.3d, the hidden lines do not clarify the drawing; they tend to confuse, and they take unnecessary time to draw. Sometimes hidden lines are necessary for clarity and should be used in such cases, especially if their use will make it possible to omit a view (Fig. 7.4).

A section-lined area is always completely bounded by a visible outline—never by a hidden line, as in Fig. 7.3e, since in every case the cut surfaces and their boundary lines will be visible. Also, a visible line can never cut across a section-lined area.

In a sectional view of an object, alone or in assembly, the section lines in all sectioned areas must be parallel, not as shown in Fig. 7.3f. The use of section lining in opposite directions is an indication of different parts, as when two or more parts are adjacent in an assembly drawing.

FIGURE 7.3   Lines in Sectioning.

FIGURE 7.4   Hidden Lines in Sections.

■ 7.4   SECTION LINING

Section-lining symbols (Fig. 7.5) have been used to indicate specific materials. These symbols represent general material types only, such as cast iron, brass, and steel. Now, however, because there are so many different types of materials, and each has so many subtypes, a general name or symbol is not enough. For example, there are hundreds of different kinds of steel. Since detailed specifications of material must be lettered in the form of a note or in the title strip, the general-purpose (cast-iron) section lining may be used for all materials on detail drawings (single parts).

Section-lining symbols may be used in assembly drawings in cases where it is desirable to distinguish different materials; otherwise, the general-purpose symbol is used for all parts.

CAD programs usually include a library that allows the user to select from a variety of section-lining patterns, making it easy to indicate various types of material rather than using the generic cast-iron symbol for all sectioned parts.

The correct method of drawing section lines is shown in Fig. 7.6a. Draw the section lines with a sharp, medium-grade pencil (H or 2H) with a conical point. Always draw the lines at 45° with horizontal as shown, unless there is some advantage in using a different angle. Space the section lines as evenly as possibly by eye from approximately 1.5 mm ($\frac{1}{16}$″) to 3 mm ($\frac{1}{8}$″) or more apart, depending on the size of the drawing or of the sectioned area. *For most drawings, space the lines about 2.5 mm ($\frac{3}{32}$″) or slightly more apart.* As a rule, space the lines as generously as possible and yet close enough to distinguish clearly the sectioned areas.

After the first few lines have been drawn, look back repeatedly at the original spacing to avoid gradually increasing or decreasing the intervals (Fig. 7.6b). Beginners almost invariably draw section lines too close together (Fig. 7.6c). This is very tedious because with small spacing the least inaccuracy in spacing is obvious.

Section lines should be uniformly thin, never varying in thickness, as in Fig. 7.6d. There should be a marked contrast in thickness of the visible outlines

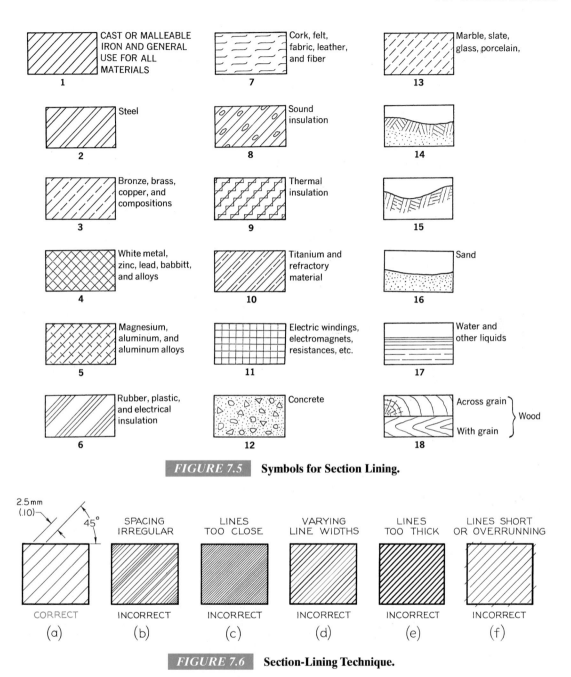

FIGURE 7.5   Symbols for Section Lining.

FIGURE 7.6   Section-Lining Technique.

and the section lines. Section lines should not be too thick, as in Fig. 7.6e. Also avoid running section lines beyond the visible outlines or stopping the lines too short, as in Fig. 7.6f.

If section lines drawn at 45° with horizontal would be parallel or perpendicular (or nearly so) to a prominent visible outline, the angle should be changed to 30°, 60°, or some other angle (Fig. 7.7).

Dimensions should be kept off sectioned areas, but when this is unavoidable the section lines should be omitted where the dimension figure is placed (see Fig. 11.13).

Section lines may be drawn adjacent to the boundaries of the sectioned areas (outline sectioning), provided that clarity is not sacrificed.

CORRECT
(a)

(c)

Direction of Section Lines.

■ 7.5 THE CUTTING PLANE

The cutting plane is indicated in a view adjacent to the sectional view (Fig. 7.8). In this view, the cutting plane appears edgewise as a line called the cutting-plane line. Alternate styles of cutting-plane lines are also shown in Fig. 7.9. The form shown in Fig. 7.9a is composed of equal dashes each about 6 mm ($\frac{1}{4}''$) or more long plus the arrowheads. This form without the dashes between the ends is especially desirable on complicated drawings. The form shown in Fig. 7.9b, composed of alternate long dashes and pairs of short dashes plus

the arrowheads, has been in general use for a long time. Both lines are drawn the same thickness as visible lines. Arrowheads indicate the direction in which the cutaway object is viewed.

Capital letters are used at the ends of the cutting-plane line when necessary to identify the cutting-plane line with the indicated section. This most often occurs in the case of multiple sections (see Fig. 7.25) or removed sections (see Fig. 7.21).

Sectional views occupy normal projected positions in the standard arrangement of views. In Fig. 7.8a, the

FIGURE 7.8 **Cutting Planes and Sections.**

FRONT VIEW IN SECTION
(a)

TOP VIEW IN SECTION
(b)

SECTION A-A   SECTION B-B
(c)

FRONT & R SIDE VIEWS IN SECTION

FIGURE 7.9 **Cutting-Plane Lines (Full Size).**

A ————————— 1.5 mm APPROX ————————— A   A ————— 3 mm APPROX ————— A

(a)   6 mm APPROX   (b) APPROX 1.5 mm   20 to 40 mm APPROX cutting plane is a frontal plane (see §6.15) and appears as a line in the top view. The front half of the object (lower half in the top view) is imagined removed. The arrows at the ends of the cutting-plane line point in the direction of sight for a front view—that is, away from the front view or section. Note that the arrows do not point in the direction of withdrawal of the re-moved portion. The resulting full section may be re-ferred to as the front view in section since it occupies the front view position.

In Fig. 7.8b, the cutting plane is a horizontal plane (see §6.15) and appears as a line in the front view. The upper half of the object is imagined removed. The ar-rows point toward the lower half in the same direction of sight as for a top view, and the resulting full section is a top view in section.

In Fig. 7.8c, two cutting planes are shown, one a frontal plane and the other a profile plane (see §6.15), both of which appear edgewise in the top view. *Each section is completely independent of the other and drawn as if the other were not present.* For section A–A, the front half of the object is imagined removed. The back half is then viewed in the direc-tion of the arrows for a front view, and the resulting section is a front view in section. For section B–B, the right half of the object is imagined removed. The left half then is viewed in the direction of the arrows for a right-side view, and the resulting sec-tion is a right-side view in section. The cutting-plane lines are preferably drawn through an exterior view

(in this case the top view, as shown) instead of a sec-tional view.

The cutting-plane lines in Fig. 7.8 are shown for purposes of illustration only. They are generally omit-ted in cases such as these, in which the location of the cutting plane is obvious. When a cutting-plane line co-incides with a center line, the cutting-plane line takes precedence.

Correct and incorrect relations between cutting-plane lines and corresponding sectional views are shown in Fig. 7.10.

■ 7.6 VISUALIZING A SECTION

Figure 7.11a shows two views of an object to be sec-tioned; it has a drilled and counterbored hole. The cutting plane is assumed to pass through the horizon-tal center line in the top view, and the front half of the object (lower half of the top view) is imagined re-moved. A pictorial drawing of the remaining back half is shown in Fig. 7.11b. The two cut surfaces pro-duced by the cutting plane are 1–2–5–6–10–9 and 3–4–12–11–7–7. However, the corresponding section shown in Fig. 7.11c is incomplete because certain vis-ible lines are missing.

If the section is viewed in the direction of sight (Fig. 7.11b), arcs A, B, C, and D will be visible. As shown in Fig. 7.11d, these arcs appear as straight lines 2–3, 6–7, 5–8, and 10–11. These lines may also be accounted for in other ways. The top and bottom surfaces of the object appear in the section as lines

FIGURE 7.10   **Cutting Planes and Sections.**

(a)
CORRECT

(b)
WRONG

(c)
WRONG

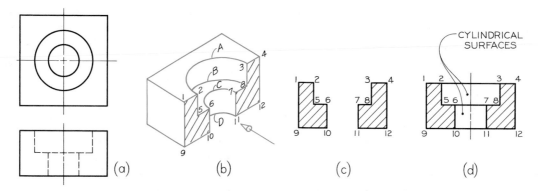

FIGURE 7.11   Visualizing a Section

1–4 and 9–12. The bottom surface of the counter-bore appears in the section as line 5–8. Also, the semicylindrical surfaces for the back half of the counterbore and of the drilled hole will appear as rectangles in the section at 2–3–8–5 and 6–7–11–10.

The front and top views of a collar are shown in Fig. 7.12a, and a right-side view in full section is required. The cutting plane is understood to pass along the center lines AD and EL. If the cutting plane were drawn, the arrows would point to the left in conformity with the direction of sight (see arrow) for the right-side view. The right side of the object is imagined removed, and the left half is viewed in the direction of the arrow, as shown pictorially in Fig. 7.12d. The cut surfaces appear edgewise in the top and front views along AD and EL; since the direction of sight for the

FIGURE 7.12   Drawing a Full Section.

section is at right angles to them, they appear in true size and shape in the sectional view. Each sectioned area is completely enclosed by a boundary of visible lines. In addition to the cut surfaces, the sectional view shows all visible parts behind the cutting plane. No hidden lines are shown.

Whenever a surface of the object (plane or cylindrical) appears as a line and is intersected by a cutting plane that also appears as a line, a new edge (line of intersection) is created that will appear as a *point* in that view. Thus, in the front view, the cutting plane creates new edges appearing as points at E, F, G, H, J, K, and L. In the sectional view (Fig. 7.12b), these are horizontal lines 31–32, 33–34, 35–36, 37–38, 39–40, 41–42, and 43–44.

Whenever a surface of an object appears as a surface (that is, not as a line) and is cut by a cutting plane that appears as a line, a new edge is created that appears as a line in the view, coinciding with the cutting-plane line, and as a line in the section.

In the top view, D is the **point view** of the vertical line KL in the front view and 41–43 in the section (Fig. 7.12b). Point C is the point view of the vertical line HJ in the front view and 37–39 in the section. Point B is the point view of two vertical lines EF and GH in the front view, and 31–33 and 35–38 in the section. Point A is the point view of three vertical lines EF, GJ, and KL in the front view, and 32–34, 36–40, and 42–44 in the section. This completes the boundaries of three sectioned areas 31–32–34–33, 35–36–40–39–37–38, and 41–42–44–43. It is only necessary now to add the visible lines beyond the cutting plane.

The semicylindrical left half F–21–G of the small hole (front view) is visible as a rectangle in the sec-

tions at 33–34–36–35 (Fig. 7.12c). The two semicircular arcs appear as straight lines in the section at 33–35 and 34–36.

Surface 24–27, a line in the front view, appears as line 11–16 in the top view and as surface 45–37–47–46, true size, in the section (Fig. 7.12c).

Cylindrical surface J–29–K, an arc in the front view, appears in the top view as 2–A–C–11–16–15 and in the section as 46–47–39–40–42–41. Thus, arc 27–29–K (front view) appears in the section (Fig. 7.12c) as straight line 46–41; and arc J–29–K appears as straight line 40–42.

All cut surfaces here are part of the same object, and the section lines must all run in the same direction, as shown.

■ 7.7 HALF SECTIONS

If a cutting plane passes halfway through an object, the result is a **half section** (Fig. 7.13). A half section has the advantage of exposing the interior of one half of the object and retaining the exterior of the other half. Its usefulness is, therefore, largely limited to symmetrical objects. It is not widely used in detail drawings (single parts) because of this limitation of symmetry and also because of difficulties in dimensioning internal shapes that are shown in part only in the sectioned half (Fig. 7.13b).

In general, hidden lines should be omitted from both halves of a half section. However, they may be used in the unsectioned half if necessary for dimensioning.

The greatest usefulness of the half section is in assembly drawing, in which it is often necessary to show both internal and external construction on the same view, but without dimensioning.

FIGURE 7.13 Half Section.

(a) CUTTING PLANE

(b) HALF SECTION

As shown in Fig. 7.13b, a center line is used to separate the halves of the half section. The American National Standards Institute recommends a center line for the division line between the sectioned half and the unsectioned half of a half-sectional view, although in some cases the same overlap of the exterior portion, as in a broken-out section, is preferred (see Fig. 7.33b). Either form is acceptable.

■ 7.8 BROKEN-OUT SECTIONS

It often happens that only a partial section of a view is needed to expose interior shapes. Such a section, limited by a break line, is called a **broken-out section**. In Fig. 7.14, a full or half section is not necessary, and a small broken-out section is sufficient to explain the construction. In Fig. 7.15, a half section would have caused the removal of half the keyway. The keyway is preserved by breaking out around it. In this case, the section is limited partly by a break line and partly by a center line.

■ 7.9 REVOLVED SECTIONS

The shape of the cross section of a bar, arm, spoke, or other elongated object may be shown in the longitudinal view by means of a revolved section (Fig. 7.16). **Revolved sections** are made by assuming a plane perpendicular to the center line or axis of the bar or other object, as shown in Fig. 7.17a, and then revolving the plane through 90° about a center line at right angles to the axis (Fig. 7.17b and 7.17c).

The visible lines adjacent to a revolved section may be broken out if desired, as shown in Figs. 7.16k and 7.17.

The superimposition of the revolved section requires the removal of all original lines covered by it

FIGURE 7.14   **Broken-Out Section.**

FIGURE 7.15   **Break Around Keyway.**

(Fig. 7.19). The true shape of a revolved section should be retained after the revolution of the cutting plane, regardless of the direction of the lines in the view (Fig. 7.20).

■ 7.10 REMOVED SECTIONS

A **removed section** is a section that is not in direct projection from the view containing the cutting plane— that is, it is not positioned in agreement with the standard arrangement of views. This displacement from

FIGURE 7.16   **Revolved Sections.**

FIGURE 7.17   Use of the Cutting Plane in Revolved Sections.

FIGURE 7.18   Conventional Breaks Used with Revolved Sections.

CORRECT

INCORRECT

FIGURE 7.19   A Common Error in Drawing Revolved Sections.

CORRECT

INCORRECT

FIGURE 7.20   A Common Error in Drawing Revolved Sections.

the normal projection position should be made without turning the section from its normal orientation.

Removed sections should be labeled, such as SECTION A–A and SECTION B–B, corresponding to the letters at the ends of the cutting-plane line (Fig. 7.21). They should be arranged in alphabetical order from left to right on the sheet. Section letters should be used in alphabetical order, but letters I, O, and Q should not be used because they are easily confused with the numeral 1 or the zero.

A removed section is often a partial section. Such a removed section is frequently drawn to an enlarged scale (Fig. 7.22). This is often desirable to show small detail clearly and to provide sufficient space for di-

mensioning. In such a case the enlarged scale should be indicated below the section title.

A removed section should be placed so that it no longer lines up in projection with any other view. It should be separated clearly from the standard arrangement of views (see Fig. 12.9). Whenever possible, removed sections should be on the same sheet as the regular views. If a section must be placed on a different sheet, cross-references should be given on the related sheets. A note should be given below the section title, such as

SECTION B–B ON SHEET 4, ZONE A3

A similar note should be placed on the sheet on which the cutting-plane line is shown, with a leader pointing to the cutting-plane line and referring to the sheet on which the section will be found. Sometimes it is convenient to place removed sections on center lines extended from the section cuts (Fig. 7.23).

7.11 OFFSET SECTIONS

In sectioning through irregular objects, it is often desirable to show features that do not lie in a straight line by "offsetting" or bending the cutting plane. Such a section is called an **offset section**. In Fig. 7.24a the cutting plane is offset in several places to include the hole at the left end, one of the parallel slots, the rectangular recess, and one of the holes at the right end. The front portion of the object is then imagined to be removed (Fig. 7.24b). The path of the cutting plane is shown by the cutting-plane line in the top view (Fig. 7.24c), and the resulting offset section is shown in the front view. The offsets or bends in the cutting plane are all 90° and are *never shown in the sectional view*.

Figure 7.24 also illustrates how hidden lines in a section eliminate the need for an additional view. In this case, an extra view would be needed to show the small boss on the back if hidden lines were not shown.

Figure 7.25 shows an example of multiple offset sections. Notice that the visible background shapes without hidden lines appear in each sectional view.

FIGURE 7.21   Removed Sections.

FIGURE 7.22   Removed Section.

FIGURE 7.23   Removed Sections.

FIGURE 7.24 Offset Section.

■ 7.12 RIBS IN SECTIONS

To avoid a false impression of thickness and solidity, ribs, webs, gear teeth, and other similar flat features are not sectioned even though the cutting plane passes along the center plane of the feature. For example, in Fig. 7.26, the cutting plane A–A passes flatwise through the vertical web, or rib, and the web is not section lined (Fig. 7.26a). *Such thin features should not be section lined, even though the cutting plane passes through them.* The incorrect section is shown in Fig. 7.26b. Note the false impression of thickness or solidity resulting from section lining the rib.

If the cutting plane passes *crosswise* through a rib or any thin member, as does the plane B–B, the member should be section lined in the usual manner, as shown in the top view (Fig. 7.26c).

If a rib is not section lined when the cutting plane passes through it flatwise, it is sometimes difficult to tell whether the rib is actually present, as, for example, ribs A in Figs. 7.27a and 7.27b. It is difficult to distinguish spaces B as open spaces and spaces A as ribs. In such cases, double-spaced *section lining* of the ribs should be used (Fig. 7.27c). This consists simply in continuing alternate section lines through the ribbed areas, as shown.

■ 7.13 ALIGNED SECTIONS

To include in a section certain angled elements, the cutting plane may be bent to pass through those features. The plane and features are then imagined to be revolved into the original plane. For example, in Fig. 7.28, the cutting plane was bent to pass through the

FIGURE 7.25 Three Offset Sections.

SECTION A-A   SECTION B-B   SECTION C-C

(c) CORRECT

A

WEB

B — B

A

(a) CORRECT   (b) INCORRECT

FIGURE 7.26   Webs in Section.

angled arm and then revolved to a vertical position (aligned), from where it was projected across to the sectional view.

In Fig. 7.29 the cutting plane is bent to include one of the drilled and counterbored holes in the sectional view. The correct section view in Fig. 7.29b gives a clearer and more complete description than does the section in Fig. 7.29c, which was taken along the vertical center line of the front view—that is, without any bend in the cutting plane. In such cases, the angle of revolution should always be less than 90°.

The student is cautioned *not to revolve* features when clearness is not improved. In some cases revolving the features results in a loss of clarity. Examples in

which revolution should not be used are Fig. 7.40 and Probs. 17 and 18.

In Fig. 7.30a, the projecting lugs are not sectioned for the same reason that ribs are not sectioned. In Fig. 7.30b, the projecting lugs are located so that the cutting plane passes through them crosswise; therefore, they are sectioned.

Another example involving rib sectioning and aligned sectioning is shown in Fig. 7.31. In the circular view, the cutting plane is offset in circular-arc bends to include the upper hole and upper rib, the keyway and center hole, the lower rib, and one of the lower holes. These features are imagined to be revolved until they line up vertically and are then projected from that position to obtain the section shown in Fig. 7.31b. Note that the ribs are not sectioned. If a regular full section of the object were drawn without using the conventions discussed here, the resulting section (Fig. 7.31c) would be incomplete and confusing and would take more time to draw.

In sectioning a pulley or any spoked wheel (Fig. 7.32a), it is standard practice to revolve the spokes if necessary (if there is an odd number) and not to section line the spokes (Fig. 7.32b). If the spoke is sectioned, the section gives a false impression of continuous metal (Fig. 7.32c). If the lower spoke is not revolved, it will be foreshortened in the sectional view, in which it presents an "amputated" and wholly misleading appearance.

Figure 7.32 also illustrates correct practice in omitting visible lines in a sectional view. Notice that spoke B is omitted in Fig. 7.32b. If it is included, as shown in Fig. 7.32c, the spoke is foreshortened, difficult and time-consuming to draw, and confusing to the reader of the drawing.

FIGURE 7.27   Alternate Section Lining.

Note use of hidden line

A   A
B   B
B   B
A   A

(a)   (b) RIBS NOT   (c) ALTERNATE
             SECTION-LINED   SECTION-LINING

FIGURE 7.28   **Aligned Section.**

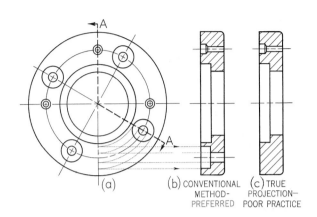

FIGURE 7.29   **Aligned Section.**

■ 7.14 PARTIAL VIEWS

If space is limited on the paper or if it is necessary to save drafting time, **partial views** may be used in connection with sectioning (Fig. 7.33). Half views are shown in Figs. 7.33a and 7.33b in connection with a full section and a half section, respectively. Note that in each case the back half of the object in the circular view is shown, in conformity with the idea of removing the front portion of the object to expose the back portion for viewing in section (see also §6.9).

Another method of drawing a partial view is to break out much of the circular view, retaining only those features that are needed for minimum representation (Fig. 7.33c).

■ 7.15 INTERSECTIONS IN SECTIONING

Where an intersection is small or unimportant in a section, it is standard practice to disregard the true pro-

jection of the figure of intersection, as shown in Figs. 7.34a and 7.34c. Larger figures of intersection may be projected, as shown in Fig. 7.34b, or approximated by circular arcs, as shown for the smaller hole in Fig. 7.34d. Note that the larger hole K is the same diameter as the vertical hole. In such cases the curves of intersection (ellipses) appear as straight lines, as shown (see also Figs. 6.38 and 6.39).

■ 7.16 CONVENTIONAL BREAKS

To shorten a view of an elongated object, conventional breaks are recommended, as shown in Fig. 7.35. For example, the two views of a garden rake in Fig. 7.36a are drawn to a small scale to fit them on the paper. In Fig. 7.36b, the handle is "broken," a long central portion is removed, and the rake is then drawn to a larger scale, producing a much clearer delineation.

Parts to be broken must have the same section throughout, or if tapered they must have a uniform

FIGURE 7.30   **Aligned Sections.**

FIGURE 7.31   Symmetry of Ribs.

FIGURE 7.32   Spokes in Section.

FIGURE 7.33   Partial Views.

FIGURE 7.34 Intersections.

taper. Note in Fig. 7.36b that the full-length dimension is given, just as if the entire rake were shown.

The breaks used on cylindrical shafts or tubes are often referred to as "S-breaks" and in industrial drafting are usually drawn entirely freehand or partly freehand and partly with an irregular curve or compass. The results of these methods are often very crude, especially when attempted by beginners. Simple construction methods for students or industrial drafters are shown in Figs. 7.37 and 7.38 and will always produce a professional result. Excellent S-breaks are also obtained with an S-break template.

Breaks for rectangular metal and wood sections are always drawn freehand, as shown in Fig. 7.35. (See also Fig. 7.18, which illustrates the use of breaks in connection with revolved sections.)

■ 7.17 COMPUTER GRAPHICS

USING CAD

You create 2D and 3D sectional views using CAD. Most CAD systems have a Hatch command to generate the section lining and hatch patterns to fill an area automatically. A wide variety of hatch patterns are

FIGURE 7.35 Conventional Breaks.

(a)   (b)

FIGURE 7.36 Use of Conventional Breaks.

generally available to show materials such as steel, bronze, sand, concrete, and many more.

Creating a full-section view from a 3D model is generally very easy. You only need to define the cutting plane. Often the hatching for the cut surfaces is generated automatically. Sectioned views other than full sections can be more difficult to create. To create good sectional drawings using CAD, you should have a clear understanding of the standards for showing section views (Fig. 7.39).

FIGURE 7.37   Steps in Drawing S-Breaks for Solid Shaft.

FIGURE 7.38   Steps in Drawing S-Breaks for Tubing.

FIGURE 7.39   Detail Drawing Produced by Using the VersaCAD Advanced System. *Courtesy of VersaCAD.*

■ KEY WORDS

SECTIONAL VIEW

CUTTING-PLANE LINE

OFFSET SECTION

REVOLVED SECTION

AUXILIARY SECTION

RIBS, SPOKES, AND WEBS

CONVENTIONAL BREAKS

SECTION LINES

FULL AND HALF SECTION

BROKEN-OUT SECTION

REMOVED SECTION

CONVENTIONS

ALIGNED SECTIONS

■ CHAPTER SUMMARY

- Sectional views show internal details without the need for hidden lines.
- Objects are imagined to be cut apart along the cutting-plane line.
- Along the cutting plane, the part of the object that is solid (cut by the cutting plane) is shown with section lines (thin lines drawn at 45°).
- In a sectional view, many hidden lines are replaced by object lines because the internal surfaces are exposed when the object is imagined to be cut open.

- The section-lining symbol denotes the material of the object.
- Ribs, webs, and spokes are not shown with section lining.
- Symmetrical features like spokes and webs are revolved so the sectional view appears symmetrical.
- Conventional breaks are used to represent various objects in shortened form.

■ REVIEW QUESTIONS

1. What does the cutting-plane line represent?
2. Sketch the section-line symbols for 10 different materials.
3. List seven different types of sections and sketch an example of each.
4. Which sectional views are used to *replace* an existing primary view? Which sectional views are used in addition to the primary views?
5. How much of an object is imagined to be cut away in a half section?

6. What type of line is used to show the boundary of a broken-out section?
7. Why are hidden lines generally omitted in a sectional view?
8. Why are some symmetrical features, like spokes and webs, revolved in the sectional view?
9. Why is a rib outlined with object lines and not filled with section lining?

■ SECTIONING PROBLEMS

Any of the following problems (Figs. 7.40–7.71) may be drawn freehand or with your instruments, as assigned by the instructor. However, the problems in Fig. 7.40 are especially suitable for sketching on 8.5" × 11.0" graph paper with appropriate grid squares. Two problems can be drawn on one sheet, using Layout A–1 similarly to Fig. 5.51, with borders drawn freehand. If desired, the

problems may be sketched on plain drawing paper. Before making any sketches, the student should study carefully §§5.1–5.9.

The problems in Figs. 7.41–7.60 are intended to be drawn with instruments, but may be drawn freehand if desired. If metric or decimal dimensions are required, you should first study §§11.1–11.25.

FIGURE 7.40 **Freehand Sectioning Problems. Using Layout A–1 or A4–1 adjusted (freehand) on graph paper or plain paper, two problems per sheet, sketch views with sections as indicated. Each grid square = 6 mm ($\frac{1}{4}''$). In Probs. 1–10, top and right-side views are given. Sketch front sectional views and then move right-side views to line up horizontally with front sectional views. Omit cutting planes except in Probs. 5 and 6.**

FILLETS AND ROUNDS R.12

Ø5.50
.75
2.12
Ø2.76
Ø4.24
4X Ø5
Ø1.498-1.500

FIGURE 7.41 Bearing. Draw necessary views, with full section (Layout A–3).*

C R S
I REQD
2.62
.62
Ø4.750
R.24
2X R.12
1.24
.56
1.12
Ø3.38
Ø2.00
3X Ø.375
⊔Ø.75 ⊤.30
Ø1.372 +.003 -.000

FIGURE 7.44 Centering Bushing. Draw necessary views, with full section (Layout A–3).*

3X Ø22 CORE EQUALLY SPACED
6X R3
METRIC
Ø133
Ø121
Ø86
Ø50
6X R2
C I
4 REQD
Ø23.72 - 23.80

FIGURE 7.42 Truck Wheel. Draw necessary views, with half section (Layout A–3).*

Ø1.436 1.438
FAO
Ø5.12
Ø4.76
Ø2.06
Ø3.12
.20
2.00
3.00
.12
C R S
I REQD
3X Ø.375
∨Ø.75×70°
EQUALLY SPACED

FIGURE 7.45 Special Bearing. Draw necessary views, with full section (Layout A–3).*

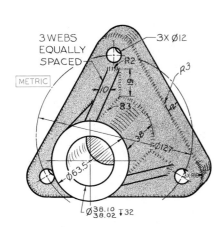

3 WEBS EQUALLY SPACED
3X Ø12
R2
R3
METRIC
8.3
Ø12T
Ø63.5
Ø 38.10 38.02 ⊤32

FIGURE 7.43 Column Support. Draw necessary views, with full section (Layout A–3).*

Ø 28.58 +.05 -.00
R2.50
2 I
R2.3
SECTION OF RIM LOOKING IN DIRECTION OF ARROW
R6
Ø40
R3
Ø143
Ø36
Ø19
METRIC

FIGURE 7.46 Idler Pulley. Draw necessary views, with full section (Layout A–3).*

* Layout A4–3 (adjusted) may be used. If dimensions are required, study §§11.1–11.25. Use metric or decimal-inch dimensions as assigned by the instructor.

FIGURE 7.47 Cup Washer. Draw necessary views, with full section (Layout A–3 or A4–3 adjusted).[*]

FIGURE 7.50 Bearing. Draw necessary views, with half section. Scale: half size (Layout B–4 or A3–4 adjusted).[*]

FIGURE 7.48 Fixed Bearing Cup. Draw necessary views, with full section (Layout A–3 or A4–3 adjusted).[*]

FIGURE 7.51 Pulley. Draw necessary views, with full section, and revolved section of spoke (Layout B–4 or A3–4 adjusted).[*]

FIGURE 7.49 Stock Guide. Draw necessary views, with half section (Layout B–4 or A3–4 adjusted).[*]

FIGURE 7.52 Step-Cone Pulley. Draw necessary views, with full section (Layout B–4 or A3–4 adjusted).[*]

[*] If dimensions are required, study §§11.1–11.25. Use metric or decimal-inch dimensions as assigned by the instructor.

3X Ø10
Ø82 BC
EQUALLY SPACED

2 ×45°CHAM

Ø114 Ø54 Ø33
Ø57 Ø43

3X 5X10
KEYWAYS
EQUALLY SPACED

3×45°CHAMFER

Ø95 Ø190
Ø54 Ø132

30°

R3
R3

R6   R6

R3
R3

2   62

18
21

27   16   19   3
78

CAST STEEL-1 REQD

METRIC

FIGURE 7.53   Sheave. Draw two views, including half
section (Layout B–4).[*]

Ø.500

Ø.69
↧.94

Ø.310 – .312

C   .59   B   A   .38
.38   .88
.12
.62   .19

A
B
C

Ø1.4590
1.4585

1.00   1.25   1.44
4.88

.38

S A E 1020 STL
1 REQD

FIGURE 7.54   Operating Valve. Given: Front, left-side,
and partial bottom views. Required: Front, right-side, and
full bottom views, plus indicated removed sections (Layout
B–4).[*]

FILLETS AND ROUNDS R.12

6.00

Ø.750   SR 1.50   Ø.25

.62

R1.00

.12

C 1
2 REQD

3.00
1.50

.25
.25
.25

.25
.25
1.25

.75
1.500
1.38

1.38

.25   1.25   .25

1.38

2X Ø.500
IN LINE

.38
Ø1.750

.998
1.000

6.00

FIGURE 7.55   Rocker Arm. Draw necessary views, with revolved
sections (Layout B–4).[*]

2X Ø10

FILLETS AND
ROUNDS R2

35
16   R12
9/20

2X R11

R8
R28
R6

2X Ø13

38

9/20

2X R12

29

Ø10

Ø22

41   81   30   R6

A

A

R6

2X R19

2X R28

29

14
R2
8
R2
22

SECTION A–A

140

C 1
1 REQD

METRIC

FIGURE 7.56   Dash Pot Lifter.
Draw necessary views, using revolved
section instead of removed section
(Layout B–4).[*]

[*] Layout A3–4 (adjusted) may be used. If dimensions are required, study §§11.1–11.25. Use metric or decimal-inch dimensions as assigned by
the instructor.

FIGURE 7.57 **Adjuster Base. Given: Front and top views. Required: Front and top views and sections A–A, B–B, and C–C. Show all visible lines (Layout B–4).**[*]

FIGURE 7.59 **Hydraulic Fitting. Given: Front and top views. Required: Front and top views and right-side view in full section (Layout B–4).**[*]

FIGURE 7.58 **Mobile Housing. Given: Front and left-side views. Required: Front view, right-side view in full section, and removed section A–A (Layout B–4).**[*]

FIGURE 7.60 **Auxiliary Shaft Bearing. Given: Front and top views. Required: Front and top views and right-side view in full section (Layout B–4).**[*]

[*] If dimensions are required, study §§11.1–11.25. Use metric or decimal-inch dimensions as assigned by the instructor.

FIGURE 7.61   Traverse Spider. Given: Front and left-side views. Required: Front and right-side views and top view in full section (Layout B–4 or A3–4 adjusted).[*]

FIGURE 7.63   Bracket. Given: Front and right-side views. Required: Take front as new top; then add right-side view, front view in full section A–A, and sections B–B and C–C (Layout B–4 or A3–4 adjusted).[*]

FIGURE 7.62   Gland. Given: Front, top, and partial left-side views. Required: Front view and right-side view in full section (Layout A–3 or A4–3 adjusted).[*]

FIGURE 7.64   Cocking Block. Given: Front and right-side views. Required: take front as new top view; then add new front view, and right-side view in full section. Draw double size on Layout C–4 or A2–4 adjusted.[*]

[*] Layout A3–4 (adjusted) may be used. If dimensions are required, study §§11.1–11.25. Use metric or decimal-inch dimensions as assigned by the instructor.

FIGURE 7.65 Packing Ring. Given: Front and top views. Required: Front view and section **A-A** (Layout A–3 or A4–3 adjusted).[*]

FIGURE 7.67 Oil Retainer. Given: Front and top views. Required: Front view and section **A-A** (Layout B–4 or A3–4 adjusted).[*]

FIGURE 7.66 Strainer Body. Given: Front and bottom views. Required: Front and top views and right-side view in full section (Layout C–4 or A2–4).[*]

FIGURE 7.68 Gear Box. Given: Front and top views. Required: Front in full section, bottom view, and right-side section **A-A**. Draw half size on Layout B–4 or A3–4 (adjusted).[*]

---

[*] If dimensions are required, study §§11.1–11.25. Use metric or decimal-inch dimensions as assigned by the instructor.

FIGURE 7.69   Slotted Disk for Threading Machine. Given: Front and left-side views. Required: Front and right-side views and top full-section view. Draw half size on Layout B–4 or A3–4 (adjusted).*

FIGURE 7.70   Web for Lathe Clutch. Given: Partial front and left-side views. Required: Full front view, right-side view in full section, and removed section A–A (Layout C–4 or A2–4).*

---

* If dimensions are required, study §§11.1–11.25. Use metric or decimal-inch dimensions as assigned by the instructor.

C H A P T E R 8

AUXILIARY VIEWS

OBJECTIVES

After studying the material in this chapter, you should be able to:

1. Create an auxiliary view from any orthographic projection using drawing instruments or CAD.

2. Draw folding lines or reference-plane lines between any two adjacent views.

3. Construct depth, height, or width auxiliary views.

4. Plot curves in auxiliary views.

5. Construct partial auxiliary views.

6. Create auxiliary sectional views.

7. Find the true length of an oblique line by constructing an auxiliary view.

8. Find the true size of an oblique plane by constructing auxiliary views.

OVERVIEW

Inclined planes and oblique lines do not appear true length or true size in any of the principal planes of projection. To determine the true length of an oblique line or the true size of an inclined plane, an auxiliary view must be created. The techniques for creating an auxiliary view are the same using traditional drawing or CAD. A line of sight and reference plane are defined. With traditional drawing, the view is manually created along line-of-sight projectors. With CAD drawing, the computer generates the view automatically if a 3D model of the object was originally created.

Many objects are shaped such that their principal faces cannot be assumed to be parallel to the regular planes of projection. For example, in Fig. 8.1a, the base of the design for the bearing is shown in its true size and shape, but the rounded upper portion is situated at an angle with the planes of projection and does not appear in its true size and shape in any of the three regular views. To show the true circular shapes, it is necessary to assume a direction of sight perpendicular to the planes of those curves, as shown in Fig. 8.1b. The resulting view is known as an *auxiliary view*. This view, together with the top view, completely describes the object. The front and right-side views are not necessary.

■ 8.1 DEFINITIONS

Any view obtained by a projection on a plane other than the horizontal, frontal, and profile projection planes is an **auxiliary view**. A *primary auxiliary view* is projected onto a plane that is perpendicular to one of the principal planes of projection and is inclined to the other two. A *secondary auxiliary view* is projected from a primary auxiliary view onto a plane that is inclined to all three principal projection planes (see §8.19).

■ 8.2 THE AUXILIARY PLANE

In Fig. 8.2a, the object shown has an inclined surface that does not appear in its true size and shape in any regular view. The auxiliary plane is assumed parallel to the inclined surface P—that is, perpendicular to the line of sight, which is at right angles to that surface. The auxiliary plane is then perpendicular to the frontal plane of projection and hinged to it.

When the horizontal and auxiliary planes are unfolded to appear in the plane of the front view (Fig. 8.2b), the folding lines represent the hinge lines joining the planes. The drawing is simplified by retaining the folding lines (H/F and F/1) and omitting the planes (Fig. 8.2c). As will be shown later, the folding lines may themselves be omitted in the actual drawing. The inclined surface P is shown in its true size and shape in the auxiliary view; the long dimension of the surface is projected directly from the front view and the depth from the top view.

The positions of the folding lines depend on the relative positions of the planes of the glass box. If the horizontal plane is moved upward, the distance Y is increased. If the frontal plane is brought forward, the distances X are increased but remain *equal*. If the auxiliary plane is moved to the right, the distance Z is increased. Note that both the top and auxiliary views show the *depth* of the object.

■ 8.3 DRAWING AN AUXILIARY VIEW: FOLDING-LINE METHOD

As shown in Fig. 8.2c, the folding lines are the hinge lines of the glass box. Distances X must be equal since they both represent the distance of the front surface of the object from the frontal plane of projection.

Although distances X must remain equal, distances Y and Z, from the front view to the respective folding lines, may or may not be equal.

The steps in drawing an auxiliary view with the aid of the folding lines, shown in Fig. 8.3, are described as follows.

1. The front and top views are given (Fig. 8.3I). It is necessary to draw an auxiliary view showing the true size and shape of inclined surface P. Draw the folding line H/F between the views at right angles to the projection lines. Distances X and Y may or may not be equal, as desired.

NOTE   In the following steps, manipulate the triangle (either triangle), as shown in Fig. 8.4, to draw lines parallel or perpendicular to the inclined face.

2. Assume a direction of sight perpendicular to surface P (Fig. 8.3II). Draw light projection lines from the front view parallel to the arrow, or perpendicular to surface P.

3. Draw folding line F/1 for the auxiliary view at right angles to the projection lines and at any convenient distance from the front view (Fig. 8.3III).

4. Draw the auxiliary view using the numbering system explained in §6.6 (Fig. 8.3IV). Locate all

FIGURE 8.1 Regular Views and Auxiliary Views.

FIGURE 8.2 An Auxiliary View.

FIGURE 8.3 Drawing an Auxiliary View—Folding-Line Method.

points the same distances from folding line F/1 as they are from folding line H/F in the top view. For example, points 1 to 5 are distance X from the folding lines in both the top and auxiliary views,

and points 6 to 10 are distance D from the corresponding folding lines. Since the object is viewed in the direction of the arrow, it will be seen that edge 5–10 will be hidden in the auxiliary view.

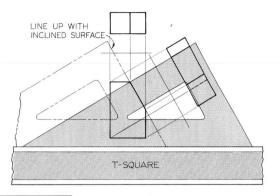

FIGURE 8.4   **Drawing Parallel or Perpendicular Lines.**

■ 8.4 REFERENCE PLANES

In the auxiliary views shown in Figs. 8.2c and 8.3, the folding lines represent the edge views of the frontal plane of projection. In effect, the frontal plane is used as a **reference plane**, or *datum plane*, for transferring distances (depth measurements) from the top view to the auxiliary view.

Instead of using one of the planes of projection as a reference plane, it is often more convenient to assume a reference plane inside the glass box parallel to the plane of projection and touching or cutting through the object. For example, in Fig. 8.5a, a reference plane is assumed to coincide with the front surface of the object. This plane appears edgewise in the top and auxiliary views, and the two reference lines are then used in the same manner as folding lines. Dimensions D in the top and auxiliary views are equal. The advantage of the reference-plane method is that fewer measurements are required since some points of the object lie in the reference plane.

The reference plane may coincide with the front surface of the object (Fig. 8.5a); it may cut through the object if the object is symmetrical (Fig. 8.5b); it may coincide with the back surface of the object (Fig. 8.5c); or it may cut through any intermediate point of the object.

The reference plane should be assumed in the position most convenient for transferring distances with respect to it. Remember the following:

1. Reference lines, like folding lines, are always at right angles to the projection lines between the views.
2. A reference plane appears as a line in two alternate views, never in adjacent views.
3. Measurements are always made at right angles to the reference lines or parallel to the projection lines.
4. In the auxiliary view, all points are at the same distances from the reference line as the corresponding points are from the reference line in the alternate view, or the *second previous view*.

■ 8.5 DRAWING AN AUXILIARY VIEW: REFERENCE-PLANE METHOD

The object in Fig. 8.6a is numbered as explained in §6.6. To draw the auxiliary view, proceed as follows:

1. Draw two views of the object, and assume an arrow indicating the direction of sight for the auxiliary view of surface A (Fig. 8.6I).
2. Draw projection lines parallel to the arrow (Fig. 8.6II).
3. Assume a reference plane coinciding with the back surface of the object, as shown in Fig. 8.6a. Draw

FIGURE 8.5   **Position of the Reference Plane.**

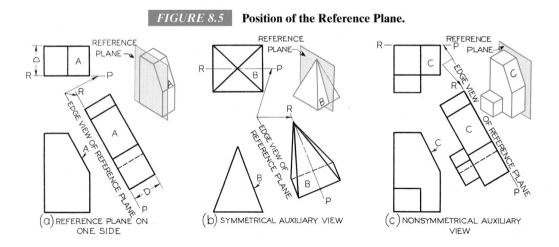

(a) REFERENCE PLANE ON ONE SIDE

(b) SYMMETRICAL AUXILIARY VIEW

(c) NONSYMMETRICAL AUXILIARY VIEW

FIGURE 8.6   **Drawing an Auxiliary View—Reference-Plane Method.**

reference lines in the top and auxiliary views at right angles to the projection lines (Fig. 8.6III). *These are the edge views of the reference plane.*

4. Draw auxiliary view of surface A (Fig. 8.6IV). It will be true size and shape because the direction of sight was taken perpendicular to that surface. Transfer depth measurements from the top view to the auxiliary view with dividers or scale. Each point in the auxiliary view will be on its projection line from the front view and the same distance from the reference line as it is in the top view to the corresponding reference line.

5. Complete the auxiliary view by adding other visible edges and surfaces of the object (Fig. 8.6V). Each numbered point in the auxiliary view lies on its projection line from the front view and is the same distance from the reference line as it is in the top view. Note

that two surfaces of the object appear as lines in the auxiliary view.

■ 8.6 CLASSIFICATION OF AUXILIARY VIEWS

Auxiliary views are classified and named according to the principal dimensions of the object shown in the auxiliary view. For example, the auxiliary view in Fig. 8.6 is a *depth auxiliary view* because it shows the principal dimension of the object, *depth*. Any auxiliary view projected from the front view, also known as a front adjacent view, will show the depth of the object and is a depth auxiliary view.

Similarly, any auxiliary view projected from the top view, also known as a top adjacent view, is a height auxiliary view; and any auxiliary view projected from the side view (either side), also known as a side adjacent view, is a width auxiliary view. For examples of height auxiliary views, see Figs. 8.1b and 8.13b. Depth auxiliary views are illustrated in Figs. 8.27 and 8.33.

■ 8.7 DEPTH AUXILIARY VIEWS

An infinite number of auxiliary planes can be assumed perpendicular to, and hinged to, the frontal plane (F) of projection. Five such planes are shown in Fig. 8.7a; the horizontal plane is included to show that it is similar to the others. All these views show the principal dimension, depth; therefore, all the auxiliary views are depth auxiliary views.

The unfolded auxiliary planes are shown in Fig. 8.7b, which also shows how the depth dimension may be projected from the top view to all auxiliary views. The arrows indicate the directions of sight for the several views, and the projection lines are respectively parallel to these arrows. The arrows may be assumed but need not be actually drawn since the projection lines determine the direction of sight. The folding lines are perpendicular to the arrows and the corresponding projection lines. Since the auxiliary planes can be assumed at any distance from the object, it follows that the folding lines may be any distance from the front view.

The complete drawing, with the outlines of the planes of projection omitted, is shown in Fig. 8.7c. This shows the drawing as it would appear on paper, in which use is made of reference planes as described in §8.4; all depth dimensions are measured perpendicular to the reference line in each view.

Note that the front view shows the height and the width of the object, but not the depth. The depth is shown in all views that are projected from the front view; thus, this rule: *The principal dimension shown in an auxiliary view is the one not shown in the adjacent view from which the auxiliary view was projected.*

■ 8.8 HEIGHT AUXILIARY VIEWS

An infinite number of auxiliary planes can be assumed perpendicular to, and hinged to, the horizontal plane (H) of projection, several of which are shown in Fig. 8.8a. The front view and all the auxiliary views show the principal dimension, height. Therefore, all the auxiliary views are height auxiliary views.

The unfolded projection planes are shown in Fig. 8.8b, and the complete drawing, with the outlines of the planes projection omitted, is shown in Fig. 8.8c. All reference lines are perpendicular to the corresponding projection lines, and all height dimensions are measured parallel to the projection lines, or perpendicular to the reference lines, in each view. Note that in the view projected from, which is the top view, the only dimension *not shown* is height.

■ 8.9 WIDTH AUXILIARY VIEWS

An infinite number of auxiliary planes can be assumed perpendicular to, and hinged to, the profile plane (P) of projection, several of which are shown in Fig. 8.9a. The front view and all the auxiliary views show the principal dimension, width. Therefore, all the auxiliary views are width auxiliary views.

The unfolded planes are shown in Fig. 8.9b, and the complete drawing, with the outlines of the planes of projection omitted, is shown in Fig. 8.9c. All refer-

FIGURE 8.7   Depth Auxiliary Views.

(a)   (b)   (c)

FIGURE 8.8   Height Auxiliary Views.

FIGURE 8.9   Width Auxiliary Views.

ence lines are perpendicular to the corresponding projection lines, and all width dimensions are measured parallel to the projection lines, or perpendicular to the reference lines, in each view. Note that in the right-side view from, which the auxiliary views are projected, the only dimension *not shown* is width.

■ 8.10 REVOLVING A DRAWING

In Fig. 8.10a is a drawing showing top, front, and auxiliary views. Figure 8.10b shows the drawing revolved, as indicated by the arrows, until the auxiliary view and the front view line up horizontally. Although the views

remain exactly the same, the names of the views are changed if drawn in this position. The auxiliary view now becomes a right-side view, and the top view becomes an auxiliary view. Some students find it easier to visualize and draw an auxiliary view when revolved to the position of a regular view in this manner. In any case, it should be understood that an auxiliary view basically is like any other view.

■ 8.11 DIHEDRAL ANGLES

The angle between two planes is a **dihedral angle**. One of the principal uses of auxiliary views is to show dihedral

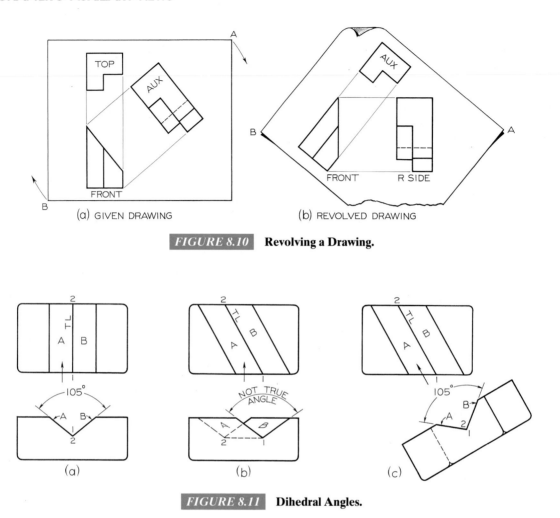

FIGURE 8.10   Revolving a Drawing.

(a) GIVEN DRAWING   (b) REVOLVED DRAWING

FIGURE 8.11   Dihedral Angles.

(a)   (b)   (c)

angles in true size, mainly for dimensioning purposes. In Fig. 8.11a, a block is shown with a V-groove situated so that the true dihedral angle between inclined surfaces A and B is shown in the front view.

Assume a line in a plane. For example, draw a straight line on a sheet of paper; then hold the paper to view the line as a point. You will observe that when the line appears as a point, the plane containing the line appears as a line. Thus, this rule applies: *To get the edge view of a plane, find the point view of any line in that plane.*

In Fig. 8.11a, line 1–2 is the line of intersection of planes A and B. Now, line 1–2 lies in both planes at the same time; therefore, a point view of this line will show both planes as lines, and the angle between them is the dihedral angle between the planes. *To get the true an-gle between two planes, find the point view of the line intersection of the planes.*

In Fig. 8.11b, the line of intersection 1–2 does not appear as a point in the front view; as a result, planes A and B do not appear as lines, and the true dihedral angle is not shown. Assuming that the actual angle is the same as in Fig. 8.11a, does the angle show larger or smaller than in Fig. 8.11a? The angle does not appear true size in Fig. 8.11b because the direction of sight (see arrow) is not parallel to the line of intersection 1–2.

In Fig. 8.11c, the direction-of-sight arrow is taken parallel to the line 1–2, producing an auxiliary view in which line 1–2 appears as a point, planes A and B appear as lines, and the true dihedral angle is shown. *To draw a view showing a true dihedral angle, assume the direction of sight parallel to the line of intersection between the planes of the angle.*

8.12 PLOTTED CURVES

As described in §6.30, when a cylinder is cut by an inclined plane, the inclined surface is elliptical in shape. In Fig. 6.34a, such a surface is produced, but the ellipse does not show true size and shape because the plane of the ellipse is not seen at right angles in any view.

In Fig. 8.12a, the line of sight is taken perpendicular to the edge view of the inclined surface, and the resulting ellipse is shown in true size and shape in the auxiliary view. The major axis is found by direct projection from the front view, and the minor axis is equal to the diameter of the cylinder. The left end of the cylinder (a circle) will appear as an ellipse in the auxiliary view, the major axis of which is equal to the diameter of the cylinder.

Since this is a symmetrical object, the reference plane is assumed to be located through the center, as shown. To plot points on the ellipses, select points on the circle of the side view, and project them across to the inclined surface or to the left-end surface, and then upward to the auxiliary view. In this manner, two points can be projected each time, as shown for points 1–2, 3–4, and 5–6. Distances *a* are equal and are transferred from the side view to the auxiliary view. A sufficient number of points must be projected to establish the curves accurately. Use the irregular curve.

Since the major and minor axes are known, any of the true ellipse methods in Figs. 4.48–4.50 and 4.52a may be used. If an approximate ellipse is adequate, the method in Fig. 4.56 can be used. The quickest and easiest method using instruments is to use an ellipse template (§4.53).

In Fig. 8.12b, the auxiliary view shows the true size and shape of the inclined cut through a piece of molding. The method of plotting points is similar to that explained for the ellipse in Fig. 8.12a.

8.13 REVERSE CONSTRUCTION

To complete the regular views, it is often necessary to construct an auxiliary view first. For example, in Fig. 8.13a, the upper portion of the right-side view cannot be constructed until the auxiliary view is drawn and points are established on the curves and then projected back to the front view, as shown.

In Fig. 8.13b, the 60° angle and the location of line 1–2 in the front view are given. To locate line 3–4 in the front view and the lines 2–4, 3–4, and 4–5 in the side view, it is necessary to first construct the 60° angle in the auxiliary view and project back to the front and side views, as shown.

8.14 PARTIAL AUXILIARY VIEWS

The use of an auxiliary view often makes it possible to omit one or more regular views and thus to simplify the shape description, as shown in Fig. 8.1b. In Fig. 8.14 three complete auxiliary-view drawings are shown. To make such drawings takes a great deal of time, particularly when ellipses are involved, as is so often the case. The completeness of detail may add nothing to clearness or may even detract from it because of the clutter of lines. However, in these cases, some portion of

FIGURE 8.12   **Plotted Curves.**

(a)

(b)

FIGURE 8.13   **Reverse Construction.**

(a)DEPTH AUXILIARY VIEW   (b) HEIGHT AUXILIARY VIEW   (c) WIDTH AUXILIARY VIEW

FIGURE 8.14   **Primary Auxiliary Views.**

every view is needed—no view can be completely eliminated.

As described in §6.9, partial views are often sufficient, and the resulting drawings are considerably simplified and easier to read. Similarly, as shown in Fig. 8.15, partial regular views and partial auxiliary views are used with the same result. Usually a break line is used to indicate the imaginary break in the views. *Do not draw a break line coinciding with a visible line or a hidden line.*

To clarify the relationship of views, the auxiliary views should be connected to the views from which they are projected, either with a center line or with one or two projection lines. This is particularly important for partial views, which are often small and appear to be "lost" and not related to any view.

■ 8.15 HALF AUXILIARY VIEWS

If an auxiliary view is symmetrical, and if it is necessary to save space on the drawing or to save time in drafting, only half of the auxiliary view may be drawn (Fig. 8.16). In this case, half of a regular view is also shown, since the bottom flange is also symmetrical (see §§6.9 and 7.14). Note that in each case the *near half* is shown.

FIGURE 8.15 **Partial Views.**

FIGURE 8.16 **Half Views.**

■ 8.16 HIDDEN LINES IN AUXILIARY VIEWS

In practice, hidden lines should be omitted in auxiliary views, unless they are needed for clearness. The beginner, however, should show all hidden lines, especially if the auxiliary view of the entire object is shown. Later, in advanced applications, it will become clearer as to when hidden lines can be omitted.

■ 8.17 AUXILIARY SECTIONS

An auxiliary section is simply an auxiliary view in section. In Fig. 8.17a, note the cutting-plane line and the terminating arrows that indicate the direction of sight for the auxiliary section. Observe that the section lines are drawn at approximately 45° with visible outlines. In an auxiliary section drawing, the entire portion of the object behind the cutting plane may be shown (Fig. 8.17a), or the cut surface alone may be shown (Fig. 8.17b and 8.17c).

An auxiliary section through a cone is shown in Fig. 8.18. This is one of the conic sections (§4.44), in this case a parabola. The parabola may be drawn by other methods (Figs. 4.57 and 4.58), but the method shown here is by projection. In Fig. 8.18, elements of the cone are drawn in the front and top views. These intersect the cutting plane at points 1, 2, 3, and so on. These points are established in the top view by projecting upward to the top views of the corresponding elements. In the auxiliary section, all points on the parabola are the same distance from the reference plane RP as they are in the top view.

A typical example of an auxiliary section in machine drawing is shown in Fig. 8.19. Here, there is not sufficient space for a revolved section, although a removed section could have been used instead of an auxiliary section.

■ 8.18 TRUE LENGTH OF LINE: AUXILIARY-VIEW METHOD

A line will show in true length when projected to a projection plane parallel to the line.

Figure 8.20 shows how to find the true length of the hip rafter 1–2 by means of a depth auxiliary view.

1. Assume an arrow perpendicular to 1–2 (front view) indicating the direction of sight, and place the H/F folding line as shown.

2. Draw the F/1 folding line perpendicular to the arrow and at any convenient distance from 1–2 (front view), and project the points 1 and 3 toward it.

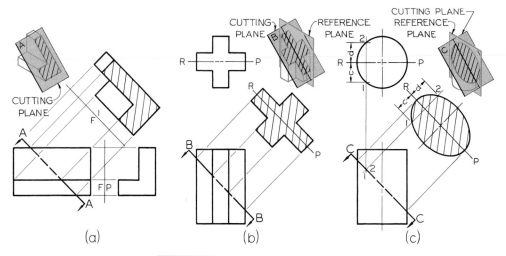

(a)   (b)   (c)

FIGURE 8.17   Auxiliary Sections.

FIGURE 8.18   Auxiliary Section.

FIGURE 8.19   Auxiliary Section.

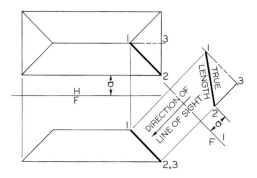

FIGURE 8.20   True Length of a Line by Means of an Auxiliary View.

3. Set off the points 1 and 2 in the auxiliary view at the same distance from the folding line as they are in the top view. The triangle 1–2–3 in the auxiliary view shows the true size and shape of the roof section 1–2–3, and the distance 1–2 in the auxiliary view is the true length of the hip rafter 1–2.

To find the true length of a line by revolution, see §9.10.

■8.19 SUCCESSIVE AUXILIARY VIEWS

Up to this point we have dealt with **primary auxiliary views**—that is, single auxiliary views projected from one of the regular views. In Fig. 8.21, auxiliary view 1 is a primary auxiliary view projected from the top view.

From primary auxiliary view 1, a **secondary auxiliary view** 2 can be drawn; then from it a **third auxiliary**

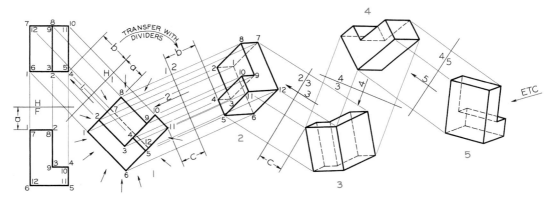

FIGURE 8.21   Successive Auxiliary Views.

view 3, and so on. An infinite number of such successive auxiliary views may be drawn. However, secondary auxiliary view 2 is not the only one that can be projected from primary auxiliary view 1. As shown by the arrows around view 1, an infinite number of secondary auxiliary views, with different lines of sight, may be projected. *Any auxiliary view projected from a primary auxiliary view is a secondary auxiliary view.* Furthermore, any succeeding auxiliary view may be used to project an infinite series of views from it.

In this example, folding lines are more convenient than reference-plane lines. In auxiliary view 1, all numbered points of the object are the same distance from folding line H/1 as they are in the front view from folding line H/F. These distances, such as distance a, are transferred from the front view to the auxiliary view.

To draw the secondary auxiliary view 2, disregard the front view and center attention on the sequence of three views: the top view, view 1, and view 2. Draw arrow 2 toward view 1 in the direction desired for view 2, and draw light projection lines parallel to the arrow. Draw folding line 1/2 perpendicular to the projection lines and at any convenient distance from view 1. Locate all numbered points in view 2 from folding line 1/2 at the same distances they are in the top view from folding line H/1, using the dividers to transfer distances. For example, transfer distance b to locate points 4 and 5. Connect points with straight lines, and determine visibility. The corner nearest the observer (11) for view 2 will be visible, and the one farthest away (1) will be hidden, as shown.

To draw views 3, 4, and so on, repeat this procedure, remembering that each time we will be concerned only with a sequence of three views. In drawing

any auxiliary view, the paper may be revolved to make the last two views line up as regular views.

■ 8.20 USES OF AUXILIARY VIEWS

Generally, auxiliary views are used to show the true shape or true angle of features that appear distorted in the regular views. Basically, auxiliary views have the following four uses:

1. True length of line, TL (§8.18).
2. Point view of line (§8.11).
3. Edge view of plane, EV (§8.21).
4. True size of plane, TS (§8.21).

■ 8.21 TRUE SIZE OF AN OBLIQUE SURFACE: FOLDING-LINE METHOD

A typical use for a secondary auxiliary view is to show the true size and shape of an oblique surface, such as surface 1–2–3–4 in Fig. 8.22. In this case folding lines are used, but the same results can be obtained with reference lines. Proceed as follows:

1. Draw the primary auxiliary view showing surface 1–2–3–4 as a line. As explained in §8.11, the edge view (EV) of a plane is found by getting the point of view of a line in that plane. To get the point view of a line, the line of sight must be assumed parallel to the line. Therefore, draw arrow P parallel to lines 1–2 and 3–4, which are true length (TL) in the front view, and draw projection lines parallel to the arrow. Draw folding line H/F between the top and front views and F/1 between the front and auxiliary views, perpendicular to the respective projection lines. All points in the auxiliary view will be the same distance from the folding line F/1 as they are in the top view from folding line

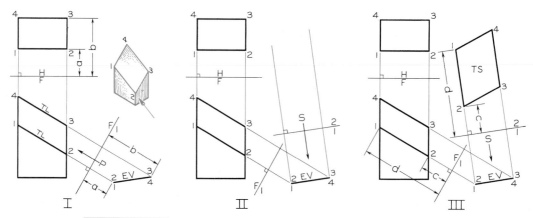

FIGURE 8.22   True Size of Oblique Surface—Folding-Line Method.

H/F. Lines 1–2 and 3–4 will appear as points in the auxiliary view, and plane 1–2–3–4 will therefore appear *edgewise*—that is, as a line.

2. Draw arrow S perpendicular to the edge view of plane 1–2–3–4 in the primary auxiliary view, and draw projection lines parallel to the arrow. Draw folding line 1/2 perpendicular to these projection lines and at a convenient distance from the primary auxiliary view.

3. Draw the secondary auxiliary view. Locate each point (transfer with dividers) the same distance from the folding line 1/2 as it is in the front view to the folding line F/1—as, for example, dimensions c and d. The true size (TS) of the surface 1–2–3–4 will be shown in the secondary auxiliary view since the direction of sight, arrow S, was taken perpendicular to it.

■ 8.22   TRUE SIZE OF AN OBLIQUE SURFACE: REFERENCE-PLANE METHOD

Figure 8.23a shows the steps in drawing an auxiliary view in which triangular surface 1–2–3 appears in true size and shape. For the true size of the surface to appear in the secondary auxiliary view, arrow S must be assumed perpendicular to the edge view of that surface; it is therefore necessary to have the edge view of surface 1–2–3 in the primary auxiliary view first. To do this, the direction of sight, arrow P, must be parallel to

FIGURE 8.23   True Size of an Oblique Surface—Reference-Plane Method.

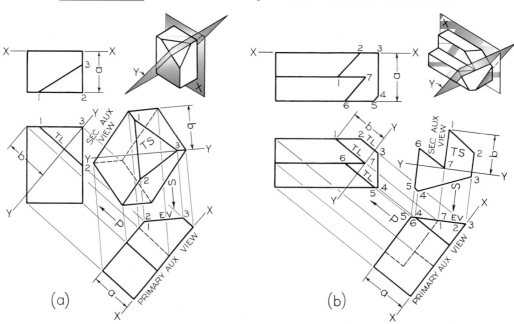

a line in surface 1–2–3 that appears true length (TL) in the front view. Therefore, arrow P is drawn parallel to line 1–2 of the front view, line 1–2 will appear as a point in the primary auxiliary view, and surface 1–2–3 must therefore appear edgewise in that view.

In this case it is convenient to use reference lines and to assume the reference plane X (for drawing the primary auxiliary view) coincides with the back surface of the object, as shown. For the primary auxiliary view, all depth measurements, as α in the figure, are transferred with dividers from the top view with respect to the reference line X–X.

For the secondary auxiliary view, reference plane Y is assumed to be cutting through the object for convenience in transferring measurements. All measurements perpendicular to Y–Y in the secondary auxiliary view are the same as between the reference plane and the corresponding points in the front view. Note that corresponding measurements must be *inside* (toward the central view in the sequence of three views) or *outside* (away from the central view). For example, dimension b is on the side of Y–Y *away* from the primary auxiliary view in both places.

Figure 8.23b shows how to determine the true size and shape of surface 1–2–3–4–5–6–7 without drawing the complete secondary auxiliary view. The method is similar to that just described.

■ 8.23 SECONDARY AUXILIARY VIEW, OBLIQUE DIRECTION OF SIGHT GIVEN

In Fig. 8.24 two views of a block are given, with two views of an arrow indicating the lines of sight for the desired secondary auxiliary views of the object. To draw these views, proceed as follows:

1. *Draw a primary auxiliary view of both the object and the assumed arrow*, which will show the true length *of the arrow.* To do this, assume a horizontal reference plane X–X in the front and auxiliary views, as shown. Then assume a direction of sight perpendicular to the given arrow. In the front view, the butt end of the arrow is a distance α higher than the arrow point, and this distance is transferred to the primary auxiliary view, as shown. All *height* measurements in the auxiliary view correspond to those in the front view.

2. *Draw a secondary auxiliary view* that shows the arrow as a point. This can be done because the arrow appears true length in the primary auxiliary view and projection lines for the secondary auxiliary view are drawn parallel to it. Draw reference line Y–Y for the secondary auxiliary view perpendicular to these pro-

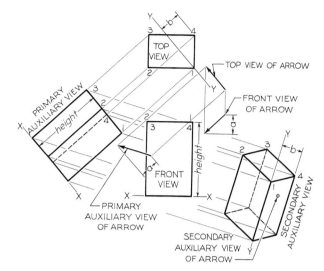

FIGURE 8.24   **Secondary Auxiliary View with Oblique Direction of Sight Given.**

jection lines. In the top view, draw Y–Y perpendicular to the projection lines to the primary auxiliary view. All measurements, such as b, with respect to Y–Y correspond in the secondary auxiliary view and the top view.

Note that the secondary auxiliary views of Figs. 8.23a and 8.24 have considerable pictorial value. These are *trimetric projections* (see §16.30). However, the direction of sight could be assumed, in the manner of Fig. 8.24, to produce either isometric or dimetric projections. If the direction of sight is assumed parallel to the diagonal of a cube, the resulting view is an *isometric projection* (§16.3).

A typical application of a secondary auxiliary view is shown in Fig. 8.25. All views are partial views, except the front view. The partial secondary auxiliary view illustrates a case in which break lines are not needed. Note the use of an auxiliary section to show the true shape of the arm.

■ 8.24 ELLIPSES

As shown in §6.30, a circle viewed obliquely appears as an ellipse. This often occurs in successive auxiliary views because of the variety of directions of sight. In Fig. 8.26a, the hole appears as a true circle in the top view. The circles appear as straight lines in the primary auxiliary view and as ellipses in the secondary auxiliary view. In the latter, the major axis AB of the ellipse is parallel to the projection lines and equal in length to the true diameter of the circle in the top view. The minor axis CD is perpendicular to the major axis, and

FIGURE 8.25 **Secondary Auxiliary View—Partial Views.**

Since the major and minor axes are easily found, any of the true-ellipse methods of Figs. 4.48–4.50 and 4.52a may be used, or an approximate ellipse (Fig. 4.56) may be found sufficiently accurate for a particular drawing. Or the ellipses may be easily and rapidly drawn with the aid of an ellipse template. The "angle" of ellipse to use is one that most closely matches the angle between the direction-of-sight arrow and the plane (EV) containing the circle, as seen in this case in the primary auxiliary view. Here the angle is $36\frac{1}{2}°$, so a 35° ellipse is selected.

In Fig. 8.26b, successive auxiliary views are shown in which the true circular shapes appear in the secondary auxiliary view, and the elliptical projections in the front and top views. It is necessary to construct the circular shapes in the secondary auxiliary view, then to project plotted points back to the primary auxiliary view, the front view, and finally to the top view, as shown in the figure for points 1, 2, 3, and 4. The final curves are then drawn with the aid of an irregular curve.

If the major and minor axes are found, any of the true-ellipse methods may be used; or better still, an ellipse template may be employed. The major and minor axes are easily established in the front view, but in the top view, they are more difficult to find. The major axis AB is at right angles to the center line GL of the hole, and equal in length to the true diameter of the hole. The minor axis ED is at right angles to the major axis. Its length is found by plotting several points in the vicinity of one end of the minor axis or by using descriptive geometry to find the angle between the line of sight and the inclined surface, and by this angle selecting the ellipse guide required.

its foreshortened length is projected from the primary auxiliary view.

The ellipse can be completed by projecting points, such as 1 and 2, symmetrically located about the reference plane RP coinciding with CD, with distances a equal in the top and secondary auxiliary views as shown, and finally, after a sufficient number of points have been plotted, by using an irregular curve.

FIGURE 8.26 **Ellipses.**

(a)

Use 35° template. (Nearest to $36\frac{1}{2}°$)

(b)

■ 8.25 COMPUTER GRAPHICS

USING CAD

Using 3D CAD, any view can be generated in one or two steps, eliminating the need to project auxiliary views manually. It is still very important to have a clear understanding which line of sight will produce a true size view or a view which shows a true dihedral angle. When measuring or dimensioning a view from a CAD screen, if the surface or angle is not true size the automatic dimension from the CAD system will be that of the apparent, or projected, distance. Incorrectly dimensioned dihedral angles can be a common error in CAD drawings created by inexperienced operators.

■ KEY WORDS

AUXILIARY VIEW	FOLDING LINES
REFERENCE PLANE	PARTIAL AUXILIARY VIEW
PRIMARY AUXILIARY	SECONDARY AUXILIARY
GLASS BOX	TRUE LENGTH
DIHEDRAL ANGLE	INCLINED SURFACE
TRUE SIZE	OBLIQUE SURFACE
OBLIQUE LINE	

■ CHAPTER SUMMARY

- An auxiliary view can be used to create a projection that shows the true length of an oblique line or true size of an inclined plane.
- Primary and secondary auxiliary views can also create the edge view of an oblique plane, the point view of an oblique line, and the true size of an oblique plane.
- An auxiliary view can be automatically created using CAD if the original object was drawn as a three-dimensional model.
- Folding lines or reference plane lines represent the edge views of projection planes.
- Points are projected between views parallel to the line of sight and perpendicular to the reference plane lines or folding lines.
- A principal use of auxiliary views is to show dihedral angles in true size.
- Curves are plotted as points in auxiliary views and are connected with an irregular curve drawing instrument or spline CAD function.
- An auxiliary view can also be drawn as a sectional view. The same sectional view conventions apply when the section is also an auxiliary view.
- A secondary auxiliary view can be constructed from a previously drawn (primary) auxiliary view.

■ REVIEW QUESTIONS

1. What is meant by *true length*? By *true size*?
2. Why is a true-length line always parallel to an adjacent reference plane line?
3. If an auxiliary view is drawn from the front view, its depth dimensions would be the same as in what other views?
4. Describe one method for transferring depth between views.
5. What is the difference between a complete auxiliary view and a partial auxiliary view?
6. How are curves drawn in an auxiliary view?
7. How many auxiliary views are necessary to draw the true size of an inclined plane? Of an oblique plane?
8. What is the angle between the reference-plane lines and the direction-of-sight lines?

■ AUXILIARY-VIEW PROBLEMS

The problems in Figs. 8.27–8.59 are to be drawn with instruments or freehand. If partial auxiliary views are not assigned, the auxiliary views are to be complete views of the entire object, including all necessary hidden lines.

It is often difficult to space properly the views of an auxiliary-view drawing. In some cases it may be necessary to make a trial blocking out on a preliminary sheet before starting the actual drawing. Al-lowances for dimensions must be made if metric or decimal dimensions are to be included. In such a case, the student should study §§11.1–11.25.

Since many of the problems in this chapter are of a general nature, they can also be solved on most computer graphics systems. If a system is available, your instructor may choose to assign specific problems to be completed by this method.

FIGURE 8.27 RH Finger. Given: Front and auxiliary views. Required: Complete front, auxiliary, left-side, and top views (Layout A–3 or A4–3 adjusted).

FIGURE 8.28 V-Block. Given: Front and auxiliary views. Required: Complete front, top, and auxiliary views (Layout A–3 or A4–3 adjusted).

FIGURE 8.29 Auxiliary View Problems. Make freehand sketch or instrument drawing of selected problem as assigned. Draw given front and right-side views, and add incomplete auxiliary view, including all hidden lines (Layout A–3 or A4–3 adjusted). If assigned, design your own right-side view consistent with given front view, and then add complete auxiliary view.

FIGURE 8.30   **Anchor Bracket. Draw necessary views or partial views (Layout A–3 or A4–3 adjusted).***

FIGURE 8.31   **Centering Block. Draw complete front, top, and right-side views, plus indicated auxiliary views (Layout B–3 or A3–3).***

FIGURE 8.32   **Clamp Slide. Draw necessary views completely (Layout B–3 or A3–3).***

FIGURE 8.33   **Guide Block. Given: Right-side and auxiliary views. Required: Right-side, auxiliary, plus front and top views—all complete (Layout B–3 or A3–3).***

FIGURE 8.34   **Angle Bearing. Draw necessary views, including a complete auxiliary view (Layout A–3 or A4–3 adjusted).***

FIGURE 8.35   **Guide Bracket. Draw necessary views or partial views (Layout B–3 or A3–3).***

* If dimensions are required, study §§11.1–11.25. Use metric or decimal-inch dimensions as assigned.

FIGURE 8.36 Rod Guide. Draw necessary views, including complete auxiliary view showing true shape of upper rounded portion (Layout B–4 or A3–4 adjusted).*

FIGURE 8.37 Brace Anchor. Draw necessary views, including partial auxiliary view showing true shape of cylindrical portion (Layout B–4 or A3–4 adjusted).*

FIGURE 8.38 45° Elbow. Draw necessary views, including a broken section and two half views of flanges (Layout B–4 or A3–4 adjusted).*

FIGURE 8.39 Angle Guide. Draw necessary views, including a partial auxiliary view of cylindrical recess (Layout B–4 or A3–4 adjusted).*

FIGURE 8.40 Holder Block. Draw front and right-side views (2.80″ apart) and complete auxiliary view of entire object showing true shape of surface A and all hidden lines (Layout A–3 or A4–3 adjusted).*

FIGURE 8.41 Control Bracket. Draw necessary views, including partial auxiliary views and regular views (Layout C–4 or A2–4).*

* If dimensions are required, study §§11.1–11.25. Use metric or decimal-inch dimensions as assigned.

FIGURE 8.42 Tool Holder Slide. Draw given views, and add complete auxiliary view showing true curvature of slot on bottom (Layout B–4 or A3–4 adjusted).[*]

FIGURE 8.44 Guide Bearing. Draw necessary views and partial views, including two partial auxiliary views (Layout C–4 or A2–4).[*]

FIGURE 8.43 Adjuster Block. Draw necessary views, including complete auxiliary view showing true shape of inclined surface (Layout B–4 or A3–4 adjusted).[*]

FIGURE 8.45 Drill Press Bracket. Draw given views and add complete auxiliary view showing true shape of inclined face (Layout B–4 or A3–4 adjusted).[*]

[*] If dimensions are required, study §§11.1–11.25. Use metric or decimal-inch dimensions as assigned.

FIGURE 8.46 Brake Control Lever. Draw necessary views and partial views (Layout B–4 or A3–4 adjusted).[*]

FIGURE 8.48 Cam Bracket. Draw necessary views or partial views as needed. (Layout B–4 or A3–4 adjusted).[*]

FIGURE 8.47 Shifter Fork. Draw necessary views, including partial auxiliary view showing true shape of inclined arm (Layout B–4 or A3–4 adjusted).[*]

FIGURE 8.49 RH Tool Holder. Draw necessary views, including partial auxiliary views showing 105° angle and square hole true size. (Layout B–4 or A3–4 adjusted).[*]

[*] If dimensions are required, study §§11.1–12.25. Use metric or decimal-inch dimensions as assigned.

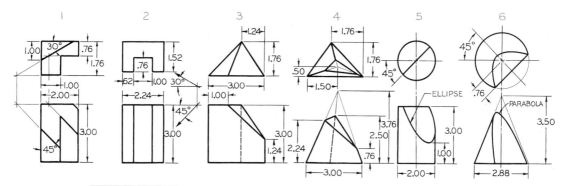

FIGURE 8.50 Draw secondary auxiliary views, complete, which (except Prob. 2) will show the true sizes of the inclined surfaces. In Prob. 2 draw secondary auxiliary view as seen in direction of arrow (Layout B–3 or A3–3).*

FIGURE 8.51 Control Bracket. Draw necessary views including primary and secondary auxiliary views so that the latter shows true shape of oblique surface A (Layout B–4 or A3–4 adjusted).*

FIGURE 8.53 Dovetail Slide. Draw complete given views and auxiliary views, including view showing true size of surface 1–2–3–4 (Layout B–4 or A3–4 adjusted).*

FIGURE 8.52 Holder Block. Draw given views and primary and secondary auxiliary views so that the latter shows true shape of oblique surface (Layout B–4 or A3–4 adjusted).*

Draw primary aux. view showing angle between planes A and B; then secondary auxiliary view showing true size of surface A.

FIGURE 8.54 Dovetail Guide. Draw given views plus complete auxiliary views as indicated (Layout B–4 or A3–4 adjusted).*

* If dimensions are required, study §§11.1–11.25. Use metric or decimal-inch dimensions as assigned.

FIGURE 8.55 **Adjustable Stop. Draw complete front and auxiliary views plus partial right-side view. Show all hidden lines (Layout C–4 or A2–4).**[*]

FIGURE 8.56 **Tool Holder. Draw complete front view, and primary and secondary auxiliary views as indicated (Layout B–4 or A3–4 adjusted).**[*]

---

[*] If dimensions are required, study §§11.1–11.25. Use metric or decimal-inch dimensions as assigned.

FIGURE 8.57 Box Tool Holder for Turret Lathe. Given: Front and right-side views. Required: Front and left-side views, and complete auxiliary view as indicated by arrow (Layout C–4 or A2–4).*

FIGURE 8.58 Pointing Tool Holder for Automatic Screw Machine. Given: Front and right-side views. Required: Front view and three partial auxiliary views (Layout C–4 or A2–4).*

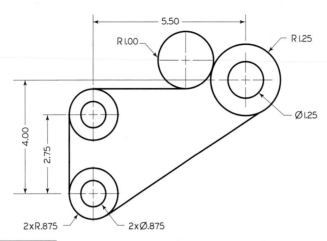

FIGURE 8.59   **Print Roller. Given: Right-side view. Design your own front and auxiliary view (Use Layout A–3 or A4–3 adjusted). If assigned, use CAD to create a partial auxiliary view.**

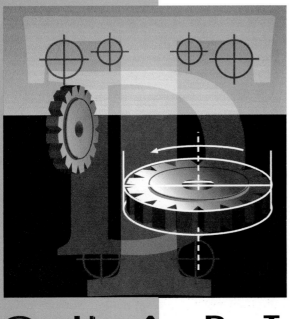

C H A P T E R 9

REVOLUTIONS

OBJECTIVES

After studying the material in this chapter, you should be able to:

1. Revolve an object about any principal axis of revolution.
2. Revolve an object to show the true length and true size of lines and planes.
3. Construct multiple revolutions to determine the true size of an oblique plane.
4. Revolve a point about a normal axis.
5. Revolve a circle to create an ellipse.
6. Revolve a three-dimensional object in space using CAD.

OVERVIEW

Revolution, like auxiliary-view projection, is a method of determining the true length and true size of inclined and oblique lines and planes. To obtain an auxiliary view, the observer changes position with respect to the object, as shown by the arrow in Fig. 9.1a. The auxiliary view shows the true size and shape of surface A. The same view of the object can be obtained by *moving the object* with respect to the observer, as shown in Fig. 9.1b. Here the object is revolved until surface A appears in its true size and shape in the right-side view. Revolution determines true length and true size without creating another view. Instead, revolution positions an object in space to create true size and shape.

■9.1 AXIS OF REVOLUTION

In Fig. 9.1b the axis of revolution is assumed perpendicular to the frontal plane of projection. The view in which the axis of revolution appears as a point (in this case the front view) *revolves but does not change shape*; in the views in which the axis is shown as a line in true length, the *dimensions of the object parallel to the axis do not change*.

To make a revolution drawing, the view on the plane of projection that is perpendicular to the axis of revolution is drawn first, since it is the only view that remains unchanged in size and shape. This view is drawn revolved either *clockwise* or *counterclockwise* about a point that is the end view, or point view, of the axis of revolution. This point may be assumed at any convenient position on or outside the view. The other views are then projected from this view.

The axis of revolution is usually considered perpendicular to one of the three principal planes of projection. Thus, an object may be revolved about an axis perpendicular to the horizontal, frontal, or profile planes of projection, and the views drawn in the new positions. Such a process is called a **primary revolution**. If this drawing is then used as a basis for another revolution, the operation is called **successive revolutions**. Obviously, this process may be continued indefinitely, which reminds us of the succession of auxiliary views shown in Fig. 8.21.

■9.2 REVOLUTION ABOUT AXIS PERPENDICULAR TO FRONTAL PLANE

A primary revolution is illustrated in Fig. 9.2. An imaginary axis XY is assumed (Fig. 9.2I), about which the object is to revolve to the desired position. In this case the axis is selected perpendicular to the frontal plane of projection, and during the revolution all points of the object describe circular arcs parallel to that plane. The axis may pierce the object at any point or may be exterior to it. In Fig. 9.2II, the front view is drawn *revolved*, but not changed in shape, through the angle desired (30° in this case), and the top and side views are obtained by projecting from the front view.

The *depth* of the top view and the side view is found by projecting from the top view of the first unrevolved position (Fig. 9.2I) *because the depth, since it is parallel to the axis, remains unchanged*. If the front view of the revolved position is drawn directly without first drawing the normal unrevolved position, the depth of the object, as shown in the revolved top and side views, may be drawn to known dimensions.

Note the similarity between the top and side views in Fig. 9.2II and some of the auxiliary views of Fig. 8.7c.

■9.3 REVOLUTION ABOUT AXIS PERPENDICULAR TO HORIZONTAL PLANE

A revolution about an axis perpendicular to the horizontal plane of projection is shown in Fig. 9.3. An imaginary axis XY is assumed perpendicular to the top plane of projection (Fig. 9.3I), and the top view is drawn revolved (but not changed in shape) to the desired position (30° in this case) (Fig. 9.3II); the other views are obtained by projecting from this view. During the revolution, all points of the object describe circular arcs parallel to the horizontal plane. The *heights* of all points in the front and side views in the revolved position remain unchanged, since they are measured parallel to the axis, and may be drawn by projecting from the initial front and side views in Fig. 9.3I.

Note the similarity between the front and side views in Fig. 9.3II and some of the auxiliary views of Fig. 8.8c.

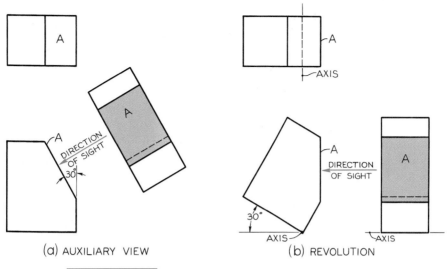

(a) AUXILIARY VIEW   (b) REVOLUTION

FIGURE 9.1   **Auxiliary View and Revolution Compared.**

FIGURE 9.2   **Primary Revolution About an Axis Perpendicular to Frontal Plane.**

FIGURE 9.3   **Primary Revolution About an Axis Perpendicular to Horizontal Plane.**

■ 9.4 REVOLUTION ABOUT AXIS PERPENDICULAR TO PROFILE PLANE

A revolution about an axis XY perpendicular to the profile plane of projection is illustrated in Fig. 9.4. During the revolution, all points of the object describe circular arcs parallel to the profile plane of projection. The widths of the top and front views in the revolved position remain unchanged, since they are measured parallel to the axis and may be obtained by projection from the top and front views in Fig. 9.4I, or may be set off by direct measurement.

Note the similarity between the top and front views in Fig. 9.4II and some of the auxiliary views of Fig. 8.9c.

■ 9.5 SUCCESSIVE REVOLUTIONS

It is possible to draw an object in an infinite number of revolved positions by making successive revolutions. Such a procedure (Fig. 9.5), limited to three or four stages, offers excellent practice in multiview projection. While it is possible to make several revolutions of a simple object without the aid of a system of numbers, it is absolutely necessary in successive revolutions to assign a number or a letter to every corner of the

FIGURE 9.4 **Primary Revolution About an Axis Perpendicular to Profile Plane.**

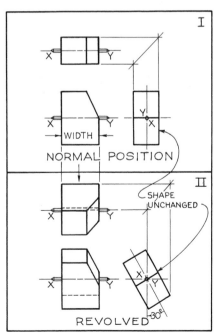

object (see §6.6). The numbering or lettering must be consistent in the various views of the several stages of revolution. Figure 9.5 shows four sets of multiview drawings numbered I, II, III, and IV, respectively. They represent the same object in different positions with reference to the planes of projection.

In Fig. 9.5I, the object is represented in its normal position with its faces parallel to the planes of projection. In (II), the object is shown revolved clockwise through an angle of 30° about an axis perpendicular to the frontal plane. The drawing in (III) is placed under (I) so that the side view, whose width remains unchanged, can be projected from space I to space II as shown.

During the revolution, all points of the object describe circular arcs parallel to the frontal plane of projection and remain at the same distance from that plane. The side view, therefore, may be projected from the side view in (I) and the front view in (II). The top view may be projected in the usual manner from the front and side views in (II).

In (III), the object from (II) has been revolved counterclockwise through an angle of 30° about an axis perpendicular to the horizontal plane of projection. During the revolution, all points describe *horizontal* circular arcs and remain at the same distance from the horizontal plane of projection. The top view from (II) is shown revolved through 30° in (III). The front and side views are obtained by projecting from the front and side views of (II) and from the top view of (III).

In Fig. 9.5IV, the object from (III) has been revolved clockwise through 15° about an axis perpendicular to the profile plane of projection. During the revolution, all points of the object describe circular arcs parallel to the profile plane of projection and remain at the same distance from that plane. The side view is copied (see §4.25) from the side view of (III), but revolved through 15°. The front and top views are projected from the side view of (IV), and from the top and front views of (III).

Another convenient method of copying a view in a new revolved position is to use tracing paper, as described in §4.26. Either a tracing can be made and transferred by rubbing, or the prick points may be made and transferred.

In Figs. 9.5III and IV, each view is an axonometric projection (see §16.2). An isometric projection can be obtained by revolution, as shown in Fig. 16.3, and a dimetric projection (see §16.28) can be constructed in a

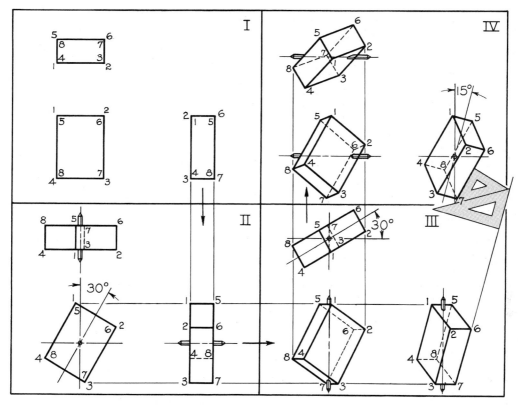

FIGURE 9.5 Successive Revolutions of a Prism.

similar manner. If neither an isometric nor a dimetric projection is specifically sought, successive revolution will produce a trimetric projection (see §16.30), as shown in Fig. 9.5.

■9.6 REVOLUTION OF A POINT: NORMAL AXIS

Examples of the revolution of a point about a straight-line axis are often found in design problems that involve pulleys, gears, cranks, linkages, and so on. For example, in Fig. 9.6a, as the disk is revolved, point 3 moves in a circular path lying in a plane perpendicular to the axis 1–2. This relationship is represented in the two views in Fig. 9.6b. Note in this instance that the axis is normal or perpendicular to the frontal plane of projection, resulting in a front view that shows a point view of the axis and a true-size view of the circular path of revolution for point 3. The top view shows the path of revolution in edge view and perpendicular to the true-length view of the axis. Similar two-view relationships would occur if the axis were perpendicular

or normal to either the horizontal or profile planes of projection.

The clockwise revolution through 150° for point 3 is illustrated in Fig. 9.6c.

■9.7 REVOLUTION OF A POINT: INCLINED AXIS

In Fig. 9.7a, the axis of revolution for point 3 is positioned parallel to the frontal plane and inclined to the horizontal and profile projection planes. Since the axis 1–2 is true length in the front view, the edge view of the path of revolution can be located as in Fig. 9.7b. To establish the circular path of revolution for point 3, an auxiliary view showing the axis in point view is required (Fig. 9.7c). The required revolution of point 3 (in this case, 210°) is now performed in this circular view. The revolved position of the point is projected to the given front and top views, as shown.

Note the similarity of the relationships of the front view and auxiliary view and the constructions shown in Fig. 9.6c.

(a)

(b)

(c)

FIGURE 9.6 **Revolution of a Point About a Normal Axis.**

■ 9.8 REVOLUTION OF A POINT: OBLIQUE AXIS

In Fig. 9.8a, the axis of revolution for point 3 is oblique to all principal planes of projection and, therefore, is shown neither in true length nor as a point view in the top, front, or profile views. To establish the necessary true length and point view of the axis 1–2 in adjacent views, two successive auxiliary views are needed (Fig. 9.8b). The required revolved position of point 3 can now be located and then projected back to complete the given front and top views.

■ 9.9 REVOLUTION OF A LINE

The procedure for the revolution of a line about an axis is very similar to that required for the revolution of a point (see § 9.6). All points on a line must revolve through the same angle or the revolved line becomes altered.

In Fig. 9.9a, the line 1–2 is to be revolved through 150° about the inclined axis 3–4. Since the axis 3–4 is given in true length in the top view, an auxiliary view is required to provide a point view of the axis (Fig. 9.9b). The necessary revolution can then be made about point view 3–4. To ensure that all points on the line rotate through the same number of degrees, a construction circle is drawn tangent to line 1–2 and a perpendicular through the tangency point becomes the reference for measuring the angle of rotation. The circular arc paths for points 1 and 2 locate the points 1_R and 2_R, as the revolved position of the line is drawn perpendicular to the radial line extending under the 150° arc of revolution and tangent to the smaller circle. The alternate-position line is used to distinguish the revolved-position line from the original given line.

■ 9.10 TRUE LENGTH OF A LINE: REVOLUTION METHOD

If a line is parallel to one of the planes of projection, its projection on that plane is equal in length to the line (see Fig. 6.20). In Fig. 9.10a, the element AB of the cone is oblique to the planes of projection; therefore, its projections are foreshortened. If AB is revolved about the axis of the cone until it coincides with either of the contour elements (for example, AB_R), it will be shown in its true length in the front view because it will then be parallel to the frontal plane of projection.

Likewise, in Fig. 9.10b, the edge of the pyramid CD is shown in its true length CD_R when it has been revolved about the axis of the pyramid until it is paral-

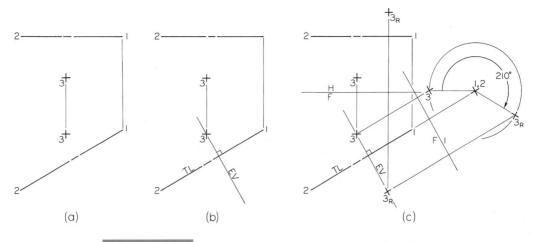

FIGURE 9.7   Revolution of a Point About an Inclined Axis.

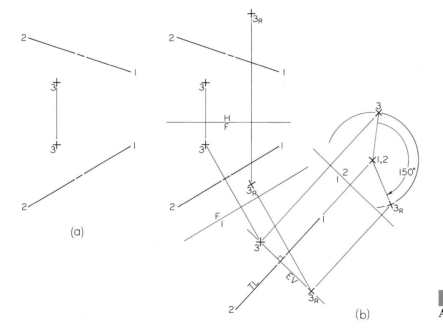

FIGURE 9.8   Revolution of a Point About an Oblique Axis.

lel to the frontal plane of projection. In Fig. 9.10c, the line EF is shown true length at EF$_R$ when it has been revolved about a vertical axis until it is parallel to the frontal plane of projection.

The true length of a line may also be found by constructing a right triangle or a true-length diagram (Fig. 9.10d) whose base is equal to the top view of the line and whose altitude is the difference in elevation of the ends. The hypotenuse of the triangle is equal to the true length of the line.

In these cases the lines are revolved until parallel to a plane of projection. The true length of a line may also be found by leaving the line stationary but shifting the position of the observer—that is, using auxiliary views (see §8.18).

■9.11 TRUE SIZE OF A PLANE SURFACE: REVOLUTION METHOD

If a surface is parallel to one of the planes of projection, its projection on that plane is true size (see

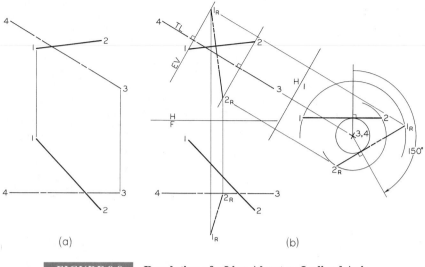

(a)   (b)

FIGURE 9.9   Revolution of a Line About an Inclined Axis.

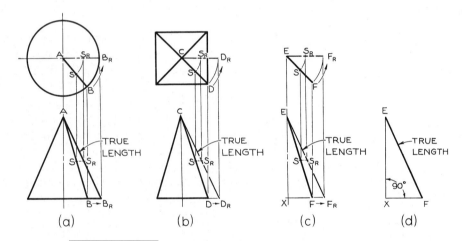

(a)   (b)   (c)   (d)

FIGURE 9.10   True Length of a Line—Revolution Method.

Fig. 6.19). In Fig. 9.11a, the inclined surface 1–2–3–4 is foreshortened in the top and side views and appears as a line in the front view. Line 2–3 is taken as the axis of revolution, and the surface is revolved clockwise in the front view to the position 4_R–3 and projected to the side view at 4_R–1_R–2–3, which is the true size of the surface. In this case the surface was revolved until parallel to the profile plane of projection.

In Fig. 9.11b, triangular surface 1–2–3 is revolved until parallel to the horizontal plane of projection so that the surface appears true size in the top view, as shown.

In Fig. 9.11c, the true size of the oblique surface 1–2–3–4–5 cannot be found by a simple primary revolution. The true size can be found by two successive revolutions or by a combination of an auxiliary view and a primary revolution (as in Fig. 9.11c). First, draw an auxiliary view that will show the edge view (EV) of the plane (see Fig. 9.22). Second, revolve the edge view of the surface until it is parallel to the folding line F/1, as shown. All points in the front view, except those in the axis of revolution line 4–5, will describe circular arcs parallel to the folding line F/1. These arcs will appear in the front view as lines parallel to the folding line, such as 2–2_R and 3–3_R . The true size of the surface is found by connecting the points with straight lines.

9.12 REVOLUTION OF CIRCLES

As shown in Figs. 4.50a to 4.50c, a circle, when viewed obliquely, appears as an ellipse. In that case the coin is

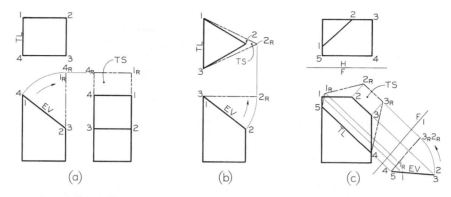

FIGURE 9.11   True Size of a Plane Surface—Revolution Method.

revolved by the fingers. The geometric construction of this revolution is shown in Fig. 9.12a. In the front view the circle appears as ACBD, and in the side view as line CD, which is really the edge view of the plane containing the circle. In the side view, CD (the side view of the circle) is revolved through any desired acute angle to $C_R D_R$.

To find points on the ellipse, draw a series of horizontal lines across the circle in the front view. Each line will cut the circle at two points, as 1 and 2. Project these points across to the vertical line representing the unrevolved circle; then revolve each point and project horizontally to the front view to establish points on the ellipse. Plot as many points as necessary to secure a smooth curve. Figure 9.12b shows an application of this construction to the representation of a revolved object with a large hole.

■ 9.13 COUNTERREVOLUTION

The reverse procedure to revolution is *counterrevolution*. For example, if the three views in Fig. 9.2–II are given, the object can be drawn in the unrevolved position in Fig. 9.2–I by counterrevolution. The front

view is simply counterrevolved back to its normal upright position, and the top and side views are drawn as shown. Similarly, in Fig. 9.5, the object may be counterrevolved from its position in Fig. 9.5–IV to its unrevolved position in Fig. 9.5–I by simply reversing the process.

In practice, it sometimes becomes necessary to draw the views of an object located on or parallel to a given oblique surface. In such an oblique position, it is very difficult to draw the views of the object because of the foreshortening of lines. The work is greatly simplified by counterrevolving the oblique surface to a simple position, completing the drawing, and then revolving to the original given position.

An example is shown in Fig. 9.13. Assume that the oblique surface 8–4–3–7, shown in three views in Fig. 9.13–I, is given and that it is required to draw the three views of a prism 13 mm high with the given oblique surface as its base. Revolve the surface about any horizontal axis XX, perpendicular to the side view, until the edges 8–4 and 3–7 are horizontal, as shown in Fig. 9.13–II. Then revolve the surface about any vertical axis YY, which appears as a point in the top view, until the edges 8–7 and 4–3 are parallel to the frontal plane,

FIGURE 9.12   Revolution of a Circle.

The Art of Making Surfboards Using CAD

With a slow surfer's drawl, John Gillis describes his creation as "unreal," an adjective not generally used by most inventors. But then, most inventors don't surf. Mr. Gillis, who makes surfboards in a Sydney suburb in Australia, hopes that his invention, the Computer Enhanced Technology board-shaping machine, changes the sport. Traditionally, surfboard shapers spend hours in poorly ventilated bays, hand-carving surfable shapes out of slabs of polyurethane foam or wood. To be a successful shaper, you need an intimate knowledge of how a surfboard interacts with waves. You also must stoop and squat continually and tolerate a lifetime of breathing foam dust.

Using Mr. Gillis's machine, along with software designed by Ian Pearce, a British surfer, shapers forgo these last two requirements. They create boards on a PC using Mr. Pearce's Deadly Accurate Template, or D.A.T., a computer-assisted design and modeling system. The information is then fed into the Computer Enhanced Technology machine, which will carve a board with one-hundredth-of-a-millimeter accuracy. The machine can also act as a board scanner, creating exact duplicates of existing boards. This means that wherever there is a PC, there's a shaping bay.

Shaping machines have been around for years and similar computer-aided technology is being developed independently in California, France, and Brazil. Mr. Gillis says the advantage of such machines is that they allow the user to design from scratch in the computer, not just replicate an existing model.

In the early 1990s, when Mr. Gillis was shaping sailboards on the Hawaiian island of Maui, he found that once he built a great board, it was almost impossible to reproduce. "Slight changes in the board made major differences," he explained. "We couldn't get it by hand."

After he returned to Australia in 1992, he stumbled across Mr. Pearce's software, which was being used to design board templates that were printed out on a blotter. Hoping Mr. Pierce would rewrite the software for his machine, Mr. Gillis rang the developer and invited him to Australia. "He came out here for four weeks and the surf was good," Mr. Gillis said with a shrug. "It inspired him to do the job."

There are those detractors, including the legendary surfer Greg Noll, who said shaping machines "took the heart and soul" out of shaping. Mr. Gillis says soul has nothing to do with shaping. "The chemicals in a board, have they got soul?" he asked. "The soul we're talking about here is when you go surfing."

Adapted from "*The Art of Making Surfboards Has Become More of a Science*," by Denis Faye, *The New York Times*, May 27, 1999.

as shown in Fig. 9.13–III. In this position the given surface is perpendicular to the frontal plane, and the front and top views of the required prism can be drawn, as shown by phantom lines in the figure, because the edges 4–1 and 3–2, for example, are parallel to the frontal plane and, therefore, are shown in their true lengths, 13 mm. When the two views in (III) have been drawn, counterrevolve the object from (III) to (II) and then from (II) to (I) to find the required views of the given object in (I).

■9.14 COMPUTER GRAPHICS

Computer graphics programs provide the user with simple and fast ways of revolving objects about any desired axis. Successive revolutions can be easily accomplished using CAD. Computer-generated revolutions also enable a drafter to readily depict circular features, which appear elliptical when viewed obliquely (Fig. 9.14).

FIGURE 9.13   **Counterrevolution of a Prism.**

FIGURE 9.14 **Pictorial Drawings With Different Viewing Angles Created by Using Computervision Designer System. The system provides complete flexibility to manipulate the original illustration to display any desired viewing orientation.** *Courtesy of Computervision Corporation, a subsidiary of Prime Computer, Inc.*

■ KEY WORDS

AXIS OF REVOLUTION

NORMAL AXIS

INCLINED AXIS

OBLIQUE AXIS

SUCCESSIVE REVOLUTIONS

COUNTERREVOLUTION

CLOCKWISE

■ CHAPTER SUMMARY

- Revolution moves an object in space, to reveal what would normally be an auxiliary view of the object in a primary view (top, front, right side).

- The main purpose of revolution is to reveal the true length and true size of inclined and oblique lines and planes in a primary view.

- A normal axis is perpendicular to one of the principal planes of projection (front, top, right side).

- Three-dimensional objects can be revolved at will with

CAD. Traditional drawing methods require projection to locate revolved points and lines. Both drawing tools use the same principles of revolution.

- Circles can be revolved to create ellipses or circles that will appear as ellipses when foreshortened on an inclined or oblique plane.

- When solving for true shape, the axis of revolution is drawn perpendicular to the plane of projection that shows the inclined or oblique surface in edge view.

■ REVIEW QUESTIONS

1. What is the purpose of revolution?

2. What is the axis of revolution? What determines where the axis is drawn?

3. How can an ellipse be created by revolution?

4. What is a normal axis? An inclined axis?

5. What are successive revolutions?

■ REVOLUTION PROBLEMS

In Figs. 9.15–9.19 are problems covering primary revolutions, successive revolutions, and counterrevolutions.

Since many of the problems in this chapter are of a general nature, they can also be solved on most computer graphics systems. If a system is available, the

instructor may choose to assign specific problems to be completed by this method.

FIGURE 9.15   Using size B or A3 sheet, divide working area into four equal parts, as shown. Draw given views of rectangle, and then the primary revolution in space II, followed by successive revolutions in spaces III and IV. Number points as shown. Omit dimensions. Use Form 3 title box.

FIGURE 9.16   Using size B or A3 sheet, divide working area into four equal parts, as shown. Draw given views of prism as shown in space I; then draw three views of the revolved prism in each succeeding space, as indicated. Number all corners. Omit dimensions. Use Form 3 title box.

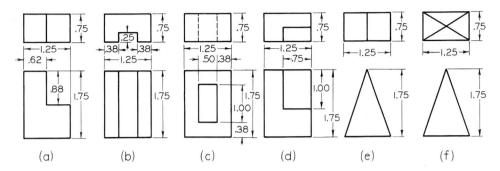

(a)   (b)   (c)   (d)   (e)   (f)

FIGURE 9.17 **Using Layout B–4 or A3–4 (adjusted) sheet, divide into four equal parts as in Fig. 9.15. In the upper two spaces, draw a simple revolution as in Fig. 9.2 and in the lower two spaces, draw a simple revolution as in Fig. 9.3, but for each problem use a block assigned from Fig. 9.17.**

Alternative Assignment: Using Layout B–4 or A3–4 (adjusted), divide into four equal parts as in Fig. 9.15. In the two left-hand spaces, draw a simple revolution as in Fig. 9.4, but use an object assigned from Fig. 9.17. In the two right-hand spaces, draw another simple revolution as in Fig. 9.4, but use a different object taken from Fig. 9.17 and revolve through 45° instead of 30°.

FIGURE 9.18 **Using Layout A–2 or A–3 or Layout A4–2 or A4–3 (adjusted), draw three views of the blocks but revolved 30° clockwise about an axis perpendicular to the top plane of projection. Do not change the relative positions of the blocks.**

FIGURE 9.19   *(opposite)* **Use Layout A–1 or A4–1 (adjusted), and divide the working area into four equal areas for four problems per sheet to be assigned by the instructor. Data for the layout of each problem are given by a coordinate system in metric dimensions. For example, in Prob. 1, point 1 is located by the scale coordinates (28 mm, 38 mm, 76 mm). The first coordinate locates the front view of the point from the left edge of the problem area. The second one locates the front view of the point from the bottom edge of the problem area. The third one locates either the top view of the point from the bottom edge of the problem area or the side view of the point from the left edge of the problem area. Inspection of the given problem layout will determine which application to use.**

1.   Revolve clockwise point 1(28, 38, 76) through 210° about the axis 2(51, 58, 94)–3(51, 8, 94).
2.   Revolve point 3(41, 38, 53) about the axis 1(28, 64, 74)–2(28, 8, 74) until point 3 is at the farthest distance behind the axis.
3.   Revolve point 3(20, 8, 84) about the axis 1(10, 18, 122)–2(56, 18, 76) through 210° and to the rear of line 1–2.
4.   Revolve point 3(5, 53, 53) about the axis 1(10, 13, 71)–2(23, 66, 71) to its extreme position to the left in the front view.
5.   Revolve point 3(15, 8, 99) about the axis 1(8, 10, 61)–2(33, 25, 104) through 180°.
6.   By revolution find the true length of line 1(8, 48, 64)–2(79, 8, 119). Scale: 1:100.
7.   Revolve line 3(30, 38, 81)–4(76, 51, 114) about axis 1(51, 33, 69)–2(51, 33, 122) until line 3–4 is shown true length and below the axis 1–2. Scale: 1:20.
8.   Revolve line 3(53, 8, 97)–4(94, 28, 91) about the axis 1(48, 23, 81)–2(91, 23, 122) until line 3–4 is in true length and above the axis.
9.   Revolve line 3(28, 15, 99)–4(13, 30, 84) about the axis 1(20, 20, 97)–2(43, 33, 58) until line 3–4 is level an above the axis.

FIGURE 9.20   **Using Layout B–3 or A3–3, draw three views of a right prism 38 mm high that has as its lower base the triangle shown above. See §9.13.**

FIGURE 9.21   **Using Layout B–3 or A3–3, draw three views of a right pyramid 51 mm high, having as its lower base the parallelogram shown above. See §9.13.**

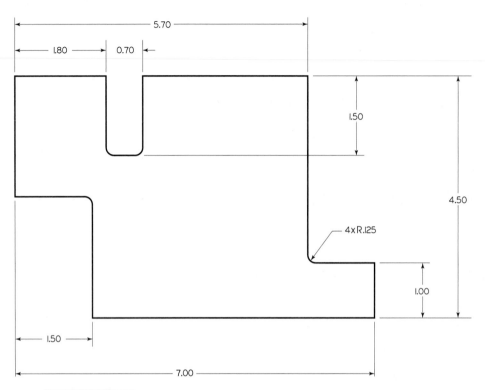

FIGURE 9.22   Using Layout A–2 or A–3 or a computer graphic system
(CAD), design a three-dimensional view of this mounting plate revolved
through 45° clockwise about an axis perpendicular to the top plane.

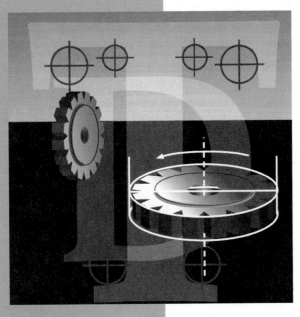

C H A P T E R   1 0

MANUFACTURING DESIGN AND PROCESSES

OBJECTIVES

After studying the material in this chapter, you should be able to:

1. Define *manufacturing* as we know it today.

2. Discuss the importance of the initial design stages in product development and manufacture.

3. Define *concurrent engineering* and show how this systematic approach integrates the design and manufacturing processes.

4. Explain the importance of computer-aided design, engineering, and manufacture in product development.

5. Explain the importance of prototypes and rapid prototyping in modern manufacturing processes.

6. Define *design for manufacture* and *design for manufacture and assembly*.

7. Explain the importance of proper material selection based on their properties, cost and availability, appearance, service life, and recycle potentials.

8. List the manufacturing processes typically used today.

9. Explain the importance of dimensional accuracy and surface finish.

10. List the typical measuring devices used in manufacturing.

11. Discuss the benefits of computer-integrated manufacturing.

OVERVIEW

Take a few moments and inspect various objects around you: your pen, watch, calculator, telephone, chair, and light fixtures. You will soon realize that all these objects had a different shape at one time. You could not find them in nature as they appear in your room. They have been transformed from various raw materials and assembled into the shapes that you now see.

Some objects are made of a single part, such as nails, bolts, wire or plastic coat hangers, metal brackets, and forks. However, most objects such as aircraft jet engines (invented in 1939), ball-point pens (1938), toasters (1926), washing machines (1910), air conditioners (1928), refrigerators (1931), photocopiers (1949), all types of machines and thousands of other products are made of an assembly of several parts made from a variety of materials. All are made by various processes that we call "manufacturing."

Manufacturing, in its broadest sense, is the process of converting raw materials into products. It encompasses (1) product design, (2) selection of raw materials, and (3) selection of processes by which manufacturing of goods take place, using various production methods and techniques.

Manufacturing is the backbone of any industrialized nation. Its importance is emphasized by the fact that, as an economic activity, it comprises approximately 20% to 30% of the value of all goods and services produced. The level of manufacturing activity is directly related to the economic health of a country. Generally, the higher the level of manufacturing activity in a country, the higher is the standard of living of its people.

Manufacturing also involves activities in which the manufactured product is itself used to make other products. Examples are large presses to shape sheet metal for car bodies, machinery to make bolts and nuts, and sewing machines for making clothing. An equally important aspect of manufacturing activities is servicing and maintaining this machinery during its useful life.

Engineering drawings, whether created with drawing instruments or CAD, are detailed instructions for manufacturing the described objects. The drawings must give information regarding shape, size, materials, finish, and, sometimes, the manufacturing process required. This chapter provides engineers with information about terms and processes used in manufacturing; information that will assist them with their drawings.

■ 10.1 "MANUFACTURING" DEFINED

The word "manufacturing" is derived from the Latin *manu factus*, meaning "made by hand." In the modern sense, manufacturing involves making products from raw materials by various processes, machinery, and operations, following a well-organized plan for each activity required. The word product means something that is produced, and the words product and production first appeared sometime during the 15th century. The word production is often used interchangeably with the word manufacturing. Whereas manufacturing engineering is the term used widely in the United States to describe this area of industrial activity, the equivalent term in other countries is production engineering.

Because a manufactured item has undergone a number of processes in which a piece of raw material has become a useful product, it has a value—defined as monetary worth or marketable price. For example, as the raw material for ceramics, clay has a certain value as mined. When the clay is used to make a ceramic cutting tool or electrical insulator, value is added to the clay. Similarly, a wire coat hanger or a nail has a value over and above the cost of a piece of wire from which it is made. Thus manufacturing has the important function of adding value.

Manufacturing may produce discrete products, meaning individual parts, or continuous products. Nails, gears, balls for bearings, beverage cans, and engine blocks are examples of discrete parts, even though they are mass produced at high production rates. On the other hand, a spool of wire, metal or plastic sheet, tubes, hose, and pipe are continuous products, which may be cut into individual lengths and thus become discrete parts.

Manufacturing is generally a complex activity involving a wide variety of resources and activities such as:

- Product design
- Purchasing
- Marketing
- Machinery and tooling
- Manufacturing
- Sales
- Process planning
- Production control
- Shipping

- Materials
- Support services
- Customer service

Manufacturing activities must be responsive to several demands and trends:

1. A product must fully meet design requirements and product specifications and standards.

2. A product must be manufactured by the most environmentally friendly and economical methods.

3. Quality must be built into the product at each stage, from design to assembly, rather than relying on quality testing after the product is made. Furthermore, quality should be appropriate to the product's use.

4. In a highly competitive environment, production methods must be sufficiently flexible so as to respond to changing market demands, types of products, production rates, production quantities, and on-time delivery to the customer.

5. New developments in materials, production methods, and computer integration of both technological and managerial activities in a manufacturing organization must constantly be evaluated with a view to their appropriate, timely, and economic implementation.

6. Manufacturing activities must be viewed as a large system, each part of which is interrelated to others. Such systems can be now modeled in order to study the effect of factors such as changes in market demands, product design, and materials. Various other factors and production methods affect product quality and cost.

7. A manufacturing organization must constantly strive for higher levels of quality and productivity (defined as the optimum use of all its resources: materials, machines, energy, capital, labor, and technology). Output per employee per hour in all phases must be maximized. Zero-based part rejection and waste are also an integral aspect of productivity.

■ 10.2 THE DESIGN PROCESS AND CONCURRENT ENGINEERING

The *design process* for a product first requires a clear understanding of the functions and the performance expected of that product. The product may be new, or

it may be a revised version of an existing product. We all have observed, for example, how the design and style of radios, toasters, watches, automobiles, and washing machines have changed. The market for a product and its anticipated uses must be defined clearly, with the assistance of sales personnel, market analysts, and others in the organization. Product design is a critical activity because it has been estimated that 70% to 80% of the cost of product development and manufacture is determined at the initial design stages. The design process is discussed at length in Chapter 14.

Traditionally, design and manufacturing activities have taken place sequentially rather than concurrently or simultaneously (Fig. 10.1a). Designers would spend considerable effort and time in analyzing components and preparing detailed part drawings; these drawings would then be forwarded to other departments in the organization, such as materials departments where, for example, particular alloys and vendor sources would be identified. The specifications would then be sent to a manufacturing department where the detailed drawings would be reviewed and processes selected for efficient production. While this approach seems logical and straightforward, in practice it has been found to be extremely wasteful or resources.

In theory, a product can flow from one department in an organization to another and directly to the marketplace, but in practice there are usually difficulties encountered. For example, a manufacturing engineer may wish to taper the flange on a part to improve its castability, or a different alloy may be desirable, thus necessitating a repeat of the design analysis stage to ensure that the product will still function satisfactorily. These iterations, also shown in Fig. 10.1a, are certainly wasteful of resources but, more importantly, of time.

There is a great desire, originally driven by the consumer electronics industry, to bring products to market as quickly as possible. The rationale is that products introduced early enjoy a greater percentage of the market and hence profits, and have a longer life before obsolescence (clearly a concern with consumer electronics). For these reasons, concurrent engineering, also called simultaneous engineering, has come to the fore.

A more modern product development approach is shown in Fig. 10.1b. While there is a general product flow from market analysis to design to manufacturing, there are recognized iterations which occur in the process. The main difference to the more modern

(a)

(b)

FIGURE 10.1   **Design and manufacturing activities traditionally have taken place sequentially rather than concurrently. With CAM, the design process can work simultaneously with the manufacturing process.**

approach is that all disciplines are involved in the early design stages, so that the iterations which naturally occur result in less wasted effort and lost time. A key to the approach is the now well-recognized importance of communication between and within disciplines. That is, while there must be communication between engineering and marketing and service functions, so too must there be avenues of interactions between engineering sub-disciplines, for example, design for manufacture, design recyclability and design for safety.

The design process begins with the development of an original product concept. An innovative approach to design is highly desirable—and even essential—at this stage for the product to be successful in the marketplace (see Chapter 14). Innovative approaches can also lead to major savings in material and production costs. The design engineer or product designer must be knowledgeable of the interrelationships among materials, design, and manufacturing, as well as the overall economics of the operation.

Concurrent engineering is a systematic approach integrating the design and manufacture of products with the view of optimizing all elements involved in the life cycle of the product. *Life cycle* means that all aspects of a product (such as design, development, production, distribution, use, and its ultimate disposal and recycling) are considered simultaneously. The basic goals of concurrent engineering are to minimize product design and engineering changes and the time and costs involved in taking the product from design concept to production and introduction of the product into the marketplace.

The philosophy of *life cycle engineering* requires that the entire life of a product be considered in the design stage (i.e., the design, production, distribution, use and disposal/recycling must be considered simultaneously). Thus a well-designed product is functional (design stage), well manufactured (production), packaged so that it safely arrives to the end user or customer (distribution), functions effectively for its intended life and has components which can be easily replaced for maintenance or repair (use), and can be disassembled so that components can be recycled (disposal).

Although the concept of concurrent engineering appears to be logical and efficient, its implementation can take considerable time and effort when those using it either do not work as a team or fail to appreciate its real benefits. It is apparent that for concurrent engineering to succeed it must:

a. Have the full support of the upper management,

b. Have multifunctional and interactive teamwork, including support groups, and

c. Utilize all available technologies.

There are numerous examples of the benefits of concurrent engineering. An automotive company, for example, has reduced the number of components in an engine by 30%, and as a result has decreased its weight by 25% and cut manufacturing time by 50%. The concurrent engineering concept can be implemented not only in large organizations but in smaller companies as well. This is particularly noteworthy in view of the fact that 98% of U.S. manufacturing establishments have fewer than 500 employees.

For both large and small companies, product design often involves preparing analytical and physical models of the product, as an aid to studying factors such as forces, stresses, deflections, and optimal part shape. The necessity for such models depends on product complexity. Today, constructing and studying analytical models is simplified through the use of computer-aided design (CAD), engineering (CAE), and manufacturing (CAM) techniques.

10.3 COMPUTER-AIDED DESIGN AND PRODUCT DEVELOPMENT

Computer-aided design (CAD) allows the designer to conceptualize objects more easily without having to make costly illustrations, models, or prototypes. These systems are now capable of rapidly and completely analyzing designs, from a simple bracket to complex structures. For example, the two-engine Boeing 777 passenger airplane was designed completely by computer (paperless design) with AutoCAD 2000 workstations linked to eight computers (Fig. 10.2). The airplane was constructed directly from the CAD/CAM software developed and no prototypes or mockups were built, unlike previous models.

10.4 COMPUTER-AIDED ENGINEERING ALLOWS FOR FUTURE MODIFICATION

Using *computer-aided engineering*, the performance of structures subjected to static or fluctuating loads and various temperatures can now be simulated, analyzed, and tested efficiently, accurately, and more quickly

FIGURE 10.2   **Boeing 777 in Flight.** *Courtesy of Boeing Co.*

than ever. The information developed can be stored, retrieved, displayed, printed, and transferred anywhere in the organization. Designs can be optimized and modifications can be made directly and easily at any time.

■ 10.5 COMPUTER-AIDED ENGINEERING LINKS ALL PHASES OF MANUFACTURING

Computer-aided manufacturing (CAM) involves all phases of manufacturing by utilizing and processing further the large amount of information on materials and processes collected and stored in the organization's database. Computers now assist manufacturing engineers and others in organizing tasks such as programming numerical control of machines; programming robots for material handling and assembly; designing tools, dies, and fixtures; and maintaining quality control.

On the basis of the models developed using the above mentioned techniques, the product designer selects and specifies the final shape and dimensions of the product, its dimensional accuracy and surface finish, and the materials to be used. The selection of materials is often made with the advice and cooperation of materials engineers, unless the design engineer is also experienced and qualified in this area. An important design consideration is how a particular component is to be assembled into the final product. Lift the hood of your car and observe how hundreds of components are put together in a limited space.

■ 10.6 THE ROLE OF PROTOTYPES AND RAPID PROTOTYPING IN PRODUCT DEVELOPMENT

The next step in the production process is to make and test a *prototype*, that is, an original working model of the product. An important development is *rapid prototyping*, which relies on CAD/CAM and various manufacturing techniques (using metallic or nonmetallic materials) to quickly produce prototypes in the form of a solid physical model of a part and at low cost. For example, prototyping new automotive components by traditional methods of shaping, forming, machining, etc. costs hundreds of millions of dollars a year; some components may take a year to produce. Rapid prototyping can cut these costs as well as development times significantly. These techniques are being advanced further so that they can be used for low-volume economical production of actual parts.

Tests of prototypes must be designed to simulate as closely as possible the conditions under which the product is to be used. These include environmental conditions such as temperature and humidity, as well as the effects of vibration and repeated use and misuse of the product. Computer-aided engineering techniques are now capable of comprehensively and rapidly performing such simulations. During this stage, modifications in the original design, materials selected, or production methods may be necessary. After this phase has been completed, appropriate process plans, manufacturing methods (Table 10.1), equipment, and tooling are selected with the cooperation of manufacturing engineers, process planners, and others involved in production.

■ 10.7 DESIGN FOR MANUFACTURE, ASSEMBLY, DISASSEMBLY, AND SERVICE

As we have seen, design and manufacturing must be intimately interrelated; they should never be viewed as separate disciplines or activities. Each part or component of a product must be designed so that it not only meets design requirements and specifications, but also can be manufactured economically and efficiently. This approach improves productivity and allows a manufacturer to remain competitive.

This broad view has become recognized as the area of *design for manufacture* (DFM). It is a comprehensive approach to production of goods and integrates the design process with materials, manufacturing methods, process planning, assembly, testing, and quality assurance. Effectively implementing design for manufacture requires that designers have a fundamental understanding of the characteristics, capabilities, and limitations of materials, manufacturing processes, and related operations, machinery, and equipment. This knowledge includes characteristics such as variability in machine performance, and dimensional accuracy and surface finish of the workpiece, processing time, and the effect of processing method on part quality.

Designers and product engineers must be able to assess the impact of design modifications on manufacturing process selection, assembly, inspection, tools and dies, and product cost. Establishing quantitative relationships is essential in order to optimize the design for ease of manufacturing and assembly at minimum product cost (also called producibility). Computer-aided design, engineering, manufacturing,

Shape of Feature	Production Method
Flat surfaces	Rolling, planing, broaching, milling, shaping, grinding
Parts with cavities	End milling, electrical-discharge machining, electrochemical machining, ultrasonic machining, casting
Parts with sharp features	Permanent mold casting, machining, grinding, fabricating, powder metallurgy
Thin hollow shapes	Slush casting, electroforming, fabricating
Tubular shapes	Extrusion, drawing, roll forming, spinning, centrifugal casting
Tubular parts	Rubber forming, expanding with hydraulic pressure, explosive forming, spinning
Curvature on thin sheets	Stretch forming, peen forming, fabricating, assembly
Opening in thin sheets	Blanking, chemical blanking, photochemical blanking
Cross-sections	Drawing, extruding, shaving, turning, centerless grinding
Square edges	Fine blanking, machining, shaving, belt grinding
Small holes	Laser, electrical discharge machining, electrochemical machining
Surface textures	Knurling, wire brushing, grinding, belt grinding, shot blasting, etching, deposition
Detailed surface feature	Coining, investment casting, permanent-mold casting, machining
Threaded parts	Thread cutting, thread rolling, thread grinding, chasing
Very large parts	Casting, forging, fabricating, assembly
Very small parts	Investment casting, machining, etching, powder metallurgy, nanofabrication, micromachining

TABLE 10.1   Shapes and Some Common Methods of Production.

and process planning techniques, using powerful computer programs, have become indispensable to those conducting such analysis. New developments include expert systems, which have optimization capabilities, thus expediting the traditional iterative process in design optimization.

After individual parts have been manufactured, they have to be assembled into a product. Assembly is an important phase of the overall manufacturing operation and requires consideration of the ease, speed, and cost of putting parts together. Also, many products must be designed so that disassembly is possible, enabling the products to be taken apart for maintenance, servicing, or recycling of their components. Because assembly operations can contribute significantly to product cost, *design for assembly* (DFA) as well as design for disassembly are now recognized as important aspects of manufacturing. Typically, a product that is easy to assemble is also easy to disassemble. The latest trend now includes design for service, ensuring that individual parts or sub-assemblies in a product are easy to reach and service.

Methodologies and computer software (CAD) have been developed for DFA utilizing 3-D conceptual designs and solid models. In this way, subassembly and assembly times and costs are minimized while maintaining product integrity and performance; the system also improves the product's ease of disassembly. The trend now is to combine design for manufacture and design for assembly into the more comprehensive *design for manufacture and assembly* (DFMA) which recognizes the inherent interrelationships between design and manufacturing.

There are several methods of assembly, such as using fasteners, adhesives, or by welding, soldering, and brazing, each with its own characteristics and requiring different operations. The use of a bolt and nut, for example, requires preparation of holes that must match in location and size. Hole generation requires operations such as drilling or punching, which take additional time, require separate operations, and produce scrap. On the other hand, products assembled with bolts and nuts can be taken apart and reassembled with relative ease.

Parts can also be assembled with adhesives. This method, which is being used extensively in aircraft and automobile production, does not require holes. However, surfaces to be assembled must match properly and be clean because joint strength is adversely affected by the presence of contaminants such as dirt, dust, oil, and moisture. Unlike mechanical fastening, adhesively joined components, as well as those that are welded, are not usually designed to be taken apart and reassembled, hence are not suitable for the important purposes of recycling individual parts in the product.

Parts may be assembled by hand or by automatic equipment and robots. The choice depends on factors such as the complexity of the product, the number of parts to be assembled, the protection required to prevent damage or scratching of finished surfaces of the parts, and the relative costs of labor and machinery required for automated assembly.

■ 10.8 MATERIAL SELECTION

An ever-increasing variety of materials is now available, each having its own characteristics, applications, advantages, and limitations. The following are the general types of materials used in manufacturing today either individually or in combination.

- Ferrous metals: carbon, alloy, stainless, and tool and die steels.
- Nonferrous metals: aluminum, magnesium, copper, nickel, titanium, superalloys, refractory metals, beryllium, zirconium, low-melting alloys, and precious metals.
- Plastics: thermoplastics, thermosets, and elastomers.
- Ceramics, glass ceramics, glasses, graphite, diamond, and diamond-like materials.
- Composite materials: reinforced plastics, metal-matrix and ceramic-matrix composites. These are also known as engineered materials.
- *Nanomaterials*, shape-memory alloys, amorphous alloys, superconductors, and various other materials with unique properties.

As new materials are developed, the selection of appropriate materials becomes even more challenging. Aerospace structures, as well as products such as sporting goods, have been at the forefront of new material usage. The trend has been to use more titanium and composites for the airframe of commercial aircraft, with a gradual decline of the use of aluminum and steel. There are constantly shifting trends in the usage of materials in all products, driven principally by economic considerations as well as other considerations.

■ 10.9 PROPERTIES OF MATERIALS

When selecting materials for products, we first consider their mechanical properties: strength, toughness, ductility, hardness, elasticity, fatigue, and creep. The strength-to-weight and stiffness-to-weight ratios of material are also important, particularly for aerospace and automotive applications. Aluminum, titanium, and reinforced plastics, for example, have higher ratios than steels and cast irons. The mechanical properties specified for a product and its components should, of course, be for the conditions under which the product is expected to function. We then consider the physical properties of density, specific heat, thermal expansion and conductivity, melting point, and electrical and magnetic properties.

Chemical properties also play a significant role in hostile as well as normal environments. Oxidation, corrosion, general degradation of properties, toxicity, and flammability of materials are among the important factors to be considered. In some commercial airline disasters, for example, many deaths have been caused by toxic fumes from burning nonmetallic materials in the aircraft cabin.

Manufacturing properties of materials determine whether they can be cast, formed, machined, welded, and heat treated with relative ease (Table 10.2). The method(s) used to process materials to the desired shapes can adversely affect the product's final properties, service life, and its cost.

■ 10.10 COST AND AVAILABILITY OF MATERIALS

Cost and availability of raw and processed materials and manufactured components are major concerns in manufacturing. Competitively, the economic aspects of material selection are as important as the technological considerations of properties and characteristics of materials.

If raw or processed materials or manufactured components are not available in the desired shapes, dimensions and quantities, substitutes and/or additional processing will be required, which can contribute significantly to product cost. For example, if we need a round bar of a certain diameter and it is not available

Alloy	Castability	Weldability	Machinability
Aluminum	E	F	G-E
Copper	F-G	F	F-G
Gray cast iron	E	D	G
White cast iron	G	VP	VP
Nickel	F	F	F
Steels	F	E	F
Zinc	E	D	E

E, excellent; G, good; F, fair; D, difficult; VP, very poor

TABLE 10.2   **General Manufacturing Characteristics of Various Alloys.**

in standard form, then we have to purchase a larger rod and reduce its diameter by some means, such as machining, drawing through a die, or grinding. It should be noted, however, that a product design can be modified to take advantage of standard dimensions of raw materials, thus avoiding additional manufacturing costs.

Reliability of supply, as well as demand, affects cost. Most countries import numerous raw materials that are essential for production. The United States, for example, imports the majority of raw materials such as natural rubber, diamond, cobalt, titanium, chromium, aluminum, and nickel from other countries. The broad political implications of such reliance on other countries are self-evident.

Different costs are involved in processing materials by different methods. Some methods require expensive machinery, others require extensive labor, and still others require personnel with special skills, a high level of education, or specialized training.

■ 10.11 APPEARANCE, SERVICE LIFE, AND RECYLING

The appearance of materials after they have been manufactured into products influences their appeal to the consumer. Color, feel, and surface texture are characteristics that we all consider when making a decision about purchasing a product.

Time- and service-dependent phenomena such as wear, fatigue, creep, and dimensional stability are important. These phenomena can significantly affect a product's performance and, if not controlled, can lead to total failure of the product. Similarly, compatibility of materials used in a product is important. Friction and wear, corrosion, and other phenomena can shorten a product's life or cause it to fail prematurely. An example is galvanic corrosion between mating parts made of dissimilar metals.

Recycling or proper disposal of materials at the end of their useful service lives has become increasingly important in an age when we are more conscious of preserving resources and maintaining a clean and healthy environment. Note, for example, the use of biodegradable packaging materials or recyclable glass bottles and aluminum beverage cans. The proper treatment and disposal of toxic wastes and materials are also a crucial consideration.

■ 10.12 MANUFACTURING PROCESSES

Before preparing a drawing for the production of a part, the drafter/designer should consider what manufacturing processes are to be used. These processes will determine the representation of the detailed feature s of the part, the choice of dimensions, and the machining of processing accuracy. Many processes are used to produce parts and shapes (Table 10.1) and there is usually more than one method of manufacturing a part from a given material. The broad categories of processing methods for materials are:

a. *Casting*: Expendable molds (i.e., sand casting) and permanent molds (Fig. 10.3).

b. *Forming and shaping*: Rolling, forging, extrusion, drawing, sheet forming, powder metallurgy, and molding (Fig. 10.4a-d).

c. *Machining*: Turning, boring, drilling, milling, planing, shaping, broaching, grinding, ultrasonic machining; chemical, electrical, and electrochemical machining; and high-energy beam machining (Fig. 10.5a-g).

Part

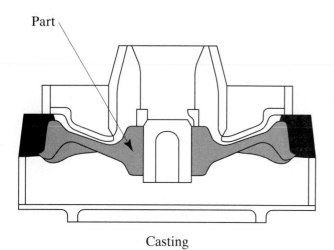

Casting

FIGURE 10.3   **This casting mold is an example of a permanent mold.**

d. *Joining*: Welding, brazing, soldering, diffusion bonding, adhesive bonding, and mechanical joining (Fig. 10.6a-b). Welding procedures and the use of standardized symbols for their representation are described in Chapters 25.

e. *Finishing*: Honing, lapping, polishing, burnishing, deburring, surface treating, coating, and plating.

Selection of a particular manufacturing process, or a series of processes, depends not only on the shape to be produced but also on many other factors pertaining to material properties (Table 10.2). Brittle and hard materials, for example, cannot be shaped easily, whereas they can be cast or machined by several methods. The manufacturing process usually alters the properties of materials. Metals that are formed at room temperature, for example, become stronger, harder, and less ductile than they were before processing.

FIGURE 10.4   **Examples of forming and shaping methods.**

(a)

(b)

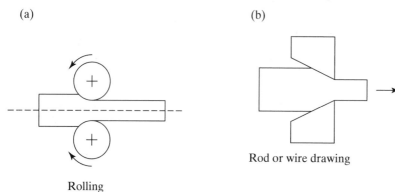

Rolling

Rod or wire drawing

(c)

(d)

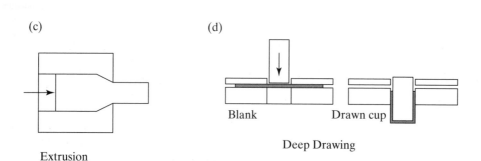

Extrusion

Blank   Drawn cup

Deep Drawing

Turning

(b)

(c)

(d)

Drilling

Milling

(e)

(f)

Dielectric
supply

Wire

(g)

Broaching

Wire electrical-discharge
machining

Grinding

FIGURE 10.5   Examples of different types of machining.

Lap
joint

Butt joint

Joining

FIGURE 10.6   Example of joining method.

(a) Casting   (b) Stamping

FIGURE 10.7   **Two steel mounting brackets (a) made by casting, (b) made by stamping.**

Two steel mounting brackets are shown in Fig. 10.7, one made by casting, and the other by stamping of sheet metal. Note that there are some differences in the designs, although the parts are basically alike. Each of these two manufacturing processes has its own advantages and limitations, as well as production rates and manufacturing cost.

Manufacturing engineers are constantly being challenged to find new solutions to manufacturing problems and cost reduction. For a long time, for example, sheet metal parts were cut and fabricated by traditional tools, punches, and dies. Although they are still widely used, some of these operations are now being replaced by laser cutting techniques (Fig. 10.8). With advances in computer technology, we can automatically control the path of the laser, thus increasing the capability for producing a wide variety of shapes accurately, repeatedly, and economically.

■ 10.13 DIMENSIONAL ACCURACY AND SURFACE FINISH

Size, thickness, and shape complexity of the part have a major bearing on the manufacturing process selected to produce it. Flat parts with thin cross-sections, for example, cannot be cast properly. Complex parts cannot be formed easily and economically, whereas they may be cast or fabricated from individual pieces.

Tolerances and surface finish obtained in hot-working operations cannot be as good as those obtained in cold-working (room temperature) operations because dimensional changes, warpage, and surface oxidation occur during processing at elevated temperatures. Some casting processes produce a better surface finish than others because of the different types of mold materials used and their surface finish.

FIGURE 10.8   **Cutting sheet metal with a laser beam.** *Courtesy of Rofin-Sinar, Inc., and Manufacturing Engineering Magazine, Society of Manufacturing Engineers.*

The size and shape of manufactured products vary widely. For example, the main landing gear for a twin-engine, 400-passenger Boeing 777 jetliner is 4.3 m (14 ft) high, with three axles and six wheels, made by forging and machining processes (Fig. 10.2). At the other extreme is the generation of a 0.05-mm (0.002-in.) diameter hole at one end of a 0.35-mm (0.014-in.) diameter needle (Fig. 10.9), using a process called electrical-discharge machining. The hole is burr-free and has a location accuracy of ±0.003 mm (0.0001 in.).

Another small-scale manufacturing example is given in Fig. 10.10, which shows microscopic gears as small as 100 m (0.004 in.) in diameter. These gears have possible applications such as powering *microrobots* to repair human cells, *microknives* in surgery, and camera shutters for precise photography. The gears are made by a special electroplating and x-ray etching technique of metal plates coated with a polymer film. The center hole in these gears is so small that a human hair cannot pass through it. Such small-scale operations are called *nanotechnology* and *nanofabrication* ("nano" meaning one billionth).

Ultraprecision manufacturing techniques and machinery are now being developed and are coming into more common use. For machining mirrorlike surfaces,

FIGURE 10.9 **A 0.05-mm hole produced in a needle, using the electrical-discharge machining process.** *Courtesy of Derata Corporation.*

Human Hair

FIGURE 10.10 **Microscopic gear with a diameter on the order of 100μm, made by a special etching process.** *Courtesy of Wisconsin Center for Applied Microelectronics, University of Wisconsin–Madison.*

for example, the cutting tool is a very sharp diamond tip and the equipment has very high stiffness and must be operated in a room where the temperature is controlled within 1 °C. Highly sophisticated techniques such as molecular-beam epitaxy and scanning-tunneling engineering are being implemented to obtain accuracies on the order of the atomic lattice (0.1 nm; 10^{-8} in.).

■ 10.14 MEASURING DEVICES USED IN MANUFACTURING

Although the machinist uses various measuring devices depending on the kind of dimensions (fractional, decimal, or metric) shown on the drawing, it is evident that to dimension correctly, the engineering designer must have at least a working knowledge of the common measuring tools. The machinists' *steel rule*, or *scale*, is a commonly used measuring tool in the shop (Fig. 10.11a). The smallest division on one scale of this rule is 0, and such a scale is used for common fractional dimensions. Also, many machinists' rules have a decimal scale with

the smallest division of .010, which is used for dimensions given on the drawing by the decimal system. For checking the nominal size of outside diameters, the *outside spring caliper* and steel scale are used, as shown in Figs. 10.11b and 10.11c. Likewise, the *inside spring caliper* is used for checking nominal dimensions, as shown in Figs. 10.11d and 10.11e. Another use for the outside caliper (Fig. 10.11f) is to check the nominal distance between holes (center to center). The *combination square* may be used for checking height (Fig. 10.11g) and for a variety of other measurements. Measuring devices are also available that have metric scales.

For dimensions that require more precise measurements, the *vernier caliper* (Figs. 10.11h and 10.11j) or the *micrometer caliper* (Fig. 10.11k) may be used. It is common practice to check measurements to 0.025 mm (.0010) with these instruments, and in some instances they are used to measure directly to 0.0025 mm (.00010).

Many of the measuring devices discussed here have been supplemented with newer, more sophisticated tools. Computerized measuring devices have broadened the range of accuracy previously attainable. Figure 10.12 illustrates an ultraprecision electronic digital readout micrometer and caliper that contain integral microprocessors. In addition to the hand-held printer/recorder providing a hard-copy output of measurements, the printer also calculates and lists statistical mean, minimum, and maximum values, as well as standard deviation.

Most measuring devices in manufacturing are adjustable so they can each be employed to measure any size within their range of designed usage. There is also a need for measuring devices designed to be used for only one particular dimension. These are called *fixed gages* because their setting is fixed and cannot be changed.

A common type of fixed gage consists of two carefully finished rounds. One might think of each of these rounds as being 25.4 mm (1.000) in diameter and 38 mm (1.5000) long. Let one of these diameters be slightly larger than the other. One can see that, for a

FIGURE 10.11   Measuring Devices Used by the Machinist.

FIGURE 10.12   **Computerized Measurement System.**
Courtesy of Fred V. Fowler Co., Inc.

certain range of hole sizes, the smaller round will enter the hole but the larger will not. If the larger round diameter is made slightly greater than the largest acceptable hole diameter and if the diameter of the smaller round is made slightly less than the smallest acceptable hole diameter, then the large round *will never go* into any acceptable hole but the small round *will go* into any acceptable hole. A fixed gage consisting of two such rounds is called a "go–no go" gage. There are, of course, many kinds of "go–no go" gages.

The subject of gages and gaging is a specialized field and involves so many technical considerations that many large companies employ highly trained workers to attend to nothing but this one feature of their operations.

■ 10.15 OPERATIONAL AND MANUFACTURING COSTS

The design and cost of tooling, the lead time required to begin production, and the effect of workpiece material on tool and die life are major considerations. Depending on its size, shape, and expected life, the cost of tooling can be substantial. For example, a set of steel dies for stamping sheet-metal fenders for automobiles may cost about $2 million.

For parts made from expensive materials, the lower the scrap rate, the more economical the production process will be; thus, every attempt should be made for *zero-base waste*. Because it generates chips, machining may not be more economical than forming operations, all other factors being the same.

Availability of machines and equipment and operating experience within the manufacturing facility are also important cost factors. If they are not available, some parts may have to be manufactured by outside firms. Automakers, for example, purchase many parts from outside vendors, or have them made by outside firms according to their specifications.

The number of parts required (quantity) and the required production rate (pieces per hour) are important in determining the processes to be used and the economics of production. Beverage cans or transistors, for example, are consumed in numbers and at rates much higher than telescopes and propellers for ships.

The operation of machinery has significant environmental and safety implications. Depending on the type of operation, some processes adversely affect the environment, such as the use of oil-base lubricants in hot metalworking processes. Unless properly controlled, such processes can cause air, water, and noise pollution. The safe use of machinery is another important consideration, requiring precautions to eliminate hazards in the workplace.

■ 10.16 CONSEQUENCES OF IMPROPER SELECTION OF MATERIALS AND PROCESSES

Numerous examples of product failure can be traced to improper selection of material or manufacturing processes or improper control of process variables. A component or a product is generally considered to have failed when:

- It stops functioning (broken shaft, gear, bolt, cable, or turbine blade).

- It does not function properly or perform within required specification limits (worn bearings, gears, tools, and dies).

- It becomes unreliable or unsafe for further use (frayed cable in a winch, crack in a shaft, poor connection in a printed-circuit board, or delamination of a reinforced plastic component).

■ 10.17 NET-SHAPE MANUFACTURING

Since not all manufacturing operations produce finished parts, additional operations may be necessary. For example, a forged part may not have the desired dimensions or surface finish; thus additional operations such as machining or grinding may be necessary. Likewise, it may be difficult, impossible, or economically undesirable to produce a part with holes using just one manufacturing process, thus necessitating additional processes such as drilling. Also, the holes produced by a particular manufacturing process may not have the proper roundness, dimensional accuracy, or surface finish, thus creating a need for additional operations such as honing.

Finishing operations can contribute significantly to the cost of a product. Consequently, the trend has been for *net-shape* or *near-net-shape manufacturing*, in which the part is made as close to the final desired dimensions, tolerances, surface finish, and specifications as possible. Typical examples of such manufacturing methods are near-net-shape forging and casting of parts, stamped sheet-metal parts, injection molding of plastics, and components made by powder-metallurgy techniques.

■ 10.18 COMPUTER-INTEGRATED MANUFACTURING

The major goals of automation in manufacturing facilities are to integrate various operations to improve productivity, increase product quality and uniformity, minimize cycle times, and reduce labor costs. Beginning in the 1940s, automation has accelerated because of rapid advances in control systems for machines and in computer technology.

Few developments in the history of manufacturing have had a more significant impact than computers. Computers are now used in a very broad range of applications, including control and optimization of manufacturing processes, material handling, assembly, automated inspection and testing of products, as well as inventory control and numerous management activities. Beginning with computer graphics and computer-aided design and manufacturing, the use of computers has been extended to *computer-integrated manufacturing* (CIM). Computer-integrated manufacturing is particularly effective because of its capability for:

- Responsiveness to rapid changes in market demand and product modification.
- Better use of materials, machinery and personnel, and reduced inventory.
- Better control of production and management of the total manufacturing operation.
- High-quality products at low cost.

The major applications of computers in manufacturing are:

a. *Computer numerical control (CNC)* is a method of controlling the movements of machine components by direct insertion of coded instructions in the form of numerical data. Numerical control was first implemented in the early 1950s and was a major advance in automation of machines.

b. *Adaptive control (AC).* The parameters in a manufacturing process are adjusted automatically to optimize production rate and product quality, and to minimize cost. Parameters such as forces, temperatures, surface finish, and dimensions of the part are monitored constantly. If they move outside the acceptable range, the system adjusts the process variables until the parameters again fall within the acceptable range.

c. *Industrial robots.* Introduced in the early 1960s, industrial robots (Figs. 10.13 and 10.14) have been replacing humans in operations that are repetitive, boring, and dangerous, thus reducing the possibility of human error, decreasing variability in product quality, and improving productivity. Robots with sensory perception capabilities are being developed (*intelligent robots*), with movements that simulate those of humans.

d. *Automated handling of materials.* Computers have allowed highly efficient handling of materials and products in various stages of completion (*work in progress*), such as from storage to machines, from machine to machine, and at the points of inspection, inventory, and shipment.

e. *Automated and robotic assembly systems* are replacing costly assembly by operators. Products are designed or redesigned so that they can be assembled more easily by machine (Fig. 10.15).

f. *Computer-aided process planning (CAPP)* is capable of improving productivity in a plant by opti-

FIGURE 10.13 **Industrial Robots.** *Courtesy of Cincinnati Milacron.*

mizing process plans, reducing planning costs, and improving the consistency of product quality and reliability. Functions such as cost estimating and work standards (time required to perform a certain operation) can also be incorporated into the system.

g. *Group technology (GT).* The concept of group technology is that parts can be grouped and produced by classifying them into families, according to similarities in design and similarities in manufacturing processes to produce the part. In this way, part designs and process plans can be standardized and families of parts can be produced efficiently and economically.

h. *Just-in-time production (JIT).* The principal of JIT is that supplies are delivered just in time to be used, parts are produced just in time to be made into subassemblies and assemblies, and products are finished just in time to be delivered to the customer. In this way, inventory-carrying costs are low, part defects are detected right away, productivity is increased, and high-quality products are made at low cost.

FIGURE 10.14   **Robotic Welding on Ford Automobile Assembly Line.**
Courtesy of Ford Motor Co.

FIGURE 10.15   **Automated Manufacturing System.** *Courtesy of Cargill Detroit.*

Digital Polish for Factory Floors

Without question, this has been the decade in which software moved irrevocably into the industrial designer's world. In corporate offices across the country, engineers have been booting up programs that let them tinker, in three dimensions, with every permutation and combination of a product's design. Be the item as lowly as a dinner plate or as complex as a Boeing 777 jet, the goal has always been the same: save time and money in getting products to market.

It was just a matter of time before engineers would aim their computers at designing and refining the assembly lines on which those products are made. Apparently, that time has come:

- These days, before it approves a design for a new car or van, the Ford Motor Company checks the plan against computer models of its factory floor. Often, through subtle changes like relocating a few seams or shaving a few millimeters from the length of a fender, Ford can lop weeks off the time it takes to prepare an old plant to make a new car.

- The Dow Chemical Company now uses computers to simulate its methods for making plastics, running what-if scenarios to fine-tune the temperatures, pressures and rates at which it feeds in raw materials. Dow can now switch production among 15 different grades of plastics in minutes, with almost no wasted material. Before computer modeling, the process took two hours and yielded lots of useless byproducts.

- The International Business Machines Corporation, the world's largest computer maker and an early convert to factory-simulation software, has learned that its assembly lines can accommodate diverse products of similar size, as long as IBM tweaked its conveyor belts to deliver different parts and products to different work areas. One early result: with almost no retooling, IBM expanded a plant in Charlotte, NC, that had made only banking systems to include voice-messaging systems, bar-code readers and devices to program pacemakers.

"No one wants to build a new assembly line, if they can re-use the one they have," said Frank Lerchenmuller, an IBM vice president for engineering technology solutions. Of course not. But until the advent of software that can simulate assembly lines and the movements of the people who run them, no one really knew a good way to gauge what they could salvage from an older factory. Now, with software from companies like Tecnomatix Technologies Inc. of Israel, Dassault Systemes of France and Aspen Technology in the United States, it is as feasible to design or remodel an entire plant as it is to reconfigure a car.

Production engineers in industries as diverse as chemicals, automobiles and aluminum smelting are manipulating virtual pictures of their plants and processes to see whether moving a clamp or adding a new ingredient will make existing equipment more productive, or will enable the same assembly line to skip freely from product to product. Some are even testing out a new virtual reality program that enables engineers wearing special goggles to detect problems by "walking through and around" a three-dimensional model of their factory designs. The entire relationship between product design and production engineering is being turned on its ear. No longer is it enough for designers to create products that can be made and maintained efficiently. Increasingly, management is asking them whether the products can be manufactured with a minimum of retooling or work disruption—and if not, whether it is worth giving up a particular feature to wring time and money from the manufacturing process.

Of course, there is little allure to the time-honored alternative to computer modeling—setting up an actual assembly line and trouble-shooting it piece by piece. "It's too risky and expensive to try new tools or methods if you have to build prototype hardware to test every change," said Rani Agarwal Finstad, director of manufacturing math-based systems for GM Powertrain, a manufacturer of car components that recently used simulation software to squeeze a month out of the process of programming robots to make new crankshafts.

The market for simulation software is growing, if slowly. Bernard Charles, Dassault's president, calculates that companies spent $300 million globally for software that simulates manufacturing operations last year. That is nothing compared with the $4 billion he estimates that industry spent on product-design software, but "there's a growing understanding that computer simulations can replace physical mockups of plants the same way they've replaced mockups of products," Mr. Charles said. Apparently, IBM agrees; it is marketing Dassault's factory-simulation software in the United States.

Testimonials to factory modeling are easy to find. The engineers who design the automation systems sold by Rockwell International have used simulation to design assembly lines that can handle different-sized items, enabling factories to produce small batches of products cost-effectively. "We're headed to where modeling will let us design plants that can efficiently build a single-lot size of one item," said Randall L. Freeman, vice president for global marketing at Rockwell Automation.

Computer simulations of the tread-etching process has enabled tire makers like Goodyear Tire and Rubber to switch production from one type of tire to another in about an hour—a process that previously took an entire work shift. And simulations have shown cookie companies like the Nabisco unit of RJR Nabisco Holdings how to use the same packaging machines to make five-pound bags for price clubs, one-pound bags for grocery stores and six-cookie packs for vending machines.

Various forces are driving the trend toward computer modeling. For one thing, computer technology has finally caught up with manufacturing pipe dreams. "Only recently have computers been powerful enough to quickly simulate what happens if you change something in a chemical reactor," said David E. Waite, Dow's manufacturing manager for information technology.

Economic and marketplace forces are at work, too. Companies that spent much of the 1990's paring ancillary product lines and work forces are now trimming capital investment, lest shareholders think they have lost their cost-cutting touch. Consumers, meanwhile, have grown increasingly picky and expect to be able to choose among myriad colors, sizes and shapes for almost any product. That means that manufacturers must mix and match parts as the orders come in. And that, in turn, means having tools that can respond to electronic commands to switch paint wells, move clamps or change packaging and labels.

Adapted from "Digital Polish for Factory Floors; Software Simulations Head to Better Assembly Lines," by Claudia H. Deutsch, *The New York Times*, March 22, 1999.

i. *Cellular manufacturing*. Cellular manufacturing involves workstations, which are *manufacturing cells* usually containing several machines and with a central robot, each performing a different operation on the part.

j. *Flexible manufacturing systems (FMS)* integrate manufacturing cells into a large unit, all interfaced with a central computer. Flexible manufacturing systems have the highest level of efficiency, sophistication, and productivity in manufacturing. Although costly, they are capable of producing parts randomly and changing manufacturing sequences on different parts quickly, thus they can meet rapid changes in market demand for various types of products.

k. *Expert systems*, which are basically intelligent computer programs, are being developed rapidly with capabilities to perform tasks and solve difficult real-life problems as human experts would.

l. *Artificial intelligence (AI)* involves the use of machines and computers to replace human intelligence. Computer-controlled systems are becoming capable of learning from experience and making decisions that optimize operations and minimize costs. *Artificial neural networks*, which are designed to simulate the thought processes of the human brain, have the capability of modeling and simulating production facilities, monitoring and controlling manufacturing processes, diagnosing problems in machine performance, conducting financial planning, and managing a company's manufacturing strategy.

■ 10.19 SHARED MANUFACTURING

Although large corporations can afford to implement modern technology and take risks, smaller companies generally have difficulty in doing so with their limited personnel, resources, and capital. More recently, the concept of *shared manufacturing* has been proposed. This consists of a regional or nationwide network of manufacturing facilities with state-of-the-art equipment for training, prototype development and small-scale production runs, and is available to help small companies develop products that compete in the global marketplace.

In view of these advances and their potential, some experts have envisaged the factory of the future. Although highly controversial and viewed as unrealistic by some, this is a system in which production will take place with little or no direct human intervention. The human role is expected to be confined to supervision, maintenance, and upgrading of machines, computers, and software.

■ KEY WORDS

ADAPTIVE CONTROL

ARTIFICIAL INTELLIGENCE

ARTIFICIAL NEURAL NETWORKS

AUTOMATED ASSEMBLY

AUTOMATED MATERIALS HANDLING

CASTING

CELLULAR MANUFACTURING

COMPUTER-AIDED DESIGN, ENGINEERING, AND
   MANUFACTURING

COMPUTER-AIDED PROCESS PLANNING

COMPUTER-INTEGRATED MANUFACTURING

COMPUTER NUMERICAL CONTROL

CONCURRENT ENGINEERING

DESIGN FOR MANUFACTURE, ASSEMBLY, DISASSEMBLY,
   AND SERVICE

DIMENSIONAL ACCURACY

EXPERT SYSTEMS

FINISHING

FIXED GAGES

FLEXIBLE MANUFACTURING SYSTEMS

FORMING

GROUP TECHNOLOGY

INDUSTRIAL ROBOTS

JOINING

JUST-IN-TIME PRODUCTION

LIFE CYCLE ENGINEERING

MACHINING

MANUFACTURING ENGINEERING

MICROKNIVES

MICROROBOTS

NANOFABRICATION

NANOTECHNOLOGY

NET-SHAPE MANUFACTURING

PRODUCIBILITY

PRODUCT COST

PROTOYTPES

RAPID PROTOTYPING

ROBOTIC ASSEMBLY

SCALE

SHAPING

SHARED MANUFACTURING

STEEL RULE

ULTRAPRECISION MANUFACTURING

■ CHAPTER SUMMARY

- Modern manufacturing involves product design, selection of materials, and selection of processes. The process of transforming raw materials into a finished product is called the manufacturing process.
- The design process requires a clear understanding of the functions and performance expected of that product.
- Concurrent engineering integrates the design process with production to optimize the life cycle of the product.
- Computer-aided design, engineering, and manufacturing are used to construct and study models (prototypes) allowing the designer to conceptualize objects more easily and more cost efficiently.
- The selection of appropriate materials is key to successful product development.
- Manufacturing processing methods have changed dramatically over the last few decades. More cost and time efficient processes can be implemented using computer-integrated manufacturing.

■ REVIEW QUESTIONS

1. List the three important phases in the manufacturing process.
2. Define concurrent engineering and explain how it can be used to enhance the design and manufacturing process.
3. Explain the benefits of rapid prototyping.
4. List four types of materials used in manufacturing today.
5. List the five broad categories of manufacturing processing.
6. Give at least two examples of nanotechnology.
7. List four types of measuring devices.
8. Give three consequences of improper selection of materials and processes.
9. List four application of computer-integrated manufacturing.

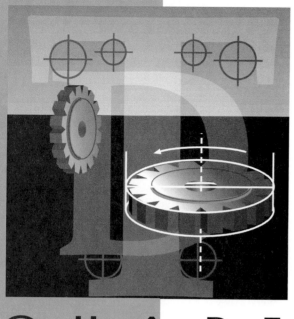

C H A P T E R   1 1

DIMENSIONING

OBJECTIVES

After studying the material in this chapter, you should be able to:

1. Use conventional dimensioning techniques to describe size and shape accurately on an engineering drawing.
2. Create and read a drawing at a specified scale.
3. Create drawings using metric, engineering, and architect scales.
4. Correctly place dimension lines, extension lines, angles, and notes.
5. Recognize aligned and unidirectional dimensioning systems.
6. Dimension circles, arcs, and inclined surfaces.
7. Apply finish symbols and notes to a drawing.

OVERVIEW

We have all heard of the "rule of thumb." Actually, at one time an inch was defined as the width of a thumb, and a foot was simply the length of a man's foot. In old England, an inch used to be "three barley corns, round and dry." In the time of Noah and the Ark, the *cubit* was the length of a man's forearm, or about 18".

In 1791, France adopted the *meter** (1 meter = 39.37"; 1" = 25.4 mm), from which the decimalized metric system evolved. In the meantime England was setting up a more accurate determination of the *yard*, which was legally defined in 1824 by act of Parliament. A foot was $\frac{1}{3}$ yard, and an inch was $\frac{1}{36}$ yard. From these specifications, graduated rulers, scales, and many types of measuring devices have been developed to achieve even more accuracy of measurement and inspection.

Until this century, common fractions were considered adequate for dimensions. Then, as designs became more complicated and it became necessary to have interchangeable parts to support mass production, more accurate specifications were required, and it became necessary to turn to the decimal-inch system or to the SI system (see §§11.9 and 11.10).

Graphical entities on engineering drawings describe shape and position. Dimensions and notes describe size and necessary manufacturing processes if the engineering drawing is to be a complete instruction for the shop technician. Objects in engineering drawings are created to scale. Large objects are drawn smaller than life size; small objects are drawn larger than life size. The ratio of drawn size to life size is the **scale**. Dimensions describe the size and location of features of an object. The correct placement of dimensions is strictly prescribed by an extensive list of drawing conventions. CAD can accurately measure the length of a drawn line, but it takes a person skilled in drawing practices to place dimensions correctly so that their interpretation is clear and unambiguous.

■ 11.1 INTERNATIONAL SYSTEM OF UNITS

The current rapid growth of worldwide science and commerce has fostered an international system of units (SI) suitable for measurements in the physical and biological sciences and in engineering. The seven basic units of measurement are the meter (length), kilogram (mass), second (time), ampere (electric current), kelvin (thermodynamic temperature), mole (amount of substance), and candela (luminous intensity).

The SI system is gradually coming into use in the United States, especially by the many multinational companies in the chemical, electronic, and mechanical industries. A tremendous effort is now under way to convert all standards of the American National Standards Institute (ANSI) to the SI units in conformity with the International Standards Organization (ISO) standards.

See inside the front cover of this book for a table converting fractional inches to decimal inches or millimeters. For the International System of Units and their United States equivalents, see Appendix 31.

■ 11.2 SIZE DESCRIPTION

In addition to a complete *shape description* of an object, as discussed in previous chapters, a drawing of the design must also give a complete *size description*; that is, it must be *dimensioned* (see ANSI/ASME Y14.5M–1994).

The need for *interchangeability* of parts is the basis for the development of modern methods of size description. Drawings today must be dimensioned so that production personnel in widely separated places can make mating parts that will fit properly when brought together for final assembly or when used as repair or replacement parts by the customer (§11.26).

The increasing need for precision manufacturing and the necessity of controlling sizes for interchangeability has shifted responsibility for size control to the designing engineer and the drafter. The production worker no longer exercises judgment in engineering matters, but only in the proper execution of instructions given on the drawings. Therefore, engineers and designers should be familiar with materials and methods of construction and with production requirements. Engineering students and designers should seize every opportunity to become familiar with the fundamental manufacturing processes.

A drawing submitted to production should show the object in its completed condition and should contain all necessary information to bring it to that final state. Therefore, in dimensioning a drawing, the de-

---

* In the SI system the meter is now defined as a length equal to the distance traveled by light of a certain wavelength in a vacuum during a time interval of 1/299,792,458 second.

signer and the drafter should keep in mind the finished piece, the production processes required, and, above all, the function of the part in the total assembly. Whenever possible—that is, when there is no conflict with functional dimensioning (§11.4)—dimensions should be given that are convenient for the individual worker or the production engineer. These dimensions should be given so that it will not be necessary to scale or assume any dimensions. No dimensions should be specified for points or surfaces that are not accessible to the worker.

Dimensions should not be duplicated or superfluous (§11.30). Only those needed to produce and inspect the part against the design specifications should be given. Students often mistakenly give the dimensions used *to make the drawing*. These are not necessarily the dimensions required. There is much more to the theory of dimensioning, as we will see.

■ 11.3 SCALE OF DRAWING

Drawings should be made to scale, and the scale should be indicated in the title block even though the worker is never expected to scale the drawing or print for a needed dimension. (See §3.31 for indications of scales.)

A heavy straight line should be drawn under any dimension that is not to scale (see Fig. 11.15), or the abbreviation *NTS* (not to scale) should be indicated. This procedure may be necessary when a change made in a drawing is not important enough to justify making an entirely new drawing.

When a drawing is prepared on a CAD system, agreement should be maintained between the defining dimensions, true size, location, and direction in all views of the object represented.

Many preprinted drawing borders include a note such as "Do not scale drawing for dimensions."

■ 11.4 LEARNING TO DIMENSION

Dimensions are given in the form of linear distances, angles, or notes regardless of the dimensioning units being used. The ability to dimension properly in millimeters, decimal inch, or fractional inch requires the following.

1. The student must learn the *technique of dimensioning*: the character of the lines, the spacing of dimensions, the making of arrowheads, and so forth. A typical dimensioned drawing is shown in Fig. 11.1.

The Increasing Complexity of Modern Designs Requires the Production of Precisely Dimensioned Drawings. *Courtesy of Diamond Star Motors.*

Note the strong contrast between the visible lines of the object and the thin lines used for the dimensions.

2. The student must learn the rules of *placement of dimensions* on the drawing. These practices assure a logical and practical arrangement with maximum legibility.

3. The student should learn the *choice of dimensions*. Formerly, manufacturing processes were considered the governing factor in dimensioning. Now function is considered first and the manufacturing processes second. The proper procedure is to dimension tentatively for function and then review the dimensioning to see if any improvements from the standpoint of production can be made without adversely affecting the functional dimensioning. A "geometric breakdown" (§11.20) will assist the beginner in selecting dimensions. In most cases dimensions thus determined will be functional, but this method should be accompanied by a logical analysis of the functional requirements.

■ 11.5 LINES USED IN DIMENSIONING

A **dimension line** (Fig. 11.2a) is a thin, dark, solid line terminated by arrowheads, which indicates the direction and extent of a dimension. In machine drawing, the dimension line is broken, usually near the middle, to provide an open space for the dimension figure. In structural and architectural drawing, it is customary to place the dimension figure above an unbroken dimension line.

As shown in Fig. 11.2b, the dimension line nearest the object outline should be spaced at least 10 mm ($\frac{3}{8}''$)

FIGURE 11.1 Dimensioning Technique. Dimensions in millimeters.

FIGURE 11.2 Dimensioning Technique.

(a)   (b)   (c)

away. All other parallel dimension lines should be at least 6 mm ($\frac{1}{4}''$) apart, and more if space is available. *The spacing of dimension lines should be uniform throughout the drawing.*

An **extension line** (Fig. 11.2a) is a thin, dark, solid line that "extends" from a point on the drawing to which a dimension refers. The dimension line meets the extension lines at right angles except in special cases (see Fig. 11.6a). A gap of about 1.5 mm ($\frac{1}{16}''$) should be left where the extension line would join the object outline. The extension line should extend about 3 mm ($\frac{1}{8}''$) beyond the outermost arrowhead (Figs. 11.2a and 11.2b).

The foregoing dimensions for lettering height, spacing, and so on should be increased approximately 50% for drawings that are to be microfilmed and then reduced to one-half size for the working print.

Otherwise the lettering and dimensioning often are not legible.

A **center line** is a thin, dark line composed of alternate long and short dashes and used to represent axes of symmetrical parts and to denote centers. As shown in Fig. 11.2c, center lines are commonly used as extension lines in locating holes and other features. When so used, the center line crosses over other lines of the drawing without gaps. A center line should always end in a long dash.

■ 11.6 PLACEMENT OF DIMENSION AND EXTENSION LINES

The correct placement of dimension lines and extension lines is shown in Fig. 11.3a. The shorter dimensions are nearest to the object outline. Dimension lines

FIGURE 11.3 Dimension and Extension Lines.

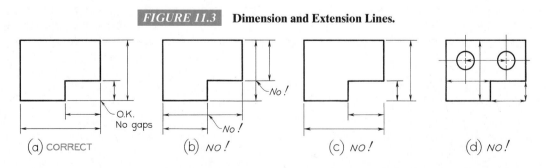

(a) CORRECT   (b) *NO!*   (c) *NO!*   (d) *NO!*

should not cross extension lines, as in Fig. 11.3b, which results from placing the shorter dimensions outside. Note that it is perfectly satisfactory to cross extension lines (Fig. 11.3a), but they should never be shortened (Fig. 11.3c). A dimension line should never coincide with, or form a continuation of, any line of the drawing (Fig. 11.3d). Avoid crossing dimension lines wherever possible.

Dimensions should be lined up and grouped together as much as possible, as in Fig. 11.4a, and not as in Fig. 11.4b.

In many cases, extension lines and center lines must cross visible lines of the object (Fig. 11.5a). When this occurs, gaps should not be left in the lines (Fig. 11.5b).

Dimension lines are normally drawn at right angles to extension lines, but an exception may be made in the interest of clarity, as in Fig. 11.6a. In crowded conditions, gaps may be left in extension lines near arrowheads so that the dimensions show clearly (Fig. 11.6b). In general, avoid dimensioning to hidden lines (Fig. 11.6c).

■ 11.7 ARROWHEADS

Arrowheads (Fig. 11.7) indicate the extent of dimensions. They should be uniform in size and style throughout the drawing and not varied according to the size of the drawing or the length of dimensions. Arrowheads should be drawn freehand, and the length and width should be in a ratio of 3:1. The length of the arrowhead should be equal to the height of the dimension whole numbers. For average use, make arrowheads about 3 mm ($\frac{1}{8}''$) long and very narrow (Fig. 11.7a). Use strokes toward the point or away from the point desired (Figs. 11.7b to 11.7d). The method in Fig. 11.7b is easier when the strokes are drawn toward the drafter. For best appearance, fill in the arrowhead, as in Fig. 11.7d.

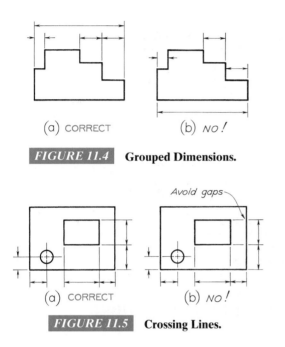

FIGURE 11.4   **Grouped Dimensions.**

FIGURE 11.5   **Crossing Lines.**

FIGURE 11.6   **Placement of Dimensions.**

FIGURE 11.7   **Arrowheads.**

■ 11.8 LEADERS

A **leader** (Fig. 11.8) is a thin, solid line leading from a note or dimension and terminating in an arrowhead or a dot touching the part to which attention is directed. Arrowheads should always terminate on a line, such as the edge of a hole; dots should be within the outline of the object. A leader should generally be an inclined straight line, if possible, except for the short horizontal shoulder (6 mm or $\frac{1}{4}''$, approx.) extending from midheight of the lettering *at the beginning or end of a note*.

A leader to a circle should be radial; that is, if extended, it would pass through the center. A drawing presents a more pleasing appearance if leaders near each other are drawn parallel. Leaders should cross as few lines as possible and should never cross each other. They should not be drawn parallel to nearby lines of the drawing, allowed to pass through a corner of the view, made unnecessarily long, or drawn horizontally or vertically on the sheet. A leader should be drawn at a large angle and terminate with the appropriate arrowhead, or with a dot (Fig. 11.8f).

■ 11.9 FRACTIONAL, DECIMAL, AND METRIC DIMENSIONS

In the early days of machine manufacturing in the United States, workers would scale the undimensioned design drawing to obtain any needed dimensions, and it was their responsibility to see that the parts fit together properly. Workers were skilled and very accurate, and excellent fits were obtained. Hand-built machines were often beautiful examples of precision craftsmanship.

The system of units and common fractions is still used in architectural and structural work, in which close accuracy is relatively unimportant and the steel tape or framing square is used to set off measurements. Architectural and structural drawings are therefore often dimensioned in this manner. Also, certain commercial commodities, such as pipe and lumber, are identified by standard nominal designations that are close approximations of actual dimensions.

As industry has progressed, there has been greater and greater demand for more accurate specifications of the important functional dimensions—more accurate than the $\frac{1}{64}''$ permitted by the engineers', architects', and machinists' scale. Since it was cumbersome to use still smaller fractions, such as $\frac{1}{128}$ or $\frac{1}{256}$, it became the practice to give decimal dimensions, such as 4.2340 and 3.815, for the dimensions requiring accuracy. However, some dimensions, such as standard nominal sizes of materials, punched holes, drilled holes, threads, keyways, and other features produced by tools that are so designated are still expressed in whole numbers and common fractions.

Thus, drawings may be dimensioned entirely with whole numbers and common fractions, or entirely with decimals, or with a combination of the two. However, more recent practice adopted the decimal-inch system, and current practice also utilizes the metric system as recommended by ANSI. Millimeters and inches in the decimal form can be added, subtracted, multiplied, and divided more easily than can fractions.

For inch-millimeter equivalents of decimal and common fractions, see inside the front cover of this book. For additional metric equivalents, see Appendix 31.

■ 11.10 DECIMAL SYSTEMS

A decimal system based on the decimal inch or the millimeter as a linear unit of measure has many advantages and is compatible with most measuring devices and machine tools. Metric measurement is based on the meter as a linear unit of measure, but the millimeter is used on most engineering drawings. To facilitate the changeover to metric dimensions, many drawings are dual-dimensioned in millimeters and decimal inches (see §11.11).

Complete decimal dimensioning employs decimals for all dimensions and designations except where cer-

FIGURE 11.8   **Leaders.**

(a)   (b)   (c)   (d)   (e)   (f)

tain commercial commodities, such as pipe and lumber, are identified by standardized nominal designations. *Combination dimensioning* employs decimals for all dimensions except the designations of nominal sizes of parts or features, such as bolts, screw threads, keyseats, or other standardized fractional designations (ANSI/ASME Y14.5M–1994).

In these systems, two-place inch or one-place millimeter decimals are used when a common fraction has been regarded as sufficiently accurate.

In the combination dimensioning system, common fractions may be used to indicate nominal sizes of materials, drilled holes, punched holes, threads, keyways, and other standard features.

One-place millimeter decimals are used when tolerance limits of ±0.1 mm or more can be permitted. Two (or more)-place millimeter decimals are used for tolerance limits less than ±0.1 mm. Fractions are considered to have the same tolerance as two-place decimal-inch dimensions when determining the number of places to retain in the conversion to millimeters. Keep in mind that 0.1 mm is approximately equal to .004 inch.

Two-place inch decimals are used when tolerance limits of ±.01″ or more can be permitted. Three or more decimal places are used for tolerance limits less than ±.01″. In two-place decimals, the second place preferably should be an even digit (for example, .02, .04, and .06 are preferred to .01, .03, or .05) so that

when the dimension is divided by 2, as is necessary in determining the radius from a diameter, the result will be a decimal of two places. However, odd two-place decimals are used when required for design purposes, such as in dimensioning points on a smooth curve or when strength or clearance is a factor.

A typical example of the use of the complete decimal-inch system is shown in Fig. 11.9. The use of the preferred decimal-millimeter system is shown in Fig. 11.10.

When a decimal value is to be rounded off to fewer places than the calculated number, regardless of the unit of measurement involved, the method prescribed is as follows.

The last figure to be retained should not be changed when the figure beyond the last figure to be retained is less than 5.

EXAMPLE 3.46325, if rounded off to three places, should be 3.463.

The last figure to be retained should be increased by 1 when the figure beyond the last figure to be retained is greater than 5 (or two figures are greater than 50).

EXAMPLE 8.37652, if rounded off to three places, should be 8.377.

The last figure to be retained should be unchanged if it is even, or increased by 1 if odd, when followed by exactly 5.

FIGURE 11.9 **Complete Decimal Dimensioning.**

FIGURE 11.10   **Complete Metric Dimensioning.**

EXAMPLE 4.365 becomes 4.36 when rounded off to two places. Also, 4.355 becomes 4.36 when cut off to two places.

The use of the metric system means not only a changeover of measuring equipment but also a changeover in thinking on the part of drafters and designers. They must stop thinking in terms of inches and common fractions and think in terms of millimeters and other SI units. Dimensioning practices remain essentially the same; only the units are changed (compare Figs. 11.9 and 11.10).

Shop scales and drafting scales for use in the decimal-inch and metric systems are available in a variety of forms. Refer to the inside of the front cover for a two-, three-, and four-place decimal equivalent table.

Once the metric system is installed, the advantages in computation, in checking, and in simplified dimensioning techniques are considerable.

■ 11.11 DIMENSION FIGURES

The importance of good lettering of dimension figures cannot be overstated. The shop produces according to the directions on the drawing, and to save time and prevent costly mistakes, all lettering should be perfectly legible. A complete discussion of numerals is given in §§4.18–4.20.

Legibility should never be sacrificed by crowding dimension figures into limited spaces. For every such case there is a practical and effective method, as shown in Fig. 11.11. In Fig. 11.11a, there is only enough room for the figure, and the arrowheads are placed outside. In Fig. 11.11b, both the arrowheads and the figure are placed outside. Other methods are shown in Figs. 11.11c and 11.11d.

If necessary, a removed partial view may be drawn to an enlarged scale to provide the space needed for clear dimensioning (Fig. 7.22).

Make all decimal points bold, allowing ample space. Where the metric dimension is a whole number, neither a decimal point nor a zero is given (Figs. 11.11a and 11.11d). Where the metric dimension is less than 1 millimeter, a zero precedes the decimal point (Fig. 11.11b). Where the dimension exceeds a whole number by a fraction of 1 millimeter, the last digit to the right of the decimal point is not followed by a zero

FIGURE 11.11   **Dimension Figures. Metric dimensions (c)–(f).**

(c)   (d)   (e)   (f)

FIGURE 11.12   Decimal Dimension figures. Metric dimensions (a)–(d).

except when expressing tolerances (Figs. 11.12c and 11.12d).

Methods of lettering and displaying decimal dimension figures are shown in Fig. 11.11. Where the decimal-inch dimension is used on drawings, a zero is not used before the decimal point of values less than 1 inch (Figs. 11.12f to 11.12j). The decimal-inch dimension is expressed to the same number of decimal places as its tolerance. Thus, zeros are added to the right of the decimal point as necessary (Fig. 11.12e).

Never letter a dimension figure over any line on the drawing, but break the line if necessary. Place dimension figures outside a sectioned area if possible (Fig. 11.13a). When a dimension must be placed on a sectioned area, leave an opening in the section lining for the dimension figure (Fig. 11.13b).

In a group of parallel dimension lines, the numerals should be staggered, as in Fig. 11.14a, and not stacked up one above the other, as in Fig. 11.14b.

DUAL DIMENSIONING

Dual dimensioning is used to show metric and decimal-inch dimensions on the same drawing. Two methods of displaying the dual dimensions are as follows.

POSITION METHOD The millimeter value is placed above the inch dimension and is separated by a dimension line or an added line for some dimensions when the unidirectional system of dimensioning is used. An alternative arrangement in a single line places the millimeter dimension to the left of the inch dimension, separated by a slash line (virgule). Each drawing should illustrate the dimension identification as $\frac{\text{MILLIMETER}}{\text{INCH}}$ or MILLIMETER/INCH. (Placement of the inch dimension above or to the left of the millimeter is also acceptable.)

EXAMPLES

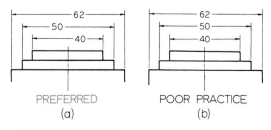

FIGURE 11.13   Dimensions and Section Lines. Metric.

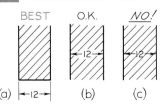

FIGURE 11.14   Staggered Numerals. Metric.

BRACKET METHOD The millimeter dimension is enclosed in square brackets, [ ]. The location of this dimension is optional but should be uniform on any drawing—that is, above or below or to the left or right of the inch dimension. Each drawing should include a note to identify the dimension values as DIMENSIONS IN [ ] ARE MILLIMETERS.

EXAMPLES

When converting a decimal-inch dimension to millimeters, multiply the inch dimension by 25.4 and round off to one less digit to the right of the decimal point than for the inch value (see §11.10). When converting a millimeter dimension to inches, divide the millimeter dimension by 25.4 and round off to one more digit to the right of the decimal point than for the millimeter value.

■ 11.12 DIRECTION OF DIMENSION FIGURES

Two systems of reading direction for dimension figures are available. In the preferred *unidirectional system*, approved by ANSI (Fig. 11.15a), all dimension figures and notes are lettered horizontally on the sheet and are read from the bottom of the drawing. The unidirectional system has been extensively adopted in the aircraft, automotive, and other industries because it is easier to use and read, especially on large drawings. In the *aligned system* (Fig. 11.15b), all dimension figures are aligned with the dimension lines so that they may be read from the right side of the sheet. Dimension lines in this system should not run in the directions included in the shaded area of Fig. 11.16, if avoidable.

In both systems, dimensions and notes shown with leaders are aligned with the bottom of the drawing. Notes without leaders should also be aligned with the bottom of the drawing.

■ 11.13 MILLIMETERS AND INCHES

Millimeters are indicated by the lowercase letters mm placed one space to the right of the numeral; thus, 12.5 mm. *Meters* are indicated by the lowercase m placed similarly; thus, 50.6 m. *Inches* are indicated by the symbol " placed slightly above and to the right of the numeral; thus, $2\frac{1}{2}$". *Feet* are indicated by the symbol ' similarly placed; thus, $3'-0$, $5'-6$, $10'-0\frac{1}{4}$. It is customary in such expressions to omit the inch marks.

It is standard practice to omit mm designations and inch marks on a drawing except when there is a possibility of misunderstanding. For example, 1 VALVE should be 1" VALVE, and 1 DRILL should be 1" DRILL or 1 mm DRILL. Where some inch dimensions are shown on a millimeter-dimensioned drawing, the abbreviation IN. follows the inch values.

In some industries, all dimensions, regardless of size, are given in inches; in others, dimensions up to 72" inclusive are given in inches, and those greater are given in feet and inches. In structural and architectural

FIGURE 11.15 Directions of Dimension Figures.

(a) UNIDIRECTIONAL SYSTEM

(b) ALIGNED SYSTEM

FIGURE 11.16   Directions of Dimensions.

drafting, all dimensions of 1′ or over are usually expressed in feet and inches.

If suitable, the drawing should contain a note stating "Unless otherwise specified, all dimensions are in millimeters" (or in inches, as applicable).

■ 11.14 DIMENSIONING ANGLES

Angles are dimensioned preferably by means of an angle in degrees and a linear dimension (Fig. 11.17a), or by means of coordinate dimensions of the two legs of a right triangle (Fig. 11.17b). The coordinate method is more suitable for work requiring a high degree of accuracy. Variations of angle (in degrees) are hard to control because the amount of variation increases with the distance from the vertex of the angle. Methods of indicating various angles are shown in Figs. 11.17c to 11.17f. Tolerances of angles are discussed in §12.18.

When degrees alone are indicated, the symbol ° is used. When minutes alone are given, the number should be preceded by 0°; thus 0°23′. In all cases,

FIGURE 11.18   Angles in Civil Engineering Projects.

whether in the unidirectional system or in the aligned system, the dimension figures for angles are lettered on horizontal guide lines. (For a general discussion of angles, see §4.2.)

In civil engineering drawings, **slope** represents the angle with the horizontal, whereas **batter** is the angle referred to the vertical. Both are expressed by making one member of the ratio equal to 1, as shown in Fig. 11.18. **Grade**, as of a highway, is similar to slope but is expressed in percentage of rise per 100′ of run. Thus a 20′ rise in a 100′ run is a grade of 20%.

In structural drawings, angular measurements are made by giving the ratio of "run" to "rise," with the larger size being 12″. These right triangles are referred to as **bevels**.

■ 11.15 DIMENSIONING ARCS

A circular arc is dimensioned in the view in which its true shape is shown by giving the numerical value of its radius preceded by the abbreviation R (Fig. 11.19). The centers may be indicated by small crosses to clarify the drawing but not for small or unimportant radii.

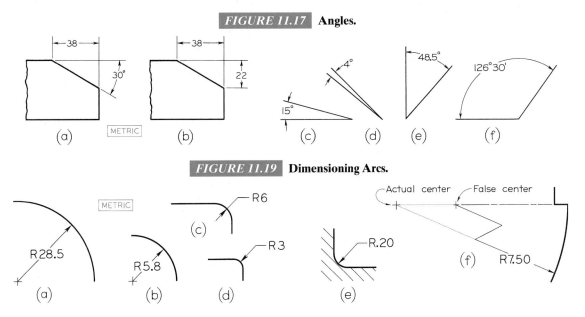

FIGURE 11.17   Angles.

FIGURE 11.19   Dimensioning Arcs.

Crosses should not be shown for undimensioned arcs. As shown in Figs. 11.19a and 11.19b, when there is room enough, both the numeral and the arrowhead are placed inside the arc. In Fig. 11.19c, the arrowhead is left inside, but the numeral had to be moved outside. In Fig. 11.19d, both the arrowhead and the numeral had to be moved outside. Figure 11.19e shows an alternate method that can be used when section lines or other lines are in the way. Note that in the unidirectional system, all of these numerals are lettered horizontally on the sheet.

For a long radius (Fig. 11.19f), when the center falls outside the available space, the dimension line is drawn toward the actual center; but a false center may be indicated and dimension line "jogged" to it, as shown.

■ 11.16 FILLETS AND ROUNDS

Individual fillets and rounds are dimensioned as any arc (Figs. 11.19c to 11.19e). If there are only a few and they are obviously the same size, as in Fig. 11.43e, one typical radius is sufficient. However, fillets and rounds are often quite numerous on a drawing, and most of them are likely to be some standard size, as R3 and R6 when dimensioning in metric or R125 and R250 when using the decimal-inch system.

In such cases it is customary to give a note in the lower portion of the drawing to cover all uniform fillets and rounds; thus,

FILLETS R6 AND ROUNDS R3 UNLESS
OTHERWISE SPECIFIED

or

ALL CASTING RADII R6 UNLESS NOTED

or simply

ALL FILLETS AND ROUNDS R6

For a discussion of fillets and rounds in the shop, see §11.5.

■ 11.17 FINISH MARKS

A **finish mark** is used to indicate that a surface is to be machined, or finished, as on a rough casting or forging. To the patternmaker or diemaker, a finish mark means that allowance of extra metal in the rough workpiece must be provided for the machining (see §11.4). On drawings of parts to be machined from rolled stock, finish marks are generally unnecessary, for it is obvious that the surfaces are finished. Similarly, it is not necessary to show finish marks when an operation is specified in a note that indicates machining, such as drilling, reaming, boring, countersinking, counterboring, and broaching, or when the dimension implies a finished surface, such as ∅6.22–6.35 (metric) or ∅2.45–2.50 (decimal-inch).

Three styles of finish marks, the general ∨ symbol, the new basic √ symbol, and the traditional ƒ symbol, are used to indicate an ordinary smooth machined surface. The ∨ symbol is like a capital V, made about 3 mm ($\frac{1}{8}$") high in conformity with the height of dimensioning lettering (Fig. 11.20a). The extended √ symbol, preferred by ANSI, is like a larger capital with the right leg extended (Fig. 11.20b). The short leg is made about 5 mm ($\frac{3}{16}$") high and the height of the long leg is about 10 mm ($\frac{3}{8}$"). The basic symbol may be altered for more elaborate surface texture specifications (see §12.22).

For best results, all finished marks should be drawn with the aid of a template or the 30° × 60° triangle. The point of the ∨ symbol should be directed inward toward the body of metal in a manner similar to that of a tool bit. The √ symbol is not shown upside down (see Figs. 11.35 and 12.46).

The preferred form and placement for the ƒ symbol are shown in Fig. 11.20e. The ƒ symbol is in

FIGURE 11.20 Finish Marks.

limited use and found mainly on drawings made in accordance with earlier drafting standards.

Figure 11.20c shows a simple casting having several finished surfaces; in Fig. 11.20d, two views of the same casting show how the finish marks are indicated on a drawing. *The finish mark is shown only on the edge view of a finished surface and is repeated in any other view in which the surface appears as a line, even if the line is a hidden line.*

The several kinds of finishes are detailed in machine shop practice manuals. The following terms are among the most commonly used: *finish all over, rough finish, file finish, sand blast, pickle, scrape, lap, hone, grind, polish, burnish, buff, chip, spotface, countersink, counterbore, core, drill, ream, bore, tap, broach,* and *knurl.* When it is necessary to control the surface texture of finished surfaces beyond that of an ordinary machine finish, the ✓ symbol is used as a base for the more elaborate surface quality symbols discussed in §12.22.

If a part is to be finished all over, finish marks should be omitted, and a general note, such as FINISH ALL OVER or FAO, should be lettered on the lower portion of the sheet.

■ 11.18 DIMENSIONS ON OR OFF VIEWS

Dimensions should not be placed on a view unless doing so promotes the clearness of the drawing. The ideal form is shown in Fig. 11.21a, in which all dimensions are placed outside the view. Compare this with the evidently poor practice in Fig. 11.21b. This is not to say that a dimension should never be placed on a view, for in many cases (particularly in complicated drawings) this is necessary (Fig. 11.21c). Certain radii and other dimensions are given on the views, but in each case investigation will reveal a good reason for placing the dimension on the view. *Place dimensions outside of views, except where directness of application and clarity are gained by placing them on the views, where they will be closer to the features dimensioned.* When a dimension must be placed in a sectioned area or on the view, leave an opening in the sectioned area or a break in the lines for the dimension figures (see Figs. 11.13b and 11.21c).

■ 11.19 CONTOUR DIMENSIONING

Views are drawn to describe the shapes of the various features of the object, and dimensions are given to define exact sizes and locations of those shapes. It follows that *dimensions should be given where the shapes are shown*—that is, in the views where the contours are delineated, as in Fig. 11.22a. Incorrect placement of the dimensions is shown in Fig. 11.22b.

Attachment of individual dimensions directly to the contours that show the shapes being dimensioned automatically prevents the attachment of dimensions to hidden lines, as shown for the depth 10 of the slot in Fig. 11.22b. It also prevents the attachment of dimensions to a visible line, the meaning of which is not clear in a particular view, such as dimension 20 for the height of the base in Fig. 11.22b.

Although the placement of notes for holes follows the contour rule wherever possible (Fig. 11.22a), the diameter of an external cylindrical shape is preferably given in the rectangular view, where it can be readily found near the dimension for the length of the cylinder (see Figs. 11.23b, 11.26, and 11.27).

■ 11.20 GEOMETRIC BREAKDOWN

Engineering structures are composed largely of simple geometric shapes, such as the prism, cylinder, pyramid,

FIGURE 11.21 **Dimensions On or Off the Views.**

(a) PREFERRED   (b) POOR PRACTICE   (c) IN COMPLICATED DRAWINGS DIMENSIONS OFTEN HAVE TO BE PLACED ON THE VIEW.

FIGURE 11.22 Contour Dimensioning.

FIGURE 11.23 Geometric Breakdown.

cone, and sphere (Fig. 11.23a). They may be exterior (positive) or interior (negative) forms. For example, a steel shaft is a positive cylinder, and a round hole is a negative cylinder.

These shapes result directly from the design necessity of keeping forms as simple as possible and from the requirements of the fundamental manufacturing operations. Forms having plane surfaces are produced by planing, shaping, milling, and so forth,

while forms having cylindrical, conical, or spherical surfaces are produced by turning, drilling, reaming, boring, countersinking, and other rotary operations (see Chapter 10, Manufacturing Design and Processes).

The dimensioning of engineering structures involves two basic steps:

1. Give the dimensions showing the sizes of the simple geometric shapes, called **size dimensions**.

2. Give the dimensions locating these elements with respect to each other, called **location dimensions**.

The process of geometric analysis is very helpful in dimensioning any object, but it must be modified when there is a conflict either with the function of the part in the assembly or with the manufacturing requirements in the shop.

Figure 11.23b is a multiview drawing of the object shown in isometric in Fig. 11.23a. Here it will be seen that each geometric shape is dimensioned with size dimensions and that these shapes are then located with respect to each other with location dimensions. Note that a *location dimension locates a three-dimensional geometric element* and not just a surface; otherwise, all dimensions would have to be classified as location dimensions.

USING CAD TO DIMENSION

Dimensions can be created somewhat automatically using CAD. The size, appearance, and dimension value can all be generated automatically. Alignment of the dimension values and whether to show metric or inch units or both can all be accomplished using CAD. Because of the complexity and intelligence that must be used in selecting which dimensions to place in the drawing, most CAD systems require you to pick what you will dimension and where to place the dimension. Some systems will generate the dimensions totally automatically, but you must review them carefully making sure that the dimensions given describe the intent for your design and the permissible tolerances.

CAD Systems Make Dimensioning Easy and Often Automatic. *Courtesy of SDRC, Milford, OH.*

■ 11.21 SIZE DIMENSIONS: PRISMS

The right rectangular prism is probably the most common geometric shape (see Fig. 4.7). Front and top views are dimensioned as shown in Figs. 11.24a and 11.24b. The height and width are given in the front view and the depth in the top view. The vertical dimensions can be placed on the left or right, provided both of them are placed in line. The horizontal dimension applies to both the front and top views and should be placed between them, as shown, and not above the top or below the front view.

Front and side views should be dimensioned as in Figs. 11.24c and 11.24d. The horizontal dimensions can be placed above or below the views, provided both are placed in line. The dimension between views applies to both views and should not be placed elsewhere without a special reason.

An application of size dimensions to a machine part composed entirely of rectangular prisms is shown in Fig. 11.25.

■ 11.22 SIZE DIMENSIONS: CYLINDERS

The right circular cylinder is the next most common geometric shape and is commonly seen as a shaft or a hole. The general method of dimensioning a cylinder is to give both its diameter and its length in the rectangular view (Fig. 11.26). If the cylinder is drawn in a vertical position, its length or altitude may be given at the right, as in Fig. 11.26a, or on the left, as in Fig. 11.26b. If the cylinder is drawn in a horizontal position, the length may be given above the rectangular view, as in Fig. 11.26c, or below, as in Fig.11.26d. An application showing the dimensioning of cylindrical shapes is shown in Fig. 11.27. The use of a diagonal diameter in

FIGURE 11.24 **Dimensioning Rectangular Prisms.**

(a)

(b)

(c)

(d)

FIGURE 11.25 **Dimensioning a Machine Part Composed of Prismatic Shapes.**

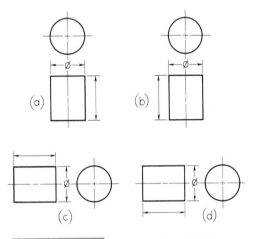

FIGURE 11.26 **Dimensioning Cylinders.**

the circular view, in addition to the method shown in Fig. 11.26, is not recommended except in special cases when clarity is improved. The use of several diagonal diameters on the same center is definitely to be discouraged, because the result is usually confusing.

The radius of a cylinder should never be given because measuring tools, such as the micrometer caliper, are designed to check diameters.

Small cylindrical holes, such as drilled, reamed, or bored holes, are usually dimensioned by means of notes specifying the diameter and the depth, with or without manufacturing operations (Figs. 11.27 and 11.32).

The diameter symbol Ø should be given before all diametral dimensions (Fig. 11.28a) (ANSI/ASME Y14.5M–1994). In some cases, the symbol Ø may be used to eliminate the circular view (Fig. 11.28b). The abbreviation DIA following the numerical value will be found on older decimal-inch drawings.

■ 11.23 SYMBOLS AND SIZE DIMENSIONS: MISCELLANEOUS SHAPES

Traditional terms and abbreviations used to describe various shapes and manufacturing processes, in addition to size specifications, are employed throughout this text. A variety of dimensioning symbols were introduced by ANSI/ASME (Y14.5M–1994) to replace traditional terms or abbreviations. These symbols are given with construction details in Fig. 11.29. Traditional terms and abbreviations are suitable for use where the symbols are not desired. Typical applications of some of these symbols are given in Fig. 11.30.

FIGURE 11.27 **Dimensioning a Machine Part That Is Composed of Cylindrical Shapes.**

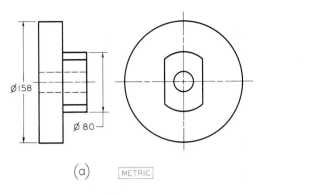

USE OF " Ø " TO INDICATE CIRCULAR SHAPE

USE OF " Ø " TO OMIT CIRCULAR VIEW

FIGURE 11.28 Use of Ø or DIA in Dimensioning Cylinders.

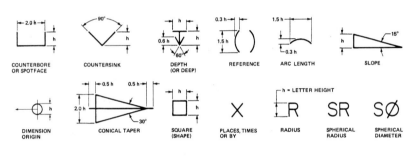

FIGURE 11.29 Form and Proportion of Dimensioning Symbols (ANSI/ASME Y14.5M–1994).

(a) BASIC DIMENSION SYMBOL

(b) COUNTERBORE OR SPOTFACE SYMBOL

(c) COUNTERSINK SYMBOL

(d) DEPTH SYMBOL

(e) SQUARE SYMBOL

(f) DIMENSION ORIGIN SYMBOL

FIGURE 11.30 Use of Dimensioning Symbols (ANSI/ASME Y14.5M–1994).

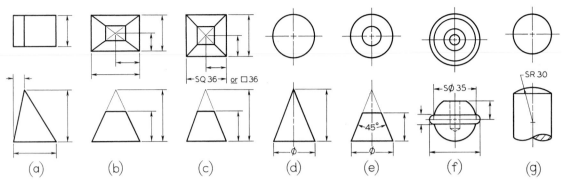

FIGURE 11.31   **Dimensioning Various Shapes.**

A triangular prism is dimensioned by giving the height, width, and displacement of the top edge in the front view and the depth in the top view (Fig. 11.31a).

A rectangular pyramid is dimensioned by giving the heights in the front view, and the dimensions of the base and the centering of the vertex in the top view (Fig. 11.31b). If the base is square, it is necessary to give the dimensions for only one side of the base, provided it is labeled SQ as shown or preceded by the square symbol □ (Fig. 11.31c).

A cone is dimensioned by giving its altitude and diameter of the base in the triangular view (Fig. 11.31d). A frustum of a cone may be dimensioned by giving the vertical angle and the diameter of one of the bases (Fig. 11.31e). Another method is to give the length and the diameters of both ends in the front view. Still another is to give the diameter at one end and the amount of taper per foot in a note (see §11.33).

Figure 11.31f shows a two-view drawing of a plastic knob. The main body is spherical and is dimensioned by giving its diameter preceded by the abbreviation and symbol for spherical diameter SØ or followed by the abbreviation SPHER. A bead around the knob is in the shape of a torus (see Fig. 4.7) and it

is dimensioned by giving the thickness of the ring and the outside diameter, as shown. In Fig. 11.31g, a spherical end is dimensioned by a radius preceded by the abbreviation SR.

Internal shapes corresponding to the external shapes in Fig. 11.31 would be dimensioned in a similar manner.

■ 11.24   SIZE DIMENSIONING OF HOLES

Holes that are to be drilled, bored, reamed, punched, cored, and so on are usually specified by symbols or standard notes, as shown in Figs. 11.29, 11.32, and 11.44. The order of items in a note corresponds to the order of procedure in the shop in producing the hole. Two or more holes are dimensioned by a single note, the leader pointing to one of the holes, as shown at the top of Fig. 11.32.

As illustrated in Figs. 6.40 and 11.32, the leader of a note should, as a rule, point to the circular view of the hole. It should point to the rectangular view only when clarity is thereby improved. When the circular view of the hole has two or more concentric circles, as for counterbored, countersunk, or tapped holes, the arrowhead should touch the outer circle (see Figs. 11.44b, 11.44c, and 11.44e to 11.44j).

FIGURE 11.32   **Dimensioning Holes.**

Notes should always be lettered horizontally on the drawing paper, and guide lines should always be used.

The use of decimal fractions to designate metric or inch drill sizes has gained wide acceptance[*] (Fig. 11.32b). For numbered or letter-size drills (Appendix 16), it is recommended that the decimal size be given in this manner, or given in parentheses; thus, #28 (.1405) DRILL, or "P" (.3230) DRILL. Metric drills are all decimal size and are not designated by number or letter.

On drawings of parts to be produced in large quantity for interchangeable assembly, dimensions and notes may be given without specification of the manufacturing process to be used. Only the dimensions of the holes are given, without reference to whether the holes are to be drilled, reamed, or punched (Figs. 11.32c and 11.32d). It should be realized that even though manufacturing operations are omitted from a note, the tolerances indicated would tend to dictate the manufacturing processes required.

■ 11.25 LOCATION DIMENSIONS

After the geometric shapes composing a structure have been dimensioned for size, as discussed, location dimensions must be given to show the relative positions of these geometric shapes, as shown in Fig. 11.32. Figure 11.33a shows that rectangular shapes, whether in the form of solids or of recesses, are located with reference to their faces. In Fig. 11.33b, cylindrical or

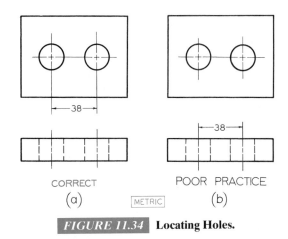

FIGURE 11.34 Locating Holes.

conical holes or bosses, or other symmetrical shapes, are located with reference to their center lines.

As shown in Fig. 11.34, location dimensions for holes are preferably given in the circular view of the holes.

Location dimensions should lead to finished surfaces wherever possible because rough castings and forgings vary in size, and unfinished surfaces cannot be relied on for accurate measurements (Fig. 11.35). Of course, the **starting dimension**, used in locating the first machined surface on a rough casting or forging, must necessarily lead from a rough surface, or from a center or a center line of the rough piece (see Figs. 13.90 and 13.91).

In general, location dimensions should be built from a finished surface as a datum plane, or from an important center or center line.

When several cylindrical surfaces have the same center line, as in Fig. 11.28b, it is not necessary to locate them with respect to each other.

FIGURE 11.33 Location Dimensions.

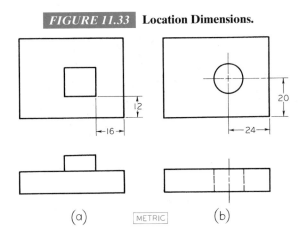

FIGURE 11.35 Dimensions to Finished Surfaces.

[*] Although drills are still listed fractionally in manufacturers' catalogs, many companies have supplemented drill and wire sizes with a decimal value. In many cases the number, letter, or common fraction has been replaced by the decimal-inch size. Metric drills are usually listed separately with a decimal-millimeter value.

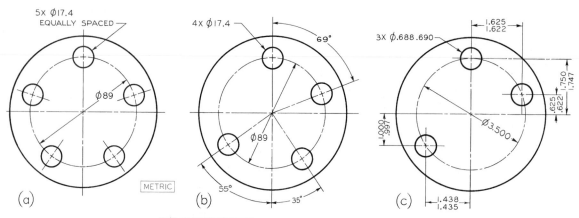

FIGURE 11.36   Locating Holes about a Center.

Holes equally spaced about a common center may be dimensioned by giving the diameter (diagonally) of the *circle of centers*, or *bolt circle* (Fig. 11.36a). Repetitive features or dimensions may be specified by the use of an X preceded with a numeral to indicate the number of times or places the feature is required. Allow a space between the letter X and the dimension as shown.

Unequally spaced holes are located by means of the bolt circle diameter plus angular measurements with reference to *only one* of the center lines (Fig. 11.36b).

Where greater accuracy is required, coordinate dimensions should be given (Fig. 11.36c). In this case, the diameter of the bolt circle is enclosed in parentheses to indicate that it is to be used only as a **reference dimension**. Reference dimensions are given for information only. They are not intended to be measured and do not govern the manufacturing operations. They represent calculated dimensions and are often useful in showing the intended design sizes (Fig. 11.36c).

When several nonprecision holes are located on a common arc, they are dimensioned by giving the radius and the angular measurements from a *baseline* (Fig. 11.37a). In this case, the baseline is the horizontal center line.

In Fig. 11.37b, the three holes are on a common center line. One dimension locates one small hole from the center; the other gives the distances between the small holes. Note the omission of a dimension at X. This method is used when (as is usually the case) the distance between the small holes is the important consideration. If the relation between the center hole and each of the small holes is more important, then include the distance at X, and denote the overall dimension as a reference dimension with parentheses.

Figure 11.37c shows another example of coordinate dimensioning. The three small holes are on a bolt circle whose diameter is given in parentheses for reference purposes only. From the main center, the small holes are located in two mutually perpendicular directions.

Another example of locating holes by means of linear measurements is shown in Fig. 11.37d. In this case, one such measurement is made at an angle to the coordinate dimensions because of the direct functional relationship of the two holes.

In Fig. 11.37e, the holes are located from two *baselines*, or *datums*. When all holes are located from a common datum, the sequence of measuring and machining operations is controlled, overall tolerance accumulations are avoided, and proper functioning of the finished part is assured, as intended by the designer. The datum surfaces selected must be more accurate than any measurement made from them, must be accessible during manufacture, and must be arranged to facilitate tool and fixture design. Thus, it may be necessary to specify accuracy of the datum surfaces in terms of straightness, roundness, flatness, and so forth (see §12.16).

Figure 11.37f shows a method of giving, in a single line, all the dimensions from a common datum. Each dimension except the first has a single arrowhead and is accumulative in value. The final and longest dimension is separate and complete.

These methods of locating holes are equally applicable to locating pins or other symmetrical features.

■ 11.26 MATING DIMENSIONS

In dimensioning a single part, its relation to mating parts, must be taken into consideration. For example, in Fig. 11.38a, a guide block fits into a slot in a base.

FIGURE 11.37 Locating Holes.

FIGURE 11.38 Mating Dimensions.

Those dimensions common to both parts are **mating dimensions**, as indicated.

These mating dimensions should be given on the multiview drawings in the corresponding locations (Figs. 11.38b and 11.38c). Other dimensions are not mating dimensions since they do not control the accurate fitting together of two parts. The actual *values* of two corresponding mating dimensions may not be ex-

actly the same. For example, the width of the slot in Fig. 11.38b may be dimensioned $\frac{1}{32}''$ (0.8 mm) or several thousandths of an inch larger than the width of the block in Fig. 11.38c, but these are mating dimensions figured from a single basic width. It will be seen that the mating dimensions shown might have been arrived at from a geometric breakdown (see §11.20). However, the mating dimensions need to be identified so that

(a) SINGLE BRACKET   (b) DOUBLE BRACKET

FIGURE 11.39 **Bracket Assembly.**

they can be specified in the corresponding locations on the two parts and so that they can be given with the degree of accuracy commensurate with the proper fitting of the parts.

In Fig. 11.39a the dimension A should appear on both the drawings of the bracket and of the frame and, therefore, is a necessary mating dimension. In Fig. 11.39b, which shows a redesign of the bracket into two parts, dimension A is not used on either part because it is not necessary to control closely the distance between the cap screws. But dimensions F are now essential mating dimensions and should appear correspondingly on the drawings of both parts. The remaining dimensions E, D, B, and C are not considered to be mating dimensions since they do not directly affect the mating of the parts.

■ 11.27 MACHINE, PATTERN, AND FORGING DIMENSIONS

In Fig. 11.38a, the base is machined from a rough casting; the patternmaker needs certain dimensions to make the pattern, and the machinist needs certain dimensions for the machining. In some cases one dimension will be used by both. Again, in most cases, these dimensions will be the same as those resulting from a geometric breakdown, but it is important to identify them to assign values to them.

Figure 11.40 shows the same part as in Fig. 11.38, with the machine dimensions and pattern dimensions identified by the letters M and P. The patternmaker is interested only in the dimensions required to make the pattern, and the machinist, in general, is concerned on-

M = MACHINE DIMENSIONS
P = PATTERN DIMENSIONS

FIGURE 11.40 **Machine and Pattern Dimensions.**

ly with the dimensions needed to machine the part. Frequently, a dimension that is convenient for the machinist is not convenient for the patternmaker, or vice versa. Since the patternmaker uses the drawing only once, while making the pattern, and the machinist refers to it continuously, the dimensions should be given primarily for the convenience of the machinist.

If the part is large and complicated, two separate drawings are sometimes made, one showing the pattern dimensions and the other the machine dimensions. The usual practice, however, is to prepare one drawing for both the patternmaker and the machinist (see §11.4).

For forgings, it is common practice to make separate forging drawings and machining drawings. A forging drawing of a connecting rod, showing only the dimensions needed in the forge shop, is shown in

Fig. 13.18. A machining drawing of the same part, but containing only the dimensions needed in the machine shop, is shown in Fig. 13.19.

Unless a decimal system is used (see §11.10), the pattern dimensions are nominal, usually to the nearest $\frac{1}{16}''$, and given in whole numbers and common fractions. If a machine dimension is given in whole numbers and common fractions, the machinist is usually allowed a tolerance (permissible in variation in size) of $\pm\frac{1}{64}''$. Some companies specify a tolerance of $\pm.010''$ on all common fractions. If greater accuracy is required, the dimensions are given in decimal form. Metric dimensions are given to one or more places, and decimal-inch dimensions are given to three or more places (see §§11.10 and 12.1). Remember that 0.1 mm is approximately .004 inch.

■ 11.28 DIMENSIONING OF CURVES

Curved shapes may be dimensioned by giving a group of radii, as shown in Fig. 11.41a. Note that in dimensioning the R126 arc whose center is inaccessible, the center may be moved inward along a center line and a jog made in the dimension line (see also Fig. 11.19f). Another method is to dimension the outline envelope of a curved shape so that the various radii are self-locating from "floating centers" (Fig. 11.41b). Either a circular or a noncircular curve may be dimensioned by means of coordinate dimensions, or datums (Fig. 11.41c; see also Fig. 11.6a).

■ 11.29 DIMENSIONING OF ROUNDED-END SHAPES

The method used for dimensioning rounded-end shapes depends on the degree of accuracy required (Fig. 11.42). When precision is not necessary, the methods used are those that are convenient for manufacturing, as in Figs. 11.42a to 11.42c.

In Fig. 11.42a, the link to be cast or to be cut from sheet metal or plate is dimensioned as it would be laid out for manufacture, by giving the center-to-center distance and the radii of the ends. Note that only one such radius dimension is necessary, but that the number of places may be included with the size dimension.

In Fig. 11.42b, the pad on a casting, with a milled slot, is dimensioned from center to center for the convenience of both the patternmaker and the machinist in layout. An additional reason for the center-to-center distance is that it gives the total travel of the milling cutter, which can be easily controlled by the machinist. The width dimension indicates the diameter of the milling cutter; hence, it is incorrect to give the radius of a machined slot. On the other hand, a cored slot (see §11.3) should be dimensioned by radius in conformity with the patternmaker's layout procedure.

In Fig. 11.42c, the semicircular pad is laid out in a similar manner to the pad in Fig. 11.42b, except that angular dimensions are used. Angular tolerances can be used if necessary (see §12.18).

When accuracy is required, the methods shown in Figs. 11.42d to 11.42g are recommended. Overall lengths of rounded-end shapes are given in each case, and radii are indicated, but without specific values. In the example in Fig. 12.42f, the center-to-center distance is required for accurate location of the holes.

In Fig. 11.42g, the hole location is more critical than the location of the radius; hence, the two are located independently, as shown.

■ 11.30 SUPERFLUOUS DIMENSIONS

All necessary dimensions must be shown, but the designer should avoid giving unnecessary or superfluous dimensions (Fig. 11.43a). Dimensions should not be repeated on the same view or on different views; nor should the same information be given in two different ways.

FIGURE 11.41 Dimensioning Curves.

FIGURE 11.42   Dimensioning Rounded-End Shapes.

Figure 11.43b illustrates a type of superfluous dimensioning that should generally be avoided, especially in machine drawing, where accuracy is important. Production personnel should not be allowed a choice between two dimensions. *Avoid "chain" dimensioning,* in which a complete series of detail dimensions is given together with an overall dimension. In such cases, one dimension of the chain should be omitted, as shown, so that the machinist is obliged to work from one surface only. This is particularly important in tol-

erance dimensioning (see §12.1), where an accumulation of tolerances can cause serious difficulties (see also §12.9).

Some inexperienced detailers have the habit of omitting both dimensions, such as those at the right in Fig. 11.43b, on the theory that the holes are symmetrically located and will be understood to be centered. One of the two location dimensions should be given.

As shown in Fig. 11.43e, when one dimension clearly applies to several identical features, it need not

FIGURE 11.43 Superfluous Dimensions.

be repeated, but the number of places should be indicated. Dimensions for fillets and rounds and other noncritical features need not be repeated nor number of places specified.

For example, the radii of the rounded ends in Figs. 11.42a to 11.42f need not be repeated, and in Fig. 11.1 both ribs are obviously the same thickness so it is unnecessary to repeat the 10-mm dimension.

■ 11.31 NOTES

It is usually necessary to supplement the direct dimensions with notes. Notes should be brief and carefully worded to allow only one interpretation. *Notes should always be lettered horizontally on the sheet, with guide lines, and arranged in a systematic manner.* They should not be lettered in crowded places, and they should not be placed between views, if possible. They should not be lettered so close together as to confuse the reader or so close to another view or detail as to suggest application to the wrong view. Leaders should be as short as possible and cross as few lines as possible. Leaders should never run through a corner of a view or through any specific points or intersections.

Notes are classified as **general notes** when they apply to an entire drawing and as **local notes** when they apply to specific items.

GENERAL NOTES General notes should be lettered in the lower right-hand corner of the drawing, above or to the left of the title block, or in a central position below the view to which they apply.

EXAMPLES

FINISH ALL OVER (FAO)
BREAK SHARP EDGES TO R0.8
G33106 ALLOY STEEL–BRINELL 340–380
ALL DRAFT ANGLES 3° UNLESS OTHERWISE SPECIFIED
DIMENSIONS APPLY AFTER PLATING

In machine drawings, the title strip or title block will carry many general notes, including material, general tolerances, heat treatment, and pattern information (see Fig. 13.14).

LOCAL NOTES Local notes apply to specific operations only and are connected by a leader to the point at which such operations are performed (Fig. 11.44). The leader should be attached at the front of the first word of a note, or just after the last word, and not at any intermediate place.

For information on notes applied to holes, see §11.24.

Certain commonly used abbreviations may be used freely in notes, such as THD, DIA, MAX. The less common abbreviations should be avoided as much as possible. All abbreviations should conform to ANSI Y1.1–1989. See Appendix 4 for American National Standard abbreviations. See Figs. 11.29 and 11.30 for form and use of alternative dimensioning symbols.

In general, leaders and notes should not be placed on the drawing until the dimensioning is substantially completed. If notes are lettered first, they will almost invariably be in the way of necessary dimensions and will have to be moved.

■ 11.32 DIMENSIONING OF THREADS

Local notes are used to specify dimensions of threads. For tapped holes the notes should, if possible, be attached to the circular views of the holes, as shown in Fig. 11.44g. For external threads, the notes are usually placed in the longitudinal views, where the threads are more easily recognized, as in Figs. 11.44v and 11.44w. For a detailed discussion of thread notes, see §13.21.

■ 11.33 DIMENSIONING OF TAPERS

A **taper** is a conical surface on a shaft or in a hole. The usual method of dimensioning a taper is to give the amount of taper in a note, such as TAPER 0.167 ON DIA (often TO GAGE added), and then give the diameter at one end, plus the length, or give the diameter at both ends and omit the length. *Taper on diameter means the difference in diameter per unit of length.*

Standard machine tapers are used on machine spindles, shanks of tools, or pins, for example, and are described in "Machine Tapers" (ANSI/ASME B5.10–1994). Such standard tapers are dimensioned on a drawing by giving the diameter, usually at the large end, the length, and a note, such as NO. 4 AMERICAN NATIONAL STANDARD TAPER (Fig. 11.45a).

For not-too-critical requirements, a taper may be dimensioned by giving the diameter at the large end, the length, and the included angle, all with proper tolerances (Fig. 11.45b). Or the diameters of both ends, plus the length, may be given with necessary tolerances.

For close-fitting tapers, the amount of *taper per unit on diameter* is indicated as shown in Figs. 11.45c and 11.45d. A gage line is selected and located by a comparatively generous tolerance, while other dimensions are given appropriate tolerances as required.

■ 11.34 DIMENSIONING OF CHAMFERS

A **chamfer** is a beveled or sloping edge, and it is dimensioned by giving the length of the offset and the angle (Fig. 11.46a). A 45° chamfer also may be dimensioned in a manner similar to that shown in Fig. 11.46a, but usually it is dimensioned by note without or with the word CHAM, as in Fig. 11.46b.

FIGURE 11.44 Local Notes. See also Figs. 7.40 and 13.32.

FIGURE 11.45   Dimensioning Tapers.

FIGURE 11.46   Dimensioning Chamfers.

■ 11.35 SHAFT CENTERS

Shaft centers are required on shafts, spindles, and other conical or cylindrical parts for turning, grinding, and other operations. Such a center may be dimensioned, as shown in Fig. 11.47. Normally the centers are produced by a combined drill and countersink.

■ 11.36 DIMENSIONING KEYWAYS

Methods of dimensioning keyways for Woodruff keys and stock keys are shown in Fig. 11.48. Note, in both

cases, the use of a dimension to center the keyway in the shaft or collar. The preferred method of dimensioning the depth of a keyway is to give the dimension from the bottom of the keyway to the opposite side of the shaft or hole, as shown. The method of computing such a dimension is shown in Fig. 11.48d. Values for A may be found in machinists' handbooks.

For general information about keys and keyways, see §13.34.

■ 11.37 DIMENSIONING OF KNURLS

A **knurl** is a roughened surface to provide a better handgrip or to be used for a press fit between two parts. For handgripping purposes, it is necessary only to give the pitch of the knurl, the type of knurling, and the length of the knurled area (Fig. 11.49a and 11.49b). To dimension a knurl for a press fit, the toleranced diameter before knurling should be given (Fig. 11.49c). A note should be added giving the pitch and type of knurl and the minimum diameter after knurling [see ANSI/ASME B94.6–1984 (R1995)].

■ 11.38 DIMENSIONING ALONG CURVED SURFACES

When angular measurements are unsatisfactory, chordal dimensions (Fig. 11.50a) or linear dimensions on the curved surfaces (Fig. 11.50b) may be given.

FIGURE 11.47   Shaft Center.

FIGURE 11.48   Dimensioning Keyways.

GRAPHICS SPOTLIGHT

Semiautomatic Dimensioning Using CAD

DIMENSIONING CONTROLS PART

Dimensioning is an important skill because the dimensions given in the drawing control how the part will be constructed and how tolerance values will be applied. Even when a drawing or model database is exported for direct machining, the machinist must know which fits and dimensions are critical, and where the part can vary. No parts are created exactly to the same size as the dimensions specified, so the designer must make it clear what allowances are possible. Dimensioning CAD drawings is accomplished using a suite of dimensioning tools provided by the software. Programs like AutoCAD 2000 call their tools semiautomatic dimensioning because the dimension lines, values, arrowheads, and extension lines are created for you automatically, but you must still choose where you will place dimensions in the drawing.

DIMENSION STYLES

AutoCAD 2000 lets you create different families of dimension appearances, called dimension styles. You use this to change the appearance of dimensions for different types of drawings. For example, architectural drawings have a different standard for their appearance than mechanical drawings, and civil drawings may still have yet another appearance. To create dimension styles and set their appearance in AutoCAD R. 14, you use the Dimension Styles dialog box. You can quickly pick it from the Dimensioning Toolbar shown in Figure A.

PARENT & CHILD STYLES

AutoCAD 2000 uses child styles to let you change the appearance of dimension types within the style; for example radial dimensions can have a different appearance than linear dimensions, or ordinate dimensions. You can have a different appearance for each of these types of dimensions: linear, radial, angular, diameter, ordinate, and leader. You can think of child styles like this. If you have a child, they generally resemble you; have brown eyes if you do, etc. But the child may decide to dye their hair. After

(A)

that, no amount of you dying your hair will change the appearance of the child's hair. This is essentially how child dimension styles work. You can set the child style for a type of dimension so that it looks different from the parent style. Once a characteristic of a child dimension style is set differently than the parent style, changing the parent no longer changes the child. You can use these styles to manage the appearance of the dimensions in your drawing so that you do not have to tweak individual dimensions. Dimension styles also allow you to have a consistent approach to controlling the appearance of the dimensions in the drawing so that you know how the dimensions will update if you make a change. Figure B shows the dialogue box you can use.

(B)

FIGURE 11.49   Dimensioning Knurls.

FIGURE 11.50   Dimensioning along Curved Surfaces.

■11.39 SHEET-METAL BENDS

In sheet-metal dimensioning, allowance must be made for bends. The intersection of the plane surfaces adjacent to a bend is called the *mold line*, and this line, rather than the center of the arc, is used to determine dimensions (Fig. 11.51). The following procedure for calculating bends is typical. If the two inner plane surfaces of an angle are extended, their line of intersection is called the IML or *inside mold line* (Figs. 11.52a to 11.52c). Similarly, if the two outer plane surfaces are extended, they produce the OML or *outside mold line*. The *center line of bend* (₵ B) refers primarily to the machine on which the bend is made and is at the center of the bend radius.

The length, or *stretchout*, of the pattern equals the sum of the flat sides of the angle plus the distance around the bend measured along the *neutral axis*. The

FIGURE 11.51   Profile Dimensioning.

distance around the bend is called the *bend allowance*. When metal bends, it compresses on the inside and stretches on the outside. At a certain zone in between, the metal is neither compressed not stretched, and this is called the neutral axis (Fig. 11.52d). The neutral axis is usually assumed to be 0.44 of the thickness from the inside surface of the metal.

The developed length of material, or bend allowance (BA), to make the bend is computed from the empirical formula

$$BA = (0.017453R + 0.0078T)N,$$

where R = radius of bend, T = metal thickness, and N = number of degrees of bend (Fig. 11.52c).

■11.40 TABULAR DIMENSIONS

A series of objects having like features but varying in dimensions may be represented by one drawing (Fig. 11.53). Letters are substituted for dimension figures on the drawing, and the varying dimensions are given in tabular form. The dimensions of many standard parts are given in this manner in catalogs and handbooks.

■11.41 STANDARDS

Dimensions should be given, wherever possible, to make use of readily available materials, tools, parts, and gages. The dimensions for many commonly used machine elements, such as bolts, screws, nails, keys, tapers, wire, pipes, sheet metal, chains, belts, ropes, pins, and rolled metal shapes, have been standardized, and the drafter must obtain these sizes from company standards manuals, from published handbooks, from American National Standards, or from manufacturers' catalogs. Tables of some of the more common items are given in the Appendix of this text.

$$BA = (0.017453R + 0.0078T)N$$

FIGURE 11.52 **Bends.**

FIGURE 11.53 **Tabular Dimensioning.**

DETAIL	A	B	C	D	E	F	UNC THD	STOCK	LBS
1	.62	.38	.62	.06	.25	.135	.312–18	Ø.75	.09
2	.88	.38	.62	.09	.38	.197	.312–18	Ø.75	.12
3	1.00	.44	.75	.12	.38	.197	.375–16	Ø.875	.19
4	1.25	.50	.88	.12	.50	.260	.437–14	Ø.1	.30
5	1.50	.56	1.00	.16	.62	.323	.5–13	Ø1.125	.46

Such standard parts are not delineated on detail drawings unless they are to be altered for use, but are drawn conventionally on assembly drawings and are listed in parts lists (see §13.14). Common fractions are often used to indicate the nominal sizes of standard parts or tools. If the complete decimal-inch system is used, all such sizes ordinarily are expressed by decimals; for example, .250 DRILL instead of $\frac{1}{4}$ DRILL. If the all-metric system of dimensioning is used, then the *preferred* metric drill of the approximate same size (.2480″) will be indicated as a 6.30 DRILL.

■ **11.42 COORDINATE DIMENSIONING**

In general, the basic coordinate dimensioning practices are compatible with the data requirements for tape or computer-controlled automatic production machines. However, to design for automated production, the designer and/or drafter should first consult the manufacturing machine manuals before making the drawings for production. Certain considerations should be noted.

1. A set of three mutually perpendicular datum or reference planes is usually required for coordinate dimensioning. These planes either must be obvious or clearly identified (Fig. 11.54).

2. The designer selects as origins for dimensions those surfaces or other features most important to the functioning of the part. Enough of these features are selected to position the part in relation to the set of mutually perpendicular planes. All related dimensions on the part are then made from these planes. An example of rectangular coordinate dimensioning without dimension lines is shown in Fig. 11.55.

3. All dimensions should be in decimals.

4. Angles should be given, where possible, in degrees and decimal parts of degrees.

5. Standard tools, such as drills, reamers, and taps, should be specified when required.

6. All tolerances should be determined by the design requirements of the part, not by the capability of the manufacturing machine.

■ **11.43 DO'S AND DON'TS OF DIMENSIONING**

The following checklist summarizes briefly most of the situations in which a beginning designer is likely to make a mistake in dimensioning. Students should check the drawing by this list before submitting it to the instructor.

FIGURE 11.54 Coordinate Dimensioning.

FIGURE 11.55 Rectangular Coordinate Dimensioning
Without Dimension Lines (ANSI/ASME Y14.5M–1994).

1. Each dimension should be given clearly so that it can be interpreted in only one way.

2. Dimensions should not be duplicated or the same information given in two different ways—dual dimensioning excluded—and no dimensions should be given except those needed to produce or inspect the part.

3. Dimensions should be given between points or surfaces that have a functional relation to each other or that control the location of mating parts.

4. Dimensions should be given to finished surfaces or important center lines, in preference to rough surfaces, wherever possible.

5. Dimensions should be so given that it will not be necessary for the machinist to calculate, scale, or assume any dimension.

6. Dimensions should be attached to the view where the shape is best shown (contour rule).

7. Dimensions should be placed in the views where the features dimensioned are shown true shape.

8. Dimensioning to hidden lines should be avoided wherever possible.

9. Dimensions should not be placed on a view unless clarity is promoted and long extension lines are avoided.

10. Dimensions applying to two adjacent views should be placed between views, unless clarity is promoted by placing some of them outside.

11. The longer dimensions should be placed outside all intermediate dimensions so that dimension lines will not cross extension lines.

12. In machine drawing, all unit marks should be omitted, except when necessary for clarity; for example, 1″ VALVE or 1 mm DRILL.

13. Production personnel should not be expected to assume that a feature is centered (as a hole on a plate), but a location dimension should be given from one side. However, if a hole is to be centered on a symmetrical rough casting, mark the center line and omit the locating dimension from the center line.

14. A dimension should be attached to only one view, not to extension lines connecting two views.

15. Detail dimensions should "line up" in chain fashion.

16. A complete chain of detail dimensions should be avoided; it is better to omit one; otherwise reference should be added to one detail dimension or the overall dimension by enclosing within parentheses.

17. A dimension line should never be drawn through a dimension figure. A figure should never be lettered over any line of the drawing. The line can be broken if necessary.

18. Dimension lines should be spaced uniformly throughout the drawing. They should be at least 10 mm (.38″) from the object outline and 6 mm (.25″) apart.

19. No line of the drawing should be used as a dimension line or coincide with a dimension line.

20. A dimension line should never be joined end to end (chain fashion) with any line of the drawing.

21. Dimension lines should not cross, if avoidable.

22. Dimension lines and extension lines should not cross, if avoidable. (Extension lines may cross each other.)

23. When extension lines cross extension lines or visible lines, no break in either line should be made.

24. A center line may be extended and used as an extension line, in which case it is still drawn like a center line.

25. Center lines should generally not extend from view to view.

26. Leaders for notes should be straight, not curved, and pointing to the center of circular views of holes wherever possible.

27. Leaders should slope at 45°, or 30°, or 60° with horizontal but may be made at any convenient angle except vertical or horizontal.

28. Leaders should extend from the beginning or from the end of a note, the horizontal "shoulder" extending from midheight of the lettering.

29. Dimension figures should be approximately centered between the arrowheads, except that in a "stack" of dimensions, the figures should be "staggered."

30. Dimension figures should be about 3 mm (.13″) high for whole numbers and 6 mm (.25″) high for fractions.

31. Dimension figures should never be crowded or in any way made difficult to read.

32. Dimension figures should not be lettered over lines or sectioned areas unless necessary, in which case a clear space should be reserved for the dimension figures.

33. Dimension figures for angles should generally be lettered horizontally.

34. Fraction bars should never be inclined except in confined areas, such as in tables.

35. The numerator and denominator of a fraction should never touch the fraction bar.

36. Notes should always be lettered horizontally on the sheet.

37. Notes should be brief and clear, and the wording should be standard in form.

38. Finish marks should be placed on the edge views of all finished surfaces, including hidden edges and the contour and circular views of cylindrical surfaces.

39. Finish marks should be omitted on holes or other features where a note specifies a machining operation.

40. Finish marks should be omitted on parts made from rolled stock.

41. If a part is finished all over, all finish marks should be omitted, and the general note FINISH ALL OVER or FAO should be used.

42. A cylinder is dimensioned by giving both its diameter and length in the rectangular view, except when notes are used for holes. A diagonal diameter in the circular view may be used in cases where clarity is gained thereby.

43. Holes to be bored, drilled, reamed, and so on are size-dimensioned by notes in which the leaders preferably point toward the center of the circular views of the holes. Indications of manufacturing processes may be omitted from notes.

44. Drill sizes are preferably expressed in decimals. For drills designated by number or letter, the decimal size must also be given.

45. In general, a circle is dimensioned by its diameter, an arc by its radius.

46. Diagonal diameters should be avoided, except for very large holes and for circles of centers. They may be used on positive cylinders when clarity is gained thereby.

47. A diameter dimension value should always be preceded by the symbol ∅.

48. A radius dimension should always be preceded by the letter R. The radial dimension line should have only one arrowhead, and it should pass through or point through the arc center and touch the arc.

49. Cylinders should be located by their center lines.

50. Cylinders should be located in the circular views, if possible.

51. Cylinders should be located by coordinate dimensions in preference to angular dimensions where accuracy is important.

52. When there are several rough, noncritical features obviously the same size (fillets, rounds, ribs, etc.), it is necessary to give only typical (abbreviation TYP) dimensions or to use a note.

53. When a dimension is not to scale, it should be underscored with a heavy straight line or marked NTS or NOT TO SCALE.

54. Mating dimensions should be given correspondingly on drawings of mating parts.

55. Pattern dimensions should be given in two-place decimals or in common whole numbers and fractions to the nearest $\frac{1}{16}''$.

56. Decimal dimensions should be used for all machining dimensions.

57. Cumulative tolerances should be avoided, especially in limit dimensioning, described in §11.9.

FIGURE 11.56 **Dimensioned Detail Drawing Produced by the Computervision CADDS 4X Production Drafting System.** *Courtesy of Computervision Corporation, a subsidiary of Prime Computer, Inc.*

■ KEY WORDS

METRIC SCALE

ARCHITECT'S SCALE

DIMENSION LINES

UNIDIRECTIONAL SYSTEM

FINISH MARKS

LOCATION DIMENSIONS

NOTES

ABBREVIATIONS

ENGINEERING SCALE

EXTENSION LINES

LEADERS

ALIGNED SYSTEM

SIZE DIMENSIONS

ANSI STANDARDS

COORDINATE DIMENSIONS

SUPERFLUOUS

■ CHAPTER SUMMARY

- To increase clarity, dimensions and notes are added to a drawing to precisely describe size, location, and manufacturing process.

- Drawings are scaled to fit on a standard sheet of paper. Drawings created by hand are drawn to scale. CAD drawings are drawn full size and scaled when they are printed.

- The three types of scales are metric, engineer's, and architect's.

- Dimensions and notes are placed on drawings according to prescribed standards.

- Dimensions that are incorrectly placed on a drawing are considered just as wrong as if the numbers in the dimension were incorrect.

- Special dimensioning techniques are used for surfaces that have been machined by one of the manufacturing processes.

■ REVIEW QUESTIONS

1. What are the different units used when a drawing is created with a metric scale? With an engineering scale? With an architect's scale?

2. Explain the concept of contour dimensioning.

3. Which type of line is *never* crossed by any other line when dimensioning an object?

4. How is geometric analysis used in dimensioning?

5. What is the difference between a size dimension and a location dimension?

6. Which dimension system allows dimensions to be read from the bottom and from the right? When can a dimension be read from the left?

7. Draw an example of dimensioning an angle.

8. When are finish marks used? Draw two types.

9. How are negative and positive cylinders dimensioned? Draw examples.

10. How are holes and arcs dimensioned? Draw examples.

11. What are notes and leaders used for?

12. Why is it important to avoid superfluous dimensions?

■ DIMENSIONING PROBLEMS

Most of a student's practice in dimensioning will be in connection with working drawings assigned from other chapters. However, a limited number of special dimensioning problems are available here in Figs. 11.57 and 11.58. The problems are designed for Layout A–3 (8.5″ × 11.0″) and are to be drawn with instruments and dimensioned to a full-size sale. Layout A4–3 (297 mm × 420 mm) may be used with appropriate adjustments in the title strip layout.

Since many of the problems in this and other chapters are of a general nature, they can also be solved on most computer graphics systems. If a system is available, the instructor may choose to assign specific problems to be completed by this method.

FIGURE 11.57 Using Layout A–3 or A4–3 (adjusted), draw assigned problem with instruments. To obtain sizes, place bow dividers on the views on this page and transfer to scale at the side to obtain values. Dimension drawing completely in one-place millimeters or two-place inches as assigned, full size. See inside back cover for decimal-inch and millimeter equivalents.

FIGURE 11.58 Using Layout A–3 or A4–3 (adjusted), draw assigned problem with instruments. To obtain sizes, place bow dividers on the views on this page and transfer to scale at the side to obtain values. Dimension drawing completely in one-place millimeters or two-place inches as assigned, full size. See inside back cover for decimal-inch and millimeter equivalents.

Ø1.00 3 HOLES

R.500

R.300

5.50

R.100

7.50

2.50

FIGURE 11.59   Using Sheet Layout A–3 of A4–3 (adjusted), draw the OML and IML. Calculate the bend allowance using the formula on p. 336.

C H A P T E R   1 2

TOLERANCING

OBJECTIVES

After studying the material in this chapter, you should be able to:

1. Read and create limit dimensions.
2. Describe the nominal size, tolerance, limits, and allowance of two mating parts.
3. Identify a clearance fit, interference fit, and transition fit.
4. Describe the basic hole and basic shaft systems.
5. Dimension two mating parts using limit dimensions, uni-lateral tolerances, and bilateral tolerances.
6. Describe the classes of fit and give examples of each.
7. Draw geometric tolerancing symbols.
8. Specify position and geometric tolerances.

OVERVIEW

Interchangeable manufacturing allows parts made in widely separated localities to be brought together for assembly. That the parts all fit together properly is an essential element of mass production. Without interchangeable manufacturing, modern industry could not exist, and without effective size control by the engineer, interchangeable manufacturing could not be achieved.

For example, an automobile manufacturer not only subcontracts the manufacture of many parts of a design to other companies but must also provide the parts for replacement. All parts in each category must be nearly enough alike so that any one of them will fit properly in any assembly. Unfortunately, *it is impossible to make anything to exact size.* Parts can be made to very close dimensions, even to a few millionths of an inch or thousandths of a millimeter (e.g., gage blocks), but such accuracy is extremely expensive.

Fortunately, *exact* sizes are not needed. The need is for varying degrees of accuracy according to functional requirements. A manufacturer of children's tricycles would soon go out of business if the parts were made with jet-engine accuracy—no one would be willing to pay the price. So what is wanted is a means of specifying dimensions with whatever degree of accuracy is required. The answer to the problem is the specification of a *tolerance* on each dimension.

The concept of quality in manufacturing is primarily a factor of machining tolerances. Products with small variations in shape and size are considered high quality and can command higher prices. Waste results when the manufacturing process cannot maintain shape and size within prescribed limits. By monitoring the manufacturing processes and reducing waste, a company can improve profits. This direct benefit to profits is why tolerancing is critical to manufacturing success. Tolerancing is an extension of dimensioning. It provides additional information about the shape, size, and position of every feature of a product. It communicates exacting directions about how to manufacture a product. Basic CAD program functionality is often supplemented with advanced dimensioning and tolerancing software that can assist with the tolerancing process. It takes a highly skilled designer to be able to apply tolerance dimensions correctly.

■ 12.1 TOLERANCE DIMENSIONING

Tolerance is the total amount that a specific dimension is permitted to vary; it is the difference between the maximum and the minimum limits for the dimension (ANSI/ASME Y14.5M–1994). For example, a dimension given as $1.625 \pm .002$ means that the manufactured part may be 1.627″ or 1.623″, or anywhere between these **limit dimensions**. The tolerance, or total amount of variation "tolerated," is .004″. Thus, it becomes the function of the detailer or designer to specify the allowance error that may be tolerated for a given dimension and still permit the satisfactory functioning of the part. Since greater accuracy costs more money, the detailer or designer will not specify the closest tolerance, but instead will specify as generous a tolerance as possible.

To control the dimensions of quantities of the two parts so that any two mating parts will be interchangeable, it is necessary to assign tolerance to the dimensions of the parts, as shown in Fig. 12.1a. The diameter of the hole may be machined not less than 1.250″ and not more than 1.251″; these two figures represent the limits and the difference between them (.001″ is the tolerance). Likewise, the shaft must be produced between the limits of 1.248″ and 1.247″; the tolerance on the shaft is the difference between these, or .001″. The metric versions for these limit dimensions for the hole and shaft are shown in Fig. 12.1b. The difference in the dimensions for either the hole or shaft is 0.03 mm, the total tolerance.

A pictorial illustration of the dimensions in Fig. 12.1a is shown in Fig. 12.2a. The maximum shaft is shown solid, and the minimum shaft is shown in phantom. The difference in diameters, .001″, is the tolerance on the shaft. Similarly, the tolerance on the hole is the difference between the two limits shown, or .001″. The loosest fit, or maximum clearance, occurs when the smallest shaft is in the largest hole (Fig. 12.2b). The tightest fit, or minimum clearance occurs when the largest shaft is in the smallest hole (Fig. 12.2c). The difference between these, .002″, is the **allowance**. The average clearance is .003″, which is the same difference as allowed in the example in Fig. 12.1a; thus, any shaft will fit any hole interchangeably.

When expressed in metric dimensions, the limits for the hole are 31.75 mm and 31.78 mm; the difference between them, 0.03 mm, is the tolerance. Similarly, the limits for the shaft are 31.70 mm and 31.67 mm;

(a) LIMIT DIMENSIONS

(b) LIMIT DIMENSIONS-METRIC

FIGURE 12.1 Fits between Mating Parts.

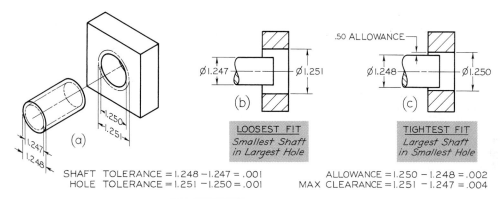

.50 ALLOWANCE

LOOSEST FIT
Smallest Shaft
in Largest Hole

TIGHTEST FIT
Largest Shaft
in Smallest Hole

SHAFT TOLERANCE = 1.248 − 1.247 = .001
HOLE TOLERANCE = 1.251 − 1.250 = .001

ALLOWANCE = 1.250 − 1.248 = .002
MAX CLEARANCE = 1.251 − 1.247 = .004

FIGURE 12.2 Limit Dimensions.

MACHINE FOR XXX
FIT AT ASSY

FIGURE 12.3 Noninterchangeable Fit.

the tolerance on the shaft is the difference between them, or 0.03 mm.

When parts are required to fit properly in assembly but not to be interchangeable, the size of one part need not be toleranced, but is indicated to be made to fit at assembly (Fig. 12.3).

■ 12.2 SIZE DESIGNATIONS

At this point, it is well to fix in mind the definitions of certain terms (ANSI/ASME Y14.5M–1994).

Nominal size is the designation used for general identification and is usually expressed in common fractions. In Fig. 12.1, the nominal size of both hole and shaft, which is $1\frac{1}{4}''$, would be 1.25″ or 31.75 mm in a decimal system of dimensioning.

Basic size, **or basic dimension**, is the theoretical size from which limits of size are derived by the application of allowances and tolerances. It is the size from

which limits are determined for the size, shape, or location of a feature. In Fig. 12.1a, the basic size is the decimal equivalent of the nominal size $1\frac{1}{4}''$, or 1.250″ or 31.75 mm in Fig. 12.1b.

Actual size is the measured size of the finished part.

Allowance is the minimum clearance space (or maximum interference) intended between the maximum material condition (MMC) of mating parts. In Fig. 12.2c, the allowance is the difference between the smallest hole, 1.250″, and the largest shaft, 1.248″, or .002″. Allowance, then, represents the tightest permissible fit and is simply the smallest hole minus the largest shaft. For clearance fits, this difference will be positive, while for interference fits it will be negative.

■ 12.3 FITS BETWEEN MATING PARTS

"Fit is the general term used to signify the range of tightness or looseness that may result from the application of a specific combination of allowances and tolerances in mating parts." [ANSI B4.1–1967 (R1994) and ANSI B4.2–1978 (R1994)]. There are four general types of fits between parts.

1. In a **clearance fit**, an internal member fits in an external member (as a shaft in a hole) and always leaves a space or clearance between the parts. In Fig. 12.2c, the largest shaft is 1.248″ and the smallest hole is 1.250″, which permits a minimum air space of .002″ between the parts. This space is the allowance, and in a clearance fit it is always positive.

2. In an **interference fit**, the internal member is larger than the external member such that there is always an actual interference of metal. In Fig. 12.4a, the smallest shaft is 1.2513″, and the largest hole is 1.2506″, so that there is an actual interference of metal amounting to at least .0007″. Under maximum material conditions the interference would be .0019″. This interference is the allowance, and in an interference fit it is always negative.

3. A **transition fit** may result in either a clearance or interference condition. In Fig. 12.4b, the smallest shaft, 1.2503″, will fit in the largest hole, 1.2506″, with .003″ to spare. But the largest shaft, 1.2509″, will have to be forced into the smallest hole, 1.2500″, with an interference of metal (negative allowance) of .0009″.

4. In a **line fit**, the limits of size are so specified that a clearance or surface contact may result when mating parts are assembled.

■ 12.4 SELECTIVE ASSEMBLY

If allowances and tolerances are properly given, mating parts can be completely interchangeable. But for close fits, it is necessary to specify very small allowances and tolerances, and the cost may be very high. To avoid this expense, either manual or computer-controlled selective assembly is often used. In **selective assembly**, all parts are inspected and classified into several grades according to actual sizes, so that "small" shafts can be matched with "small" holes, "medium" shafts with "medium" holes, and so on. In this way, very satisfactory fits may be obtained at much less expense than by machining all mating parts to very accurate dimensions. Since a transition fit may or may not represent an interference of metal, interchangeable assembly generally is not as satisfactory as selective assembly.

■ 12.5 BASIC HOLE SYSTEM

Standard reamers, broaches, and other standard tools are often used to produce holes, and standard plug gages are used to check the actual sizes. On the other hand, shafting can easily be machined to any size desired. Therefore, toleranced dimensions are commonly figured on the so-called **basic hole system**, in which the *minimum hole is taken as the basic size*, an allowance is assigned, and tolerances are applied on both sides of, and away from, this allowance.

In Fig. 12.5a, the minimum size of the hole, .500″, is taken as the basic size. An allowance of .002″ is decided on and subtracted from the basic hole size, making the maximum shaft .498″. Tolerances of .002″ and .003″, respectively, are applied to the hole and shaft to obtain the maximum hole of .502″ and the minimum shaft of .495″. Thus, the minimum clearance between the parts becomes .500″ − .498″ = .002″ (smallest hole minus largest shaft), and the maximum clearance is .502″ − .495″ = .007″ (largest hole minus smallest shaft).

In the case of an interference fit, the maximum shaft size would be found by *adding the desired allowance* (maximum interference) to the basic hole size. In Fig. 12.4a, the basic size is 1.2500″. The maximum interference decided on was .0019″, which added to the basic size gives 1.2519″, the largest shaft size.

The basic hole size can be changed to the basic shaft size by subtracting the allowance for a clearance fit, or adding it for an interference fit. The result is the largest shaft size, which is the new basic size.

■ 12.6 BASIC SHAFT SYSTEM

In some branches of industry, such as textile machinery manufacturing, in which use is made of a great deal of cold-finished shafting, the **basic shaft system** is often

FIGURE 12.4 **Fits between Parts.**

(a) INTERFERENCE FIT   (b) TRANSITION FIT

BASIC HOLE FIT   BASIC SHAFT FIT

FIGURE 12.5 **Basic-Hole and Basic-Shaft Systems.**

used. This system should be used only when there is a reason for it. For example, it is advantageous when several parts having different fits, but one nominal size, are required on a single shaft. In this system, *the maximum shaft is taken as the basic size*, an allowance for each mating part is assigned, and tolerances are applied on both sides of, and away from, this allowance.

In Fig. 12.5b, the maximum size of the shaft, .500″, is taken as the basic size. An allowance of .002″ is decided on and added to the basic shaft size, giving the minimum hole, .502″. Tolerances of .003″ and .001″, respectively, are applied to the hole and shaft to obtain the maximum hole, .505″, and the minimum shaft, .499″. Thus, the minimum clearance between the parts is .502″ − .500″ = .002″ (smallest hole minus largest shaft), and the maximum clearance is .505″ − .499″ = .006″ (largest hole minus smallest shaft).

In the case of an interference fit, the minimum hole size would be found by *subtracting the desired allowance from the basic shaft size*.

The basic shaft size may be changed to the basic hole size by adding the allowance for a clearance fit or by subtracting it for an interference fit. The result is the smallest hole size, which is the new basic size.

■ 12.7 SPECIFICATIONS OF TOLERANCES

A tolerance of a decimal dimension must be given in decimal form to the same number of places (see Fig. 12.8).

General tolerances on decimal dimensions in which tolerances are not given may also be covered in a printed note, such as

DECIMAL DIMENSION TO BE HELD TO ± .001.

Thus, if a dimension 3.250 is given, the worker machines between the limits 3.249 and 3.251 (see Fig. 12.9).

Tolerances for metric dimensions may be covered in a note, such as the commonly used

METRIC DIMENSIONS TO BE HELD TO ± 0.08.

Thus, when the given dimension of 3.250″ is converted to millimeters, the worker machines between the limits of 82.63 mm and 82.74 mm.

Every dimension on a drawing should have a tolerance, either direct or by general tolerance note, except that commercial material is often assumed to have the tolerances set by commercial standards.

It is customary to indicate an overall general tolerance for all common fraction dimensions by means of a printed note in or just above the title block (see Fig. 12.9).

EXAMPLE

ALL FRACTIONAL DIMENSIONS ± $\frac{1}{64}$″
UNLESS OTHERWISE SPECIFIED.

General angular tolerances also may be given as

ANGULAR TOLERANCE ± 1°.

Several methods of expressing tolerances in dimensions are approved by ANSI (ANSI/ASME Y14.5M–1994) as follows.

1.   Limit dimensioning. In this preferred method, the maximum and minimum limits of size and location are specified, as shown in Fig. 12.6. The high limit (maximum value) is placed above the low limit (minimum value) (Fig. 12.6a). In single-line note form, the low limit precedes the high limit separated by a dash (Fig. 12.6b).

2.   Plus-or-minus dimensioning. In this method the basic size is followed by a plus-or-minus expression of tolerance resulting in either a unilateral or bilateral tolerance (Fig. 12.7). If two unequal tolerance numbers are given, one plus and one minus, the plus is placed above the minus. One of the numbers may be zero, if desired. If a single tolerance value is given, it is preceded by the plus-or-minus symbol (±) (Fig. 12.8). This method should be used when the plus and minus values are equal.

FIGURE 12.6 **Method of Giving Limits.**

(a)   (b)

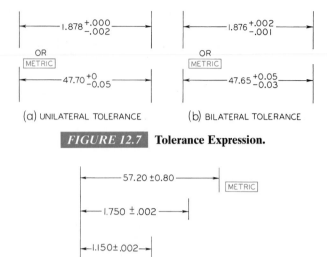

(a) UNILATERAL TOLERANCE   (b) BILATERAL TOLERANCE

FIGURE 12.7   **Tolerance Expression.**

FIGURE 12.8   **Bilateral Tolerances.**

The **unilateral system of tolerances** allows variations in only one direction from the basic size. This method is advantageous when a critical size is approached as material is removed during manufacture, as in the case of close-fitting holes and shafts. In Fig. 12.7a the basic size is 1.878″ (47.70 mm). The tolerance .002″ (0.05 mm) is all in one direction—toward the smaller size. If this is a shaft diameter, the basic size 1.878″ (47.70 mm) is the size nearest the critical size because it is nearest to the tolerance zone; hence the tolerance is taken *away* from the critical size. A unilateral tolerance is always all plus or all minus; that is, either the plus or the minus value must be zero. However, the zeros should be given as shown in Fig. 12.7a.

The **bilateral system of tolerances** allows variations in both directions from the basic size. Bilateral tolerances are usually given with location dimensions or with any dimensions that can be allowed to vary in either direction. In Fig. 12.7b, the basic size is 1.876″ (47.65 mm), and the actual size may be larger by .002″ (0.05 mm) or smaller by .001″ (0.03 mm). If it is desired to specify an equal variation in both directions, the combined plus-or-minus symbol ($\pm$) is used with a single value, as shown in Fig. 12.8

A typical example of limit dimensioning is given in Fig. 12.9.

FIGURE 12.9   **Limit Dimensions.**

3. **Single-limit dimensioning**. It is not always necessary to specify both limits. MIN or MAX is often placed after a number to indicate minimum or maximum dimensions desired where other elements of design determine the other unspecified limit. For example, a thread length may be dimensioned as: $|\leftarrow 1.500 \rightarrow|$ MIN FULL THD or a radius dimensioned as .05 R MAX ⌐ . Other applications include depths of holes, chamfers, and so on

4. **Angular tolerances** are usually bilateral and in terms of degrees, minutes, and seconds.

> **EXAMPLES** $25° \pm 1°$, $25° \, 0' \pm 0° \, 15'$, or $25° \pm 0.25°$ (see also §12.18).

■ 12.8 AMERICAN NATIONAL STANDARD LIMITS AND FITS

The American National Standards Institute has issued the ANSI B4.1–1967 (R1994), "Preferred Limits and Fits for Cylindrical Parts," defining terms and recommending preferred standard sizes, allowances, tolerances, and fits in terms of the decimal inch. This standard gives a series of standard types and classes of fits on a unilateral hole basis such that the fit produced by mating parts in any one class will produce approximately similar performance throughout the range of sizes. These tables prescribe the fit for any given size or type of fit; they also prescribe the standard limits for the mating parts which will produce the fit.

The tables are designed for the basic hole system (§12.5; see Appendixes 5–9). For coverage of the metric system of tolerances and fits, see §§12.11–12.13 and Appendixes 11–14.

Letter symbols to identify the five types of fits are as follows:

RC	Running or Sliding Clearance Fits
LC	Locational Clearance Fits
LT	Transition Clearance or Interference Fits
LN	Locational Interference Fits
FN	Force or Shrink Fits

These letter symbols, plus a number indicating the class of fit within each type, are used to indicate a complete fit. Thus, FN 4 means a Class 4 Force Fit. The fits are described [ANSI B4.1–1967 (R1994)] as follows.

RUNNING AND SLIDING FITS

Running and sliding fits, for which description of classes of fits and limits of clearance are given (Appendix 5), are intended to provide a similar running performance, with suitable lubrication allowance, throughout the range of sizes. The clearances for the first two classes, used chiefly as slide fits, increase more slowly with diameter than the other classes, so that accurate location is maintained even at the expense of free relative motion.

LOCATIONAL FITS

Locational fits (Appendixes 6–8) are fits intended to determine only the location of the mating parts; they may provide rigid or accurate location, as with interference fits, or provide some freedom of location, as with clearance fits. Accordingly, they are divided into three groups: clearance fits, transition fits, and interference fits.

FORCE FITS

Force or shrink fits (Appendix 9) constitute a special type of interference fit, normally characterized by maintenance of constant bore pressures throughout the range of sizes. The interference therefore varies almost directly with diameter, and the difference between its minimum and maximum value is small to maintain the resulting pressures within reasonable limits.

In the tables for each class of fit, the range of nominal sizes of shafts or holes is given in inches. To simplify the tables and reduce the space required to present them, the other values are given in thousandths of an inch. Minimum and maximum limits of clearance are given; the top number is the least clearance, or the allowance, and the lower number the maximum clearance, or the greatest looseness of fit. Then, under the heading "Standard Limits" are given the limits for the hole and for the shaft that are to be applied algebraically to the basic size to obtain the limits of size for the parts, using the basic hole system.

For example, take a 2.0000″ basic diameter with a Class RC 1 fit. This fit is given in Appendix 5. In the column headed "Nominal Size Range, Inches," find 1.97–3.15, which embraces the 2.0000″ basic size. Reading to the right, we find under "Limits of Clearance" the values 0.4 and 1.2, representing the maximum clearance between the parts *in thousandths of an inch*. To get these values in inches, simply multiply by one thousandth; thus, $\frac{4}{10} \times \frac{1}{1000} = .0004″$. To convert 0.4 thousandths to inches, simple move the decimal point three places to the left; thus, .0004″. Therefore, for this 2.0000″ diameter, with a Class RC 1 fit, the minimum clearance, or allowance, is .0004″, and the maximum clearance, representing the greatest looseness, is .0012″.

Reading farther to the right, we find under "Standard Limits" the value + 0.5, which when converted to inches is .0005″. Add this to the basic size thus: 2.0000″ + .0005″ = 2.0005″, the upper limit of the hole. Since the other value given for the hole is zero, the lower limit of the hole is the basic size of the hole, or 2.0000″. The hole would then be dimensioned as

$$\begin{matrix} 2.0005 \\ 2.0000 \end{matrix} \quad \text{or} \quad 2.0000 \genfrac{}{}{0pt}{}{+.0005}{-.0000}.$$

The limits for the shaft are read as −.0004″ and −.0007″. To get the limits of the shaft, subtract these values from the basic size; thus,

$$2.000″ − .0004″ = 1.9996″ \text{ (upper limit)}$$

$$2.000″ − .0007″ = 1.9993″ \text{ (lower limit).}$$

The shaft would then be dimensioned in inches as follows:

$$\begin{matrix} 1.9996 \\ 1.9993 \end{matrix} \quad \text{or} \quad 1.9996 \genfrac{}{}{0pt}{}{+.0000}{-.0003}.$$

■ 12.9 ACCUMULATION OF TOLERANCES

In tolerance dimensioning, it is very important to consider the effect of one tolerance on another. When the location of a surface in a given direction is affected by more than one tolerance figure, the tolerances are *cumulative*. For example, in Fig. 12.10a, if dimension Z is omitted, surface A will be controlled by both dimensions X and Y, and there can be a total variation of .010″ instead of the variation of .005″ permitted by dimension Y, which is the dimension directly applied to

surface A. Furthermore, if the part is made to all the minimum tolerances of X, Y, and Z, the total variation in the length of the part will be .015″, and the part can be as short as 2.985″. However, the tolerance on the overall dimension W is only .005″, permitting the part to be only as short as 2.995″. The part is superfluously dimensioned.

In some cases, for functional reasons, it may be desired to hold all three small dimensions X, Y, and Z closely without regard to the overall length. In such a case the overall dimension is just a **reference dimension** and should be denoted with parentheses. In other cases it may be desired to hold two small dimensions X and Y and the overall closely without regard to dimension Z. In that case, dimension Z should be omitted, or denoted as a reference with parentheses.

As a rule, it is best to dimension each surface so that it is affected by only one dimension. This can be done by referring all dimensions to a single datum surface, such as B, as shown in Fig. 12.10b (see also Figs. 11.37d to 11.37f).

■ 12.10 TOLERANCES AND MACHINING PROCESSES

As has been repeatedly stated in this chapter, tolerances should be as coarse as possible and still permit satisfactory use of the part. If this is done, great savings can be effected from the use of less expensive tools, lower labor and inspection costs, and reduced scrapping of material.

Figure 12.11 shows a chart of tolerance grades obtainable in relation to the accuracy of machining processes that may be used as a guide by the designer. Metric values may be ascertained by multiplying the given decimal-inch values by 25.4 and rounding off the product to one less place to the right of the decimal point than given for the decimal-inch value (see

 FIGURE 12.10   **Cumulative Tolerances.**

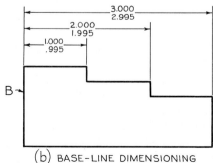

(a) CUMULATIVE TOLERANCES   (b) BASE-LINE DIMENSIONING

Range of Sizes		Tolerances								
From	To and Including									
.000	.599	.00015	.0002	.0003	.0005	.0008	.0012	.002	.003	.005
.600	.999	.00015	.00025	.0004	.0006	.001	.0015	.0025	.004	.006
1.000	1.499	.0002	.0003	.0005	.0008	.0012	.002	.003	.005	.008
1.500	2.799	.00025	.0004	.0006	.001	.0015	.0025	.004	.006	.010
2.800	4.499	.0003	.0005	.0008	.0012	.002	.003	.005	.008	.012
4.500	7.799	.0004	.0006	.001	.0015	.0025	.004	.006	.010	.015
7.800	13.599	.0005	.0008	.0012	.002	.003	.005	.008	.012·	.020
13.600	20.999	.0006	.001	.0015	.0025	.004	.006	.010	.015	.025

FIGURE 12.11 Tolerances Related to Machining Processes.

§11.10). For detailed information on manufacturing processes and measuring devices, see Chapter 10.

■ 12.11 METRIC SYSTEM OF TOLERANCES AND FITS

The preceding material on limits and fits between mating parts is suitable, without need of conversion, for the decimal-inch system of measurement. A system of preferred metric limits and fits by the International Organization for Standardization (ISO) is in the ANSI B4.2 standard. The system is specified for holes, cylinders, and shafts, but it is also adaptable to fits between parallel surfaces of such features as keys and slots. The following terms for metric fits, although somewhat similar to those for decimal-inch fits, are illustrated in Fig. 12.12.

1. **Basic size** is the size from which limits or deviations are assigned. Basic sizes, usually diameters, should be selected from a table of preferred sizes (see Fig. 12.17).

2. **Deviation** is the difference between the basic size

FIGURE 12.12 Terms Related to Metric Limits and Fits [ANSI B4.2– 1978 (R1994)].

and the hole or shaft size. This is equivalent to the tolerance in the decimal-inch system.

3. **Upper deviation** is the difference between the basic size and the permitted maximum size of the part.

This is comparable to maximum tolerance in the decimal-inch system.

4. Lower deviation is the difference between the basic size and the minimum permitted size of the part. This is comparable to minimum tolerance in the decimal-inch system.

5. Fundamental deviation is the deviation closest to the basic size. This is comparable to minimum allowance in the decimal-inch system.

6. Tolerance is the difference between the permitted minimum and maximum sizes of a part.

7. International tolerance grade (IT) is a set of tolerances that varies according to the basic size and

provides a uniform level of accuracy within the grade. For example, in the dimension 50H8 for a close-running fit, the IT grade is indicated by the numeral 8. (The letter H indicates that the tolerance is on the hole for the 50-mm dimension.) In all, there are 18 IT grades—IT01, IT0, and IT1 through IT16 (Figs. 12.13 and 12.14)—for IT grades related to machining processes and for the practical use of the IT grades (see also Appendix 10).

8. Tolerance zone refers to the relationship of the tolerance to basic size. It is established by a combination of the fundamental deviation indicated by a letter and the IT grade number. In the dimension 50H8, for the close-running fit, the H8 specifies the tolerance zone (see Fig. 12.14).

9. The **hole-basis system of preferred fits** is a system in which the basic diameter is the minimum size. For the generally preferred hole-basis system, the fundamental deviation is specified by the uppercase letter H (Fig. 12.15a).

10. The **shaft-basis system of preferred fits** is a system in which the basic diameter is the maximum size of the shaft. The fundamental deviation is given by the lowercase letter f (Fig. 12.15b).

11. An **interference fit** results in an interference between two mating parts under *all* tolerance conditions.

12. A **transition fit** results in either a clearance or an interference condition between two assembled parts.

13. Tolerance symbols are used to specify the tolerances and fits for mating parts (Fig. 12.15c). For the hole-basis system, the 50 indicates the diameter in millimeters; the fundamental deviation for the hole is in-

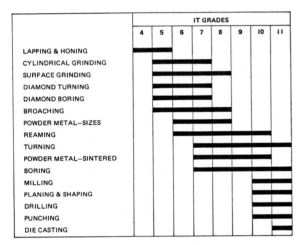

FIGURE 12.13 International Tolerance Grades Related to Machining Processes [ANSI B4.2–1978 (R1994)].

FIGURE 12.14 Practical Use of International Tolerance Grades.

FIGURE 12.15 Application of Definitions and Symbols to Holes and Shafts [ANSI B4.2–1978 (R1994)].

50 H8   50H8$\left(\dfrac{50.039}{50.000}\right)$ $\dfrac{50.039}{50.000}$(50H8)

(a) PREFERRED   (b)   (c)

FIGURE 12.16 **Acceptable Methods of Giving Tolerance Symbols (ANSI/ASME Y14.5M–1994).**

dicated by the capital letter H, and for the shaft it is indicated by the lowercase letter f. The numbers following the letters indicate this IT grade. Note that the symbols for the hole and shaft are separated by the slash. Tolerance symbols for a 50-mm-diameter hole may be given in several acceptable forms (Fig. 12.16). The values in parentheses are for reference only and may be omitted. The upper and lower limit values may be found in Appendix 11.

12.12 PREFERRED SIZES

The preferred basic sizes for computing tolerances are given in Table 12.1. Basic diameters should be selected

Basic Size, mm		Basic Size, mm		Basic Size mm	
First Choice	Second Choice	First Choice	Second Choice	First Choice	Second Choice
1		10		100	
	1.1		11		110
1.2		12		120	
	1.4		14		140
1.6		16		160	
	1.8		18		180
2		20		200	
	2.2		22		220
2.5		25		250	
	2.8		28		280
3		30		300	
	3.5		35		350
4		40		400	
	4.5		45		450
5		50		500	
	5.5		55		550
6		60		600	
	7		70		700
8		80		800	
	9		90		900
				1000	

TABLE 12.1 **Preferred Sizes [ANSI B4.2–1978 (R1994)]**

from the first choice column since these are readily available stock sizes for round, square, and hexagonal products.

12.13 PREFERRED FITS

The symbols for either the hole-basis or shaft-basis preferred fits (clearance, transition, and interference) are given in Table 12.2. Fits should be selected from this table for mating parts where possible.

The values corresponding to the fits are found in Appendixes 11–14. Although second and third choice basic size diameters are possible, they must be calculated from tables not included in this text. For the generally preferred hole-basis system, note that the ISO symbols range from H11/c11 (loose running) to H7/u6 (force fit). For the shaft-basis system, the preferred symbols range from C11/h11 (loose fit) to U7/h6 (force fit).

Suppose that you want to use the symbols to specify the dimensions for a free-running fit (hole basis) for a proposed diameter of 48 mm. Since 48 mm is not listed as a preferred size in Table 12.1, the design is altered to use the acceptable 50-mm diameter. From the preferred fits descriptions in Table 12.2, the free-running fit (hole-basis) is H9/d9. To determine the upper and lower deviation limits of the hole as given in the preferred hole-basis table (Appendix 11), follow across from the basic size of 50 to H9 under "Free running." The limits for the hole are 50.000 and 50.062 mm. Then the upper and lower limits of deviation for the shaft are found in the d9 column under "Free running." They are 49.920 and 49.858 mm, respectively. Limits for other fits are established in a similar manner.

Limits for the shaft-basis dimensioning are determined similarly from the preferred shaft basis table in Appendix 12. See Figs. 12.16 and 12.17 for acceptable methods of specifying tolerances by symbols on drawings. A single note for the mating parts (free-running fit, hole basis) would be Ø50 H9/d9 (Fig. 12.17).

12.14 GEOMETRIC TOLERANCING

Geometric tolerances state the maximum allowable variations of a form or its position from the perfect geometry implied on the drawing. The term "geometric" refers to various forms, such as a plane, a cylinder, a cone, a square, or a hexagon. Theoretically these are perfect forms, but, because it is impossible to produce perfect forms, it may be necessary to specify the

ISO Symbol		Description
Hole Basis	**Shaft[a] Basis**	

<table>
<tr><td rowspan="4">Clearance Fits</td><td>H11/c11</td><td>C11/h11</td><td>Loose-running fit for wide commercial tolerances or allowances on external members.</td></tr>
<tr><td>H9/d9</td><td>D9/h9</td><td>Free-running fit not for use where accuracy is essential, but good for large temperature variations, high running speeds, or heavy journal pressures.</td></tr>
<tr><td>H8/f7</td><td>F8/h7</td><td>Close-running fit for running on accurate machines and for accurate location at moderate speeds and journal pressures.</td></tr>
<tr><td>H7/g6</td><td>G7/h6</td><td>Sliding fit not intended to run freely, but to move and turn freely and locate accurately.</td></tr>
<tr><td rowspan="3">Transition Fits</td><td>H7/h6</td><td>H7/h6</td><td>Locational clearance fit provides snug fit for locating stationary parts; but can be freely assembled and disassembled.</td></tr>
<tr><td>H7/k6</td><td>K7/h6</td><td>Locational transition fit for accurate location, a compromise between clearance and interference.</td></tr>
<tr><td>H7/n6</td><td>N7/h6</td><td>Locational transition fit for more accurate location where greater interference is permissible.</td></tr>
<tr><td rowspan="3">Interference Fits</td><td>H7/p6</td><td>P7/h6</td><td>Locational interference fit for parts requiring rigidity and alignment with prime accuracy of location but without special bore pressure requirements.</td></tr>
<tr><td>H7/s6</td><td>S7/h6</td><td>Medium drive fit for ordinary steel parts or shrink fits on light sections, the tightest fit usable with cast iron.</td></tr>
<tr><td>H7/u6</td><td>U7/h6</td><td>Force fit suitable for parts which can be highly stressed or for shrink fits where the heavy pressing forces required are impractical.</td></tr>
</table>

More clearance →

More interference →

[a] The transition and interference shaft-basis fits shown do not convert to exactly the same hole-basis fit conditions for basic sizes in the range from Q through 3 mm. Interference fit P7/h6 converts to a transition fit H7/p6 in the above size range.

TABLE 12.2   Preferred Fits [ANSI B4.2–1978 (R1994)]

FREE RUNNING FIT – HOLE BASIS

(a) PREFERRED   (b) ACCEPTABLE   (c) ACCEPTABLE

FIGURE 12.17   Methods of Specifying Tolerances with Symbols for Mating Parts.

amount of variation permitted. These tolerances specify either the diameter or the width of a tolerance zone within which a surface or the axis of a cylinder or a hole must be if the part is to meet the required accuracy for proper function and fit. When tolerances of form are not given on a drawing, it is customary to assume that, regardless of form variations, the part will fit and function satisfactorily.

Tolerances of form and position or location control such characteristics as straightness, flatness, parallelism, perpendicularity (squareness), concentricity, roundness, angular displacement, and so on.

Methods of indicating geometric tolerances by means of *geometric characteristic symbols* are recommended rather than by traditional notes and are discussed and illustrated subsequently. See the latest Dimensioning and Tolerancing Standard (ANSI/ASME Y14.5M–1994) for more complete coverage.

12.15 SYMBOLS FOR TOLERANCES OF POSITION AND FORM

Since traditional narrative notes for specifying tolerances of *position* (location) and *form* (shape) may be confusing or unclear, may require too much space, and may not be understood internationally, most multinational companies have adopted symbols for such specifications (ANSI/ASME Y14.5M–1994). These ANSI symbols provide an accurate and concise means of specifying geometric characteristics and tolerances in a

minimum of space (Table 12.3). The symbols may be supplemented by notes if the precise geometric requirements cannot be conveyed by the symbols. For construction details of the geometric tolerancing symbols, see Appendix 37.

Combinations of the various symbols and their meanings are given in Fig. 12.18. Application of the symbols to drawing are illustrated in Fig. 12.43. The geometric characteristic symbols plus the supplementary symbols are further explained and illustrated with material adapted from ANSI/ASME Y14.5M–1994, as follows.

1. The **basic dimension symbol** is identified by the enclosing frame symbol (Fig. 12.18a). The basic dimension (size) is the value used to describe the theoretically exact size, shape, or location of a feature. It is the basis from which permissible variations are

Geometric characteristic symbols				Modifying symbols	
	Type of Tolerance	Characteristic	Symbol	Term	Symbol
For individual features	Form	Straightness	—	At maximum material condition	Ⓜ
		Flatness	▱	At least material condition	Ⓛ
		Circularity (roundness)	○	Projected tolerance zone	Ⓟ
		Cylindricity	⌭	Free state	Ⓕ
For individual or related features	Profile	Profile of a line	⌒	Tangent plane	Ⓣ
		Profile of a surface	⌓	Diameter	⌀
For related features	Orientation	Angularity	∠	Spherical diameter	S⌀
		Perpendicularity	⊥	Radius	R
		Parallelism	∥	Spherical radius	SR
				Controlled radius	CR
	Location	Position	⌖	Reference	( )
		Concentricity	◎	Arc length	⌒
		Symmetry	=	Statistical tolerance	⟨ST⟩
	Runout	Circular runout	↗*	Between	↔
		Total runout	↗↗*		

*ARROWHEADS MAY BE FILLED OR NOT FILLED

TABLE 12.3   Geometric Characteristic and Modifying Symbols *(ASME Y14.5M–1994)*

(a) BASIC DIMENSION SYMBOL

DIA (DIAMETER) ——————————— ⌀
MMC (MAXIMUM MATERIAL CONDITION) — Ⓜ
RFS (REGARDLESS OF FEATURE SIZE) — Ⓢ

(c) MODIFYING SYMBOLS

(b) DATUM SYMBOL

— Datum reference letter

— Geometric characteristic symbol

— Tolerance

— Modifier

(d) FEATURE CONTROL SYMBOLS

— Symbol   — Tolerance

⊥ 0.05 A

— Datum reference

↗ 0.05 A-B

— Reference to two datums

Modifier applicable to tolerance — Modifier of datum —

⊕ ⌀0.05 Ⓜ A Ⓜ

Datum reference —

(e) FEATURE CONTROL SYMBOLS WITH DATUM REFERENCES

FIGURE 12.18 Use of Symbols for Tolerance of Position and Form (ASME Y14.5M–1994).

established by tolerances on other dimensions in notes, or in feature control frames.

2. The **datum identifying symbol** consists of a capital letter in a square frame and a leader line extending from the frame to the concerned feature, terminating with a triangle. The triangle may be filled or not filled (see Fig. 12.18b). Letters of the alphabet (except I, O, and Q) are used as datum-identifying letters. A point, line, plane, cylinder, or other geometric form assumed to be exact for purposes of computation may serve as

a datum from which the location or geometric relationship of features of a part may be established, as shown in Fig. 12.19.

3. Supplementary symbols include the symbols for MMC (maximum material condition, i.e., minimum hole diameter, maximum shaft diameter) and LMC (least material condition, i.e., maximum hole diameter, minimum shaft diameter) (Fig. 12.18c). The abbreviations MMC and LMC are also used in notes (see also Table 12.3).

FIGURE 12.19 Placement of Datum Feature Symbol (ASME Y14.5M–1994).

(a) Feature Surface and an extension line

(b) Feature Size - ⌀

(c) Feature Size - ⌀

(d) Feature Size

(e) Feature Size - ⌀

(f) Feature Size - ⌀

(g) Feature Size - ⌀

(h) Feature Control Frame

The symbol for diameter is used instead of the abbreviation DIA to indicate a diameter, and it precedes the specified tolerance in a feature control symbol (Fig. 12.18d). This symbol for diameter instead of the abbreviation DIA is used on a drawing, and it should precede the dimension. For narrative notes, the abbreviation DIA is preferred.

4. Combined symbols are found when individual symbols, datum reference letters, needed tolerances, and so on are found in a single frame (Fig. 12.18e).

A position of form tolerance is given by a feature control symbol made up of a frame about the appropriate geometric characteristic symbol plus the allowable tolerance. A vertical line separates the symbol and the tolerance (Fig. 12.18d). Where needed, the tolerance should be preceded by the symbol for the diameter and followed by the symbol for MMC or LMC.

A tolerance of position or form related to a datum is so indicated in the feature control symbol by placing the datum reference letter following either the geometric characteristic symbol or the tolerance. Vertical lines separate the entries, and, where applicable, the datum reference letter entry includes the symbol for MMC or LMC (Fig. 12.18).

■ 12.16 POSITIONAL TOLERANCES

In §12.25 there are a number of examples of the traditional methods of locating holes—that is, by means of rectangular coordinates or angular dimensions. Each dimension has a tolerance, either given directly or indicated on the completed drawing by a general note.

Figure 12.20a shows a hole located from two surfaces at right angles to each other. In Fig. 12.20b, the center may lie anywhere within a square tolerance zone, the sides of which are equal to the tolerances.

Thus, the total variations along either diagonal of the square by the coordinate method of dimensioning will be 1.4 times greater than the indicated tolerance. Hence, a .014-diameter tolerance zone would increase the square tolerance zone area 57% without exceeding the tolerance permitted along the diagonal of the square tolerance zone.

Features located by toleranced angular and radial dimensions will have a wedge-shaped tolerance zone. (see Fig. 12.29).

If four holes are dimensioned with rectangular coordinates as in Fig. 12.21a, acceptable patterns for the square tolerance zones for the holes are shown in Figs. 12.21b and 12.21c. The locational tolerances are actually greater than indicated by the dimensions.

Feature control symbols are related to the feature by one of several methods illustrated in Fig. 12.44. The following methods are preferred:

1. Adding the symbol to a note or dimension pertaining to the feature.
2. Running a leader from the symbol to the feature.
3. Attaching the side, end, or corner of the symbol frame to an extension line from the feature.
4. Attaching a side or end of the symbol frame to the dimension line pertaining to the feature.

In Fig. 12.21a, hole A is selected as a datum, and the other three are located from it. The square tolerance zone for hole A results from the tolerances on the two rectangular coordinate dimensions locating hole A. The sizes of the tolerance zones for the other three holes result from the tolerances between the holes, while their locations will vary according to the actual location of the datum hole A. Two of the many possible zone patterns are shown in Figs. 12.21b and 12.21c.

FIGURE 12.20 Tolerance Zones.

(a)   (b)   (c)

FIGURE 12.21   Tolerance Zones.

Thus, with the dimensions shown in Fig. 12.21a, it is difficult to say whether the resulting parts will actually fit the mating parts satisfactorily even though they conform to the tolerances shown on the drawing.

These disadvantages are overcome by giving exact theoretical locations by untoleranced dimensions and then specifying by a note how far actual positions may be displaced from these locations. This is called **true-position dimensioning**. It will be seen that the tolerance zone for each hole will be a circle, with the size of the circle depending on the amount of variation permitted from true position.

A true-position dimension denotes the theoretically exact position of a feature. The location of each feature, such as a hole, slot, or stud, is given by untoleranced basic dimensions identified by the enclosing frame or symbol. To prevent misunderstandings, true position should be established with respect to a datum.

In simple arrangements, the choice of a datum may be obvious and not require identification.

Positional tolerancing is identified by a characteristic symbol directed to a feature, which establishes a circular tolerance zone (Fig. 12.22).

Actually, the "circular tolerance zone" is a cylindrical tolerance zone (the diameter of which is equal to the positional tolerance while its length is equal to the length of the feature unless otherwise specified), and its axis must be within this cylinder (Fig. 12.23).

The center line of the hole may coincide with the center line of the cylindrical tolerance zone (Fig. 12.23a); it may be parallel to it but displaced so as to remain within the tolerance cylinder (Fig. 12.23b); or it may be inclined while remaining within the tolerance cylinder (Fig. 12.23c). In this last case we see that the positional tolerance also defines the limits of squareness variation.

FIGURE 12.22   True-Position Dimensioning [ANSI Y14.5M–1982 (R1988)].

(a)   (b)

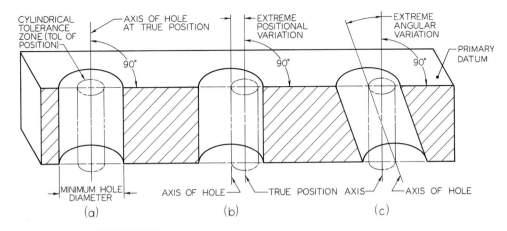

FIGURE 12.23   Cylindrical Tolerance Zone (ASME Y14.5M–1994).

In terms of the cylindrical surface of the hole, the positional tolerance specification indicates that all elements on the hole surface must be on or outside a cylinder whose diameter is equal to the minimum diameter (MMC; §12.17) or the maximum diameter of the hole minus the positional tolerance (diameter, or twice the radius), with the center line of the cylinder located at true position (Fig. 12.24).

The use of basic untoleranced dimensions to locate features at true position avoids one of the chief difficulties in tolerancing—the accumulation of tolerances (§12.9), even in a chain of dimensions (Fig. 12.25).

While features, such as holes and bosses, may vary in any direction from the true-position axis, other features, such as slots, may vary on either side of a true-position plane (Fig. 12.26).

FIGURE 12.24   True Position Interpretation (ASME Y14.5M–1994).

FIGURE 12.25   No Tolerance Accumulation.

Since the exact locations of the true positions are given by untoleranced dimensions, it is important to prevent the application of general tolerances to these. A note should be added to the drawing, such as

GENERAL TOLERANCES DO NOT APPLY TO BASIC TRUE-POSITION DIMENSIONS.

■ 12.17 MAXIMUM MATERIAL CONDITION

Maximum material condition, usually abbreviated MMC, means that a feature of a finished product contains the maximum amount of material permitted by the toleranced size dimensions shown for that feature. Thus, we have MMC when holes, slots, or other internal features are at minimum size, or when shafts, pads, bosses, and other external features are at their maximum size. We have MMC for both mating parts when the largest shaft is in the smallest hole and there is the least clearance between the parts.

In assigning positional tolerance to a hole, it is necessary to consider the size limits of the hole. If the hole is at MMC (smallest size), the positional

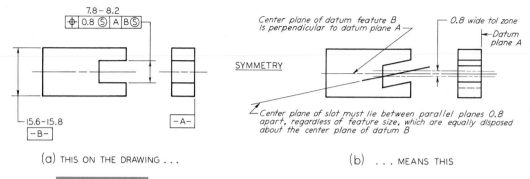

FIGURE 12.26   **Positional Tolerancing for Symmetry (ASME Y14.5M–1994).**

FIGURE 12.27   **Maximum and Minimum Material Conditions—Two-Hole Pattern (ASME Y14.5M–1994).**

tolerance is not affected, but if the hole is larger, the available positional tolerance is greater. In Fig. 12.27a, two half-inch holes are shown. If they are exactly .500″ in diameter (MMC, or smallest size) and are exactly 2.000″ apart, they should receive a gage made of two round pins .500″ in diameter fixed in a plate 2.000″ apart (Fig. 12.27b). However, the center-to-center distance between the holes may vary from 1.993″ to 2.007″.

If the .500″ diameter holes are at their extreme positions (Fig. 12.27c), the pins in the gage would have to be .007″ smaller, or .493″ diameter, to enter the holes. Thus, if the .500″ diameter holes are located at the maximum distance apart, the .493″ diameter gage pins

would contact the inner sides of the holes; and if the holes are located at the minimum distance apart, the .493″ diameter pins would contact the outer surfaces of the holes, as shown. If gagemakers' tolerances are not considered, the gage pins would have to be .493″ diameter and exactly 2.000 apart if the holes are .500 diameter, or MMC.

If the holes are .505″ diameter—that is, at maximum size (Fig. 12.27d)—they will be accepted by the same .493″ diameter gage pins at 2.000″ apart if the inner sides of the holes contact the inner sides of the gage pins and the outer sides of the holes contact the outer sides of the gage pins, as shown. Thus the holes may be 2.012″ apart, which is beyond the tolerance permitted for the center-to-center distance between the holes. Similarly, the holes may be as close together as 1.988″ from center to center, which again is outside the specified positional tolerance.

Thus, when the holes are at maximum size, a greater positional tolerance becomes available. Since all features may vary in size, it is necessary to make clear on the drawing at what basic dimension the true position applies. In all but a few exceptional cases, the additional positional tolerance available when holes are larger than minimum size is acceptable and desirable. Parts thus accepted can be freely assembled whether or not the holes or other features are within the specified positional tolerance. This practice has been recognized and used in manufacturing for years, as is evident from the use of fixed-pin gages, which have been commonly used to inspect parts and control the least favorable condition of assembly. Thus it has become common practice for both manufacturing and inspection to assume that positional tolerance applies to MMC and that greater positional tolerance becomes permissible when the part is not at MMC.

To avoid possible misinterpretation as to whether maximum material condition (MMC) applies, it should be clearly stated on the drawing by the addition of MMC symbols to each applicable tolerance or by suitable coverage in a document referenced on the drawing.

When MMC is not specified on the drawing with respect to an individual tolerance, datum reference, or both, the following rules apply:

1. True-position tolerances and related datum references apply at MMC. For a tolerance of position, RFS (regardless of feature size) may be specified on the drawing with respect to the individual tolerance, datum reference, or both, as applicable.

2. All applicable geometric tolerances, such as angularity, parallelism, perpendicularity, concentricity, and symmetry tolerances, including related datum references, or both, apply at RFS, where no modifying symbol is specified. Circular runout, total runout, concentricity, and symmetry are applicable only on an RFS basis and cannot be modified to MMC or LMC. No element of the actual feature will extend beyond the envelope of the perfect form at MMC. MMC or LMC must be specified on the drawing where it is required.

■ 12.18 TOLERANCES OF ANGLES

Bilateral tolerances have traditionally been given on angles (Fig. 12.28). Consequently, the wedge-shaped tolerance zone increases as the distance from the vertex of the angle increases. Thus, the tolerance had to be figured after considering the total displacement at the point farthest from the vertex of the angle before a tolerance could be specified that would not exceed the allowable displacement. The use of angular tolerances may be avoided by using gages. Taper turning is often handled by machining to fit a gage or by fitting to the mating part.

If an angular surface is located by a linear and an angular dimension (Fig. 12.29a), the surface must lie within a tolerance zone (Fig. 12.29b). The angular zone will be wider as the distance from the vertex increases. To avoid the accumulation of tolerances—that is, to decrease the tolerance zone—the *basic angle* tolerancing method (Fig. 12.29c) is recommended (ASME Y14.5M–1994). The angle is indicated as basic with the proper symbol and no angular tolerance is specified. The tolerance zone is now defined by two parallel planes, resulting in improved angular control (Fig. 12.29d).

■ 12.19 FORM TOLERANCES FOR SINGLE FEATURES

Straightness, flatness, roundness, cylindricity, and, in some instances, profile are form tolerances applicable to single features regardless of feature size (RFS).

1. A **straightness tolerance** specifies a tolerance zone within which an axis or all points of the considered

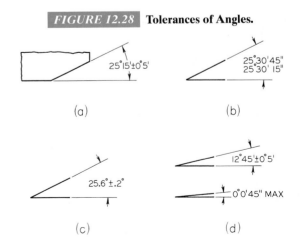

FIGURE 12.28   Tolerances of Angles.

(a)

(b)

(c)

(d)

FIGURE 12.29 **FIGURE 12.29** **Angular Tolerance Zones (ASME Y14.5M–1994).**

FIGURE 12.30 **Specifying Straightness (ASME Y14.5M–1994).**

element must lie (Fig. 12.30). Straightness is a condition in which an element of a surface or an axis is a straight line.

2. A **flatness tolerance** specifies a tolerance zone defined by two parallel planes within which the surface must lie (Fig. 12.31). Flatness is the condition of a surface having all elements in one plane.

3. A **roundness (circularity) tolerance** specifies a tolerance zone bounded by two concentric circles within which each circular element of the surface must lie (Fig. 12.32). Roundness is a condition of a surface of revolution in which, for a cone or cylinder, all points of the surface intersected by any plane perpendicular to a common axis are equidistant from that axis. For a sphere, all points of the surface intersected by any

plane passing through a common center are equidistant from that center.

4. A **cylindricity tolerance** specifies a tolerance zone bounded by two concentric cylinders within which the surface must lie (Fig. 12.33). This tolerance applies to both circular and longitudinal elements of the entire surface. Cylindricity is a condition of a surface of revolution in which all points of the surface are equidistant from a common axis. When no tolerance of form is given, many possible shapes may exist within a tolerance zone, as illustrated in Fig. 12.34.

5. A **profile tolerance** specifies a uniform boundary or zone along the true profile within which all elements of the surface must lie (Figs. 12.35 and 12.36). A profile is the outline of an object in a given plane (two-

THIS ON THE DRAWING . . . . .

FLATNESS

. . . . . MEANS THIS

0.25 wide tolerance zone

The surface must be within the specified tolerance of size and must lie between two parallel planes 0.25 apart.

FIGURE 12.31 **Specifying Flatness (ASME Y14.5M–1994).**

dimensional) figure. Profiles are formed by projecting a three-dimensional figure onto a plane or by taking cross sections through the figure, with the resulting profile composed of such elements as straight lines, arcs, or other curved lines.

■ 12.20 FORM TOLERANCES FOR RELATED FEATURES

Angularity, parallelism, perpendicularity, and in some instances, profile are form tolerances applicable to related features. These tolerances control the attitude of features to one another (ASME Y14.5M–1994).

1. An **angularity tolerance** specifies a tolerance zone defined by two parallel planes at the specified basic angle (other than 90°) from a datum plane or axis

THIS ON THE DRAWING . . . . MEANS THIS

CYLINDER   CONE   SECTION A-A

0.25 wide tolerance zone

ROUNDNESS

Each circular element of the surface in any plane perpendicular to a common axis must be within the specified tolerance of size and must lie between two concentric circles — one having a radius 0.25 larger than the other.

FIGURE 12.32 **Specifying Roundness for a Cylinder or Cone (ASME Y14.5M–1994).**

THIS ON THE DRAWING . . . . MEANS THIS

0.25 wide tolerance zone

CYLINDRICITY

The cylindrical surface must be within the specified tolerance of size and must lie between two concentric cylinders — one having a radius 0.25 larger than the other.

FIGURE 12.33 **Specifying Cylindricity (ASME Y14.5M–1994).**

THIS ON THE DRAWING . . . . MEANS THIS

Tolerance zone or boundary within which forms
may vary when no tolerance of form is given.

FIGURE 12.34 **Acceptable Variations of Form—No Specified Tolerance of Form.**

THIS ON THE DRAWING . . . . MEANS THIS

(UNTOLERANCED DIMENSIONS ARE BASIC)

ALL CORNERS R0.2 MAX

Surfaces all around must lie within two parallel
boundaries 0.6 apart equally disposed about
the true profile which are perpendicular to
datum plane A. Radii of part corners must
not exceed 0.2.

FIGURE 12.35 **Specifying Profile of a Surface All Around (ASME Y14.5M–1994).**

THIS ON THE DRAWING . . . . MEANS THIS

(UNTOLERANCED DIMENSIONS ARE BASIC)

The surface between points X & Y must lie
between the two profile boundaries 0.25 apart,
equally disposed about the true profile, which
are perpendicular to datum plane A and positioned with respect to datum planes B & C.

FIGURE 12.36 **Specifying Profile of a Surface between Points (ASME Y14.5M–1994).**

THIS ON THE DRAWING . . . . .

ANGULARITY

. . . . . MEANS THIS

The surface must be within the specified tolerance of size and must lie between two parallel planes 0.4 apart which are inclined at 30° to the datum plane A.

FIGURE 12.37 **Specifying Angularity for a Plane Surface (ASME Y14.5M–1994).**

within which the surface or the axis of the feature must lie (Fig. 12.37).

2. A **parallelism tolerance** specifies a tolerance zone defined by two parallel planes or lines parallel to a datum plane or axis, respectively, within which the surface or axis of the feature must lie, or the parallelism tolerance may specify a cylindrical tolerance zone parallel to a datum axis within which the axis of the feature must lie (Figs. 12.38–12.40).

3. Perpendicularity tolerance. Perpendicularity is a condition of a surface, median plane, or axis at 90° to a datum plane or axis. A perpendicularity tolerance specifies one of the following:

a. A tolerance zone is defined by two parallel planes perpendicular to a datum plane, datum axis, or axis within which the surface of the feature must lie (Fig. 12.41).

b. A cylindrical tolerance zone perpendicular to a datum plane within which the axis of the feature must lie (Fig. 12.42).

4. Concentricity tolerance. Concentricity is the condition in which the axes of all cross-sectional elements of a feature's surface of revolution are common to the axis of a datum feature. A concentricity tolerance specifies a cylindrical tolerance zone whose axis coincides with a datum axis and within which all cross-sectional axes of the feature being controlled must lie (Fig. 12.43).

■ 12.21 APPLICATION OF GEOMETRIC TOLERANCING

The use of various feature control symbols in lieu of notes for position and form tolerance dimensions as abstracted from ASME Y14.5M–1994 is illustrated in Fig. 12.44. For a more detailed treatment of geometric tolerancing, consult the latest ASME Y14.5M dimensioning and tolerancing standard.

■ 12.22 SURFACE ROUGHNESS, WAVINESS, AND LAY

The modern demands of the automobile, the airplane, and other modern machines that can stand heavier loads and higher speeds with less friction and wear have increased the need for accurate control of surface quality by the designer regardless of the size of the

THIS ON THE DRAWING . . . . MEANS THIS

PARALLELISM

The surface must be within the specified tolerance of size and must lie between two planes 0.12 apart which are parallel to the datum plane A.

FIGURE 12.38 **Specifying Parallelism for a Plane Surface (ASME Y14.5M–1994).**

THIS ON THE DRAWING . . . . MEANS THIS

PARALLELISM

Datum plane A

0.12 wide
tolerance
zone

Possible orientation
of the feature axis

The feature axis must be within the specified
tolerance of location and must lie between two
planes 0.12 apart which are parallel to the
datum plane, regardless of feature size.

FIGURE 12.39 **Specifying Parallelism for an Axis Feature RFS (ASME Y14.5M–1994).**

THIS ON THE DRAWING . . . . MEANS THIS

PARALLELISM

Ø10.000 - 10.022 (10H8)

// Ø0.05 Ⓜ A

-A-

Possible orientation
of feature axis

0.05 diameter
tolerance zone

Datum axis A

The feature axis must be within the specified
tolerance of location. Where the feature is at
maximum material condition (10.00), the maxi-
mum parallelism tolerance is 0.05 diameter.
Where the feature departs from its MMC size,
an increase in the parallelism tolerance is al-
lowed which is equal to the amount of such
departure.

FIGURE 12.40 **Specifying Parallelism for an Axis Feature at MMC (ASME Y14.5M–1994).**

feature. Simple finish marks are not adequate to specify surface finish on such parts.

Surface finish is intimately related to the functioning of a surface, and proper specification of finish of such surfaces as bearings and seals is necessary. Surface quality specifications should be used only where needed, since the cost of producing a finished surface becomes greater as the quality of the surface called for is increased. Generally, the ideal surface finish is the roughest one that will do the job satisfactorily.

The system of surface texture symbols recommended by ANSI/ASME (Y14.36M–1996) for use on drawings, regardless of the system of measurement used, is now broadly accepted by American industry. These symbols are used to define *surface texture, roughness,* and *lay.* See Fig. 12.45 for the meaning and construction of these symbols. The basic surface texture symbol in Fig. 12.46a indicates a finished or machined surface by any method, just as does the general V symbol (Fig. 12.20a). Modifications to the basic surface texture symbol (Figs. 12.44b to 12.44d), define restrictions on material removal for the finished surface. Where surface texture values other than roughness average (R_a) are specified, the symbol must be drawn with the horizontal extension, as shown in Fig. 12.45e. Construction details for the symbols are given in Fig. 12.45f.

The surface must be within the specified tolerance of size and must lie between two parallel planes 0.12 apart which are perpendicular to the datum plane A.

PERPENDICULARITY FOR A PLANE SURFACE

(a)

The feature center plane must be within the specified tolerance of location and must lie between two parallel planes 0.12 apart, regardless of feature size, which are perpendicular to the datum plane A.

PERPENDICULARITY FOR A MEDIAN PLANE

(b)

The feature axis must be within the specified tolerance of location and must lie between two planes 0.2 apart, regardless of feature size, which are perpendicular to the datum axis A.

PERPENDICULARITY FOR AN AXIS

(c)

FIGURE 12.41 Specifying Perpendicularity (ASME Y14.5M–1994).

Applications of the surface texture symbols are given in Fig. 12.46a. Note that the symbols read from the bottom and/or the right side of the drawing and that they are not drawn at any angle or upside down.

Measurements for roughness and waviness, unless otherwise specified, apply in the direction that gives the maximum reading, usually across the lay (Fig. 12.46b). The recommended roughness height values are given in Table 12.4.

When it is necessary to indicate the roughness-width cutoff values, the standard values to be used are listed in Table 12.5. If no value is specified, the 0.80 value is assumed.

THIS ON THE DRAWING . . . . MEANS THIS

PERPENDICULARITY

The feature axis must be within the specified tolerance of location. Where the feature is at MMC (15.984) the maximum perpendicularity tolerance is 0.05 diameter. Where the feature departs from its MMC size, an increase in the perpendicularity tolerance is allowed which is equal to the amount of such departure.

FIGURE 12.42 Specifying Perpendicularity for an Axis, Pin, or Boss (ASME Y14.5M–1994).

THIS ON THE DRAWING . . . . MEANS THIS

CONCENTRICITY

The feature axis must be within a cylindrical zone of 0.1 diameter, regardless of feature size, and whose axis coincides with the datum axis.

FIGURE 12.43 Specifying Concentricity (ASME Y14.5M–1994).

FIGURE 12.44 Application of Symbols to Position and Form Tolerance Dimensions (ASME Y14.5M–1994).

Symbol	Meaning
(a)	Basic Surface Texture Symbol. Surface may be produced by any method except when the bar or circle, (b) or (d), is specified.
(b)	Material Removal By Machining Is Required. The horizontal bar indicates that material removal by machining is required to produce the surface and that material must be provided for that purpose.
(c) 3.5	Material Removal Allowance. The number indicates the amount of stock to be removed by machining in millimeters (or inches). Tolerances may be added to the basic value shown or in a general note.
(d)	Material Removal Prohibited. The circle in the vee indicates that the surface must be produced by processes such as casting, forging, hot finishing, cold finishing, die casting, powder metallurgy or injection molding without subsequent removal of material.
(e)	Surface Texture Symbol. To be used when any surface characteristics are specified above the horizontal line or to the right of the symbol. Surface may be produced by any method except when the bar or circle, (b) or (d), is specified.

(f)

* This dimension is adjusted by +1 for each line of values beyond the two lines shown below the horizontal line.

FIGURE 12.45 **Surface Texture Symbols and Construction (ANSI/ASME Y14.36M–1996).**

(a)

UNLESS OTHERWISE SPECIFIED:
ALL SURFACES 3.2

(b)

FIGURE 12.46 **Application of Surface Texture Symbols and Surface Characteristics (ANSI/ASME Y14.36M–1996).**

GRAPHICS SPOTLIGHT

Geometric Tolerances With AutoCAD 2000

AutoCAD 2000 has built in dialog boxes which allow you to create feature control frames for geometric dimensioning and tolerancing. You can create a feature control frame by picking the Tolerance icon from AutoCAD's Dimensioning toolbar. When you do so the dialog box shown in Figure A will appear on your screen. It shows the standard tolerance symbols.

To begin creating a feature control frame all you need to do is double click on the symbol you want to use. For example, you could double-click on the posi-

(A)

tional tolerance symbol shown in the upper left hand corner of the dialog box. When you have selected the symbol a new dialog box shown in Figure B will appear on the screen. You use it to create a single feature control frame, or a stacked feature control frame. You can also add diameter symbols, modifiers, datum references, or datum identifiers. The diameter symbol

shown in the Geometric Tolerance dialog box was added just by picking in the empty box below the heading Dia. A diameter symbol appears automatically. The area to the right of the diameter symbol is a text entry box that you use to type in the value you want to show for the tolerance.

To add a modifier symbol pick in the next empty box to the right. The Material Condition dialog box shown in Figure C pops up on the screen. You can quickly pick the modifier you want to add from the dialog box.

Datum references can be created just as quickly by picking in the appropriate box and typing in the letter you want to use. Datum references can also have a modifier when used with certain types of tolerances. Again, just pick in the empty box below the modifier and use the dialog box that appears to add a symbol.

If you want stacked tolerances or a datum identifier, you continue on with the same basic procedure. When you pick OK at the end of the process, you will be prompted to pick a location to place the tolerance in the drawing. You can also use the Leader command and select the options to place a tolerance at the end of a leader line. Using these dialog boxes you can quickly add geometric tolerance symbols as shown in Figure D to your drawings. Creating the symbols is easy, but you must give careful consideration to what the placement of the symbols in the

(B)

drawing means and make sure to reflect the intent of the design and the tolerances that are required for the part to function correctly in the assembly. Specifying needlessly restrictive tolerances just increases the cost of the part, without adding more functionality to the design.

(C)

(D)

Micro-meters[a] (μm)	Micro-inches (μin.)	Micro-meters[a] (μm)	Micro-inches (μin.)
0.012	0.5	1.25	50
0.025	1	1.60	63
0.050	2	2.0	80
0.075	3	2.5	100
0.10	4	3.2	125
0.125	5	4.0	180
0.15	6	5.0	200
0.20	8	6.3	250
0.25	10	8.0	320
0.32	13	10.0	400
0.40	16	12.5	500
0.50	20	15	600
0.63	25	20	800
0.80	32	25	1000
1.00	40		

[a] Micrometers are the same as thousandths of a millimeter (1μm = 0.001 mm)

TABLE 12.4 **Preferred Series Roughness Average Values (R_a) (ANSI/ASME Y14.36–1996).** *Recommended values are in color.*

Millimeters (mm)	Inches (in.)	Millimeters (mm)	Inches (in.)
0.08	.003	2.5	.1
0.25	.010	8.0	.3
0.80	.030	25.0	1.0

TABLE 12.5 **Standard Roughness Sampling Length (Cutoff) Values (ANSI/ASME Y14.36–1996).**

Millimeters (mm)	Inches (in.)	Millimeters (mm)	Inches (in.)
0.0005	.00002	0.025	.001
0.0008	.00003	0.05	.002
0.0012	.00005	0.08	.003
0.0020	.00008	0.12	.005
0.0025	.0001	0.20	.008
0.005	.0002	0.25	.010
0.008	.0003	0.38	.015
0.012	.0005	0.50	.020
0.020	.0008	0.80	.030

TABLE 12.6 **Preferred Series Maximum Waviness Height Values (ANSI/ASME Y14.36–1996).**

When maximum waviness height values are required, the recommended values to be used are as given in Table 12.6.

When it is desired to indicate lay, the lay symbols in Fig. 12.48 are added to the surface texture symbols as per the examples given. Selected applications of the surface texture values to the symbols are given and explained in Fig. 12.49.

A typical range of surface roughness values that may be obtained from various production methods is shown in Fig. 12.50. Preferred roughness-height values are shown at the top of the chart.

■ 12.23 USING GEOMETRIC DIMENSIONING AND TOLERANCING

Geometric dimensioning and tolerancing (GDT) has evolved over the last forty years to become an indispensable tool for defining parts and features more accurately. GDT not only considers an individual part and its dimensions and tolerances, but views that part in relations to its related parts. This allows the designer more latitude in defining the parts feature's more accurately by not only considering the part's dimensions, but its tolerances at the initial design stage. GDT also simplifies the inspection process. This is accomplished through the use of ASME standards (ASME--Y14.5M), as we have discussed previously.

Individually manufactured parts and components must eventually be assembled in to products. We take for granted that each part of a lawnmower, for example, will mate properly with its other components when assembled. The wheels will slip into their axles, the pistons will fit properly into their cylinders, etc. Nothing should be too tight or too loose.

Geometric dimensioning and tolerancing, therefore, is important to both the design and manufacturing processes.

Applying GDT principles to the design process requires five steps:

Step 1: Define the part's functions. It is best to break the part down to its simplest functions. Be as specific as possible. For example, a lawnmower wheel's functions is to: (a). Give the product mobility: (b). Lift the mowing deck off the ground; (c) Add rigidity to the body, etc.

Step 2: List the functions by priority. Only one function should have top priority This step can be difficult since many parts are designed to incorporate multiple functions. In our lawnmower wheels example, the function with top priority would be to give the product mobility.

Step 3: Define the datum reference frame. This step should be based on your list of priorities This may mean creating several reference frames, each based on a priority on your list. The frame should be set up in either one, two, or three planes.

Step 4: Control selection. (See §§12.19, 12.21, 12.22). In most cases, several controls will be needed (e.g.,runout, position, concentricity, roughness, etc.). Begin with the simplest control. By "simplest" we mean least restrictive. Work from the least restrictive to the most restrictive set of controls.

Step 5: Calculate tolerances. Most tolerances are mathematically based. This step should be the easiest. Apply MMC, RFS, or LMC where indicated. (See §§12.15, 12.17, 12.19.) Avoid completing this step first, it should always be your last. See Fig. 12.47 for a worksheet outlining these five steps.

CAD programs generally allow the user to add tolerances to dimension values in the drawings. Geometric dimensioning and tolerancing symbols, finish marks, and other standard symbols are typically available as a part of the CAD program or as a symbol library.

Geometric dimensioning and tolerancing has become an essential part of today's manufacturing industry. To compete in today's marketplace, companies are required to develop and produce products of the highest quality, at lowest cost, and guarantee on-time delivery. Although considered by most to be a design specification language, GDT is a manufacturing and inspection language as well, providing a means for uniform interpretation and understanding by these various groups. It provides both a national and international contract base for customers and suppliers. See Chapter 10 for a more in-depth discussion of how GDT can be used in both the manufacturing and inspection processes.

1. DEFINE THE PART'S (FEATURE'S) FUNCTION:

Basic function _____

_____

Additional function(s) _____

_____

2. LIST THE FUNCTIONS IN ORDER OF PRIORITY

Function# _____   Function# _____   Function# _____

3. DEFINE DATUM REFERENCE FRAME

Part # _____   Function _____

Primary Datum Feature _____   Secondary Datum Feature _____

Part # _____   Function _____

Primary Datum Feature _____   Secondary Datum Feature _____

Part # _____   Function _____

Primary Datum Feature _____   Secondary Datum Feature _____

4. SELECT CONTROL TYPE

Part# _____   Part # _____

Control _____   Control _____

5. CALCULATE THE TOLERANCES

Part # _____   Part# _____   Part# _____

_____

FIGURE 12.47   **Geometric Dimensioning and Tolerancing Design Worksheet.**

LAY SYMBOLS

SYM	DESIGNATION	EXAMPLE	SYM	DESIGNATION	EXAMPLE
—	Lay parallel to the line representing the surface to which the symbol is applied.	DIRECTION OF TOOL MARKS	X	Lay angular in both directions to line representing the surface to which symbol is applied.	DIRECTION OF TOOL MARKS
⊥	Lay perpendicular to the line representing the surface to which the symbol is applied.	DIRECTION OF TOOL MARKS	M	Lay multidirectional	
C	Lay approximately circular relative to the center of the surface to which the symbol is applied.		R	Lay approximately radial relative to the center of the surface to which the symbol is applied.	

FIGURE 12.48 Lay Symbols (ANSI/ASME Y14.36M–1996).

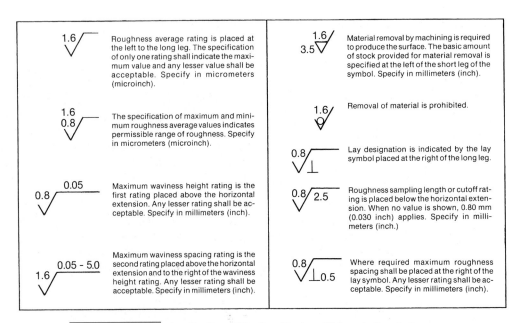

FIGURE 12.49 Application of Surface Texture Values to Symbol (ANSI/ASME Y14.36M–1996).

FIGURE 12.50 **Surface Roughness Produced by Common Production Methods (ANSI/ASME B46.1–1985). The ranges shown are typical of the processes listed. Higher or lower values may be obtained under special conditions.**

FIGURE 12.51 **Application of Surface Finish Symbols with Computervision CADDS 4X Production Drafting System.** *Courtesy of Design Pacifica.*

GENERAL TOLERANCE SYMBOLS

Symbol	Name
⌀	Diameter
XX.XX	Basic
Ⓜ	Maximum Material Condition (MMC)
Ⓛ	Least Material Condition (LMC)
Ⓢ	Regardless of Feature Size
SYMBOL NOT DEFINED	Full Indicator Movement (FIM)
Ⓟ	Projected Tolerance Zone
⊕→	Dimension Origin
⌀	All–Around
R	Radius
( )	Reference Dimension (REF)
S⌀	Spherical Diameter (SD)
SYMBOL NOT DEFINED	Spherical Radius (SR)
⌒	Arc Length
– – –	Chain Line
▷	Conical Taper
◁	Slope
⊔	Counterbore/Spotface
∨	Countersink
↧	Depth/Deep (DP)
X̲X̲.X̲X̲	Dimension Not To Scale
X	Times/Places

FORM AND ORIENTATION TOLERANCE SYMBOLS

Symbol	Name
—	Straightness
▱	Flatness
○	Circularity
⌭	Cylindricity
⊥	Perpendicularity
∠	Angularity
//	Parallelism
⌓	Surface Profile
⌒	Line Profile
⌰	Total Runout
∕	Circular Runout
SYMBOL NOT DEFINED	Unit Control

TOLERANCE SYMBOLS OF LOCATION

Symbol	Name
◎	Concentricity
⊕	Position
⬌	Symmetry

FIGURE 12.52 Geometric Dimensioning and Tolerancing Symbols Available in Computervision's CADDS 4X Production Drafting System. *Courtesy of Computervision Corporation, a subsidiary of Prime Computer, Inc.*

■ KEY WORDS

TOLERANCE	LIMIT DIMENSION
ALLOWANCE	NOMINAL SIZE
BASIC-HOLE SYSTEM	LIMITS
CLEARANCE FIT	INTERFERENCE FIT
TRANSITION FIT	BASIC-SHAFT SYSTEM
UNILATERAL TOLERANCE	BILATERAL TOLERANCE
GEOMETRIC TOLERANCING	MAXIMUM MATERIAL CONDITION
PERPENDICULAR	PARALLEL
RUNOUT	CONCENTRIC
CYLINDRICITY	CIRCULARITY
CONTROL	GEOMETRIC DIMENSIONING AND TOLERANCING (GDT)
FUNCTION	

■ CHAPTER SUMMARY

- Tolerance dimensioning describes the minimum and maximum limits for a size or location of a feature.
- There are several ways of dimensioning tolerances, including limit dimensions, unilateral tolerances, bilateral tolerances, and geometric tolerancing.
- Basic-hole tolerance systems are the most commonly used tolerance system because they assume the hole is nominal size and adjust the shaft to accommodate the tolerance.
- The amount of space between two mating parts at maximum material condition is called the allowance.
- Mating parts with large allowances are classified as having a clearance fit or running and sliding fit.
- Mating parts with negative allowances are classified as having an interference fit or force fit.
- Mating parts are designed around a nominal size and class of fit. All other tolerances are calculated from these two values.
- High-quality parts are often dimensioned with geometric tolerancing to ensure that the size, shape, and relative geometric characteristics are properly defined.
- GDT has become an essential part of today's manufacturing industry. GDT is not only a design language, but an inspection language as well.

■ REVIEW QUESTIONS

1. What do the two numbers of a limit dimension mean?
2. Draw three different geometric tolerances that reference a datum. Label the information in each box.
3. Why is the basic-hole system more common than the basic-shaft system?
4. Give five examples of nominal sizes in everyday life. What is the purpose of a nominal size?
5. Give an example of two parts that would require a running and sliding fit. A force fit.
6. List five classes of fit.
7. Can one part have an allowance? Why?
8. Can two parts have a tolerance? Why?
9. Give an example of how GDT could be used as both a design and inspection tool.
10. List the five steps required to apply GDT to the design process.

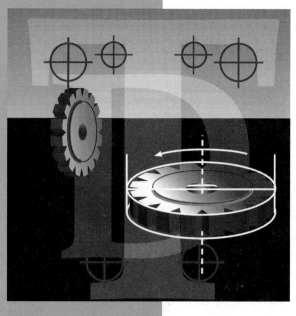

CHAPTER 13

THREADS, FASTENERS, AND SPRINGS

OBJECTIVES

After studying the material in this chapter, you should be able to:

1. Define and label the parts of a screw thread.
2. Identify various screw thread forms.
3. Draw detailed, schematic, and simplified threads in section and elevation.
4. Define typical thread specifications.
5. Identify various fasteners and describe their use.
6. Draw various screw head types.
7. Draw springs in elevation using break conventions.

OVERVIEW

The concept of the screw thread seems to have occurred first to Archimedes, the third-century B.C. mathematician who wrote briefly on spirals and invented or designed several simple devices applying the screw principle. By the first century B.C., the screw was a familiar element but was crudely cut from wood or filed by hand on a metal shaft. Nothing more was heard of the screw thread until the fifteenth century.

Leonardo da Vinci understood the screw principle, and he created sketches showing how to cut screw threads by machine. In the sixteenth century, screws appeared in German watches and were used to fasten suits of armor. In 1569, the screw-cutting lathe was invented by the Frenchman Besson, but this method of screw production did not take hold for another century and a half; nuts and bolts continued to be made largely by hand. In the eighteenth century, screw manufacturing started in England during the Industrial Revolution.

Threads and fasteners are the principal fastening devices used for assembling component parts. The shape of the helical thread is called the **thread form**. The metric thread form is the international standard, although the unified thread form is common in the United States. Other thread forms are used in specific applications. CAD drawing programs often use software that automatically depicts threads. The thread specification is a special leader note that defines the type of thread or fastener. This is an instruction for the shop technician so the correct type of thread is created during the manufacturing process. To speed production time and reduce costs, many new types of fasteners are created every year. Existing fasteners are also modified to improve their insertion in mass production.

■ 13.1 STANDARDIZED SCREW THREADS

In early times, there was no such thing as standardization. Nuts made by one manufacturer would not fit the bolts of another. In 1841 Sir Joseph Whitworth started crusading for a standard screw thread, and soon the Whitworth thread was accepted throughout England.

In 1864 the United States adopted a thread proposed by William Sellers of Philadelphia, but the Sellers nuts would not screw onto a Whitworth bolt, or vice versa. In 1935 the American Standard thread, with the same 60° V form of the old Sellers thread, was adopted in the United States. Still there was no stan-

(a)   (b)

(a) Springs. (b) Screws and fasteners. *From* **Machine Design: An Integrated Approach** *by Robert Norton,* © *1996. Reprinted by permission of Prentice-Hall, Inc.*

dardization among countries. In peacetime it was a nuisance; in World War I it was a serious inconvenience; and in World War II the obstacle was so great that the Allies decided to do something about it. Talks began among the Americans, British, and Canadians, and in 1948 an agreement was reached on the unification of American and British screw threads. The new thread was called the *Unified screw thread*, and it represents a compromise between the American Standard and Whitworth systems, allowing complete interchangeability of threads in three countries.

In 1946 an International Organization for Standardization (ISO) committee was formed to establish a single international system of metric screw threads. Consequently, through the cooperative efforts of the Industrial Fasteners Institute (IFI), several committees of the American National Standards Institute, and the ISO representatives, a metric fastener standard was prepared.[*]

Today screw threads are vital to our industrial life. They are designed for hundreds of different purposes; the three basic applications are (1) to *hold parts* together, (2) to *adjust parts* with reference to each other, and (3) to *transmit power*.

■ 13.2 SCREW THREAD TERMS

The following definitions apply to screw threads in general (Fig. 13.1). For additional information regarding specific Unified and metric screw thread terms and definitions, refer to the following standards:

ANSI/ASME B1.1–1989
ANSI/ASME B1.7M–1984 (R1992)

---

[*] For a listing of ANSI standards for threads, fasteners, and springs, see Appendix 1.

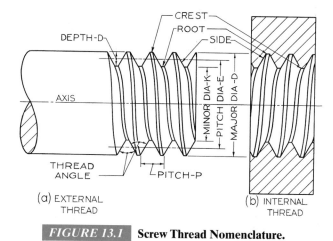

DEPTH-D

CREST

ROOT

SIDE

AXIS

MINOR DIA-K

PITCH DIA-E

MAJOR DIA-D

THREAD ANGLE

PITCH-P

(a) EXTERNAL THREAD

(b) INTERNAL THREAD

FIGURE 13.1   **Screw Thread Nomenclature.**

ANSI/ASME B1.13M–1983 (R1989)

ANSI/ASME Y14.6–1978 (R1993)

ANSI/ASME Y14.6aM–1981 (R1993).

SCREW THREAD   A ridge of uniform section in the form of a helix (§4.60) on the external or internal surface of a cylinder.

EXTERNAL THREAD   A thread on the outside of a member, as on a shaft.

INTERNAL THREAD   A thread on the inside of a member, as in a hole.

MAJOR DIAMETER   The largest diameter of a screw thread (applies to both internal and external threads).

MINOR DIAMETER   The smallest diameter of a screw thread (applies to both internal and external threads).

PITCH   The distance from a point on a screw thread to a corresponding point on the next thread measured parallel to the axis. The pitch P is equal to 1 divided by the number of threads per inch.

PITCH DIAMETER   The diameter of an imaginary cylinder passing through the threads to make equal the widths of the threads and the widths of the spaces cut by the cylinder.

LEAD   The distance a screw thread advances axially in one turn.

ANGLE OF THREAD   The angle included between the sides of the thread measured in a plane through the axis of the screw.

CREST   The top surface joining the two sides of a thread.

ROOT   The bottom surface joining the sides of two adjacent threads.

SIDE   The surface of the thread that connects the crest with the root.

AXIS OF SCREW   The longitudinal center line through the screw.

DEPTH OF THREAD   The distance between the crest and the root of the thread measured normal to the axis.

FORM OF THREAD   The cross section of thread cut by a plane containing the axis.

SERIES OF THREAD   Standard number of threads per inch for various diameters.

■ 13.3 SCREW THREAD FORMS

Various forms of threads are used to hold parts together, to adjust parts with reference to each other, or to transmit power (Fig. 13.2). The 60° *Sharp-V thread* was originally called the United States Standard thread, or the Sellers thread. For purposes of certain adjustments, the Sharp-V thread is useful with the increased friction resulting from the full thread face. It is also used on brass pipe work.

The *American National thread* with flattened roots and crests is a stronger thread. This form replaced the Sharp-V thread for general use.

The *Unified thread* is the standard thread agreed upon by the United States, Canada, and Great Britain in 1948, and has replaced the American National form. The crest of the external thread may be flat or rounded, and the root is rounded; otherwise, the thread form is essentially the same as the American National.

The *metric thread* is the standard screw thread agreed upon for international screw thread fasteners. The crest and root are flat, but the external thread is often rounded if formed by a rolling process. The form is similar to the American National and Unified threads but with less depth of thread.

The *square thread* is theoretically the ideal thread for power transmission, since its face is nearly at right angles to the axis, but due to the difficulty of cutting it with dies and because of other inherent disadvantages (such as the fact that split nuts will not readily disengage), the square thread has been displaced to a large extent by the Acme thread. The square thread is not standardized.

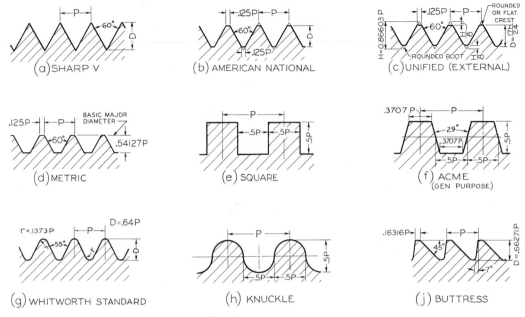

FIGURE 13.2   Screw Thread Forms.

The *Acme thread* is a modification of the square thread and has largely replaced it. It is stronger than the square thread, is easier to cut, and has the advantage of easy disengagement from a split nut, as on the lead screw of a lathe.

The *standard worm thread* (not shown) is similar to the Acme thread but is deeper. It is used on shafts to carry power to worm wheels.

The *Whitworth thread* was the British standard and has been replaced by the Unified thread. Its uses correspond to those of the American National thread.

The *knuckle thread* is usually rolled from sheet metal but is sometimes cast; in modified forms it is used in electric bulbs and sockets, bottle tops, etc.

The *buttress thread* is designed to transmit power in one direction only and is used in large guns, in jacks, and in other mechanisms having similar high-strength requirements.

■ 13.4 THREAD PITCH

The **pitch** of any thread form is the distance parallel to the axis between corresponding points on adjacent threads (Figs. 13.1a–13.3). For metric threads, this distance is specified in millimeters.

The pitch for a metric thread that is included with the major diameter in the thread designation determines the size of the thread—for example, M10 × 1.5, as shown in Fig. 13.3b. See also §13.21 or Appendix 15 for more information.

FIGURE 13.3   Pitch of Threads.

For threads dimensioned in inches, the pitch is equal to 1 divided by the number of threads per inch. The thread tables give the number of threads per inch for each standard diameter. Thus, a Unified coarse thread (Appendix 15) of 1″ diameter has eight threads per inch, and the pitch P equals $\frac{1}{8}″$ (.125).

If a thread has only four threads per inch, the pitch and the threads themselves are quite large (Fig. 13.3a). If there are, say, 16 threads per inch, the pitch is only $\frac{1}{16}″$ (.063), and the threads are relatively small, similar to those in Fig. 13.3b.

The pitch or the number of threads per inch can be measured with a scale (Fig. 13.3c) or with a *thread-pitch gage* (Fig. 13.3d).

■ 13.5 RIGHT-HAND AND LEFT-HAND THREADS

A *right-hand thread* is one that advances into a nut when turned clockwise, and a left-hand thread is one that advances into a nut when turned counterclockwise (Fig. 13.4). A thread is always considered to be right-handed (RH) unless otherwise specified. A *left-hand thread* is always labeled LH on a drawing (see Fig. 13.19a).

■ 13.6 SINGLE AND MULTIPLE THREADS

A *single thread*, as the name implies, is composed of one ridge, and the lead is therefore equal to the pitch. *Multiple threads* are composed of two or more ridges running side by side. As shown in Figs. 13.5a to 13.5c, the *slope line* is the hypotenuse of a right triangle whose short side equals .5P for single threads, P for double threads, 1.5P for triple threads, and so on. This applies to all forms of threads. In *double threads*, the lead is twice the pitch; in *triple threads*, the lead is three times the pitch, and so on. On a drawing of a single or triple thread, a root is opposite a crest; in the case of a double or quadruple thread, a root is drawn opposite a root. Therefore, in one turn, a double thread advances twice as far as a single thread, and a triple thread advances three times as far. RH double square and RH triple Acme threads are shown in Figs. 13.5d and 13.5e, respectively.

Multiple threads are used wherever quick motion, but not great power, is desired, as on fountain pens, toothpaste caps, valve stems, etc. The threads on a valve stem are frequently multiple threads, to impart quick action in opening and closing the valve. Multiple threads on a shaft can be recognized and counted by observing the number of thread endings on the end of the screw.

■ 13.7 THREAD SYMBOLS

There are three methods of representing screw threads on drawings—the *schematic*, *simplified*, and *detailed* methods. For clarity of representation and where good judgment dictates, schematic, simplified, and detailed thread symbols may be combined on a single drawing.

FIGURE 13.4   **Right-Hand and Left-Hand Threads.**

FIGURE 13.5   **Multiple Threads.**

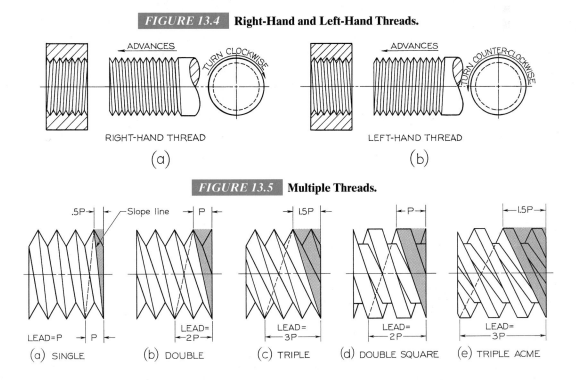

Two sets of thread symbols, the schematic and the more common simplified, are used to represent the threads of small diameter, under approximately 1″ or 25-mm diameter on the drawing. The symbols are the same for all forms of threads, such as metric, Unified, square, and Acme.

The detailed representation is a close approximation of the exact appearance of a screw thread. The true projection of the helical curves of a screw thread (see Fig. 13.1) presents a pleasing appearance, but this does not compensate for the laborious task of plotting the helices. Consequently, the true projection is rarely used in practice.

When the diameter of the thread on the drawing is more than 1″ or 25 mm, a pleasing drawing may be made by the *detailed* representation method, in which the true profiles of the threads (any form of thread) are drawn; but the helical curves are replaced by straight lines (Fig. 13.6).* Whether the crests or roots are flat or rounded, they are represented by single

---

* A thread 42 mm or $1\frac{5}{8}$″ diameter, if drawn half size, would be less than 25 mm or 1″ diameter on the drawing and hence would be too small for this method of representation.

lines and not double lines, as in Fig. 13.1; consequently, American National and Unified threads are drawn in exactly the same way.

■ 13.8 EXTERNAL THREAD SYMBOLS

Simplified external thread symbols are shown in Figs. 13.7a and 13.7b. The threaded portions are indicated by hidden lines parallel to the axis at the approximate depth of the thread, whether in section or in elevation. [Use the schematic depth of thread in the table in Fig. 13.9a to draw these lines (Fig. 13.7d)].

When the schematic form is shown in section (Fig. 13.7c), it is necessary to show the Vs; otherwise no threads would be evident. However, it is not necessary to show the Vs to scale or according to the actual slope of the crest lines. To draw the Vs, use the schematic thread depth (Fig. 13.9a), and let the pitch be determined by the 60° Vs.

Schematic threads in elevation (Fig. 13.7d) are indicated by alternate long and short lines at right angles to the center line, with the root lines being preferably thicker than the crest lines. Although the crest lines should theoretically be spaced according to actual pitch, the lines would often be very crowded

---

FIGURE 13.6   Detailed Metric, American National, and Unified Threads.

(a) EXTERNAL DETAILED THREADS   (b) INTERNAL DETAILED THREADS

FIGURE 13.7   External Thread Symbols.

(a) (b) SIMPLIFIED

(c) (d) SCHEMATIC

and tedious to draw, thus defeating the purpose of the symbol, which is to save drafting time. In practice, the experienced drafter spaces the crest lines carefully by eye, and then adds the heavy root lines spaced by eye halfway between the crest lines. In general, the spacing should be proportionate for all diameters. For convenience in drawing, proportions for the schematic symbol are given in Fig. 13.9.

■ 13.9 INTERNAL THREAD SYMBOLS

Internal thread symbols are shown in Fig. 13.8. Note that the only differences between the schematic and simplified internal thread symbols occur in the sectional views. The representation of the schematic thread in section in Figs. 13.8m, 13.8o, and 13.8p is exactly the same as the external symbol in Fig. 13.7d. Hidden threads, by either method, are represented by pairs of hidden lines. The hidden dashes should be staggered, as shown.

In the case of blind tapped holes, the drill depth normally is drawn at least three schematic pitches beyond the thread length, as shown in Figs. 13.8d, 13.8e, 13.8n, and 13.8o. The symbols in Figs. 13.8f and 13.8p represent the use of a bottoming tap, when the length of thread is the same as the depth of drill (see also §13.24).

■ 13.10 DRAWING THREAD SYMBOLS

Figure 13.9a shows a table of values of depth and pitch to use in drawing thread symbols. These values are selected to produce a well-proportioned symbol and to be convenient to set off with the scale. An experienced drafter can carefully space the lines by eye, but a student should use the scale. Note that values of D and P are for the diameter *on the drawing*. Thus, a $1\frac{1}{2}''$ diameter thread at half-scale would be $\frac{3}{4}''$ diameter on the drawing, and values of D and P for a $\frac{3}{4}''$ major diameter would be used. Nominal diameters for decimal-inch or metric threads are treated in a similar manner.

SIMPLIFIED SYMBOLS   The steps for drawing the simplified symbols for an external thread in elevation and in section are shown in Figs. 13.9b to 13.9e. The thread depth from the table is used for establishing the pairs of hidden lines that represent the threads in elevation and in section. No pitch measurement is needed. The completed symbols are shown in Figs. 13.9d and 13.9e.

The steps for drawing the simplified symbol for an internal thread in section are shown in Figs. 13.9f to 13.9h. The simplified representation for the internal thread in elevation is identical to that used for schematic representation, as the threads are indicated by pairs of hidden lines (Fig. 13.9g). The simplified

FIGURE 13.8 Internal Thread Symbols.

MAJOR DIAMETER	#5 (.125) TO #12 (.216)	.25	.3125	.375	.4375	.5	.5625	.625	.6875	.75	.8125	.875	.9375	l.
(a)	DEPTH, D	.03125	.03125	.03125	.0468	.0468	.0625	.0625	.0625	.0625	.0781	.0937	.0937	.0937	.0937
PITCH, P	.0468	.0625	.0625	.0625	.0625	.0937	.0937	.0937	.0937	.125	.125	.125	.125	.125

(For metric values: I" = 25.4 mm or see inside front cover.)

FIGURE 13.9   To Draw Thread Symbols—Simplified and Schematic.

symbol for an internal thread in section is shown in Fig. 13.9h. The major diameter of the thread is represented by hidden lines across the sectioned area.

SCHEMATIC SYMBOLS   The steps for drawing the schematic symbols for an external thread in elevation and in section are shown in Figs. 13.9j to 13.9n. Note that when the pitches P are set off in Fig. 13.9k, the final crest line for a full pitch may fall beyond the actual thread length, as shown. The completed schematic symbol for an external thread in elevation is shown in Fig. 13.9m. The completed schematic symbol for an external thread in section is shown in Fig. 13.9n. The schematic thread depth is used for drawing the Vs, and the pitch is established by the 60° Vs.

The steps for drawing the schematic symbols for an internal thread in elevation and in section are shown in Figs. 13.9o to 13.9q. Here again the symbol thread length may be slightly longer than the actual given thread length. If the tap drill depth is known or given, the drill is drawn to that depth, as shown. If the thread note omits this information, as is often done in practice, the drafter merely draws the hole three thread pitches (schematic) beyond the thread length. The tap drill diameter is represented approximately, as shown, and not to actual size. The completed schematic symbol for an internal thread in elevation is shown (Fig. 13.9p). Pairs of hidden lines represent the threads, and the hidden-line dashes are staggered. The completed schematic symbol for an internal thread in section is shown in Fig. 13.9q. The schematic internal thread in section is represented in the same manner as for the schematic external thread.

■ 13.11 DETAILED REPRESENTATION: METRIC, UNIFIED, AND AMERICAN NATIONAL THREADS

The detailed representation for metric, Unified, and American National threads is the same, since the flats, if any, are disregarded. The steps in drawing these threads are shown in Fig. 13.10.

1.   Draw center line and lay out length and major diameter (Fig. 13.10a).

2.   Find the number of threads per inch in Appendix 15 for American National and Unified threads (Fig. 13.10b). This number depends on the major diameter of the thread, whether the thread is internal or external. Find P (pitch) by dividing 1 by the number of

threads per inch (§13.4). The pitch for metric threads is given directly in the thread designation. For example, the M14 × 2 thread has a pitch of 2 mm (see Appendix 15). Establish the slope of the thread by offsetting the slope line $\frac{1}{2}$P for single threads, P for double threads, $1\frac{1}{2}$P for triple threads, and so on. (These offsets are the same in terms of P for any form of thread.) For right-hand external threads, the slope line slopes upward to the left; for left-hand external threads, the slope line slopes upward to the right. If the number of threads per inch conforms to the scale, the pitch can be set off directly. For example, eight threads per inch can easily be set off with the architects' scale, and ten threads per inch with the engineers' scale. Otherwise, use the bow dividers or use the parallel-line method shown in Fig. 13.10b.

3.   From the pitch points, draw crest lines parallel to the slope line (Fig. 13.10c). These should be dark, thin lines. Slide your triangle along a T-square (or another triangle) to make parallel lines. Draw two Vs to establish the depth of thread, and draw guide lines for the root of thread, as shown.

4.   Draw 60° Vs finished weight (Fig. 13.10d). These Vs should stand vertically; that is, they should not "lean" with the thread.

5.   Draw root lines dark at once (Fig. 13.10e). Root lines will *not* be parallel to crest lines. Slide the triangle on the straightedge to make root lines parallel.

6.   When the end is chamfered (usually 45° with end of shaft, sometimes 30°), the chamfer extends to the thread depth (Fig. 13.10f). The chamfer creates a new crest line, which is then drawn between the two new crest points. It is not parallel to the other crest lines. In the final drawing, all thread lines should be approximately the same weight—thin, but dark.

The corresponding internal detailed threads, in section, are drawn as shown in Fig. 13.11. Notice that for LH threads the lines slope upward to the left (Figs. 13.11a to 13.11c), while for RH threads the lines slope upward to the right (Figs. 13.11d to 13.11f). Make all final thread lines medium-thin but dark.

■ 13.12 DETAILED REPRESENTATION OF SQUARE THREADS

The steps in drawing the detailed representation of an external square thread when the major diameter is over 1″ or 25 mm (approx.) on the drawing are shown in Fig. 13.12.

FIGURE 13.10 Detailed Representation—External Metric, Unified, and American National Threads.

SINGLE, L H INTERNAL

DOUBLE, R H INTERNAL

FIGURE 13.11 Detailed Representation—Internal Metric, Unified, and American National Threads.

1. Draw the center line, and lay out the length and major diameter of the thread (Fig. 13.12a). Determine P by dividing 1 by the number of threads per inch (see Appendix 22). For a single RH thread, the lines slope upward to the left, and the slope line is offset *as for all single threads of any form*. On the upper line, set off spaces equal to $\frac{P}{2}$, as shown, using a scale if possible; otherwise, use the bow dividers or the parallel-line method to space the points.

2. From the $\frac{P}{2}$ points on the upper line, draw fairly thin lines (Fig. 13.12b). Draw guide lines for root of thread, making the depth $\frac{P}{2}$ as shown.

3. Draw parallel visible back edges of threads (Fig. 13.12c).

4. Draw parallel visible root lines (Fig. 13.12d). Note enlarged detail in Fig. 13.12g.

5. Accent the lines (Fig. 13.12e). All lines should be thin and dark.

Note the end view of the shaft in Fig. 13.12f. The root circle is hidden; no attempt is made to show the true projection. If the end is chamfered, a solid circle would be drawn instead of the hidden circle.

Figure 13.13 is an assembly drawing showing an external square thread partly screwed into a nut. The detail of the square thread at A is the same as shown in Fig. 13.12. But when the external and internal threads are assembled, the thread in the nut overlaps and covers up half of the V, as shown at B.

$$P = \frac{1''}{NO.\ THDS\ PER\ IN.\ (SEE\ TABLE)}$$

SLOPE OF THREAD

SINGLE, R H EXTERNAL THREAD

MAJOR DIA

L

(a)

(b)

(c)

ROOT LINES PARALLEL

2.5–2 SQUARE

SEE ENLARGED DETAIL

ALL LINES THIN AND DARK

END

To ℄ of shaft

(d)

(e)

(f)

(g)

FIGURE 13.12   **Detailed Representation—External Square Threads.**

SCREW ONLY | SCREW & NUT | NUT ONLY

A

B

FIGURE 13.13   **Square Threads in Assembly.**

The internal thread construction is the same as in Fig. 13.14. Note that the thread lines representing the back half of the internal threads (since the thread is in section) slope in the opposite direction from those on the front side of the screw.

Steps in drawing a single internal square thread in section are shown in Fig. 13.14. Note in Fig. 13.14b that a crest is drawn opposite a root. This is the case for both single and triple threads. For double or quadruple threads, a crest is opposite a crest. Thus, the construction in Figs. 13.14a and 13.14b is the same for any multiple of thread. The differences appear in Fig. 13.14c,

where the threads and spaces are distinguished and outlined.

The same internal thread is shown in elevation (external view) in Fig. 13.14e. The profiles of the threads are drawn in their normal position, but with hidden lines, and the sloping lines are omitted for simplicity. The end view of the same internal thread is shown in Fig. 13.14f. Note that the hidden and solid circles are opposite those for the end view of the shaft (see Fig. 13.12f).

■ 13.13 DETAILED REPRESENTATION OF ACME THREAD

The steps in drawing the detailed representation of Acme threads when the major diameter is larger than 1″ or 25 mm (approx.) on the drawing are shown in Fig. 13.15.

1. Draw the center line, and lay out the length and major diameter of the thread (Fig. 13.15a). Determine P by dividing 1 by the number of threads per inch (see Appendix 22). Draw construction lines for the root diameter, making the thread depth $\frac{P}{2}$. Draw construction lines halfway between crest and root guide lines.

2. On the intermediate construction lines, lay off $\frac{P}{2}$ spaces (Fig. 13.15b). Setting off spaces directly with a scale is possible (for example, if $\frac{P}{2} = \frac{1}{10}''$, use the

FIGURE 13.14 **Detailed Representation—Internal Square Threads.**

FIGURE 13.15 **Detailed Representation—Acme Threads.**

engineers' scale); otherwise, use bow dividers or the parallel-line method.

3. Through alternate points, draw construction lines for sides of threads (draw 15° instead of $14\frac{1}{2}°$) (Fig. 13.15c).

4. Draw construction lines for other sides of threads (Fig. 13.15d). Note that for single and triple threads, a crest is opposite a root, while for double and quadruple threads, a crest is opposite a crest. Heavy in tops and bottoms of threads.

5. Draw parallel crest lines, final weight at once (Fig. 13.15e).

6. Draw parallel root lines, final weight at once, and heavy in the thread profiles (Fig. 13.15f). All lines should be thin and dark. Note that the internal threads in the back of the nut slope in the opposite direction to the external threads on the front side of the screw.

End views of Acme threaded shafts and holes are drawn exactly like those for the square thread (Figs. 13.12 and 13.14).

■ 13.14 USE OF PHANTOM LINES

In representing objects having a series of identical features, phantom lines may be used to save time

FIGURE 13.16   **Use of Phantom Lines.**

(Fig. 13.16). Threaded shafts and springs thus represented may be shortened without the use of conventional breaks, but must be correctly dimensioned. The use of phantom lines is limited almost entirely to detailed drawings.

■ 13.15 THREADS IN SECTION

Detailed representations of large threads in section are shown in Figs. 13.6 and 13.10–13.15. As indicated by the note in Fig. 13.6b, the root lines and crest lines may be omitted in internal sectional views, if desired.

External thread symbols are shown in section in Fig. 13.7. Note that in the schematic symbol, the Vs must be drawn. Internal thread symbols in section are shown in Fig. 13.8.

Threads in an assembly drawing are shown in Fig. 13.17. It is customary not to section a stud or a nut, or any solid part, unless necessary to show some internal shapes (see §13.23). Note that when external and internal threads are sectioned in assembly, the Vs are required to show the threaded connection.

■ 13.16 AMERICAN NATIONAL THREAD

The old American National thread was adopted in 1935. The *form*, or profile (Fig. 15.2b), is the same as the old Sellers' profile, or U.S. Standard, and is known as the *National form*. The methods of representation are the same as for the Unified and metric threads. As noted earlier, American National threads have been replaced by the Unified and metric threads. However, they may still be found on earlier drawings. Five series of threads were embraced in the old ANSI standards.

1. *Coarse thread*—A general-purpose thread for holding purposes. Designated NC (National Coarse).

2. *Fine thread*—A greater number of threads per inch; used extensively in automotive and aircraft construction. Designated NF (National Fine).

3. *8-pitch thread*—All diameters have 8 threads per inch. Used on bolts for high-pressure pipe flanges, cylinder-head studs, and similar fasteners. Designated 8N (National form, 8 threads per inch).

4. *12-pitch thread*—All diameters have 12 threads per inch; used in boiler work and for thin nuts on shafts and sleeves in machine construction. Designated 12N (National form, 12 threads per inch).

5. *16-pitch thread*—All diameters have 16 threads per inch; used where necessary to have a fine thread regardless of diameter, as on adjusting collars and bearing retaining nuts. Designated 16N (National form, 16 threads per inch).

■ 13.17 UNIFIED EXTRA FINE THREADS

The *Unified extra fine thread* series has many more threads per inch for given diameters than any series of the American National or Unified. The form of thread is the same as the American National. These small threads are used in thin metal where the length of thread engagement is small, in cases where close adjustment is required, and where vibration is great. They are designated UNEF (extra fine).

■ 13.18 AMERICAN NATIONAL THREAD FITS

For general use, three classes of screw thread fits between mating threads (as between bolt and nut) have been established by ANSI.

(a) SIMPLIFIED   (b) SCHEMATIC   **FIGURE 13.17**   **Threads in Assembly.**

These fits are produced by the application of tolerances listed in the standard and are described as follows.

1. *Class 1 fit*—Recommended only for screw thread work where clearance between mating parts is essential for rapid assembly and where shake or play is not objectionable.
2. *Class 2 fit*—Represents a high quality of commercial thread product and is recommended for the great bulk of interchangeable screw thread work.
3. *Class 3 fit*—Represents an exceptionally high quality of commercially threaded product and is recommended only in cases where the high cost of precision tools and continual checking are warranted.

The class of fit desired on a thread is indicated in the thread note, as shown in §13.21.

■ 13.19 METRIC AND UNIFIED THREADS

The preferred metric thread for commercial purposes conforms to the International Organization for Standardization (ISO) publication basic profile M for metric threads. This M profile design is comparable to the Unified inch profile, but the two are not interchangeable. For commercial purposes, two series of metric threads are preferred—coarse (general purpose) and fine—thus drastically reducing the number of previously used thread series (see Appendix 15).

The Unified thread constitutes the present American National standard. Some earlier American National threads are still included in the new standard. The standard lists 11 different series of numbers of threads per inch for the various standard diameters, together with the selected combinations of special diameters and pitches.

The 11 series are the *coarse thread series* (UNC or NC), recommended for general use corresponding to the old National coarse thread; the *fine thread* series (UNF or NF), for general use in automotive and aircraft work and in applications where a finer thread is required; the *extra fine* series (UNF or NF), which is the same as the SAE extra fine series, used particularly in aircraft and aeronautical equipment and generally for threads in thin walls; and the eight series of 4, 6, 8, 12, 16, 20, 28, and 32 threads with constant pitch. The 8UN or 8N, 12UN or 12N, and 16UN or 16N series are recommended for the uses corresponding to the old 8-, 12-, and 16-pitch American National threads. In addition, there are three special thread series—UNS, NS, and UN—that involve special combinations of diameter, pitch, and length of engagement.

■ 13.20 METRIC AND UNIFIED THREAD FITS

For some specialized metric thread applications, the tolerances and deviations are specified by tolerance grade, tolerance position, class, and length of engagement. Two classes of metric thread fits are generally recognized. The first class of fits is for general-purpose applications and has a tolerance class of 6H for internal threads and a class of 6g for external threads. The second class of fits is used where closer fits are necessary and has a tolerance class of 6H for internal threads and a class of 5g6g for external threads. Metric thread tolerance classes of 6H/6g are generally assumed if not otherwise designated and are used in applications comparable to the 2A/2B inch classes of fits.

The single-tolerance designation of 6H refers to both the tolerance grade and position for the pitch diameter and the minor diameter for an internal thread. The single-tolerance designation of 6g refers to both the tolerance grade and position for the pitch diameter and the major diameter of the external thread. A double designation of 5g6g indicates separate tolerance grades for the pitch diameter and for the major diameter of the external thread.

The standard for Unified screw threads specifies tolerances and allowances defining the several classes of fit (degree of looseness or tightness) between mating threads. In the symbols for fit, the letter A refers to the external threads and B to internal threads. There are three classes of fit each for external threads (1A, 2A, 3A) and internal threads (1B, 2B, 3B). Classes 1A and 1B have generous tolerances, facilitating rapid assembly and disassembly. Classes 2A and 2B are used in the normal production of screws, bolts, and nuts, as well as a variety of general applications. Classes 3A and 3B provide for applications needing highly accurate and close-fitting threads.

■ 13.21 THREAD NOTES

Thread notes for metric, Unified, and American National screw threads are shown in Fig. 13.18. These same notes or symbols are used in correspondence, on shop and storeroom records, and in specifications for parts, taps, dies, tools, and gages.

FIGURE 13.18 Thread Notes.

Metric screw threads are designated basically by the letter M for metric profile followed by the nominal size (basic major diameter) and the pitch, both in millimeters and separated by the symbol ×. For example, the basic thread note M10 × 1.5 is adequate for most commercial purposes (Fig. 13.18b).

If the generally understood tolerances need to be specified, the tolerance class of 6H for the internal thread or the tolerance class of 6g for the external thread is added to the basic note (Fig. 13.18g). Where closer mating threads are desired, a tolerance of 6H for the internal thread and tolerance classes of 5g6g for the external thread are added to the basic note.

When the thread note refers to mating parts, a single basic note is adequate with the addition of the internal and external thread tolerance classes separated by the slash. The basic note for mating threads now becomes M10 × 1.5–6H/6g for the general-purpose thread or M10 × 1.5–6H/5g6g for the close-fitting thread (Fig. 13.18h).

For a left-hand thread, LH is added to the thread note. (Absence of LH indicates an RH thread.)

If it is necessary to indicate the length of the thread engagement, the letter S (short), N (normal), or L (long) is added to the thread note. For example, the single note M10 × 1.5–6H/6g–N–LH combines the specifications for internal and external mating left-hand metric threads of 10-mm diameter and 1.5-mm pitch with general-purpose tolerances and normal length of engagement.

A thread note for a blind tapped hole is shown in Fig. 13.18a. In a complete note, the tap drill and depth should be given, though in practice they are often omitted and left to the shop. For tap drill sizes, see Appendix 15. If the LH symbol is omitted, the thread is understood to be RH. If the thread is a multiple thread, the word DOUBLE, TRIPLE, or QUADRUPLE should precede the thread depth; otherwise, the thread is understood to be single. Thread notes for holes are preferably attached to the circular views of the holes, as shown.

Thread notes for external threads are preferably given in the longitudinal view of the threaded shaft, as shown in Figs. 13.18b to 13.18f. Examples of 8-, 12-, and 16-pitch threads, not shown in the figure, are 2–8N–2, 2–12N–2, and 2–16N–2. A sample special thread designation is $1\frac{1}{2}$–7N–LH.

General-purpose Acme threads are indicated by the letter G, and centralizing Acme threads by the letter C. Typical thread notes are $1\frac{3}{4}$–4 ACME–2G or $1\frac{3}{4}$–6 ACME–4C.

Thread notes for Unified threads are shown in Figs. 13.18j and 13.18k. Unified thread notes are distinguished from American National threads by the insertion of the letter U before the series letters, and by the letters A and B (for external or internal, respectively)

after the numeral designating the class of fit. If the letters LH are omitted, the thread is understood to be RH. Some typical thread notes are:

$\frac{1}{4}$–20 UNC–2A TRIPLE

$\frac{9}{16}$–18 UNF–2B

$1\frac{3}{4}$–16 UN–2A

■ 13.22 AMERICAN NATIONAL STANDARD PIPE THREADS

The American National Standard for pipe threads, originally known as the Briggs standard, was formulated by Robert Briggs in 1882. Two general types of pipe threads have been approved as American National Standard: *taper pipe threads* and *straight pipe threads*.

The profile of the taper pipe thread is illustrated in Fig. 13.19. The taper of the standard tapered pipe thread is 1 in 16 or .75″ per foot measured on the diameter and along the axis. The angle between the sides of the thread is 60°. The depth of the sharp V is .8660p, and the basic maximum depth of the truncated thread is .800p, where p = pitch. The basic pitch diameters, E_0 and E_1, and the basic length of the effective external taper thread, L_2, are determined by the formulas

$$E_0 = D - (.050D + 1.1)\frac{1}{n}$$

$$E_1 = E + .0625 L_1$$

$$L_2 = (.80D + 6.8)\frac{1}{n},$$

were D = basic outer diameter (O.D.) of pipe, E_0 = pitch diameter of thread at end of pipe, E_1 = pitch diameters of thread at large end of internal thread, L_1 = normal engagement by hand, and n = number of threads per inch.

The ANSI also recommended two modified taper pipe threads for (1) dryseal pressure-tight joints (.88″

FIGURE 13.19 **American National Standard Taper Pipe Thread [ANSI/ASME B1.20.1–1983 (R1992)].**

per foot taper) and (2) rail fitting joints. The former is used to provide a metal-to-metal joint, eliminating the need for a sealer, and is used in refrigeration, marine, automotive, aircraft, and ordnance work. The latter is used to provide a rigid mechanical thread joint, as required in rail fitting joints.

While taper pipe threads are recommended for general use, there are certain types of joints in which straight pipe threads are used to advantage. The number of threads per inch, the angle, and the depth of thread are the same as on the taper pipe thread, but the threads are cut parallel to the axis. Straight pipe threads are used for pressure-tight joints for pipe couplings, fuel and oil line fittings, drain plugs, free-fitting mechanical joints for fixtures, loose-fitting mechanical joints for locknuts, and loose-fitting mechanical joints for hose couplings.

Pipe threads are represented by detailed or symbolic methods in a manner similar to the representation of Unified and American National threads. The symbolic representation (schematic or simplified) is recommended for general use regardless of diameter (Fig. 13.20). The detailed method is recommended only when the threads are large and when it is desired to show the profile of the thread, as, for example, in a sectional view of an assembly.

As shown in Fig. 13.20, it is not necessary to draw the taper on the threads unless there is some reason to emphasize it, since the thread note indicates whether the thread is straight or tapered. If it is desired to show the taper, it should be exaggerated, as shown in Fig. 13.21, where the taper is drawn $\frac{1}{16}''$ per $1''$ *on radius* (or $6.75''$ per $1'$ *on diameter*) instead of the actual taper of $\frac{1}{16}''$ *on diameter*. American National Standard taper pipe threads are indicated by a note giving the nominal diameter followed by the letters NPT (National pipe taper), as shown in Fig. 13.21. When straight pipe threads are specified, the letters NPS (National pipe straight) are used. In practice, the tap drill size is normally not given in the thread note.

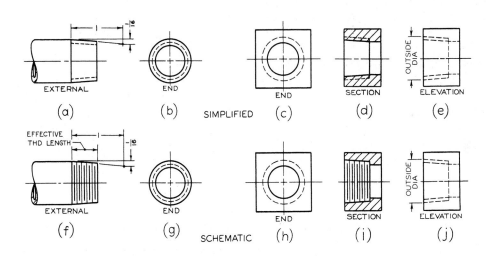

FIGURE 13.20   Conventional Pipe Thread Representation.

FIGURE 13.21   Conventional Representation of Pipe Threads.

G R A P H I C S   S P O T L I G H T

Fastener Libraries

ENGINEERS SPEND TWENTY HOURS PER MONTH REDRAWING PARTS

Many engineers spend up to twenty hours each month redrawing standard parts or parts they purchase from outside vendors. They need to show how the parts fit in assembly or in order to specify which part to use. Using a library of these standard parts can save considerable time in creating engineering drawings and specifications. Some vendors are willing to provide free drawings for their parts in standard drawing format. Many resources are available on the World Wide Web. You can also purchase libraries of standard symbols.

THOUSANDS OF PARTS AVAILABLE IN PARTSPEC

One place you can go for standard fasteners and vendor part drawings is Autodesk's PartSpec software. PartSpec is an application that runs with AutoCAD

Manufacturer:	FASTENERS
Product:	(Selection Available)
Model:	

(Selection Available)
BINDING HEAD SCREW
BUTTON HEAD CAP SCREW
DOWEL PIN
FILLISTER HEAD SCREW
FLAT HEAD 100
FLAT HEAD 82
FLAT SOCKET
FLAT WASHER (A NARROW)
FLAT WASHER (A WIDE)
FLAT WASHER (B NARROW)
FLAT WASHER (B REGULAR)
FLAT WASHER (B WIDE)
HEX BOLT
HEX NUT
HEX NUT (HEAVY JAM)
HEX NUT (HEAVY)
HEX NUT (JAM)
HEX NUT (THICK)
HEX SCREW
HEX WASHER SCREW
LOCK WASHER (EXTRA DUTY)

(A)

Manufacturer:	FASTENERS
Product:	FILLISTER HEAD SCREW
Model:	ANSI-FRACTION

⦿ Drawing
◯ Picture
◯ Text

Sch T
Back L F R
Sect B

Insert

Front View

SIZE: 1/4-20

Part Number:
Part Description: 1/4-20 FILLISTER HEAD SCREW

Previous

(B)

Release 12 or 13. You can use it to search through a part database containing thousands of parts on two CD-ROMs. The PartSpec window with standard fasteners selected is shown in Fig. A.

As you see in the figure above, you can select from various standard libraries and manufacturer databases. Once you have a library or manufacturer selected, you can choose from the list of products and the desired model for which drawings are available in the PartSpec database. Figure B shows a fillister head screw, model ANSI-fraction, size 1/4-20, is shown as the selection. The front view drawing of the fillister head screw of that size is shown at the right of the dialog box. If you want to insert that view into your current AutoCAD drawing you can pick on the icon labeled Insert in the upper right. To select from other available views, you can pick on the T, F, B, L, R, Back, Sch, and Sect. buttons for the view desired. Drawings provided with PartSpec follow a set of standards to ensure their usability.

MANUFACTURER DRAWINGS AND ORDERING INFORMATION

Over twenty different manufactures are represented in the PartSpec database. You can select a manufac-

turer from the list available, and then pick a particular product and model or type in a part number or description used to search the database. You can also qualify the search by detailed information appropriate to the part. Once you have selected a part, you can get ordering information or manufacturer's specifications in text format. Figure C shows Penn Engineering's Self-Clinching Flush Head Stud.

SAVE TIME SEARCHING FOR MATERIAL DATA WITH MATERIALSPEC

PartSpec has a counterpart for specifying materials, called MaterialSpec. It is a searchable text database on CD-ROM containing materials from five categories: plastics, metals, composites, ceramics, and military specifications (MIL5). You can choose materials by type, manufacturer, part name or number, description, property, or application. Add-on applications can provide a valuable resource for engineering. One of the biggest advantages of using CAD is that drawings can be re-used, re-scaled, or re-oriented for different purposes resulting in a valuable time savings. Remember the World Wide Web is also a valuable engineering resource for drawings and material information.

(C)

■ 13.23 BOLTS, STUDS, AND SCREWS

The term **bolt** is generally used to denote a "through bolt" that has a head on one end, is passed through clearance holes in two or more aligned parts, and is threaded on the other end to receive a nut to tighten and hold the parts together (Fig. 13.22a; see also §§13.25 and 13.26).

A hexagon head *cap screw* (Fig. 13.22b) is similar to a bolt except that it generally has greater length of thread for when it is used without a nut; in such cases, one of the members being held together is threaded to act as a nut. The cap screw is screwed on with a wrench. Cap screws are not screwed into thin materials if strength is desired (see §13.29).

A *stud* (Fig. 13.22c) is a steel rod threaded on both ends. It is screwed into place with a pipe wrench or, preferably, with a stud driver. As a rule, a stud is passed through a clearance hole in one member and screwed into another member; a nut is used on the free end, as shown.

A *machine screw* (Fig. 13.32) is similar to the slotted-head cap screws but, in general, is smaller. It may be used with or without a nut.

A *set screw* (Fig. 13.33) is a screw with or without a head that is screwed through one member and whose special point is forced against another member to prevent relative motion between the two parts.

It is not customary to section bolts, nuts, screws, and similar parts when drawn in assembly, as shown in Figs. 13.22 and 13.31, because they do not themselves require sectioning for clearness (see §13.23).

■ 13.24 TAPPED HOLES

The bottom of a drilled hole is conical in shape, as formed by the point of the twist drill (Figs. 13.23a and 13.23b). When an ordinary drill is used in connection with tapping, it is referred to as a **tap drill**. On drawings, an angle of 30° is used to approximate the actual 31°.

The thread length is the length of full or perfect threads. The tap drill depth is the depth of the cylindrical portion of the hole and does not include the cone point. The portion A of the drill depth shown beyond the threads in Figs. 13.23c and 13.23d includes the several imperfect threads produced by the chamfered end of the tap. This distance A varies according to drill size and whether a plug tap (see Fig. 11.19h) or a bottom-

(a) BOLT (b) CAP SCREW (c) STUD

FIGURE 13.22 **Bolt, Cap Screw, and Stud.**

FIGURE 13.23 **Drilled and Tapped Holes.**

ing tap is used to finish the hole. For drawing purposes, when the tap drill depth is not specified, the distance A may be drawn equal to three schematic thread pitches (see Fig. 13.9).

A tapped hole finished with a bottoming tap is drawn as shown in Fig. 13.23e. Blind bottoming holes should be avoided wherever possible. A better procedure is to cut a relief with its diameter slightly greater than the major diameter of the thread (Fig. 13.23f).

One of the chief causes of tap breakage is insufficient tap drill depth, in which the tap is forced against a bed of chips in the bottom of the hole. Therefore, the drafter should never draw a blind hole when a through hole of not much greater length can be used. When a blind hole is necessary, however, the tap drill depth should be generous. Tap drill sizes for Unified, American National, and metric threads are given in Appendix 15. It is good practice to give the tap drill size in the thread note (see §13.21).

The thread length in a tapped hole depends on the major diameter and the material being tapped. In Fig. 13.24, the minimum engagement length X, when both parts are steel, is equal to the diameter D of the thread. When a steel screw is screwed into cast iron, brass, or bronze, $X = 1\frac{1}{2}D$; when it is screwed into aluminum, zinc, or plastic, $X = 2D$.

Since the tapped thread length contains only full threads, it is necessary to make this length only one or two pitches beyond the end of the engaging screw. In simplified or schematic representation, the threads are omitted in the bottoms of tapped holes to show the ends of the screws clearly (Fig. 13.24).

When a bolt or a screw is passed through a clearance hole in one member, the hole may be drilled 0.8 mm ($\frac{1}{32}''$) larger than the screw up to $\frac{3}{8}''$ or 10 mm diameter and 1.5 mm ($\frac{1}{16}''$) larger for larger diameters. For more precise work, the clearance hole may be only 0.4 mm ($\frac{1}{64}''$) larger than the screw up to $\frac{3}{8}''$ or 10 mm diameter and 0.8 mm ($\frac{1}{32}''$) larger for larger diameters. Closer fits may be specified for special conditions.

The clearance spaces on each side of a screw or bolt need not be shown on a drawing unless it is necessary to show that there is no thread engagement, in which case the clearance spaces are drawn about 1.2 mm ($\frac{3}{64}''$) wide for clarity.

13.25 STANDARD BOLTS AND NUTS

American National Standard bolts and nuts,[*] metric and inch series, are produced in hexagon form, while the square form is only produced in the inch series (Fig. 13.25). Square heads and nuts are chamfered at 30°, and hexagon heads and nuts are chamfered at 15–30°. Both are drawn at 30° for simplicity.

BOLT TYPES Bolts are grouped according to use: *regular* bolts for general service, and *heavy* bolts for heavier service or easier wrenching. Square bolts come only in the regular type; hexagon bolts, screws, and nuts and square nuts are standard in both types.

Metric hexagon bolts are grouped according to use: regular and heavy bolts and nuts for general service and high-strength bolts and nuts for structural bolting.

[*] The ANSI standards cover several bolts and nuts. For complete details, see the standards.

FIGURE 13.24 Tapped Holes.

HEXAGON BOLT AND NUT
(a)

SQUARE BOLT AND NUT
(b)

FIGURE 13.25 **Standard Bolts and Nuts.** *Courtesy of Cordova Bolt Inc., Buena Park, CA.*

FINISH   Square bolts and nuts, hexagon bolts, and hexagon flat nuts are unfinished. *Unfinished* bolts and nuts are not machined on any surface except for the threads. Traditionally, hexagon bolts and hexagon nuts have been available as unfinished, semifinished, or finished. According to the latest standards, hexagon cap screws and finished hexagon bolts have been consolidated into a single product—*hex cap screws*—thus eliminating the regular semifinished hexagon bolt classification. Heavy semifinished hexagon bolts and heavy finished hexagon bolts also have been combined into a single product called *heavy hex screws.* Hexagon cap screws, heavy hexagon screws, and all hexagon nuts, except hexagon flat nuts, are considered *finished* to some degree and are characterized by a "washer face" machined or otherwise formed on the bearing surface. The washer face is $\frac{1}{64}$" thick (drawn $\frac{1}{32}$"), and its diameter is equal to $1\frac{1}{2}$ times the body diameter D for the inch series.

For nuts the bearing surface also may be a circular surface produced by chamfering. Hexagon screws and hexagon nuts have closer tolerances and may have a more finished appearance but are not completely machined. There is no difference in the drawing for the degree of finish on finished screws and nuts.

Metric bolts, cap screws, and nuts are produced in the hexagon form (Fig. 13.25a). The hexagon heads and nuts are chamfered at 15–30°. Both are drawn at 30° for simplicity.

PROPORTIONS   Sizes based on diameter D of the bolt body (including metric) (Fig. 13.26), which are either exact formula proportions or close approximations for drawing purposes, are as follows.
Regular hexagon and square bolts and nuts:

$$W = 1\tfrac{1}{2}D \qquad H = \tfrac{2}{3}D \qquad T = \tfrac{7}{8}D,$$

where W = width across flats, H = head height, and T = nut height.
Heavy hexagon bolts and nuts and square nuts:

$$W = 1\tfrac{1}{2}D + \tfrac{1}{8}\text{" (or + 3 mm)}$$

$$H = \tfrac{2}{3}D \qquad T = D$$

The washer face is always included in the head or nut height for finished hexagon screw heads and nuts.

THREADS   Square and hex bolts, hex cap screws, and finished nuts in the inch series are usually Class 2 and may have coarse, fine, or 8-pitch threads. Unfinished nuts have coarse threads, Class 2B. For diameter and pitch specifications for metric threads, see Appendix 18.

THREAD LENGTHS
For bolts or screws up to 6" (150 mm) in length:

$$\text{Thread length} = 2D + \tfrac{1}{4}\text{" (or + 6 mm)}$$

For bolts or screws over 6" in length,

$$\text{Thread length} = 2D + \tfrac{1}{2}\text{" (or + 12 mm)}$$

Fasteners too short for these formulas are threaded as close to the head as practicable. For drawing purposes, this may be taken as approximately three pitches. The threaded end may be rounded or chamfered, but is usually drawn with a 45° chamfer from the thread depth (Fig. 13.26).

BOLT LENGTHS   Lengths of bolts have not been standardized because of the endless variety required by industry. Short bolts are typically available in standard length increments of $\frac{1}{4}$" (6 mm), while long bolts come in increments of $\frac{1}{2}$ to 1" (12 to 25 mm). For dimensions of standard bolts and nuts, see Appendix 18.

■ 13.26 DRAWING STANDARD BOLTS

In practice, standard bolts and nuts are not shown in detail drawings unless they are to be altered, but they appear so frequently on assembly drawings that a suitable but rapid method of drawing them must be used. Time-saving templates are available, or they may be drawn from exact dimensions taken from tables (see Appendix 18) if accuracy is important, as in figuring clearances. However, in the great majority of cases the conventional representation, in which proportions based on the body diameter are used, will be sufficient, and a considerable amount of time may be saved. Three typical bolts illustrating the use of these proportions for the regular bolts are shown in Fig. 13.26.

Although the curves produced by the chamfer on the bolt heads and nuts are hyperbolas, in practice these curves are always represented approximately by means of circular arcs (Fig. 13.26).

FIGURE 13.26 Bolt Proportions (Regular).

Generally, bolt heads and nuts should be drawn "across corners" in all views, regardless of projection. This conventional violation of projection is used to prevent confusion between the square and hexagon heads and nuts and to show actual clearances. Only when there is a special reason should bolt heads and nuts be drawn across flats. In such cases, the conventional proportions are used (Fig. 13.27).

Steps in drawing hexagon bolts, cap screws, and nuts are illustrated in Fig. 13.28, and those for square bolts and nuts in Fig. 13.29. Before drawing a bolt, the diameter of the bolt, the length (from the underside of the bearing surface to the tip), the style of head (square or hexagon), and the type (regular or heavy), as well as the finish, must be known.

If only the longitudinal view of a bolt is needed, it is necessary to draw only the lower half of the top views in Figs. 13.28 and 13.29 with light construction lines to project the corners of the hexagon or square to

the front view. These construction lines may then be erased if desired.

The head and nut heights can be spaced off with the dividers on the shaft diameter and then transferred as shown in both figures, or the scale may be used as in Fig. 5.15. The heights should not be determined by arithmetic.

The $\frac{1}{64}''$ (0.4 mm) washer face has a diameter equal to the distance across flats of the bolt head or nut. It appears only on the metric and finished hexagon screws or nuts, and the washer face thickness is drawn at $\frac{1}{32}''$ (1 mm) for clearness. The $\frac{1}{32}''$ (1 mm) is included in the head or nut height.

Threads should be drawn in simplified or schematic form for body diameters of 1″ (25 mm) or less on the drawing (Fig. 13.9b or 13.9d) and by detailed representation for larger diameters (§§13.7 and 13.8). The threaded end of the screw should be chamfered at 45° from the schematic thread depth (Fig. 13.9a).

FIGURE 13.27 Bolts "Across Flats."

On drawings of small bolts or nuts under approximately $\frac{1}{2}''$ diameter (12 mm), where the chamfer is hardly noticeable, the chamfer on the head or nut may be omitted in the longitudinal view.

Many styles of templates are available for saving time in drawing bolt heads and nuts.

■ 13.27 SPECIFICATIONS FOR BOLTS AND NUTS

In specifying bolts in parts lists, in correspondence, or elsewhere, the following information must be covered in order.

1. Nominal size of bolt body.
2. Thread specification or thread note (see §13.21).
3. Length of bolt.
4. Finish of bolt.
5. Style of head.
6. Name.

> **EXAMPLE** (Complete Decimal-Inch)
>
> .75–10 UNC-2A × 2.50 HEXAGON CAP SCREW

> **EXAMPLE** (Abbreviated Decimal-Inch)
>
> .75 × 2.50 HEX CAP SCR

> **EXAMPLE** (Metric)
>
> M8 X 1.25–40, HEX CAP SCR

Nuts may be specified as follows.

> **EXAMPLE** (Complete)
>
> $\frac{5}{8}$–11 UNC–2B SQUARE NUT

FIGURE 13.28 Steps in Drawing (a) Finished Hexagon Head Bolt (Cap Screw) and Hexagon Nut, and (b) Square-Itead Bolt and Square Nut.

FIGURE 13.29 Steps in Drawing Square-Head Bolt and Square Nut.

EXAMPLE (Abbreviated)

$\frac{5}{8}$SQ NUT

EXAMPLE (Metric)

M8 × 1.25 HEX NUT

For either bolts or nuts, the words REGULAR or GENERAL PURPOSE are assumed if omitted from the specification. If the heavy series is intended, the word HEAVY should appear as the first word in the name of the fastener. Likewise, HIGH STRENGTH STRUCTURAL should be indicated for such metric fasteners. However, the number of the specific ISO standard is often included in the metric specifications—for example, HEXAGON NUT ISO 4032 M12 × 1.75. Similarly, finish need not be mentioned if the fastener or nut is correctly named (see §13.25).

■ 13.28 LOCKNUTS AND LOCKING DEVICES

Many types of special nuts and devices to prevent nuts from unscrewing are available, some of the most common of which are illustrated in Fig. 13.30. The American National Standard *jam nuts* (Figs. 13.30a and 13.30b) are the same as the hexagon or hexagon flat nuts, except that they are thinner. The application shown in Fig. 13.30b, where the larger nut is on top and is screwed on more tightly, is recommended. They are the same distance across flats as the corresponding hexagon nuts ($1\frac{1}{2}D$ or $1\frac{1}{2}D + \frac{1}{8}''$). They are slightly over $\frac{1}{2}D$ in thickness but are drawn $\frac{1}{2}D$ for simplicity. They are available with or without the washer face in the regular and heavy types. The tops of all are flat and chamfered at 30°, and the finished forms have either a washer face or a chamfered bearing surface.

The lock washer, shown in Fig. 13.30c, and the cotter pin, shown in Figs. 13.30e, 13.30g, and 13.30h, are very common (see Appendixes 27 and 30). The set screw (Fig. 13.30f) is often made to press against a plug of softer material, such as brass, which in turn presses against the threads without deforming them. For use with cotter pins (see Appendix 30), a hex slotted nut (Fig. 13.30g) and a hex castle nut (Fig. 13.30h), as well as a hex thick slotted nut and a heavy hex thick slotted nut, are recommended.

Similar metric locknuts and locking devices are available. See fastener catalogs for details.

REGULAR UNFINISHED
JAM NUT (AMER STD)

REGULAR SEMI-FINISHED
JAM NUT (AMER STD)

FINISHED SLOTTED
NUT (AMER STD)

FINISHED CASTLE
NUT (AMER STD)

ESNA
STOP NUT

FIGURE 13.30   **Locknuts and Locking Devices.**

■ 13.29 STANDARD CAP SCREWS

Five types of American National Standard cap screws are shown in Fig. 13.31. The first four of these have standard heads, while the socket head cap screws (Fig. 13.31e) have several different shapes of round heads and sockets. Cap screws are regularly produced in finished form and are used on machine tools and other machines for which accuracy and appearance are important. The ranges of sizes and exact dimensions are given in Appendixes 18 and 19. The hexagon head cap screw and hex socket head cap screw in several forms are available in metric (see Appendix 18).

Cap screws ordinarily pass through a clearance hole in one member and screw into another (§13.24). The clearance hole need not be shown on the drawing when the presence of the unthreaded clearance hole is obvious.

Cap screws are inferior to studs if frequent removal is necessary; hence, they are used on machines requiring few adjustments. The slotted or socket-type heads are best under crowded conditions.

The actual standard dimensions may be used in drawing the cap screws whenever exact sizes are necessary, but this is seldom the case. In Fig. 13.31 the dimensions are given in terms of body diameter D, and they closely conform to the actual dimensions. The resulting drawings are almost exact reproductions and

are easy to draw. The hexagonal head cap screw is drawn in the manner shown in Fig. 13.28. The points are drawn chamfered at 45° from the schematic thread depth.

For correct representation of tapped holes, see §13.24. For information on drilled, countersunk, or counterbored holes, see §6.33.

In an assembly section, it is customary not to section screws, bolts, shafts, or other solid parts whose center lines lie in the cutting plane. Such parts in themselves do not require sectioning and are, therefore, shown "in the round" (Fig. 13.31).

Note that screwdriver slots are drawn at 45° in the circular views of the heads, without regard to true projection, and that threads in the bottom of the tapped holes are omitted so that the ends of the screws may be clearly seen. A typical cap screw note is as follows:

EXAMPLE (Complete)

$\frac{3}{8}$–16 UNC-2A × $2\frac{1}{2}$HEXAGON HEAD CAP SCREW

EXAMPLE (Abbreviated)

$\frac{3}{8}$ × $2\frac{1}{2}$HEX HD CAP SCR

EXAMPLE (Metric)

M20 × 2.5 × 80 HEX HD CAP SCR

a

A fully rendered and
assembled turbine display.
(All courtesy of Autodesk, Inc.)

b

An exploded wireframe
display.

c

A surface-rendered
exploded display.

d

A surface-rendered,
color-coded display.

a, b, c

VRML images found at the Dynojet Research Incorporated web site. When viewed with a VRML browser, these images have a 3D quality. *(All courtesy of Dynojet Research, Inc.)*

a, b

Use of CAD speeds the
design process and reduces
costs. These models of a
robot welder and a Zip
drive let manufacturers
simulate their products
before they were even built.
*(Reproduced by permission of
SDRC, Inc.)*

A Finite Element Model
of diesel engine compo-
nents created with I-DEAS
software. *(Courtesy of SDRC, Inc.)*

A structural stress analysis
of the Sudbury Neutrino
Observatory created with
Auto FEA by ANSYS.
(Courtesy of ANSYS)

a

An engineer using virtual reality to help in autmobile design. A special helmet, goggles, and glove allow the engineer to simulate the driving experience as seen below. *(Courtesy of Ford Motor Company)*

b

CAD software and virtual reality equipment allow users to experience "virtual rooms" and decide whether they like the design before construction. *(Courtesy of Truevision)*

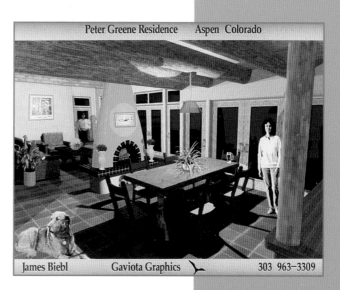

Peter Greene Residence   Aspen Colorado

James Biebl   Gaviota Graphics   303 963–3309

An automated cutting system uses patterns designed with CAD software to produce precise designs. *(Courtesy of Gerber Scientific, Inc.)*

Modern manufacturing depends heavily on computer controlled robots. At this Chrysler plant, 66 robots apply spot welds. *(Courtesy of Chrysler Motor Corp.)*

a, b, c

Examples of solid models
created with I-DEAS soft-
ware. Solid modelling can
help bring designs to life.
(All courtesy of SDRC, Inc.)

PLATE 8

a, b, c

CAD software is very useful as a tool to visualize architectural designs. All these images were created in AutoCAD. *(All courtesy of Autodesk, Inc.)*

(a) HEXAGON HEAD   (b) FLAT HEAD   (c) ROUND HEAD   (d) FILLISTER HEAD   (e) HEX SOCKET

Hexagon Head Screws   Coarse, Fine, or 8-Thread Series, 2A. Thread length = $2D + \frac{1}{4}''$ up to 6″ long and $2D + \frac{1}{2}''$ if over 6″ long. For screws too short for formula, threads extend to within $2\frac{1}{2}$ threads of the head for diameters up to 1″. Screw lengths not standardized. For suggested lengths for metric Hexagon Head Screws, see Appendix 15.

Slotted Head Screws   Coarse, Fine, or 8-Thread Series, 2A. Thread length = $2D + \frac{1}{4}''$. Screw lengths not standardized. For screws too short for formula, threads extend to within $2\frac{1}{2}$ threads of the head.

Hexagon Socket Screws   Coarse or Fine Threads, 3A. Coarse thread length = $2D + \frac{1}{2}''$ where this would be over $\frac{1}{2}L$; otherwise thread length = $\frac{1}{2}L$. Fine thread length = $1\frac{1}{2}D + \frac{1}{2}''$ where this would be over $\frac{3}{8}L$; otherwise thread length = $\frac{3}{8}L$. Increments in screw lengths = $\frac{1}{8}''$ for screws $\frac{1}{4}''$ to 1″ long, $\frac{1}{4}''$ for screws 1″ to 3″ long, and $\frac{1}{2}''$ for screws $3\frac{1}{2}''$ to 6″ long.

FIGURE 13.31   Standard Cap Screws. See Appendixes 18 and 19.

■ 13.30 STANDARD MACHINE SCREWS

Machine screws are similar to cap screws but are in general smaller (.060″ to .750″ dia). There are eight ANSI-approved forms of heads shown in Appendix 20. The hexagonal head may be slotted if desired. All others are available in either slotted or recessed-head forms. Standard machine screws are regularly produced with a naturally bright finish, not heat treated, and are regularly supplied with plain-sheared ends, not chamfered. For similar metric machine screw forms and specifications, see Appendix 20.

Machine screws are particularly adapted to screwing into thin materials, and all the smaller-numbered screws are threaded nearly to the head. They are used extensively in firearms, jigs, fixtures, and dies. Machine screw nuts are used mainly on the round head, pan head, and flat head types and are usually hexagonal in form.

Exact dimensions of machine screws are given in Appendix 20, but they are seldom needed for drawing purposes. The four most common types of machine screws are shown in Fig. 13.32, in which proportions based on diameter D conform closely to the actual dimensions and produce almost exact drawings. Clearance holes and counterbores should be made slightly larger than the screws, as explained in §13.24.

FIGURE 13.32   Standard Machine Screws. See Appendix 20.

(a) ROUND HEAD   (b) FLAT HEAD   (c) OVAL HEAD   (d) FILLISTER HEAD

Note that the threads in the bottom of the tapped holes are omitted so that the ends of the screws will be clearly seen. Observe also that it is conventional practice to draw the screwdriver slots at 45° in the circular view without regard to true projection.

A typical machine screw note is as follows:

EXAMPLE (Complete)

No. 10 (.1900)–32 NF-3 × $\frac{5}{8}$ FILLISTER HEAD MACHINE SCREW

EXAMPLE (Abbreviated)

No. 10 (.1900) × $\frac{5}{8}$ FILL HD MACH SCR

EXAMPLE (Metric)

M8 × 1.25 × 30 SLOTTED PAN HEAD MACHINE SCREW

■ 13.31 STANDARD SET SCREWS

The function of set screws (Fig. 13.33) is to prevent relative motion, usually rotary, between two parts, such as the movement of the hub of a pulley on a shaft. A set screw is screwed into one part so that its point bears firmly against another part. If the point of the set screw is cupped (Fig. 13.33e), or if a flat is milled on the shaft (Fig. 13.33a), the screw will hold much more firmly. Obviously, set screws are not efficient when the load is heavy or is suddenly applied. Usually they are manufactured of steel and case hardened.

The American National Standard square head set screw and slotted headless set screw are shown in Figs. 13.33a and 13.33b. Two American National Standard socket set screws are illustrated in Figs. 13.33c and 13.33d. American National Standard set screw points are shown in Figs. 13.33e to 13.33k. Headless set screws have come into greater use because the projecting head of headed set screws has caused many industrial casualties; this has resulted in legislation prohibiting their use in many states.

Most of the dimensions in Fig. 13.33 are American National Standard formula dimensions, and the resulting drawings are almost exact representations.

Metric hexagon socket headless set screws with the full range of points are available and are represented in the same manner as shown in Fig. 13.33. Nominal diameters of metric hex socket set screws are 1.6, 2, 2.5, 3, 4, 5, 6, 8, 10, 12, 16, 20, and 24 mm.

Square head set screws have coarse, fine, or 8-pitch threads, Class 2A, but are usually furnished with coarse threads since the square head set screw is generally used on the rougher grades of work. Slotted headless and socket set screws have coarse or fine threads, Class 3A.

Nominal diameters of set screws range from number 0 up through 2″; set screw lengths are standardized in increments of $\frac{1}{32}″$ to 1″ depending on the overall length of the set screw.

Metric set screw length increments range from 0.5 to 4 mm, again depending on overall screw length.

FIGURE 13.33 **American National Standard Set Screws.**

Set screws are specified as follows.

EXAMPLE (Complete)

$\frac{3}{8}$-16 UNC-2A × $\frac{3}{4}$SQUARE HEAD
FLAT POINT SET SCREW

EXAMPLE (Abbreviated)

$\frac{3}{8}$- × 1$\frac{1}{4}$ SQ HD FL PT SS
$\frac{7}{16}$ × $\frac{3}{4}$ HEX SOC CUP PT SS
$\frac{1}{4}$-20 UNC 2A × $\frac{4}{8}$ SLOT. HDLS CONE PT SS

EXAMPLE (Metric)

M10 × 1.5 × 12 HEX SOCKET HEAD SET SCREW

■ 13.32 AMERICAN NATIONAL STANDARD WOOD SCREWS

Wood screws with three types of heads—flat, round, and oval—have been standardized (Fig. 13.34). The dimensions shown closely approximate the actual dimensions and are more than sufficiently accurate for use on drawings.

The Phillips-style recessed head is also available on several types of fasteners as well as wood screws. Three styles of cross recesses have been standardized by the ANSI. A special screwdriver is used, as shown in Fig. 13.35q, and results in rapid assembly without damage to the head.

■ 13.33 MISCELLANEOUS FASTENERS

Many other types of fasteners have been devised for specialized uses. Some of the more common types are shown in Fig. 13.35. A number of these are American National Standard round-head bolts, including carriage, button head, step, and countersunk bolts.

Helical coil threaded inserts (Fig. 13.35p) are shaped like a spring except that the cross section of the wire conforms to threads on the screw and in the hole. These are made of phosphor bronze or stainless steel, and they provide a hard, smooth protective lining for tapped threads in soft metals and plastics.

■ 13.34 KEYS

Keys are used to prevent relative movement between shafts and wheels, couplings, cranks, and similar

FIGURE 13.34 American National Standard Wood Screws.

FIGURE 13.35 Miscellaneous Bolts and Screws.

FIGURE 13.36 Square and Flat Keys.

FIGURE 13.37 Woodruff Keys and Key-Slot Cutter.

machine parts attached to or supported by shafts (Fig. 13.36).

For heavy-duty functions, rectangular keys (flat or square) are suitable, and sometimes two rectangular keys are necessary for one connection. For even stronger connections, interlocking *splines* may be machined on the shaft and in the hole (see Fig. 13.9).

A *square key* is shown in Fig. 13.36a and a *flat key* in Fig. 13.36b. The widths of keys generally used are about one fourth the shaft diameter. In either case, one half the key is sunk into the shaft. The depth of the keyway or the keyseat is measured on the side—not the center (Fig. 13.36a). Square and flat keys may have the top surface tapered $\frac{1}{8}''$ per foot, in which case they become square taper or flat taper keys.

A rectangular key that prevents rotary motion but permits relative longitudinal motion is a *feather key* and is usually provided with *gib heads*, or otherwise fastened so it cannot slip out of the keyway. A *gib head key* is shown in Fig. 13.36c. It is exactly the same as the square taper or flat taper key except that a gib head, which provides for easy removal, is added. Square and flat keys are made from cold-finished stock and are not machined. For dimensions, see Appendix 21.

The *Pratt & Whitney key* (P & W) (Fig. 13.36d) is rectangular in shape, with semicylindrical ends. Two thirds of the height of the P & W key is sunk into the shaft keyseat (see Appendix 25).

The *Woodruff key* is semicircular in shape (Fig. 13.37). The key fits into a semicircular key slot cut with a Woodruff cutter, as shown, and the top of the key fits into a plain rectangular keyway. Sizes of keys

for given shaft diameters are not standardized, but for average conditions it will be found satisfactory to select a key whose diameter is approximately equal to the shaft diameter. For dimensions, see Appendix 23.

A **keyseat** is in a shaft; a **keyway** is in the hub or surrounding part.

Typical specifications for keys are as follows:

$\frac{1}{4} \times 1\frac{1}{2}$SQ KEY
No. 204 WOODRUFF KEY
$\frac{1}{4} \times \frac{1}{16} \times 1\frac{1}{2}$FLAT KEY
No. 10 P & W KEY

Notes for nominal specifications of keyways and keyseats are shown in Figs. 11.44o, 11.44p, 11.44r, and 11.44x. For production work, keyways and keyseats should be dimensioned as shown in Fig. 11.48. See manufacturers' catalogs for specifications for metric counterparts.

■ 13.35 MACHINE PINS

Machine pins include taper pins, straight pins, dowel pins, clevis pins, and cotter pins. For light work, the taper pin is effective for fastening hubs or collars to shafts (Fig. 13.38) in which the hole through the collar and shaft is drilled and reamed when the parts are assembled. For slightly heavier duty, the taper pin may be used parallel to the shaft as for square keys (see Appendix 29).

Dowel pins are cylindrical or conical in shape and are used for a variety of purposes, chief of which is to keep two parts in a fixed position or to preserve alignment. The dowel pin is most commonly used and is

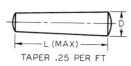

TAPER .25 PER FT

FIGURE 13.38 Taper Pin.

recommended where accurate alignment is essential. Dowel pins are usually made of steel and are hardened and ground in a centerless grinder.

The clevis pin is used in a clevis and is held in place by a cotter pin. For the latter, see Appendix 30.

■ 13.36 RIVETS

Rivets are regarded as permanent fastenings as distinguished from removable fastenings, such as bolts and screws. Rivets are generally used to hold sheet metal or rolled steel shapes together and are made of wrought iron, carbon steel, copper, or occasionally other metals.

To fasten two pieces of metal together, holes are punched, drilled, or punched and then reamed, slightly larger in diameter than the shank of the rivet. Rivet diameters in practice are made from $d = 1.2 \sqrt{t}$ to $d = 1.4 \sqrt{t}$, where d is the rivet diameter and t is the metal thickness. The larger size is used for steel and single-riveted joints, and the smaller may be used for multiple-riveted joints. In structural work it is common practice to make the hole 1.6 mm ($\frac{1}{16}''$) larger than the rivet.

When the red-hot rivet is inserted, a "dolly bar," having a depression the shape of the driven head, is held against the head. A riveting machine is then used to drive the rivet and to form the head on the plain end. This action causes the rivet to swell and fill the hole tightly.

Large rivets or heavy hex structural bolts were commonly used in structural work of bridges and buildings and in ship and boiler construction. Although not used in modern construction, an engineer could be involved in updating existing structures using rivets. They are shown in their exact formula proportions in Fig. 13.39. The button head (Fig. 13.39a) and countersunk head (Fig. 13.39e) types are the rivets most commonly used in structural work. The button head and cone head are commonly used in tank and boiler construction.

Typical riveted joints are illustrated in Fig. 13.40. Notice that the longitudinal view of each rivet shows the shank of the rivet with both heads made with circular arcs, and the circular view of each rivet is represented by only the outside circle of the head. In structural drafting, where there may be many such circles to draw, the drop spring bow (Fig. 3.53) is a convenient instrument.

Since many engineering structures are too large to be built in the shop, they are built in the largest units possible and then are transported to the desired location. Trusses are common examples of this. The rivets driven in the shop are called *shop rivets*, and those driven on the job are called *field rivets*. However, heavy steel bolts are commonly used on the job for structural work. Solid black circles are used to represent field rivets, and other standard symbols are used to show other features, as shown in Fig. 13.41.

For light work, small rivets are used. American National Standard small solid rivets are illustrated with dimensions showing their standard proportions in Fig. 13.42 [ANSI/ASME B18.1.1–1972 (R1995)]. Included in the same standard are tinners', coppers', and belt rivets. Metric rivets are also available. Dimensions for large rivets can be found in ANSI/ASME B18.1.2–1972 (R1995). See manufacturers' catalogs for additional details.

FIGURE 13.39 Standard Large Rivets.

| BUTTON HEAD (a) | HIGH BUTTON HEAD (ACORN) (b) | CONE HEAD (c) | PAN HEAD (d) | FLAT TOP COUNTERSUNK HD (e) | ROUND TOP COUNTERSUNK HD (f) |

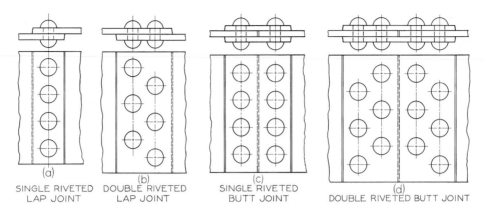

SINGLE RIVETED LAP JOINT (a)   DOUBLE RIVETED LAP JOINT (b)   SINGLE RIVETED BUTT JOINT (c)   DOUBLE RIVETED BUTT JOINT (d)

FIGURE 13.40 **Common Riveted Joints.**

FIGURE 13.41 **Conventional Rivet Symbols.**

FIGURE 13.42 **American National Standard Small Solid Rivet Proportions.**

FLAT HEAD   COUNTERSUNK HEAD   BUTTON HEAD   PAN HEAD   TRUSS OR WAGON BOX HEAD

Blind rivets, commonly known as Pop Rivets™ (Fig. 13.43), are often used for fastening together thin sheet-metal assemblies. Blind rivets are hollow and are installed with manual or power-operated rivet guns which grip a center pin or mandrel, pulling the head into the body and expanding the rivet against the sheet metal. They are available in aluminum, steel, stainless steel, and plastic. As with any fastener, the designer should be careful to choose an appropriate material to avoid corrosive action between dissimilar metals.

■ 13.37 SPRINGS

A **spring** is a mechanical device designed to store energy when deflected and to return the equivalent amount of energy when released [ANSI Y13.13M–1981 (R1992)]. Springs are commonly made of *spring steel*, which may be music wire, hard-drawn wire, or oil-tempered wire. Other materials used for compression springs include stainless steel, beryllium copper, and phosphor bronze. In addition, compression springs made of urethane plastic are used in applications where conventional springs would be

FIGURE 13.43 Blind Rivets (a) Before Installation, and (b) Installed.

(a) DETAILED ROUND-WIRE SPRING

(b) DETAILED SQUARE-WIRE SPRING

(c) SMALL SPRING IN SECTION

(d) USE OF PHANTOM LINES

(e) SCHEMATIC COMPRESSION SPRING

(f) SCHEMATIC TENSION SPRING

FIGURE 13.44 Helical Springs.

FL = Free length D = Controlling dia inside or outside
t = Dia of wire L_1 = Comp length (Min) L_2 = Comp length (Max)

(a) No. of coils PLAIN ENDS

(b) SQUARED ENDS

(c) PLAIN END GROUND

(d) SQUARED AND GROUND

FIGURE 13.45 Compression Springs.

affected by corrosion, vibration, or acoustic or magnetic forces. Springs are classified as *helical springs* (Fig. 13.44) or *flat springs* (Fig. 13.48). Helical springs may be cylindrical or conical but are usually the former.

There are three types of helical springs: *compression springs*, which offer resistance to a compressive force (Fig. 13.45); *extension springs*, which offer resistance to a pulling force (Fig. 13.46); and *torsion springs*, which offer resistance to a torque or twisting force (Fig. 13.47).

On working drawings, true projections of helical springs are never drawn because of the labor involved.

Instead, as in the drawing of screw threads, the detailed and schematic methods are used, where straight lines replace helical curves (Fig. 13.44).

The elevation view of the square-wire spring is similar to the square thread with the core of the shaft removed (Fig. 13.12). Standard section lining is used if the areas in section are large, as in Figs. 13.44a and 13.44b. If these areas are small, the sectioned areas may be made solid black (Fig. 13.44c). In cases where a complete picture of the spring is not necessary, phantom lines may be used to save time in drawing the coils (Fig. 13.44d). If the drawing of the spring is too small

MATERIAL: 2.00 OIL TEMPERED SPRING STEEL WIRE
14.5 COILS RIGHT HAND
MACHINE LOOP AND HOOK IN LINE
SPRING MUST EXTEND TO 110 WITHOUT SET
FINISH: BLACK JAPAN

FIGURE 13.46 **Extension Spring Drawing.**

MATERIAL : .059 MUSIC WIRE
6.75 COILS RIGHT HAND NO INITIAL TENSION
TORQUE : 2.50 INCH LB AT 155° DEFLECTION SPRING MUST
DEFLECT 180° WITHOUT PERMANENT SET AND
MUST OPERATE FREELY ON .75 DIAMETER SHAFT
FINISH : CADMIUM OR ZINC PLATE

FIGURE 13.47 **Torsion Spring Drawing.**

to be represented by the outlines of the wire, it may be drawn by the schematic method, in which single lines are used (Figs. 13.44e and 13.44f).

Compression springs have *plain ends* (Fig. 13.45a) or *squared (closed) ends* (Fig. 13.45b). The ends may be *ground* (Fig. 13.45c) or both *squared and ground* (Fig. 13.45d). Required dimensions are indicated in the figure. When required, RH or LH is specified.

Many companies use standard printed spring drawings with a printed form to be filled in by the drafter, providing the necessary information, plus load at a specified deflected length, the load rate, finish, type of service, and other data.

An extension spring may have any one of many types of ends, and it is therefore necessary to draw the spring or at least the ends and a few adjacent coils (Fig. 13.46). Note the use of phantom lines to show the continuity of coils. Printed forms are used when a given form of spring is produced with differences in verbal specification only.

MATERIAL : 1.20 X 14.0 SPRING STEEL
HEAT TREAT : 44-48 C ROCKWELL
FINISH : BLACK OXIDE AND OIL

FIGURE 13.48 **Flat Spring.**

A typical torsion spring drawing is shown in Fig. 13.47. Here also printed forms are used when there is sufficient uniformity in product to permit a common representation.

A typical flat spring drawing is shown in Fig. 13.48. Other types of flat springs are *power springs* (or flat coil springs), *Belleville springs* (like spring washers), and *leaf springs* (commonly used in automobiles).

■ 13.38 DRAWING HELICAL SPRINGS

The construction for a schematic elevation view of a compression spring having six total coils is shown in Fig. 13.49a. Since the ends are closed, or squared, two of the six coils are "dead" coils, leaving only four full pitches to be set off along the top of the spring, as shown.

If there are $6\frac{1}{2}$ total coils (Fig. 13.49b), the $\frac{P}{2}$ spacings will be on opposite sides of the spring. The construction of an extension spring with six active coils and loop ends is shown in Fig. 13.49c.

Figure 13.50 shows the steps in drawing a sectional view and an elevation view of a compression spring by detailed representation. The given spring is shown pictorially in Fig. 13.50a. In Fig. 13.50b, a cutting plane has passed through the center line of the spring, and the front portion of the spring has been removed. In Fig. 13.50c, the cutting plane has been removed. Steps in

6 TOTAL COILS
COMPRESSION SPRING
(a)

6.5 TOTAL COILS
COMPRESSION SPRING
(b)

6 TOTAL COILS
EXTENSION SPRING
(c)

FIGURE 13.49 Schematic Spring Representation. *Courtesy of SDRC, Milford, OH.*

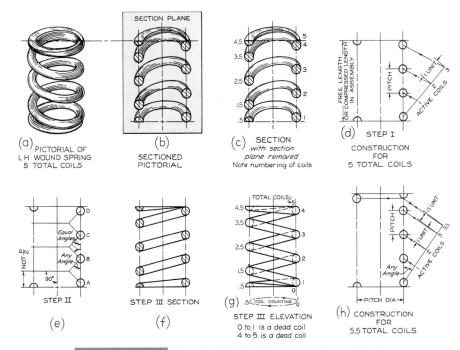

FIGURE 13.50 Steps in Detailed Representation of Spring.

constructing the spring through several stages to obtain the sectional view are shown in Figs. 13.50d to 13.50f. The corresponding elevation view is shown in Fig. 13.50g.

If there is a fractional number of coils, such as $5\frac{1}{2}$ coils in Fig. 13.50h, note that the half-rounds of sectional wire are placed on opposite sides of the spring.

■ 13.39 COMPUTER GRAPHICS

Standard representations of threaded fasteners and springs, in both detailed and schematic forms, are available in CAD symbol libraries. Use of computer graphics frees the drafter from the need to draw time-consuming repetitive features by hand and also make it easy to modify drawings if required.

In 3D modeling, thread is not usually represented because it can be difficult to create and computer intensive to view and edit. Instead the nominal diameter of a threaded shaft or hole is usually created along with notation calling out the thread. Sometimes the depth of the thread is shown in the 3D drawing, to call attention to the thread and to help in determining fits and clearances.

FIGURE 13.51 Examples of Fastener Symbols Available for Use with AutoCAD in SPOCAD's Autofasteners Library. (*Courtesy SPOCAD*).

FIGURE 13.52 CAD-Generated Drawing Showing Detailed Thread Representation. *Courtesy of Computervision Corporation, a Subsidiary of Prime Computer, Inc.*

■ KEY WORDS

THREAD FORM	MAJOR DIAMETER
MINOR DIAMETER	INTERNAL THREAD
EXTERNAL THREAD	PITCH
LEAD	THREAD ANGLE
CREST	ROOT
CLASS OF FIT	UNIFIED THREAD FORM
METRIC THREAD FORM	SCHEMATIC THREAD REPRESENTATION
MULTIPLE LEAD	SIMPLIFIED THREAD REPRESENTATION
PHANTOM LINES	CAP SCREWS
MACHINE SCREWS	SET SCREWS
KEYS	PINS
HELIX	BOLTS
STUDS	SPRINGS
RIVETS	NUTS

■ CHAPTER SUMMARY

- There are many types of thread forms; however, metric and Unified are the most common.

- The method of showing threads on a drawing is called the thread representation. The three types of thread representation are detailed, schematic, and simplified.

- The major diameter, pitch, and form are the most important parts of a thread specification.

- Thread specifications are a special type of leader note. The thread specification tells the manufacturing technician what kind of thread needs to be created.

- The nut and bolt is still the most common type of fastener. Many new types of fasteners are being created to streamline the production process.

- Keys and pins are special fasteners that attach a pulley to a shaft.

- The screw head determines what kind of tool will be necessary to install the fastener.

■ REVIEW QUESTIONS

1. Draw a typical screw thread and label the parts of the thread.

2. Sketch a long spring and show how phantom lines are used to represent the middle part of the spring.

3. Draw several types of screw heads.

4. List five types of screws.

5. Why is the simplified thread representation the most commonly used drawing style?

6. List five fasteners that do *not* have any threads.

7. Write out a metric thread specification and a Unified thread specification and label each part of the specification.

8. Which type of thread form is used on a light bulb?

■ THREAD AND FASTENER PROBLEMS

Students are expected to make use of the information in this chapter and in various manufacturers' catalogs in connection with the working drawings at the end of the next chapter, where many different kinds of threads and fasteners are required. However, several problems are included here for specific assignment in this area (Figs. 13.53 to 13.56). All are to be drawn on tracing paper or detail paper, size B or A3 sheet (see inside back cover).

FIGURE 13.53 Draw specified detailed threads arranged as shown. Using Layout B–3 or A3–3. Omit all dimensions and notes given in inclined letters. Letter only the thread notes and the title strip.

FIGURE 13.54 Draw specified detailed threads, arranged as shown. using Layout B–3 or A3–3. Omit all dimensions and notes given in inclined letters. Letter only the thread notes and the title strip.

FIGURE 13.55 Draw specified thread symbols, arranged as shown. Draw simplified or schematic symbols, as assigned by instructor. Using Layout B–5 or A3–5. Omit all dimensions and notes given in inclined letters. Letter only the drill and thread notes, the titles of the views, and the title strip.

FIGURE 13.56 Draw fasteners, arranged as shown. Using Layout B–3 or A3–3. At (a) draw $\frac{7}{8}$–9 UNC-2A × 4 Hex Cap Screw. At (b) draw $1\frac{1}{8}$–7 UNC-2A × $4\frac{1}{4}$ Sq Hd Bolt. At (c) draw $\frac{3}{8}$–16 UNC-2A × $1\frac{1}{2}$ Flat Hd Cap Screw. At (d) draw $\frac{7}{16}$–14 UNC-2A × 1 Fill Hd Cap Screw. At (e) draw $\frac{1}{2}$ × 1 Headless Slotted Set Screw. At (f) draw front view of No. 1010 Woodruff Key. Draw simplified or schematic thread symbols as assigned. Letter titles under each figure as show.

C H A P T E R   1 4

DESIGN
AND WORKING
DRAWINGS

OBJECTIVES

After studying the material in this chapter, you should be able to:

1. Define the different types of design.
2. Define engineering design and examine how the proper objectives and motivation can turn any one into a good designer.
3. Discuss the different sources for design ideas for both the individual designer as well as a design team.
4. Describe the stages of the design process.
5. Discuss solid modeling, parametric modeling, prototyping and rapid prototyping.
6. Use a case study to illustrate of each stage of the design process.
7. Identify the elements of a detail drawing and create a simple detail drawing.
8. List the common elements of a title block and record strip.
9. Create a typical drawing sequence of numbers.
10. Describe the process for revising drawings.
11. List the parts of an assembly drawing.
12. Describe the special requirements of a patent drawing.

OVERVIEW

The many products, systems, and services that enrich our standard of living are largely the result of the design activities of engineers. It is principally this design activity that distinguishes engineering from science and research; the engineer is a designer, a creator, or a "builder."

The design process is an exciting and challenging effort, and the engineer-designer relies heavily on graphics as a means to create, record, analyze, and communicate to other design concepts or ideas. The ability to communicate verbally, symbolically, and graphically is essential.

The design team progresses through five stages in the design process. To be a successful member of the design team, every member must understand the process and know how to fulfill his or her role. Various types of drawings are required at each stage of the design process. CAD can help the drafter create drawings, but it takes a skilled drafter to know which drawings are required at each design stage. Much of the design process is refinement of existing products. Refinement creates improved products, lowers cost, and increases profit for the company that manufacturers the product. Models are an important part of the design process. Some models are created to scale in a model shop. Other models are generated by the computer and printed or displayed in virtual reality. All models allow interaction with the design to further improve the design. Revising a drawing is an important part of the design process. Revisions must be tracked, identified, logged, and saved for future reference. Both paper and electronic storage is an important part of the drafter's responsibility on the design team. Assembly and working drawings show how multiple parts fit together. They describe the end result of creating individual pieces that must fit together to work.

FIGURE 14.1   **Aesthetic and functional design combine to give this sports car not only a look of elegance, but of speed. Although pleasing to the eye, this car is the superb product of aerodynamic and mechanical engineering.** *Reprinted with permission from Bavarian Autosport.*

■ 14.1 "DESIGN" DEFINED

Design is a process, a series of linked steps with stated objectives. It is a way of conceiving and creating new ideas and then communicating those ideas to others in a way that can be easily understood. This is accomplished most efficiently through the use of graphics. Design can be used to reflect personal expressions or to enhance product development. This reflection of personal expression is most often referred to as *aes-*

thetic design while the enhancement of product development is considered *functional design*. Aesthetics and function can work hand in hand to create a product that is not only appealing to the senses, but fulfills specific product demands. A well-designed automobile is a good example of how aesthetics and function can work together. (See Fig. 14.1.)

There are two general types of design: *empirical design*, sometimes referred to as conceptual design, and *scientific design*. In scientific design, use is made of the principles of physics, mathematics, chemistry, mechanics, and other sciences in the new or revised design of devices, structures, or systems intended to function under specific conditions. In empirical design, much use is made of the information in handbooks, which in turn has been learned by experience. Nearly all technical design is a combination of scientific and empirical design. Therefore, a competent designer has both adequate engineering and scientific knowledge and access to the many handbooks related to the field.

■ 14.2 "ENGINEERING DESIGN" DEFINED

Engineering design is also a process. This process is used to solve society's needs, desires, and problems through the application of scientific principles, experience, and creativity. Some people are creative and are naturally gifted at design, but everyone can become a designer if they learn to use the proper tools and techniques involved with the design process. Becoming a designer is much like learning to play a musical instrument; some people are better at it then others, but everyone can learn to play if they learn the steps involved.

Two key elements to any successful design plan is gaining the proper *motivation* and stating the *objectives* to the plan. Design is the single most important activity practiced by engineers. Design separates engineering from the rest of the sciences in that it is the application of scientific principles to create solutions. Your motivation in any design plan should be to create the most efficient solution to any given problem. The objective statement will provide a framework within which any engineering design problem can be addressed in a methodical manner. Proper planning and scheduling are also key to successful designs plans. Setting a deadline for the completion of each design phase is imperative. We will the discuss the steps in the design process at length in §14.4

■ 14.3 DESIGN CONCEPTS— SOURCES FOR NEW IDEAS

INDIVIDUAL CREATIVITY TECHNIQUES   New ideas or design concepts usually begin in the mind of a single individual—the designer. But how does one go about developing new ideas? There is an old saying in the engineering industry:

> "Good design is to borrow. Genius design is to steal."

Unlike your other courses of study where plagiarism is considered bad and should be subject to punishment, copying good ideas is highly advisable in design. Students are urged to copy not only from existing products and classmates, but they should study catalogs, manufacturers' patents, and nature.

Look through industry catalogs and handbooks for existing designs. Think of ways in which these existing designs can be used or modified to work in your design plan. Manipulate them through freehand sketches (see Chapter 3) or through the use of computer software (CAD).

STUDY PATENT DRAWINGS (See Fig. 14.2)   A patent is issued by the U.S. government granting the holder the "right to exclude others from making, using or selling" a specific product. The patent process was first developed as a way of disclosing technical advances by granting a period of protection for a limited

FIGURE 14.2   **Pictorial Patent Drawing.**

amount of time (a patent is issued for 17 years). The U.S. Patent and Trademark Office has extremely strict regulations as to the presentation of materials (i.e., no freehand sketches are accepted and all patent drawings must be made with drafting instruments or by a process which will make them easily reproducible). You cannot use or copy any existing patents, but they can be a great source of ideas. The U.S. Patent Office, therefore, can be a valuable resource in quest for design ideas. A discussion of how to apply for a patent for a new design appears in §14.26

EXAMINE MANUFACTURED PRODUCTS.   Dismantle them, evaluate them, and study how their parts are designed to work together. This is referred to a *reverse engineering*. Sophisticated reverse engineering involves evaluating a product using a machine called a *coordinate measuring machine* (CMM). (See Fig. 14.3.) The machine is a electromechanical devices containing a probe on one end. The probe measures the object and then places all of the pertinent information into a CAD database where it can be manipulated. Although you may not have access to such a complicated machine, examine manufactured products that are available to you. Think of ways to improve or change these existing designs. Where could they be improved? What would you do differently?

Study a product that is no longer performing to the manufacturer's existing or upgraded standards, referred to as *functional decomposition*. How could you expand/change the design to guarantee better performance? What could you do to expand the life of the product? How could you make it more efficient, more cost effective, etc.?

FIGURE 14.3 **Coordinate Measuring Machine (CMM). Used to Accurately Measure a Part for Reverse Engineering or Quality Control.**

STUDYING THE NATURAL WORLD. Noting how other creatures interact with their surroundings can provide a wealth of information and creativity. Such things as bee hives or spiders' webs are masterpieces of structural design. A hummingbird's wings are aerodynamic wonders. (See Figs. 14.4 and 14.5.) Study them and expand on their designs.

Use all computer hardware and software available to you. Animation and CAD programs have become numerous in recent years. Although you may not have

FIGURE 14.4 **Studying designs in nature, such as this spider's web, can provide the designer with new information and ideas.** *Courtesy of Peter Arnold, Inc.*

FIGURE 14.5 **The wings of a hummingbird are aerodynamic wonders. Study of such designs in nature can be enlightening to any designer.** *Courtesy of Photo Researchers, Inc.*

the resources to invest in numerous new software programs, be sure to make use of those readily available at your school. Even programs such as Adobe Illustrator® or Photoshop® can help in your search for new ways of viewing and conceiving objects.

Excellent resources for engineering and design are available on the World Wide Web. Search for terms like design, engineering, technology, or for more specific terms, depending on your interests. The following Web sites are useful for engineering design:

- http://www.yahoo.com/headlines/
  Yahoo's site for the latest technology news and a one-week archive

- http://www.techweb.com/
  TechWeb site from CMP media

- http://www.uspto.gov/
  U.S. Patent Office on-line search site

Using the techniques discussed above and listed in Fig. 14.6, the designer should have a few ideas as to where to begin. In order to capture, preserve, and develop these ideas, the designer makes liberal use of freehand sketches of views and pictorials (see Chapter 3). These sketches are revised or redrawn as the concept is developed. All sketches should be preserved for reference and dated as a record of the development of the design.

GROUP CREATIVITY TECHNIQUES At some point in the development of the idea, you will probably find it to your advantage to pool your ideas with those of others and begin working in a team effort; such a team may include others familiar with problems of materials, production, marketing, and so on. In industry, the project becomes a team effort long before the product is produced and marketed. Obviously, the design process is not a haphazard operation of an inventor working in a garage or basement, although it might well begin in that manner. Industry could not long survive if its products were determined in a haphazard manner. Hence, nearly all successful companies support a well-organized design effort, and the vitality of the company depends, to a large extent, on the *planned* output of its designers and design teams. Groups play an important role in the creative design process.

The two most commonly used group creativity techniques are brainstorming and storyboarding. *Brainstorming* occurs when a group of individuals come to together to discuss new ideas. A brainstorming session can stimulate, enlighten, and motivate designers to look at their product designs in a different light based upon input from other team members. The most important rule to follow during a brainstorming session is that no criticism of others' work should be tolerated. Criticism only serves to stymie the creative process. A second rule for any good brainstorming session is to come prepared with as many new ideas as possible. This is not the time to be conservative; be open to presenting new ideas.

Storyboarding is a technique often used by designers to graphically illustrate the progression of their designs, as well as the manufacturing process required to create a final product. Storyboards are rough sketches, usually created freehand by the designer. Storyboards are a valuable tool in any brainstorming session as they can be used as a base to be built on creatively by group members during the session. These freehand sketches should be rough so that they can be updated, revised, or modified based on input from team members.

Reintegration of the ideas generated during the brainstorming session into an individual's design is of utmost importance. Once the design team has settled on a specific design, it is imperative that the individual designer incorporate this input into his/her design. (See Fig. 14.6.)

Since it is important for you to be able to work effectively with others in a group or team, you must be able to express yourself clearly and concisely. Do not underestimate the importance of your communication skills, your ability to express your ideas verbally (written and spoken), symbolically (equations, formulas, etc.), and *graphically*.

INDIVIDUAL CREATIVITY TECHNIQUES INCLUDE:

Studying Industry Catalogs/Handbooks

Examining Manufactured Items

Studying Patent Drawings

Conducting Reverse Engineering

Examining Functional Decomposition

Studying the Natural World

Using Software Products

Utilizing Design, Engineering, and Technology Web Sites

GROUP CREATIVITY TECHNIQUES INCLUDE:

Brainstorming

Storyboarding

Reintegration

FIGURE 14.6 **Individual and group creativity techniques.**

These graphical skills include the ability to present information and ideas clearly and effectively in the form of sketches, drawings, graphs, and so on. This textbook is dedicated to helping you develop your communication skills in graphics.

■ 14.4 THE DESIGN PROCESS

Design is the ability to combine ideas, scientific principles, resources, and often existing products into a solution of a problem. This ability to solve problems in design is the result of an organized and orderly approach to the problem known as the *design process*.

The design process leading to manufacturing, assembly, marketing, service, and the many activities necessary for a successful product is composed of several easily recognized phases. Although many industrial groups may identify them in their own particular way, a convenient procedure for the design of a new or improved product is in five stages as follows:

1. Identification of problem, need, or "customer."
2. Concepts and ideas.
3. Compromise solutions.
4. Models and/or prototypes.
5. Production and/or working drawings.

Ideally, the design moves through the stages as shown in Fig. 14.7, but if a particular stage proves

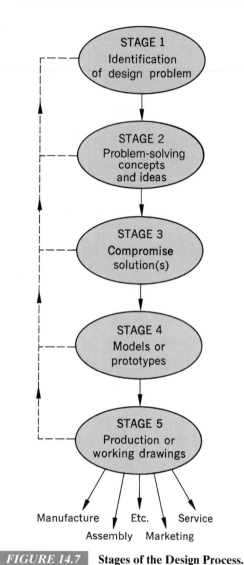

FIGURE 14.7 Stages of the Design Process.

unsatisfactory, it may be necessary to return to a previous stage and repeat the procedure as indicated by the dashed-line paths. This repetitive procedure is often referred to as *looping*.

■ 14.5 STAGE 1—IDENTIFICATION OF THE PROBLEM AND THE CUSTOMER

The design activity begins with the recognition of a *problem* and/or the determination of a *need* or want for a product, service, or system and the economic feasibility of fulfilling this need.

The designer not only must identify the problem or need but also the *customer*. Who will be affected or influenced by the design? The creation of any new de-

sign and the related design process ultimately should be driven by its end users. Determine if the design should be geared toward a single, very specific user, a specific purchaser or purchasers, a manufacturer or group of manufacturers, or to the general public. A part to be used in the space shuttle, for example, would not need to be designed or manufactured for operation by the general public. It has a limited market and customer base. But a design for a new home gym, which requires the user to complete the final assembly, should take into account a wide range of users and mechanical abilities. It is important that the designer identify the end user before beginning the design process.

It is also important to determine if the product to be designed must meet with any government standards/regulations or adhere to any professional organizations' standards or codes before starting the design process.

Any design process will involve compromises such that all of the designer's original requirements cannot be met. Government standards may limit the use of certain materials, for example, and the design may have to take a different form than that originally conceived by the designer. Materials or manufacturing processes may become too costly, resources may become unavailable, etc. It is important for the designer to approach the design process knowing that compromises may have to be made. Prioritize the design requirements. It is a good idea to break the *design requirements* into four categories: essential, important, desirable, or beneficial. If the designer has the requirements broken into these categories before implementing the design, decision making as to what to change and when will become easier when the need arises.

Engineering design problems may range from the simple and inexpensive container opener such as the pull tab (Fig. 14.8) commonly used on beverage cans to the more complex problems associated with the needs of air and ground travel, space exploration, environmental control, and so forth. Although the product may be very simple, such as the pull tab on a beverage can, the production tools and dies require considerable engineering and design effort. The airport automated transit system design, Fig. 14.9, meets the need of moving people efficiently between the terminal areas. The system is capable of moving 3300 people every 10 minutes.

The Lunar Roving Vehicle, Fig. 14.10, is a solution to a need in the space program to explore larger areas

FIGURE 14.8 **Pull-Tab Can Opener.** *John Schultz— PAR/NYC.*

FIGURE 14.9 **Airport Transit System.** *Courtesy of Westinghouse Electric Corp.*

FIGURE 14.10 **Lunar Roving Vehicle.** *Courtesy of NASA.*

of the lunar surface. This vehicle is the end result of a great deal of design work associated with the support systems and the related hardware.

At the problem identification stage, either the designer recognizes that there does exist a need requiring a design solution or, perhaps more often, a directive is received to that effect from management. No attempt is made at this time to set goals or criteria for the solution.

Information concerning the identified problem becomes the basis for a problem proposal, which may be a paragraph or a multipage report presented for formal consideration. A proposal is a plan for action that will be followed to solve the problem. The proposal, if approved, becomes an agreement to follow the plan. In the classroom, the agreement is made between you and your instructor on the identification of the problem and your proposed plan of action.

Following approval of the proposal, further aspects of the problem are explored. Available information related to the problem is collected, and parameters or guidelines for time, cost, function, and so on are defined within which you will work. For example: What is the design expected to do? What is the estimated cost limit? What is the market potential? What can it be sold for? When will the prototype be ready for testing? When must production drawings be ready? When will production begin? When will the product be available on the market?

The parameters of a design problem, including the time schedule, are established at this stage. Nearly all designs represent a compromise, and the amount of time budgeted to a project is no exception.

■ 14.6 STAGE 2—CONCEPTS AND IDEAS

At this stage, many ideas are collected—reasonable and otherwise—for possible solutions to the problem. The ideas are broad and unrestricted to permit the possibility of new and unique solutions. The ideas may be from individuals, or they may come from group or team brainstorming sessions where one suggestion often generates many more ideas from the group. As the ideas are elicited, they are recorded for future consideration and refinement. No attempt is made to evaluate ideas at this stage. All notes and sketches are signed, dated, and retained for possible patent proof.

The larger the collection of ideas, the greater are the chances of finding one or more ideas suitable for further refinement. All sources of ideas, such as technical literature, reports, design and trade journals, patents, and existing products are explored. Ideas can come from such sources as the Greenfield Village Museum in Dearborn, Michigan, the Museum of Science and Industry in Chicago, trade exhibitions, the World Wide Web, large hardware and supply stores, mail order catalogs. Even the user of an existing product is an excellent source, because that person often has suggestions for improvement. The potential user may be helpful with specific reactions to the proposed solution.

No attempt is made to evaluate ideas at this stage. All notes and sketches are signed, dated, and retained for possible patent proof.

■ 14.7 STAGE 3—COMPROMISE SOLUTIONS

Various features of the many conceptual ideas generated in the preceding stages are selected after careful consideration and combined into one or more promising compromise solutions. At this point the best solution is evaluated in detail, and attempts are made to simplify it so that it performs efficiently and is easy to manufacture, repair, and even dispose of when its lifetime is over.

Refined design sketches are often followed by a study of suitable materials and of motion problems that may be involved. What source of power is to be used—manual, electric motor, or what? What type of motion is needed? Is it necessary to translate rotary motion into linear motion or vice versa? Many of these problems are solved graphically using schematic drawings in which various parts are shown in skeleton form. For example, pulleys and gears are represented by circles, an arm by a single line, and a path of motion by centerlines. Certain basic calculations, such as those related to velocity and acceleration, may also be made at this time.

Preliminary studies are followed by a design layout—usually an accurate CAD drawing, showing actual sizes so that proportions and fits can be clearly visualized—or by a clearly dimensioned layout sketch. An example is shown in Fig. 14.11. At this time all parts are carefully designed for strength and function. Costs are constantly kept in mind, because no matter how well the device performs, it must sell at a profit; otherwise the time and development costs will have been a loss.

During the layout process, experience provides a sense of proportion, size, and fit that permits noncritical features to be designed by eye or with the aid of empirical data. Stress analysis and detailed computation may be necessary in connection with high speeds, heavy loads, or special requirements or conditions.

Figure 14.12 shows the layout of basic proportions of parts and how they fit together in an assembly drawing. Special attention is given to clearances of moving parts, ease of assembly, and serviceability. Standard parts are used wherever possible, because they are less expensive than custom parts. Most companies maintain some form of an engineering standards manual, which contains much of the empirical data and detailed information that is regarded as "company standard." Materials and costs are carefully considered. Although functional considerations must come first, manufacturing problems must be kept constantly in mind.

■ 14.8 STAGE 4—MODELS AND PROTOTYPES

A model to scale is often constructed to study, analyze, and refine a design. To instruct the model-shop craftsperson in the construction of the prototype or model, dimensioned sketches or three dimensional computer models are required. A full-size working model made to final specifications, except possibly for materials, is known as a prototype. The prototype is tested and modified where necessary, and the results are noted in the revision of the sketches and working drawings. Figure 14.13 shows a prototype of the magnetic levitation train.

If the prototype is unsatisfactory, it may be necessary to return to a previous stage in the design process and repeat the procedures. It must be remembered that time and expenses always limit the duration of this looping. Eventually a decision must be reached for the production model.

MI0 ×1.5 HEX LOCK NUT

1.5

40°

8 CIR GROOVES

0.76

SF

HONE & HARD CHROME PL

R14

SF

STROKE

60°

14

#608 WOODRUFF CUTTER REWORKED TO 45° INCL ∠

Ø 4.75
4.70

11

45°

BRZ

.5-NPT

M20×2.5

6X Ø10 TIE RODS EQ SP

SF

30°

METRIC

60.5 STROKE

AIR CYLINDER
100 mm BORE – STY. #1

FIGURE 14.11   **Design Layout.**

(a) INDICATING HEAD

Lexan window

Sheet-metal parts

Sheet-metal part

Sheet-Metal Prototype

(b) SHEET-METAL HOUSING

Die-cast cover

Lexan window

Balancing springs

Dashpot

Pointer

Jewel bearing

Die-cast base

Link to scale

(c) DIECAST HOUSING

FIGURE 14.12   **Improved Design of Indicating Head.** *Courtesy of Ohaus
Scale Corp. and Machine Design.*

FIGURE 14.14   **Examples of Solids Created with CAD.**
Courtesy of American Small Business Computers.

FIGURE 14.13   **A Prototype of the Magnetic Levitation Train Car During a Test Run.**

SOLID OR 3D MODELING   CAD systems that offer solid modeling usually have options or commands for creating complex solids using primitive shapes, including boxes, prisms, cylinders, spheres, cones, tori, and sometimes wedges and pyramids. Figure 14.14 shows an example of some solids generated using CAD. Many CAD systems also have a primitive command which creates any regular solid. If there is not a specific command to create the solid you want, you usually have the option of creating new solid objects through processes called extrusion and revolution (both generally referred to as sweeping solids).

Extrusion is named for the manufacturing process which forms material by forcing it through a shaped opening. You can also think of extrusion as taking the cross-sectional shape of the object and sweeping it along a path to enclose a solid volume. Features which have a continuous cross section along a straight axis can be created using extrusion. Some CAD software can only extrude shapes along a straight-line path, while others can do straight or curved paths. Most have the option to taper the extruded feature as it is created. An example of an extruded solid model is shown in Fig. 14.15.

Revolution is the process of forming a solid by revolving the cross-sectional shape of the object along a circular path to enclose a solid volume. Many objects that cannot be created by extrusion can be created by revolution. A solid object created by revolving a shape by 270° is shown in Fig. 14.16.

Complex solid models can be formed by joining primitives and solids formed by extrusion and revolution using *Boolean operators*. Boolean operators are named for 18th century mathematician and logician, Charles Boole. Most CAD programs that allow solid modeling support three Boolean operators: *union* (sometimes called addition), *difference* (sometimes called subtraction), and *intersection*. Venn diagrams are often used to show how sets are joined together using Boolean operators. Figure 14.17 shows Venn diagrams for union, difference, and intersection. Boolean operators can also be used to join solids you create by extruding or revolving other solids or solid primitives.

The union of solid A and solid B forms a single new solid that is their combined volume without any duplication where they have overlapped. Solid A difference solid B is similar to subtracting B from A. The order of the operation does make a difference in the result (unlike union). For A difference B, any volume from solid B that overlaps solid A is eliminated and

Venn diagrams depicting Boolean operators

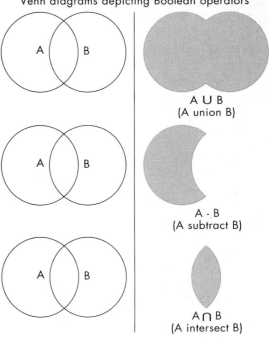

A ∪ B
(A union B)

A - B
(A subtract B)

A ∩ B
(A intersect B)

FIGURE 14.15 Extruded Solid.

Results of Boolean operators on solids

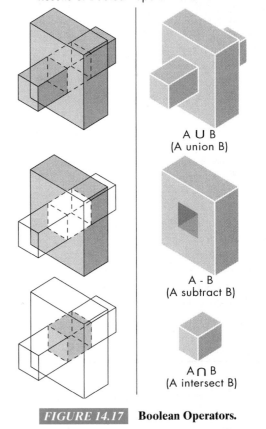

A ∪ B
(A union B)

A - B
(A subtract B)

A ∩ B
(A intersect B)

FIGURE 14.16 Revolved Solid.

FIGURE 14.17 Boolean Operators.

the result forms a new solid. A intersect B results in a new solid where only the volume common both to solid A and solid B is retained. You can use these primitives, extrusion, revolution, and Boolean operators to create solid models for a variety of objects. Objects that cannot be created in this way are warped surfaces, such as those on the exteriors of automobiles and airplanes.

PARAMETRIC SOLID MODELING CAD systems, especially those allowing parametric solid modeling (where design parameters control the model geometry), provide many benefits for shortening the design cycle time. (In parametric design, the curve paths are controlled by mathematical functions rather than a set of coordinates.) In this way, parametric solid modeling allows concurrent design, where members of the design team along with members from the company's manufacturing and marketing divisions can work together at the same time to provide a total design solution. In parametric models, constraints and parametric dimensions control the model geometry. As the design changes, so can the constraints and dimensions; the model and drawings update automatically. Three-dimensional models can also be exported to rapid prototyping equipment and to direct manufacturing to allow quick progress from design to product.

RAPID PROTOTYPING While refining the design ideas, engineers often work concurrently with manufacturing to determine the best ways to make an assemble the necessary parts. After several cycles of refining, analyzing, and synthesizing the best ideas, the final design is ready to go into production. *Rapid prototyping* systems allow parts to quickly be generated directly from 3D models for mockup and testing. Rapid prototyping can also be used in situations were prototypes are still deemed necessary for various reasons (i.e., customer request). Many companies are designing their products with 3D design packages an then feeding the CAD data into separate software programs that not only evaluate the design but also generate a separate set of data, which is then usable in a variety of ways. The new data can be forwarded to a CNC mill and a sample model can then be cut from the data. Data can also be forwarded to rapid prototyping equipment using such technologies as *stereolithography* (SLA), *selective laser sintering* (SLS), *ballistic particle manufacturing* (BPM), and *laminated object manufacturing* (LOM).

SLA builds part from layers of laser-cured photopolymer. The SLS process builds parts layer by layer with a laser from powdered materials such as nylon, polycarbonate, or a composite glass-nylon material. Some rapid prototyping machines build objects by spraying molten particles of a thermoplastic. The LOM process builds layer by layer from rolls of sheet goods similar to paper. (Refer to the Graphics Spotlight on pages 436 to 437 for a good example of rapid prototyping in action.)

■ 14.9 STAGE 5—PRODUCTION OR WORKING DRAWINGS

To produce or manufacture a product, a final set of production or working drawings is made, checked, and approved.

In industry the approved production design layouts are turned over to the engineering department for the production drawings. The drafter, or detailers, "pick off" the details from the layouts with the aid of the scale or dividers. The necessary views are drawn for each part to be made, and complete dimensions and notes, Chapter 11, are added so that the drawings will describe these parts completely. These working drawings of the individual parts are also known as *detail drawings*, §14.11.

Unaltered standard parts do not require a detail drawing but are shown conventionally on the assembly drawing and listed with specifications in the parts list, §14.15.

A detail drawing of one of the parts from the design layout of Fig. 14.11 is shown in Fig. 14.19. For details concerning working drawings, see §§14.11–14.19.

After the parts have been detailed, an *assembly drawing* is made, showing how all the parts go together in the complete product. The assembly may be made by tracing the various details in place directly from the detail drawings, or the assembly may be traced from the original design layout, but if either is done, the value of the assembly for checking purposes, §14.25, will be largely lost. The various types of assemblies are discussed in §§14.20–14.25.

Finally, in order to protect the manufacturer, a *patent drawing*, which is often a form of assembly, is prepared and filed with the u.s. patent office. patent drawings are line shaded, often lettered in script, and otherwise follow rules of the patent office, §14.25.

FIGURE 14.18 Solid modeling allows you to quickly get from design to product. *Courtesy of Solid Concepts, Inc.*

FIGURE 14.19 A Detail Drawing.

■ 14.10 DESIGN OF A NEW PRODUCT

An example of the design and development of a new product is that of IBM's ThinkPad 701C subnotebook computer, shown in Fig. 14.20.

STAGE 1 Problem Identification. When a company wants to determine the feasibility of a new product, it solicits opinions and ideas from many sources, including engineers, designers, drafters, managers, and potential consumers. Price ranges and estimated sales are also carefully explored.

In the case of the ThinkPad, IBM wanted to produce a subnotebook-size computer with a full-size keyboard—that is, a keyboard with the same size keys and the same spacing between keys as in a desktop computer. They also wanted the computer to have the largest available display, but the end product had to be thin, lightweight, and inexpensive enough to be competitive.

STAGE 2 Concepts and Ideas. In order to fit a full-size keyboard into a subnotebook case, a mechanical engineer working on the project came up with the idea of splitting the keyboard into two pieces that would interlock when the computer case was open. The two pieces could hang over the sides of the open case, thereby giving a little extra space for the relatively large keyboard. To close the computer case, the two pieces of the keyboard would need to separate and slide inward into new positions.

Once the idea of the split keyboard was accepted, the team moved from rough sketches and mockups to solid modeling.

STAGE 3 Compromise Solution. Using IBM's CATIA CAD/CAM software and an IBM RISC System/6000 workstation, the development team created a variety of possible keyboard designs for the ThinkPad. This system enabled them to produce virtual prototypes without building and rebuilding a series of actual 3D models. For example, they had to design a system to move the two parts of the keyboard when the computer case was opened and closed. However, the keyboard halves could not simply be moved by the case itself because if the system jammed, forcing the case open would break the keyboard. One feature of the CATIA software is a system that can identify areas of possible physical interference between parts of a model. Thus, the team could see on a computer screen where solid parts of the new computer might hit each other.

When the ThinkPad case is opened, the Track-Write keyboard is driven into position by a spring-loaded mechanism that moves the two halves of the keyboard asymmetrically. Closing the computer case moves the two halves of the keyboard back into their storage position by way of an axial cam and resets the spring (see Figs. 14.21 and 14.22).

FIGURE 14.21 **IBM ThinkPad.** *Courtesy of International Business Machines Corporation. Unauthorized use not permitted.*

FIGURE 14.20 **IBM ThinkPad 701 C Subnotebook.** *Courtesy of International Business Machines Corporation. Unauthorized use not permitted.*

FIGURE 14.22 **IBM ThinkPad.** *Courtesy of International Business Machines Corporation. Unauthorized use not permitted.*

STAGE 4   Prototypes Although in the past prototypes referred to actual working models, in the production of the ThinkPad computer, many of the prototypes existed only as 3D computer images. For example, early prototype designs for the keyboard—in the form of CATIA files—were given to the IBM unit that was developing other elements of the computer so that all the parts could be integrated into a functional whole.

STAGE 5   Production In the final stages of the design process, completed CATIA models were sent to outside vendors who used them to program numerically control (NC) tools that created the molds for parts of the computer. The same models created by the design process functioned throughout the various stages of the project. (See the Graphics Spotlight for a real-life example of a team using the design process.)

■ 14.11 WORKING DRAWINGS

Working drawings, which normally include assembly and details, are the specifications for the manufacture of a design. Therefore, they must be neatly made and

carefully checked. The working drawings of the individual parts are also referred to as *detail drawings*, §§14.12–14.19.

■ 14.12 NUMBER OF DETAILS PER SHEET

Two general methods are followed in industry regarding the grouping of details on sheets. If the machine or structure is small or composed of few parts, all the details may be shown on one large sheet, Fig. 14.23.

When larger or more complicated mechanisms are represented, the details may be drawn on several large sheets, several details to the sheet, and the assembly is drawn on a separate sheet. Most companies have now adopted the practice of drawing only one detail per sheet, however simple or small. The basic 8.50 × 11.00 or 210 mm × 297 mm sheet is most commonly used for details, multiples of these sizes being used for larger details or the assembly. For standard sheet sizes.

When several details are drawn on one sheet, careful consideration must be given to spacing. The drafter should determine the necessary views for each detail and *block in all views lightly before beginning to draw any view*, as shown in Fig. 14.23. Ample space

FIGURE 14.23   **Blocking in the Views.**

The rules for Cannonball Run, the final competition at Ideo University, are simple: To win, a team needs to:

1. Build a device that will propel a steel "cannonball" farther than contraptions built by the three opposing teams.
2. Make the ball signal the end of its journey by setting off a buzzer in the designated "cannonball catcher," a round target with the approximate circumference of a coffee cup.
3. Use the provided material, which consists of a bundle of wooden dowels, a chunk of cushiony foam, a roll of electrical tape, a stack of index cards, some paint sticks, a fistful of rubber bands, an extrememly long piece of black string, a mousetrap, and the tubes all this came in.
4. Complete a cannonball launcher within 90 minutes.

Not the simplest of tasks, but then again, no one ever said that learning creativity was easy. In fact, the compeition at Ideo U. consisted of one journalist and 15 engineers from the networking giant Cisco Systems. At the beginning of the competition, they were all skeptical. Creativity couldn't possibliy be taught, let alone at a one-day innovation and design workshop.

Ideo U. Design Workshops
Ideo, the Silicon Valley firm that's famous for the designing products like Apple's first mouse, a no-mess toothpaste tube for Procter & Gamble's Crest, and, most recently, the Palm V, the silvery, wafer-thin, light-as-a feather addition to 3Com's blockbuster line of hand held organizers.

Founded in 1978 by Standford design professor, David Kelley, Ideo has designed more than 3,000 products for a roster of clients, which include a sizeable portion of the FORTUNE 500. Ideo began offering design workshops for its customers and potential customers after many began clamouring to know exactly how they came up with there designs. Since then, companies ranging from NEC to Kodak to Steelcase have been sending employees to Ideo U.

Can Creativity be Taught?
"They say that genius is 99% perspiration and 1% inspiration," says Dennis Boyle, the Ideo principal leading the Cannonball Run Workshop. "Most companies have that 99%. It's the 1% that's really hard, and that's why our clients are asking us to work with their people and not just their product."

To home in on that elusive 1%, Ideo's employees explain the techniques they use to design products and then force participants to put them into practice. That's where Cannonball Run comes in.

Brainstorming
The first step: brainstorming. Earlier that afternoon, Brendan Boyle, head of Ideo's toy-invention studio had explained brainstorming the Ideo way. Ideo takes its rules for brainstorming so seriously that they are printed on a large banner that runs across the top of the classroom's whiteboards They are:

- Defer judgment (otherwise you'll interrupt the flow of ideas);
- Build on the ideas of others (it's far more productive than hogging the glory of your own insights);
- Stay focused on the topic (no tangents);

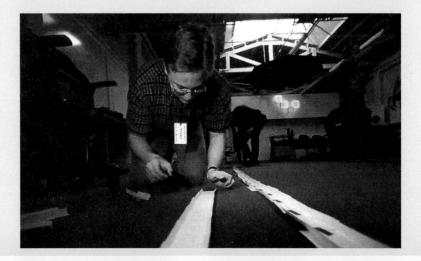

STAGE 4 Prototypes Although in the past prototypes referred to actual working models, in the production of the ThinkPad computer, many of the prototypes existed only as 3D computer images. For example, early prototype designs for the keyboard—in the form of CATIA files—were given to the IBM unit that was developing other elements of the computer so that all the parts could be integrated into a functional whole.

STAGE 5 Production In the final stages of the design process, completed CATIA models were sent to outside vendors who used them to program numerically control (NC) tools that created the molds for parts of the computer. The same models created by the design process functioned throughout the various stages of the project. (See the Graphics Spotlight for a real-life example of a team using the design process.)

■ 14.11 WORKING DRAWINGS

Working drawings, which normally include assembly and details, are the specifications for the manufacture of a design. Therefore, they must be neatly made and carefully checked. The working drawings of the individual parts are also referred to as *detail drawings*, §§14.12–14.19.

■ 14.12 NUMBER OF DETAILS PER SHEET

Two general methods are followed in industry regarding the grouping of details on sheets. If the machine or structure is small or composed of few parts, all the details may be shown on one large sheet, Fig. 14.23.

When larger or more complicated mechanisms are represented, the details may be drawn on several large sheets, several details to the sheet, and the assembly is drawn on a separate sheet. Most companies have now adopted the practice of drawing only one detail per sheet, however simple or small. The basic 8.50 × 11.00 or 210 mm × 297 mm sheet is most commonly used for details, multiples of these sizes being used for larger details or the assembly. For standard sheet sizes.

When several details are drawn on one sheet, careful consideration must be given to spacing. The drafter should determine the necessary views for each detail and *block in all views lightly before beginning to draw any view*, as shown in Fig. 14.23. Ample space

FIGURE 14.23   Blocking in the Views.

A Day at Ideo U

The rules for Cannonball Run, the final competition at Ideo University, are simple: To win, a team needs to:

1. Build a device that will propel a steel "cannonball" farther than contraptions built by the three opposing teams.
2. Make the ball signal the end of its journey by setting off a buzzer in the designated "cannonball catcher," a round target with the approximate circumference of a coffee cup.
3. Use the provided material, which consists of a bundle of wooden dowels, a chunk of cushiony foam, a roll of electrical tape, a stack of index cards, some paint sticks, a fistful of rubber bands, an extrememly long piece of black string, a mousetrap, and the tubes all this came in.
4. Complete a cannonball launcher within 90 minutes.

Not the simplest of tasks, but then again, no one ever said that learning creativity was easy. In fact, the compeition at Ideo U. consisted of one journalist and 15 engineers from the networking giant Cisco Systems. At the beginning of the competition, they were all skeptical. Creativity couldn't possibliy be taught, let alone at a one-day innovation and design workshop.

Ideo U. Design Workshops
Ideo, the Silicon Valley firm that's famous for the designing products like Apple's first mouse, a no-mess toothpaste tube for Procter & Gamble's Crest, and, most recently, the Palm V, the silvery, wafer-thin, light-as-a feather addition to 3Com's blockbuster line of hand held organizers.

Founded in 1978 by Standford design professor, David Kelley, Ideo has designed more than 3,000 products for a roster of clients, which include a sizeable portion of the FORTUNE 500. Ideo began offering design workshops for its customers and potential customers after many began clamouring to know exactly how they came up with there designs. Since then, companies ranging from NEC to Kodak to Steelcase have been sending employees to Ideo U.

Can Creativity be Taught?
"They say that genius is 99% perspiration and 1% inspiration," says Dennis Boyle, the Ideo principal leading the Cannonball Run Workshop. "Most companies have that 99%. It's the 1% that's really hard, and that's why our clients are asking us to work with their people and not just their product."

To home in on that elusive 1%, Ideo's employees explain the techniques they use to design products and then force participants to put them into practice. That's where Cannonball Run comes in.

Brainstorming
The first step: brainstorming. Earlier that afternoon, Brendan Boyle, head of Ideo's toy-invention studio had explained brainstorming the Ideo way. Ideo takes its rules for brainstorming so seriously that they are printed on a large banner that runs across the top of the classroom's whiteboards They are:

- Defer judgment (otherwise you'll interrupt the flow of ideas);
- Build on the ideas of others (it's far more productive than hogging the glory of your own insights);
- Stay focused on the topic (no tangents);

- One person at a time (so you don't drown out that quiet, brilliant mumbler in the corner);
- Go for quantity (when Ideo staffers brainstorm, they shoot for 150 ideas in 30 to 45 minutes);
- Encourage wild ideas (to paraphrase Einstein, "If the first idea doesn't sound absurd, then there's no hope for it); and
- Be visual (sketch ideas to help people understand them).

Team 2 stuck to these rules and within a few minutes came up with 15-20 ideas for the launcher.

Rapid Prototyping

To narrow their ideas down, Team 2 used rapid proto-typing, another Ideo technique. The idea behind rapid prototyping is that it's easier to discuss a model of something, no matter how primitive, than to talk about a bunch of ideas. "If a picture is worth a thousand words," says Ideo's Steve Vassallo, "a prototype is worth ten thousand."

Rapid prototyping consists of three Rs: Rough, Rapid, and Right. The first two Rs are fairly self-explanatory—make your models rough and make them rapidly. In the early stages perfecting a model is a waste of time. "You learn just as much from a models that's wrong as you do from one that's right," says Vassalo. Even the final R (Right), doesn't mean that your model has to work. Instead it refers to building lots of small models that focus on specific problems. For Team 2's Cannonball Run project, the three Rs worked.

After making a few rough models with the mouse-trap, they were certain that they could never fire the cannonball through the air with any precision. That nudged them towards a safer option—building a ramp that would guide the ball from a table top to its target on the floor via two guide rails made out of the wooden dowels. They got busy building their device. Thirty minutes before deadline, they realized that one of the other teams were doing the exact same thing, with one crucial difference: They were taping togeth-er the index cards (the most useless looking of all the provided materials) to create a 30-foot long track that would guide the cannonball from their ramp to their cannonball catcher at the far end of the room. What's more they were carefully folding up the sides of each card to make sure the ball didn't get derailed on its way to the destination. Brilliant!

Teams 3 and 4 had gone with different designs that don't look nearly as impressive. So what did Team 2 do? They stole the idea. Suddenly, the competition was reduced to which team, Team 1 or Team 2, would be able to tape the index cards together faster.

Using Brainstorming and Rapid Prototyping Techniques in Real Life

Of course, in real life, you can't always glance across the room and steal your competitor's ideas. But the Cannonball Run project drove home Ideo's philosophy about brainstorming and rapid prototyping methods: They get you to stop dithering and start doing. What you can come up with on the fly won't be nearly as bad as you think—in fact it'll often be better that what you come up with working slowly and deliberately. Besides, coming up with something—anything—is often half the battle.

All 15 participants walked away from the experience with changed ideas of how to approach even the simplest of projects. "I like how it showed that you don't have to spend tons of money to prototype. You can do a lot of trial-and-error modeling on your own without paying a lot of money to go outside just to find something that doesn't work," stated one Team 2 participant. Another teammate added, "When I went to work the next day, I called an emergency brainstorming session and set a goal of 100 ideas in an hour. I thought maybe we'd get 50. We got 103." Would he recommend the workshop to his colleagues? "Oh man, are you kidding me? Absolutely!" But they could be biased. After all, Team 2 won.

Adapted from "Staying Smart: A Day at Innovation U.," by Ed Brown, *Fortune*, April 12, 1999, pp. 163-165.

should be allowed for dimensions and notes. A simple method to space the views is to cut out rectangular scraps of paper roughly equal to the sizes of the views and to move these around on the sheet until a suitable spacing is determined. The corner locations are then marked on the sheet, and the scraps of paper are discarded.

The same scale should be used for all details on a single sheet, if possible. When this is not possible, the scales for the dissimilar details should be clearly noted under each.

■ 14.13 TITLE AND RECORD STRIPS

The function of the title and record strip is to show, in an organized manner, all necessary information not given directly on the drawing with its dimensions and notes. Obviously, the type of title used depends on the filing system in use, the processes of manufacture, and the requirements of the product. The following information should generally be given in the title form:

1. Name of the object represented.
2. Name and address of the manufacturer.
3. Name and address of the purchasing company, if any.
4. Signature of the drafter who made the drawing and the date of completion.
5. Signature of the checker and the date of completion.
6. Signature of the chief drafter, chief engineer, or other official, and the date of approval.

7. Scale of the drawing.
8. Number of the drawing.

Other information may be given, such as material, quantity, heat treatment, finish, hardness, pattern number, estimated weight, superseding and superseded drawing numbers, symbol of machine, and many other items, depending on the plant organization and the peculiarities of the product. Some typical commercial titles are shown in Figs. 14.24, 14.25, and 14.26. See the inside back cover for traditional title forms and ANSI-approved sheet sizes.

The title form is usually placed along the bottom of the sheet, Fig. 14.24, or in the lower right-hand corner of the sheet, Fig. 14.26, because drawings are often filed in flat, horizontal drawers, and the title must be easily found. However, many filing systems are in use, and the location of the title form is governed by the system employed.

Lettering should be single-stroke vertical or inclined Gothic capitals. The items in the title form should be lettered in accordance with their relative importance. The drawing number should receive the greatest emphasis, closely followed by the name of the object and the name of the company. The date, scale, and drafter's and checker's names are important, but they do not deserve prominence. Greater importance of items is indicated by heavier lettering, larger lettering, wider spacing of letters, or by a combination of these methods. See Table 14.1 for recommended letter heights.

FIGURE 14.24   Title Strip.

		NO. REQUIRED	MATERIAL	HEAT TREATMENT	PART NAME		DRAWN BY		
		1	SAE 3115	SEE NOTE	FEED WORM SHAFT		H.F.	UNIT 3134	
		REPLACED BY	REPLACES	OLD PART NO.	DRAWN FOR SIMPLEX & DUPLEX (1200)		TRACED BY E.E.Z.	ALSO USED ON ABOVE MACHINES	
				563-310	ENGINEERING DEPARTMENT KEARNEY & TRECKER		CHECKED BY C.STB.	FIRST USED ON LOT	LAST USED ON LOT
				SCALE FULL SIZE	CORPORATION MILWAUKEE, WISCONSIN, U. S. A.		APPROVED BY		
ALTERATIONS	DATE OF CHG						DATE 8-10-1996	17840 B	

REPORT ALL ERRORS TO FOREMAN

FIGURE 14.25   Title Strip.

DO NOT SCALE THIS DRAWING FOR DIMENSIONS.   MACHINE FRACTIONAL DIMENSIONS ± 1/64   ALL DIMENSIONS IN INCHES UNLESS OTHERWISE SPECIFIED.

HEAT TREATMENT	SCALE FULL	CATERPILLAR TRACTOR CO.
		EXECUTIVE OFFICES — SAN LEANDRO, CALIF.
SAE VIII HDN ROCKWELL C-50-56 NOTE 3 TEST LOCATIONS	DATE 8-10-1996	NAME FIRST, FOURTH & THIRD
	DRAWN BY S.G.	SLIDING PINION
	TRACED BY L.R.	MATERIAL C.T. #1E36 STEEL ② ①
	CHECKED BY n.w.	UPSET FORGING 3.875 ROUND MAX
	APPROVED BY amB.	
	REDRAWN FROM	1A4045

(left side columns): CHGD MATL ETC 10-22-83 / WAS #2345 ETC 5-21-83 — DATE — CHANGE NOTICE — 2 / 1 SYM

FIGURE 14.26 **Identification of Details with Parts List.**

| Use | Minimum Letter Heights | | Drawing Size |
	Freehand	Instrumental	
Drawing number in title block	.312″ ($\frac{5}{16}$) 7 mm	.290″ 7 mm	Larger than 17″ × 22″
	.250″ ($\frac{1}{4}$) 7 mm	.240″ 7 mm	Up to and including 17″ × 22″
Drawing title	.250″ ($\frac{1}{4}$) 7 mm	.240″ 7 mm	All
Section and tabulation letters	.250″ ($\frac{1}{4}$) 7 mm	.240″ 7 mm	
Zone letters and numerals in borders	.188″ ($\frac{3}{16}$) 5 mm	.175″ 5 mm	
Dimensions, tolerances, limits, notes, subtitles for special views, tables, revisions, and zone letters for the body of the drawing	.125″ ($\frac{1}{8}$) 3.5 mm	.120″ 3.5 mm	Up to and including 17″ × 22″
	.156″ ($\frac{5}{32}$) 5 mm	.140″ 5 mm	Larger than 17″ × 22″

[a] ANSI Y14.2M–1979 (R1987).

TABLE 14.1 **Recommended[a] Minimum Letter Heights.**

Many companies have adopted their own title forms or those preferred by ANSI and have them printed on standard-size sheets, so that the drafters need merely fill in the blank spaces.

Drawings constitute important and valuable information regarding the products of a manufacturer. Hence, carefully designed, well-kept, systematic files are generally maintained for the filing of drawings.

■ 14.14 DRAWING NUMBERS

Every drawing should be numbered. Some companies use serial numbers, such as 60412, or a number with a prefix or suffix letter to indicate the sheet size, as A60412 or 60412-A. The size A sheet would probably be the standard 8.50 × 11.00 or 9.00 × 12.00, and the B size a multiple thereof. Many different numbering schemes are in use in which various parts of the drawing number indicate different things, such as model number of the machine and the general nature or use of the part. In general, it is best to use a simple numbering system and not to load the number with too many indications.

The drawing number should be lettered 7 mm (.2500) high in the lower-right and upper-left corners of the sheet.

FIGURE 14.27   **Identification Numbers.**

14.15 PARTS LISTS

A bill of material, or *parts list*, consists of an itemized list of the several parts of a structure shown on a detail drawing or an assembly drawing [ANSI Y14.34M–1982 (R1988)]. This list is often given on a separate sheet, but is frequently lettered directly on the drawing. The title strip alone is sufficient on detail drawings of only one part, Fig. 14.25, but a parts list is necessary on detail drawings of several parts, Fig. 14.26.

Parts lists on machine drawings contain the part numbers or symbols, a descriptive title of each part, the number required, the material specified, and frequently other information, such as pattern numbers, stock sizes of materials, and weights of parts.

Parts are listed in general order of size or importance. The main castings or forgings are listed first, parts cut from cold-rolled stock second, and standard parts such as fasteners, bushings, and roller bearings third. If the parts list rests on top of the title box or strip, the order of the items should be from the bottom upward, Figs. 14.26 and 14.32, so that new items can be added later, if necessary. If the parts list is placed in the upper-right corner, the items should read downward.

Each detail on the drawing may be identified with the parts list by the use of a small circle containing the part number, placed adjacent to the detail, as in Fig. 14.26. One of the sizes in Fig. 14.27 will be found suitable, depending on the size of the drawing.

Standard parts whether purchased or company produced, are not drawn but are included in the parts list. Bolts, screws, bearings, pins, keys, and so on are identified by the part number from the assembly drawing and are specified by name and size or number.

14.16 ZONING

To facilitate locating an item on a large or complex drawing, regular ruled intervals are labeled along the margins, often in the right and lower margins only. The intervals on the horizontal margin are labeled from right to left with numerals, and the intervals on the vertical margin are labeled from bottom to top with letters.

14.17 CHECKING

The importance of accuracy in technical drawing cannot be overestimated. In commercial offices, errors sometimes cause tremendous unnecessary expenditures. *The drafter's signature on a drawing identifies who is responsible for the accuracy of the work.*

In small offices, checking is usually done by the designer or by one of the drafters. In large offices, experienced engineers are employed who devote a major part of their time to checking drawings.

The pencil drawing, upon completion, is carefully checked and signed by the drafter who made it. The drawing is then checked by the designer for function, economy, practicability, and so on. Corrections, if any, are then made by the original drafter.

The final checker should be able to discover all remaining errors, and, to be effective, the work must be done in a systematic way. The checker should study the drawing with particular attention to the following points.

1. Soundness of design, with reference to function, strength, materials, economy, manufacturability, serviceability, ease of assembly and repair, lubrication, and so on.
2. Choice of views, partial views, auxiliary views, section line work, lettering, and so on.
3. Dimensions, with special reference to repetition, ambiguity, legibility, omissions, errors, and finish marks. Special attention should be given to tolerances.
4. Standard parts. In the interest of economy, as many parts as possible should be standard.
5. Notes, with special reference to clear wording and legibility.
6. Clearances. Moving parts should be checked in all possible positions to assure freedom of movement.
7. Title form information.

14.18 DRAWING REVISIONS

Changes on drawings are necessitated by changes in design, changes in tools, desires of customers, or errors in design or in production. In order that the sources of all changes of information on drawings may be understood, verified, and accessible, an accurate record of all changes should be made on the drawings. The record should show the character of the change, by whom, when, and why made.

FIGURE 14.28   **Revisions.**

The changes are made by erasures directly on the original drawing or by means of erasure fluid on a reproduction print. Additions are simply drawn in on the original. The removal of information by crossing out is not recommended. If a dimension is not noticeably affected by a change, it may be underlined with a heavy line to indicate that it is not to scale. In any case, prints of each issue or microfilms are kept on file to show how the drawing appeared before the revision. New prints are issued to supersede old ones each time a change is made.

If considerable change on a drawing is necessary, a new drawing may be made and the old one then stamped OBSOLETE and placed in the "obsolete" file. In the title block of the old drawing, the words "SUPERSEDED BY ..." or "REPLACED BY ..." are entered followed by the number of the new drawing. On the new drawing, under "SUPERSEDES ..." or "REPLACES ...," the number of the old drawing is entered.

Various methods are used to reference the area on a drawing where the change is made, with the entry in the revision block. The most common is to place numbers or letters in small circles near the places where the changes were made and to use the same numbers or letters in the revision block, Fig. 14.28. On zoned drawings, §14.16, the zone of the correction would be shown in the revision block. In addition, the change should be described briefly, and the date and the initials of the person making the change should be given.

◼ 14.19 SIMPLIFIED DRAFTING

Drafting time is a considerable element of the total cost of a product. Consequently, industry attempts to reduce drawing costs by simplifying its drafting practices, but without loss of clarity to the user.

The American National Standard Drafting Manual, published by the American National Standards Institute, incorporates the best and the most representative practices in this country, and the authors are in full accord with them. These standards advocate simplification in many ways, for example, partial views, half views, thread symbols, piping symbols, and single-line spring drawings. Any line or lettering on a drawing that is not needed for clarity should be omitted.

A summary of practices to simplify drafting is as follows.

1. Use word description in place of drawing wherever practicable.

2. Never draw an unnecessary view. Often a view can be eliminated by using abbreviations or symbols such as HEX, SQ, DIA, Ø, , and cL.

3. Draw partial views instead of full views wherever possible. Draw half views of symmetrical parts.

4. Avoid elaborate, pictorial, or repetitive detail as much as possible. Use phantom lines to avoid drawing repeated features.

5. List rather than draw, when possible, standard parts such as bolts, nuts, keys, and pins.

6. Omit unnecessary hidden lines.

7. Use outline section lining in large sectioned areas wherever it can be done without loss of clarity.

8. Omit unnecessary duplication of notes and lettering.

9. Use symbolic representation wherever possible, such as piping symbols and thread symbols.

10. Draw freehand, or mechanically plus freehand, wherever practicable.

11. Avoid hand lettering as much as possible. For example, parts lists should be typed on a separate sheet.

12. Use labor saving devices wherever feasible, such as templates and plastic overlays.

13. Use electronic devices or computer graphics systems wherever feasible for design, drawing, and repetitive work.

Some industries have attempted to simplify their drafting practices even more. Until these practices are accepted generally by industry and in time find their way into ANSI standards, the students should follow the ANSI standards as exemplified throughout this book. Fundamentals should come first—shortcuts perhaps later.

■ 14.20   ASSEMBLY DRAWINGS

An assembly drawing shows the assembled machine or structure, with all detail parts in their functional positions. Assembly drawings vary in character according to use, as follows: (1) design assemblies, or layouts, discussed in §14.7, (2) general assemblies, (3) working drawing assemblies, (4) outline or installation assemblies, and (5) check assemblies.

■ 14.21   GENERAL ASSEMBLIES

A set of working drawings includes the *detail drawings* of the individual parts and the *assembly drawing* of the assembled unit. The detail drawings of an automobile

connecting rod are shown in Figs. 14.29 and 14.30, and the corresponding assembly drawing is shown in Fig. 14.31. Such an assembly, showing only one unit of a larger machine, is often referred to as a *subassembly*.

An example of a complete general assembly appears in Fig. 14.32, which shows the assembly of a hand grinder. Another example of a subassembly is shown in Fig. 14.33.

1. Views. In selecting the views for an assembly drawing, the purpose of the drawing must be kept in mind: to show how the parts fit together in the assembly and to suggest the function of the entire unit, not to describe the shapes of the individual parts. The assembly worker receives the actual finished parts. If more information is needed about a part that cannot be obtained form the part itself, the detail drawing must be checked. Thus, the assembly drawing purports to show

FIGURE 14.29   Forging Drawing of Connecting Rod. *Courtesy of Cadillac Motor Car Division.*

FIGURE 14.30 Detail Drawing of Connecting Rod. *Courtesy of Cadillac Motor Car Division.*

FIGURE 14.31 Assembly Drawing of Connecting Rod. *Courtesy of Cadillac Motor Car Division.*

FIGURE 14.32 Assembly Drawing of Grinder.

FIGURE 14.33 Subassembly of Accessory Shaft Group.

relationships of parts, *not shapes*. The view or views selected should be the minimum views or partial views that will show how the parts fit together. In Fig. 14.31, only one view is needed, while in Fig. 14.32 only two views are necessary.

2. Sections. Since assemblies often have parts fitting into or overlapping other parts, hidden-line delineation is usually out of the question. Hence, in assemblies, sectioning can be used to great advantage. For example, in Fig. 14.32, try to imagine the right-side view drawn in elevation with interior parts represented by hidden lines. The result would be completely unintelligible.

Any kind of section may be used as needed. A broken-cut section is shown in Fig. 14.32, a half section in Fig. 14.33, and several removed sections are shown in Fig. 14.29. For general information on assembly sectioning, see §14.22. For methods of drawing threads in sections, see §14.16.

3. Hidden lines. As a result of the extensive use of sectioning in assemblies, hidden lines are often not needed. However, they should be used wherever necessary for clearness.

4. Dimensions. As a rule, dimensions are not given on assembly drawings, since they are given completely on the detail drawings. If dimensions are given, they are limited to some function of the object as a whole, such as the maximum height of a jack, or the maximum opening between the jaws of a vise. Or when machining is required in the assembly operation, the necessary dimensions and notes may be given on the assembly drawing.

5. Identification. The methods of identification of parts in an assembly are similar to those used in detail drawings where several details are shown on one sheet, as in Fig. 14.26. Circles containing the part numbers are placed adjacent to the parts, with leaders terminated by arrowheads touching the parts as in Fig. 14.32. The circles shown in Fig. 14.27 are, with the addition of radial leaders, satisfactory for assembly drawings. Note, in Fig. 14.32, that these circles are placed in orderly horizontal or vertical rows and not scattered over the sheet. Leaders are never allowed to cross, and adjacent leaders are parallel or nearly so.

The parts list includes the part numbers or symbols, a descriptive title of each part, the number required per machine or unit, the material specified, and frequently other information, such as pattern numbers, stock sizes, weights, and so on. Frequently the parts list is lettered or typed on a separate sheet.

Another method of identification is to letter the part names, numbers required, and part numbers, at the end of leaders as shown in Fig. 14.33. More commonly, however, only the part numbers are given, together with ANSI-approved straight-line leaders.

6. Drawing revisions. Methods of recording changes are the same as those for detail drawings, Fig. 14.29, for example. See §14.18.

■ 14.22 ASSEMBLY SECTIONING

In assembly sections it is necessary not only to show the cut surfaces but also to distinguish between adjacent parts. This is done by drawing the section lines in opposing directions, as shown in Fig. 14.34. The first

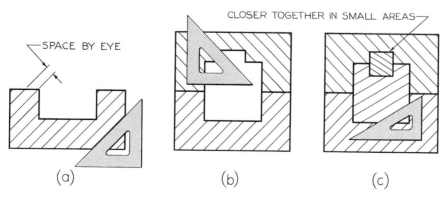

FIGURE 14.34 **Section Lining (Full Size).**

FIGURE 14.35   **Symbolic Section Lining.**

FIGURE 14.37   **Assembly Section.** *Courtesy of Hewitt-Robins, Inc.*

FIGURE 14.36   **Sectioning Thin Parts.**

large area, (a), is section-lined at 458. The next large area, (b), is section-lined at 458 in the opposite direction. Additional areas are then section-lined at other angles, such as 308 or 608 with horizontal, as shown at (c). If necessary, "odd" angles may be used. Note at (c) that in small areas it is necessary to space the section lines closer together. The section lines in adjacent areas should not meet at the visible lines separating the areas.

For general use, the cast-iron general-purpose section lining is recommended for assemblies. Wherever it is desired to give a general indication of the materials used, symbolic section lining may be used, as in Fig. 14.35.

In sectioning relatively thin parts in assembly, such as gaskets and sheet-metal parts, section lining is ineffective, and such parts should be shown in solid black, Fig. 14.36.

Often solid objects, or parts that themselves do not require sectioning, lie in the path of the cutting plane. It is customary and standard practice to show such parts unsectioned, or "in the round." These include bolts, nuts, shafts, keys, screws, pins, ball or roller

bearings, gear teeth, spokes, and ribs among others. Many are shown in Fig. 14.37, and similar examples are shown in Figs. 14.32 and 14.33.

■ 14.23 WORKING DRAWING ASSEMBLY

A working drawing assembly, Fig. 14.38, is a combined detail and assembly drawing. Such drawings are often used in place of separate detail and assembly drawings when the assembly is simple enough for all its parts to be shown clearly in the single drawing. In some cases, all but one or two parts can be drawn and dimensioned clearly in the assembly drawing, in which event these parts are detailed separately on the same sheet. This type of drawing is common in valve drawings, locomotive subassemblies, aircraft subassemblies, and drawings of jigs and fixtures.

■ 14.24 INSTALLATION ASSEMBLIES

An assembly made specifically to show how to install or erect a machine or structure is an *installation assembly*. This type of drawing is also often called an *outline assembly*, because it shows only the outlines and the relationships of exterior surfaces. A typical installation assembly is shown in Fig. 14.39. In aircraft drafting, an installation drawing (assembly) gives complete information for placing details or subassemblies in their final positions in the airplane.

FIGURE 14.38   Working Drawing Assembly of Drill Jig.

■ 14.25 CHECK ASSEMBLIES

After all detail drawings of a unit have been made, it may be necessary to make a *check assembly*, especially if a number of changes were made in the details. Such an assembly is drawn accurately to scale in order to check graphically the correctness of the details and their relationship in assembly. After the check assembly has served its purpose, it may be converted into a general assembly drawing.

■ 14.26 PATENT DRAWINGS

The patent application for a machine or device must include drawings to illustrate and explain the invention. It is essential that all patent drawings be mechanically correct and constitute complete illustrations of every feature of the invention claimed. The strict re-

quirements of the U.S. Patent Office in this respect serve to facilitate the examination of applications and the interpretation of patents issued thereon. A typical patent drawing is shown in Fig. 14.40.

The drawings for patent applications are pictorial and explanatory in nature; hence, they are not detailed as are working drawings for production purposes. Center lines, dimensions, notes, and so forth are omitted. Views, features, and parts, for example, are identified by numbers that refer to the descriptions and explanations given in the specification section of the patent application.

Patent drawings are made with India ink on heavy, smooth, white paper, exactly 10.00 × 15.00 with 1.00 borders on all sides. A space of not less than 1.250 from the shorter border, which is the top of the drawing, is left blank for the heading of title, name, number, and other data to be added by the Patent Office.

DWG NO. B-2463   WORK ORDER NO. 43625   CITY DROP FORGE & TOOL CORPORATION UTICA, NEW YORK   DWG NO. B-2463

FIGURE 14.39   **Installation Assembly.**

5,511,508
PONTOON RUNNER SYSTEM
John M. Wilson, Sr., and Dean R. Wilson, both of Marrero,
La., assignors to Wilco Marsh Buggies & Draglines, Inc., La.
Filed Apr. 21, 1994, Ser. No. 230,618
Int. Cl.^{6} B63B *3/00*

U.S. Cl. 114—356   10 Claims

FIGURE 14.40   **Pictorial Patent Drawing.**

All lines must be solid black and suitable for reproduction at a smaller size. Line shading is used whenever it improves readability.

The drawings must contain as many figures as necessary to show the invention clearly. There is no restriction on the number of sheets. The figures may be plan, elevation, section, pictorial, and detail views of portions or elements, and they may be drawn to an enlarged scale if necessary. The required signatures must be placed in the lower right-hand corner of the drawing, either inside or outside the border line.

Because of the strict requirements of the Patent Office, applicants are advised to employ competent drafters to make their drawings. To aid drafters in the preparation of drawings for submission in patent applications, the *Guide for Patent Draftsmen* has been prepared by and can be obtained from the Superintendent of Documents, U.S. Government Printing Office, Washington, D.C. 20402.

■ KEY WORDS

STAGES OF DESIGN	CUSTOMER
DESIGN REQUIREMENTS	CONCEPTS
MODELS	REFINEMENT
VIRTUAL REALITY	PARAMETRIC SOLID MODELING
DETAIL DRAWING	COMPUTER SIMULATION
3D MODELING	WORKING DRAWING
SOLID MODELING	PROTOTYPE
ASSEMBLY DRAWING	RAPID PROTOTYPING
PRODUCTION DRAWINGS	TITLE BLOCKS
BOOLEAN OPERATORS	DRAWING NUMBERS
DIFFERENCE INTERSECTION	PATENT DRAWINGS
RECORD STRIPS	REVERSE ENGINEERING
EXTRUSION REVOLUTION	COORDINATE MEASURING MACHINE
CHECKING AND PROOFING	FUNCTIONAL DECOMPOSITION
FUNCTIONAL DESIGN	BRAINSTORMING
AESTHETIC DESIGN	STORYBOARDING
MOTIVATION	REINTEGRATION
OBJECTIVES	BOOLEAN OPERATORS
CREATIVITY TECHNIQUES	REVOLVED SOLID
EXTRUDED SOLID	VENN DIAGRAMS

■ CHAPTER SUMMARY

- The design team moves through five stages during the design process. Each stage helps the team refine the design until it meets all product requirements.
- The final drawings created during the design process include assembly drawings, working drawings, design drawings, and patent drawings.
- There are many revisions to drawings during the design process. The drafter must keep track of each version and what changes were made.

- Models are an important way of testing the way parts are assembled. Both scale models created in a model shop and computer-generated virtual reality models are used by the design team to test their design.
- During the design process, all members of the team must understand their specific roles and how they relate and interact with the rest of the team. Effective teamwork is an essential part of the design process.

■ REVIEW QUESTIONS

1. What are the special requirements of a patent drawing?
2. What kinds of information are included in an assembly drawing?
3. Name three individual creativity techniques. Name two group creativity techniques.
4. Define SLA, SLS, BPM, and LOM and give an example of each used in a manufacturing setting.
5. What are the five stages of the design process? Describe each stage.
6. How is a detail drawing different from an assembly drawing?
7. Why are drawings numbered? Why is this numbering so important?
8. Describe the drawing revision process. Why is it so important to keep track of revisions?
9. How are revised paper drawings stored? How are revised CAD drawings stored?
10. What are the advantages of computer modeling? What are the disadvantages?

■ DESIGN AND WORKING DRAWING PROBLEMS

DESIGN PROBLEMS

The following suggestions for project assignments are of a general and very broad nature, and it is expected that they will help generate many ideas for specific design projects. Much design work is undertaken to improve an existing product or system by utilization of new materials, new techniques, or new systems or procedures. In addition to the design of the product itself, another large amount of design work is essential for the tooling, production, and handling of the product. You are encouraged to discuss with your instructor any ideas you may have for a project.

Prob. 14.1 Design new or improved playground, recreational, or sporting equipment. For example, a new child's toy could be both recreational and educational.

Prob. 14.2 Design new or improved health equipment. For example, physically handicapped people need special equipment.

Prob. 14.3 Design security or safety devices. Fire, theft, or poisonous gases are a threat to life and property.

Prob. 14.4 Design devices and/or systems for waste handling. Home and factory waste disposal needs serious consideration.

Prob. 14.5 Design new or improved educational equipment. Both teacher and student would welcome more efficient educational aids.

Prob. 14.6 Design improvements in our land, sea, and air transportation systems. Vehicles, controls, highways, and airports need further refinement.

Prob. 14.7 Design new or improved devices or material handling. A dispensing device for a powdered product is an example.

Prob. 14.8 Improve the design of an existing device or system.

Prob. 14.9 Design or redesign devices for improved portability.

Prob. 14.10 Design an airport luggage handling system that will reduce damage to all types of baggage.

Prob. 14.11 Break up into design teams. See how many different ideas each team can come up with for a new layout of your classroom. Time limit is 20 minutes.

Prob. 14.12 Design a new or improved bike safety lock and chain. Integrate the locking devices into the bike's frame, if possible.

Each solution to a design problem, whether prepared by an individual student or formulated by a group, should be in the form of a *report*, which should be typed or carefully lettered, assembled, and bound. It is suggested that the report contain the following (or variations of the following, as specified by your instructor).

1. A title sheet. The title of the design project should be placed in approximately the center of the sheet, and your name or the names of those in the group in the lower right-hand corner. The symbol PL should follow the name of the project leader.

2. Table of contents with page numbers.

3. Statement of the purpose of the project with appropriate comments.

4. Preliminary design sketches, with comments on advantages and disadvantages of each, leading to the final selection of the *best* solution. All work should be signed and dated.

5. An accurately made pictorial and/or assembly drawing(s), using traditional drawing methods or CAD as assigned, if more than one part is involved in the design.

6. Detail working drawings, freehand, mechanical, or CAD-produced as assigned. The 8.5″ × 11.0″ sheet size is preferred for convenient insertion in the report. Larger sizes may be bound in the report with appropriate folding.

7. A bibliography or credit for important sources of information, if applicable.

WORKING DRAWING PROBLEMS

The problems in Figs. 14.41–14.102 are presented to give you practice in making regular working drawings of the type used in industry. Many problems, especially those of the assemblies, offer an excellent opportunity for you to exercise your ability to redesign or improve on the existing design. Due to the variations in sizes and in scales that may be used, you are required to select the sheet sizes and scales, when these are not specified, subject to the approval of the instructor. Standard sheet layouts are shown inside the front cover of this book.

The statements for each problem are intentionally brief, so that the instructor may amplify or vary the requirements when making assignments. Use the preferred metric system or the acceptable complete decimal-inch system, as assigned. Either the preferred unidirectional or acceptable aligned dimensioning may be assigned.

It should be clearly understood that in problems presented in pictorial form, the placement of dimensions and finish marks cannot always be followed in the drawing. *The dimensions given are in most cases those needed to make the parts, but due to the limitations of pictorial drawings they are not in all cases the dimensions that should be shown on the working drawing.* In the pictorial problems the rough and finished surfaces are shown, but finish marks are usually omitted. You should add all necessary finish marks and place all dimensions in the preferred places in the final drawings.

Each problem should be preceded by a sketch, fully dimensioned. Any of the title blocks shown inside the back cover of this book may be used, with modification if de-

sired, or you may design the title block if so assigned by the instructor.

Since many of the problems in this chapter are of a general nature, they can also be solved on most CAD systems. If a system is available, the instructor may choose to assign specific problems to be completed by this method.

FIGURE 14.41   Table Bracket.
Prob. 14.13: Make detail drawing using size B or A3 sheet.

FIGURE 14.42   RH Tool Post.
Prob. 14.14: Make detail drawing using size B or A3 sheet.
If assigned, convert dimensions to metric system.

FIGURE 14.43 Drill Press Base.
Prob. 14.15: Make detail drawing using size C or A2 sheet. Use unidirectional metric or decimal-inch dimensions.

FIGURE 14.44 Shifter Fork.
Prob. 14.16: Make detail drawing using size B or A3 sheet. If assigned, convert dimensions to metric system.

FIGURE 14.45 Idler Arm.
Prob. 14.17: Make detail drawing using size B or A3 sheet.

FIGURE 14.46 **Drill Press Bracket.**
Prob. 14.18: Make detail drawing using size C or A2 sheet. If assigned, convert dimensions to decimal inches or redesign the part with metric dimensions.

FIGURE 14.47 **Dial Holder.**
Prob. 14.19: Make detail drawing using size C or A2 sheet. If assigned, convert dimensions to decimal inches or redesign the part with metric dimensions.

FIGURE 14.48   Rack Slide.
Prob. 14.20: Make detail drawings half size on size B or A3 sheet. If assigned, convert dimensions to decimal inches or redesign the part with metric dimensions.

FIGURE 14.49   Automatic Stop Box.
Prob. 14.21: Make detail drawing half size on size B or A3 sheet. If assigned, redesign the part with metric dimensions.

2×Ø$\frac{1.250}{1.252}$ (IN LINE)   4×.375–16UNC–2B↧.5   *Some dimensions of each part are given on mating part.*   WALL THICKNESS.375 UNLESS OTHERWISE SPECIFIED FILLETS & ROUNDS R.125

Ø2.25

1.75

.375

R.438

4×Ø.406 (FOR .375 HEX HD CAP SCREWS)

2
1.5

40° A

R2.125

Ø2.5

45°

90°

.875

R.75

3.625
7.5
3.25

40°

6.75

Ø4.5

.75
R.75
.375

Ø6.5

Ø1.625

Ø$\frac{1.375}{1.377}$

3.75
2.5
4.5

2×Ø.531

Ø7

Ø5.75

.438

2×.125 NPT ↧.375

.75
1.5

.75

8.3

Ø.188 –.125 NPT

2.25

Ø2.5

45° R&F

2×Ø.531

2.5 1.125

1.75

5.75

4
2

VIEW AT A   C 1–1 EACH REQD

R.75

R.25

2

4

5.5

(To ℄ of central web)

FIGURE 14.50 **Conveyor Housing.**
Prob. 14.22: Make detail drawings half size on size C or A2 sheets. If assigned, convert dimensions to decimal inches or redesign the parts with metric dimensions.

50
R6   17 16
R10
16   27

M6×1–16 DEEP 3 HOLES EQUALLY SPACED AT EACH END

Ø 38.10–38.15

R54
R14
R3   10
172   10
RIO   86   R3
R3   R8   RIO 76
R6   60°   RIO
R8
10
254   127

C 1
1 REQD   METRIC

6
DETAIL OF GROOVES
20°   20°

R6   A

R10   10   10

Ø$\frac{89.99}{89.91}$ R3

Ø127   Ø80   3   Ø58

R6

224

140

6   R6

35

32   16

25   R6   A   305

10   54   168

4× Ø16   35   241

R6

102

25

204

R6

10   10   10

FIGURE 14.51 **Spindle Housing.**
Prob. 14.23: Given: Front, left-side, and bottom views, and partial removed section.
Required: Front view in full section, top view, and right-side view in half section on A-A. Draw half size on size C or A2 sheet. If assigned, dimension fully.

CI – I REQD

—The note for this should
read — to be removed
after machining.

ARBOR SUPPORT
BRACKET

FIGURE 14.52   **Arbor Support Bracket.**
Prob. 14.24: Given: Front and right-side views.
**Required: Front, left-side, and bottom views, and a detail section A-A. Use
American National Standard tables for indicated fits and if required convert
to metric values (see Appendixes 5–14). If assigned, dimension in the metric
or decimal-inch system.**

FIGURE 14.53   **Pump Bracket for a
Thread Milling Machine.**
**Prob. 14.25: Given: Front and left-side views.
Required: Front and right-side views, and
top view in section on A-A. Draw full size
on size B or A3 sheet. If assigned, dimension
fully.**

WALLS 5 THICK – FILLETS
& ROUNDS R3 UNLESS
OTHERWISE SPECIFIED

METRIC

FIGURE 14.54 Support Base for
Planer.
Prob. 14.26: Given: Front and top views.
Required: Front and top views, left-side
view in full section A-A, and removed
section B-B. Draw full size on size C or
A2 sheet. If assigned, dimension fully.

Some hidden lines
have been intentionally
omitted from side view.

DIE FORGING
SAE 1020 – NORMALIZE & HARDEN

10 THDS PER IN.

Lead — used to
create friction, yet
soft enough not to
ruin the threads

Set Screw
Oiler

SECTION A-A
(IN ASSEMBLY)

FIGURE 14.55 Jaw
Base for Chuck Jaw.
Prob. 14.27: Given: Top,
right-side, and partial
auxiliary views.
Required: Top, left-side
(beside top), front, and
partial auxiliary views
complete with dimensions,
if assigned. Use metric or
decimal-inch dimensions.
Use American National
Standard tables for
indicated fits or convert for
metric values. See
Appendixes 5–14.

MILLIMETER
INCH

FILLETS AND ROUNDS R3

METRIC

CAST STEEL
1 REQ D

PLACE DIMENSIONS
IN PREFERRED PLACES
ON NEW DRAWING

FIGURE 14.56 **Fixture Base for 60-Ton Vertical Press.**
Prob. 14.28: Given: Front and right-side views.
Required: Revolve front view 90° clockwise; then add top and left-side views. Draw half size on size C or A2 sheet. If assigned, complete with dimensions.

SECTION AT B-B
(DOUBLE SIZE)

METRIC

FILLETS AND ROUNDS R3
UNLESS OTHERWISE SPECIFIED

C 1
1 REQD

FIGURE 14.57 **Bracket.**
Prob. 14.29: Given: Front, left-side, and bottom views, and partial removed section.
Required: Make detail drawing. Draw front, top, and right-side views, and removed sections A-A and B-B. Draw half size on size C or A2 sheet. Draw section B-B full size. If assigned, complete with dimensions.

FIGURE 14.58   Roller Rest Bracket for Automatic Screw Machine.
Prob. 14.30: Given: Front and left-side views.
Required: Revolve front view 90° clockwise; then add top and left-side views.
Draw half size on size C or A2 sheet. If assigned, complete with dimensions.

FIGURE 14.59   Guide Bracket for Gear Shaper.
Prob. 14.31: Given: Front and right-side views.
Required: Front view, a partial right-side view, and two partial auxiliary views taken in direction of arrows. Draw half size on size C or A2 sheet. If assigned, complete with unidirectional dimensions.

FIGURE 14.60 **Rear Tool Post.**
Prob. 14.32: Given: Front and left-side views.
Required: Take left-side view as new top view; add front and left-side views,
approx. 215 mm apart, a primary auxiliary view, then a secondary view taken
so as to show true end view of 19-mm slot. Complete all views, except show
only necessary hidden lines in auxiliary views. Draw full size on size C or A2
sheet. If assigned, complete with dimensions.

FIGURE 14.61 **Bearing for a Worm
Gear.**
Prob. 14.33: Given: Front and right-side
views.
Required: Front, top, and left-side
views. Draw full size on size C or A2
sheet. If assigned, complete with
dimensions.

2 × Ø.188

R.25

.188

R.125   .562

SECT B-B

Ø.203 -.25-20 UNC-2 B
0.2183
0.2175 PITCH DIA – 4 HOLES
SYMMETRICALLY SPACED
WITH RESPECT TO ℄₁ & ℄₂

0.188
0.187 FOR 5 GROOVES
SMOOTH FINISH

R.125   .290°
        .64
.312   .60°
        .094
20°
Ø.109 -8 HOLES
EQUALLY SPACED,
BOTTOM GROOVE

SECT A-A

FLATS ON OPP
SIDES OF PISTON
5.395
5.385 APART –
EACH 2.6975
     2.6925 TO
℄ OF PISTON

FLATS ON OPP
SIDES OF PISTON
4.750
4.745 APART

5.482 GRIND
5.480
5.062 TURN ALL RING GROOVES
5.051

Ø 4.625

SMOOTH
FINISH

60°

R0.63

Ø.125

.25 SR

.032 × 45°
CHAMFER

R.125
Ø4.688

.25
2 CORE

R.25
R.125

Ø 5.125

R.188

20°

.094

GRIND TAPER

1.875

2.312

3.6875
3.6835

RELIEF

4.75

.407

R.063

.501
.500
.251
.250

2.3750
2.3725

.4"

5°

R.125

5.437 TURN BOTTOM R.032 GROOVE
5.432
5.513 TURN FULL LENGTH OF PISTON
5.510
5.495 GRIND STRAIGHT FOR LENGTH "A"
5.494

Ø 4.877
Ø 4.875

(5 GROOVES)

Ø 5.188

R.125

.50
.063
30°

.375

.50

.813

1.125

1.438

R.018
.012

22.5°

SEE
SECT A-A

6.062

STRAIGHT "A"

SQUARE
CORNER

Ø1.9380
 1.9375 MUST BE REAMED SQUARE WITH SKIRT

THIS SURFACE RECESSED .014 TO 45° ON
                      .010
EACH SIDE OF ℄ OF WRIST PIN HOLES

GRAY IRON CASTING
6-REQD

FIGURE 14.62   **Caterpillar Tractor Piston.**
**Prob. 14.34: Make detail drawing full size on size C or A2 sheet. If assigned,
use unidirectional decimal-inch system, converting all fractions to two-place
decimal dimensions, or convert all dimensions to metric.**

FIGURE 14.63   **Generator Drive Housing.**
Prob. 14.35: Given: Front and left-side views.
**Required: Front view, right-side view in full section, and top view in full
section on A-A. Draw full size on size C or A2 sheet. If assigned, complete
with dimensions.**

FIGURE 14.64   **Machinist's Clamp.**
**Prob. 14.36: Draw details and assembly. If assigned, use unidirectional two-
place decimal-inch dimensions or redesign for metric dimensions.**

① COLUMN
CAST IRON

Ø12.5

③ M12 × 1.75 − 65LG
HEX CAP SCREW

R30

42

Ø42

Ø30 SF

② CAP
CAST IRON

④ HEX
NUT

R6   Ø32

⑤ HEX
LOCK NUT

R12   Ø42

METRIC

Ø48
Ø66
M24 × 3
▼22

FIGURE 14.65   **Hand Rail Column.**
Prob. 14.37: (1) Draw details. If assigned, complete with dimensions. (2) Draw assembly.

② HANDLE
MALL. IRON

⑤ PIN

Ø10.0 ▼18

R14

R28

R3   R15

Ø2.9 GIVE TOL.
FOR Ø3 × 28 LG PIN
GIVE TOL.

③ SCREW
CRS

④ BUSHING
BRONZE   R3

Ø28

M14 × 2

R18

Ø7.94

Ø10

Ø12

45°

① BLOCK
CAST IRON

METRIC

FIGURE 14.66   **Drill Jig.**
Prob. 14.38: (1) Draw details. If assigned, complete with dimensions. (2) Draw assembly.

FIGURE 14.67 Tool Post.
Prob. 14.39: (1) Draw details. (2) Draw assembly. If assigned, use
unidirectional two-place decimals for all fractional dimensions or redesign
for all metric dimensions.

FIGURE 14.68   Belt Tightener.

Prob. 14.40: (1) Draw details. (2) Draw assembly. It is assumed that the parts are to be made in quantity and they are to be dimensioned for interchangeability on the detail drawings. Use tables in Appendixes 11–14 for limit values. Design as follows.

a. **Bushing fit in pulley: Locational interference fit.**
b. **Shaft fit in bushing; Free running fit.**
c. **Shaft fits in frame: Sliding fit.**
d. **Pin fit in frame: Free running fit.**
e. **Pulley hub length plus washers fit in frame: Allowance 0.13 and tolerances 0.10.**
f. **Make bushing 0.25 mm shorter than pulley hub.**
g. **Bracket fit in frame: Same as e above.**

FIGURE 14.69 **Milling Jack.**
Prob. 14.41: (1) Draw details. (2) Draw assembly. If assigned, convert dimensions to metric or decimal-inch system.

FIGURE 14.70 **Connecting Bar.**
Prob. 14.42: (1) Draw details. (2) Draw assembly. If assigned, convert dimensions to metric or decimal-inch system.

FIGURE 14.71 Clamp Stop.
Prob. 14.43: (1) Draw details. (2) Draw assembly. If assigned, convert dimensions to decimal-inch system or redesign for metric dimensions.

FIGURE 14.72 Pillow Block Bearing.
Prob. 14.44: (1) Draw details. (2) Draw assembly. If assigned, complete with dimensions.

467

FAO ALL PARTS EXCEPT ① BASE

METRIC

CENTERING REST

PARTS LIST							
NO.	PART NAME	MATL	REQD	NO.	PART NAME	MATL	REQD
1	BASE	C I	1	5	CLAMP SCREW	S A E 1020	1
2	REST	S A E 1020	1	6	CLAMP HANDLE	S A E 1020	1
3	CLAMP	S A E 1020	1	7	M6 X 1-25 LG FIL HD CAP SCREW		2
4	ADJUSTING NUT	S A E 1020	1	8	5.5 X 5.5 X 3.2 - 25 LG KEY	S A E 1030	1

FIGURE 14.73 **Centering Rest.**
Prob. 14.45: (1) Draw details. (2) Draw assembly. If assigned, complete with dimensions.

(4) SCREW
S A E 1040-HEAT TR
.375-16UNC-3A

(6) SET SCREW
S A E 1040
HEAT TREAT

(7) CUSHION
PHOSPHOR
BRONZE

Ø.297
(TO HOLE)
.375-16UNC-3B
⊥.312

.625 ACROSS FLATS

.375-16UNC-3A

(5) WASHER
S A E 1040
HEAT TREAT

(3) ADJUST
SCREW
S A E 1040
HEAT TREAT

.375-16UNC-3B
CLEAR THROUGH

(1) CAP
C I

(2) WEDGE
CRS

FIGURE 14.71 Clamp Stop.
Prob. 14.43: (1) Draw details. (2) Draw assembly. If assigned, convert dimensions to decimal-inch system or redesign for metric dimensions.

2× Ø 5.3
2X R
R6 R21
R18
R22
R22
86
18
43
132
56
28
86 25
R10
(4) HEX NUT
(1) PILLOW
BLOCK
CAST IRON
Ø44
Ø 56
Ø76
R6

(2) BEARING CAP
CAST IRON

METRIC

32
45° X 2.5 CHAM
BOTH ENDS
Ø21 (CAP ONLY)

(3) STUD M20 x 2.5
82 LONG-S A E 1040

Ø17.5 ⊤32
M20x2.5 ⊤28

16
35
5
94
48
60°
30 R6 12 R10
R6
82
28
BABBITT
142

FIGURE 14.72 Pillow Block Bearing.
Prob. 14.44: (1) Draw details. (2) Draw assembly. If assigned, complete with dimensions.

467

FAO ALL PARTS EXCEPT ① BASE

METRIC

CENTERING REST

NO.	PART NAME	MATL	REQD	NO.	PART NAME	MATL	REQD
1	BASE	C I	1	5	CLAMP SCREW	S A E 1020	1
2	REST	S A E 1020	1	6	CLAMP HANDLE	S A E 1020	1
3	CLAMP	S A E 1020	1	7	M6 X 1-25 LG FIL HD CAP SCREW		2
4	ADJUSTING NUT	S A E 1020	1	8	5.5 X 5.5 X 3.2 – 25 LG KEY	S A E 1030	1

PARTS LIST

FIGURE 14.73 **Centering Rest.**
Prob. 14.45: (1) Draw details. (2) Draw assembly. If assigned, complete with dimensions.

PIPE VISE

⑥ HANDLE
STD PIPE

⑦ HANDLE CAP
STD CAP

② VISE SCREW
S.A.E. 1045

⑨ HEX NUT
S.A.E. 1020

⑩ GUIDE LINK
S.A.E. 1020

③ GUIDE BAR
S.A.E. 1020

① VISE BASE
CAST STEEL

④ UPPER JAW
S.A.E. 1045
HARDENED

⑤ LOWER JAW
S.A.E. 1045
HARDENED

⑧ HEX CAP SCR
S.A.E. 1020

MILLIMETERS
INCHES

FIGURE 14.74 **Pipe Vise.**
**Prob. 14.46: (1) Draw details. (2) Draw assembly. To obtain dimensions, take
distances directly from figure with dividers; then set dividers on printed scale
and read measurements in millimeters or decimal inches as assigned. All
threads are general-purpose metric threads (see Appendix 15) or Unified
coarse threads except the American National Standard pipe threads on
handle and handle caps.**

FIGURE 14.75 Tap Wrench.
Prob. 14.47: (1) Draw details. (2) Draw assembly. If assigned, use
unidirectional two-place decimals for all fractional dimensions or redesign
for metric dimensions.

FIGURE 14.76 Machinist's Vise.
Prob. 14.48: (1) Draw details. (2) Draw assembly. If assigned, use
unidirectional two-place decimals for all fractional dimensions or redesign
for metric dimensions.

FIGURE 14.77   Screw Jack.

Prob. 14.49: (1) Draw details. See Fig. 14.21, showing "boxed-in" views on sheet layout C–678 or A2–678 (see inside front cover). (2) Draw assembly. If assigned, convert dimensions to decimal inches or redesign for metric dimensions.

FIGURE 14.78   **Stock Bracket for Cold Saw Machine.**
Prob. 14.50: (1) Draw details. (2) Draw assembly. If assigned, use
unidirectional decimal dimensions or redesign for metric dimensions.

FIGURE 14.79   Front Circular Forming Cutter Holder.
Prob. 14.51: (1) Draw details. (2) Draw assembly. To obtain dimensions, take distances directly from figure with dividers and set dividers on printed scale. Use metric or decimal-inch dimensions as assigned.

FIGURE 14.80   **Machine Vise.**
Prob. 14.52: (1) Draw details. (2) Draw assembly. If assigned, convert dimensions to the decimal-inch system or redesign with metric dimensions.

GRINDER WHEEL

STOCK

FIGURE 14.81   Grinder Vise.
Prob. 14.53: See Figs. 14.82 and 14.83.

SPHERICAL CORNER

VIEW IN DIRECTION
OF ARROW A

Ø.626
.625
⊔Ø1.062 FACE
ON BOTH SIDES
THICKNESS TO BE .750

2.5 MAX CUTTER

SHARP
CORNER
LOOKING
IN THIS
DIRECTION

FILLETS AND
ROUNDS R.125

4×.438−14UNC−2B
⊤.875

2×#10−32UNF−2B
⊤.437

① VISE BASE
C I I REQD

CUTTER

#10−32UNF−2A

.062 X .062 SLOT

⑮ PROTRACTOR
SCREW SAE 1115
2 REQD

#10−32UNF−2A

.062 X.031 SLOT

⑯ JAW PLATE SCREW
SAE 1115 −4 REQD

Ø.20
⊤.5

PIN

(FN 1 fit)

.031 X 45°
CHAMFER
(PIN)

Ø.500
.499

CUT FOR ⑲
#204 WOODRUFF KEY

⑩ COMPOUND REST HANDLE
SAE 3140 − I REQD

.562−8 ACME
L H −CLEAR
THROUGH

PARTIAL
TOP VIEW

SPHERICAL
CORNER

SIDE
VIEW−
LOOKING
IN THE
DIRECTION
OF ARROW A

2×#10−32UNF−2B
⊤.438

② SLIDING JAW
C I −I REQD

2×.5−12UNC−2B ⊤.688
BOTTOM TAP

90 80 70 60 50 40 30 20

Ø.626
.625

2×Ø.219 ⊔Ø.344 ⊤.125

⑥ PROTRACTOR
SA E 3140−I REQD

FIGURE 14.82 Grinder Vise.
Prob. 14.53, continued: (1) Draw details. (2) Draw assembly. See Figs. 14.81
and 14.83. If assigned, convert dimensions to decimal inches or redesign with
metric dimensions.

4 × Ø.469 ⊔Ø.656 ↧.25

.687

R.125

1.5   Ø1.312

3.25

1.5

1.125

.25

.125

R2.25

R.0

LOCATE ZERO AND
MARK IN ASSEMBLY

R1.515

R.875

.562

Ø.500
.501

R.687

4.687

.75

1.749
1.748

.75

④ SECONDARY BASE
C I – I REQD

.031   30°   .093

Ø1.187   Ø.562

⑧ WASHER
S A E 1020 – 2 REQD

Ø.499
.498 –12UNC–2A

4.5   1

.375

Ø.624
.623

R.062

USE ⑱
STANDARD
FIN HEX
NUT & WASHER
⑧

45°
CHAMFER
TO BOTTOM
OF THD

⑦ HINGE BOLT
S A E 1040 – I REQD

REAM FOR ⑰
#O TAPER PIN

.28

.437

Ø.626
.625

⑪ COLLAR
S A E 1020 – I REQD

45°CHAMFER TO BOTTOM
OF THD

.437–14UNC–2A

.062

1.25

.25

Ø.625

.093

⑬ SEC BASE SCREW
S A E 1020 – 4 REQD

45° CHAMFER TO BOTTOM
OF THD

.5–12UNC–2A

.062

1.25

.25

Ø.75

.093

⑭ CLAMP PLATE SCREW
S A E 3140 C H – 2 REQD

2 × Ø.218 –⊔Ø.343– ↧.062

2.75   .5

3.5

.062

.375

45°   .187

1.125

⑫ JAW PLATE
S A E 1030 – 2 REQD

2 × Ø.531 –⊔Ø.781– ↧.25

.437

.625

1.25

.625   1.5

2.75

③ CLAMP PLATE
S A E 3140 – I REQD

Ø.563–CLEAR THROUGH
⊔Ø1.25

(No tapped holes
on this side)

.687   1.5   3.25

R.125

.75

R.125

.25

.375

1.375

1.75

.625

.5

1.75
1.750

3.5   .75

R.125

2.25

.500
.501

.75

4.687

1.25

⑤ HINGE BASE
C I – I REQD

#10–32 UNF–2B –.375 DEEP
2 HOLES ON 1"DIA BC

Ø.09 COMB.
DRILL AND
CSK–BOTH
ENDS

CUT FOR ⑲
#204 WOODRUFF KEY

REAM IN PLACE
WITH PART #11 FOR ⑰
#O TAPER PIN

4.75

.375

Ø.624
.623

.498
.497

2.375

.937

Ø.437

.562–8 ACME L H

.125

.375

⑨ VISE SCREW
S A E 3140 – I REQD

FIGURE 14.83   **Grinder Vise.**

Prob. 14.53, continued: See Fig. 14.82 for instructions.

4 AXLE
C R S–2 REQD

X 45°CHAM

0.625 × 45° CHAM

STOCK ITEMS:
10 .875 × 8.25 SF HEX HD BOLT – 2 REQD
DRILL .187 COTTER PIN HOLE .187 FROM TIP
11 .875 SF SLOTTED HEX NUT–2 REQD
12 .875 S A E PLAIN WASHER–8 REQD
13 .156 × 1.5 S A E COTTER PIN–2 REQD
14 #10 (.190) × .625 ROUND HD MACH SCR–4 REQD

DETAIL SHOWING
BEARING ASSY

8 BALLS Ø.312

7 #99504 NEW
DEPARTURE BALL BEARING
2 REQ'D. (Stock item).

6 KEEPER PLATE
C R S –2 REQD

3 CROSS HEAD
H R S – I REQD

Ø.5 CORE–3 HOLES
EQUALLY SPACED

5 ADJUSTING SHIM
H R S – 2 REQD

TUMBLE
TO RE-
MOVE
BURRS

Ø.190–24 NC–2 B
–2 HOLES
(Through)

8 AXLE SNAP RING
SPRING STEEL–2 REQD

(Stock item)

1 TROLLEY WHEEL
C I – 2 REQD

9 WHEEL SNAP RING
SPRING STEEL–4 REQD

(Stock item)

2 SIDE PLATE
H R S – 2 REQD

FIGURE 14.84 **Trolley.**
Prob. 14.54: (1) Draw details, omitting parts 7–14. (2) Draw assembly. If
assigned, convert dimensions to decimal inches or redesign for metric
dimensions.

FIGURE 14.85 Arbor Press.

Prob. 14.55: (1) Draw details. (2) Draw assembly. If assigned, convert dimensions to decimal inches or redesign for metric dimensions.

479

FIGURE 14.86   **Forming Cutter Holder.**
**Prob. 14.56: (1) Draw details using decimal or metric dimensions. (2) Draw
assembly. Above layout is half size. To obtain dimensions, take distances
directly from figure with dividers and double them. At left is shown the top
view of the forming cutter holder in use on the lathe.**

Item	NAME	Amt	MATL	REMARKS	Item	NAME	Amt	MATL	REMARKS
1	BASE PLATE	1	CRS	1×5×9.5	9	SLEEVE	1	BRONZE	O D.718–1 D.640
2	GAGE BLOCK	1	CRS	1.5×2.875×4.875	10	STUD	1	CRS	.625 DIA × 3
3	LOCATING PLUG	1	CRS	2.005 DIA × 2.25	11	KEY	2	CRS	.5 ×.812 ×1.5
4	C-WASHER	1	CRS	2.875 DIA ×.5	12	SOC HD CAP SCR	2	STK	.312×.75
5	REST BLOCK	1	CRS	1.375 × 2 ×2.75	13	PIN	1	DR	.375×2
6	CLAMP	1	CRS	1×1×3.625	14	SOC HD CAP SCR	3	STK	.5 × 1.25
7	.625 STD HEX NUT	2	STK		15	DOWEL PIN	2	STK	.312 DIA × 1.5
8	SPRING	1	MUSIC WIRE	WIRE .054 –O D.875	16	SOC HD CAP SCR	2	STK	.5×1

FIGURE 14.87 **Milling Fixture for Clutch Arm.**
Prob. 14.57: (1) Draw details using the decimal-inch system or redesign for
metric dimensions, if assigned. (2) Draw assembly.

JACOBS CHUCK

MILLIMETERS
INCHES

FIGURE 14.88   **Drill Speeder.**
Prob. 14.58: See Figs. 14.89 and 14.90.

FIGURE 14.89   **Drill Speeder.**

Prob. 14.58, continued: (1) Draw details. (2) Draw assembly. See Fig. 14.88. If assigned, convert dimensions to decimal inches or redesign with metric dimensions.

FIGURE 14.90 Drill Speeder.
Prob. 14.58, continued: See Fig. 14.89 for instructions.

FIGURE 14.91 Vertical Slide Tool.

Prob. 14.59: (1) Draw details. If assigned, convert dimensions to decimal inches or redesign for metric system. (2) Draw assembly. For part 2: Take given top view as front view in the new drawing; then add top and right-side views. See also Fig. 14.92. If assigned, use unidirectional dimensions.

FIGURE 14.92 **Vertical Slide Tool.**
Prob. 14.59, continued: See Fig. 14.91 for instructions. For part 1: Take top view as front view in the new drawing; then add top and right-side views.

FIGURE 14.93   **Slide Tool.**
Prob. 14.60: Make assembly drawing. See Figs. 14.95–14.97.

PARTS LIST	NO. OF SHEETS 2 SHEET NO. 1	MACHINE NO. M-219
NAME NO. 4 SLIDE TOOL (SPECIFY SIZE OF SHANK REQ'D.)		LOT NUMBER
		NO. OF PIECES

TOTAL ON MACH.	NO. PCS.	NAME OF PART	PART NO.	CAST FROM PART NO.	TRACING NO.	MATERIAL	ROUGH WEIGHT PER PC.	DIA.	LENGTH	MILL	PART USED ON	NO. REQ. FINISH
	1	Body	219-12		D-17417	A-3-S D F						
	1	Slide	219-6		D-19255	A-3-S D F					219-12	
	1	Nut	219-9		E-19256	#10 BZ					219-6	
	1	Gib	219-1001		C-11129	S A E 1020					219-6	
	1	Slide Screw	219-1002		C-11129	A-3-S					219-12	
	1	Dial Bush.	219-1003		C-11129	A-1-S					219-1002	
	1	Dial Nut	219-1004		C-11129	A-1-S					219-1002	
	1	Handle	219-1011		E-18270	(Buy from Cincinnati Ball Crank Co.)					219-1002	
	1	Stop Screw (Short)	219-1012		E-51950	A-1-S					219-6	
	1	Stop Screw (Long)	219-1013		E-51951	A-1-S					219-6	
	1	Binder Shoe	219-1015		E-51952	#5 Brass					219-6	
	1	Handle Screw	219-1016		E-62322	X-1315 C F					219-1011	
	1	Binder Screw	219-1017		E-63927	A-1-S					219-6	
	1	Dial	219-1018		E-39461	A-1-S					219-1002	
	2	Gib Screw	219-1019		E-52777	A-1-S		$\frac{1}{4}$-20	1		219-6	
	1	Binder Screw	280-1010		E-24962	A-1-S					219-1018	
	2	Tool Clamp Screws	683-F-1002		E-19110	D-2-S					219-6	
	1	Fill Hd Cap Scr	1-A			A-1-S		$\frac{3}{8}$	$1\frac{3}{8}$		219-6 219-9	
	1	Key	No.404 Woodruff								219-1002	

FIGURE 14.94   **Prob. 14.61: Slide Tool Parts List.**

FIGURE 14.95 Slide Tool.
Prob. 14.61, continued: (1) Draw details using decimal-inch dimensions or redesign with metric dimensions, if assigned. (2) Draw assembly. See Fig. 14.93.

FILLETS & ROUNDS
R.125 UNLESS
OTHERWISE
SPECIFIED

GIB SCREW 219-1019
S A E X 1315 STEEL (COLD FINISHED) - .5 BAR
TREAT P55Z

I-BINDER SHOE 219-1015
NO. 5 BRASS .266 BAR

FORGING DETAIL NO. 219-6
A-3 STEEL

I-DIAL NUT 219-1004
S A E x-1315 STEEL-COLD FINISHED.
.781 HEX BAR
TREAT - P55Z

DRILL JIG $\frac{300-B}{1608.}$

DOVE TAIL GAGE $\frac{300-B}{3004}$

USE GAGE WITH
MASTER GIB $\frac{300-B}{3009}$

I-SLIDE-219-6
A-3-STEEL DROP FORGING.

.250 TAPER PER FT.

STAMP HERE
THE WARNER & SWASEY CO.
CLEVELAND, O. U.S.A.
M-219.

I-HANDLE SCREW-219-1016
S A E X-1315 STEEL-COLD FINISHED - .188 BAR
TREAT P55Z

COLLET $\frac{21-D}{54}$

DRILL JIG $\frac{300-B}{1610}$

TAPPING FIX $\frac{300-B}{1611}$

SPECIAL TAP $\frac{300-B}{1612}$

TO MATCH BODY

I-NUT-219-9
NO. 10 BRONZE

FIGURE 14.96 Slide Tool.
Prob. 14.61, continued: See. Fig. 14.95 for instructions.

FIGURE 14.97 Slide Tool.
Prob. 14.61, continued: See Fig. 14.95 for instructions.

STOCK SIZE .437 R.062
.062×45° CHAM 30°

⑩ CLAMP PLUG
.312 BRASS ROD–2 REQD

Ø.125 DRILL WITH
PC #8 IN ASSY
R.25 .312 .156
R.3.5
SYM ON ₵
R.062
Ø.254 / .251
R.3.5 R.125
.125
FAO
1.5

⑦ LOCKING HANDLE
CRS– 4 REQD
CHROME PLATE

STANDARD PARTS
NO. REQD
4 –.375–16UNC–2A x 1.5 HEX SOCKET CUP PT SET SCR
2 –.375–16UNC–2A x.562 HEX SOCKET FLAT PT SET SCR
8 –.25–20UNC–2A x.625 FILLISTER HD CAP SCR
12 – Ø.125 x.75 DRILL ROD
2 – #4 (.112)–40UNC–2A x .25 ROUND HD MACH SCR
4 – Ø.125 x .187 DRILL ROD

THICKNESS OF LINE APPROX .015
.093 .25 .109
ONE REQD–ALUMINUM PURCHASE
.062 DOUBLE SIZE
2 × Ø.136 #20 (.032) B & S GAUGE
.90 80 70 60 50 40 30 20 10 O 10 20 30 40 50 60 70 80 90 .25
5.504
5.942
DEVELOPMENT

⑨ PROTRACTOR SCALE

(Holes same as on opposite side)
FILLETS AND ROUNDS R.125
R.375 3.5 3 .562
.562
75°
.062 R.2.000
3.503 / 3.500 G 1.5
.625
.500 / .495
1.687 (To bottom of 2.000 R)
4x #7(.201)DRILL–.812 DEEP
.25–20UNC–2B, .625DEEP
3.375 3.25 6.5
.181
4x Ø.120–.125 REDRILL .562 DEEP
IN ASSEMBLY WITH
PLATES FOR .125 DOWEL PINS

① SADDLE
C I –1 REQD

.1281 .625
Ø.3120 –GRIND
Ø.250 / .241
.031×45° CHAMFER
.015
.125 DRILL .062 DEEP
WITH PC #7 IN ASSY

⑧ ECCENTRIC
.312 CRS #1112 –4 REQD
CYANIDE HARDEN

FIGURE 14.98 "Any Angle" Tool Vise.
**Prob. 14.62: (1) Draw details using decimal-inch dimensions or redesign with
metric dimensions, if assigned. (2) Draw assembly. See also Fig. 14.99.**

FIGURE 14.99   **"Any-Angle" Tool Vise.**
Prob. 14.62, continued: See Fig. 14.98 for instructions.

FIGURE 14.100 **Fixture for Centering Connecting Rod.**
Prob. 14.63: (1) Draw details using decimal-inch dimensions or redesign with metric dimensions, if assigned. (2) Draw assembly. See also Figs. 14.101 and 14.102.

FIGURE 14.101 **Fixture for Centering Connecting Rod. Prob. 14.63, continued: See Fig. 14.100 for instructions.**

(8) HAND LEVER "AAA" STEEL FORGING-WT 0.5# I REQD

TOP VIEW

SPHERICAL

.125 DRILL IN PLACE WITH (7) FOR (39) .125×1 PIN

.093×.046 OIL GROOVE

(2) CRADLE "AAA" STEEL CASTING WT 22#-HEAT TREAT "B" I REQD

4×Ø.6240-6245 REQD

(26) BUSHING PHOSPHOR BRONZE STK 1.5 DIA×.75CORE-WT .63# I REQD

.03×45° CHAMFER

(27) BUSHING PHOSPHOR BRONZE STK 1.5 DIA×.75CORE-WT .8# I REQD .093×.046 OILGROOVE

.03×45°CHAMFER

Ø.624-625 FOR (41) .625×.225 PIN

(3) CLAMP "AAA" STEEL CASTING WT 8.4#-HEAT TREAT "B" I REQD

(24) CAM "RR" STEEL-STK .625×2.5 WT 2#-HEAT TREAT "Q" I REQD

.062×45° CHAMFER

.75-16UN-3A SQ

WASHERFACE 2.5 DIA×.015

NECK .125×.062 DEEP

TO WASHERFACE

(18) SPRING "S"STEEL-STK Ø.062 HEAT TREAT"SP" 8 COILS-ENDS CLOSED & GROUND-I REQD

FILLETS & ROUNDS R.062

FREE

Ø.625-.626

(40) .625×3.5 PIN 2 REQD

ENDS CLOSED & GROUND

—11 COILS

1.812 FREE

(17) SPRING "S"STEEL-STK.093DIA HEAT TREAT "SP" I REQD

.375-16UNC-2B TO .750 HOLE FOR (33) .375×.875 SOCKET SET SCR

Ø.749-.750 THRU

(25) CAM "RR" STEEL-STK 1.5×2.75 WT 4#-HEAT TREAT "Q" I REQD

Ø.626-628

45°

45°

Ø"DIA

(29) PLUNGER "RR" STEEL-STK .75 DIA WT .28#-HEAT TREAT "Q" I REQD

SR.187

Ø.9990 Ø.9985

NECK .063×.032 DEEP

(15) ROUGH LOCATER "RR" STEEL-STK 2.5 WT 3.82#- HEAT TREAT "Q" I REQD

R.937

Ø2.375

(5) CLAMP "AAA" STEEL STK 1.5×2 WT 3.5#-HEAT TREAT"B"-I REQD

60°

FIGURE 14.102 **Fixture for Centering Connecting Rod.** Prob. 14.63, continued: See Fig. 14.100 for instructions.

495

FIGURE 14.103   Alignment Wheel.
Prob. 14.64. (1) Draw top and left-side views.
(2) Redesign with metric dimensions.

Ø.25 THRU
2 HOLES EQ SP
ON Ø1.50 B.C

.75 DIA
THRU

.25

Ø1.00

Ø2.00

1.50

.12 X .12 CHAMFER

FIGURE 14.104   Rubber Bushing.
Prob. 14.65. (1) Draw top and left-side views.
(2) Redesign with metric dimensions.

FIGURE 14.105 Problem 14.66. 8-Port Nylon Manifold. Draw bottom and left-side view. Redesign with metric dimensions.

CHAPTER 15

REPRODUCTION AND CONTROL OF DRAWINGS

OBJECTIVES

After studying the material in this chapter, you should be able to:

1. Describe blueprinting and digital engineering printing.
2. Discuss the differences between Diazo-Moist and Diazo-Dry Processes.
3. Understand the differences between CD-ROM and Optical Disk Storage Systems.
4. Discuss how the processes of Xerography and fax technology work.
5. Discuss how documents may be handled in a "paperless office."

OVERVIEW

An essential part of designers' or drafters' education is a thorough knowledge of reproduction techniques and processes and drawing storage. Specifically, they should be familiar with the various processes available for the reproduction of drawings: *blueprint, diazo, microfilm, microfiche*, etc.

Because the average engineering drawing requires a considerable economic investment, adequate control and protection of the original drawing are mandatory. Such items as drawing numbers, §15.13, methods of filing, microfilming, security files, print making and distribution, drawing changes, and retrieval of drawings are all important. A proper drawing-control system will enable those in charge of drawings (1) to know the location and status of the drawing at all times; (2) to minimize the damage to original drawings from the handling required for revisions, printing, and so on; and (3) to provide distribution of prints to proper persons.

Those organizations with computer-aided design (CAD) systems often use computer storage of finished drawings. In addition, digitized drawing information about frequently required components and elements, such as standard bolts, nuts, screws, pins, and piping valves, is stored in the computer for recall and replacement on drawings as needed. CAD systems of this type have obvious advantages for production, storage, control, and recall of drawings. However, design documentation requirements generally dictate that all of the approved drawing revisions be stored in a permanent record. Many companies fail to properly store the design history of their drawings in a suitable fashion. Because CAD drawings stored on a hard drive or tape can be edited, they are not considered a permanent record. WORM (write once read many) CD-ROM drives make a good permanent storage medium for CAD drawing. Most small and medium-size companies and a substantial number of large firms may not be able to justify the acquisition of high-capacity permanent storage systems for their CAD documents and thus will continue to use the conventional methods of reproduction, storage, retrieval, and control of drawings described in this chapter. But technologies such as WORM CD-ROMs are becoming more compact and less expensive, and as advancing technology makes such systems more affordable, it is expected that many companies will make the change to storing their permanent drawings on a computer storage system.

■ 15.1 STORAGE OF DRAWINGS

Drawings may be stored flat in large flat-drawer files or hung vertically in cabinets especially designed for the purpose. Exceptionally large drawings are often rolled and stored in tubes in racks or cabinets. Prints are often folded and stored in standard office file cases. Proper control procedures will enable the user of the drawing to find it in the file, to return it to its proper place, and to know where the drawing is when not in the file.

■ 15.2 REPRODUCTION OF DRAWINGS

After the drawings of a machine or structure have been completed, it is usually necessary to supply copies to many different persons and firms. Obviously, therefore, some means of exact, rapid, and economical reproduction must be used. Even when a drawing is plotted from a CAD system, it is frequently faster to use a reproduction process to distribute the drawing. Plots can be created on mylar, or on specialty papers that allow prints to be made directly from the plot. Large format copy machines are also popular for creating distribution drawings of a print. Networks, groupware, internet and intranet, and modems are allowing many workplaces to go to a paperless office, where drawings are distributed electronically (Fig. 15.1). However, when there is a need to take drawings into the field, printing is still frequently required.

■ 15.3 BLUEPRINT PROCESS AND DIGITAL ENGINEERING PRINTING/COPYING

Of the several processes in use for reproduction, the *blueprint* is the oldest process used for making prints of large drawings. It is essentially a photographic process in which the original drawing is the negative.

The blueprint process, which was the common method used for the reproduction of drawings for many years, has now been replaced to a large extent by other more convenient and efficient processes.

High-speed digital engineering printers, such as the one shown in Fig. 15.2, are most widely used in the engineering and manufacturing industry. Such printers can produce output from either CAD files, hard copy, or a mixture of both. These printers can also produce multi-media products and digital sorting for automated set production.

Zimco Plant

Zimco Enterprises

Acme Company

Intracompany networking

Intercompany networking

FIGURE 15.1   **Intracompany and Intercompany Networking.** *From Computers, 4/E by Long/Long. © Copyright 1996. Reprinted by permission of Prentice-Hall, Inc.*

FIGURE 15.2   **Digital Engineering Printer.** *Courtesy of Océ-USA, Inc., Chicago, IL.*

■ 15.4 DIAZO-MOIST PRINTS

A black-and-white print, composed of nearly black lines on a white background, may be made from ordinary pencil or ink tracings by exposure in the same manner as for blueprints, directly on special blackprint paper, cloth, or film.

Exposure may be made in a blueprint machine or any machine using light in a similar way. However, the prints are not washed as in blueprinting, but must be fed through a special developer that dampens the coated side of the paper with a developing solution.

Colored-line prints in red, brown, or blue lines on white backgrounds may be made on the same machine simply by using the appropriate paper in each case. These prints, together with diazo-dry prints, §15.5, are still used today, put recent improvements in digital printing has made that the most common form of outputting today.

■ 15.5 THE DIAZO-DRY PROCESS

The *diazo-dry* process is based on the sensitivity to light of certain dyestuff intermediates that have the characteristic of decomposing into colorless substances if exposed to ultraviolet light, and of reacting with coupling components to form an azo dyestuff upon exposure to ammonia vapors. It is a contact method of reproduction, and depends on the transmission of light through the original for the reproduction of positive prints. The subject matter may be pen or pencil lines, typewritten or printed matter, or any opaque image. There is no negative step involved; positives are used to obtain positive prints. Sensitized materials can be handled under normal illumination.

The diazo whiteprint method of reproduction consists of two simple steps—exposure and dry development by means of ammonia vapors. Exposure is made in a printer equipped with a source of ultraviolet light, a mercury vapor lamp, fluorescent lamp, or carbon arc. The light emitted by these light sources brings about a

FIGURE 15.3 **Diazit Omnitrac EFP Model Machine.** *Courtesy of Diazit Company, Inc.*

photochemical decomposition of the light-sensitive yellow coating of the paper except in those places where the surface is protected by the opaque lines of the original. The exposed print is developed dry in a few seconds in a dry-developing machine by the alkaline medium produced by ammonia vapors.

A popular combination printer (exposer) and developer, Diazit Omnitrac printer, is shown in Fig. 15.3. The tracing and the sensitized paper are fed into the machine, and when they emerge, the print is practically dry and ready for use.

Another exposer and developer combined in one machine is the Ozalid Whiteprinter. Two operations are involved: (1) the tracing and the sensitized paper are fed into the printer slot for exposure to light, as shown in Fig. 15.4 (a), and (2) the paper is then fed through the developer slot for exposure to ammonia vapors, as shown at (b). If it is desired to remove the ammonia odor completely, the print is then fed through the printer with the back of the sheet next to the warm glass surrounding the light.

■ 15.6 XEROGRAPHY

Xerox prints are positive prints with black lines on a white background (Fig. 15.5). A selenium-coated and electrostatically charged plate is used. A special camera is used to project the original onto the plate; hence, reduced or enlarged reproductions are possible. A negatively charged plastic powder is spread across the

(a) EXPOSURE

(b) AMMONIA DEVELOPMENT

FIGURE 15.4 **Exposure and Development.** *Courtesy of Ozalid Corporation.*

plate and adheres to the positively charged areas of the image. The powder is then transferred to paper by means of a positive electric charge and is baked onto the surface to produce the final print. Full-sized prints

FIGURE 15.5 **Xerox Engineering Document Systems.** *Courtesy of the Xerox Corporation.*

or reductions can be made inexpensively and quickly in the fully automated Xerox or other similar copy machines. The process is dry and sensitive to all types of copy. The Xerox process is used also to produce mats for the Multilith offset duplicating method, §15.12.

Recent application of xerography includes volume print making from original drawings or microfilms, §15.16.

■ 15.7 FAX TECHNOLOGY

Telecopiers, also called facsimile or fax machines, Fig. 15.10, can receive or send documents (usually $8\frac{1}{2}'' \times 11''$) over standard telephone lines in the office or in the field. Most fax machines can transmit data at 9,600 bits per second (bps). After the telephone circuit is established, the document is fed into the sending machine. The copy is read and translated into signals for the receiving machine, which reproduces the document. A computer can send and receive documents directly, generally as a raster or bitmap type image, avoiding the need for a paper copy of the drawing.

■ 15.8 DIGITAL IMAGE PROCESSING

Modern digital techniques have made possible the direct production of drawings on a laser printer from a variety of input sources, including computers and electronic video equipment.

In addition to drawings produced with the assistance of a CAD program, Chapter 2, conventional hand-produced drawings may be stored in computer memory through the use of digital scanning techniques or by manually digitizing the drawing. Also, color laser copiers can reproduce drawings in four colors, with black lettering (Fig. 15.6), and some are available with optional built-in computer processing unit and monitor, video player, and film projector to permit convenient viewing and editing of drawings.

■ 15.9 RECORDABLE CD-ROM STORAGE SYSTEMS

Recordable CD-ROM systems (Fig. 15.7) let you store digital information such as CAD drawings, digital audio and video, data, multimedia projects, and other digitally stored records. Write-once-read-many (WORM) CD-ROM storage devices provide excellent storage for CAD documentation. Once the CD has been written it cannot be erased or re-written. The shelf life for storage of the media is at least 100 years, so it qualifies as an archival media for permanent storage. CDs are compact and easy to store, and CD-ROM players are standard equipment on many CAD systems. Another advantage of CD-ROM systems is that they are random access storage systems, so that you can go directly to the document you wish to retrieve, unlike tape systems, which must wind through all of the previous tape. Systems that can automatically retrieve from a selection of multiple CDs, called juke

FIGURE 15.6 **Internal Components of a Xerox Digital Color Production System.** *Courtesy of the Xerox Corporation.*

box systems, are available for quickly retrieving documents in a network storage situation.

■15.10 OPTICAL DISK STORAGE SYSTEMS

Optical disk storage systems, Fig. 15.8, use optical magnetic media to store capacities up to 4.6 GB (gigabytes) on a single removable disk. They are rewritable media. This means that they are not suitable for archival storage of permanent records. However, the fast retrieval speeds of up to 6 MB/sec, which is as fast as most hard drives, low cost per megabyte of storage, thirty year shelf life, and high capacities make them a useful storage system for CAD documentation.

■15.11 DOCUMENT MANAGEMENT SOFTWARE

Specialized software is available to help manage document revision history, approval, storage, file naming, and other issues of managing digital documentation, such as that produced by CAD systems. Automanager Workflow™® is one such software package. In order to have an effective document management system, a lot of planning and setup needs to be done to ensure success. A software package alone will not provide instant success in managing the large number of files and meeting legal requirements for document storage. It requires setup time, training, and on-going effort to make it effective. If you are unsure how long different documents must be retained, ARMA (the American Records Management Association) is a good place to go for information.

■ 15.12 OFFSET PRINTING

The Photolith, Multilith, and Planograph methods are generally known as *offset printing*. A camera is used to reproduce the original, enlarged or reduced if necessary, upon an aluminum or zinc sheet. This master plate is then mounted on a rotary drum that revolves in contact with a rubber roller that picks up the ink from the image and transfers it to the paper. The prints are excellent positive reproductions.

■ 15.13 PHOTOGRAPHIC CONTACT PRINTS

Either transparent or opaque drawings may be reproduced the same size as the original by means of *contact printing*. The original is pressed tightly against a sheet of special photographic paper, either by mechanical spring pressure or by means of suction as in the "vacuum printer." The paper is exposed by the action of the transmitted or reflected light, and the print is developed in the manner of a photograph in a dark or semi-dark room.

Excellent duplicate tracings can be made on paper, on film, and on either opaque map cloth or transparent tracing cloth through this process. Poor pencil drawings or tracings can be duplicated and improved by intensifying the lines so as to be much better than the original. Pencil drawings can be transformed into "ink-line" tracings. Also, by this process, a reproduction can be made directly from an existing print.

■ 15.14 PHOTOSTATS

The Visual Graphics Total Camera II, Fig. 15.9, is essentially a highly specialized camera. It is a completely modular daylight graphic reproduction system that includes a precision black-and-white stat camera with self-contained lighting, automatic focusing and processing, and programmable memory and microprocessor control. Various plug-in modular components are also available for special-purpose photo reproductions, such as enlargements or reductions, line or halftone stats, offset plates, reverses, dropouts, color prints and film transparencies, and other special effects for a multitude of applications.

A photostat print may be the same size or larger or smaller than the original, while photographic

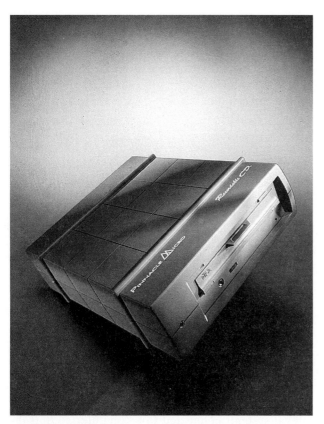

FIGURE 15.7 **This Pinnacle Recordable CD-Rom System is Priced for Market Sales to both the Consumer and Commercial.** *Courtesy of Pinnacle Micro, Inc.*

FIGURE 15.8 **An Affordable Pinnacle Optical Hard Drive and Disk.** *Courtesy of Pinnacle Micro, Inc.*

FIGURE 15.9   Visual Graphics Total Camera II.
Courtesy of Visual Graphics Corporation.

contact prints, §15.13, must be the same size. The original may be transparent or opaque. It is simply fastened in place, the camera is adjusted to obtain the desired type and size of print, and the print is made, developed, and dried in the machine (no darkroom is required). For black-and-white stats, the result is a negative print with white lines on a near-black background. A positive print having near-black lines on a white background is made by photostating the negative print.

■ 15.15 LINE ETCHING

Line etching is a photographic method of reproduction. The drawing, in black lines on white paper or on tracing cloth or film, is placed in a frame behind a glass and photographed. This photographic negative is then mounted on a pane of glass and is printed on a sheet of planished zinc or copper. After the print has been specially treated to render the lines acid resistant, the plate is washed in a nitric acid solution, which eats away the metal between the lines, leaving them standing above the surface of the plate, like type. The plate is then mounted upon a hardwood base, which can be used in any printing press, as are blocks of type.

■ 15.16 MICROFILM AND MICROFICHE

A microfilm is a photographic image of information, records, or drawings that is stored on film at a greatly reduced scale.

Microfilm has come into considerable use, especially where large numbers of drawings are involved, to furnish complete duplication of all drawings in a small filing space. Microfilm makes a good permanent storage media because of its long archival period and its relatively small size. Microfilm also provides duplicate copies for security reasons. Enlargement copies can be made from the film through photographic, electrostatic, or photocopy methods. The films may be 16, 35, or 70 mm and may be produced in rolls, jacketed film, or individually mounted on aperture cards, Fig. 15.10.

The individual cards may be viewed in a reader and, if desired, a full-size print may be had from a reader-printer unit. Many readers use automated retrieval systems connected to a computer so that the operator only has to search for the desired record on the computer screen. Marks are created on the film as it is photographed to allow the computer system to index the exact spot on the film for retrieval.

Since the aperture equipment is essentially a standard data card used for electronic computers, mechanized equipment is capable of sorting, filing, and retrieving the cards. Duplicate aperture cards and reproductions of the drawings to the size desired may be

FIGURE 15.10   A Standard Aperture Card. Courtesy of C. S. Barber.

ORIGINAL DOCUMENT
TRANSMITTED TO STORAGE
VAULT & NOT USED TO
PRODUCE WORKING COPY

AUTOMATIC MICROFILM
PROCESSOR

FILM TO CARD CONVERTER

ENLARGED PRINTS FROM
THE MICROFILM INSERT OR
DUPLICATE PUNCHED CARDS
WITH A MICROFILM INSERT
WILL BE ORDERED THROUGH
THE TELEPHONE SYSTEM BY
DIALING AN IDENTIFICATION
CODE AND THE DOCUMENT
NUMBER

ENGINEERING

PRODUCTION

ACCOUNTING

MANUFACTURING

BANK OF ELECTRONIC
FILES & SORTERS

FLO-FILM CAMERA
CONVERTS DRAWINGS
UP TO 42" WIDE TO
35 MM MICROFILM AT
SPEED OF 40 FT. PER
MIN.

CARD
REPRODUCERS

FILMSORT CARDS,
COMPLETE WITH DRAW
ING, MACHINE OPERA-
TIONS, ROUTING, LABOR
RATES, ETC.

DRAFTER - DESIGNER

DESK READERS
ENGINEERS
DESIGNERS
CUSTOMERS, ETC.

BUILT-IN READERS ON
MACHINE TOOLS

WORKING COPY

COPY-FLOW MACHINE
REPRODUCES MICROFILM INSERT
TO WORKING COPY ON PLAIN
PAPER AT RATE OF 20 FT. PER MIN.

FIGURE 15.11   **A Mechanized Engineering Data Handling System.**
Courtesy of United Technology Center, Sunnyvale, CA.

produced on specialized equipment. A typical mechanized engineering data handling system is shown in Fig. 15.11.

A *microfiche* is a cardlike film containing many rows of images or records or drawings. Card sizes used for storage are $3'' \times 5''$, $4'' \times 6''$, and $5'' \times 8''$. A typical $4'' \times 6''$ microfiche will contain the equivalent of 270 pages of information. The individual cards may be viewed on a reader and, if desired, a full-size copy may be made by using a reader-printer (Fig. 15.12).

Computer-output microfilm (COM) refers to a process used to produce drawings and records on microfilm, with the aid of a computer. A COM unit will produce a microfilm from database information converted to an image on a high-resolution screen that is then photographed. The main advantages of COM are storage capability and speed.

FIGURE 15.12   **Microfilm Reader-Printer.** *Courtesy of 3M Co.*

■ KEY WORDS

BLUEPRINT	DIGITAL IMAGING
DIAZO	OFFSET PRINTING
OPTICAL DISK STORAGE	MICROFILM
WORM	MICROFICHE
XEROGRAPHY	PHOTOSTAT

■ CHAPTER SUMMARY

- Technical drawings are detailed and often very expensive to create. It is important to undertand how to reproduce and manage them safely.

- Past management systems involved physically filing drawings. Most new systems now archive and distribute electronically.

- The blueprint, Diazo-Moist and Diazo-Dry processes of reproduction are older but still used in many companies.

- Xerography, Fax Technology and Digital Image Processing are processes now commonly used which allow great flexibility in control of the drawing.

- Microfilm and Microfiche methods store information on a greatly reduced scale and allow for large numbers of drawings to be stored in a small space.

- Digital printers have become the most widely used output devices in the engineering industry.

■ REVIEW QUESTIONS

1. How do the Diazo-Dry and the Diazo-Moist processes differ?

2. What are some of the benefits and the dangers of using an electronic system to transfer and archive drawings?

3. Explain how CD-ROMs are used in the field of Technical Drawing.

4. Explain how the Xerography process works.

5. Describe how your class archives and manages its drawings?

6. What are some advantages to using digital printers versus other output devices?

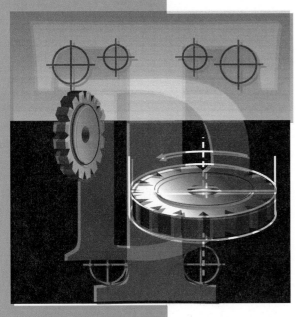

C H A P T E R   1 6

AXONOMETRIC PROJECTION

OBJECTIVES

After studying the material in this chapter, you should be able to:

1. Describe the differences between multiview projection, axonometric projection, oblique projection, and perspective.

2. Sketch examples of an isometric cube, a dimetric cube, and a trimetric cube.

3. List the advantages of multiview projection, axonometric projection, oblique projection, and perspective.

4. Create an isometric drawing given a multiview drawing.

5. Measure along each isometric axis.

6. Draw inclined and oblique surfaces in isometric.

7. Draw angles, ellipses, and irregular curves in isometric.

OVERVIEW

As described in Chapter 6, multiview drawing makes it possible to represent accurately the most complex forms of a design by showing a series of exterior views and sections. This type of representation has two limitations, however: Its execution requires a thorough understanding of the principles of multiview projection, and its reading requires a definite exercise of the constructive imagination. Although multiview drawings are common in most technical drawings, they do not show length, width, and height in a silngle view.

For communication of design ideas, it is often necessary to prepare accurate and scientifically correct than can be easily understood by persons without technical training. **Axonometric projection** rotates the object with respect to the observer so that all three dimensions can be seen in one view, approximately as they appear to an observer. These projections are often called *pictorial drawings* [ANSI/ASME Y14.4M–1989 (R1994)] because they look more like a picture than multiview drawings. Since pictorial drawing shows only the appearance of an object, it is not satisfactory for completely describing complex or detailed forms.

Various types of pictorial drawing are used extensively in catalogs, sales literature, and technical work to supplement and amplify multiview drawings. For example, pictorial drawing is used in Patent Office drawings; in piping diagrams; in machine, structural, and architectural designs; and in furniture design.

The most common axonometric projection is *isometric*, which means "equal measure." When a cube is drawn in isometric, the axes are equally spaced (120° apart). Though not as photorealistic as perspective drawings, isometric drawings are much easier to draw. CAD software is particularly effective at creating isometric drawings, which are often called 3D models. Dimetric and trimetric are more realistic than isometric but are much harder to draw and are therefore used less frequently in engineering work.

■ 16.1 METHODS OF PROJECTION

The four principal types of projection are illustrated in Fig. 16.1, and all except the regular multiview projection (Fig. 16.1a) are pictorial types since they show several sides of the object in a single view. In all cases, the views, or projections, are formed by the piercing points in the plane of projection of an infinite number of visual rays of projectors.

In both multiview projection and *axonometric projection* (Fig. 16.1b), the observer is considered to be at infinity, and the visual rays are parallel to each other and perpendicular to the plane of projection. Therefore, both are classified as *orthographic projections* (§1.10).

In *oblique projection* (Fig. 16.1c), the observer is considered to be at infinity, and the visual rays are parallel to each other but oblique to the plane of projection (see Chapter 17).

In *perspective* (Fig. 16.1d), the observer is considered to be at a finite distance from the object, and the visual rays extend form the observer's eye, or station point (SP), to all points of the object to form a "cone of rays" (see Chapter 18).

■ 16.2 TYPES OF AXONOMETRIC PROJECTION

The distinguishing feature of axonometric projection, as compared to multiview projection, is the inclined position of the object with respect to the plane of projection. Since the principal edges and surfaces of the object are inclined to the plane of projection, the lengths of the lines, the sizes of the angles, and the general proportions of the object vary with the infinite number of possible positions in which the object may be placed with respect to the plane of projection. Three of these are shown in Fig. 16.2.

In these cases the edges of the cube are inclined to the plane of projection and are therefore foreshortened (see Fig. 6.20c). The degree of foreshortening of any line depends on its angle with the plane of projection; the greater the angle, the greater the foreshortening. If the degree of foreshortening is determined for each of the three edges of the cube that meet at one corner, scales can be easily constructed for measuring along these edges or any other edges parallel to them (see Figs. 16.41a and 16.46).

It is customary to consider three edges of the cube that meet at the corner nearest the observer as the *axonometric axes*. In Fig. 16.1b, the axonometric axes, or simply the *axes*, are OA, OB, and OC. As shown in Fig. 16.2, axonometric projections are classified as (a) isometric projection, (b) dimetric projection, and (c) trimetric projection, depending on the number of scales of reduction required.

FIGURE 16.1   Four Types of Projection.

FIGURE 16.2   Axonometric Projections.

ISOMETRIC PROJECTION

■ 16.3 THE ISOMETRIC METHOD OF PROJECTION

An **isometric projection** as one in which all angles between the axonometric axes are equal. To produce an isometric projection (again, isometric means "equal measure"), it is necessary to place the object so that its principal edges, or axes, make equal angles with the plane of projection and are therefore foreshortened equally (see Fig. 5.21). In this position the edges of a cube would be projected equally and would

Isometric projection of cube

Diagonal of cube

Isometric projection of cube

Diagonal projects as a point

Diagonal of cube

Isometric projection of cube

Diagonal of cube

35° 16′

(a)
THREE VIEWS
OF A CUBE

(b)
ISOMETRIC PROJECTION BY
REVOLUTION AND AN AUXILIARY VIEW

(c)
ISOMETRIC OBTAINED
BY REVOLUTION

FIGURE 16.3   Isometric Projection.

make equal angles with each other (120°), as shown in Fig. 16.2a.

Figure 16.3a shows a multiview drawing of a cube. In Fig. 16.3b, the cube is shown revolved through 45° about an imaginary vertical axis. Now an auxiliary view in the direction of the arrow will show the cube diagonal ZW as a point, and the cube appears as a true isometric projection. The cube may be further revolved (Fig. 16.3c). This time the cube is titled forward about an imaginary horizontal axis until the three edges OX, OY, and OZ make equal angles with the frontal plane of projection and are therefore foreshortened equally. Here again, a diagonal of the cube, in this case OT, appears as a point in the isometric view. The front view thus obtained is a true isometric projection. In this projection the 12 edges of the cube make angles of about 35° 16′ with the frontal plane of projection. The lengths of their projections are equal to the lengths of the edges multiplied by $\sqrt{\frac{2}{3}}$, or by 0.816, approximately. Thus the projected lengths are about 80% of the true lengths, or still more roughly, about three fourths of the true lengths. The projections of the axes OX, OY, and OZ make angles of 120° with each other and are called the *isometric axes*. Any line parallel to one of these is called a *nonisometric line*. The angles in the isometric projection of the cube are either 120° or 60°, and all are projections of 90° angles. In an isometric projection of a cube, the faces of the cube, and any planes parallel to them, are called *isometric planes*.

■ 16.4 THE ISOMETRIC SCALE

A correct isometric projection may be drawn with the use of a special isometric scale, prepared on a strip of paper or cardboard (Fig. 16.4). All distances in the isometric scale are $\sqrt{\frac{2}{3}}$ times true size, or approximately 80% of true size. The use of the isometric scale is illustrated in Fig. 16.5a. A scale of 9″ = 1′–0, or $\frac{3}{4}$-size scale (or metric equivalent), could be used to approximate the isometric scale.

■ 16.5 ISOMETRIC DRAWING

When a drawing is prepared with an isometric scale, or when the object is actually *projected* on a plane of projection, it is an *isometric projection* (Fig. 16.5a). When a drawing is prepared with an ordinary scale, it is an *isometric drawing* (Fig. 16.5b). The isometric drawing is

FIGURE 16.4   Isometric Scale.

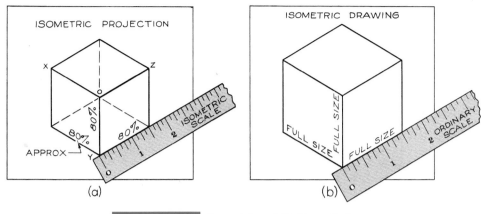

FIGURE 16.5 **Isometric and Ordinary Scales.**

about 25% larger than the isometric projection, but the pictorial value is obviously the same in both.

Since the isometric projection is foreshortened and an isometric drawing is full-scale size, it is usually advantageous to make an isometric drawing rather than an isometric projection. The drawing is much easier to execute and, for all practical purposes, is just as satisfactory as the isometric projection.

■ 16.6 MAKING AN ISOMETRIC DRAWING

The construction of an isometric drawing of an object composed only of normal surfaces (§6.19) is illustrated in Fig. 16.6. Notice that all measurements are made parallel to the main edges of the enclosing box—that is, parallel to the isometric axes. No measurement along a diagonal (nonisometric line) on any surface or through the object can be set off directly with the scale. The object may be drawn in the same position by beginning at the corner Y, or any other corner, instead of at the corner X.

The construction of an isometric drawing of an object composed partly of inclined surfaces (and oblique edges) is shown in Fig. 16.7. Notice that inclined surfaces are located by *offset*, or *coordinate*, *measurements* along the isometric lines. For example, dimensions E and F are set off to locate the inclined surface M, and dimensions A and B are used to locate surface N.

Sketching in isometric is discussed in §§5.11–5.13.

■ 16.7 OBLIQUE SURFACES IN ISOMETRIC

Oblique surfaces in isometric may be drawn by establishing the intersections of the oblique surface with the isometric planes. For example, in Fig. 16.8a, the oblique plane is known to contain points A, B, and C. To establish the plane (Fig. 16.8b), line AB is extended to X and Y, points that are in the same isometric planes as C. Lines XC and YC locate points E and F. Finally, AD and ED are drawn, using the rule of parallelism of lines. The completed drawing is shown in Fig. 16.8c.

■ 16.8 OTHER POSITIONS OF THE ISOMETRIC AXES

The isometric axes may be placed in any desired position according to the requirements of the problem (Fig. 16.9), but the angle between the axes must remain 120°. The choice of the directions of the axes is determined by the position from which the object is usually viewed (Fig. 16.10), or by the position that best describes the shape of the object. If possible, both requirements should be met.

If the object is characterized by considerable length, the long axis may be placed horizontally for best effect (Fig. 16.11).

■ 16.9 OFFSET LOCATION MEASUREMENTS

The method of locating one point with respect to another is illustrated in Figs. 16.12 and 16.13. In each

FIGURE 16.6   **Isometric Drawing of Normal Surfaces.**

FIGURE 16.7   **Inclined Surfaces in Isometric.**

case, after the main block has been drawn, the offset lines CA and BA in the multiview drawing are drawn full size in the isometric drawing, thus locating corner A of the small block or rectangular recess. These measurements are called *offset measurements*, and since they are parallel to certain edges of the main block in the multiview drawings, they will be parallel, respec-

tively, to the same edges in the isometric drawings (see §6.25).

■ 16.10 HIDDEN LINES

The use of hidden lines in isometric drawing is governed by the same rule as in all other types of projec-

FIGURE 16.8 Oblique Surfaces in Isometric.

FIGURE 16.9 Positions of Isometric Axes.

(a) CORRECT   (b) INCORRECT

FIGURE 16.10 An Object Naturally Viewed from Below.

FIGURE 16.11 Long Axis Horizontal.

FIGURE 16.12 Offset Location Measurements.

FIGURE 16.13 Offset Location Measurements.

16.11 CENTER LINES

The use of center lines in isometric drawing is governed by the same rules as in the multiview drawing: *Center lines are drawn if they are needed to indicate symmetry or if they are needed for dimensioning* (Fig. 16.14). In general, center lines should be used sparingly and omitted in cases of doubt. The use of too many

tion: *Hidden lines are omitted unless they are needed to make the drawing clear.* Figure 16.14 shows a case in which hidden lines are needed because a projecting part cannot be clearly shown without them.

FIGURE 16.14   **Use of Hidden Lines.**

center lines may produce a confusion of lines. Examples in which center lines are not needed are shown in Figs. 16.10 and 16.11. Examples in which they are needed are seen in Figs. 16.14 and 16.39a.

◼ 16.12 BOX CONSTRUCTION

Objects of rectangular shape may be more easily drawn by means of *box construction*, which consists simply in imagining the object to be enclosed in a rectangular box whose sides coincide with the main faces of the object. For example, the object shown in two views (Fig. 16.15) is imagined to be enclosed in a construction box. This box is then drawn lightly with con-

struction lines (Fig. 16.15I), the irregular features are then constructed (Fig. 16.15II), and finally, the required lines are made heavy (Fig. 16.15III).

◼ 16.13 NONISOMETRIC LINES

Since the only lines of an object that are drawn true length in an isometric drawing are the isometric axes or lines parallel to them, nonisometric lines cannot be set off directly with the scale. For example, in Fig. 16.16a, the inclined lines BA and CA are shown in their true lengths (54 mm) in the top view, but since they are not parallel to the isometric axes, they are not true length in the isometric. Such lines are drawn in isometric by means of box construction and offset measurements. First, as shown in Fig. 16.16b, the measurements 44 mm, 18 mm, and 22 mm can be set off directly since they are made along isometric lines. The nonisometric 54 mm dimension cannot be set off directly, but if one half of the given top view is constructed full size to scale (Fig. 16.16I), the dimension X can be determined. This dimension is parallel to an isometric axis and can be transferred with dividers to the isometric (Fig. 16.16II). The dimensions 24 mm and 9 mm are parallel to isometric lines and can be set off directly (Fig. 16.16III).

FIGURE 16.15   **Box Construction.**

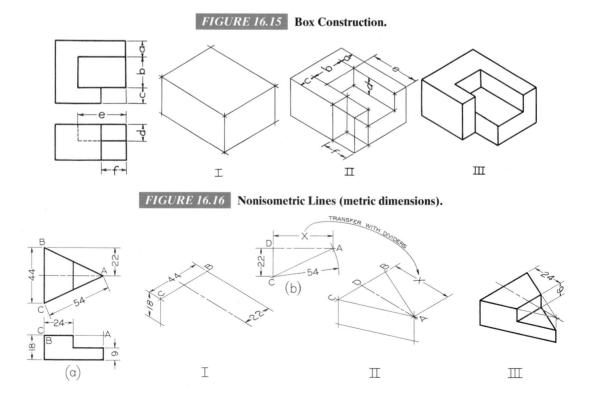

FIGURE 16.16   **Nonisometric Lines (metric dimensions).**

FIGURE 16.8   **Oblique Surfaces in Isometric.**

FIGURE 16.9   **Positions of Isometric Axes.**

FIGURE 16.10   **An Object Naturally Viewed from Below.**

FIGURE 16.11   **Long Axis Horizontal.**

FIGURE 16.12   **Offset Location Measurements.**

FIGURE 16.13   **Offset Location Measurements.**

tion: *Hidden lines are omitted unless they are needed to make the drawing clear.* Figure 16.14 shows a case in which hidden lines are needed because a projecting part cannot be clearly shown without them.

■ 16.11 CENTER LINES

The use of center lines in isometric drawing is governed by the same rules as in the multiview drawing: *Center lines are drawn if they are needed to indicate symmetry or if they are needed for dimensioning* (Fig. 16.14). In general, center lines should be used sparingly and omitted in cases of doubt. The use of too many

FIGURE 16.14   Use of Hidden Lines.

center lines may produce a confusion of lines. Examples in which center lines are not needed are shown in Figs. 16.10 and 16.11. Examples in which they are needed are seen in Figs. 16.14 and 16.39a.

■ 16.12 BOX CONSTRUCTION

Objects of rectangular shape may be more easily drawn by means of *box construction*, which consists simply in imagining the object to be enclosed in a rectangular box whose sides coincide with the main faces of the object. For example, the object shown in two views (Fig. 16.15) is imagined to be enclosed in a construction box. This box is then drawn lightly with con-

struction lines (Fig. 16.15I), the irregular features are then constructed (Fig. 16.15II), and finally, the required lines are made heavy (Fig. 16.15III).

■ 16.13 NONISOMETRIC LINES

Since the only lines of an object that are drawn true length in an isometric drawing are the isometric axes or lines parallel to them, nonisometric lines cannot be set off directly with the scale. For example, in Fig. 16.16a, the inclined lines BA and CA are shown in their true lengths (54 mm) in the top view, but since they are not parallel to the isometric axes, they are not true length in the isometric. Such lines are drawn in isometric by means of box construction and offset measurements. First, as shown in Fig. 16.16b, the measurements 44 mm, 18 mm, and 22 mm can be set off directly since they are made along isometric lines. The nonisometric 54 mm dimension cannot be set off directly, but if one half of the given top view is constructed full size to scale (Fig. 16.16I), the dimension X can be determined. This dimension is parallel to an isometric axis and can be transferred with dividers to the isometric (Fig. 16.16II). The dimensions 24 mm and 9 mm are parallel to isometric lines and can be set off directly (Fig. 16.16III).

FIGURE 16.15   Box Construction.

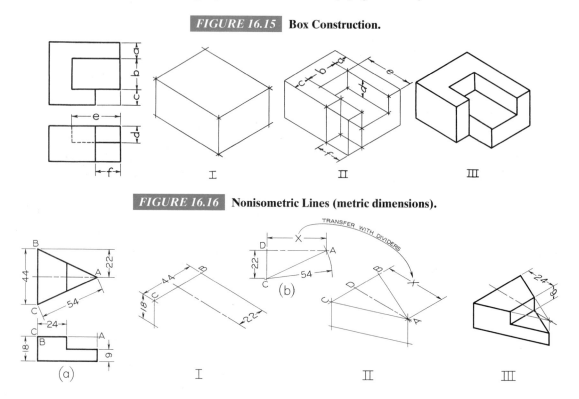

FIGURE 16.16   Nonisometric Lines (metric dimensions).

To realize the fact that nonisometric lines will not be true length in the isometric drawing, set your dividers on BA in (II) and then compare with BA on the given top view in Fig. 16.16a. Do the same for line CA. It will be seen that BA is shorter and CA is longer in the isometric than the corresponding lines in the given views.

■ 16.14 ANGLES IN ISOMETRIC

As shown in §6.26, angles project true size only when the plane of the angle is parallel to the plane of projection. An angle may project larger or smaller than true size, depending on its position. Since in isometric the various surfaces of the object are usually inclined to the plane of projection, it follows that angles generally will not be projected true size. For example, in the multiview drawing in Fig. 16.17a, none of the three 60° angles will be 60° in the isometric drawing. To realize this fact, measure each angle in the isometric in Fig. 16.17II with the protractor and note the number of degrees compared to the true 60°. No two angles are the same; two are smaller and one is larger than 60°.

As shown in Fig. 16.17I, the enclosing box can be drawn from the given dimensions, except for dimen-

sion X, which is not given. To find dimension X, draw triangle BDA from the top view full size, as shown in Fig. 16.17b. Transfer dimension X to the isometric in (I) to complete the enclosing box.

To locate point A in Fig. 16.17II, dimension Y must be used, but this is not given in the top view (Fig. 16.17a). Dimension Y is found by the same construction (Fig. 16.17b) and then transferred to the isometric, as shown. The completed isometric is shown in Fig. 16.17III, where point E is located by using dimension K, as shown.

A regular protractor cannot be used to set off angles in isometric.[*] *Angular measurements must be converted to linear measurements along isometric lines.*

Figure 16.18a shows two views of an object to be drawn in isometric. Point A can easily be located in the isometric by measuring .88″ down from point O (Fig. 16.18I). However, in the given drawing, the location of point B depends on the 30° angle, and to locate B in the isometric linear dimension X must be known. This distance can be found graphically by drawing the right triangle BOA attached to the isometric, as shown. The

[*] Isometric protractors for setting off angles on isometric surfaces are available from drafting supplies dealers.

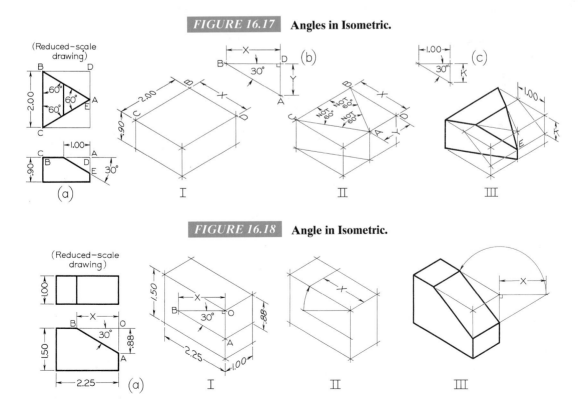

FIGURE 16.17   **Angles in Isometric.**

FIGURE 16.18   **Angle in Isometric.**

distance X is then transferred to the isometric with the compass or dividers (Fig. 16.18II). Actually, the triangle could be attached in several different positions. One of these is shown in Fig. 16.18III.

When angles are given in degrees, it is necessary to convert the angular measurements into linear measurements. This is best done by drawing a right triangle separately, as in Fig. 16.17b, or attached to the isometric (Fig. 16.18).

16.15 IRREGULAR OBJECTS

If the general shape of an object does not conform somewhat to a rectangular pattern (Fig. 16.19), it may be drawn using the box construction discussed previously (Fig. 16.19a). Various points of the triangular base are located by means of offsets a and b along the edges of the bottom of the construction box. The vertex is located by means of offsets OA and OB on the top of the construction box.

However, it is not necessary to draw the complete construction box. If only the bottom of the box is drawn (Fig. 16.19b), the triangular base can be constructed as before. The orthographic projection of the vertex O′ on the base can then be located by offsets O′A and O′B, as shown, and from this point, the vertical line O′O can be erected, using measurement C.

An irregular object may be drawn by means of a series of sections. The edge views of a series of imaginary cutting planes are shown in the top and front views of the multiview drawing in Fig. 16.20a. In Fig. 16.20I, the various sections are constructed in isometric, and in Fig. 16.20II, the object is completed by drawing lines through the corners of the sections. In the isometric in Fig. 16.20I, all height dimensions are taken from the front view in Fig. 16.20a, and all depth dimensions from the top view.

16.16 CURVES IN ISOMETRIC

Curves may be drawn in isometric by means of a series of offset measurements similar to those discussed in §16.9. In Fig. 16.21 any desired number of points, such as A, B, and C, are selected at random along the curve in the given top view in Fig. 16.21a. Enough points should be chosen to fix accurately the path of the curve; the more points used, the greater the accuracy. Offset grid lines are then drawn from each point parallel to the isometric axes.

Offset measurements a and b are laid off in the isometric to locate point A on the curve (Fig. 16.21I). Points B, C, and D are located in a similar manner (Fig. 16.21II). A light freehand curve is sketched smoothly through the points (Fig. 16.21III). Points A′, B′, C′,

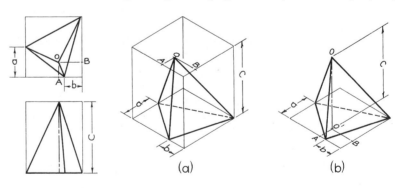

FIGURE 16.19 **Irregular Object in Isometric.**

(a)   (b)

FIGURE 16.20 **Use of Sections in Isometric.**

(a)   I   II

FIGURE 16.21   Curves in Isometric.

and D′ are located directly under points A, B, C, and D by drawing vertical lines downward, making all equal to dimension c, the height of the block (Fig. 16.21IV). A light freehand curve is then drawn through the points. The final curve is heavied in with the aid of the irregular curve, and all straight lines are darkened to complete the isometric (Fig. 16.21V).

■ 16.17 TRUE ELLIPSES IN ISOMETRIC

As shown in §§4.48, 5.12, and 6.30, if a circle lies in a plane that is not parallel to the plane of projection, the circle will be projected as a true ellipse. The ellipse can be constructed by the method of offsets (§16.16). As shown in Fig. 16.22a, draw parallel lines spaced at random across the circle; then transfer these lines to the isometric with the aid of the dividers (Fig. 16.22b). To

locate points in the lower ellipse, transfer points of the upper ellipse down a distance equal to the height d of the block and draw the ellipse, part of which will be hidden, through these points. Draw the final ellipses with the aid of the irregular curve.

A variation of the method of offsets, which provides eight points on the ellipse, is illustrated in Figs. 16.22c and 16.22d. If more points are desired, parallel lines, as in Fig. 16.22a, can be added. As shown in Fig. 16.22c, circumscribe a square around the given circle, and draw diagonals. Through the points of intersection of the diagonals and the circle, draw another square, as shown. Draw this construction in the isometric, as shown in Fig. 16.22d, transferring distances a and b with the dividers.

A similar method that provides 12 points on the ellipse is shown in Fig. 16.22e. The given circle is divided

FIGURE 16.22   True Isometric Ellipse Construction.

into 12 equal parts, using the 30° × 60° triangle. Lines parallel to the sides of the square are drawn through these points. The entire construction is then drawn in isometric, and the ellipse is drawn through the points of intersection.

When the center lines shown in the top view in Fig. 16.22a are drawn in isometric (Fig. 16.22b), they become the conjugate diameters of the ellipse. The ellipse can then be constructed on the conjugate diameters by the methods of Figs. 4.51 and 4.52b.

When the 45° diagonals (Fig. 16.22c) are drawn in isometric (Fig. 16.22d), they coincide with the major and minor axes of the ellipse, respectively. Note that the minor axis is equal in length to the sides of the inscribed square in Fig. 16.22c. The ellipse can be constructed on the major and minor axes by any of the methods in §§4.45 and 4.48.

Remember the rule: *The major axis of the ellipse is always at right angles to the center line of the cylinder, and the minor axis is at right angles to the major axis and coincides with the center line.*

Accurate ellipses may be drawn with the aid of ellipse guides (§§4.53 and 16.21) or with a special *ellipsograph.*

If the curve lies in a nonisometric plane, not all offset measurements can be applied directly. For example, in Fig. 16.23a, the elliptical face shown in the auxiliary view lies in an inclined nonisometric plane. The cylinder is enclosed in a construction box, and the box is then drawn in isometric (Fig. 16.23I). The base is drawn by the method of offsets, as shown in Fig. 16.22. The inclined ellipse is constructed by locating a

number of points on the ellipse in the isometric and drawing the final curve by means of the irregular curve.

Measurements a, b, c, and so on are parallel to an isometric axis and can be set off in the isometric on each side of the center line X–X (Fig. 16.23I). Measurements e, f, g, and so on are not parallel to any isometric axis and cannot be set off directly in isometric. However, when these measurements are projected to the front view and down to the base (Fig. 16.23a), they can then be set off along the lower edge of the construction box, as shown in (I). The completed isometric is shown in (II).

The ellipse may also be drawn with the aid of an appropriate ellipse template selected to fit the major and minor axes established along X–X and Y–Y, respectively.

■ 16.18 APPROXIMATE FOUR-CENTER ELLIPSE

An approximate ellipse is sufficiently accurate for nearly all isometric drawings. The method commonly used, called the *four-center ellipse,* is illustrated in Figs. 16.24 to 16.26. It can be used only for ellipses in isometric planes.

To apply this method (Fig. 16.24), draw, or conceive to be drawn, a square around the given circle in the multiview drawing; then do the following:

I. Draw the isometric of the square, which is an equilateral parallelogram whose sides are equal to the diameter of the circle (Fig. 16.24I).

FIGURE 16.23   **Ellipse in Inclined Plane.**

FIGURE 16.24 Steps in Drawing Four-Center Ellipse.

FIGURE 16.25 Isometric Drawing of a Bearing.

II. Erect perpendicular bisectors to each side, using the 30° × 60° triangle (Fig. 16.24II). These perpendiculars will intersect at four points, which will be centers for the four circular arcs.

III. Draw the two large arcs, with radius R, from the intersections of the perpendiculars in the two closest corners of the parallelogram (Fig. 16.24III).

IV. Draw the two small arcs, with radius r, from the intersections of the perpendiculars within the parallelogram, to complete the ellipse (Fig. 16.24IV). As a check on the accurate location of these centers, a long diagonal of the parallelogram may be drawn, as shown. The midpoints of the sides of the parallelogram are points of tangency for the four arcs.

A typical drawing with cylindrical shapes is illustrated in Fig. 16.25. Note that the centers of the larger ellipse cannot be used for the smaller ellipse, though the ellipses represent concentric circles. Each ellipse has its own parallelogram and its own centers. Observe also that the centers of the lower ellipse are obtained by projecting the centers of the upper large

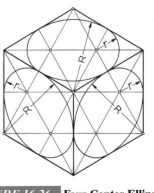

FIGURE 16.26 Four-Center Ellipses.

ellipse down a distance equal to the height of the cylinder.

The construction of the four-center ellipse on the three visible faces of a cube is shown in Fig. 16.26, a study of which shows that all diagonals are horizontal or 60° with horizontal; hence, the entire construction is made with the T-square and 30° × 60° triangle.

Actually, the four-center ellipse deviates considerably from the true ellipse. As shown in Fig. 16.27a, the

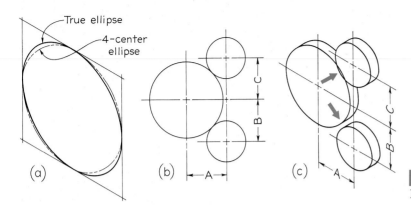

(a)   (b)   (c)

FIGURE 16.27   Faults of Four-Center Ellipse.

four-center ellipse is somewhat shorter and "fatter" than the true ellipse. In constructions where tangencies or intersections with the four-center ellipse occur in the zones of error, the four-center ellipse is unsatisfactory (Figs. 16.27b and 16.27c).

For a much closer approximation to the true ellipse, the Orth four-center ellipse (Fig. 16.28), which requires only one more step than the regular four-center ellipse, will be found sufficiently accurate for almost any problem.

When it is more convenient to start with the isometric center lines of a hole or cylinder in drawing the ellipse, rather than the enclosing parallelogram, the *alternate four-center ellipse* is recommended (Fig. 16.29).

A completely constructed ellipse is shown in Fig. 16.29a, and the steps followed are shown in Figs. 16.29b to 16.29d.

1.   Draw the isometric center lines (Fig. 16.29I). From the center, draw a construction circle equal to the actual diameter of the hole or cylinder. The circle will intersect the center lines at four points A, B, C, and D.

2.   From the two intersection points on one center line, erect perpendiculars to the other center line (Fig. 16.29II); then from the two intersection points on the other center line, erect perpendiculars to the first center line.

FIGURE 16.28   **Orth Four-Center Ellipse.** *Courtesy of Professor H. D. Orth.*

I   II   III   IV

FIGURE 16.29   **Alternate Four-Center Ellipse.**

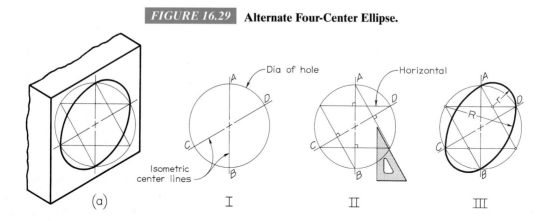

(a)   I   II   III

3. With the intersections of the perpendiculars as centers, draw two small arcs and two large arcs (Fig. 16.29III).

NOTE   The preceding steps are exactly the same as for the regular four-center ellipse of Fig. 16.24 except for the use of the isometric center lines instead of the enclosing parallelogram.

■ 16.19   SCREW THREADS IN ISOMETRIC

Parallel partial ellipses spaced equal to the symbolic thread pitch (Fig. 13.9a) are used to represent the crests only of a screw thread in isometric (Fig. 16.30). The ellipses may be drawn by the four-center method of §16.18, or with the ellipse template, which is much more convenient.

■ 16.20   ARCS IN ISOMETRICS

The four-center ellipse construction is used in drawing circular arcs in isometric. Figure 16.31a shows the complete construction. However, it is not necessary to draw the complete constructions for arcs, as shown in Figs. 16.31b and 16.31c. In each case the radius R is set off from the construction corner; then at each point, perpendiculars to the lines are erected, and their intersection is the center of the arc. Note that the R distances are equal in Figs. 16.31b and 16.31c, but that the actual radii used are quite different.

If a truer elliptic arc is required, the Orth construction (Fig. 16.28) can be used, or a true elliptic arc may be drawn by the method of offsets (§16.17) or with the aid of an ellipse template (§16.21).

■ 16.21   ELLIPSE TEMPLATES

One of the principal time-consuming elements in pictorial drawing is the construction of ellipses. A wide variety of ellipse templates is available for ellipses of various sizes and proportions. They are not available in every possible size, of course, and it may be necessary to "use the fudge factor," such as leaning the pencil or pen when inscribing the ellipse, or shifting the template slightly for drawing each quadrant of the ellipse.

The design of the ellipse template in Fig. 16.32 combines the angles, scales, and ellipses on the same instrument. The ellipses are provided with markings to coincide with the isometric center lines of the holes—a convenient feature in isometric drawing.

■ 16.22   INTERSECTIONS

To draw the elliptical intersection of a cylindrical hole in an oblique plane in isometric (Fig. 16.33a), draw the ellipse in the isometric plane on top of the construction box (Fig. 16.33b); then project points down to the oblique plane as shown. It will be seen that the construction for each point forms a trapezoid, which is produced by a slicing plane parallel to a lateral surface of the block.

FIGURE 16.30   Screw Threads in Isometric.

FIGURE 16.32   Instrumaster Isometric Template.

FIGURE 16.31   Arcs in Isometric.

D = DIAMETER
R = RADIUS

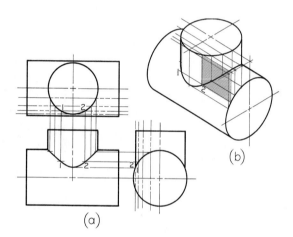

FIGURE 16.33 **Oblique Plane and Cylinder.**

FIGURE 16.34 **Intersection of Cylinders.**

To draw the curve of intersection between two cylinders (Fig. 16.34), pass a series of imaginary cutting planes through the cylinders parallel to their axes, as shown. Each plane will cut elements on both cylinders that intersect at points on the curve of intersection (Fig. 16.33b). As many points should be plotted as necessary to assure a smooth curve. For most accurate work, the ends of the cylinders should be drawn by the Orth construction, with ellipse guides, or by one of the true-ellipse constructions.

■ 16.23 THE SPHERE IN ISOMETRIC

The isometric drawing of any curved surface if evidently the envelope of all lines that can be drawn on that surface. For the sphere, the great circles (circles cut by any plane through the center) may be selected as the lines on the surface. Since all great circles, except those that are perpendicular or parallel to the plane of projection, are shown as ellipses having equal major axes, it follows that their envelope is a circle whose diameter is the major axis of the ellipses.

In Fig. 16.35a, two views of a sphere enclosed in a construction cube are shown. The cube is drawn in (I) together with the isometric of a great circle that lies in a plane parallel to one face of the cube. Actually, the ellipse need not be drawn, for only the points on the diagonal located by measurements a are needed. These points establish the ends of the major axis from which the radius R of the sphere is determined. The resulting drawing shown in (II) is an *isometric drawing*, and its diameter is, therefore, $\sqrt{\frac{3}{2}}$ times the actual diameter of the sphere. The *isometric projection* of the

FIGURE 16.35 **Isometric of a Sphere.**

ISOMETRIC
PROJECTION
OF A SPHERE

sphere is simply a circle whose diameter is equal to the true diameter of the sphere, as shown in (III).

■ 16.24 ISOMETRIC SECTIONING

In drawing objects characterized by open or irregular interior shapes, isometric sectioning is as appropriate as in multiview drawing. An *isometric full section* is shown in Fig. 16.36. In such cases it is usually best to draw the cut surface first and then to draw the portion of the object that lies behind the cutting plane. Other examples of isometric full sections are shown in Figs. 6.92, 7.11b, and 7.12d.

FIGURE 16.36   **Isometric Full Section.**

FIGURE 16.37   **Isometric Half Section.**

An *isometric half section* is shown in Fig. 16.37. The simplest procedure in this case is to make an isometric drawing of the entire object and then the cut surfaces. Since only a quarter of the object is removed in a half section, the resulting pictorial drawing is more useful than full sections in describing both exterior and interior shapes together. Other typical isometric half sections are shown in Figs. 7.13, 7.41, and 7.42.

Isometric broken-out sections are also sometimes used. Examples are shown in Figs. 6.99 and 7.51.

Section lining in isometric drawing is similar to that in multiview drawing. Section lining at an angle of 60° with horizontal (Figs. 16.36 and 16.37) is recommended, but the direction should be changed if at this angle the lines would be parallel to a prominent visible line bounding the cut surface, or to other adjacent lines of the drawing.

■ 16.25 ISOMETRIC DIMENSIONING

Isometric dimensions are similar to ordinary dimensions used on multiview drawings but are expressed in pictorial form. Two methods of dimensioning are approved by ANSI—namely, the pictorial plane (aligned) system and the unidirectional system (Fig. 16.38). Note that vertical lettering is used for either system of dimensioning. Inclined lettering is not recommended for pictorial dimensioning. The method of drawing numerals and arrowheads for the two systems is shown in Figs. 16.38a and 16.38b. For the 64-mm dimension in the aligned system in Fig. 16.38a, the extension lines, dimension lines, and lettering are all drawn in the isometric plane of one face of the object. The "horizontal" guide lines for the lettering are drawn parallel to the dimension line, and the "vertical" guide lines are drawn parallel to the extension lines. The

FIGURE 16.38   **Numerals and Arrowheads in Isometric (metric dimensions).**

(a) ALIGNED   (b) UNIDIRECTIONAL   (c) INCORRECT barbs of the arrowheads should line up parallel to the extension lines.

For the 64-mm dimension in the unidirectional system (Fig. 16.38b), the extension lines and dimension lines are all drawn in the isometric plane of one face of the object, and the barbs of the arrowheads should line up parallel to the extension lines, as in Fig. 16.38a. However, the lettering for the dimensions is vertical and reads from the bottom of the drawing. This simpler system of dimensioning is often used on pictorials for production purposes.

As shown in Fig. 16.38c, the vertical guide lines for the letters should not be perpendicular to the dimension lines. The example in Fig. 16.38c is incorrect because the 64-mm and 32-mm dimensions are lettered neither in the plane of corresponding dimension and extension lines nor in a vertical position to read from the bottom of the drawing. The 20-mm dimension is awkward to read because of its position.

Correct practice in isometric dimensioning using the aligned system of dimensioning is shown in Fig. 16.39a. Incorrect practice is shown in Fig. 16.39b, where the $3\frac{1}{8}''$ dimension runs to a wrong extension line at the right, and consequently the dimension does not lie in an isometric plane. Near the left side, a number of lines cross one another unnecessarily and terminate on the wrong lines. The upper $\frac{1}{2}''$ drill hole is located from the edge of the cylinder when it should be dimensioned from its center line. Study these two drawings carefully to discover additional mistakes in Fig. 16.39b.

The dimensioning methods described apply equally to fractional, decimal, and metric dimensions.

Many examples of isometric dimensioning are given in the problems at the ends of Chapters 6, 7, 8, and 14, and you should study these to find samples of almost any special case you may encounter.

■ 16.26 EXPLODED ASSEMBLIES

Exploded assemblies are often used in design presentations, catalogs, sales literature, and in the shop to show all the parts of an assembly and how they fit together. They may be drawn by any of the pictorial methods, including isometric (Fig. 16.40). Other isometric exploded assemblies are shown in Chapter 14.

■ 16.27 PIPING DIAGRAMS

Isometric and oblique drawings are well suited for representation of piping layouts, as well as for all other structural work to be represented pictorially.

DIMETRIC PROJECTION
■ 16.28 THE DIMETRIC METHOD OF PROJECTION

A **dimetric projection** is an axonometric projection of an object so placed that two of its axes make equal angles with the plane of projection and the third axis makes either a smaller or a greater angle. Hence, the two axes making equal angles with the plane of projection are foreshortened equally, while the third axis is foreshortened in a different ratio.

Generally, the object is so placed that one axis will be projected in a vertical position. However, if the relative positions of the axes have been determined, the

FIGURE 16.39   **Correct and Incorrect Isometric Dimensioning (Aligned System).**

(a)

(b)

FIGURE 16.40 Exploded
Assembly of Power Module for Zero-
Emission Automobiles. *Courtesy of
SDRC, Milford, OH.*

projection may be drawn in any revolved position, as in isometric drawing (see §16.8).

The angles between the projection of the axes must not be confused with the angles which the axes themselves make with the plane projection.

The positions of the axes may be assumed such that any two angles between the axes are equal and over 90°, and the scales are determined graphically, as shown in Fig. 16.41a, in which OP, OL, and OS are the projections of the axes or converging edges of a cube. In this case, angle POS = angle LOS. Lines PL, LS, and SP are the lines of intersection of the plane of projection with the three visible faces of the cube. From descriptive geometry we know that since line LO is perpendicular to the plane POS, in space, its projection LO is perpendicular to PS, the intersection of the plane POS and the plane of projection. Similarly, OP is perpendicular to SL, and OS is perpendicular to PL.

FIGURE 16.41 Dimetric Projection.

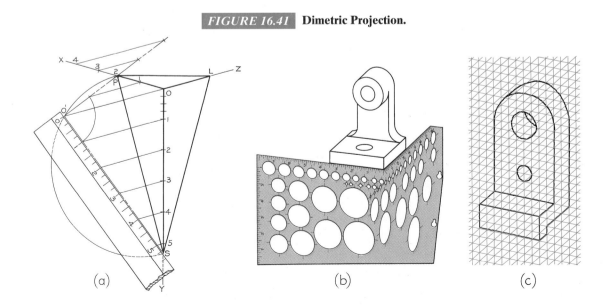

(a)   (b)   (c)

If the triangle POS is revolved about the line PS as an axis into the plane of projection, it will be shown in its true size and shape as PO'S. If regular full-size scales are marked along the lines O'P and O'S, and the triangle is counterrevolved to its original position, the dimetric scales may be laid off on the axes OP and OS, as shown.

To avoid the preparation of special scales, use can be made of available scales on the architects' scale by assuming the scales and calculating the positions of the axes, as follows:

$$\cos a = - \frac{\sqrt{2h^2v^2 - v^4}}{2hv},$$

where a is one of the two equal angles between the projections of the axes, h is one of the two equal scales, and v is the third scale. Examples are shown in the upper row of Fig. 16.42, in which the assumed scales, shown encircled, are taken from the architects' scale. One of these three positions of the axes will be found suitable for almost any practical drawing.

The Instrumaster Dimetric Template (Fig. 16.41b) has angles of approximately 11° and 39° with horizontal, which provides a picture similar to that in Fig. 16.42III. In addition, the template has ellipses corresponding to the axes and accurate scales along the edges. For other information on drawing of ellipses, see §16.32.

The Instrumaster Dimetric Graph paper (Fig. 16.41c) can be used to sketch in dimetrics as easily as to sketch isometrics on isometric paper. The grid lines slope in conformity to the angles on the Dimetric Template in Fig. 16.41b, and when printed on vellum, the grid lines do not reproduce on prints.

■16.29 APPROXIMATE DIMETRIC DRAWING

Approximate dimetric drawings, which closely resemble true dimetrics, can be constructed by substituting for the true angles shown in the upper half of Fig. 16.42 angles that can be obtained with the ordinary triangles and compass, as shown in the lower half of the figure. The resulting drawings will be sufficiently accurate for all practical purposes.

The procedure in preparing an approximate dimetric drawing, using the position in Fig. 16.42VI, is shown in Fig. 16.43. The offset method of drawing a curve is shown in the figure. Other methods for drawing ellipses are the same as in trimetric drawing (§16.32).

FIGURE 16.42 **Angles of Axes Determined by Assumed Scales.**

FIGURE 16.43 Steps in Dimetric Drawing.

FIGURE 16.44 Steps in Dimetric Sketching.

The steps in making a dimetric sketch, using a position similar to that in Fig. 16.42V, are shown in Fig. 16.44. The two angles are equal. Angles of about 20° with the horizontal will produce the most pleasing effect.

An exploded approximate dimetric drawing of an adding machine is shown in Fig. 16.45. The dimetric axes used are those in Fig. 16.42IV. Pictorials such as this are often used in service manuals.

TRIMETRIC PROJECTION

■ 16.30 THE TRIMETRIC METHOD OF PROJECTION

A **trimetric projection** is an axonometric projection of an object so placed that no two axes make equal angles with the plane of projection. In other words, each of the three axes and the lines parallel to them, respectively, have different ratios of foreshortening when projected to the plane of projection. If the three axes are assumed in any position on paper such that none

of the angles is less than 90°, and if neither an isometric nor a dimetric position is deliberately arranged, the result will be a trimetric projection.

■ 16.31 TRIMETRIC SCALES

Since the three axes are foreshortened differently, three different trimetric scales must be prepared and used. The scales are determined as shown in Fig. 16.46a, the method being the same as explained for the dimetric scales in §16.28. As shown, any two of the three triangular faces can be revolved into the plane of projection to show the true lengths of the three axes. In the revolved position, the regular scale is used to set off inches or fractions thereof. When the axes have been counterrevolved to their original positions, the scales will be correctly foreshortened, as shown. These dimensions should be transferred to the edges of three thin cards and marked OX, OZ, and OY for easy reference.

A special trimetric angle may be prepared from Bristol Board or plastic, as shown in Fig. 17.46b.

G R A P H I C S   S P O T L I G H T

3D Pictorials Aid Designers of Future Electric Cars

They rode on rockets to the moon and proved they can generate enough electricity to power an automobile. But fuel cells are still years away from widespread use in the automobile industry.

Standing in their path are high costs and the problems of a complex technology. Together, these forces ensure large numbers of fuel-cell-powered vehicles will not hit showroom floors for a decade or more.

"There's a lot of serious work going into it, and there's a lot of potential there," says Bernard Robertson, DaimlerChrysler's vice president of engineering technologies. "It's just that the challenges are pretty formidable."

FUEL CELLS POSE THORNY PROBLEMS FOR DESIGN TEAM

A fuel cell uses sophisticated membranes to strip electrons from hydrogen atoms creating a charge imbalance and electrical current. The cell recombines the hydrogen with oxygen to form water vapor. DaimlerChrysler is trying to lead the industry in fuel cells by forming joint ventures with Ford Motor Co. and Ballard Powers Systems, Inc. of Vancouver, British Columbia, a supplier of fuels cell stacks. The goal is to be the first to manufacture complete fuel-cell powertrains for sale in the world market.

The task is daunting. At DaimlerChrysler's fuel-cell development center near Stuttgart, Germany, 900

3D pictorial of Necar 4 fuel-cell-powered car. Such 3D images aid designers in overcoming current design problems.

technical people are devoted exclusively to fuel-cell research. Necar 4, the fourth generation of the center's New Electric Car series of fuel-cell concepts, was unveiled to the public in March 1999. Necar is technically impressive because it crams the entire fuel-cell system in a 6-inch-deep space under the floor, but also illustrated the shortcomings of current fuel-cell technology.

DaimlerChrysler officials admit the vehicle is overweight by more than 600 pounds and is astronomically expensive. A mass-produced fuel cell system would cost $30,000 using today's technology, although Necar 4's hand-built engine is estimated to have cost $350,000. Gasoline engines typically cost $3,000. Specialized hardware is what drives the fuel cell's costs. The largest expense is the row of electricity-conducting bipolar plates in the fuel cell stack. These plates, made from ultra hard carbon-graphite, have dozens of intricate channels that must be individually cut by computer-controlled machine tools. For maximum efficiency, the channels must be machined to the high tolerance usually reserved for jet engine turbines.

CAD HELPS DESIGNER SEE POSSIBILITIES

With all of this precision machining involved, the engineers at DaimlerChrsyler have been assigned two separate tasks: (1) develop a fuel cell that is small and light enough to meet size and weight restrictions; and (2) develop manufacturing equipment capable of mass producing such a product at a reasonable cost.

Since making even one model of such a cell or vehicle is cost restrictive, the design teams have turned to computer-design and computer-manufacturing software programs for help. 3D pictorials let them see not only how they can better design the fuel cell for each vehicle, but what is needed in the way of retooling for mass production of such cells. By keeping costs down, engineers are hopeful that they will be able to design and develop an efficient electric car by the year 2004. Retooling of assembly lines could take a few years longer, but DaimlerChrysler is confident that they will have an efficient, reliable, fuel-cell powered vehicle on the world market within the next decade.

Adapted from "Fuel Cells Still Pose Thorny Problems," by Aaron Robinson, "Automotive News," March 29, 1999.

Perhaps six or seven such guides, using angles for a variety of positions of the axes, would be sufficient for all practical requirements. [*]

■ 16.32 TRIMETRIC ELLIPSES

The trimetric center lines of a hole, or on the end of a cylinder, become the conjugate diameters of the ellipse when drawn in trimetric. The ellipse may be drawn on the conjugate diameters (Figs. 4.51 or 4.52b), or the major and minor axes may be determined from the conjugate diameters (Fig. 4.53c) and the ellipse constructed on them by any of the methods of Figs. 4.48–4.50 and 4.52a, or with the aid of an ellipse template (Fig. 4.55).

[*] Plastic templates of this type are available from drafting supplies dealers.

One advantage of trimetric projection is the infinite number of positions of the object available. The angles and scales can be handled without too much difficulty, as shown in §16.31. However, the infinite variety of ellipses has been a discouraging factor.

In drawing any axonometric ellipse, keep the following in mind:

1. On the drawing, the major axis is always perpendicular to the center line, or axis, of the cylinder.

2. The minor axis is always perpendicular to the major axis; that is, on the paper it coincides with the axis of the cylinder.

3. The length of the major axis is equal to the actual diameter of the cylinder.

Thus we know at once the directions of both the major and minor axes, and the length of the major axis.

ITEM	NO. REQ'D	DESCRIPTION	SPUDNIK PART NO.
1	1	AXLE 4HOLE 1 x 12 WITH HUB PLATE	201034
2	8	BOLT 1/2 x 1-1/2 UNC-13 GRADE 5	501087
3	2	BOLT 3/8 x 1 UNC-16 GRADE 5	501049
4	4	BOLT 3/8 x 1-1/2 UNC-16 GRADE 5	501051
5	4	BOLT 3/8 x 3/4 UNC-16 GRADE 5	501216
6	1	BOLT 5/8 x 3 UNC-11 GRADE 5	501129
7	4	CAR BOLT 3/8 x 1	501349
8	4	CAR BOLT 3/8 x 1-1/2	501351
9	2	CASTER 1DIA x 3 WIDE 820LB RIGID	951145
10	1	FLAT BAR 3/8 x 3 x 18 LG	1115M38A-B1
11	2	FLNG_BRNG.2BLT.SCJT.1	231042
12	1	IDLER 60 PITCH 5/8 BORE 15 THOOTH #709	881079
13	1	KEY 1/4 x 1 1/2 SQUARE	502203
14	4	LUG BOLT 1/2-20 x 1-5/8	951028
15	4	LUG NUT 1/2-20	951116
16	1	MTR HYD 22.6 CU/IN 1DIA SHAFT 101-1016	601507
17	14	NUT 3/8-16NC	501809
18	8	NUT LOCK 1/2-13NC	501708
19	1	NUT LOCK 5/8-11NC	501275
20	1	PLANTER FILLER SWING DRIVE SHEILD	841084
21	1	RLR CHN 60 PITCH x 32-1/4 LG	351005A
22	1	RLR CHN MASTER LINK 60 PITCH	351010
23	2	SHEET 10GA x 10 x 10	1115M37A-B1
24	1	SPRCKT 60BS11 x 1 BORE	881033
25	1	SPRCKT 60BS18 x 1 BORE	881039
26	1	SWIVEL FRAME, WELDMENT	1115M32A
27	1	TIRE & RIM 480 x TUBELESS MOUNTED	951106
28	8	WSHR FLT 1/2	501906
29	6	WSHR FLT 3/8	501904
30	11	WSHR FLT 5/8	501907
31	18	WSHR LCK 3/8	501932

SPUDNIK EQUIPMENT COMPANY
P.O. Box 1045 Telephone 208-785-0480
Blackfoot, Idaho 83221

This drawing is the sole property of the above named. All rights of design and/or formation are reserved. No part of this document may be reproduced without prior.

PROJECT TITLE:
PLANTER FILLING CONVEYOR, MODEL 1115
SPECIAL NOTE: TEARSLEY
23 JAN 96
DRAWING TITLE:
SWIVEL FRAME ASSEMBLY

FIGURE 16.45 **Exploded Diametric of Planter Filling Conveyor.**
Courtesy of Spudnik Equipment Company, Inc.

We do not know the length of the minor axis. If we can find it, we can easily construct the ellipse with the aid of an ellipse template or any of a number of ellipse constructions mentioned earlier.

In Fig. 16.47a, center O is located as desired, and horizontal and vertical construction lines that will contain the major and minor axes are drawn through O. Note that the major axis will be on the horizontal line perpendicular to the axis of the hole, and the minor axis will be perpendicular to it, or vertical.

Set the compass for the actual radius of the hole and draw the semicircle, as shown, to establish the ends A and B of the major axis. Draw AF and BF parallel to the axonometric edges WX and YX, respectively, to locate F, which lies on the ellipse. Draw a vertical line through F to intersect the semicircle at F′ and join

F′ to B′, as shown. From D′, where the minor axis, extended, intersects the semicircle, draw D′E and ED parallel to F′B and BF, respectively. Point D is one end of the minor axis. From center O, strike arc DC to locate C, the other end of the minor axis. On these axes, a true ellipse can be constructed, or drawn with the aid of an ellipse template. A simple method for finding the "angle" of ellipse template to use is shown in Fig. 4.55c. If an ellipse template is not available, an approximate four-center ellipse (Fig. 4.56) will be found satisfactory in most cases.

In constructions where the enclosing parallelogram for an ellipse is available or easily constructed, the major and minor axes can be readily determined, as shown in Fig. 16.47b. The directions of both axes and the length of the major axis are known. Extend

FIGURE 16.46 **Trimetric Scales.**

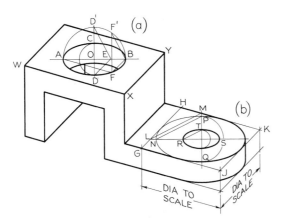

FIGURE 16.47 **Ellipses in Trimetric.** *Method (b)*
courtesy of Professor H. E. Grant.

the axes to intersect the sides of the parallelogram at L
and M, and join the points with a straight line. From
one end N of the major axis, draw a line NP parallel to
LM. The point P is one end of the minor axis. To find
one end T of the minor axis of the smaller ellipse, it is
only necessary to draw RT parallel to LM or NP.

The method of constructing an ellipse on an
oblique plane in trimetric is similar to that shown for
isometric in Fig. 16.33.

■16.33 AXONOMETRIC PROJECTION
BY THE METHOD OF INTERSECTIONS

Instead of constructing axonometric projections with
the aid of specially prepared scales, as explained in the
preceding paragraphs, an axonometric projection can
be obtained directly by projection from two orthographic views of the object. This method, called the
method of intersections, was developed by Profs. L.
Eckhart and T. Schmid of the Vienna College of Engineering and was published in 1937.

To understand this method, let us assume that the
axonometric projection of a rectangular object is giv-
en, and it is necessary to find the three orthographic
projections: the top view, front view, and side view
(Fig. 16.48).

Assume that the object is placed so that its principal edges coincide with the coordinate axes, and assume that the plane of projection (the plane on which
the axonometric projection is drawn) intersects the
three coordinate planes in the triangle ABC. From descriptive geometry, we know that lines BC, CA, and AB
will be perpendicular, respectively, to axes OX, OY,
and OZ. Any one of the three points A, B, or C may be
assumed anywhere on one of the axes, and the triangle
ABC may be drawn.

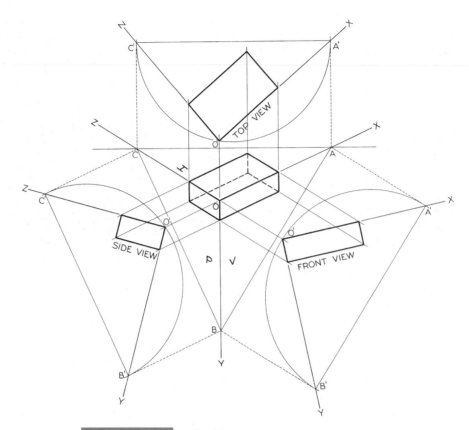

FIGURE 16.48   **Views from an Axonometric Projection.**

To find the true size and shape of the top view, re-volve the triangular portion of the horizontal plane AOC, which is in front of the plane of projection, about its base CA, into the plane of projection. In this case, the triangle is revolved *inward* to the plane of projection through the smallest angle made with it. The triangle will then be shown in its true size and shape, and the top view of the object can be drawn in the triangle by projection from the axonometric pro-jection, as shown, since all width dimensions remain the same. In the figure, the base CA of the triangle has been moved upward to C'A' so that the revolved posi-tion of the triangle will not overlap its projection.

In the same manner, the true sizes and shapes of the front view and side view can be found, as shown.

It is evident that if the three orthographic projec-tions, or in most cases any two of them, are given in their relative positions, as shown in Fig. 16.48, the di-rections of the projections could be reversed so that the intersections of the projecting lines would deter-mine the required axonometric projection.

To draw an axonometric projection by the method of intersections, it is helpful to make a sketch of the desired general appearance of the projection (Fig. 16.49). Even if the object is a complicated one, this sketch need not be complete, but only an enclosing box. Draw the projections of the coordinate axes OX, OY, and OZ parallel to the principal edges of the ob-ject, as shown in the sketch, and the three coordinate planes with the plane of projection.

Revolve the triangle ABO about its base AB as the axis into the plane of projection. Line OA will revolve to O'A, and this line, or one parallel to it, must be used as the baseline of the front view of the object. The pro-jecting lines from the front view to the axonometric must be drawn parallel to the projection of the unre-volved Z-axis, as indicated in the figure.

Similarly, revolve the triangle COB about its base CB as the axis into the plane of projection. Line CO will revolve to CO", and this line, or one parallel to it, must be used as the baseline of the side view. The direction of the projecting lines must

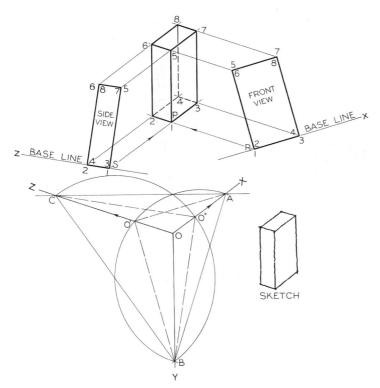

FIGURE 16.49   Axonometric Projection.

be parallel to the projection of the unrevolved X-axis, as shown.

Draw the front-view baseline at a convenient location, but parallel to O'X, and with it as the base, draw the front view of the object. Draw the side-view baseline also at a convenient location, but parallel to O"C, and with it as the base, draw the side view of the object, as shown. From the corners of the front view, draw projecting lines parallel to OZ, and from the corners of the side view, draw projecting lines parallel to OX. The intersections of these two sets of projecting lines determine the desired axonometric projection. It will be an isometric, a dimetric, or a trimetric projection, depending on the form of the sketch used as the basis for the projections (§16.2). If the sketch is drawn so that the three angles formed by the three coordinate axes are equal, the resulting projection will be an isometric projection; if two of the three angles are equal, the resulting projection will be a dimetric projection; and if no two of the three angles are equal, the resulting projection will be a trimetric projection.

To place the desired projection on a specific location on the drawing (Fig. 16.49), select the desired projection P of the point 1, for example, and draw two projecting lines PR ands PS to intersect the two baselines and thereby to determine the locations of the two views on their baselines.

Another example of this method of axonometric projection is shown in Fig. 16.50. In this case, it was deemed necessary only to draw a sketch of the plan or base of the object in the desired position, as shown. The axes are then drawn with OX and OZ parallel, respectively, to the sides of the sketch plan, and the remaining axis OY is assumed in a vertical position. The triangles COB and AOB are revolved, and the two baselines are drawn parallel to O"C and O'A, as shown. Point P, the lower front corner of the axonometric drawing, is then chosen at a convenient place, and projecting lines are drawn toward the baselines parallel to axes OX and OZ to locate the positions of the views on the baselines. The views are drawn on the baselines or cut apart from another drawing and fastened in place with drafting tape.

FIGURE 16.50   **Axonometric Projection.**

To draw the elliptical projection of the circle, assume any points, such as A, on the circle in both front and side views. Note that point A is the same altitude d above the baseline in both views. The axonometric projection of point A is found simply by drawing the projecting lines from the two views. The major and minor axes may be easily found by projecting in this manner or by methods shown in Fig. 16.47; the true ellipse may be drawn by any of the methods of Figs. 4.48–4.50 and 4.52a, or with the aid of an ellipse template. An approximate ellipse is satisfactory for most drawings and may be used.

■ 16.34 USING CAD

Pictorial drawings of all sorts can be created using 3D CAD. To create pictorials using 2D CAD, you would use similar projection techniques to those presented in this chapter. The advantage of 3D CAD is that once you make a 3D model of a part or assembly you can change the viewing direction at any time for orthographic, isometric, or perspective views. You can also apply different materials to the drawing objects and shade them to produce a high degree of realism in the pictorial view.

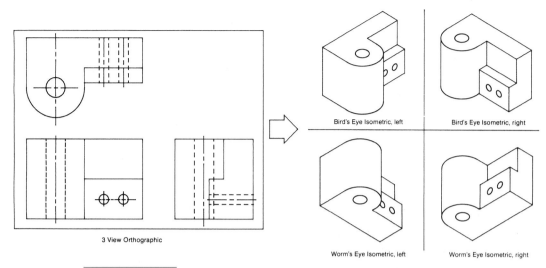

3 View Orthographic

Bird's Eye Isometric, left

Bird's Eye Isometric, right

Worm's Eye Isometric, left

Worm's Eye Isometric, right

FIGURE 16.51 **Orthographic to Isometric Conversion. The Auto-trol Orthographic to Axonometric Package (OTAP) system can be used to convert an orthographic drawing to axonometric.** *Courtesy of Auto-trol Technology Corporation.*

FIGURE 16.52 **Isometric Assembly Drawing Produced by Using the Computervision Designer System.** *Courtesy of Computervision Corporation, a subsidiary of Prime Computer, Inc.*

FIGURE 16.53 **3D Pictorial Drawing of a Zip Drive.** *Courtesy of SDRC, Milford, OH.*

▪ KEY WORDS

AXONOMETRIC	ISOMETRIC
DIMETRIC	TRIMETRIC
PERSPECTIVE	INFINITY
LINE OF SIGHT	VISUAL RAYS
PLANE OF PROJECTION	FINITE
INCLINED SURFACE	OBLIQUE
ISOMETRIC AXES	BOX CONSTRUCTION
FOUR-CENTER ELLIPSE	

▪ CHAPTER SUMMARY

- Axonometric projection is a method of creating a pictorial representation of an object. It shows all three dimensions of length, width, and height in one view.
- Isometric is the easiest of the axonometric projections to draw and is therefore the most common pictorial drawing. Isometric drawings created with CAD are often called 3D models.
- The spaces between the axes of an isometric drawing each are 120°. Isometric axes are drawn at 30° to the horizontal and vertical.
- The only lines on an isometric drawing that are to scale are parallel to the three isometric axes.
- An axonometric drawing is created by rotating an object about imaginary vertical and horizontal axes until three adjacent views, usually the top, front, and right side view, can all be seen at the same time.
- Inclined surfaces and oblique surfaces must determined by plotting the endpoints of each edge of the surface.
- Angles, irregular curves, and ellipses require special construction techniques for accurate representation.
- A common method of drawing an object in isometric is by creating as isometric box and drawing the features of the object within the box.
- Unlike perspective drawing, in which parallel lines converge on a vanishing point, parallel lines are drawn parallel in axonometric drawings.

▪ REVIEW QUESTIONS

1. Why is isometric drawing more common than perspective drawing in engineering work?
2. What are the differences between axonometric projection and perspective?
3. What type of projection is used when creating a 3D model with CAD?
4. At what angles are the isometric axes drawn?
5. What are the three views that are typically shown in an isometric drawing?
6. Which type of projection places the observer at a finite distance from the object? Which types place the observer at an infinite distance?
7. Why is isometric easier to draw than dimetric or trimetric?
8. Is the four-circle ellipse a true ellipse or an approximation?
9. Is an ellipse in CAD a four-circle ellipse or a true conic section?

▪ AXONOMETRIC PROBLEMS

Figures 16.54–16.58 consist of problems to be drawn axonometrically. The earlier isometric sketches may be drawn on isometric paper (§5.13), and later sketches should be made on plain drawing paper. On drawings to be executed with instruments, show all construction lines required in the solutions.

For additional problems, see Figs. 6.52–6.54, 17.23–17.26, and 18.34.

Since many of the problems in this chapter are of a general nature, they can also be solved on most computer graphics systems. If a system is available, the instructor may choose to assign specific problems to be completed by this method.

1 KEY PLATE ✓

2 BASE

3 STRAP

METRIC

METRIC

4 BRACKET

5 CUTTER BLOCK

6 BRACKET

7 HOUSE MODEL

METRIC

8 GUIDE BLOCK

9 FINGER

FIGURE 16.54 **(1) Make freehand isometric sketches. (2) Make isometric drawings with instruments on Layout A–2 or A4–2 (adjusted). (3) Make dimetric drawings with instruments, using Layout A–2 or A4–2 (adjusted), and position assigned from Fig. 16.42. (d) Make trimetric drawings, using instruments, with axes chosen to show the objects to best advantage. If dimensions are required, study §16.25.**

FIGURE 16.55 **(1) Make freehand isometric sketches. (2) Make isometric drawings with instruments on Layout A–2 or A4–2 (adjusted). (3) Make dimetric drawings with instruments, using Layout A–2 or A4–2 (adjusted), and position assigned from Fig. 16.42. (4) Make trimetric drawings, using instruments, with axes chosen to show the objects to best advantage. If dimensions are required, study §16.25.**

FIGURE 16.56 (1) Make isometric freehand sketches. (2) Make isometric drawings with instruments, using Size A or A4 sheet or Size B or A3 sheet, as assigned. (3) Make dimetric drawings with instruments, using Size A or A4 sheet or Size B or A3 sheet, as assigned, and position assigned from Fig. 16.42. (4) Make trimetric drawings, using instruments, with axes chosen to show the objects to best advantage. If dimensions are required, study §16.25.

FIGURE 16.57 (1) Make isometric freehand sketches. (2) Make isometric drawings with instruments, using Size A or A4 sheet or Size B or A3 sheet, as assigned. (3) Make dimetric drawings with instruments, using Size A or A4 sheet or Size B or A3 sheet, as assigned, and position assigned from Fig. 16.42. (4) Make trimetric drawings, using instruments, with axes chosen to show the objects to best advantage. If dimensions are required, study §16.25.

FIGURE 16.58 (1) Make isometric freehand sketches. (2) Make isometric drawings with instruments, using Size A or A4 sheet or Size B or A3 sheet, as assigned. (3) Make dimetric drawings with instruments, using Size A or A4 sheet or Size B or A3 sheet, as assigned, and position assigned from Fig. 16.42. (4) Make trimetric drawings, using instruments, with axes chosen to show the objects to best advantage. If dimensions are required, study §16.25.

FIGURE 16.59 *Nylon Collar Nut.* **(1) Make isometric freehand sketch. (2) Make isometric drawing with instruments, using Size A or A4 sheet or Size B or A3 sheet, as assigned.**

FIGURE 16.60 *Plastic T-Handle Plated Steel Stud.* **(1) Make dimetric drawing with instruments, using Size A or A4 sheet as assigned. (2) Make trimetric drawing, using instruments. Use Size A or A4 sheet as assigned.**

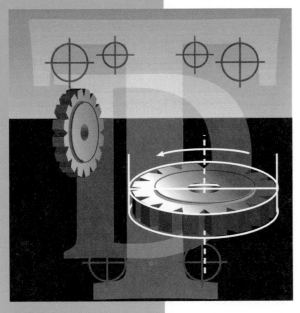

C H A P T E R 1 7

OBLIQUE
PROJECTION

OVERVIEW

If an observer is considered to be stationed at an infinite distance from an object and looking toward the object so that the projectors are parallel to each other and oblique to the plane of projection, the resulting drawing is an **oblique projection** (see Fig. 16.1c). As a rule, the object is placed with one of its principal faces parallel to the plane of projection. This is equivalent to holding the object in your hand and viewing it approximately as shown in Fig. 5.27.

Oblique projection provides an easy method for drawing circular features that are parallel to the plane of projection. Axonometric circles are tedious constructions using paper and pencil. With oblique projection, the front view is the same as the front view in a multiview drawing. Circles and angles parallel to the projection plane are true size and shape and are therefore easy to construct. Oblique projection is not as photorealistic as axonometric projection. Depth is distorted and must be compensated for to approximate a realistic appearance for the object. There is little reason to create oblique drawing with CAD since isometric drawings are created automatically once a 3D model is created. While circles in the front view are easy to draw, they are very difficult to create in the top or side views. Therefore, oblique is primarily used on manually constructed drawings, where the majority of circles appear in the front view. Sometimes an object is rotated to position circles in the front view.

■ 17.1 OBLIQUE AND OTHER PROJECTIONS COMPARED

A comparison of oblique projection and orthographic projection is shown in Fig. 17.1. In the oblique projection, the front face A′B′C′D′ is identical with the front view, or orthographic projection, $A^V B^V C^V D^V$. Thus, if an object is placed with one of its faces parallel to the plane of projection, that face will be projected true size and shape in oblique projection as well as in orthographic or multiview projection. This is why oblique is preferable to axonometric projection in the pictorial representation of certain objects. Note that surfaces of the object that are not parallel to the plane of projection will not project in true size and shape. For example, surface ABFE on the object (a square) projects as a parallelogram A′B′F′E′ in the oblique projection.

In axonometric projection, circles on the object nearly always lie in the surfaces inclined to the plane of projection and project as ellipses. In oblique projection, the object may be positioned so that those surfaces are parallel to the plane of projection, in which case the circles will project as true circles and can be easily drawn with the compass.

A comparison of the oblique and orthographic projections of a cylindrical object is shown in Fig. 17.2. In both cases, the circular shapes project as true circles. Note that although an observer looking in the direction of the oblique arrow sees these shapes as ellipses, the drawing, or projection, represents not what is seen but what is projected on the plane of projection. This curious situation is peculiar to oblique projection.

Observe that the axis AB of the cylinder projects as a point $A^V B^V$ in the orthographic projection, since the line of sight is parallel to AB. But in the oblique projection, the axis projects as a line A′B′. The more nearly the direction of sight approaches the perpendicular with respect to the plane of projection—that is, the larger the angle between the projectors and the plane—the closer the oblique projection moves toward the orthographic projection, and the shorter A′B′ becomes.

■ 17.2 DIRECTIONS OF PROJECTORS

In Fig. 17.3, the projectors make an angle of 45° with the plane of projection; hence, the line CD′, which is perpendicular to the plane, projects true length at C′D′. If the projectors make a greater angle with the plane of projection, the oblique projection is shorter, and if the projectors make a smaller angle with the plane of projection, the oblique projection is longer. Theoretically, CD′ could project in any length from zero to infinity. However, the line AB is parallel to the plane and will project in true length regardless of the angle the projectors make with the plane of projection.

In Fig. 17.1, the lines AE, BF, CG, and DH are perpendicular to the plane of projection and project as parallel inclined lines A′E, B′F, C′G, and D′H′ in the oblique projection. These lines on the drawing are called the **receding lines**. As we have seen, they may be any length, from zero to infinity, depending on the direction of the line of sight. Our next concern is this: What angle do these lines make on paper with respect to horizontal?

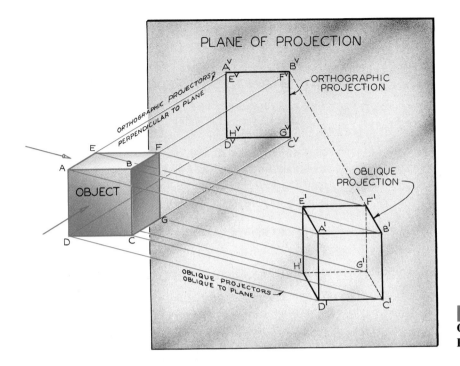

FIGURE 17.1 Comparison of Oblique and Orthographic Projections.

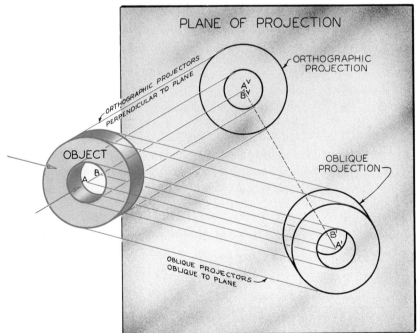

FIGURE 17.2 Circles Parallel to Plane of Projection.

In Fig. 17.4, the line AO is perpendicular to the plane of projection, and all the projectors make angles of 45° with it; therefore, all the oblique projections BO, CO, DO, and so on are equal in length to the line AO. It can be seen from the figure that the projectors may be selected in any one of an infinite number of directions and yet maintain any desired angle with the plane of projection. It is also evident that the directions of the projections BO, CO, DO, and so on are independent of the angles the projectors make with the plane of projection. Ordinarily, this inclination of the projection is 45° (CO in the figure), 30°, or 60° with

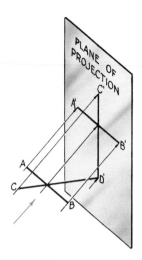

FIGURE 17.3   **Lengths of Projections.**

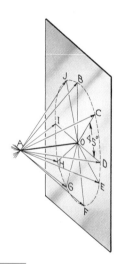

FIGURE 17.4   **Directions and Projections.**

FIGURE 17.5   **Variation in Direction of Receding Axis.**

horizontal since these angles may be easily drawn with the triangles.

■ 17.3 ANGLES OF RECEDING LINES

The receding lines may be drawn at any convenient angle. Some typical drawings with the receding lines in various directions are shown in Fig. 17.5. The angle that should be used in an oblique drawing depends on the shape of the object and the location of its significant features. For example, in Fig. 17.6a a large angle was used to obtain a better view of the rectangular recess on the top, while in Fig. 17.6b a small angle was chosen to show a similar feature on the side.

■ 17.4 LENGTH OF RECEDING LINES

Since the eye is accustomed to seeing objects with all receding parallel lines appearing to converge, an oblique projection presents an unnatural appearance, with more or less serious distortion depending on the object shown. For example, the object shown in Fig. 17.7a is a cube, and the receding lines are full length, but the receding lines appear to be too long and to diverge toward the rear of the block. A striking example of the unnatural appearance of an oblique drawing when compared with the natural appearance of a perspective is shown in Fig. 17.8. This example points up one of the chief limitations of oblique projection: Objects characterized by great length should not be drawn in oblique with the long dimension perpendicular to the plane of projection.

The appearance of distortion may be reduced by decreasing the length of the receding lines (remember, we established in §17.2 that they could be any length). In Fig. 17.7 a cube is shown in five oblique drawings with varying degrees of foreshortening of the receding

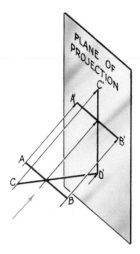

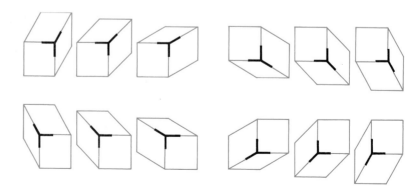

FIGURE 17.5   Variation in Direction of Receding Axis.

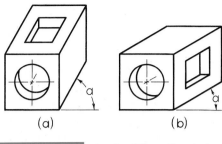

FIGURE 17.6   **Angle of Receding Axis.**

these fortifications the central portion was higher than the rest, and it was called *cavalier* because of its dominating and commanding position.

When the receding lines are drawn to half size (Fig. 17.7d), the drawing is commonly known as a **cabinet projection**. The term is attributed to the early use of this type of oblique drawing in the furniture industries. A comparison of cavalier projection and cabinet projection is shown in Fig. 17.9.

lines. The range of scales chosen is sufficient for almost all problems, and most of the scales are available on the architects', engineers', or metric scales.

When the receding lines are true length—that is, when the projectors make an angle of 45° with the plane of projection—the oblique drawing is called a **cavalier projection** (Fig. 17.7a). Cavalier projections originated in the drawing of medieval fortifications and were made on horizontal planes of projection. On

■ 17.5 CHOICE OF POSITION

The face of an object showing the essential contours should generally be placed parallel to the plane of projection (Fig. 17.10). If this is done, distortion will be kept to a minimum and labor reduced. For example, in Figs. 17.10a and 17.10c, the circles and circular arcs are shown in their true shapes and may be quickly drawn with the compass, while in Figs. 17.10b and 17.10d these curves are not shown in their true shapes and must be plotted as free curves or in the form of ellipses.

FIGURE 17.7   **Foreshortening of Receding Lines.**

FIGURE 17.8   **Unnatural Appearance of Oblique Drawing.**

(a) CAVALIER PROJECTION (b) CABINET PROJECTION

FIGURE 17.9 **Comparison of Cavalier and Cabinet Projections.**

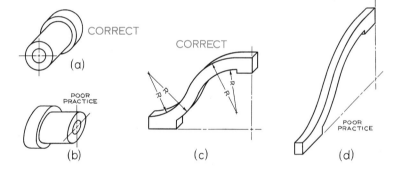

FIGURE 17.10 **Essential Contours Parallel to Plane of Projection.**

The longest dimension of an object should generally be placed parallel to the plane of projection, as shown in Fig. 17.11.

FIGURE 17.11 **Long Axis Parallel to Plane of Projection.**

■17.6 STEPS IN OBLIQUE DRAWING

The steps in drawing a cavalier drawing of a rectangular object are shown in Fig. 17.12. Being by drawing the axes OX and OY perpendicular to each other and the receding axis OZ at any desired angle with horizontal (Fig. 17.12I). On these axes, construct an enclosing box, using the overall dimension of the object. Block in the various shapes in detail (II), and heavy in all final lines (III).

Many objects most adaptable to oblique representation are composed of cylindrical shapes built on axes

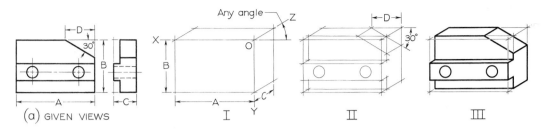

FIGURE 17.12   Steps in Oblique Drawing—Box Construction.

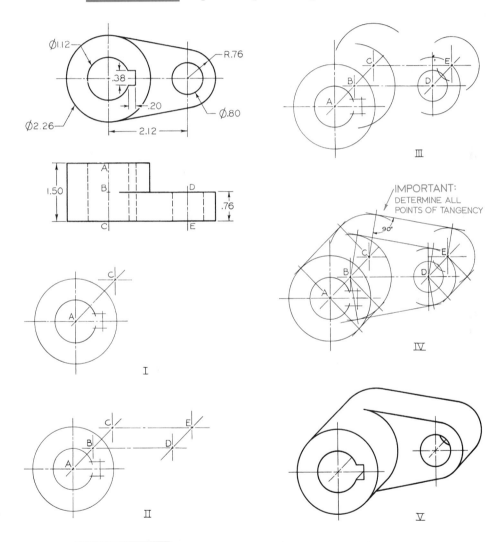

FIGURE 17.13   Steps in Oblique Drawing—Skeleton Construction.

or center lines. In such cases, the oblique drawing is best constructed on the projected center lines, as shown in Fig. 17.13. The object is positioned so that the circles shown in the given top view are parallel to the plane of projection and, hence, can be readily

drawn with the compass to their true shapes. The general procedure is to draw the center-line skeleton, as shown in (I) and (II), and then to build the drawing on these center lines. It is very important to construct all points of tangency, as shown in (IV), especially if the drawing is to be inked. For a review of tangencies, see §§4.30–4.38. The final cavalier drawing is shown in (V).

■ 17.7 FOUR-CENTER ELLIPSE

It is not always possible to place an object so that all its significant contours are parallel to the plane of

FIGURE 17.14 **Circles and Arcs Not Parallel to Plane of Projection.**

(a) OBJECT WITH CIRCLES IN DIFFERENT PLANES

PARALLELOGRAM MUST BE EQUILATERAL TO USE 4-CENTER ELLIPSE

PERPENDICULAR BISECTORS TO SIDES OF PARALLELOGRAM

(b) USE OF 4-CENTER ELLIPSE

projection. For example, the object shown in Fig. 17.14a has two sets of circular contours in different planes, and both cannot be placed parallel to the plane of projection.

In the oblique drawing in Fig. 17.14b, the regular four-center method of Fig. 16.24 was used to construct ellipses representing circular curves not parallel to the plane of projection. This method can be used only in cavalier drawing, in which case the enclosing parallelogram is equilateral—that is, the receding axis is drawn to full scale. The method is the same as in the isometric: Erect perpendicular bisectors to the four sides of the parallelogram; their intersections will be centers for the four circular arcs. If the angle of the receding lines is other than 30° with horizontal, as in this case, the centers of the two large arcs will not fall in the corners of the parallelogram.

The regular four-center method is not convenient in oblique drawing unless the receding lines make 30° with horizontal so that the perpendicular bisectors may be drawn easily with the 30° × 60° triangle and the T-square, parallel rule, or drafting machine without the necessity of first finding the midpoints of the sides. A more convenient method is the alternate four-center ellipse drawn on the two center lines, as shown in Fig. 17.15. This is the same method as used in isometric (Fig. 16.29), but in oblique drawing it varies slightly in appearance according to the different angles of the receding lines.

First, draw the two center lines. Then, from the center, draw a construction circle equal in diameter to the actual hole or cylinder. The circle will intersect each center line at two points. From the two points on

FIGURE 17.15 **Alternate Four-Center Ellipse.**

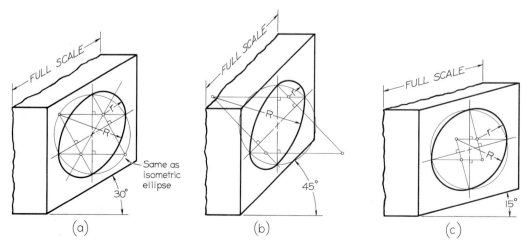

(a)   (b)   (c)

one center line, erect perpendiculars to the other center line. Then, from the two points on the other center line, erect perpendiculars to the first center line. From the intersections of the perpendiculars, draw four circular arcs, as shown.

It must be remembered that the four-center ellipse can be inscribed only in an *equilateral* parallelogram; hence, it cannot be used in any oblique drawing in which the receding axis is foreshortened. Its use is limited, therefore, to cavalier drawing.

■ 17.8 OFFSET MEASUREMENTS

Circles, circular arcs, and other curved or irregular lines may be drawn by means of offset measurements, as shown in Fig. 17.16. The offsets are first drawn on the multiview drawing of the curve (Fig. 17.16a), and these are transferred to the oblique drawing (Fig. 17.16b). In this case, the receding axis is full scale, and therefore all offsets can be drawn full scale. The four-center ellipse could be used, but the method here is more accurate. The final curve is drawn with the aid of the irregular curve.

If the oblique drawing is a cabinet drawing (Fig. 17.16c) or any oblique drawing in which the receding axis is drawn to a reduced scale, the offset measurements parallel to the receding axis must be drawn to the same reduced scale. In this case, there is no choice of methods since the four-center ellipse cannot be used. A method of drawing ellipses in a cabinet drawing of a cube is shown in Fig. 17.16d.

As shown in Fig. 17.17, a free curve may be drawn in oblique by means of offset measurements. This figure also illustrates a case in which hidden lines are used to make the drawing clearer.

FIGURE 17.17   **Use of Offset Measurements.**

The use of offset measurements in drawing an ellipse in a plane inclined to the plane of projection is shown in Fig. 17.18. In Fig. 17.18a, a number of parallel lines are drawn to represent imaginary cutting planes. Each plane will cut a rectangular surface between the front end of the cylinder and the inclined surface. These rectangles are drawn in oblique, as shown in Fig. 17.18b, and the curve is drawn through corner points, as indicated. The final cavalier drawing is shown in Fig. 17.18c.

■ 17.9 ANGLES IN OBLIQUE PROJECTION

If an angle that is specified in degrees lies in a receding plane, it is necessary to convert the angle into linear measurements to draw the angle in oblique. For example, in Fig. 17.19a, an angle of 30° is given. To draw the angle in oblique, we need to know dimensions AB and

FIGURE 17.16   **Use of Offset Measurements.**

(a)

(b) CAVALIER   (c) CABINET   (d) CABINET

FIGURE 17.18   Use of Offset Measurements.

FIGURE 17.19   Angles in Oblique Projection.

BC. The distance AB is given as 32 mm and can be set off directly in the cavalier drawing (Fig. 17.19b). Distance BC is not known, but can easily be found by constructing the right triangle ABC (Fig. 17.19c) from the given dimensions in the top view in Fig. 17.19a. The length BC is then transferred with dividers to the cavalier drawing, as shown.

In cabinet drawing, it must be remembered that *all receding dimensions* must be reduced to half size. Thus, in the cabinet drawing in Fig. 17.19d, the distance BC must be half the side BC of the right triangle in Fig. 17.19e.

FIGURE 17.20   Oblique Half Section.

■ 17.10 OBLIQUE SECTIONS

Sections are often useful in oblique drawing, especially in the representation of interior shapes. An **oblique half section** is shown in Fig. 17.20. Other examples are shown in Figs. 7.41, 7.42, and 7.45. **Oblique full sections**, in which the plane passes completely through the object, are seldom used because they do not show enough of the exterior shapes. In general, all the types of sections discussed in §16.24 for isometric drawing may be applied equally to oblique drawing.

■ 17.11   SCREW THREADS IN OBLIQUE

Parallel partial circles spaced equal to the symbolic thread pitch (see Fig. 13.9a) are used to represent the crests only of a screw thread in a cavalier oblique (Fig. 17.21). For cabinet oblique the space would be one half of the symbolic pitch. If the thread is so positioned to require ellipses, they may be drawn by the four-center method of §17.7.

■ 17.12   OBLIQUE DIMENSIONING

An oblique drawing may be dimensioned in a manner similar to that described in §16.25 for isometric drawing (Fig. 17.22). The general principles of dimensioning, as outlined in Chapter 11, must be followed. As shown in Fig. 17.22, all dimension lines, extension lines, and arrowheads must lie in the planes of the object to which they apply. The dimension figures also will lie in the plane when the aligned dimensioning system is used (Fig. 17.22a). For the unidirectional system of dimensioning, all dimension figures are set horizontal and read form the bottom of the drawing (Fig. 17.22b). This simpler system is often used on pictorials for production purposes. Vertical lettering should be used for all pictorial dimensioning.

Dimensions should be placed outside the outlines of the drawing except when greater clarity or directness of application results from placing the dimensions directly on the view. The dimensioning methods described apply equally to fractional, decimal, and metric dimensions. For many other examples of oblique dimensioning, see Figs. 6.61, 6.65, 6.66, and others on following pages.

■ 17.13   OBLIQUE SKETCHING

Methods of sketching in oblique on plain paper are illustrated in Fig. 5.27. Ordinary graph paper is very useful in oblique sketching (see Fig. 5.28). The height and width proportions can be easily controlled by simply counting the squares. A very pleasing depth proportion can be obtained by sketching the receding lines at 45° diagonally through the squares and through half as many squares as the actual depth would indicate.

■ 17.14   COMPUTER GRAPHICS

Using computer graphics, the drafter can easily create an oblique drawing that will provide the desired amount of foreshortening along the receding axis as well as the preferred direction of the axis. CAD programs also permit curves and circular features, which are not parallel to the frontal plane, to be readily shown on the drawing. Oblique sections (§17.10) and repetitive features such as screw threads (§17.11) may be quickly and accurately depicted.

FIGURE 17.21   Screw Threads in Oblique.

FIGURE 17.22   Oblique Dimensioning.

(a) ALIGNED

(b) UNIDIRECTIONAL

G R A P H I C S   S P O T L I G H T

High Technology Is First Mate In the Race for America's Cup[*]

A klaxon sounds and the sleek hull of the racing yacht begins knifing through cool, calm waters at increasing speed. The bow heaves as it pushes through the flat water, raising a wave as it moves faster and sending ripples fanning from the waterline. People riding along feel the breeze in their faces as the hull glides at speeds of up to 14 knots, but the motion and sensations last only a few seconds. This dash by a 25-foot-long scale model covers only about 800 feet and takes place in a huge water tank, not the open ocean. But it nonetheless signals a beginning of the next race for the America's Cup, the world's most prestigious sailing competition.

Challengers hoping to capture the America's Cup from New Zealand in 2000 have already begun extensive research and testing directed toward designing and buiding the fastest sailboats in their class. Months, even years, before construction begins on the boats, teams of naval architects, designers, computer scientists, model builders and engineers engage in a technological competition to create machines that can complete a two-hour race a few minutes or seconds ahead of rivals. It is this competition that brings yacht builders to the David Taylor Model Basin at the Naval Surface Warfare Center. Here, where the Navy tows and tests models of its future destroyers, frigates and other warships in the world's largest towing tanks, John K. Marshall, president of the New York Yacht Club, watches as fiberglass models of different racing hulls go through their paces.

"This is our surface warfare, so perharps it's appropriate that we are here," said Mr. Marshall, director of the Young America campaign, a $40 million effort by the New York Yacht Club to build the boat that wins the right to challenge Team New Zealand for the oldest trophy in international sport.

"Sailing in a sport, an athletic competition for which people must train and develop their skills," Mr. Marshall said. "But the America's Cup is also a technology competition and it's always been that way".

"If your boat is as fast, you can win sailing skill," said Bob Billingham of America One, the group organizing the entry for the St. Francis Yacht Club of San Francisco. "But you can't win with a slower boat."

So team worldwide labor to refine their designs, jealously guarding studies of hull shapes, sails and even rigging hardware to deny the smallest secret to competitors. Yachts in this class are so closely matched that no advantage is insignificant. Veterans remember when an Australian challenger in 1983 snatched the cup from the United States for the first time with help from a radical innovation, a winged keel. The Australians kept the keel secret until the last moment to prevent competitors from trying to copy it.

Getting the fastest boat requires working within the strictures of tight rules governing the overall design of this class of vessels. From 1958 to 1987, sailors competed for the America's Cup in 12-Meter Class yachts. But in 1989, a multinational group of yacht designers developed rules for a new International America's Cup Class, which first appeared in the 1992 competition.

The new America's Cup boats are lighter, faster, narrower and longer and carry more sail than their predecessors, with canoe-like bodies made of carbon fiber material instead of aluminum. The design is based on a mathematical formula that balances a boat's waterline length, sail area and displacement so that adding significantly to one dimension requires decreasing others. Generally, an America's Cup contender in about 75 feet long, supports a mast that stands 115 feet off the water, has a keel 14 feet deep and weighs 45,000 to 48,000 pounds. More than 40,000 pounds are in a lead ballast bulb at the base of the keel.

Registering to challenge Team New Zealand, who gained the prize in 1995 sailing Black Magic, 16 yacht clubs and syndicates from 10 nations, including 5 from the United States, have so far paid their $200,000 entry fees. Experts estimate that 10 or 12 of these groups will raise enough money to build at least one boat and that perhaps 4 or 5 of the competitors will muster the talent and expertise to produce first-rate vessels with a chance of winning. The competitors are to assemble in the harbor off Auckland in October 1999 and begin a series of match races to determine the best boat to be named the official challenger for the America's Cup. The winning boat will then race Team New Zealand's best new yacht in a best-of-seven series held in February and March of 2000 in the Hauraki Gulf, northeast of Auckland.

With such intense competition, any weight reduction or change in hull shape, sail design, or the placement of components, like the keel or rudder, that resluts in even a 1 percent increase in performance is significant.

Increasingly, the teams rely on computer simulation and the ability to test many design ideas in the cyberseas of a mathematical model before building and trying them in the real word. "Engineers use sophistcated software, known as *computational fluid dynamics programs*", said John Kuhn, a naval architect at Science Applications International Corporation in San Diego, a technical firm supporting the San Francisco group. The programs simulate the fluid flow around hulls and appendages, like rudders, keels and ballast bulbs, or the movement of air around masts or sails. Results from the programs, which calculate pressure and drag, give engineers the information they need to design components that are then tested in tanks or wind tunnels.

Information from these tests the *fluid dynamics programs* then go into a larger computer simulation called a *velocity prediction program*, or VPP. This program combines design specifications with environmental variables like wind, wave and temperature to make predictions on how fast a boat will sail in specific conditions. "A VPP integrates the work of different people working on different parts of a boat and predicts how an overall design will perform on water," said Mr. Kuhn, technical coordinator for the San Francisco group. "These programs are not perfect, but they help tell you how basic elements contribute to a design".

With each competition, said Duncan MacLane, technology project manager for the New York group, the designers are seeing better matches between computer predictions and actual performance. Still, advice from naval architects and other experts like Bruce Farr, the principal designer for the New York group, remains crucial.

"There is still a lot of art in the design process," Mr. MacLane said, "with many of the improvements we are considering coming from the intuition of designers. There is still a designer in front of the computer screen dealing with the nuances, making very subtle alignments in the design that produces a winner".

Tom Schnackenberg, who heads the design team for the New Zealand group, said that although computational and model testing made significant contributions to producing a boat, only full-scale testing and analysis of a real vessel could confirm its design performance. "In the real world", Mr. Scknackenberg said, "we often find full-scale results at variance with predictions". Team New Zealand plans to build at least one boat and use its older championship yachts in its preparations, said Alan Sefton, a spokesman for the group.

Many of the teams preparing new boats are paying extra attention to the sails and riggings, partly because of differences in these areas that appeared in the last cup race, said Mr. Kuhn of the San Francisco group. The mast and rigging on Black Magic, the New Zealand boat, was set farther back than those on other races, and the New Zealanders displayed sails with unusual shapes.

"Everyone in looking at sails and rigging because sail aerodynamics is one of the least understood elements of design," Mr. Kuhn said. "This is where we may be able to squeeze out some more performance". He and other experts said any group that wished to seek the America's Cup but had yet to start this kind of research and planning was probably out of luck. "The race," Mr. Kuhn said, "has already begun".

---

*Adapted from "High Technology is First Mate in the Race for America's Cup," by Warren E. Leary, *New York Times*, July 21, 1998.

■ KEY WORDS

OBLIQUE PROJECTION	PROJECTORS
PLANE OF PROJECTION	RECEDING LINES
CAVALIER	CABINET
SKELETON CONSTRUCTION	OFFSET MEASUREMENT

■ CHAPTER SUMMARY

- Oblique projection makes drawing circles in the projection plane easier than with other pictorial projection methods.
- There are two commonly used types of oblique projection: cavalier and cabinet.
- Width and height are drawn true size and true shape in oblique projection. The depth axis for cavalier (full depth) is usually 30°, while the depth axis for cabinet (half depth) is usually 45°.
- Oblique drawings of circular features are often created by first drawing a skeleton of center lines.
- There is usually no reason for creating oblique drawings using CAD, since isometric drawings are easier to make with CAD and appear more photorealistic.
- Oblique projection is a common sketching method because the front view is true size and true shape and easier to draw.

■ REVIEW QUESTIONS

1. What is the primary advantage of an oblique projection?
2. Which is the most photorealistic: isometric, perspective, or oblique projection? Which is the least photorealistic?
3. If a hockey puck were to be drawn using oblique projection, how should it be positioned to appear as a circle?
4. Can an angle on an oblique drawing be measured in the front view? In the right side view? In the top view?
5. Why are oblique drawings seldom created with CAD software?
6. What is the first thing that should be drawn when creating an oblique drawing?
7. Describe how to plot an irregular curve in an oblique drawing.

■ OBLIQUE PROJECTION PROBLEMS

Many problems to be drawn in oblique—either cavalier or cabinet—are given in Figs. 17.23–17.26. They may be drawn freehand (§5.14) using graph paper or plain drawing paper as assigned by the instructor, or they may be drawn with instruments. In the latter case, all construction lines should be shown on the completed drawing.

Many additional problems suitable for oblique projection will be found in Figs. 6.52–6.54, 8.27–8.29, 16.54–16.57, and 18.34.

Since many of the problems in this chapter are of a general nature, they can also be solved on most computer graphics systems. If a system is available, the instructor may choose to assign specific problems to be completed by this method.

1 ROD GUIDE

2 ADJUSTABLE ARM

3 FOLLOWER

4 GUIDE ARM

5 HOUSING CAP

6 GLAND

7 CONTROL ARM

8 RACK

9 STEP CONE

10 ANGLE BEARING

11 WORKBENCH

FIGURE 17.23 **(1) Make freehand oblique sketches. (2) Make oblique drawings with instruments, using Size A or A4 sheet, or Size B or A3 sheet, as assigned. If dimensions are required, study §17.12.**

FIGURE 17.24 Make oblique drawings with instruments, using Size A or A4 sheet, or Size B or A3 sheet, as assigned. If dimensions are required, study §17.12.

1 CLEVIS

2 ADJUSTABLE ORDER

METRIC

3 TURRET LATHE STOCK REST

4 CLUTCH BRACKET

5 RAIL SUPPORT

FIGURE 17.25 **Make oblique drawings with instruments, using Size A or A4 sheet, or Size B or A3 sheet, as assigned. If dimensions are required, study §17.12.**

1 GUIDE

2 TERMINAL BLOCK

3 STACK BLOCK

4 SLIDE

5 ADAPTER PLATE

6 DRIVE SLEEVE

7 SAW GUIDE BLOCK

8 TRAVERSE STOP PISTON

9 OIL PUMP BODY

10 CUTTING OFF TOOL HOLDER

FIGURE 17.26 Make oblique drawings with instruments, using Size A or A4 sheet, or Size B or B3 sheet, as assigned. If dimensions are required, study §17.12.

C H A P T E R 1 8

PERSPECTIVE

OBJECTIVES

After studying the material in this chapter, you should be able to:

1. Identify a drawing created using perspective projection.
2. List the differences between perspective projection and axonometric projection.
3. Create a drawing using multiview perspective.
4. Describe three types of perspective.
5. Measure distances in perspective projection.

OVERVIEW

Perspective, or **central projection**, excels over all other types of projection in the pictorial representation of objects because it more closely approximates the view produced by the human eye (Fig. 18.1). Geometrically, an ordinary photograph is a perspective. While perspective is of major importance to architects, industrial designers, and illustrators, engineers at one time or another are also certain to be concerned with the pictorial representation of objects and should understand the basic principles of perspective (see ANSI/ASME Y14.4M-1989 (R1994)).

Unlike axonometric projection, which places the observer at an infinite distance from the object, perspective projection defines the observer at a finite distance. This projection technique causes parallel edges to converge at vanishing points, as in a photograph. This technique duplicates the image produced by the human eye of the real world. To accomplish this image accuracy, every point and edge of an object must be projected from a multiview drawing.

The three types of perspective are one-point, two-point, and three-point perspective. Perspective projection is complicated and requires both theoretical understanding of projection and proficiency in construction techniques. This complexity exceeds the capabilities of many engineering CAD software programs for personal computers. Advanced CAD software programs that run on faster workstation computers can easily render perspective projection.

■ 18.1 GENERAL PRINCIPLES

As explained in §1.9, a perspective involves four main elements: (1) the observer's eye, (2) the object being viewed, (3) the plane of projection, and (4) the projectors from the observer's eye to all points on the object. With rare exceptions (see §18.6), the plane of projection is placed between the observer and the object, as shown in Fig. 1.9, and the collective piercing points in the plane of projection of all the projectors produce the perspective.

In Fig. 18.2, the observer is shown looking along a boulevard and through an imaginary plane of projection. This plane is called the **picture plane**, or PP. The position of the observer's eye is called the **station point**, or SP. The lines from SP to the various points in the scene are the projectors, or more properly in per-

spective, **visual rays**. The points where the visual rays pierce PP are the **perspectives** of the respective points. Collectively, these piercing points form the perspective of the object or the scene as viewed by the observer. The perspective thus obtained is shown in Fig. 18.3.

In Fig. 18.2, the perspective of lamp post 1–2 is shown at 1′–2′, on the picture plane; the perspective of lamp post 3–4 is shown at 3′– 4′, and so on. Each succeeding lamp post, as it is farther from the observer, will be projected smaller than the one preceding. A lamp post at an infinite distance from the observer would appear as a point on the picture plane. A lamp post in front of the picture plane would be projected taller than it is, and a lamp post in the picture plane would be projected in true length. In the perspective (Fig. 18.3), the diminishing heights of the posts are apparent.

In Fig. 18.2, the line representing the *horizon* is the edge view of the *horizon plane*, which is parallel to the ground plane and passes through SP. In Fig. 18.3, the horizon is the line of intersection of this plane with the picture plane and represents the eye level of the observer, or SP. Also, in Fig. 18.2, the *ground plane* is the edge view of the ground on which the object usually rests. In Fig. 18.3, the *ground line*, or GL, is the intersection of the ground plane with the picture plane.

In Fig. 18.3, it will be seen that lines that are parallel to each other but not parallel to the picture plane, such as curb lines, sidewalk lines, and lines along the tops and bottoms of the lamp posts, all converge toward a single point on the horizon. This point is called the **vanishing point**, or VP, of the lines. Thus, the first rule to learn in perspective is this: *All parallel lines that are not parallel to* PP *vanish at a single vanishing point*, and *if these lines are parallel to the ground, the vanishing point will be on the horizon.* Parallel lines that are also parallel to PP, such as the lamp posts, remain parallel and do not converge toward a vanishing point.

■ 18.2 MULTIVIEW PERSPECTIVE

A perspective can be drawn by the ordinary methods of multiview projection, as shown in Fig. 18.4. The upper portion of the drawing shows the top view of the station point, the picture plane, the object, and the visual rays. At the right are the right-side view of the same station point, picture plane, object, and visual rays. In the front view, the picture plane coincides with the plane of the paper, and the perspective is drawn on it. Note the method of projecting from the top view to

FIGURE 18.1   A CAD-produced Perspective of an Airport. *The material has been reprinted with permission from and under the copyright of Autodesk, Inc.*

FIGURE 18.2   Looking Through the Picture Plane.

FIGURE 18.3   A Perspective.

the side view, which conforms to the usual multiview methods shown in Fig. 6.7.

To obtain the perspective of point 1, a visual ray is drawn in the top view from SP_T to point 1 on the object. From the intersection 1′ of this ray with the picture plane, a projection line is drawn downward until it

meets a similar projection line from the side view. This intersection is the perspective of point 1, and the perspectives of all other points are found in a similar manner.

Observe that all parallel lines that are also parallel to the picture plane (the vertical lines) remain parallel

Parallel Railroad Tracks Seem to Converge in the Distance. *Willard Clay; Tony Stone Worldwide.*

and do not converge, whereas the other two sets of parallel lines converge toward vanishing points. Because the vanishing points are not needed in the multiview construction of Fig. 18.4, they are not shown. But if the converging lines were extended, it would be found that they meet at two vanishing points (one for each set of parallel lines).

The perspective of any object may be constructed in this way, but if the object is placed at an angle with the picture plane, as is usually the case, the method is a bit cumbersome because of the necessity of constructing the side view in a revolved position. The revolved side view can be dispensed with, as shown in the following section.

FIGURE 18.4   **Multiview Method of Drawing Perspective.**

■ 18.3 THE SETUP FOR A SIMPLE PERSPECTIVE

The construction of a perspective of a simple form is shown in Fig. 18.5. The upper portion of the drawing, as in Fig. 18.4, shows the top views of SP, PP, and of the object. The lines SP–1, SP–2, SP–3, and SP–4 are the top views of the visual rays.

In the side view, a departure from Fig. 18.4 is made, in that a revolved side view is not required. All that is needed is any elevation view that will provide the necessary elevation or height measurements. If these dimensions are known, no view is required.

The perspective itself is drawn in the front-view position, the picture plane being considered as the plane of the paper on which the perspective is drawn. The ground line is the edge view of the ground plane or the intersection of the ground plane with the picture plane. The horizon is a horizontal line in the picture plane that is the line of intersection of the horizon plane with the picture plane. Since the horizon plane passes through the observer's eye, or SP, the horizon is drawn at the level of the eye—that is, at the distance above the ground line representing, to scale, the altitude of the eye above the ground.

The *center of vision*, or CV, is the orthographic projection (or front view) of SP on the picture plane, and since the horizon is at eye level, CV will always be on the horizon, except in three-point perspective (see §18.11). In Fig. 18.5, the top view of CV is CV′, found by dropping a perpendicular from SP to PP. The front view CV is found by projecting downward from CV′ to the horizon.

FIGURE 18.5   **Perspective of a Prism.**

■ 18.4 DRAWING AN ANGULAR PERSPECTIVE

Since objects are defined principally by edges that are straight lines, the drawing of a perspective resolves itself into drawing the *perspective of a line*. A drafter who can draw the perspective of a line can draw the perspective of any object, no matter how complex.

To draw the perspective of any horizontal straight line not parallel to PP—for example, the line 1–2 in Fig. 18.5—proceed as follows.

I. *Find the piercing point in PP of the line.* In the top view, extend line 1–2 until it pierces PP at T; then project downward to the level of the line 1–2 projected horizontally from the side view. The point S is the piercing point of the line.

II. *Find the vanishing point of the line.* The vanishing point of a line is the piercing point in PP of a line drawn through SP parallel to that line. Hence, the vanishing point VPR of the line 1–2 is found by drawing a line from SP parallel to that line and finding the top view of its piercing point O, and then projecting downward to the horizon. The line SP–O is actually a visual ray drawn toward the infinitely distant point on line 1–2 of the object, extended, and the vanishing point is the intersection of this visual ray with the picture plane. The vanishing point is, then, the perspective of the infinitely distant point on the line extended

III. *Join the piercing point and the vanishing point with a straight line.* The line S–VPR is the line joining these two points, and it is the perspective of a line of infinite length containing the required perspective of the line 1–2.

IV. *Locate the endpoints of the perspective of the line.* The endpoints 1′ and 2′ can be found by projecting down from the piercing points of the visual rays in PP, or by simply drawing the perspectives of the remaining horizontal edges of the object. In practice, it is best to use both methods as a check on the accuracy of the construction. To locate the endpoints by projecting from the piercing points, draw visual rays from SP to the points 1 and 2 on the object in the top view. The top views of the piercing points are X and Z. Since the perspectives of points 1 and 2 must lie on the line S–VPR, project downward from X and Z to locate points 1′ and 2′.

After the perspectives of the horizontal edges have been drawn, the vertical edges and inclined edges can be drawn, as shown, to complete the perspective of the object. Note that *vertical heights can be measured only in the picture plane.* If the front vertical edge 1–5 of the object was actually PP—that is, if the object was situated with the front edge in PP—the vertical height could be set off directly full size. If the vertical edge is behind PP, a plane of the object, such as surface 1–2–5–6, can be extended forward until it intersects PP in line TQ. The line TQ is called a *measuring line*, and the true height SQ of line 1–5 can be set off with a scale or projected from the side view as shown.

If a large drawing board is not available, one vanishing point, such as VPR, may fall off the board. By using one vanishing point VPL and projecting down from the piercing points in PP, vanishing point VPR may be eliminated. However, a valuable means of checking the accuracy of the construction will be lost.

■ 18.5 POSITION OF THE STATION POINT

The center line of the cone of visual rays should be directed toward the approximate center, or center of interest, of the object. In two-point perspective, the type shown in Fig. 18.5, the location of the station point (SP) in the plan view should be slightly to the left, not directly in front of the center of the object, and at such a distance that the object can be viewed at a glance without turning the head. This is accomplished if a cone of rays with its vertex at SP and a vertical angle of about 30° entirely closes the object, as shown in Fig. 18.6.

In the perspective portion of Fig. 18.5, SP does not appear because the station point is in front of the pic-

FIGURE 18.6   **Distance from Station Point to Object.**

ture plane. However, the orthographic projection CV of SP in the picture plane does show the height of the station point with respect to the ground plane. Since the horizon is at eye level, it also shows the altitude of the station point. Therefore, in the perspective portion of the drawing, the horizon is drawn a distance above the ground line at which it is desired to assume the station point. For most small and medium-size objects, such as machine parts or furniture, the station point is best assumed slightly above the top of the object. Large objects, such as buildings, are usually viewed from a station point about the altitude of the eye above the ground, or about 5′–6″.

■ 18.6 LOCATION OF THE PICTURE PLANE

In general, the picture plane is placed in front of the object, as in Fig. 18.7b and Fig. 18.7c. However, it may be placed behind the object, as in Fig. 18.7a, and it may even be placed behind SP, as in Fig. 18.7d, in which event the perspective is reversed, as is the case of a camera. Of course, the usual position of the picture plane is between SP and the object. The perspectives in Fig. 18.7 differ in size but not in proportion. As in Figs. 18.7b and 18.7c, with the picture plane between SP and the object, the farther that plane is from the object, the smaller the perspective will be. This distance may be assumed, therefore, with the thought of controlling the scale of the perspective. In practice, however, the object is usually assumed with the front corner in the picture plane to facilitate vertical measurements (see Fig. 18.12).

■ 18.7 POSITION OF THE OBJECT WITH RESPECT TO THE HORIZON

To compare the elevation of the object with that of the horizon is equivalent to referring it to the level of the eye (SP) because the horizon is on a level with the eye, except in three-point perspective (see §18.11). The differences in effect produced by placing the object on, above, or below the horizon are shown in Fig. 18.8.

If the object is placed above the horizon, it is above the level of the eye, or above SP, and will appear as seen from below. Likewise, if the object is below the horizon, it will appear as seen from above.

■ 18.8 THE THREE TYPES OF PERSPECTIVES

Perspective drawings are classified according to the number of vanishing points required, which in turn de-

pends on the position of the object with respect to the picture plane.

If the object is situated with one face parallel to the plane of projection, only one vanishing point is required, and the result is a *one-point perspective*, or *parallel perspective* (§18.9).

If the object is situated at an angle with the picture plane but with vertical edges parallel to the picture plane, two vanishing points are required, and the result is a *two-point perspective*, or an *angular perspective*. This is the most common type of perspective drawing and is the one described in §18.4 (see also §18.10).

If the object is situated so that no system of parallel edges is parallel to the picture plane, three vanishing points are necessary, and the result is a *three-point perspective* (see §18.11).

■ 18.9 ONE-POINT PERSPECTIVE

In one-point perspective (see Fig. 16.1d), the object is placed so that two sets of its principal edges are parallel to PP and the third set is perpendicular to PP. This third set of parallel lines will converge toward a single vanishing point in perspective, as shown.

In Fig. 18.9, the view shows the object with one face parallel to the picture plane. If desired, this face could be placed in the picture plane. The piercing points of the eight edges perpendicular to PP are found by extending them to PP and then projecting downward to the level of the lines as projected across from the elevation view.

To find the VP of these lines, a visual ray is drawn from SP parallel to them (the same as in step II of §18.4), and it is found that the *vanishing point of all lines perpendicular to* PP *is in* CV. By connecting the eight piercing points with the vanishing point CV, the indefinite perspectives of the eight edges are obtained.

To cut off on these lines the definite lengths of the edges of the object, horizontal lines are drawn from the ends of one of the edges in the top view and at any desired angle with PP—45°, for example, as shown. The piercing points and the vanishing point VPR of these lines are found, and the perspectives of the lines are drawn. The intersections of these with the perspectives of the corresponding edges of the object determine the lengths of the receding edges. The perspective of the object may then be completed as shown.

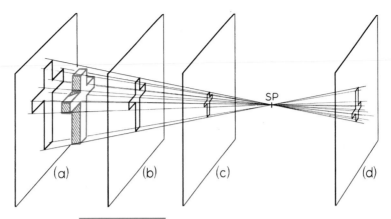

FIGURE 18.7   Location of Picture Plane.

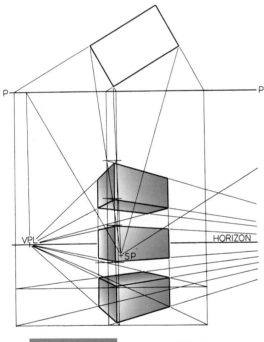

FIGURE 18.8   Object and Horizon.

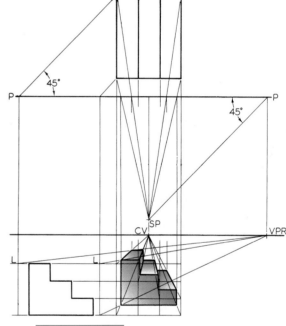

FIGURE 18.9   One-Point Perspective.

One of the most common uses of parallel perspective is in the representation of interiors of buildings, as illustrated in Fig. 18.10.

An adaptation of one-point perspective, which is simple and effective in representing machine parts, is shown in Fig. 18.11. The front surface of the cylinder is placed in PP, and all circular shapes are parallel to PP; hence, these shapes will be projected as circles and circular arcs in the perspective. SP is located in front and to one side of the object, and the horizon is placed well above the ground line. The single vanishing point is on the horizon in CV.

The two circles and the keyway in the front surface of the object will be drawn true shape because they lie in PP. The circles are drawn with the compass on center O′. To locate R′, the perspective center of the large arc, draw visual ray SP–R; then, from its intersection X with PP, project down to the center line of the large cylinder, as shown.

To find the radius T′W′ at the right end of the perspective, draw visual rays SP–T and SP–W, and from their intersections with PP, project down to T′ and W′ on the horizontal center line of the hole.

FIGURE 18.10 One-Point Perspective. *Courtesy of Autodesk, Inc.*

■ 18.10 TWO-POINT PERSPECTIVE

In two-point perspective, the object is placed so that one set of parallel edges is vertical and has no vanishing point, while the two other sets have vanishing points. This is the most common type and is the method discussed in §18.4. It is suitable especially for representing buildings in the architectural drawing, or large structures in civil engineering, such as dams or bridges.

The perspective drawing of a small building is shown in Fig. 18.12. It is common practice (1) to assume a vertical edge of an object in PP so that direct measurements may be made on it and (2) to place the object so that its faces make unequal angles with PP; for example, one angle may be 30° and the other 60°. In practical work, complete multiview drawings are usually available, and the plane and elevation may be fastened in position, used in the construction of the perspective, and later removed.

Since the front corner AB lies in PP, its perspective A′B′ may be drawn full size by projecting downward from the plan and across from the elevation. The lengths of the receding lines from this corner are cut off by vertical lines SC′ and RE′ drawn from the intersections S and R, respectively, of the visual rays to these points of the object. The perspectives of the tops of the windows and the door are determined by the lines A′–VPR and A′–VPL, and their widths and lateral spacings are determined by projecting downward from the intersections with PP of the respective visual rays. The bottom lines of the windows are determined by the lines V′–VPR and V′–VPL.

FIGURE 18.11   **One-Point Perspective.**

The perspective of the line containing the ridge of the roof is found by joining N′, the point where the ridge line pierces the picture plane, and VPR. The ridge ends O′ and Q′ are found by projecting downward from the intersections of the visual rays with PP, or by drawing the perspectives of any two lines intersecting at the points. The perspective of the roof is completed by joining the points O′ and Q′ to the end of the eaves.

■ 18.11 THREE-POINT PERSPECTIVE

In three-point perspective, the object is placed so that none of its principal edges is parallel to the picture plane (PP); therefore, each of the three sets of parallel edges will have a separate vanishing point (VP) (Fig. 18.13). The picture plane is assumed approximately perpendicular to the center line of the cone of rays.

In this figure, think of the paper as the picture plane, with the object behind the paper and placed so that all its edges make an angle with the picture plane. If a point CV is chosen, it will be the orthographic projection of your eye, or the station point, on the picture plane. The vanishing points P, Q, and R are found by conceiving lines to be drawn from a station point in

space parallel to the principal axes of the object and finding their piercing points in the picture planes. It will be recalled that the basic rule for finding the vanishing point of a line in any type of perspective is to draw a visual ray, or line, from the station point parallel to the edge of the object whose vanishing point is required and finding the piercing point of this ray in the picture plane. Since the object is rectangular, these lines to the vanishing points are at right angles to each other in space exactly as the axes are in axonometric projection (see Fig. 17.48). The lines PQ, QR, and RP are perpendicular, respectively, to CV–R, CV–P, and CV–Q and are the *vanishing traces*, or horizon lines, of planes through SP parallel to the principal faces of the object.

The imaginary corner O is assumed in the picture plane and may coincide with CV; but as a rule the front corner is placed at one side near CV, thus determining how nearly the observer is assumed to be directly in front of this corner.

In this method the perspective is drawn directly from measurements and not projected from views. The dimensions of the object are given by the three views, and these will be set off on *measuring lines* GO, EO, and OF (see §18.13). The measuring lines EO and OF are drawn parallel to the vanishing trace PQ, and the measuring line GO is drawn parallel to RQ. These measuring lines are actually the lines of intersection of principal surfaces of the object, extended, with PP. Since these lines are in PP, true measurements of the object can be set off along them.

Three *measuring points* M_1, M_2, and M_3 are used in conjunction with the *measuring lines*. To find M_1, revolve triangle CV–R–Q about RQ as an axis. Since it is a right triangle, it can be easily constructed true size with the aid of a semicircle, as shown. With R as center and R–SP_1 as radius, strike arc SP_1 –M_1, as shown. M_1 is the measuring point for the measuring line GO. Measuring points M_2 and M_3 are found in a similar manner.

Height dimensions, taken from the given views, are set off full size or to any desired scale, along measuring line GO, at points 3, 2, and 1. From these points, lines are drawn to M_1, and heights on the perspective are the intersections of these lines with the perspective front corner OT of the object. Similarly, the true depth of the object is set off on measuring line EO from 0 to 5, and the true width is set off on measuring line OF from 0 to 8. Intermediate points can be constructed in a similar manner.

FIGURE 18.12   Perspective Drawing of a Small Building.

■ 18.12 THE PERSPECTIVE LINEAD AND TEMPLATE

The **perspective linead** consists of three straight-edged blades that can be clamped to each other at any desired angles (Fig. 18.14a). This instrument is conve-

nient in drawing lines toward a vanishing point outside the limits of the drawing.

Before starting such a drawing, a small-scale diagram should be made in which the relative positions of the object, PP, and SP are assumed, and the

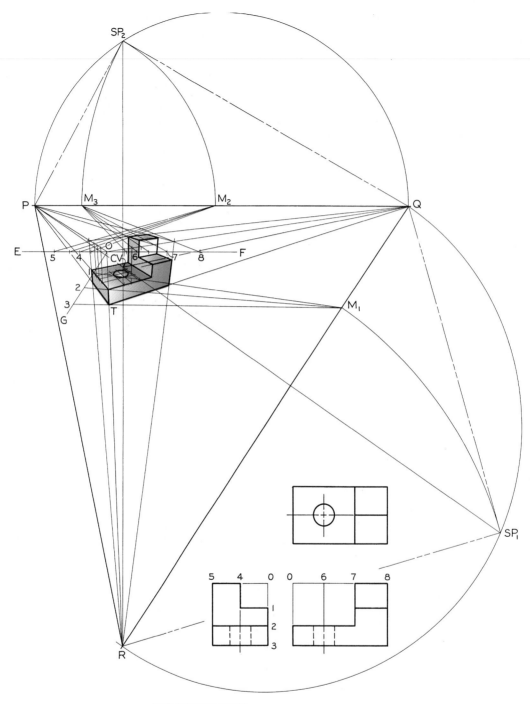

FIGURE 18.13 **Three-Point Perspective.**

distances of the vanishing points from CV determined (Fig. 18.14b). Draw any line LL through a vanishing point as shown; then on the full-size drawing, assume CV and locate LL, as shown in Fig. 18.14a.

To set the linead, clamp the blades in any convenient position; set the edge of the long blade along the horizon; and draw the lines BA and BC along the short blades. Then set the edge of the long the blade along line LL, and draw the lines DE and DF to intersect the lines first drawn at points G and H. Set pins at these points. If the linead is moved so that the short blades touch the pins, all lines drawn along the edge of the long blade will pass through VPL. This method is based on the principle that an angle inscribed in a circle is measured by half the arc it subtends.

A **perspective template** (Fig. 18.15) of thin wood or heavy cardboard, cut in the form of a circular arc, may be used instead of a perspective linead. If the template is attached to the drawing board so that the inaccessible VP is at the center of the circular arc and the T-square is moved so that the head remains in contact with the template, lines drawn along the edge of the blade will, if extended, pass through the inaccessible VP.

If the edge of the blade does not pass through the center of the head, the lines drawn will be tangent to a circle whose center is at VP and whose radius is equal to the distance from the center of the head to the edge of the blade.

■ 18.13 MEASUREMENTS IN PERSPECTIVE

As explained in §18.1, all lines in PP are shown in their true lengths, and all lines behind PP are foreshortened.

Let it be required to draw the perspective of a line of telephone poles (Fig. 18.16). Let OB be the line of intersection of PP with the vertical plane containing the poles. In this line, the height AB of a pole is set off directly to the scale desired, and the heights of the perspectives of all poles are determined by drawing lines from A and B to VPR.

To locate the bottoms of the poles along the line B–VPR, set off along PP the distances 0–1, 1–2, 2–3, . . . ,

FIGURE 18.15 Perspective Template.

equal to the distance from pole to pole; draw the lines 1–1, 2–2, 3–3, . . . , forming a series of isosceles triangles 0–1–1, 0–2–2, 0–3–3, ... The lines 1–1, 2–2, 3–3, . . . , are parallel to each other and, therefore, have a common vanishing point MP, which is found in the usual manner by drawing from SP a line SP–T parallel to the lines 1–1, 2–2, 3–3, . . . , and finding its piercing point MP (*measuring point*) in PP.

Since the line SP–X is parallel to the line of poles 1–2–3, . . . , the triangle SP–X–T is an isosceles triangle, and T is the top view of MP. The point T may be determined by setting off the distance X–T equal to SP–X or simply by drawing the arc SP–T with center at X and radius SP–X.

Having the measuring point MP, find the piercing points in PP of the lines 1–1, 2–2, 3–3, . . . , and draw their perspectives as shown. Since these lines are horizontal lines, their piercing points fall in a horizontal line BZ in PP, at the bottom of the drawing. Along BZ the true distances between the poles are set off; hence, BZ is called a *measuring line*. The intersections 1′, 2′,

FIGURE 18.14 Perspective Linead.

(a) FULL-SIZE DRAWINGS, SHOWING SETTINGS OF LINEAD

(b) SMALL-SCALE DIAGRAM TO LOCATE VANISHING POINTS AND LINE LL

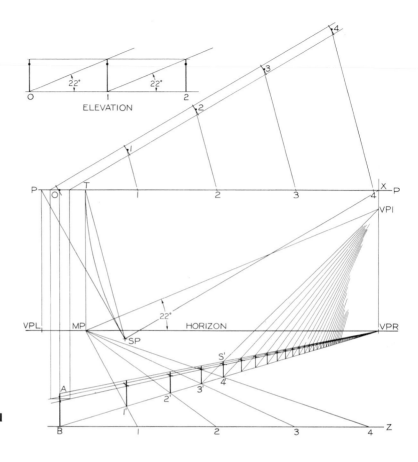

FIGURE 18.16 **Measurement of Vertical and Horizontal Lines.**

3′, ..., of the perspectives of the lines 1–1, 2–2, 3–3, ..., with the line B–VPR determine the spacing of the poles.

It will be seen that only a few measurements may be made along the measuring line BZ within the limits of the drawing. For additional measurements, the *diagonal method* of spacing may be employed, as shown. Since all diagonals from the bottom of each pole to the top of the succeeding pole are parallel, they have a common vanishing point VPI, which may be found as explained in §18.14. It is evident that the diagonal method exclusively may be used in the solution of this problem.

The method of direct measurements may also be applied to lines inclined to PP and to the ground plane, as illustrated in Fig. 18.17 for the line XE, which pierces PP at X. If the end of the house is conceived to be revolved about a vertical axis XO into PP, the line XE will be shown in its true length and inclination at XY. This line XY may be used as the measuring line for XE; it remains only to find the corresponding measuring point MP. The line YE is the horizontal base of an isosceles triangle having its vertex at X, and a line drawn parallel to it through SP will determine MP, as described for Fig. 18.16.

■ 18.14 VANISHING POINTS OF INCLINED LINES

The vanishing point of an inclined line is determined, as for all other lines, by finding the piercing point in PP of a line drawn from SP parallel to the given line.

Fig. 18.18 shows the perspective of a small building. The vanishing point of the inclined roof line C′E′ can be determined as follows: If a plane is conceived to be passed through the station point and parallel to the end of the house (plan view), it would intersect PP in the line XY, through VPL, and perpendicular to the horizon. Since the line drawn from SP parallel to C′E′ (in space) is in the plane SP–X–Y, it will pierce PP at some point T in XY. To find the point T, conceive the plane SP–X–Y revolved about the line XY as an axis in-

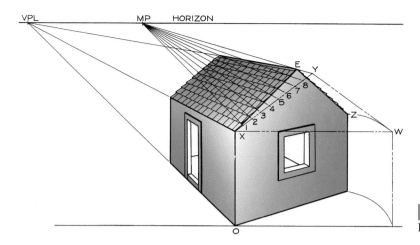

FIGURE 18.17 Measurement of Inclined Lines.

to PP. The point SP will then fall on the horizon at a point shown by O in the top view and by MR in the front view. From the point MR draw the revolved position of the line SP–T (now MR–T) making an angle of 30° with the horizon and thus determining the point T, which is the vanishing point of the line C′E′ and of all lines parallel to that line. The vanishing point S of the line D′E′ is evidently in the line XY, because D′E′ is in the same vertical plane as the line C′E′. The vanishing point S is as far below the horizon as T is above the horizon, because the line E′D′ slopes downward at the same angle at which the line C′E′ slopes upward.

The perspectives of inclined lines can generally be found without finding the vanishing points, by finding the perspectives of the endpoints and joining them. *The perspective of any point may be determined by finding the perspectives of any two lines intersecting at the point.* Obviously, it would be best to use horizontal lines, parallel, respectively, to systems of lines whose vanishing points are already available. For example, in Fig. 18.18, to find the perspective of the inclined line EC, the point E′ is the intersection of the horizontal lines R′–VPR and B′–VPL. The point C′ is already established, since it is in PP; but if it were not in PP, it could be easily found in the same manner. The perspective of the inclined line EC is, therefore, the line joining the perspectives of the endpoints E′ and C′.

■ 18.15 CURVES AND CIRCLES IN PERSPECTIVE

If a circle is parallel to PP, its perspective is a circle. If the circle is inclined to PP, its perspective may be any one of the conic sections in which the base of the cone is the given circle, the vertex is SP, and the cutting

plane is PP. But since the center line of the cone of rays should be approximately perpendicular to the picture plane, the perspective will generally be an ellipse. The ellipse may be constructed by means of lines intersecting the circle, as shown in Fig. 18.19. The radial lines in the elevation view at the left can be easily drawn with the 45° and 30° × 60° triangles. A convenient method for determining the perspective of any plane curve is shown in Fig. 18.20.

■ 18.16 THE PERSPECTIVE PLAN METHOD

A perspective may be drawn by drawing first the perspective of the plan of the object (Fig. 18.21a), then the vertical lines (Fig. 18.21b), and finally the connecting lines (Fig. 18.21c). However, in drawing complicated structures, the superimposition of the perspective on the perspective plan causes a confusion of lines. For this reason, the perspective of the plan from which the location of vertical lines is determined is drawn either above or below its normal location. A suggestion of the range of possible positions of the perspective plan is given in Fig. 18.22; use of the perspective plan below the perspective is shown in Fig. 18.23.

The chief advantages of the perspective plan method over the ordinary plan method are that the vertical lines of the perspective can be spaced more accurately and that a considerable portion of the construction can be made above or below the perspective drawing, so that a confusion of lines on the required perspective is avoided.

When the perspective plan method is used, the ordinary plan view can be omitted and measuring points used to determine distances along horizontal edges in the perspective.

FIGURE 18.18   **Vanishing Points of Inclined Lines.**

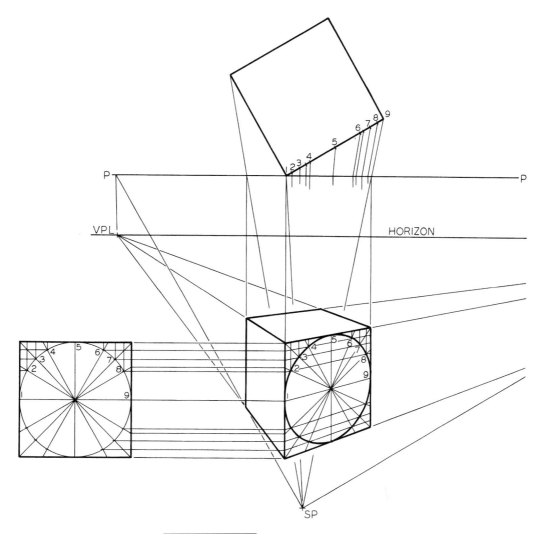

FIGURE 18.19   Circles in Perspective.

FIGURE 18.20   Curves in Perspective.

■ 18.17 PERSPECTIVE DIAGRAM

The spacing of vanishing points and measuring points may be determined graphically or may be calculated. In Fig. 18.24 a simple diagram of the plan layout shows the position of the object, the picture plane, the station point, and the constructions for finding the vanishing points and measuring points for the problem in Fig. 18.23. As indicated in the figure, the complete plan need not be drawn. The diagram should be drawn to any small convenient scale, and vanishing points and measuring points should be set off in the perspective to the larger scale desired.

In practice, structures are usually considered in one of a limited number of simple positions with reference to the picture plane, such as $30° \times 60°$, $45° \times 45°$, and $20° \times 70°$. Therefore, a table of measurements for locating vanishing points and measuring points may be easily prepared, to avoid the necessity of a special construction for each drawing.

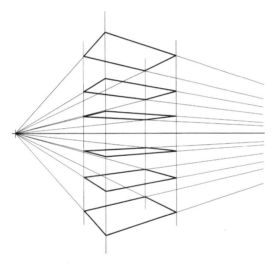

FIGURE 18.21 **Building upon the Perspective Plan.**

FIGURE 18.22 **Positions of Perspective Plan.**

FIGURE 18.23 **Perspective Plan Method.**

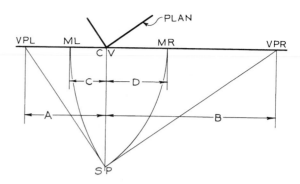

FIGURE 18.24 **Perspective Diagram.**

■ 18.18 SHADING

The effect of light can be utilized advantageously in describing the shapes of objects and in the finish and embellishment of such drawings as display drawings, patent drawings, and industrial pictorial drawings. Ordinary working drawings are not shaded.

Since the purpose of an industrial pictorial drawing is to show clearly the shape and not to be artistic, the shading should be simple and limited to producing a clear picture. Some of the common types of shading are shown in Fig. 18.25. Pencil or ink lines are drawn mechanically (Fig. 18.25a) or freehand (Fig. 18.25b). Two methods of shading fillets and rounds are shown in Figs. 18.25c and 18.25d. Shading produced with pen dots is shown in Fig. 18.25e, and pencil "tone" shading is shown in Fig. 18.25f. Pencil shading applied to pictorial drawings on tracing paper may be reproduced with good results by making a whiteprint or a blueprint.

Examples of line shading on pictorial drawings often used in industrial sales literature are shown in Figs. 18.25 to 18.27.

■ 18.19 COMPUTER GRAPHICS

Perspective drawings, which provide pictorials most resembling photographs, are also the most time-consuming types of pictorials to draw. CAD programs are available that will produce either wireframe (Fig. 18.28), or solid perspective representations, with user selection of viewing distance, focal point, z-axis convergence, and arc resolution scale. Historically, perspectives have seen far greater application in architectural than in engineering drawing. Now the availability of these computer graphics routines makes perspective drawing a viable alternative for the drafter wishing to employ a pictorial representation of an object.

FIGURE 18.25   Methods of Shading.

FIGURE 18.26   Surface Shading Applied to Pictorial Drawing of Display Case.

FIGURE 18.27   A Line-Shaded Drawing of an Adjustable Support for Grinding. *Courtesy of A. M. Byers Co.*

Modeled by Computervision Corporation
for I.M.Pei & Partners, Architects and Planners
and Paul Stevenson Oles, Architectural Perspectivist

FIGURE 18.28   **Perspective Drawing Produced by Using the Computervision Designer System for Building and Management (BDM).** *Courtesy of Computervision Corporation, a subsidiary of Prime Computer, Inc.*

FIGURE 18.29   **Wireframe CAD Perspective of a Car.** *Courtesy of Ford Motor Company.*

■ KEY WORDS

PERSPECTIVE PROJECTION

CENTER OF VISION (CV)

GROUND LINE (GL)

HORIZON

VISUAL RAYS

OBSERVER'S POINT OF VIEW

VANISHING POINT (VP)

PICTURE PLANE (PP)

STATION POINT (SP)

ANGULAR PERSPECTIVE

■ CHAPTER SUMMARY

- The most photorealistic projection is perspective.
- There are three types of perspective projection: one-point, two-point, and three-point perspective.
- In perspective projection, parallel edges converge to one or more vanishing points, which replicate the image of objects as seen by the human eye.
- Object edges are projected onto a picture plane via a straight line to the observer's eye (station point).
- Perspective projection requires two orthographic views (usually top and right side) to construct the perspective view.

- The location and relationship between the vanishing points, the picture plane, and the object determine the appearance of the perspective view.
- In one-point perspective, the object is placed so that two of the three primary axes of the object are parallel to the picture plane.
- In two-point perspective, the object is placed so that only one of the three primary axes of the object are parallel to the picture plane.
- In three-point perspective, the object is placed so that none of the three primary axes of the object are parallel to the picture plane.

■ REVIEW QUESTIONS

1. What is the primary advantage of a perspective projection?
2. Why is perspective projection rarely used in engineering?
3. What is the purpose of the picture plane?
4. What is the station point?
5. How does the distance between the station point and the ground line affect the final perspective drawing?

6. What is the relationship between the station point and the horizon?
7. What type of perspective is often used for rendering interior spaces in architectural drawings?
8. What tools are available to assist the drafter in creating perspective drawings on paper?

■ PERSPECTIVE PROBLEMS

Layouts for perspective problems are given in Figs. 18.30–18.32. Draw on a size B or A3 sheet of paper, vellum, or film, with your name, date, class, and other information lettered below the border as specified by the instructor. Omit dimensions.

Draw problems from Fig. 18.33 on size B or A3 paper. Determine the arrangement on the sheet to produce the most effective perspective in each case. For problems in Fig. 18.34, select both sheet size and scale.

Since many of the problems in this chapter are of a general nature, they can also be solved on most computer graphics systems. If a system is available, the instructor may choose to assign specific problems to be completed by this method.

In addition to these problems, many suitable problems for perspective are found among the axonometric and oblique problems at the ends of Chapters 16 and 17.

FIGURE 18.30 Draw views and perspective. Omit dimensions. Use Size B or A3 sheet.

FIGURE 18.31 Draw views and perspective. Omit dimensions. Use Size B or A3 sheet.

FIGURE 18.32   Draw views and perspective. Omit dimensions. Use Size
B or A3 sheet.

FIGURE 18.33   Draw front elevation, plan, and perspective. Omit
dimensions. Scale: $\frac{1}{8}'' = 1' - 0$. Use Size B or A3 sheet.

1 TOOL BLOCK

2 VISE BASE CASTING

3 SPECIAL CLIP

4 ROD GUIDE

5 SPECIAL CAM

FIGURE 18.34   Draw side or front elevation, plan, and perspective of
assigned problem. Omit dimensions. Use Size B or A3 sheet.

FIGURE 18.35   Draw side or front elevation, plan, and perspective of assigned problem. Omit dimensions. Select sheet size and scale

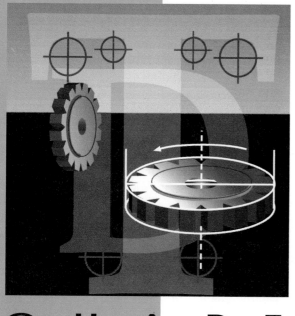

C H A P T E R 1 9

INTERSECTION
AND
DEVELOPMENTS

OBJECTIVES

After studying the material in this chapter, you should be able to:

1. Construct the development of prisms, pyramids, cylinders, and cones.

2. Use triangulation to transfer surface shapes to a development.

3. Create the development of transition pieces.

4. Graphically solve for the intersection of solids.

OVERVIEW

Some of the most complex drawing constructions are intersections and developments. A **development** is a flat representation of a three-dimensional solid that when folded together portrays the solid object. An intersection is the result of two solids that intersect each other. Sheet-metal construction is the most common application for developments and intersections. Even using computers, the graphic solution of developments and intersections is a complex computational task.

A machine part or structure often consists of a number of geometric shapes. Easily represented geometric forms frequently meet in lines of intersection that require knowledge and skill to produce in multiview projection. Accurate representation of the intersecting surfaces is very important since precision fit is necessary for function and appearance. The development of these surfaces, such as those found in sheet-metal fabrication, is a flat pattern that represents the unfolded or unrolled surface of the form. The resulting plane figure gives the true size of each area of the form so connected that when fabricated the desired part or structure is produced.

■ 19.1 SURFACES

A **surface** is a geometric magnitude having two dimensions. A surface may be generated by a line, called the **generatrix** of the surface. Any position of the generatrix is an **element** of the surface (see Fig. 6.31a).

A **ruled surface** is one that may be generated by a straight line and may be a plane, a single-curved surface, or a warped surface.

A *plane* is a ruled surface that may be generated by a straight line, one point of which moves along another straight line while the generatrix remains parallel to its original position. Many of the geometric solids are bounded by plane surfaces (see Fig. 4.7).

A *single-curved surface* is a developable ruled surface; that is, it can be unrolled to coincide with a plane. Any two adjacent positions of the generatrix lie in the same plane. Examples are the cylinder and the cone (see Fig. 4.7).

A *warped surface* is a ruled surface that is not developable (Fig. 19.1). No two adjacent positions of the generatrix lie in the same plane. Many exterior surfaces on an airplane or automobile are warped surfaces.

A double-curved surface may be generated only by a curved line and has no straight-line elements. Such a surface, generated by revolving a curved line about a straight line in the plane of the curve, is called a *double-curved surface of revolution*. Common examples are the *sphere, torus, ellipsoid* (Fig. 4.7), and *hyperboloid* (Fig. 19.1d).

A **developable surface** is one that may be unfolded or unrolled to coincide with a plane (§19.4). Surfaces composed of single-curved surfaces, or of planes, or of combinations of these types are developable. Warped surfaces and double-curved surfaces are not developable. They may be developed approximately by dividing them into sections and substituting for each section a developable surface—that is, a plane or a single-curved surface. If the material used is sufficiently pliable, the flat sheets may be stretched, pressed, stamped, spun, or otherwise forced to assume the desired shape. Nondevelopable surfaces are often produced by a combination of developable surfaces, which are then formed slightly to produce the required shape.

■ 19.2 SOLIDS

Solids bounded by plane surfaces are *polyhedra*, the most common of which are the pyramid and prism. Convex solids whose faces are all equal regular polygons are *regular polyhedra*. The simple regular polyhedra are the *tetrahedron, cube, octahedron, dodecahedron*, and *icosahedron*, known as the five *Platonic solids*.

Plane surfaces that bound polyhedra are *faces* of the solids. Lines of intersection of faces are *edges* of the solids.

A solid generated by revolving a plane figure about an axis in the plane of the figure is a *solid of revolution*.

Solids bounded by warped surfaces have no group name. The most common example of such solids is the screw thread.

INTERSECTIONS AND DEVELOPMENTS OF PLANES AND SOLIDS

■ 19.3 PRINCIPLES OF INTERSECTIONS

The principles involved in intersections of planes and solids have their practical application in the cutting of openings in roof surfaces for flues and stacks; in wall surfaces for pipes, chutes, and so on; and in the building of sheet-metal structures (tanks, boilers, etc.).

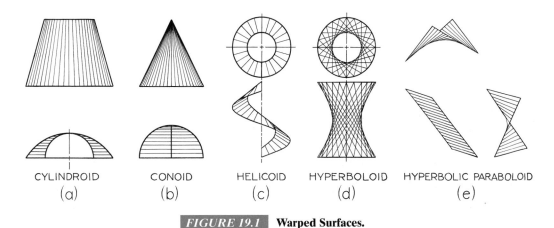

FIGURE 19.1   Warped Surfaces.

In such cases, the problem is generally one of determining the true size and shape of the intersection of a plane and one of the more common geometric solids. The intersection of a plane and a solid is the locus of the points of intersection of the elements of the solid with the plane. For solids bounded by plane surfaces, it is necessary only to find the points of intersection of the edges of the solid with the plane and to join these points, in consecutive order, with straight lines. For solids bounded by curved surfaces, it is necessary to find the points of intersection of several elements of the solid with the plane and to trace a smooth curve through these points. The curve of intersection of a plane and a circular cone is a *conic section* (see §4.44 and Fig. 4.46).

■ 19.4 DEVELOPMENTS

The **development** of a surface is that surface laid out on a plane (Fig. 19.2). Practical applications of developments occur in sheet-metal work, stone cutting, pattern making, packaging, and package design.

Single-curved surfaces and the surfaces of polyhedra can be developed. Warped surfaces and double-curved surfaces can be developed only approximately (see §19.1).

FIGURE 19.2   Development of Surfaces.

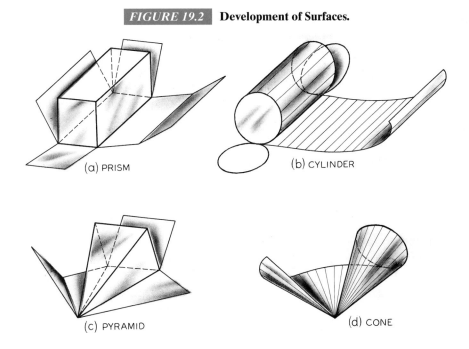

In sheet-metal layout, extra material must be provided for laps and seams. If the material is heavy, the thickness may be a factor, and the crowding of metal in bends must be considered (see §11.39). The drafter must also take stock sizes into account and should make layouts to economize in the use of material and of labor. In preparing developments, it is best to put the seam at the shortest edge and to attach the bases at edges where they match, to economize in soldering, welding, or riveting.

It is common practice to draw development layouts with the *inside surfaces up*. In this way, all fold lines and other markings are related directly to inside measurements, which are the important dimensions in all ducts, pipes, tanks, and other vessels, and in this position they are also convenient for use in the fabricating shop.

■ 19.5 HEMS AND JOINTS FOR SHEET METAL AND OTHER MATERIALS

A wide variety of hems and joints are used in the fabrication of sheet-metal developments and other materials (Fig. 19.3). Hems are used to eliminate the raw edge as well as to stiffen the material. Joints and seams may be made for sheet metal by bending, welding, riveting, and soldering and by gluing and stapling for package materials.

Sufficient material as required for hems and joints must be added to the layout or development. The amount of allowance depends on the thickness of the material and the production equipment; therefore, no specific dimensions for allowances are given in this chapter (see §11.39).

■ 19.6 FINDING THE INTERSECTION OF A PLANE AND A PRISM AND DEVELOPING THE PRISM

The true size and shape of the intersection of a plane and a prism is shown in the auxiliary view (Fig. 19.4a). The length AB is the same as AB in the front view, and the width AD is the same as AD in the top view.

The development of a prism is shown in Fig. 19.4b. On the straight line 1–1, called the *stretchout line* (SOL), set off the widths of the faces 1–2, 2–3, . . ., taken from the top view. At the division points, erect perpendiculars to 1–1, and set off on each the length of the respective edge, taken from the front view. The lengths can be projected across from the front view, as shown. Join the points thus found by straight lines to complete the development of the lateral surface. Attach to this development the lower base and the upper base, or auxiliary view, to obtain the development of the entire surface of the frustum of the prism.

■ 19.7 FINDING THE INTERSECTION OF A PLANE AND A CYLINDER AND DEVELOPING THE CYLINDER

The intersection of a plane and a cylinder is an ellipse whose points are the piercing points in the secant plane of the elements of the cylinder (Fig. 19.5a). In spacing the elements, it is best, though not necessary, to divide the circumference of the base into *equal* parts and to draw an element at each division point. In the auxiliary view, the widths BC, DE, . . ., are taken from the top view at 2–16, 3–15, . . ., respectively, and the curve is traced through the points thus determined, with the aid of the irregular curve.

FIGURE 19.3   Sheet-Metal Hems and Joints.

(a) SINGLE FLANGE   (b) DOUBLE FLANGE   (c) ROLLED EDGE   (d) SINGLE HEM   (e) DOUBLE HEM   (f) WIRED EDGE

Soldered, welded, riveted, etc.

(g) LAP SEAM   (h) PLAIN FLAT SEAM   (j) GROOVED SEAM   (k) SINGLE SEAM   (m) DOUBLE SEAM   (n) STANDING SEAM

FIGURE 19.4 Plane and Prism.

The major axis AH and the minor axis JK are shown true length in the front view and the top view, respectively. Therefore, the ellipse may also be constructed as explained in §§4.45–4.48 or with the aid of an ellipse template (§4.53).

The development of a cylinder is shown in Fig. 19.5b. The base of the cylinder develops into a straight line 1–1, the stretchout line (SOL), equal to the circumference of the base, whose length may be determined by calculation (πd), by setting off with the bow dividers, or by rectifying the arcs of the base 1–2, 2–3, ... (see §4.42). Divide the stretchout line into the same number of equal parts as the circumference of the base, and draw an element through each division perpendicular to the line. Set off on each element its length, projected from the front view, as shown; then trace a smooth curve through the points A, B, D, ..., and attach the bases.

■ 19.8 FINDING THE INTERSECTION OF A PLANE AND AN OBLIQUE PRISM AND DEVELOPING THE PRISM

The intersection of a plane and an oblique prism is shown in Fig. 19.6a. The right section cut by the plane WX is a regular hexagon, as shown in the auxiliary

view; the oblique section, cut by the horizontal plane YZ, is shown in the top view.

The development of an oblique prism is shown in Fig. 19.6b. The right section develops into the straight line WX, the stretchout line (SOL). On the stretchout line, set off the widths of the faces 1–2, 2–3, ..., taken from the auxiliary view, and draw a line through each division perpendicular to the line. From the stretchout line, set off the lengths of the respective edges measured from WX in the front view. Join the points A, B, C, ... with straight lines, and attach the bases, which are shown in their true sizes in the top view.

■ 19.9 FINDING THE INTERSECTION OF A PLANE AND AN OBLIQUE CYLINDER

The intersection of a plane and an oblique cylinder is shown in Fig. 19.7a. As shown in the auxiliary view, the right section cut by the plane WX is a circle. The intersection of the horizontal plane YZ with the cylinder is an ellipse shown in the top view, whose points are found as explained for the auxiliary view in Fig. 19.5a (§19.7). The major axis AH is shown true length in the top view, and the minor axis JK is equal to the diameter of the cylinder. Therefore, the ellipse may be constructed as explained in §§4.45–4.48 or with the aid of an ellipse template (§4.53).

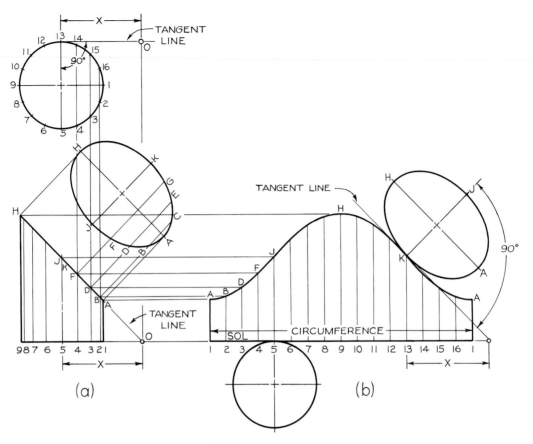

FIGURE 19.5   Plane and Cylinder.

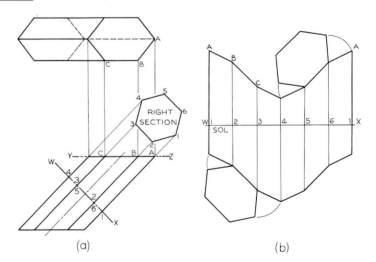

FIGURE 19.6   Plane and Oblique Prism.

For the development of an oblique cylinder (Fig. 19.7b), the cylinder may be considered as a prism having an infinite number of edges. Therefore, the development is found in a manner similar to that of the oblique prism shown in Fig. 19.6.

The circle of the right section cut by plane WX develops into a straight line 1–1, the stretchout line (SOL), equal in length to the circumference of the circle (πd). Divide the stretchout line into the same number of equal parts as the circumference of the circle as

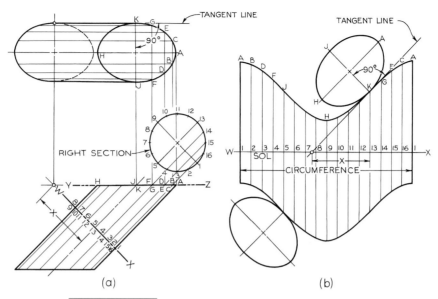

FIGURE 19.7   Plane and Oblique Circular Cylinder.

shown in the auxiliary view, and draw elements through these points perpendicular to the line. Set off on each element its length, taken from the front view with dividers, as shown; then trace a smooth curve through the points A, B, D, . . . and attach the bases.

■ 19.10   FINDING THE INTERSECTION OF A PLANE AND A PYRAMID AND DEVELOPING THE RESULTING TRUNCATED PYRAMID

The intersection of a plane and a pyramid is a trapezoid (Fig. 19.8a) whose vertices are the points in which the edges of the pyramid pierce the secant plane. In the auxiliary view, the altitude of the trapezoid is projected from the front view, and the widths AD and BC are transferred from the top view with dividers.

The development of a truncated pyramid is shown in Fig. 19.8b. With O in the development as center and 0–1′ in the front view (the true length of one of the edges) as radius, draw the arc 1′–2′–3′ . . . . Inscribe the cords 1′–2′, 2′–3′, . . . , equal, respectively, to the sides of the base, as shown in the top view. Draw the lines 1′–O, 2′–O, . . . , and set off the true lengths of the lines OD′, OA′, OB′, . . . , respectively, taken from the true lengths in the front view (see §9.10).

To complete the development, join the points D′, A′, B′, . . . , by straight lines, and attach the bases to their corresponding edges. To transfer an irregular figure, such as the trapezoid shown here, refer to §§4.25 and 4.26.

■ 19.11   FINDING THE INTERSECTION OF A PLANE AND A CONE AND DEVELOPING THE LATERAL SURFACE OF THE CONE

The intersection of a plane and a cone is an ellipse (Fig. 19.9a). If a series of horizontal cutting planes is passed perpendicular to the axis, as shown, each plane will cut a circle from the cone that will shown in true size and shape in the top view. Points in which these circles intersect the original secant plane (see Fig. 4.6) are points on the ellipse. Since the secant plane is shown edgewise in the front view, all of these piercing points may be found in that view and projected to the others, as shown.

The method of finding an intersection shown in Fig. 19.9b is most suitable when a development also is required, since it utilizes elements that are also needed in the development. The piercing points of these elements in the secant plane are points on the intersection. Divide the base into any number of equal parts, and draw an element at each division point. These elements pierce the secant plane in points A, B, C, ... The top views of these points are found by projecting upward from the front view, as shown. In the auxiliary view, the widths BL, CK, . . . , are taken from the top view. The ellipse is then drawn with the aid of the irregular curve.

The major axis of the ellipse, shown in the auxiliary view, is equal to AG in the front view. The minor axis

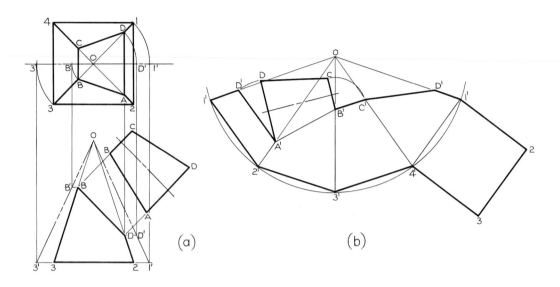

FIGURE 19.8   Plane and Pyramid.

FIGURE 19.9   Plane and Cone.

MN bisects the major axis and is equal to the minor axis of the ellipse in the top view. With these axes, the ellipse may also be constructed as explained in §§4.45–4.48 or with the aid of an ellipse template (§4.53).

For the development of the lateral surface of a cone (Fig. 19.9c), the cone may be considered as a pyramid having an infinite number of edges; hence, the development is found in a manner similar to that explained for the pyramid in §19.10. The base of the cone develops into a circular arc, with the slant height of the cone as its radius and the circumference of the base as its length (see §4.42). The lengths of the elements in the development are taken from the element O–7 or O–1 in the front view (Fig. 19.9b). Instead of

our finding the true circumference of the base, the vertical angle 1–O–1 in the development can be set off equal to $\frac{r}{s}$ 360° (where r is the radius of the base and s is the slant height of the cone).

■ 19.12 FINDING THE DEVELOPMENT OF A HOOD AND FLUE

The development of a hood and flue is shown in Fig. 19.10. Since the hood is a conical surface, it may be developed as described in §19.11. The two end sections of the elbow are cylindrical surfaces and may be developed as described in §19.7. The two middle sections of the elbow are cylindrical surfaces, but since their bases are not perpendicular to the axes, they will not develop into straight lines. They will be developed in a manner similar to that for an oblique cylinder (§19.9, Fig. 19.7b). If the auxiliary

planes AB and DC are passed perpendicular to the axes, they will cut right sections from the cylinders, which will develop into the straight lines AB and CD in the developments.

If the developments are arranged as shown in Fig. 19.10, the elbow can be constructed from a rectangular sheet of metal without wasting material. The patterns are shown separated after cutting. Before cutting, the adjacent curves coincided.

■ 19.13 FINDING THE DEVELOPMENT OF A TRUNCATED OBLIQUE RECTANGULAR PYRAMID

None of the four lateral surfaces is shown true size or shape in the multiview drawing in Fig. 19.11. Using the method of §9.10, revolve each edge until it appears in

FIGURE 19.10 **A Hood and Flue.**

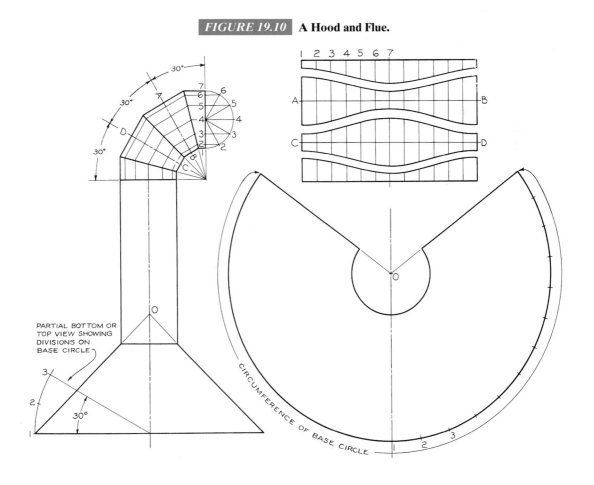

true length in the front view, as shown. Thus, O–2 revolves to O–2′, O–3 revolves to O–3′, and so on. These true lengths are transferred, from the front view to the development, with a compass, as shown. Notice that true lengths OD′, OA′, OB′, . . . , are found and transferred. The true lengths of the edges of the bases are given in the top view and are transferred directly to the development.

■ 19.14 TRIANGULATION

Triangulation is simply a method of dividing a surface into a number of triangles and transferring them to the development. A triangle is said to be "indestructible" because if its sides are of given lengths, it can be only one shape. A triangle can be easily transferred by transferring the sides with the aid of the compass (§4.28).

■ 19.15 FINDING THE DEVELOPMENT OF AN OBLIQUE CONE BY TRIANGULATION

To find the development of an oblique cone by triangulation, divide the base of the cone in the top view into any number of equal parts, and draw an element at each division point (Fig. 19.12). Find the true length of each element (§9.10). If the divisions of the base are

comparatively small, the lengths of the chords may be set off in the development as representing the lengths of the respective subtending arcs. In the development, set off O–1′ equal to O–1 in the front view, where it is shown true length. With 1′ in the development as center and the chord 1–2 taken from the top view as radius, strike an arc at 2′. With O as center and 0–2′, the true length of the element O–2 from the "true-length" diagram, as radius, draw the arc at 2′. The intersection of these arcs is a point on the development of the base of the cone. The points 3′, 4′, . . . , in the curve are found in a similar manner, and the curve is traced through these points with the aid of an irregular curve. Since the development is symmetrical about element O–7′, it is necessary to lay out only half the development, as shown.

■ 19.16 TRANSITION PIECES

A **transition piece** is one that connects two differently shaped, differently sized, or skewed-position openings. In most cases, transition pieces are composed of plane surfaces and conical surfaces, the latter being developed by triangulation (Fig. 19.13). Triangulation can also be used to develop, approximately, certain warped surfaces. Transition pieces are used extensively in air conditioning, heating, ventilating, and similar construction.

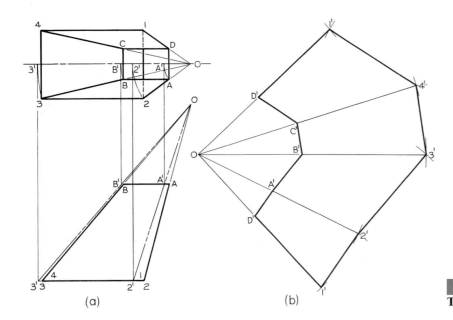

(a)   (b)

FIGURE 19.11   **Development of a Transition Piece.**

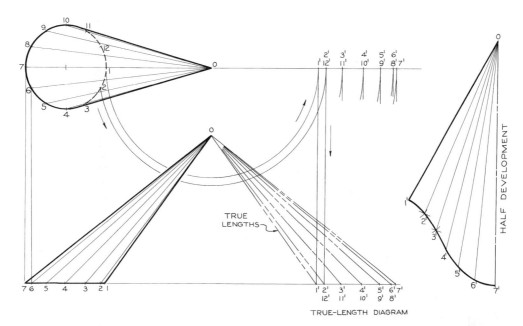

FIGURE 19.12   **Development of an Oblique Cone by Triangulation.**

FIGURE 19.13   **Transition Pieces.**

■ 19.17 FINDING THE DEVELOPMENT OF A TRANSITION PIECE CONNECTING RECTANGULAR PIPES ON THE SAME AXIS

The transition piece can be a frustum of a pyramid that connects rectangular pipes on the same axis (Fig. 19.14a). Find the vertex O of the pyramid by extending its edges to their intersection. Find the true lengths of the edges by any one of the methods in §9.10. The development can then be found as explained in §19.10.

If the transition piece is not a frustum of a pyramid (Fig. 19.14b), it can best be developed by triangulation (§19.14), as shown for the faces 1–5–8–4 and 2–6–7–3, or by extending the sides to form triangles, as shown for faces 1–2–6–5 and 3–4–8–7, and then finding the true lengths of the sides of the triangles and setting them off as shown (see §9.10).

As a check on the development, lines parallel on the surface must also be parallel on the development;

for example, 8′–5′ must be parallel to 4′–1′ on the development.

■ 19.18 FINDING THE DEVELOPMENT OF A TRANSITION PIECE CONNECTING A CIRCULAR PIPE AND A RECTANGULAR PIPE ON THE SAME AXIS

The transition piece connecting a circular pipe and a rectangular pipe on the same axis is composed of four isosceles triangles and four conical surfaces (Fig. 19.15). The seam is along line S–1. Begin the development on the line 1′–S, and draw the right triangle 1′–S–A, whose base SA is equal to half the side AD and whose hypotenuse A–1′ is equal to the true length of side A–1.

The conical surfaces are developed by triangulation, as explained in §§19.14 and 19.15.

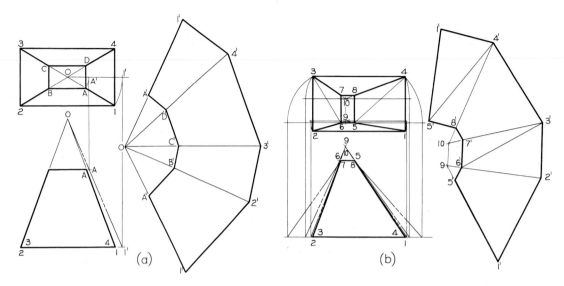

FIGURE 19.14   Development of a Transition Piece. Connecting Rectangular Pipes on the Same Axis.

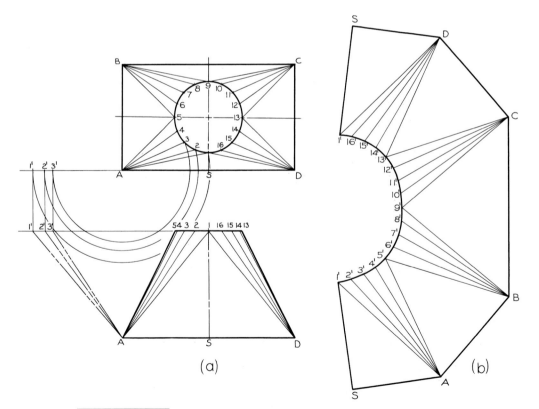

FIGURE 19.15   Development of a Transition Piece. Connecting a Circular Pipe to a Rectangular Pipe on the Same Axis.

■ 19.19 FINDING THE DEVELOPMENT OF A TRANSITION PIECE CONNECTING TWO CYLINDRICAL PIPES ON DIFFERENT AXES

The transition piece connecting two cylindrical pipes in different axes can be a frustum of a cone, the vertex of which may be found by extending the contour elements of their intersection A (Fig. 19.16).

The development can be found by triangulation, as explained in §§19.14 and 19.15. The sides of each triangle are the true lengths of two adjacent elements of the cone, and the base is the true length of the curve of the base of the cone between the two elements. This curve is not shown in its true length in either view, and the plane of the base of the frustum must therefore be revolved until it is horizontal to find the distance from the foot of one element to the foot of the next. When the plane of the base is thus revolved, the foot of any element, such as 7, revolved to 7′, and the curve 6′–7′ (top view) is the true length of the curve of the base between the elements 6 and 7. In practice, the chord distances between these points are generally used to approximate the curved distances.

After the conical surface has been developed, the true lengths of the elements on the truncated section of the cone are set off from the vertex A of the development to secure points on the upper curve of the development.

If the transition piece is not a frustum of a cone, its development is found by another variation of triangulation, as shown in Fig. 19.17. The circular intersection with the large vertical pipe is shown true size in the top view, and the circular intersection with the small inclined pipe is shown true size in the auxiliary view. Since both intersections are true circles and the planes containing them are not parallel, the lateral surface of the transition piece is a warped surface and not conical (single curved). It is theoretically nondevelopable but may be approximately developed by considering it to be made up of plane triangles, alternate ones of which are inverted, as shown in the development. The true lengths of the sides of the triangles are found by the method of Fig. 9.10d, but in a systematic manner to form true-length diagrams, as shown in Fig. 19.17.

■ 19.20 FINDING THE DEVELOPMENT OF A TRANSITION PIECE CONNECTING A SQUARE PIPE AND A CYLINDRICAL PIPE ON DIFFERENT AXES

The development of the transition piece connecting a square pipe and a cylindrical pipe on different axes is made up of five plane triangular surfaces and four triangular conical surfaces similar to those in Fig. 19.15 (Fig. 19.18). The development is made in a similar manner to those described in §§19.15 and 19.18.

FIGURE 19.16 Development of a Transition Piece. Connecting Two Cylindrical Pipes on Different Axes.

FIGURE 19.17   Development of a Transition Piece.

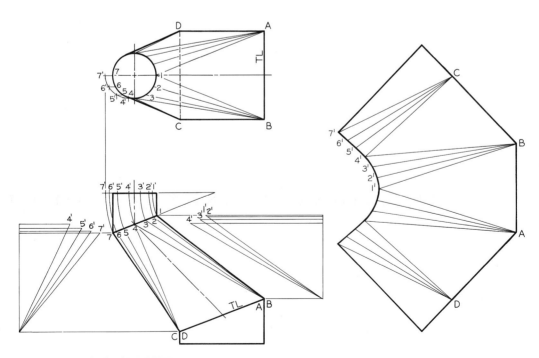

FIGURE 19.18   Development of a Transition Piece. Connecting a Square Pipe to a Cylindrical Pipe on Different Axes.

■ 19.21 FINDING THE INTERSECTION OF A PLANE AND A SPHERE AND FINDING THE APPROXIMATE DEVELOPMENT OF THE SPHERE

The intersection of a plane and a sphere is a circle (top views, Fig. 19.19), with the diameter of the circle depending on where the plane is passed. Any circle cut by a plane through the center of the sphere is called a **great circle**. If a plane passes through the center and perpendicular to the axis, the resulting great circle is called the **equator**. If a plane contains the axis, it will cut a great circle called a **meridian**.

The surface of a sphere is double curved and is not developable (§19.1). The surface may be developed approximately by dividing it into a series of zones and substituting for each zone a frustum of a right-circular cone. The development of the conical surfaces is an approximate development of the spherical surface (Fig. 19.19a). If the conical surfaces are inscribed within the sphere, the development will be smaller than the spherical surface, while if the conical surfaces are circumscribed about the sphere, the development will be larger. If the conical surfaces are partly within and partly without the sphere, as indicated in Fig. 19.19, the resulting development very closely approximates the spherical surface. This method of developing a spherical surface is the *polyconic* method. It is used on government maps of the United States.

Another method of making an approximate development of the double-curved surface of a sphere is to divide the surface into equal sections with meridian planes and substitute cylindrical surfaces for the spherical sections (Fig. 19.19b). The cylindrical surfaces may be inscribed within the sphere, or circumscribed about it, or located partly within and partly without. The development of the series of cylindrical surfaces is an approximate development of the spherical surface. This method is the *polycylindric* method, sometimes designated as the *gore* method.

INTERSECTIONS AND DEVELOPMENTS OF SOLIDS

■ 19.22 PRINCIPLES OF INTERSECTIONS

Intersections of solids are generally regarded as a province of descriptive geometry. For information on the more complicated intersections, any standard text on that subject will be helpful. However, most of the intersections encountered in drafting practice do not require a knowledge of descriptive geometry, and some of the more common solutions may be found in the following paragraphs.

An intersection of two solids is referred to as a **figure of intersection**. Two plane surfaces intersect in a straight line; hence, if two solids that are composed of plane surfaces intersect, the figure of intersection will

FIGURE 19.19   **Approximate Development of a Sphere.**

(a) POLYCONIC METHOD

PARTIAL DEVELOPMENT

QUARTER DEVELOPMENT

(b) POLYCYLINDRIC METHOD

be composed of straight lines, as shown in Figs. 19.20–19.23. The method generally consists of finding the piercing points of the edges of one solid in the surfaces of the other solid and joining these points with straight lines.

If curved surfaces intersect, or if curved surfaces and plane surfaces intersect, the figure of intersection will be composed of curves, as shown in Figs. 19.5, 19.9, and 19.24–19.29. The method generally consists of finding the piercing points of *elements* of one solid in the surfaces of the other. A smooth curve is then traced through these points, with the aid of the irregular curve.

■ 19.23 FINDING THE INTERSECTION AND DEVELOPMENTS OF TWO PRISMS

In the intersection of two prisms shown in Fig. 19.20a, the points in which the edges A, B, C, and D of the horizontal prism pierce the vertical prism are vertices of the intersection. The edges D and B of the horizontal prism intersect the edges 3 and 7 of the vertical prism at the points E, F, L, and M. The edges A and C of the horizontal prism intersect the faces of the vertical prism at the points G, H, J, and K. The intersection is completed by joining these points in order by straight lines.

To develop the lateral surface of the horizontal prism (Fig. 19.20b), set off on the vertical stretchout line A-A the widths of the faces AB, BC, . . . , taken from the end view, and draw the edges through these points, as shown. Set off, from the stretchout line, the lengths of the edges AG, BL, . . . , taken from the front view or from the top view, and join the points G, L, J, . . . , by straight lines.

To develop the lateral surface of the vertical prism, set off on the stretchout line 1–1 the widths of the faces 1–2, 3–5, . . . , taken from the top view, and draw the edges through these points, as shown. Set off on the stretchout line the distances 1–2, 5–4, 5–6, and 1–8, taken from the top view, and draw the intermediate elements parallel to the principal edges. Take the lengths of the principal edges and of the intermediate elements from the front view, and join the points E, G, L, . . . , in order with straight lines, to complete the development.

■ 19.24 FINDING THE INTERSECTION AND DEVELOPMENTS OF TWO PRISMS

In the intersection of two prisms shown in Fig. 19.21a, the points in which the edges ACEH of the horizontal prism pierce the surfaces of the vertical prism pierce the surfaces of the horizontal prism are found in the

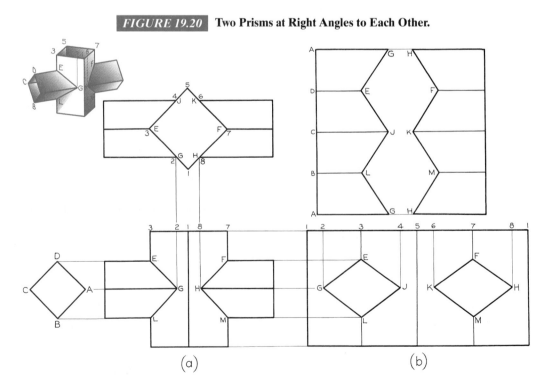

FIGURE 19.20 **Two Prisms at Right Angles to Each Other.**

(a)   (b)

543 216 1278 91011

A   BC D   E   GH J   A
1 2   3   45   6   7 8   9 1011   12   1

(a)   (b)

FIGURE 19.21 **Two Prisms at Right Angles to Each Other.**

top view and are projected downward to the corresponding edges ACEH in the front view. The points in which the edges 5 and 11 of the vertical prism are found in the left-side view at G, D, J, and B and are projected horizontally to the front view, intersecting the corresponding edges as shown. The intersection is completed by joining these points in order by straight lines.

The lateral surfaces of the two prisms in Fig. 19.21b are developed as explained in §19.23 (see Fig. 19.20b). True lengths of all lateral edges and lines parallel to them are shown in the front view of Fig. 19.21a.

■ 19.25 FINDING THE INTERSECTION AND DEVELOPMENTS OF TWO PRISMS

In the intersection of two prisms in Fig. 19.22a, the points in which edges 1–2–3–4 of the inclined prism pierce the surfaces of the vertical prism are vertices of the intersection. These points, found in the top view, are projected downward to the corresponding edges 1–2–3–4 in the front view, as shown. The intersection is completed by joining these points in order by straight lines.

The lateral surfaces of the two prisms (Fig. 19.22b) are developed as explained in §19.23 (see Fig. 19.20b). True lengths of all edges of both prisms are shown in the front view of Fig. 19.22a.

■ 19.26 FINDING THE INTERSECTION AND DEVELOPMENTS OF TWO PRISMS

In the intersection of two prisms shown in Fig. 19.23, the edges of the oblique prism are oblique to the planes of projection, and in the front and top views none of the edges is shown true length (see §6.24), and none of the faces is shown true size (see §6.23). Furthermore, none of the angles, including the angle of inclination, is shown true size (see §6.26). Therefore, it is necessary to draw a secondary auxiliary view (see §8.19) to obtain the true size and shape of the right section of the oblique prism.

The direction of sight, indicated by arrow A, is assumed perpendicular to the end face 1–2–3—that is, parallel to the principal edges of the prism. The primary auxiliary view, taken in the direction of arrow B, shows the true lengths of the edges, the true inclination of the prism with respect to the horizontal, and

FIGURE 19.22   Two Prisms Oblique to Each Other.

incidentally, the true length and inclination of arrow A. In the secondary auxiliary view, arrow A is shown as a point, and the end face 1–2–3 is shown in its true size.

In the intersection of two prisms shown in Fig. 19.23a, the points in which the edges 1–2–3 of the oblique prism pierce the surfaces of the vertical prism are vertices of the intersection, found first in the top view and then projected downward to the front view.

The lateral surfaces of the two prisms are developed as explained in §19.23 (Fig. 19.20b). True lengths of the edges of the vertical prism are shown in the front view (Fig. 19.23b). True lengths of the edges of the oblique prism can be shown in the primary auxiliary view; true lengths to the vertices of the intersection may be found in this view, as shown for line X–5.

■ 19.27 FINDING THE INTERSECTION AND DEVELOPMENTS OF TWO CYLINDERS AT RIGHT ANGLES

In the intersection of two cylinders shown in Fig. 19.24a, assume a series of elements (preferably equally spaced) on the horizontal cylinder, numbered 1, 2, 3, . . . , in the side view, and draw their top and front views. Their points of intersection with the surface of the vertical cylinder are shown in the top view at A, B, C, . . . , and may be found in the front view by projecting downward to their intersections with the corresponding elements 1, 2 , 3, . . . , in the front view. When a sufficient number of points have been found to determine the intersection, the curve is traced through the points with the aid of an irregular curve (see also Fig. 6.38c).

FIGURE 19.23 Two Prisms Oblique to Each Other.

The lateral surfaces of the two cylinders are developed as explained in §19.7. True lengths of all elements of both cylinders are shown in the front view. Since both cylinders have bases at right angles to the center lines, the circles will develop as straight lines, and the developments will be rectangular, as shown (Fig. 19.24b). The length XY of the stretchout line for the development of the vertical cylinder is equal to the circumference of the cylinder, or πd, and the length 1–1 of the stretchout line for the development of the horizontal cylinder is determined in the same way. Those elements of the large cylinder that pierce the small cylinder can be identified in the top view as elements A, B, C, ... When these are drawn in the development, the points of intersections are found at their intersections with the corresponding elements of the horizon-tal cylinder taken from the front view, thus determining one of the figures of intersection, as shown in Fig. 19.24b.

■ 19.28 FINDING THE INTERSECTION AND DEVELOPMENTS OF TWO CYLINDERS OBLIQUE TO EACH OTHER

In the intersection of two cylinders shown in Fig. 19.25a, a revolved right section of the inclined cylinder is divided into a number of equal parts, and an element is drawn at each of the division points, 1, 2, 3, ... The points of intersection of these elements with the surface of the vertical cylinder are shown in the top view at B, C, D, . . . , and are found in the front view by projecting downward to intersect the corresponding

CIRCUMFERENCE = 3.1416 x DIA

CIRCUMFERENCE = 3.1416 x DIA

(a)

(b)

FIGURE 19.24 Two Cylinders at Right Angles to Each Other.

HALF DEVELOPMENT

HALF DEVELOPMENT

(b)

(a)

(b)

FIGURE 19.25 Two Cylinders Oblique to Each Other.

elements 1, 2, 3, ... The curve is traced through these points with the aid of an irregular curve.

The lateral surfaces of the two cylinders (Fig. 19.25b) are developed as explained in §§19.7 and 19.9. True lengths of all elements of both cylinders are shown in the front view.

■ 19.29 FINDING THE INTERSECTION AND DEVELOPMENTS OF A PRISM AND A CONE

In the intersection of a prism and a cone shown in Fig. 19.26a, points in which the edges of the prism intersect the surface of the cone are shown in the side view at A, C, and F. Intermediate points such as B, D, E, and G are piercing points of any lines on the lateral surface of the prism parallel to the edges. Through all of the piercing points in the side view, elements of the cone

are drawn and then drawn in the top and front views. The intersections of the elements of the cone with the edges of the prism (and lines along the prism drawn parallel thereto) are points of the intersections. The figures of intersections are traced through these points with the aid of an irregular curve.

The elements 6, 5, 4, ..., in the side view of the cone may be regarded as the edge views of cutting planes that cut these elements on the cone and edges or elements on the prism. The intersections of corresponding edges or elements on the two solids are points on the figure of intersection.

Another method of finding the figure of intersection is to pass a series of horizontal parallel planes through the solids in the manner of Fig. 19.9a. The plane will cut circles on the cone and straight lines on the prism, and their intersections will be points on the figure of intersection (see also Fig. 19.27b).

FIGURE 19.26 Prism and Cone.

The lateral surface of the prism is developed as explained in §19.23 (Fig. 19.20). True lengths of all edges and lines parallel thereto are shown in both the front and top views (Fig. 19.26b).

The lateral surface of the cone (Fig. 19.26c) is developed as explained in §19.11. True lengths of elements from the vertex to points on the intersections are found as shown in Fig. 9.10a.

■ 19.30 FINDING THE INTERSECTION OF A PRISM AND A CONE WITH PRISM EDGES PARALLEL TO CONE AXIS

Since the lateral surfaces of the prism in Fig. 19.27a are parallel to the axis of the cone, the figure of intersection will be composed of a series of hyperbolas (see §§4.44 and 4.47). If a series of planes is assumed containing the axis of the cone, each plane will contain edges of the prism, or will cut lines parallel to them along the prism and will cut elements on the cone that intersect these points on the figure of intersection.

The intersection in Fig. 19.27b is the same as in Fig. 19.27a, but it is found in a different manner. Here a series of parallel planes perpendicular to the axis of the cone cut circles of varying diameters on the cone.

These circles are shown true size in the top view, where the piercing points of these circles in the vertical plane surfaces of the prism are also shown. The front views of these piercing points are found by projecting downward to the corresponding cutting-plane lines.

The chamfer of an ordinary hexagon bolt head or hexagon nut is actually a conical surface that intersects the six vertical sides of a hexagonal prism to form hyperbolas. In Fig. 19.27c, the methods of both Figs. 19.27a and 19.27b are shown to illustrate how points may be found by either method.

In machine drawings of bolts and nuts, these hyperbolic curves are approximated by means of circular arcs, as shown in Fig. 13.27.

■ 19.31 FINDING THE INTERSECTIONS AND THE DEVELOPMENTS OF A CYLINDER AND A CONE

Points in which elements of the cylinder (preferably equally spaced to facilitate the development) intersect the surface of the cone are shown in the side view at A, B, C, . . . in Fig. 19.28a. The elements of the cylinder are shown here as points. Elements of the cone are

FIGURE 19.27 **Prisms and Cones.**

(a)   (b)   (c)

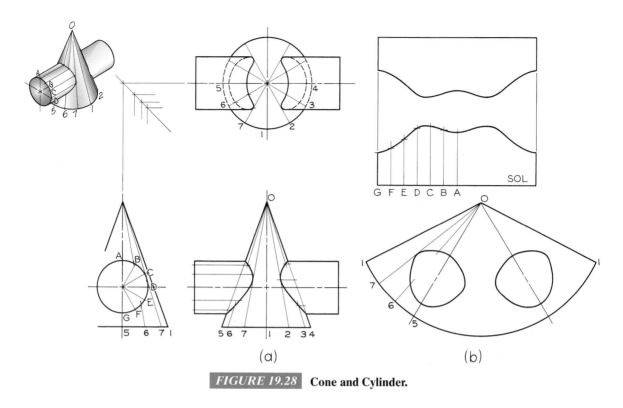

FIGURE 19.28 Cone and Cylinder.

then drawn from the vertex through each of these points, and then drawn in their correct locations in the top and front views. The intersections of these elements with the elements A, B, C ... of the cylinder are points on the figures of intersection. The curves are then traced through these points with the aid of an irregular curve.

As explained in §19.29, the elements 5, 6, 7, . . . , in the side view of Fig. 19.28a could be regarded as edge views of cutting planes that cut elements from both the cone and the cylinder, the elements meeting at points on the figure of intersection. Or a series of horizontal parallel planes can be passed through the solids that will cut circles from the cone and elements from the cylinder that intersect at points on the figure of intersection.

As shown in Fig. 19.28b, the lateral surface of the cylinder is developed as explained in §19.7. True lengths of all elements are shown in both the front and top views. The lateral surface of the cone is developed

as explained in §19.11. True lengths of elements from the vertex to points on the intersections are found as shown in Fig. 9.10a.

19.32 FINDING THE INTERSECTION OF A CYLINDER AND A SPHERE

In the intersection of a cylinder and a sphere in Fig. 19.29, horizontal planes 1, 2, 3, . . . , which appear edgewise in the front and side views, cut elements A, B, C, ..., from the cylinder and circular arcs 1′, 2′, 3′, ..., from the sphere. The intersections of the elements with the arcs produced by the corresponding planes are points on the figure of intersection. Join the points with a smooth curve.

19.33 USING CAD

Determining the intersections and developments of planes and solids that contain plane, curved, or warped surfaces can be very time consuming if done

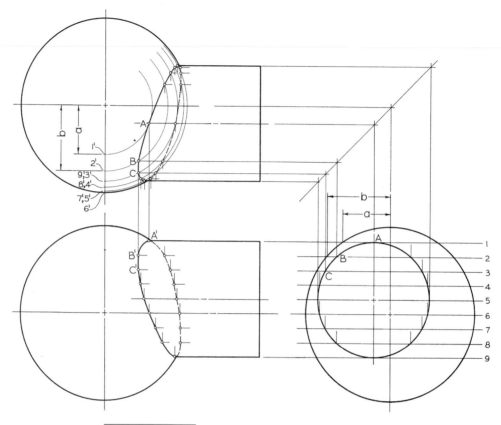

FIGURE 19.29 Intersection of Sphere and Cylinder.

by traditional methods as shown in Figs. 19.23, 19.25, and 19.28. 3D CAD software can let you quickly create 3D models joined together to create complex shapes. Once the solids or surfaces are defined, many programs have the additional capability to generate the flat pattern, or development, directly from the model. Also the code to control 3D NC machines can be generated from the CAD database.

■ KEY WORDS

DEVELOPMENT

CURVED SURFACE

GENERATRIX

STRETCHOUT LINE

TRUNCATED

INTERSECTION

WARPED SURFACE

RULED SURFACE

TRANSITION PIECE

GREAT CIRCLE

MERIDIAN

POLYCYLINDRIC

■ CHAPTER SUMMARY

- The technique for creating the development of solids is determined by the basic geometric shape. Prisms, pyramids, cylinders, and cones each have a particular development technique.

- The intersection of two solids is determined by plotting the intersection of each surface and transferring the intersection points to each development.

- Cones and pyramids use radial development. Prisms and cylinders use parallel development.

- Truncated solids, cones, and pyramids are created by developing the whole solid and then plotting the truncated endpoints on each radial element.

- Transition pieces are developed by creating triangular surfaces that approximate the transition from rectangular to circular. The smaller the triangular surfaces, the more accurate the development.

■ REVIEW QUESTIONS

1. How is the development of a pyramid similar to the development of a cone?

2. When developing a truncated cone or pyramid, why is the complete solid developed first?

3. What descriptive geometry techniques are used to determine the intersection points between two solids?

4. What is a transition piece?

5. What is a stretchout line?

6. Which parts of a development are true size and true shape?

7. What building trades use developments and intersections?

■ INTERSECTION AND DEVELOPMENT PROBLEMS

A wide selection of intersection and development problems is provided in Figs. 19.30–19.37. These problems are designed to fit size B (11.0″ × 17.0″) or A3 (297 mm × 420 mm) sheets. Dimensions should be included on the given views. Take extra effort to be accurate in these drawings and to draw smooth curves as required.

Since many of the problems in this chapter are of a general nature, they can also be solved on most computer graphics systems. If a system is available, the instructor may choose to assign specific problems to be completed by this method.

FIGURE 19.30   Draw given views and develop lateral surface (Layout A3–3 or B–3).

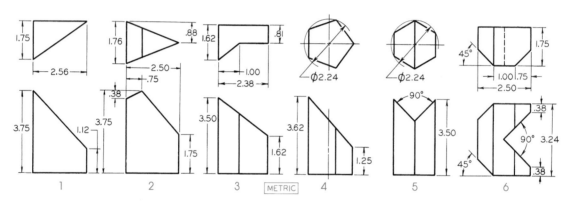

FIGURE 19.31   Draw given views and develop lateral surface (Layout A3–3 or B–3).

FIGURE 19.32   Draw given views and develop lateral surface (Layout A3–3 or B–3).

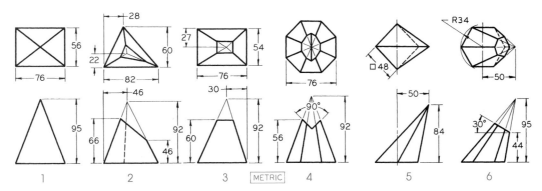

FIGURE 19.33   Draw given views and develop lateral surface (Layout A3–3 or B–3).

FIGURE 19.34   Draw given views and develop lateral surface (Layout A3–3 or B–3).

FIGURE 19.35   Draw given views of the forms and develop lateral surfaces (Layout A3–3 or B–3).

FIGURE 19.36 Draw the given views of assigned form and complete the intersection. Then develop lateral surfaces (Layout A3–3 or B–3).

FIGURE 19.37   Draw the given views of assigned form and complete the intersection. Then develop lateral surfaces (Layout A3–3 or B–3).

CHAPTER 20

GEARING AND CAMS

OBJECTIVES

After studying the material in this chapter, you should be able to:

1. Define the characteristics of a spur gear, worm gear, and bevel gear.
2. Calculate the gear ratio and rpm of two mating gears, given the pitch diameters.
3. Define the principal spur gear terms.
4. Draw a spur gear.
5. Describe the relationship between a cam profile and a displacement diagram.
6. Draw a cam profile, given a displacement profile drawing.
7. List the types of cam followers.

OVERVIEW

In machine design and drafting, various devices are used to transmit power and motion from one machine member to another. *Gears, pulleys and belts, chains and sprockets, cams, linkages,* and other devices are commonly used. In the layout of these machines and in making detail drawings of these elements, certain standards must be followed, and a knowledge of the function of these devices is important.

Gears are one of the most common drive transfer mechanisms. Gears can change rotation direction, rotation speed, and axis orientation. The complex shape of a gear tooth is the result of mathematical computation. Drawing gears on paper or with CAD requires considerable theoretical knowledge. Advanced CAD software programs can make gear drawing easier once the parameters of the gear are determined. Gear terminology must be clearly understood before drawing a gear on paper or with CAD. Cams change rotational motion into reciprocating motion. Both gears and cams are commonly used in automobile engines and transmissions.

■20.1 GEARS

Gears[*] are used to transmit power and rotating or reciprocating motion from one machine part to another (Fig. 20.1). They may be classified according to the position of the shafts that they connect. Parallel shafts, for example, may be connected by *spur gears, helical gears*, or *herringbone gears*. Intersecting shafts may be connected by *bevel gears* having either straight, skew, or spiral teeth. Nonparallel, nonintersecting shafts may be connected by *helical gears, hypoid gears*, or a *worm* and *worm gear*. A spur gear meshed with a *rack* will convert rotary motion to reciprocating motion.

■20.2 SPUR GEARS

The *friction wheels* shown in Fig. 20.2a transmit motion and power from one shaft to another parallel shaft. However, friction wheels are subject to slipping, and excessive pressure is required between the wheels to obtain the necessary frictional force; therefore, they are usually used for low-power applications, such as phonograph turntable drives. If teeth of the proper shape are provided on the cylindrical surfaces, the re-

[*] See ANSI/AGMA 115.01–1989, ANSI/AGMA 1012–F90, and other ANSI/AGMA standards for additional information.

sulting spur gears (Fig. 20.2b) transmit the same motion and power without slipping and with greatly reduced bearing pressures.

If a friction wheel of diameter D turns at n rpm (revolutions per minute), the linear velocity, v, of a point of its periphery will be $\pi D n$, since $\pi D = c$ (circumference).

EXAMPLE Let

$$D = 3 \text{ in.}$$

$$n = 100 \text{ rpm}$$

Then

$$v = \pi D n = \pi(3)(100) \text{ in./min}$$

$$= 942 \text{ in./min}$$

or

$$\frac{942}{12} = 78.5 \text{ ft/min.}$$

But the pitch circles of a pair of mating spur gears correspond exactly to the outside diameters of the friction wheels, and since the gears turn in contact without slipping, they must have the same linear velocity at the pitch line. Therefore,

$$\pi D_G n_G = \pi D_P n_P$$

or

$$\frac{D_G}{D_P} = \frac{n_P}{n_G} = m_G,$$

where D_G = pitch diameter of larger gear (called *wheel*)

   D_P = pitch diameter of smaller gear (called *pinion*)

   n_G = rpm of gear

   n_P = rpm of pinion

   m_G = gear ratio.

The gear ratio is also expressed as n_P/n_G or D_G/D_P.

EXAMPLE Let

$$D_G = 27'' \quad \text{and} \quad D_P = 9''.$$

FIGURE 20.1   An Assortment of Gears. *Courtesy Charles Bond Co.*

EQUAL PITCH CIRCLES

D

d

(a)

D_G

D_P

(b)

FIGURE 20.2   Friction Gears and Toothed Gears.

Then

Gear ratio $= m_G = 27 : 9$

$= 3 : 1$ (read as 3 to 1).

EXAMPLE For the same gear pair, let

$n_P = 1725$ rpm.

Find n_G.

$$\frac{n_P}{n_G} = \frac{D_G}{D_P}, \frac{n_G}{n_P} = \frac{D_P}{D_G}$$

$$n_G = n_P \frac{D_P}{D_G} = 1725 \cdot \frac{9}{27}$$

$$= \frac{1725}{3}$$

$$= 575 \text{ rpm}$$

The teeth on mating gears must be of equal width and spacing; hence, the number of teeth on each gear, N, is directly proportional to its pitch diameter, or

$$\frac{N_G}{N_P} = \frac{D_G}{D_P} = \frac{n_P}{n_G} = m_G.$$

■ 20.3 SPUR GEAR DEFINITIONS AND FORMULAS[*]

Proportions and shapes of gear teeth are well standardized, and the terms illustrated and defined in Fig. 20.3 are common to all spur gears. The dimensions relating to tooth height are for full-depth $14\frac{1}{2}°$ or $20°$ involute teeth.

■ 20.4 THE SHAPE OF THE TOOTH

If gears are to operate smoothly with a minimum of noise and vibration, the curved surface of the tooth profile must be of a definite geometric form. The most common form in use today is the *involute profile*.

In the involute system, the form of the tooth depends basically on the *pressure angle*, which is ordinarily $14\frac{1}{2}°$ or $20°$. This pressure angle determines the size of the *base circle*; from this the involute curve is generated.

The base circle is constructed in the following manner. At any point on the pitch circle, such as point P (the pitch point) (Fig. 20.4), a line is drawn tangent to the pitch circle; a second line is drawn through P at the required pressure angle ($14\frac{1}{2}°$ is frequently approximated at $15°$ on the drawing). This line is called the *line of contact*. A line is then drawn perpendicular to the line of contact from the center, C. The base circle is then drawn with radius CJ tangent to the line of contact at J.

[*] See also ANSI/AGMA 1012–F90 and other ANSI/AGMA (American Gear Manufacturers Association) standards for more details.

If the exact shape of the tooth is desired, the portion of the profile from the base circle to the addendum circle can be drawn as the involute of the base circle. In Fig. 20.5, the tooth profile from A to O is an involute of the base circle. The method of construction is shown in Figs. 4.64d and 4.64e. That part of the profile which is below the base circle, line OB, is drawn as a radial line (a straight line drawn from the gear center) that terminates in the fillet at the root circle. The fillet should be equal in radius to one and one half times the clearance.

For display drawings and more rapid construction, the involute curve can be closely approximated with two circular arcs, as shown in Fig. 20.6. This method, originally devised by Grant,[*] employs a table of arc radii, an involute odontograph, for gears having various numbers of teeth. The base circle is drawn as described previously, and the spacing of the teeth is set off along the pitch circle. Then the face of the tooth from P to A is drawn with the *face radius* R, and the portion of the flank from P to O is drawn with the *flank radius* r. Both arcs are drawn from centers located on the base circle. The table gives the correct face and flank radii for gears of *one* diametral pitch. For other pitches, the values in the table must be divided by the diametral pitch. For gears with more than 90 teeth, use a single radius (let R = r) computed from the appropriate formula given in Fig. 20.6, and then divide by diametral pitch. Below the base circle, the flank of the tooth is completed with a radial line OB and a fillet.

EXAMPLE Suppose that $N = 20$ and $P = 4$ (the diametral pitch) for a $14\frac{1}{2}°$ involute tooth. The values from the table are $R = 4.02$ and $r = 1.56$. These must be divided by P; then $R = 4.02/4 = 1.005''$ and $r = 1.56/4 = 0.39''$. (Note that these values are for a full-size drawing. If the drawing is reduced or enlarged, the values must be adjusted accordingly.) Templates are also available for drawing gear tooth profiles and can increase the speed of drawing considerably.

[*] G.B. Grant, "Teeth of Gears," 1891. Grant's tabulated radii, which have been used for many years, were based on a pressure angle of $15°$ and were empirically shortened to correct for interference at the tooth tips. The new radii given in Fig. 20.6 have been computed for both $14\frac{1}{2}°$ and $20°$ to approximate more closely the true involute profile. To distinguish between the two tables, the new values are called *Wellman's involute odontograph*.

Term	Symbol	Definition	Formula
Addendum	a	Radial distance from pitch circle to top of tooth.	$a = 1/P$
Base Circle		Circle from which involute profile is generated.	
Chordal addendum	a_c	Radial distance from top of a tooth to the chord of pitch circle.	$a_c = a + \frac{1}{2}D[1 - \cos(90°/N)]$
Chordal thickness	t_c	Thickness of a tooth measured along a chord of pitch circle.	$t_c = D\sin(90°/N)$
Circular pitch	p	Distance measured along pitch circle from a point on one tooth to corresponding point on the adjacent tooth; includes one tooth and one space.	$p = \pi D/N$ $p = \pi/P$
Circular thickness	t	Thickness of a tooth measured along the pitch circle: equal to one-half the circular pitch.	$t = p/2 = \pi/2P$
Clearance	c	Distance between top of a tooth and bottom of mating space: equal to the dedendum minus the addendum.	$c = b - a = 0.157/P$
Dedendum	b	Radial distance from pitch circle to bottom of tooth space.	$b = 1.157/P$
Diametral pitch	P	A ratio equal to number of teeth on the gear per inch of pitch diameter.	$P = N/D$
Number of teeth	N_G or N_P	Number of teeth on the gear or pinion.	$N = P \times D$
Outside diameter	D_o	Diameter of addendum circle: equal to pitch diameter plus twice the addendum.	$D_o = D + 2a = (N + 2)/P$
Pitch circle		An imaginary circle that corresponds to circumference of the friction gear from which the spur gear is derived.	
Pitch diameter	D_G or D_P	Diameter of pitch circle of gear or pinion.	$D = N/P$
Pressure angle	ϕ	Angle that determines direction of pressure between contacting teeth and designates shape of involute teeth—e.g. $14\frac{1}{2}°$ involute; also determines size of base circle.	
Root diameter	D_R	Diameter of the root circle; equal to pitch diameter minus twice the dedendum.	$D_R = D - 2b =$ $(N - 2.314)/P$
Whole depth	h_t	Total height of the tooth; equal to the addendum plus the dedendum.	$h_t = a + b = 2.157/P$
Working depth	h_k	Distance a tooth projects into mating space; equal to twice the addendum.	$h_k = 2a = 2/P$

FIGURE 20.3   **Spur Gear Nomenclature.**

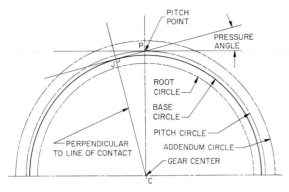

FIGURE 20.4   **Construction of a Base Circle.**

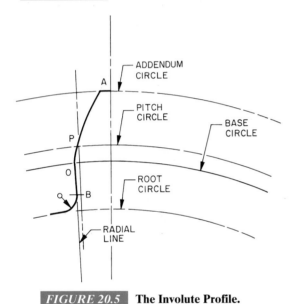

FIGURE 20.5   **The Involute Profile.**

The teeth may be spaced around the periphery by laying off equal angles (Fig. 20.7). The number of spaces should be 2*N*, twice the number of teeth, to make the space between teeth equal to the tooth thickness at the pitch circle. In the example, since $N = 20$, $a = 360°/2N = 360°/40 = 9°$, the angle subtended by each tooth and each space.

When the pressure angle is 20° and the height of the tooth is reduced, the teeth are called *stub teeth*. Stub teeth are drawn in the same manner as other teeth except that $a = 0.8/P$, $b = 1/P$, and the pressure angle is made 20°. The major advantage of stub teeth is that they are stronger than the $14\frac{1}{2}°$ standard full-depth teeth.

When the gear teeth are formed on a flat surface, the result is a rack (Fig. 20.8). In the involute system, the sides of rack teeth are straight and are inclined at

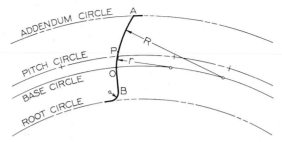

No. of Teeth (N)	$14\frac{1}{2}°$		20°	
	R (in.)	r (in.)	R (in.)	r (in.)
12	2.87	0.79	3.21	1.31
13	3.02	0.88	3.40	1.45
14	3.17	0.97	3.58	1.60
15	3.31	1.06	3.76	1.75
16	3.46	1.16	3.94	1.90
17	3.60	1.26	4.12	2.05
18	3.74	1.36	4.30	2.20
19	3.88	1.46	4.48	2.35
20	4.02	1.56	4.66	2.51
21	4.16	1.66	4.84	2.66
22	4.29	1.77	5.02	2.82
23	4.43	1.87	5.20	2.98
24	4.57	1.98	5.37	3.14
25	4.70	2.08	5.55	3.29
26	4.84	2.19	5.73	3.45
27	4.97	2.30	5.90	3.61
28	5.11	2.41	6.08	3.77
29	5.24	2.52	6.25	3.93
30	5.37	2.63	6.43	4.10
31	5.51	2.74	6.60	4.26
32	5.64	2.85	6.78	4.42
33	5.77	2.96	6.95	4.58
34	5.90	3.07	7.13	4.74
35	6.03	3.18	7.30	4.91
36	6.17	3.29	7.47	5.07
37–39	6.36	3.46	7.82	5.32
40–44	6.82	3.86	8.52	5.90
45–50	7.50	4.46	9.48	6.76
51–60	8.40	5.28	10.84	7.92
61–72	9.76	6.54	12.76	9.68
73–90	11.42	8.14	15.32	11.96
91–120	0.118N		0.156N	
121–180	0.122N		0.165N	
Over 180	0.125N		0.171N	

FIGURE 20.6   **Wellman's Involute Odontograph.**

an angle equal to the pressure angle. To mesh with a gear, the linear pitch of the rack must be the same as the circular pitch of the gear, and the rack teeth must have the same height proportions as the gear teeth.

EQUAL ANGLES

FIGURE 20.7   **Spacing Gear Teeth.**

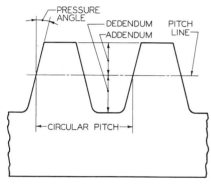

PRESSURE ANGLE

DEDENDUM

ADDENDUM

PITCH LINE

CIRCULAR PITCH

FIGURE 20.8   **Involute Rack Teeth.**

20.5 WORKING DRAWINGS OF SPUR GEARS

A typical working drawing of a spur gear is shown in Fig. 20.9. Since the teeth are cut to standard shape with special cutters, it is not necessary to show individual teeth on the drawing. Instead, the addendum and root circles are drawn as phantom lines and the pitch circle as a center line. Thus, the drawing actually shows only a gear blank—a gear complete except for teeth. Since the machining of the blank and the cutting of the teeth are separate operations in the shop, the necessary dimensions are arranged in two groups: the blank dimensions are shown on the views, and the cutting data are given in a note or table.

Before laying out the working drawing, the drafter must calculate the gear dimensions. For example, if the gear must have 48 teeth of 4 diametral pitch, with $14\frac{1}{2}^{\circ}$ full-depth involute profile, as in Fig. 20.9, then the following items should be calculated in this order: pitch diameter, addendum, dedendum, outside diameter, root diameter, whole depth, chordal thickness, and chordal addendum. The dimensions shown in Fig. 20.9 are the minimum requirements for the spur gear. The chordal addendum and chordal thickness are given to aid in checking the finished gear. Other special data may be given in the table, according to the degree of precision required and the method of manufacture.

20.6 DESIGN OF SPUR GEARS

The design of spur gears normally begins with the selection of pitch diameters to suit the required speed ratio, center distance, and space limitations. The size of the teeth—that is, the diametral pitch—depends on the gear speeds, gear materials, horsepower to be transmitted, and the selected tooth form. The complete analysis and design of precision gears is complex and beyond the scope of this textbook, but the chart in

FIGURE 20.9   **Working Drawing of a Spur Gear.**

.5x.25 KWY

ALL FILLETS AND ROUNDS R.24

Ø4.00

Ø3.50

Ø1.877
1.875

3.00

Ø10.24

Ø12.500

.50

.12

1.76

2.00

CUTTING DATA	
NO. OF TEETH	48
DIA PITCH	4.00
TOOTH FORM	$14\frac{1}{2}^{\circ}$ INV.
WHOLE DEPTH	0.5393
CHORDAL ADD	0.2532
CHORD. THICK.	0.3926
PITCH DIA	12.000
CIRC. THICK.	0.3927
WORK. DEPTH	0.5000

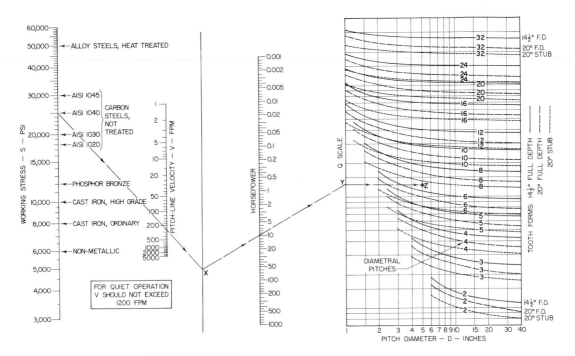

FIGURE 20.10   **Chart for Design of Cut Spur Gears.**

Fig. 20.10 will quickly yield a suitable diametral pitch for ordinary cut spur gears.[*]

EXAMPLE Determine the diametral pitch and face width for a 5″ pitch diameter (G10400 carbon steel) pinion having $14\frac{1}{2}°$ full-depth teeth that must transmit 10 hp (horsepower) at 200 rpm.

Calculate the pitch-in line velocity V as follows:

$$V = \frac{\pi}{12} D_P n_P$$

$$= 0.262 \times 5 \times 200 = 262 \text{ fpm}.$$

On the chart, draw a straight line from 25,000 psi on the working stress scale through 262 fpm on the velocity scale to intersect the pivot line at X. From X, draw a second straight line through 10 on the horsepower scale to intersect the Q scale at Y. From this point, enter the graph of pitches and go to the ordinate for 5″ pitch diameter. The junction point Z falls slightly above the curve for $14\frac{1}{2}°$ full-depth teeth of 6 diametral pitch; hence, choose 6 diametral pitch for the gears.

For good proportions the face width of a spur gear should be about three times the circular pitch, and this proportion is incorporated in the chart. Therefore, for 6 diametral pitch the circular pitch is $\pi/6$ or .5236″, and the face width is $3 \times .5236$ or 1.5708″. This width should be rounded off to $1\frac{5}{8}″$ (1.625).

When pinion and gear are of the same material, the smaller gear is the weaker, and the design should be based on the pinion. When the materials are different, the chart should be used to determine the horsepower capacity of each gear.

■ 20.7 WORM GEARS

Worm gears[*] are used to transmit power between nonintersecting shafts that are at right angles to each other. The **worm** is a screw having a thread of the same shape as a rack tooth. The *worm wheel* is similar to a helical gear that has been cut to conform to the shape of the worm for more contact. A large speed ratio is obtainable with worm gearing since a *single-thread worm* in one revolution advances the worm wheel only one tooth and a space.

In Fig. 20.11, a worm and a worm wheel are shown engaged. The section taken through the center of the

[*] The chart is based on the Lewis equation, with the Barth velocity modification, and assumes gear-face width equal to three times the circular pitch.

[*] See ANSI/AGMA 1012–F90 and other standards for more details.

FACE LENGTH–F
LEAD | PITCH
ADDENDUM
WHOLE DEPTH
PITCH DIA–D$_W$
OUTSIDE DIA–D$_O$
CENTER DISTANCE
OUTSIDE DIA – D$_O$
THROAT DIA – D$_t$
PITCH DIA – D$_G$
FACE
FACE RADIUS
RIM RADIUS

FIGURE 20.11 **Double Thread Worm and Worm Gear.**

worm and perpendicular to the axis of the worm wheel shows that the worm section is identical to a rack and that the wheel section is identical to a spur gear. Consequently, in this plane the height proportions of thread and gear teeth are the same as for a spur gear of corresponding pitch.

PITCH (p) The axial pitch of the worm is the distance from a point on one thread to the corresponding point on the next thread measured parallel to the worm axis. The pitch of the worm must exactly equal the circular pitch of the gear.

LEAD (L) The lead is the distance that the thread advances axially in one turn. The lead is always a multiple of the pitch. Thus, for a single-thread worm, the lead equals the pitch; for a double-thread worm, the lead is twice the pitch, and so on.

LEAD ANGLE (λ) The lead angle is the angle between a tangent to the helix at the pitch diameter and a plane perpendicular to the axis of the worm. The lead angle can be calculated from the formula

$$\tan \lambda = \frac{L}{\pi D_W},$$

where D_W = pitch diameter of the worm.

The speed ratio of worm gears depends only on the *number of threads* on the worm and the *number of teeth* on the gear. Therefore,

$$m_G = \frac{N_G}{N_W},$$

where N_G = number of teeth on the gear
  N_W = number of threads on the worm.

For $14\frac{1}{2}°$ standard involute teeth and single-thread or double-thread worms, the following proportions are the recommended practice of the AGMA. All formulas are expressed in terms of circular pitch p instead of diametral pitch P. It is easier to machine the worm and the hob used to cut the gear if the circular pitch has an even rational value such as $\frac{5}{8}''$.

For the worm:

Pitch diameter	$D_W = 2.4p + 1.1^*$
Whole depth	$h_t = 0.686p$
Outside diameter	$D_o = D_W + 0.636p$
Face length	$F = p(4.5 + N_G/50)$

For the gear:

Pitch diameter	$D_G = p(N_G/\pi)$
Throat diameter	$D_t = D_G + 0.636p$
Outside diameter	$D_o = D_t + 0.4775p$
Face radius	$R_f = \frac{1}{2}D_W - 0.318p$
Rim radius	$R_r = \frac{1}{2}D_W + p$
Face width	$F = 2.38p + 0.25$
Center distance	$C = \frac{1}{2}(D_G + D_W)$

*Recommended value, but may be varied.

▪ 20.8 WORKING DRAWINGS OF WORM GEARS

In an assembly drawing, the engaged worm and gear can be shown as in Fig. 20.11, but it is customary to omit the gear teeth and represent the gear blank conventionally, as shown in the lower half of the circular view. On detail drawings, the worm and gear are usually drawn separately, as shown in Figs. 20.12 and 20.13. Although dimensioning of these parts is again largely dependent on the method of production, it is standard practice to dimension the blanks on the views and to give the cutting data in tabular form, as shown. Note that those dimensions that closely affect the engagement of the gear and worm have been given as three-place decimal or limit dimensions; other dimensions, such as rim radius, face lengths, and gear outside diam-

FIGURE 20.12	Working Drawing of a Worm.

CUTTING DATA	
NO. OF THREADS	2
PITCH DIA	2.533
AXIAL PITCH	0.625
LEAD–R H	1.250
LEAD ANGLE	8° 56'
PRESSURE ANGLE	$14\frac{1}{2}°$
WHOLE DEPTH	0.429

MILL TO 50% THREAD WIDTH

F A O –GRIND THREAD FLANKS

FIGURE 20.13	Working Drawing of a Worm Gear.

CUTTING DATA	
NO. OF TEETH	30
PITCH DIA	5.967
ADDENDUM	0.199
WHOLE DEPTH	0.429
NO. OF THREADS	2
AXIAL PITCH	0.625
LEAD – R H	1.250
LEAD ANGLE	8° 56'
PRESSURE ANGLE	$14\frac{1}{2}°$

eter, have been rounded to convenient two-place decimal values.

■ 20.9 BEVEL GEARS

Bevel gears are used to transmit power between shafts whose axes intersect. The analogous friction drive would consist of a pair of cones having a common apex at the point of intersection of the axes, as in Fig. 20.14. The axes may intersect at any angle, but axes at right angles are most common, and this is the only case that will be considered here. Bevel gear teeth have the same involute shape as teeth on spur gears, but the bevel gear teeth are tapered toward the cone apex; hence, the height and width of a bevel gear tooth vary as the distance from the cone apex. Whereas spur gears are interchangeable—a spur gear of given pitch will run properly with any other spur gear of the same pitch and tooth form—this is not true of bevel gears, which must be designed in pairs and will run only with each other.

The speed ratio of bevel gears can be calculated from the same formulas given for spur gears in §20.2.

■ 20.10 BEVEL GEAR DEFINITIONS AND FORMULAS

The design of bevel gears is very similar to that of spur gears;[*] therefore, many of the spur gear terms are applied with slight modification to bevel gears. The *pitch diameter D* of a bevel gear is the diameter of the base of the pitch cone, and the *circular pitch p* to the teeth is measured along this circle. The *diametral pitch P* is also based on this circle; hence, the relationship of these three terms is the same as for spur gears.

FIGURE 20.14   Friction Cones.

[*] In the simplified formulas given here, tooth proportions are assumed equal on both gears, but in modern practice bevel gears are often designed with unequal addenda and unequal tooth thicknesses to balance the strength of gear and pinion. (See ANSI/AGMA 2005–B88.)

FIGURE 20.15   **Bevel Gear Nomenclature.**

The important dimensions and angles of a bevel gear are illustrated in Fig. 20.15. The *pitch cone* is shown as the triangle AOB, and the pitch angle is $\frac{1}{2}$ angle AOB. The root and face angle lines do not actually converge at point O but are often drawn as if they do for simplicity. It can be seen from Fig. 20.16 that the pitch angle of each gear depends on the relative diameters of the gears. When the shafts are at right angles, the sum of the pitch angles for the two mating gears equals 90°.

Therefore, the pitch angles, Γ (gamma), are determined from the following equations:

$$\tan \Gamma_G = \frac{D_G}{D_P} = \frac{N_G}{N_P}$$

and

$$\tan \Gamma_P = \frac{D_P}{D_G} = \frac{N_P}{N_G}.$$

Other terms are defined in Table 20.1.

■ 20.11 WORKING DRAWINGS OF BEVEL GEARS

As in the case of spur gears, a working drawing of a bevel gear gives only the dimensions of the gear blank. The necessary data for cutting the teeth are given in a note or table. A single sectional view usually will provide all necessary information (Fig. 20.16). If a second

CUTTING DATA

	GEAR	PINION
NO. OF TEETH	27	18
DIA PITCH	3	
TOOTH FORM	$14\frac{1}{2}°$ STD INVOL	
ADDENDUM	0.333	
ROOT ANGLE	52°14′	29°36′
WHOLE DEPTH	0.719	
CHORDAL ADD.	0.3409	0.3447
CHORD. THICK.	0.5233	0.5229

FIGURE 20.16 Working Drawing of Bevel Gears.

view is required, only the gear blank is drawn, and the tooth profiles are omitted. Two gears are shown in their operating relationship. On detail drawings, each gear is usually drawn separately, as in Fig. 20.15 and fully dimensioned. Proper placing of the gear-blank dimensions is largely dependent on the manufacturing methods used in producing the gear, but the scheme shown is commonly followed.

20.12 CAMS

Cams provide a simple means for obtaining unusual and irregular motions that would be difficult to produce otherwise. Figure 20.17a illustrates the basic principle of the cam. A shaft rotating at uniform speed carries an irregularly shaped disk called the **cam**; a reciprocating member, called the **follower**, presses a small roller against the curved surface of the cam. Rotation of the cam thus causes the follower to reciprocate with a definite cyclic motion according to the shape of the cam profile. The roller is held in contact with the cam by gravity or a spring. The problem of the drafter is to construct the cam profile necessary to obtain the desired motion of the follower.

An automobile valve cam that operates a flat-faced follower is shown in Fig. 20.17b. Figure 20.17c shows a disk cam with the roller follower attached to a linkage to transmit motion to another part of the device.

20.13 DISPLACEMENT DIAGRAMS

Since the motion of the follower is of primary importance, its rate of speed and its various positions should be carefully planned in a displacement diagram before the cam profile is constructed. A displacement diagram (Fig. 20.18) is a curve showing the displacement of the follower as ordinates erected on a base line that represents one revolution of the cam. The follower displacement should be drawn to scale, but any convenient length can be used to represent the 360° of cam rotation.

The motion of the follower as it rises or falls depends on the shape of the curves in the displacement diagram. In this diagram, four commonly employed types of curves are shown. If a straight line is used, such as the dashed line AD in the figure, the follower will move with a uniform velocity, but it will be forced to start and stop very abruptly, producing high acceleration and unnecessary force on the follower and other members. This straight-line motion can be

Term	Symbol	Definition	Formula
Addendum	a	Distance from pitch cone to top of tooth; measured at large end of tooth.	$a = 1/P$
Addendum angle	α	Angle subtended by addendum; same for gear and pinion.	$\tan \alpha = a/A$
Back angle		Usually equal to the pitch angle.	
Backing	Y	Distance from base of pitch cone to rear of hub.	
Chordal addendum	a_c	For bevel gears, the formulas given for spur gears can be used if D is replaced by $D/\cos \Gamma$ and N is replaced by $N \cos \Gamma$.	
Chordal thickness	t_c		
Crown backing	Z	More practical than backing for shop use; dimension Z given on drawings instead of Y.	$Z = Y + a \sin \Gamma$
Crown height	X	Distance, parallel to gear axis, from cone apex to crown of the gear.	$X = \frac{1}{2}D_o/\tan \Gamma_o$
Dedendum	b	Distance from pitch cone to bottom of tooth; measured at large end of tooth.	$b = 1.188/P$
Dedendum angle	δ	Angle subtended by dedendum; same for gear and pinion.	$\tan \delta = b/A$
Face angle	Γ_o	Angle between top of teeth and the gear axis.	$\Gamma_o = \Gamma + \alpha$
Face width	F	Should not exceed $\frac{1}{3}A$ or $10/P$, whichever is smaller.	
Mounting distance	M	A dimension used primarily for inspection and assembly purposes.	$M = Y + \frac{1}{2}D/\tan \Gamma$
Outer cone distance	A	Slant height of pitch cone; same for gear and pinion.	$A = D/2 \sin \Gamma$
Outside diameter	D_o	Diameter of outside or crown circle of the gear.	$D_o = D + 2a \cos \Gamma$
Pitch diameter	D_G or D_P	Diameter of base of pitch cone of gear or pinion.	$D_G = N_G/P$ $D_P = N_P/P$
Root angle	Γ_R	Angle between the root of the teeth and the gear axis.	$\Gamma_R = \Gamma - \delta$

TABLE 20.1   *Bevel Gear Terms, Definitions, and Formulas.*

(a)   (b)   (c)

FIGURE 20.17   Disk Cams.

FIGURE 20.18 **Displacement Diagram with Typical Curves.**

modified as shown in the curve ABCD, where arcs have been introduced at the beginning and at the end of the period.

The curve shown at EF is one that gives harmonic motion to the follower. To construct this curve, a semicircle is drawn whose diameter is equal to the desired rise. The circumference of the semicircle is divided into equal arcs, the number of divisions being the same as the number of horizontal divisions. Points on the curve are then found by projecting horizontally from the divisions on the semicircle to the corresponding ordinates.

The parabolic curve shown at GHK gives the follower constantly accelerated and decelerated motion. The half of the curve from G to H is exactly the reverse of the half from H to K. To construct the curve HK, the vertical height from K to J is divided into distances proportional to $1^2, 2^2, 3^2, \ldots$, or $1, 4, 9, \ldots$, the number of such divisions being the same as the number of horizontal divisions (see §§4.16 and 4.58). Points on the curve are found by projecting horizontally from the divisions on the line JK to the corresponding ordinates. The parabolic curve and curves of higher polynomial equations produce smoother follower motion than those of the other curves discussed.

■**20.14 THE CAM PROFILE**

The general procedure in constructing a cam profile is shown in Fig. 20.19. The disk cam rotating counterclockwise on its shaft raises and lowers the roller follower that is constrained to move along the straight line AB. The displacement diagram at the bottom of the figure shows the desired follower motion.

With the follower in its lowest or initial position, the center of the roller is at A, and OA is the radius of the *base circle*. The diameter of the base circle is determined from design parameters, which are not discussed here.

Since the cam must remain stationary while it is being drawn, an equivalent rotative effect is obtained by imagining that the cam stands still while the follower rotates about the cam in the opposite direction. Therefore, the base circle is divided into 12 equiangular divisions corresponding to the divisions used in the displacement diagram. These divisions begin at zero and are numbered in an opposite direction to the cam rotation.

The points $1, 2, \ldots$, on the follower axis AB indicate successive positions of the center of the roller and are located by transferring ordinates such as x and y from the displacement diagram. Thus, when the cam has rotated 60°, the follower roller must rise a distance x to position 2, and after 90° of rotation, a distance y to position 3, and so on.

It should now be observed that while the center of the roller moved from its initial position A to position 2, for example, the cam rotated 60° *counterclockwise*. Therefore, point 2 must be revolved *clockwise* about the cam center O to the corresponding 60° tangent line to establish point 2′. In this position, the complete follower would appear as shown by the phantom outline. Points 1′, 2′, 3′, . . . , represent consecutive positions of the roller center, and a smooth curve drawn through these points is called the *pitch curve*. To obtain the actual cam profile, the roller must be drawn in a number of positions, and the cam profile drawn tangent to the roller circles, as shown. The best results are obtained by first drawing the pitch curve very carefully and then drawing several closely spaced roller circles with

FIGURE 20.19 Disk Cam Profile Construction.

G R A P H I C S   S P O T L I G H T

CAD Design of Gears and Cams

CAD DESIGN OF GEARS AND CAMS

Once you know the design requirements for a particular gear or cam, a CAD software package can be used to automatically generate the drawing. It can be very time consuming to create drawings of gears and cams by hand. Using CAD frees the designer to spend more time on other aspects of the design.

AUTOMATIC DRAWING GENERATION

One program you can use to automatically generate drawings for gears and cams is Cimlogic™ Toolbox Power Transmission software. It is designed to run with AutoCAD® and AutoCAD Mechanical Desktop®. Toolbox Power Transmission software lets you type the data defining the motions for the cam or the details for the gear into user friendly dialog boxes.

The first step in creating a cam is to choose whether you will design a circular cam or a linear cam. Figure A shows a circular cam selected and follower diameter of .75.

ONE PICK SPECIFIES CAM MOTION

Once you have selected the type of cam and entered the default radius and starting point for the motion, you use a new dialog box shown in Figure B to define the various motions for the cam. You can choose constant acceleration, cycloidal, harmonic, double harmonic, dwell, modified sine, modified trapezoid, polynomial, and uniform motions. To define a motion, you just pick on the type of motion desired, type in the ending radius (if appropriate) and the number of degrees to perform this motion. Once you have the dialog box filled out to draw the portion of the cam, just pick on create. You can add additional motions for circular cams up to 360° of travel.

DISPLACEMENT DIAGRAM AND SUMMARY CREATED FOR YOU

The cam drawing shown in Figure C was created in minutes using AutoCAD Mechanical Desktop and

Toolbox Power Transmission software. You can select whether or not to show the follower path (it is shown in the figure). The displacement diagram and the cam summary were generated automatically, just by picking where to place the information. Toolbox Power Transmission software also will generate gear and sprocket drawings in a similar fashion. In addition, the regular toolbox software can be used to automatically create fasteners, keys, seals, standard symbols, and other useful items.

(A)

(B)

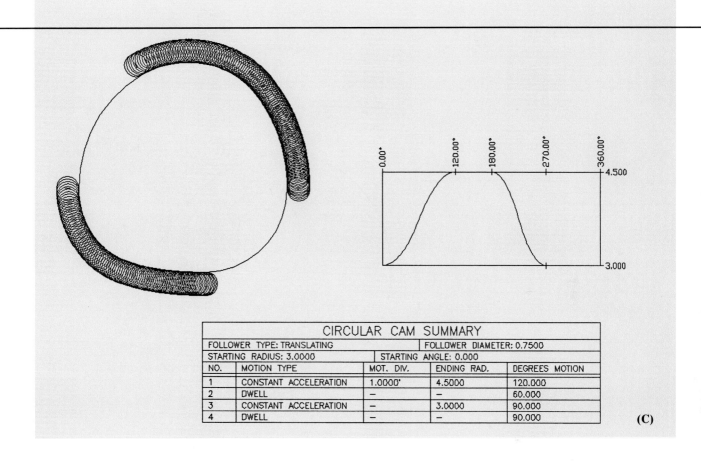

CIRCULAR CAM SUMMARY				
FOLLOWER TYPE: TRANSLATING		FOLLOWER DIAMETER: 0.7500		
STARTING RADIUS: 3.0000		STARTING ANGLE: 0.000		
NO.	MOTION TYPE	MOT. DIV.	ENDING RAD.	DEGREES MOTION
1	CONSTANT ACCELERATION	1.0000'	4.5000	120.000
2	DWELL	–	–	60.000
3	CONSTANT ACCELERATION	–	3.0000	90.000
4	DWELL	–	–	90.000

(C)

centers on the pitch curve, as shown between points 5′ and 6′.

If the follower is offset as shown in Fig. 20.20, an offset circle is drawn with center O and radius equal to the amount of offset. As the cam turns, the extended center line of the follower will always be tangent to this offset circle. The equiangular spaces are stepped off on the offset circle, and tangent lines are then drawn from each point on the offset circle, as shown.

If the roller is on a pivoted arm, as shown in Fig. 20.21a, then the displacement of the roller center is along the circular arc AB. The height of the displacement diagram (not shown) should be made equal to the rectified length of arc AB. Ordinates from the diagram are then transferred to arc AB to locate the roller positions 1, 2, 3, ... As the follower is revolved about the cam, pivot point C moves in a circular path of radius OC to the consecutive positions C_1, C_2, ... Length AC is constant for all follower positions;

hence, from each new position of point C, the follower arc of radius R is drawn as shown at the 90° position. The roller centers 1, 2, 3, . . . , are now revolved about the cam center O to intersect the follower arcs at 1′, 2′, 3′, ... After the pitch curve is completed, the cam profile is drawn tangent to the roller circles.

The construction for a flat-faced follower is shown in Fig. 20.21b. The initial point of contact is at A, and points 1, 2, 3, . . . , represent consecutive positions of the follower face. Then for the 90° position, point 3 must be revolved 90°, as shown, to position 3′, and the flat face of the follower is drawn through point 3′ at right angles to the cam radius. When this procedure has been repeated for each position, the cam profile will be enveloped by a series of straight lines, and the cam profile is drawn inside and tangent to these lines. Note that the point of contact, initially at A, changes as the follower rises: At 90°, for example, contact is at D, a distance X to the right of the follower axis.

Disk Cam Profile with Offset Follower Construction.

■ 20.15 CYLINDRICAL CAMS

When the follower movement is in a plane parallel to the cam shaft, some form of cylindrical cam must be employed. In Fig. 20.22, for example, the follower rod moves vertically parallel to the cam axis as the attached roller follows the groove in the rotating cam cylinder.

A cylindrical cam of diameter D is required to lift the follower rod a distance AB with harmonic motion in 180° of cam motion and to return the rod in the remaining 180° with the same motion. The displacement diagram is drawn first and conveniently placed directly opposite the front view. The 360° length of the dia-

gram must be made equal to πD so that the resulting curves will be a true development of the outer surface of the cam cylinder. The pitch curve is drawn to represent the required motion, and a series of roller circles is then drawn to establish the sides of the groove tangent to these circles. This completes the development of the outer cylinder and actually provides all information needed for making the cam; hence, it is not uncommon to omit the curves in the front view.

To complete the front view, points on the curves are projected horizontally from the development. For example, at 60° in the development, the width of the groove measured parallel to the cam axis is X, a distance slightly greater than the actual roller diameter.

FIGURE 20.21 Pivoted and Flat-Faced Followers.

FIGURE 20.22 Cylindrical Cam.

This width X is projected to the front view directly below point 2, the corresponding 60° position in the top view, to establish two points on the outer curves. The inner curves for the bottom of the groove can be established in the same manner, except that the groove width X is located below point 2′, which lies on the inner diameter. The inner curves are only approximate because the width at the bottom of the groove is actually slightly greater than X, but the exact bottom width can only be determined by drawing a second development for the inner cylinder.

■20.16 OTHER DRIVE DEVICES

When the distance between drive and driven shafts makes the use of gears impractical, devices such as belt and pulley or chain and sprocket drives are often employed. Layout and detailing standards vary somewhat from one company to another, but design procedures and specification methods may be obtained from almost any good textbook or handbook on mechanical design.

■20.17 COMPUTER GRAPHICS

Once the designer has determined the particular requirements of a gearset, CAD software is available that will permit the user to generate drawings of single gears or two gears in mesh quickly (Fig. 20.23), varying the pressure angle and number of teeth as desired.

FIGURE 20.23 **Pictorial of Geared Window Crank Assembly.** *Courtesy of CADKEY, Inc.*

Features such as pitch circle center line and root and outer phantom circles can be shown or omitted from the drawing as desired.

■KEY WORDS

SPUR GEAR	PITCH DIAMETER
RPM	GEAR RATIO
INVOLUTE PROFILE	BASE CIRCLE
CIRCULAR PITCH	DIAMETRAL PITCH
PITCH CIRCLE	ROOT DIAMETER
WORKING DEPTH	ADDENDUM
DEDENDUM	ROOT CIRCLE
ADDENDUM CIRCLE	CAM PROFILE
DISPLACEMENT DIAGRAM	CAM FOLLOWER

■ CHAPTER SUMMARY

- Gears transmit power from one rotating shaft to another. The purpose of a gear is to change the rpm, direction, or axis orientation.

- Gears are one of the more difficult objects to draw on paper or with CAD because the image requires mathematical calculation and a thorough understaning of gear theory.

- Once the mathematical calculations for a gear are complete, the construction of a gear profile is begun by constructing four circles: the addendum circle, pitch circle, base circle, and root circle.

- The involute profile is the most common gear tooth profile.
- Advanced CAD programs can automate the construction of gear teeth.
- The most common gear type is the spur gear. Spur gear axes are parallel to each other.
- The axes of worm gears and bevel gears are positioned 90° to each other.
- Cams change rotating motion into reciprocating motion. The displacement curve defines the linear follower movement as the cam rotates through 360° of rotary motion.

■ REVIEW QUESTIONS

1. What is the purpose of a gear?
2. What is the geometric shape most commonly used for a gear tooth profile?
3. What are the four circles used to draw a gear?
4. Which types of gears have shafts that are perpendicular to each other?
5. Describe how to draw a cam profile, given a displacement diagram.

6. What is the purpose of a cam follower?
7. How many total degrees of rotation are shown on a cam displacement diagram?
8. Why is the cam follower position always the same at the starting point and the ending point?

■ PROBLEMS ON GEARING AND CAMS

The following problems will provide practice in laying out and making working drawings of the common types of gears and cams. Where paper sizes are not given, select both scale and sheet layout. If assigned, convert the design layouts to metric dimensions. If a CAD system is available, the instructor may choose to assign specific problems to be completed by this method.

GEARING

Prob. 20.1 A 12-tooth IDP pinion engages a 15-tooth gear. Make a full-size drawing of a segment of each gear showing how the teeth mesh. Construct the $14\frac{1}{2}°$ involute teeth exactly, noting any points where the teeth appear to interfere. Label gear ratio m_G on the drawing. Include dimensions, notes, and cutting data as assigned by your instructor. *Alternate Assignment:* Use 13 or 14 teeth, or any number of teeth as assigned by your instructor.

Prob. 20.2 Follow instructions for Prob. 20.1, but use 20° stub teeth instead of $14\frac{1}{2}°$ involute teeth.

Prob. 20.3 Follow instructions for Prob. 20.1, but use a rack in place of the 12-tooth pinion.

Prob. 20.4 Make a display drawing of the pinion in Fig. 20.24. Show two views, drawing the teeth by the odontograph method shown in Fig. 20.6. Draw double size. Omit dimensions.

Prob. 20.5 Make a pictorial display of the intermediate pinion shown in Fig. 14.89 (part 6). Show the gear as an oblique half section (see §17.10), similar to Fig. 20.24. Draw four-times size, reducing the 30° receding lines by one half, as in cabinet projection (see §17.4). Draw the teeth by the odontograph method.

Prob. 20.6 A spur gear has 60 teeth of 5 diametral pitch. The face width is 1.50″. The shaft is 1.19″ in diameter. Make

FIGURE 20.24   Pinion (Prob. 20.4).

the hub 2.00″ long and 2.25″ in diameter. Calculate accurately all dimensions, and make a working drawing of the gear. Show six spokes, each 1.12″ wide at the hub, tapering to .75″ wide at the rim and .50″ thick. Use your own judgment for any dimensions not given. Draw half size on Layout A–3 or A4–3 (adjusted) or full size on Layout B–3 or A3–3.

Prob. 20.7   Make a working drawing of the intermediate pinion shown in Fig. 14.89 (part 6). Check the gear dimensions by calculation.

Prob. 20.8   Follow instructions for Prob. 20.7, but use the intermediate gear shown in Fig. 14.89 (part 5).

Prob. 20.9   Follow instructions for Prob. 20.7, but use the pinion shown in Fig. 20.24.

Prob. 20.10   Follow instructions for Prob. 20.7, but use the spur gear shown in Fig. 20.25.

Prob. 20.11   A pair of bevel gears has teeth of 4 diametral pitch. The pinion has 13 teeth, the gear 25 teeth. The face width is 1.12″. The pinion shaft is .94″ in diameter, and the gear shaft is 1.19″ in diameter. Calculate accurately all dimensions, and make a working drawing showing the gears engaged as in Fig. 20.16. Make the hub diameters approximately twice the shaft diameters. Select key sizes from Appendix 21. The backing for the pinion must be .62″, for the gear 1.25″. Use your own judgment for any dimensions not given.

Prob. 20.12   Make a working drawing of the pinion in Prob. 20.11.

Prob. 20.13   Make a working drawing of the gear in Prob. 20.11.

Prob. 20.14   Show two views of the pinion in Prob. 20.12. Follow the general instructions in that problem.

Prob. 20.15   Follow instructions in Prob. 20.11 but use 5 diametral pitch and 30 and 15 teeth. The face is 1.00″. Shafts: pinion, 1.00″ diameter; gear, 1.50″ diameter. Backing: pinion, .50″; gear, 1.00″.

FIGURE 20.25   Spur Gear (Prob. 20.10).

(a)

17"x 22"
sheet
.5"border

6.0

6.5

6.0

4.25

(b)

FIGURE 20.26 **Countershaft End (Prob. 20.17).** *Courtesy of Link-Belt Co.*

Prob. 20.16 Follow instructions in Prob. 20.11 but use 4 diametral pitch, both gears 20 teeth. Select the correct face width. Shafts: 1.38″ diameter. Backing: 0.75″.

Prob. 20.17 Figure 20.26a shows a countershaft end used on a trough conveyor. Figure 20.26b shows the layout for an assembly drawing of a similar unit. Using a scale of half size, make an assembly drawing of the complete unit (given that the layout dimensions are full size). The following full-size dimensions are sufficient to establish the position and general outline of the parts; the minor detail dimensions, web and rib shapes, and fillets and rounds should be designed with the help of the photograph.

The gears are identical in size and are similar in shape to the one in Fig. 20.15. There are 24 teeth of 3 diametral pitch in each gear. Face width, 1.50″. Shafts, 2.00″ diameter, extending 7.00″ beyond left bearing, 4.00″ beyond rear (break shafts as shown). Hub diameters, 2.75″. Backing, 1.00″. Hub lengths, 3.25″. Front gear is held by a square gib key and a .38″ set screw. Collar on front shaft next to right bearing is .75″ thick, 2.25″ outside diameter, with a .38″ set screw.

On the main casting, the split bearings are 2.75″ diameter, 3.00″ long, and 10.00″ apart. Each bearing cap is held by two $\frac{1}{2}$″ bolts, 3.50″ apart, center to center. Oil holes have a $\frac{1}{4}$″ pipe tap for plug or grease cup. Shaft center lines are 6.50″ above bottom surface, 8.00″ from rear surface of casting. Main casting is 11.50″ high, and its base is 16.00″ long, 8.75″ wide, and .75″ thick. All webs, ribs, and walls are uniformly

.50″ thick. In the base are eight holes (not shown in the photograph) for $\frac{1}{2}$″ bolts, two outside each end, and two inside each end.

Proceed by first blocking in the gears in each view, and then block in the principal main casting dimensions. Fill in details only after principal dimensions are clearly established.

Prob. 20.18 The worm and worm gear shown in Fig. 20.11 have a circular pitch of .62″, and the gear has 32 teeth of $14\frac{1}{2}$° involute form. The worm is double threaded. Make an assembly drawing similar to Fig. 20.11. Draw the teeth on the gear by the odontograph method of Fig. 20.6. Calculate dimensions accurately, and use AGMA proportions. Shafts: worm, 1.12″ diameter; gear, 1.62″ diameter.

Prob. 20.19 Make a working drawing of the worm in Prob. 20.18.

Prob. 20.20 Make a working drawing of the gear in Prob. 20.18.

Prob. 20.21 Make a working drawing of the worm in Prob. 20.18, but make the worm single threaded.

Prob. 20.22 A single-thread worm has a lead of .75″. The worm gear has 28 teeth of standard form. Make a working drawing of the worm. The shaft is 1.25″ in diameter.

Prob. 20.23 Make a working drawing of the gear in Prob. 20.22. The shaft is 1.50″ in diameter.

CAMS

Prob. 20.24 For the setup in Fig. 20.27a, draw the displacement diagram and determine the cam profile that will give the radial roller follower this motion: up 1.50″ in 120°, dwell 60°, down in 90°, dwell 90°. Motions are to be unmodified straight line and of uniform velocity. The roller is .75″ in diameter, and the base circle is 3.00″ in diameter. Note that the follower has zero offset. The cam rotates clockwise.

Prob. 20.25 Follow instructions for Prob. 20.24 except that the straight-line motions are to be modified by arcs whose radii are equal to one half the rise of the follower.

Prob. 20.26 Follow instructions for Prob. 20.24 except that the upward motion is to be harmonic and the downward motion parabolic.

Prob. 20.27 Follow instructions for Prob. 20.26 except that the follower is offset 1.00″ to the left of the cam center line.

(a)   (b)   (c)

FIGURE 20.27   Cam Problems (Probs. 20.24–20.31). Use Size A or A4 sheet.

Prob. 20.28   For the setup in Fig. 20.27b, draw the displacement diagram, and determine the cam profile that will give the flat-faced follower this motion: dwell 30°, up 1.50″ on a parabolic curve in 180°, dwell 30°, down with harmonic motion in 120°. The base circle is 3.00″ in diameter. After completing the cam profile, determine the necessary width of face of the follower by finding the position of the follower where the point of contact with the cam is farthest from the follower axis. The cam rotates counterclockwise.

Prob. 20.29   For the setup in Fig. 20.27c, draw the displacement diagram, and determine the cam profile that will swing the pivoted follower through an angle of 30° with the same motion as prescribed in Prob. 20.28. The radius of the follower arm is 2.75″, and in its lowest position the center of the roller is directly over the center of the cam. The base circle is 2.50″ in diameter, and the roller is .75″ in diameter. The cam rotates counterclockwise.

Prob. 20.30   Follow instructions for Prob. 20.29 except that the motion is to be that given in Probs. 20.24 and 20.25.

Prob. 20.31   Follow instructions for Prob. 20.29 except that the motion is to be that given in Probs. 20.24 and 20.26.

Prob. 20.32   Using an arrangement like Fig. 20.22, construct a *half* development, and complete the front view for the following cylindrical cam. Cam, 2.50″ diameter, 2.50″ high. Roller, .50″ diameter; cam groove, .38″ deep. Cam shaft, .62″ diameter; follower rod, .62″ wide, .31″ thick. Motion: up 1.50″ with harmonic motion in 180°, down with the same motion in remaining 180°. Cam rotates counterclockwise. Assume lowest position of the follower at the front center of cam. Use Layout A–3 or A4–3 (adjusted).

Prob. 20.33   Follow instructions for Prob. 20.32, but construct a *full* development for the following motion: up $1\frac{1}{2}$″ with parabolic motion in 120°, dwell 90°, down with harmonic motion in 150°. Use Layout B–3.

C H A P T E R   2 1

ELECTRONIC DIAGRAMS

After studying the material in this chapter, you should be able to:

1. Identify common component symbols on an electronic schematic diagram.
2. Draw a schematic diagram using standardized symbols.
3. Trace the signal path for simple schematic diagrams.
4. Identify interrupted and uninterrupted lines.
5. Designate terminals and numerical values of components.

OVERVIEW

Working drawings for the fabrication of electrical machinery, switching devices, chassis for electronic equipment, cabinets, housings, and other "mechanical" elements associated with electrical equipment are based on the same principles as given in Chapter 14, "Design and Working Drawings." A working drawing of a chassis for an electronic device is shown in Fig. 21.1.

While more and more circuits are contained within integrated circuit chips, point-to-point connections are still required on most electronic devices. Such connections are represented on schematic diagrams, block diagrams, and wiring diagrams. Every discrete component is represented with a unique graphic symbol. Components with terminals or numeric values are labeled. Many CAD programs include a library of graphic electronic symbols to make drawing schematic diagrams easier and less time consuming. On paper drawings, plastic templates are available to shorten drawing time.

■ 21.1 SOURCES OF STANDARDIZED SYMBOLS

The symbols approved by the American National Standards Institute (ANSI) are published in "Graphic Symbols for Electrical and Electronic Diagrams," ANSI/IEEE 200–1975 (R1989). In addition, modern printed circuitry techniques, which are used extensively in today's electronic equipment, require specially prepared diagrams or drawings (see §21.15).

Recommendations for the preparation of electrical and electronic diagrams using the American National Standard symbols appear in "Electrical and Electronics Diagrams," ANSI Y14.15. Figure 21.2 is a typical schematic diagram. Much of the material in this chapter is extracted or adapted from that standard.

In addition to the ANSI standards, other standards should be referred to if applicable or required. The U.S. government has developed a series of standards to be used by military contractors, including the following:

MIL–STD–275	Printed Wiring for Electronic Equipment
MIL–STD–429	Printed Wiring and Printed Circuits—Terms and Definitions
MIL–STD–454	Standard General Requirements for Electronic Equipment
MIL–STD–681	Identification Coding and Application of Hook Up and Lead Wire
MIL–STD–1495	Multilayer Printed Wiring Boards for Electronic Equipment

In other applications, adherence to standards developed by Underwriters' Laboratory (UL) may be required, particularly where safety considerations may dictate a special printed circuit board layout or component spacing.

CAD SYMBOL LIBRARIES

You can create or purchase libraries of standard electronic symbols that can be quickly inserted to create electronic diagrams. CAD symbol libraries should follow approved standards just as manually created drawings would. When creating CAD drawings showing electronic symbols, consider the final size of the plotted drawing. Make sure that the symbols you create and add to the drawing will meet the minimum size standards for the symbols as set out in ANSI Y14.15.

■ 21.2 TYPES OF ELECTRONIC DIAGRAMS

The following types of diagrams are commonly used in the electronics industry. Definitions are quoted from ANSI Y14.15.

SCHEMATIC DIAGRAMS   The type of drawing used by those concerned with the design, construction, and maintenance of electronic equipment, defined as

> a diagram which shows, by means of graphic symbols, the electrical connections and functions of a specific circuit arrangement. The schematic diagram facilitates tracing the circuit and its functions without regard to the actual physical size, shape, or location of the component devices or parts.

SINGLE-LINE OR ONE-LINE DIAGRAM   Frequently this type of diagram is called a block diagram; it is used to simplify the representation of complex equipment by using blocks or rectangles to depict stages, units, or groups of components in a system. ANSI defines it as

> a diagram which shows, by means of single lines and graphic symbols, the course of an electric circuit or system of circuits and the component devices or parts used therein.

A—⁷⁄₆₄″ (3mm) DIA.	J—¼″ (6mm)	P—⅝″ (16mm)	Z—1⅜″ (34mm)	KK—3″ (76mm)
B—⁹⁄₆₄″ (4mm) DIA.	K—⁵⁄₁₆″ (8mm)	S—¾″ (19mm)	BB—1½″ (38mm)	LL—4⅜″ (111mm)
C—³⁄₁₆″ (5mm) DIA.	L—⅜″ (10mm)	U—⅞″ (22mm)	CC—1¾″ (44mm)	MM—4¹¹⁄₁₆″ (119mm)
D—¼″ DIA.	M—⁷⁄₁₆″ (11mm)	V—1″ (25mm)	DD—2″ (51mm)	OO—7″ (178mm)
E—½″ DIA.	N—½″ (13mm)	Y—1¼″ (32mm)	HH—2½″ (64mm)	PP—7⅜″ (187mm)
F—¾″ DIA.	O—⁹⁄₁₆″ (14mm)			

FIGURE 21.1 **Working Drawing for Chassis Fabrication (top plate of Bud Mfg. Co. CU247 chassis box).** *Courtesy of American Radio Relay League.*

BT1—Battery, 9-volt rectangular.
D1—Zener diode, 6.2-V.
J1-J4, incl.—Standard tip jacks.
M1—Panel meter, 0-50 uA dc; Radio Shack
  22-051 or equiv.
P1-P3, incl.—Standard tip plugs.
P5, P6—Standard test probe.
Q1, Q2—Motorola MPF102; do not substitute.
S1—Spst toggle.
S2—2-pole, 3-position rotary.
S3—2-pole, 5-position rotary.

FIGURE 21.2 **Schematic Diagram of a FET (field-effect transistor) VOM (volt-ohm-milliammeter).** *Courtesy of American Radio Relay League.*

CONNECTION OR WIRING DIAGRAM Such a diagram is used to represent the wiring between component devices in electrical or electronic equipment. It is defined as follows.

A diagram which shows the connections of an installation or its component devices or parts. It may cover internal or external connections, or both, and contains such detail as is needed to make or trace connections that are involved. The connection diagram usually shows general physical arrangement of the component devices or parts.

INTERCONNECTION DIAGRAM　This diagram is similar to the connection diagram; both serve to supplement schematic diagrams. It is described as follows:

A form of connection or wiring diagram which shows only external connections between unit assemblies or equipment. The internal connections of the unit assemblies or equipment are usually omitted.

■ 21.3 DRAWING SIZE, FORMAT, AND TITLE

The sizes and formats for drawings of electrical and electronic diagrams should conform to ANSI/ASME Y14.1–1995 or ANSI/ASME Y14.1M–1995.

The title of a drawing of one of the types defined in §21.2 should include the standardized wording in the definition and a description of the application—for example,

SINGLE-LINE DIAGRAM—AM–FM RECEIVER
SCHEMATIC DIAGRAM—
　　　　　　　250-WATT AMATEUR TRANSCEIVER

It is often useful to include some basic wiring information on schematic diagrams, such as connection details of coils and switches. The title of such a combined form is not altered, however, but describes the primary function of the diagram.

■ 21.4 LINE CONVENTIONS AND LETTERING

As in any drawing intended for reproductions, line thicknesses and letter sizes should be selected according to the amount of reduction or enlargement involved so that legibility will not be adversely affected.

ANSI recommends a line of medium thickness for general use on electrical diagrams. A thin line may be used for brackets, leader lines, and so on. To emphasize special features such as main signal paths, a thicker line may be used to provide the desired contrast. For recommended line thickness and lettering, refer to ANSI/ASME Y14.2M.

Line conventions for electrical diagrams are shown in Fig. 21.3.

FOR GENERAL USE	MEDIUM
MECHANICAL CONNECTION, SHIELDING, & FUTURE CIRCUITS LINE	MEDIUM
BRACKET–CONNECTING DASH LINE	MEDIUM

USE OF THESE LINE THICKNESSES OPTIONAL

BRACKETS, LEADER LINES, ETC.	THIN
BOUNDARY OF MECHANICAL GROUPING	THIN
FOR EMPHASIS	THICK

FIGURE 21.3　Line Conventions for Electronic Diagrams (ANSI Y14.15).

■ 21.5 CONVENTIONAL PRACTICES IN ELECTRONIC DIAGRAMS

SYMBOLS　As stated earlier, symbols used should conform to ANSI/IEEE 200–1975 (R1989) or to some other nationally approved standard. If no symbol is available, a special symbol may be devised (or a standard symbol augmented), provided that an explanatory note is included. Examples of commonly used schematic symbols are shown in Appendix 36.

SIZE OF SYMBOLS　It is recommended in ANSI Y14.15 that symbols be drawn roughly 1.5 times the size of the samples shown in the ANSI/IEEE standard, provided that the anticipated reduction is no greater than 2.5 to 1. Following this recommendation, circular envelopes for semiconductors will be about 16 mm or .62″ to 19 mm or .75″ in diameter, although the envelope for semiconductors may be omitted if no confusion results. Some textbooks on this subject contain much more detailed recommendations about symbol sizes, as well as spacing and arrangements.

SWITCHES AND RELAYS　These in general should be shown in the "normal" position—with no operating force or applied energy. If exceptions are necessary, as for switches that may operate in several positions with no applied force, an explanatory note should describe the conditions shown.

ABBREVIATIONS　As in other fields of technical drawing, abbreviations on electrical diagrams should conform to ANSI/ASME Y1.1. (See Appendix 4.)

FIGURE 21.4   Single-Line Diagram (ANSI Y14.15).

GROUPING OF PARTS   When certain parts or components are naturally grouped, as in separately obtained subassemblies or assembled components such as relays, tuned circuit transformers, hermetically sealed units, and printed circuit boards, this grouping may be indicated by means of an enclosing dashed-line "box," as in Fig. 21.6, or by extra space from adjacent circuitry.

■ 21.6 SINGLE-LINE DIAGRAMS

The single-line diagram is intended to describe the basic functions of a circuit or system. As such, it normally includes little of the detailed information and individual-parts identification of the schematic diagram. The individual lines connecting the symbols may represent single conductors or multiple conductors. The emphasis is on the function of each stage of a device rather than on the composition of the stage. A single-line diagram as used in electronics and communications is shown in Fig. 21.4.

Layout of a single-line diagram involves essentially the same principles and procedures (except for lesser detail) suggested for schematic diagrams (§21.7).

■ 21.7 SCHEMATIC DIAGRAMS

A convenient procedure for making a schematic (or single-line) diagram is to begin with a freehand sketch

on grid paper (Fig. 21.5). It is frequently desirable to make the final drawing (Fig. 21.6) on tracing paper or film placed over similar grid paper. Note that some

FIGURE 21.5   **A Portion of a Preliminary Freehand Sketch of a Schematic Diagram.**

FIGURE 21.6 **Maintenance-Type Schematic Diagram of FM Weather Monitor Radio.** *Copyright Motorola, Inc. 1980. All rights reserved. Reprinted with permission of Motorola, Inc.*

FIGURE 21.6 (cont.)

FIGURE 21.7   Electronic Symbol Templates.

FIGURE 21.8   CAD Generated Schematic Layout.
Courtesy of IBM.

Circuit courtesy of Intersil Inc.

FIGURE 21.9   Computer-Generated Schematic Diagram. *Courtesy of Chessel-Robocom Corp.*

details are rearranged in Fig. 21.6 to improve the final diagram.

The use of templates, such as those shown in Fig. 21.7, is a convenient time-saver in drawing symbols.

Computer-aided drafting techniques, as described in Chapter 2, may also be used to produce complicated schematic drawings efficiently. Using appropriate software, the drafter/designer can lay out and revise a schematic on the monitor (Fig. 21.8) and then have a drawing, produced by a printer (Fig. 21.9).

The various parts or symbols should be arranged to provide a pleasing balance between blank areas and lines. It is very important that sufficient blank spaces be provided adjacent to symbols for insertion of reference designations and notes. Exceptionally large spaces will, of course, give an unbalanced effect and should be avoided unless it is necessary to provide for possible later circuit additions.

SIGNAL PATH It is standard practice to arrange schematic and single-line diagrams so that the signal or transmission path from input to output proceeds from left to right and from top to bottom if it is necessary to draw the diagram in successive "layers." Supplementary circuits, such as a power supply and an oscillator circuit, are usually drawn below the main circuit.

Stages of an electronic device are groups of components, usually associated with an electronic tube or transistor or other semiconductor, which together perform one function of the device.

For example, the sketch in Fig. 21.5 shows the RF (radio frequency) amplifier stage of the FM Weather Monitor Radio, whose schematic is shown in Fig. 21.6. Some other stages that may be seen in Fig. 21.6 are the first and second mixer stages associated with transistors Q2 and Q3, the limiter/detector stage containing integrated circuit U1, and finally the audio output stage, U2, and speaker. The power supply, which rectifies alternating current through diodes CR2–CR5 to produce direct current voltage, regulated through integrated circuit U3, is shown at the lower left, along with a rechargeable battery backup power supply, E1.

Also shown in the lower portion of the diagram is the circuitry contained on a separate tone decoder printed circuit board (within the dashed lines).

The experienced electronic drafter is able to visualize fairly accurately the space required by the circuitry involved in each state. The drafter generally keeps the semiconductor symbols in horizontal lines and groups the associated circuitry in reasonably symmetrical arrangement about them. Thus, each stage is fairly well confined to an assigned area of the drawing. Note again that *the signal path from input to output*

follows the general path from left to right and top to bottom. The input is at the upper left and the output at the lower right in Fig. 21.6. Note that the signal path is clearly designated by a heavier than normal line. This is typical of maintenance-type schematic diagrams, which are drawn to be easily read and interpreted by service technicians. Supplementary circuitry (the power supply) is in the lower portion of the diagram.

Connecting lines (for conductors) are drawn horizontally or vertically, for the most part, minimizing bends and crossovers. Long interconnecting lines should be avoided. *Interrupted paths* may be used in place of long, awkward interconnecting lines or where a diagram occupies more than one sheet. When parallel connecting lines must be drawn close together, the spacing between lines should not be less than .06″ after reduction. As a further visual aid, parallel lines should be grouped with consideration of function and with at least double spacing between groups.

Crossovers are not usually completely avoidable. When they are necessary, they should be handled with care. The looped crossovers of Fig. 21.10a are not American National Standard but are still employed when there is possibility of confusion. A simpler practice recognized by ANSI is shown in Fig. 21.10b. Connection of more than three lines at one point, shown at X, is not recommended and can usually be avoided by moving or "staggering" one or more lines at Y.

The ANSI-recommended practice (ANSI Y14.15) is shown in Fig. 21.10c. In this system it is understood that termination of a line signifies a connection. If more than three lines come together, as at Z, the dot symbol becomes necessary. This is avoidable, however, by staggering the connecting lines.

Interrupted paths, for either a single line or groups of lines, may be used where desirable for overall simplification of a diagram (Figs. 21.11 and 21.12). These

FIGURE 21.10 Crossovers.

(a)   (b)   (c)

CONNECTOR INPUT   CIRCUIT ARRANGEMENT

FIGURE 21.11   **Identification of Interrupted Lines (ANSI Y14.15).**

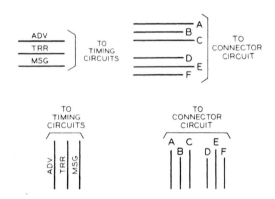

FIGURE 21.12   **Typical Arrangement of Line Identifications and Destinations (ANSI Y14.15).**

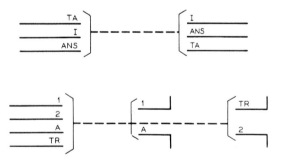

FIGURE 21.13   **Interrupted Lines Interconnected by Dashed Lines (ANSI Y14.15).**

must be carefully labeled with letters, numbers, abbreviations, or other identification so that their destinations are unmistakable. Grouped lines are also bracketed as well as labeled (Fig. 21.12). When convenient, interrupted grouped lines may be connected by dashed lines (Fig. 21.13).

■ 21.8 TERMINALS

Terminal circles need not be shown unless they are needed for clarity and identification. Switches S101 and S102 of Fig. 21.6 illustrate the use of terminal symbols and their identification.

When actual physical markings appear on or near terminals of a component, these may be shown on the electrical diagram. Otherwise, for convenient reference it is helpful to assign arbitrary numbers or letters to the terminals. These designations must then be explained by a simple diagram that associates the arbitrarily assigned numbers or letters with the actual physical arrangement of terminals on the component (Figs. 21.14, 21.15, and 21.16b). Figure 21.16a is a pictorial explanation of fig. 21.16b.

Terminals or leads are frequently identified by colors or symbols, which should be indicated on the diagram. In Fig. 21.6, color coding is shown for transformer T2, and the colors of the insulated wire leads attached to the decoder board subchassis are noted near each terminal.

Terminal identification for rotary variable resistors follows practices similar to the foregoing, except that in addition it is frequently desirable to indicate

FIGURE 21.14   **Terminal Identification—Toggle Switch (ANSI / IEEE).**

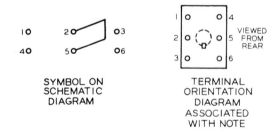

FIGURE 21.15   **Terminal Identification—Rotary Switch (ANSI / IEEE).**

(a)   (b)

FIGURE 21.16 Terminal Identification—Lever-Type Key (ANSI / IEEE).

the direction of rotation. This is normally described as clockwise or counterclockwise as viewed from the knob or actuator end of the control. Any contrary arrangement must be explained by a note or diagram. The letters CW placed near the terminal adjacent to the movable contact identify the extreme clockwise position of the movable terminal (Fig. 21.17a). When terminals are numbered, number 2 is assigned to the movable contact (Fig. 21.17b). Additional fixed taps are assigned sequential numbers, as in Fig. 21.17c.

Switch position, as it affects function, should also be shown on a schematic diagram. Depending on complexity, the designation may range from the simple ON–OFF of switch S101 in Fig. 21.6 to the functional labeling of the terminals in Fig. 21.18a or to the tabular form of function listing (Fig. 21.19b). The tabular forms indicate by dashes which terminals are connected for each position. For example, in Fig. 21.19b,

FIGURE 21.17 Terminal Identification—Variable Resistor (ANSI / IEEE).

(a)   (b)   (c)

FIGURE 21.18 Position-Function Relationship for Rotary Switches—Optional Methods (ANSI / IEEE).

(a)   (b)

FIGURE 21.19 Position-Function Relationships for Rotary Switches—Tabular Method Only (ANSI / IEEE).

(a)   (b)

TYPICAL SWITCH SECTION

(a)

GRAPHICAL SYMBOL

(b)

FIGURE 21.20 Development of a Graphical Symbol—Rotary Switch (ANSI / IEEE).

FIGURE 21.21 Identification of Parts by Suffix Letters (ANSI / IEEE).

position 2 connects terminal 1 to terminal 3, terminal 5 to terminal 7, and terminal 9 to terminal 11.

■ 21.9 DIVISION OF PARTS

For clarity, sections of multielement parts may be drawn separately in a schematic diagram, with the subdivisions indicated by suffix letters. Thus, for the rotary switch of Fig. 21.20, the first portion S1A of switch S1 is identified as S1A FRONT and S1A REAR, viewed as usual from the actuator end. Note in Fig. 21.6 that sections of integrated circuit U104 are designated as U104A, U104B, U104C, U104D, and U104E and are separated from each other by other components in the drawing.

Another example of suffixing is shown in Fig. 21.21. Here the two piezoelectric crystals A and B are enclosed in one unit, Y1. They are then referred to as Y1A and Y1B.

Another method of identifying parts of components that are functionally separated on the diagram is with the PART OF prefix (Fig. 21.22a). If the portion is

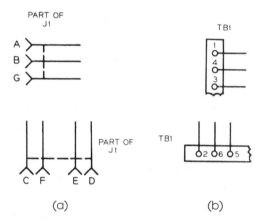

(a)

(b)

FIGURE 21.22 Identification of Portions of Items (ANSI / IEEE).

indicated as incomplete by a short-break line, as in Fig. 21.22b, the words PART OF may be omitted.

■ 21.10 ELECTRON TUBE PIN IDENTIFICATION

Electron tube pins are conventionally numbered clockwise from the tube base key or other point of reference, with the tube viewed from the bottom. In the recommended method of pin identification on a diagram, the corresponding numbers are shown immediately outside the tube envelope and adjacent to the connecting line (Fig. 21.23).

Electron tubes, while generally not used in new designs, are still commonly seen in high-power amplifiers. Their symbols will be seen in maintenance diagrams used while troubleshooting or modifying existing equipment.

FIGURE 21.23 Terminal Identification for Electron Tube Pins (ANSI / IEEE).

■21.11 REFERENCE DESIGNATIONS

An essential part of any electrical diagram is the identification of each separately replaceable part, shown with appropriate combinations of letters and numbers. In addition, portions not separately replaceable are frequently identified, as in previous examples. In electronics and communications, the recognized form is the appropriate letter followed by a number of the same size and on the same line, with no separating hyphen or space. This in turn is followed by any required suffix, again with no hyphen.

The assignment of numbers for each category (resistances, capacitances, inductances, etc.) should start in the upper left corner of the diagram and proceed from left to right, then top to bottom, ending at the lower right corner. If some parts are deleted in revision, the remaining components should not be renumbered. The numbers not used should be listed in a table (Fig. 21.24). If the circuit contains many parts, it may also be helpful to include, as shown, the highest numbers used in each category.

Electron tubes and semiconductors, such as transistors and integrated circuits, are identified by the reference designation and by the type number. It is frequently desirable also to include the tube function below the type number. All this information should be placed near the tube symbol—above it, if convenient (Fig. 21.25). Additional examples of transistor reference designations are shown in Figs. 21.2 and 21.6, although sometimes the transistor types are identified on a separate sheet.

■21.12 NUMERICAL VALUES

Along with reference designations, numerical values for resistance, capacitance, and inductance should be shown, preferably in the form employing the fewest numerals. This may be done by a judicious combination of the multipliers shown in Fig. 21.26a and the symbols in Figs. 21.26b and 21.26c. Note that commas

HIGHEST REFERENCE DESIGNATIONS	
R65	C35
REFERENCE DESIGNATIONS NOT USED	
R7, R9 R60, R62	C11, C14 C19, C23

FIGURE 21.24 Highest and Omitted Reference Designations (ANSI / IEEE).

FIGURE 21.25 Reference Designation, Type Number, and Function for Electron Tubes and Semiconductors (ANSI / IEEE).

are not used in four-digit numbers: 4700 is recommended, not 4,700.

INDUCTANCE According to magnitude, inductance may be expressed in henries (H), millihenries (mH or MILLI H), or microhenries (μH or UH). Following the principle of minimizing the number of numerals, 2μH is preferable to .002 mH, and 5 mH is better than either .005H or 5000 UH.

NOTE Much repetition of units of measurement may be avoided by notes such as the following: UNLESS OTHERWISE SPECIFIED, RESISTANCE VALUES ARE IN OHMS AND CAPACITANCE VALUES ARE IN MICROFARADS.

PART VALUE PLACEMENT For clarity, numerical values should be immediately adjacent to the symbol. Suggested forms are shown in Fig. 21.27.

■21.13 FUNCTIONAL IDENTIFICATION AND OTHER INFORMATION

It sometimes contributes to the readability of a diagram to include special functional identification of

Multiplier	Prefix	Symbol	
		Method 1	Method 2
10^{12}	tera	T	T
10^9	giga	G	G
10^6 (1,000,000)	mega	M	M
10^3 (1000)	kilo	k	K
10^{-3} (.001)	milli	m	MILLI
10^{-6} (.000001)	micro	μ	U
10^{-9}	nano	n	N
10^{-12}	pico	p	P
10^{-15}	femto	f	F
10^{-18}	atto	a	A

(a) MULTIPLIERS

Range in Ohms	Express as	Example
Less than 1000	ohms	.031 470
1000 to 99,999	ohms or kilohms	1800 15,853 10 k 22 K
100,000 to 999,999	kilohms or megohms	380 k .38 M
1,000,000 or more	megohms	3.3 M

(b) RESISTANCE

Range in Picofarads	Express as	Example
Less than 10,000	picofarads	152.4 pF 4700 PF
10,000 or more	microfarads	.015 μF 30 UF

(c) CAPACITANCE

FIGURE 21.26 Numerical Values for Components.

FIGURE 21.27 Methods of Reference Designation and Part Value Placement (ANSI / IEEE).

certain parts or stages. In particular, where functional designations (TUNER, OUTPUT, etc.) are to be shown on a panel or chassis surface, they should also be shown on the electrical diagram in an appropriate place.

Test points may be identified by the words TEST POINT on the drawing. If several are to be shown, the abbreviated form TP1, TP2, or M1, M2, and so on may be used (Fig. 21.6).

Still other information that may be shown on schematic diagrams, if desired, includes the following.

1. DC resistance of transformer windings and coils
2. Critical input or output impedance values
3. Voltage or current wave shapes at selected points
4. Wiring requirements for critical ground points, shielding pairing, and so on
5. Power or voltage ratings of parts
6. Indication of operational controls or circuit functions

21.14 INTEGRATED CIRCUITS

The integrated circuit is a semiconductor wafer or "chip" that has been processed to produce a microminiature replacement for discrete components, such as transistors, diodes, resistors, capacitors, and connecting wiring.

Integrated circuits are widely used in consumer products, such as pocket calculators, personal computers, radios, and television sets, as well as in mainframe computers, microprocessors, and many other industrial applications.

A typical integrated circuit, housed in a "DIP" (dual in-line package) less than an inch in length (Fig. 21.28a), contains circuitry replacing all the discrete components shown in Fig. 21.28b. To simplify the representation of such circuitry, a schematic symbol is used (Fig. 21.28c).

21.15 PRINTED CIRCUITS

In the interests of miniaturization and mass production, printed circuit boards are widely used in the

(a) PICTORIAL
REPRESENTATION OF
COMPONENT

(b) SCHEMATIC REPRESENTATION
(¼ of circuit shown)

(c) SYMBOLIC
REPRESENTATION

FIGURE 21.28 **A Typical Dual In-Line Package Integrated Circuit Representation.** *(b) Courtesy of Motorola, Inc.*

electronics industry, replacing expensive and tedious hand-wiring manufacturing methods.

A variety of procedures have been developed for fabricating these boards. Their name is derived from an early method of production, depositing (printing) a pattern of conductive ink on a base of insulating material. The method now most commonly used consists of etching a wiring pattern on copper-coated phenolic, glass-polyester, or glass-epoxy material.

Single-sided printed circuit (PC) boards have a component side and a foil side. The component side often has part designations silk-screened on the board; on the foil side, the component leads are soldered onto the copper foil.

If CAD is not being used, once the electronic designer has decided on the physical arrangement of components to be mounted on the printed circuit board, a freehand layout sketch is made. The layout shown in Fig. 21.29a was made double size on tracing paper over a .1″-square-grid graph-paper guide.

Several traditional hand methods may be used to make the finished artwork from which the production master (Fig. 21.29b) is derived. These include pen-and-ink drafting, the application of dry-transfer material, or preprinted self-adhesive material. The pen-and-ink method is tedious and less accurate than the other two methods since it requires drawing all conductor paths by hand on vellum or film.

Use of preprinted self-adhesive symbols and tapes is the preferred traditional method, providing an accurate, fast, and easily made master, such as the example in Fig. 21.30. It is important to maintain close tolerances in the production of printed circuit artwork, so that the various electronic components' leads will fit properly in the spaces provided for them on the finished board. CAD circuit design software, however, should be utilized whenever possible to provide optimum PC board designs with minimal effort.

■21.16 COMPUTER GRAPHICS

The production of printed circuit artwork has been greatly simplified through the use of computer-aided drafting (CAD). Sophisticated programs such as P-CAD's Master Designer have been developed for personal computers that aid the drafter or designer in

(a)   (b)

FIGURE 21.29 Printed Circuit Layout Sketch and Master Drawing.
Courtesy of Godbout Electronics.

reducing the physical size of the board and minimizing the need for crossover jumper wires.

Double-sided printed circuit boards are common, and many compact designs require multilayer boards, in which the conductive paths are sandwiched between insulating layers. These board layouts (Fig. 21.31) re-

quire precise registration of the artwork for each layer to ensure proper alignment of corresponding features, such as holes that are to be "plated through" from side to side.

A CAD component layout program such as Master Placer allows the designer to create the best

FIGURE 21.30 Printed Circuit Master Made with Self-Adhesive Material.

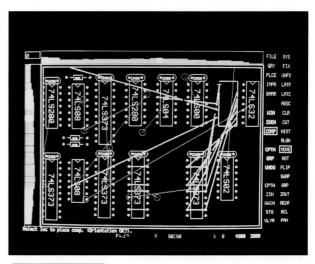

FIGURE 21.32 Computer-Assisted Component Layout. *Courtesy of CADAM, an IBM company.*

FIGURE 21.31 Multilayer Printed Circuit Board Layout Produced with P-CAD Software. *Courtesy of CADAM, an IBM company.*

possible parts placement in the shortest possible time (Fig. 21.32).

Increased use is being made of microminiature surface-mount components, which have short solder tab connections instead of wire leads and so do not require drilled mounting holes. The small size of these parts requires the high degree of accuracy in board layout and design that CAD systems can easily provide.

Interactive CAD systems (Chapter 7) are capable of providing full-size or scaled artwork along with other data required to set up automated soldering and drilling equipment required to produce a finished printed circuit board.

■KEY WORDS

SCHEMATIC DIAGRAM	SINGLE-LINE DIAGRAM
WIRING DIAGRAMS	CAPACITOR
TERMINALS	TRANSISTOR
INTERRUPTED PATH	SEMICONDUCTOR
INTEGRATED CIRCUITS	MIL-STD
CHASSIS	SIGNAL PATH

CROSSOVERS

NUMERICAL VALUES

PRINTED CIRCUIT BOARD LAYOUT

GROUND

RESISTOR

INDUCTOR

DIODE

TRANSFORMER

■ CHAPTER SUMMARY

- Schematic diagrams show the signal path between discrete components.
- Wiring diagrams show point-to-point wiring connections.
- Block diagrams show simplified representations of subsystems. Each subsystem is designated by a separate rectangular box.
- Unique graphic symbols are assigned to every electronic component. CAD programs store these symbols in a library. Pencil schematic drawings can be created using plastic template guides.
- Computer graphics programs can automate much of the drawing work when using the computer to generate a printed circuit board layout.
- Letters and numbers are placed next to components to indicate connection points, terminal pin designations, and reference values.

■ REVIEW QUESTIONS

1. In what direction does the signal path flow in a schematic diagram?
2. What is the difference between a block diagram and a schematic diagram?
3. What does each box represent in a block diagram?
4. In a schematic diagram, what does a large dot mean when two lines cross?
5. How are a component's terminal pins identified in a schematic diagram?
6. Draw the representation of a wire that stops and then continues at a different location.
7. What type of electronic drawing shows parts in three dimensions?
8. What are the names of each side of a printed circuit board? Which side contains the soldered connections?
9. Draw the schematic symbols for 10 electronic components.
10. What is the schematic symbol for chassis ground?

■ ELECTRONIC DIAGRAM PROBLEMS

The following exercises in the construction of schematic diagrams are designed for Layout A–3 or A4-3 (adjusted). If freehand sketches are assigned, 8.5″ × 11.0″ grid paper with .25″ grid squares is suggested. For a mechanical drawing, tracing paper or film is convenient; the drawing is preceded by a sketch on grid paper to work out the details of arrangement and spacing. Refer to Appendix 36 for standard graphical symbols. All of the following problems may also be solved using a CAD system.

Prob. 21.1   The circuit shown in Fig. 21.33 is suitable for classroom or laboratory demonstrations. After a local radio station is tuned with a regular 9-volt battery in place, other devices, such as photoelectric cells and homemade batteries, are substituted.

Make a freehand, mechanical, or CAD schematic diagram of the circuit, approximately twice the size of Fig. 21.33. Use standard symbols and show component values and reference designations, following recommended practices (Layout A–3).

Components List

C1	10-365 PF variable capacitor
D1	Germanium diode
L1	Loopstick antenna coil with center tap
T1	Output transformer: 2500 ohm primary, 3–4 ohm secondary
Q1	NPN type RF transistor (*B = base*, *C = collector, E = emitter*)
Q2	PNP type audio transistor

Prob. 21.2   The unit shown in Fig. 21.34 is used to calibrate the tuning dials of short-wave communications receivers by providing a check signal every 100 kilohertz throughout the commonly used bands.

FIGURE 21.33   **Circuit Demonstrating the Generation of Electrical Energy (Prob. 21.1).**

FIGURE 21.34 **Crystal Calibrator (Prob. 21.2).**

Components List

Capacitors
C1   1000 PF
C2   7–45 PF trimmer
C3   10 PF

Crystal
Y1   100 kHz

Resistors (ohms)
R1   56K
R2   56K

Integrated Circuit
U1   HEP 570 (quad 2-input gate)

Reproduce the schematic diagram approximately double size, freehand, mechanically, or using CAD, as assigned. Add standard symbols and include reference designations, component values, and other data following recommended practices (Layout A–3 or A4–3 adjusted).

Prob. 21.3 The circuit of Fig. 21.35 is that of a variable frequency oscillator (VFO) that may be used with transmitters operating in the 80-meter amateur radio ("ham") band. Make a freehand, mechanical, or CAD schematic diagram, approximately twice the size of Fig. 21.35. Use standard sym-

bols and include reference designations and component values, following recommended practices (Layout A–3 or A4–3 adjusted).

Components List

Capacitors
C1   100 PF trimmer
C2   50 PF
C3   150 PF variable
C4   470 PF
C5, C6   1000 PF
C7, C8   .1 UF

Resistors (ohms)
R1, R2, R3   22K
R4   270

Coils
L1   6 UH ceramic or air core
L2   1 MH RF choke

Semiconductors
D1   1N914 silicon diode
D2   6 V, 1 W zener diode
Q1   40673 dual-gate MOSFET transistor

FIGURE 21.35 **Variable Frequency Oscillator (Prob 21.3.).** *Circuit courtesy of American Radio Relay League.*

FIGURE 21.36 **Transistor Pocket Radio (Prob. 21.4).**

(Chassis Grd)

Prob. 21.4 Make a freehand, mechanical, or CAD schematic diagram of the circuit shown in Fig. 21.36 approximately double size. Use standard symbols and show reference designations and component values, following recommended practices (Layout A–3 or A4–3 adjusted).

Note: By rearranging slightly a few connecting lines, you can eliminate the three dot symbols.

Components List

Capacitors		Resistors (ohms)	
C1	10 PF	R1	47K
C2	10–365 PF	R2	82K
	variable	R3	2200
C3	90 UF	R4	1000
C4	.005 UF	R5	10K
C5	5 UF	R6	82
C6	.001 UF	R7	10K variable
C7	5 UF		(potentiometer)
C8	.01 UF	R8	82K
C9	.005 UF	R9	5600
C10	.005 UF	R10	3900
C11	90 UF		
C12	.005 UF		

Coils
L1   Loopstick antenna (same symbol as
       magnetic core transformer)
L2   Magnetic core, .5 MILLI H
L3   Magnetic core, 1.0 MILLI H

Transistors
(*E* = emitter, *B* = base, *C* = collector)
Q1   PNP type, RF-AF amplifier
Q2   PNP type, audio amplifier

Miscellaneous
S1   On-off switch (mounted on R7)
D1   Diode detector

Prob. 21.5 Figures 21.37a and 21.37b are pictorial wiring diagrams of a transistorized code practice oscillator. The unit provides for practicing International Morse Code either by listening to an audible tone over headphones or speaker or by watching a flashing light.

Study the illustrations and the components list carefully, making preliminary sketches of connections. Then make a complete schematic diagram of the circuit following recommended practices and including component values and reference designations (Layout A–3 or A4–3 adjusted).

Note: Terminal strips TS–1 and TS–2 and the battery holder are for mechanical function and convenience in wiring. They should *not* be shown in a schematic diagram.

Components List

Capacitors
C1   .068 UF

Resistors (ohms)
R1   100K
R2   100
R3   220
R4   50K variable (potentiometer)
R5   10
R6   10

Transistors
($E = emitter, B = base, C = collector$)
Q1   NPN type, oscillator
Q2   PNP type, amplifier

Miscellaneous
Battery   "C" Type, $1\frac{1}{2}$ volt
Battery holder
Jack   2-conductor (for headphones)
Key   Telegraph key (not shown—
            connected between terminals 1 and
            2 of TS–2)
Lamp, 1.5 V
Lamp socket
Speaker
Switch   3-position slide switch
Connections
    Position one (OFF-LIGHT)—terminals
        1–5, 3–4
    Position two (SPEAKER)—terminals 1–6,
        2–4
    Position three (PHONES)—terminals 2–5
Terminal strips TS–1 and TS–2

(a) FIRST WIRING

(b) FINAL WIRING

FIGURE 21.37 **Code Practice Oscillator (Prob. 21.5).**

C H A P T E R   2 2

STRUCTURAL DRAWING

OBJECTIVES

After studying the material in this chapter, you should be able to:

1. Create a structural truss or floor plan drawing.
2. Label and specify the size and shape of steel structural members.
3. Identify, draw, and label various structural steel shapes.
4. Identify, draw, and label high-strength bolts used in structural joints.
5. Identify welding symbols used in steel fabrication of structural components.
6. Identify and read concrete and brick construction details.

OVERVIEW

Structural drawing consists of the preparation of design and working drawings for buildings, bridges, domes, tanks, towers, and other civil structures. It comprises a very large field for the drafter. Although the basic drawing principles are the same as for those of machines and machine parts, certain methods of representation are different in structural drafting.

Ordinarily, the structural engineer determines the form and shape of a structure, as well as the sizes of the main members to be used. The drafter then makes the detail drawings, frequently under the engineer's supervision. Thus, the drafter is the engineer's first assistant and has the opportunity to learn something about design. In many cases, the drafter's position is a stepping-stone to greater responsibility.

Structural drawing can appear in plan or elevation. The location, size, shape, material, and fastening details must be clearly defined. Inaccurate or ambiguous structural drawings can cause building failure and endanger human life. Structural engineers and experienced structural drafters are essential members of the engineering team. Nearly every commercial building uses structural steel in its construction. Many computer graphics programs can enhance the drawing process by providing structural strength calculations for each structural element in a drawing. To ensure safety, meticulous proofing and checking is performed by every member of the team.

■ 22.1 STRUCTURE AND MATERIALS

A spider web is one of nature's fine examples of a structure. The web is made of many parts connected to form a unit strong enough to support the spider. Most of our structures also have many interconnecting parts, such as beams, girders, and columns, that form a framework strong enough to support loads (Figs. 22.1 and 22.2).

The materials most commonly used in construction are wood, glass, structural steel, aluminum, concrete (plain, reinforced, and prestressed), structural clay products, and stone masonry (plain and reinforced).

■ 22.2 WOOD CONSTRUCTION

Many different types of wood are used as structural timber, including ash, birch, cedar, cypress, Douglas fir, elm, oak, pine, poplar, redwood, and spruce. Information concerning the strength properties of the various types and grades can be obtained from *Design Values for Wood Construction*, published by the National Forest Products Association (NFPA), Washington, DC. For design of different members and connections, refer to the NFPA's *National Design Specifications for Wood Construction*, NDS Supplement, *Design Values for Wood Construction*, 1991.

Wood is commonly used for sills, columns, studs, joists, rafters, purlins, trusses, and sheathing in homes and other buildings. Typical drawings of wood structures and construction details may be obtained from the various publications of the NFPA. Common methods of fastening timber members include nails, screws, lag screws, drift bolts, bolts, steel plates, and various special timber connectors. Ordinarily, a structural timber is cut so that the wood fibers, or grain, runs parallel to the length. The strength resistance of wood is not the same in a direction perpendicular to the grain as it is parallel to the grain. Therefore, in designing connections, the direction of the force to be transmitted must be taken into account. Also, proper spacing, edge distance, and end distance must be maintained for screws, bolts, and other connectors.

Typical bolted joints are shown in Fig. 22.3. Either steel or wood splice plates may be used to transmit the forces (Figs. 22.3a and 22.3b). A detail without splice plates is shown in Fig. 22.3c.

Each type of connection requires a different design. The use of *split-ring metal connectors* (Fig. 22.4) is now common. Figure 22.5 shows a drawing of the left half of a timber root truss in which this type of connector is used. Only the left half is drawn, since the truss is symmetrical. By referring to the views of the top and bottom chords, the relative positions of the connecting members of the structure are shown. In drawings of trusses, the view of the top chord is simply an auxiliary view. However, it is customary to show the lower chord by means of a section taken just above the lower chord with the *line of sight downward*. The lower chord, therefore, is shown in first-angle projection.

Ordinarily, wood is surfaced or finished by milling or planing. Because of the wood loss in surfacing, a nominal $1''$ thickness is reduced to a minimum of $\frac{3}{4}''$ for dressed thickness if dry, and $\frac{25}{32}''$ if the wood is green. For nominal dimensions from $2''$ to $4''$, the dressed sizes, dry, are less in each case by $\frac{1}{2}''$, or by $\frac{7}{16}''$ if green.

FIGURE 22.1   **A CAD Drawing Showing Structure.** *Courtesy of Autodesk, Inc.*

For 5″, 6″, and 7″ dimensions, the dressed-size reduction is $\frac{1}{2}$″ for dry wood and $\frac{3}{8}$″ for green wood. For 8″ and greater sizes, the reduction is $\frac{3}{4}$″ for dry and $\frac{1}{2}$″ for green wood. Lumber is considered "green" if its moisture content exceeds 19%. The symbols S2S and S2E indicate, respectively, surfacing of two sides and two edges. If all four faces are to be surfaced, the symbol S4S is used. The working drawings must show whether standard dressed, standard rough, or special sizes are to be used.

■ 22.3 METAL RING CONNECTORS

If properly installed by skilled workers in wood of proper grade and moisture content, the metal ring connector is a very satisfactory and useful device. The method consists of using either a toothed ring, called an *alligator*, or a *split ring* (Fig. 22.4a). If the toothed ring (Fig. 22.4d) is used, it is placed between two members to be connected, and these are drawn together by tightening the bolt so that the teeth of the ring are

FIGURE 22.2   Model of Lamella Dome of Light-Weight Standard Steel Trusses. *Courtesy of Autodesk, Inc.*

FIGURE 22.3   Typical Bolted Joints.

forced into the two members, and the ring thus assists in transmitting stress from one member to the other. If the split ring is used, a groove is cut into each of the two members to be connected, the ring is placed in the grooves, and the two members are held together by means of a bolt, as shown in Fig. 22.6. The open joint of the ring should be in a direction at right angles to that of the stress, so that as the stress is applied the ring is deformed slightly and transmits the pressure to the wood within the ring as well as to that without. With this connection, the tensile and shearing strengths of wood are developed to a higher degree than by other methods of connection, and it is possible to use timber in tension much more economically.

It is standard practice to show ring connectors by solid lines in order to save time, as shown in Fig. 22.5.

■ 22.4 STRUCTURAL STEEL DRAFTING

Structural steel drawings are ordinarily of two types: *engineering design drawings* made in the design engineer's office and *manufacturing (shop) drawings* usu-

FIGURE 22.4 **Metal Connectors for Timber Structures.**

FIGURE 22.5 **A Roof Truss.** *Based on a design by Timber Engineering Company.*

The structure of this church is almost entirely wood and glass. *Photo by R. Greg. Hursley.*

FIGURE 22.6   **Method of Installing Split-Ring Connectors.**

ally made in the office of the steel fabricator. For a more complete treatment of this subject, consult *Detailing for Steel Construction* (published by the American Institute of Steel Construction, Chicago, IL).

Design drawings are concerned primarily with showing clearly the overall dimensions of the structure, such as the location of columns, beams, angles, and other structural shapes, and the listing of the sizes of these members. It is necessary to show a certain amount of detail, usually in the form of typical cross sections, special connections required, various notes, and so on.

In the case of a building floor, for example, a *floor plan* is drawn, showing the steel columns in cross section and the beam or girder framing by the use of single heavy lines, as shown in Fig. 22.7. Members framing from column to column, providing end support for other beams, are called *girders*, while smaller beams framing between girders are called *filler beams*. The designer's plans are sent to the steel fabricator who is to furnish the steel for the job. From these plans the fabricator makes the necessary detailed shop drawings and erection plans. However, before shop work is begun, the fabricator's drawings are sent to the design engineer for final checking, because the engineer has the authority to make any changes necessary to conform to the required strength and safety of connections. As soon as the fabricator has received the shop drawings approved by the engineer, the shop work can begin.

Shop drawings consist of detail drawings of all parts of the entire structure, showing exactly how the parts are to be made (see Figs. 22.11–22.15 and 22.17). Essentially, such drawings show all dimensions necessary for fabrication calculated to the nearest $\frac{1}{16}''$, the location of all holes for connections, details of connection parts, and the required sizes of all material. In addition, fabrication or construction methods may be specified by appropriate notes on the detail drawings whenever such items are not covered by separate specifications. Obviously, fabrication and shop methods, as well as suitable field construction methods, must be fully understood by the detailer.

The design of details and connections is an important part of the engineering of the structure and should not be neglected, since the connections of the various members must be adequate to transmit the forces in these members. Connection details should be drawn to a scale sufficiently large to show them clearly without crowding, although overall lengths of members need not be drawn to scale. All dimensions should be shown, since detail drawings should never be scaled in the shop or in the field by the workers making the piece. An adequate system of piece marking should be employed. Each piece that is separately handled should have its own piece mark, and this piece mark should be shown wherever the member appears on the drawings. This mark also is painted on the member in the shop and later serves as a shipping mark and erection mark in the field for final assembly of the member in the structure.

(a)

Split-Ring Connector

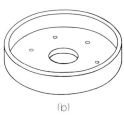

(b)

Pressed Steel
Shear Plate

(c)

Malleable Iron
Shear Plate

(d)

Toothed Ring Connector

FIGURE 22.4 **Metal Connectors for Timber Structures.**

FIGURE 22.5 **A Roof Truss.** *Based on a design by Timber Engineering Company.*

The structure of this church is almost entirely wood and glass. *Photo by R. Greg. Hursley.*

FIGURE 22.6   Method of Installing Split-Ring Connectors.

ally made in the office of the steel fabricator. For a more complete treatment of this subject, consult *Detailing for Steel Construction* (published by the American Institute of Steel Construction, Chicago, IL).

Design drawings are concerned primarily with showing clearly the overall dimensions of the structure, such as the location of columns, beams, angles, and other structural shapes, and the listing of the sizes of these members. It is necessary to show a certain amount of detail, usually in the form of typical cross sections, special connections required, various notes, and so on.

In the case of a building floor, for example, a *floor plan* is drawn, showing the steel columns in cross section and the beam or girder framing by the use of single heavy lines, as shown in Fig. 22.7. Members framing from column to column, providing end support for other beams, are called *girders*, while smaller beams framing between girders are called *filler beams*. The designer's plans are sent to the steel fabricator who is to furnish the steel for the job. From these plans the fabricator makes the necessary detailed shop drawings and erection plans. However, before shop work is begun, the fabricator's drawings are sent to the design engineer for final checking, because the engineer has the authority to make any changes necessary to conform to the required strength and safety of connections. As soon as the fabricator has received the shop drawings approved by the engineer, the shop work can begin.

Shop drawings consist of detail drawings of all parts of the entire structure, showing exactly how the parts are to be made (see Figs. 22.11–22.15 and 22.17). Essentially, such drawings show all dimensions necessary for fabrication calculated to the nearest $\frac{1}{16}''$, the location of all holes for connections, details of connection parts, and the required sizes of all material. In addition, fabrication or construction methods may be specified by appropriate notes on the detail drawings whenever such items are not covered by separate specifications. Obviously, fabrication and shop methods, as well as suitable field construction methods, must be fully understood by the detailer.

The design of details and connections is an important part of the engineering of the structure and should not be neglected, since the connections of the various members must be adequate to transmit the forces in these members. Connection details should be drawn to a scale sufficiently large to show them clearly without crowding, although overall lengths of members need not be drawn to scale. All dimensions should be shown, since detail drawings should never be scaled in the shop or in the field by the workers making the piece. An adequate system of piece marking should be employed. Each piece that is separately handled should have its own piece mark, and this piece mark should be shown wherever the member appears on the drawings. This mark also is painted on the member in the shop and later serves as a shipping mark and erection mark in the field for final assembly of the member in the structure.

FIGURE 22.7 Typical Steel Floor Design Plan.

Erection plans, ordinarily made by the steel fabricator, are essentially skeleton assembly drawings showing the relationship of the various members or parts to be fitted together in the finished structure in the field. In all cases, the piece marks of the individual members are shown on the erection plans. Only sufficient detail to enable the complete assembly of the various members by skilled workers is required, because the detail drawings, already made, fully describe each member and its connections. In most cases, line diagrams in which members are represented simply by heavy straight lines are adequate, although when complex assemblies are required, these should be shown in greater detail. Assembly views should be drawn to scale but, like the detail shop drawings, are never scaled by workers to obtain dimensions. Appropriate notes on these drawings may be used to indicate how the structure is to be assembled.

An erection plan for roof steel framing that is an addition to an existing building is shown in Fig. 22.8. This industrial structure houses a pulp mill for the manufacture of paper roofing products. New steel is shown by full lines, whereas existing roof members are shown by dashed lines. Connections to existing steel members are shown in sectional views, and timber framing for the support of large roof ventilators is also shown.

22.5 STRUCTURAL STEEL SHAPES

Although aluminum and magnesium shapes are available for use in construction, only steel shapes are within the scope of this chapter. Structural steel is available in many standard shapes that are formed by the mill

by rolling steel billets under high temperatures. The shapes available are square, flat, or round bars; plates; equal-leg and unequal-leg angles; American Standard and miscellaneous channels; S, W, M, and HP shapes for use as beams, columns, and bearing piles; structural tees, mill cut from W, S, or M shapes; pipe, in standard, strong, and extra-strong weights; and tubing, in square, rectangular, or circular cross sections. Figure 22.9 shows some typical cross sections of these shapes with the conventional manner of designation or billing in each case. The correct designations must be used on both the design and the detailed drawings in every case where the structural member appears. As a typical example, a wide flange section of 14″ nominal depth, weighing 53 lb per ft and having an overall length of $26'-2\frac{1}{8}''$, would be designated as W14 × 53 × $26'-2\frac{1}{8}$.

The use of templates such as those shown in Fig. 22.10 is a convenient timesaver in drawing structural symbols. Most CAD programs have structural shapes symbol libraries available.

22.6 SCALES FOR DETAILING

Details should be drawn to a scale of $\frac{3}{4}'' = 1'-0$, or $1'' = 1'-0$, using the architects' scale.. Overall lengths of members, however, need not be drawn to scale.

22.7 SPECIFICATIONS

Detailed information concerning dimensions, weights, and properties of rolled steel structural shapes, rolling mill practice, and miscellaneous data

FIGURE 22.8   Roof Steel Erection Plan.

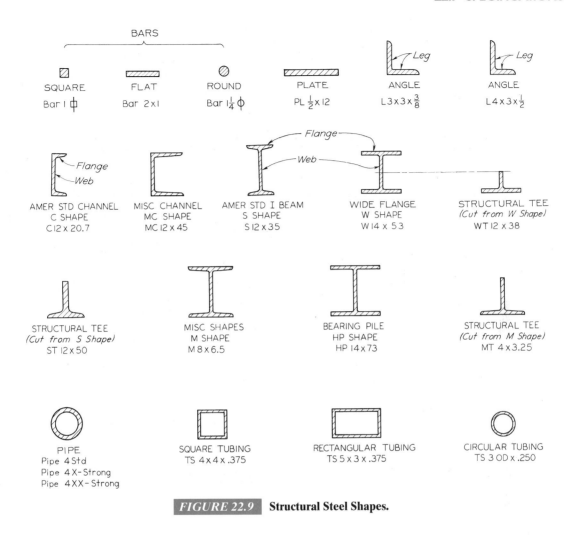

FIGURE 22.9 Structural Steel Shapes.

for designing and estimating may be found in the *Manual of Steel Construction* (American Institute of Steel Construction, AISC). The information contained in this manual is essential to structural steel drafting.

Currently, 15 different types or grades of structural steel are available. These differ in chemical composition and physical properties. Each is controlled in its manufacture by a separate ASTM (American Society for Testing Materials) specification, and there are considerable variations in the strengths and costs of the various grades. The design engineer must be aware of the various physical properties of steels, such as

strengths, ductilities, corrosion resistance, and costs, to make an economical selection of the grade of steel. The types used, in any case, must be specified by ASTM designation on the drawings. The grade most commonly used now is ASTM A36; the number 36 specifies that the guaranteed minimum yield strength is 36 ksi (36,000 lb/in.^{2}). Many light-weight cold-formed shapes in the form of C and Z sections are also available.

Main members of a steel structure must be joined together to form the complete structure in the field. In the modern steel fabricating shop, the most common

FIGURE 22.10 Structural Cross-Sections Template.

method of forming suitable connections is by welding of connection material to the main members, with the provision of open holes for insertion of field bolts to join with other members of the assembly. The connection material, consisting, for example, of angles or connection plates, may also be attached to the main members by riveting or by bolting with either ordinary or high-strength steel bolts in either bearing-type or slip-critical-type connections. Formerly, shop riveting and field riveting were used exclusively in structural work. Now rarely used, the riveted connection has been widely replaced by welding or high-strength bolting. High-strength bolts must be field tightened by a definite amount of torque applied to the wrench.

■ 22.8 RIVETING

Although riveting is seldom used now, structural drafters and designers will often find reference to riveted joints in original plans of structures that require new additions or modifications. The following material is presented to provide a familiarity with this form of structural joining.

Structural rivets are made of soft carbon steel and are available in diameters ranging from $\frac{1}{2}''$ to $1\frac{1}{4}''$. Rivets driven in the shop are called *shop rivets*, and those driven in the field (at the construction site) are called *field rivets*. Rivets are usually of the button-head type and are driven hot, into holes $\frac{1}{16}''$ larger than the rivet diameter. The length of a rivet is the thickness (grip) of the parts being connected, plus the length of the shank necessary to form the driven head and to fill the hole. Excess shank length will produce capped heads, whereas lengths too short will not permit the formation of a full head. Shop rivets are ordinarily driven by large riveting machines that are part of the permanent shop equipment.

Field rivets are heated in a forge at the construction site. When properly heated, the rivet is held firmly in the hole with a dolly bar while the pneumatic hammer or rivet gun forms a round, smooth head.

A shop drawing for a riveted roof truss is shown in Fig. 22.11. Only the left half is drawn, since the truss is symmetrical about the center line. The use of the gage lines of the members should be noted. Gage lines should be located as closely as possible to the centroidal axes of the members, and at the joints where members intersect, these gage lines should intersect at a single point to avoid unnecessary moment stresses due to eccentricities. It is noted that the locations of the open holes indicate where the field splices are to be—namely, at the center line of the truss ($¢$) for the top chord and at $5'-2\frac{5}{16}$ from the center line for the bottom chord.

■ 22.9 FRAME BEAM CONNECTIONS

Because of their common usage, the AISC recommends certain standard connections for attaching beams to other members. These connections are ordi-

FIGURE 22.11 **A Riveted Truss.** *Based on a design by Fort Worth Structural Steel Company.*

narily adequate to transmit the end forces that beams carry. However, the drafter should know the strength of these connections and use them only when they are sufficient. For complete information, see the AISC *Manual of Steel Construction*, Allowable Stress Design (ASD) and Load Resistance Factor Design (LRFD) versions. This manual shows details of standard framed beam connections using $\frac{3}{4}''$, $\frac{7}{8}''$, and 1" diameter

bolted or riveted connections, and allowable loads for both slip-critical-type and bearing-type connections. The fasteners may have a regular or a staggered arrangement. The holes may be either standard round or oversized slotted ones.

The use of angles for standard two-angle framed beam connections in a typical detail drawing of a floor beam is shown in Fig. 22.12. This drawing illustrates

FIGURE 22.12 **Floor Beam Shop Drawing.**

several important features: Shop rivets are shown as open circles on shop drawings, whereas holes for field rivets or bolts are blacked in solid (see Fig. 13.12), *gage lines* (lines passing through rivets or holes like center lines) are always shown, and it is desirable to line up holes or rivets on these lines where possible, rather than to "break the gage." It is necessary to locate the gage line of an angle for each leg in all cases, unless it has already been shown for the identical angle elsewhere on the drawing. The edge distance, from end rivet or hole to the end of the angle, must be given at one end; the billed length of the piece is worked out to provide the necessary edge distance at the other end. It is not necessary that the beam extend the full length of the distance back-to-back of end angles. In this case, as is customary, it is shown "set back" at both ends; the length of beam called for is 1″ less than the $13'-7\frac{3}{4}$ distance. Below the drawing, the mark B25 is the piece or shipping mark that appears on the erection plan and is to be painted on the member in the shop for identification. The end connection angles are fully detailed at the left end of the beam and are given the assembly mark аа. Therefore, at the right end where these same angles are again used, only the assembly mark 2–аа, to indicate two angles, is given. The figure $10'-1\frac{1}{4}$ is called an *extension figure*, as this is the distance from the back of the left-end angles to the center of the group of four holes. Note that this dimension is on the same horizontal line as the $3'-4\frac{1}{2}$ figure just to the left. It is customary, in giving feet and inches, to give the foot mark (′) after dimensions in feet, but not to give the (″) mark, designating inches.

■ 22.10 WELDING

Welding is a common method for connecting steel members of buildings and bridges. Most steel fabricators have riveting, bolt, and welding equipment avail-

able, although a few are equipped to handle only welded fabrication. The metal-arc process is used; energy is supplied through an electrode to unite both the metal of the electrode and the parent or base metal. Electrodes may be either bare or coated, although most welding today is done with coated electrodes. Of all types of welds, the *fillet weld* is most common in structural steel fabrication. For additional information, refer to Chapter 25 and to the specifications of the AISC *Manual of Steel Construction*. When a structure is to be welded, it should be designed throughout for this method of fabrication, as it is not possible to obtain the maximum economy of construction by merely substituting welding for riveting. The designations of welds by the use of standard symbols (see Fig. 25.3) have greatly simplified the making of shop drawings.

A beam with end connection angles shop welded to the beam web is shown in Fig. 22.13. The outstanding legs of the angles are to be welded to the connecting columns in the field, as shown in the end view. This view pertains only to field erection. Open holes in the outstanding legs are for bolts, to facilitate positioning.

A shop drawing of a diagonal bracing between two columns is shown in Fig. 22.14. Here the diagonal members are shop welded to gusset plates that are to be bolted to the column flanges as a permanent installation in the field.

Figure 22.15 is the complete shop drawing for a symmetrical welded roof truss. Because it is symmetrical, it is only necessary to draw the left half of the structure; symmetry is shown on the drawing by the note Sym. abt. ₵. The clip angles marked аа are to be used for the attachment of roof purlins to the truss. In this structure the only plate material needed is the small gusset plate marked pb; most of the connections of web members to chords are made by simply fillet welding the angles against the webs of the chords. The chords are of structural tee (WT) type. The top chords

FIGURE 22.13 Detail of Welded Beam.

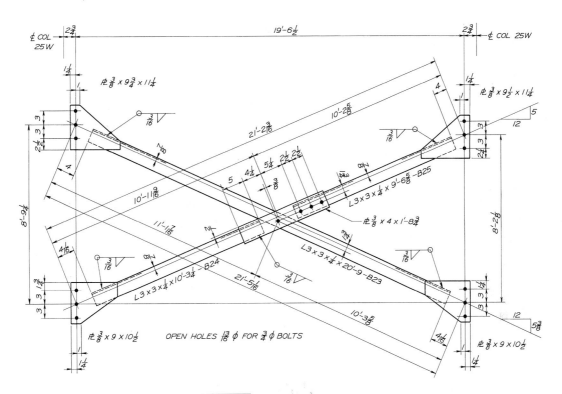

FIGURE 22.14 Details of Column Bracing.

FIGURE 22.15 A Welded Roof Truss. *Courtesy of American Institute of Steel Construction.*

are joined at the ridge by butt welding, which is also used at the end of the truss where the chords join. Note the use of welding symbols, the marking of members, and the listing of all sizes and quantities in the Bill of Material. The drawing is uncluttered and clear, with considerable important information conveyed under the heading General Notes.

■ 22.11 HIGH-STRENGTH BOLTING FOR STRUCTURAL JOINTS

The two basic types of high-strength steel bolts in common use are known as ASTM A325 and A490. The type A449 is similar in physical properties to A325, except that ordinary rather than special nuts may be used with this type. These bolts are treated by quenching and tempering. The A325 bolt is made of medium-carbon steel, whereas the A490 is of alloy steel. Metric high-strength structural bolts, nuts, and washers are available. Consult a manufacturer's catalog or Appendix 18 for specifications. At the time of installation, such bolts are tightened a prescribed amount either by the "turn of the nut method" or by use of a calibrated torque wrench.

The use of a high-strength steel bolt to transmit a force from the center plate into the two outside plates is shown in Fig. 22.16. When fully tightened, the connecting parts are held together by friction, thus preventing joint slip. Fatigue failures due to impact or stress reversals are then minimized. The slip resistance depends not only on the amount of clamping force but also on the nature of the contact surfaces. Figure 22.16 shows hardened washers under both head and nut. Whether one or two washers are needed, or none, depends on the method of tightening used, the yield stress of the material being joined, and whether the joint is to be the "slip-critical" or "bearing" type. In the bearing-type connection, no allowance is made for friction due to clamping action, and the strength of the bolt shank bearing against the material is relied on.

FIGURE 22.16 **High-Tensile-Strength Steel Bolt.**

HIGH STRENGTH HEX HEAD BOLT
HEAVY HEX NUT
HARDENED WASHERS

Numerous specifications govern accepted practice. These, together with installation and inspection procedures, design examples, and reference tables, are well covered in *High Strength Bolting for Structural Joints* (published by Bethlehem Steel Corporation, Bethlehem, PA).

Figure 22.17 represents the complete shop drawing of a steel column of two-floor height; the floors are indicated by reference lines Ⓑ, ①, and ② of the drawing. Here, high-strength bolts are used to attach connection material to the W12 × 96 column shaft. The top views at levels ① and ② show the outstanding legs of the angles in sectional plan views, with open holes shown by the round dots located by dimensions taken from the column center lines. The open holes are for the insertion of field bolts in beam connections when the entire assembly is erected.

Faces Ⓐ, Ⓑ, Ⓒ, and Ⓓ are designated. Viewing a column from above, we designate the faces in that order counterclockwise, with faces Ⓐ and Ⓒ designating the flanges. With regard to web faces Ⓑ and Ⓓ, only face Ⓑ needs to be drawn in the usual case. However, when the connections on face Ⓓ are exceptionally complicated this face also should be drawn as an additional elevation view.

Note the manner of showing the shop bolts and their designation "HSB" (high-strength bolts).

At the top of this column, splice connection material is provided by Bars (b), for attachment of the shaft above. All material for this column is listed in the bill of material on the drawing.

■ 22.12 CALCULATION OF DIMENSIONS

Perhaps the most important part of the structural drafter's work is the accurate calculation of dimensions. If there are incorrect dimensions on the drawings, they will result in serious errors and misfits when members are assembled in the field. Correction of such errors not only entails considerable expense but often delays the completion of the work. Since in ordinary steel work dimensions are given to the closest $\frac{1}{16}''$, considerable precision is demanded. For skewed members, such as those in a truss, some trigonometry is involved. The dimensions may be easily and accurately determined with trigonometry and a calculator with natural functions. For example, to calculate the dimensions for the truss of Fig. 22.18 that has point B at the midpoint of AC and BD perpendicular to top chord AC, proceed as follows:

FIGURE 22.17 Steel Column Detail—Bolted Connections. *Courtesy of American Institute of Steel Construction.*

FIGURE 22.18 Calculation of Truss Dimensions.

For dimensions in feet plus inches with inch fractions to the closest $\frac{1}{16}$″, convert feet and inches to inches and decimals and reconvert final results to feet, inches, and fractions.

Bevel = angle tangent × 12; sixteenths = inch decimals × 16.

$$\tan \theta = \frac{90''}{180''} = 0.5$$

and

$$\theta = \text{arc} \tan 0.5 = 26.565°$$

Bevel (AC and BD):

$$0.5 \times 12'' = 6''$$

Bevel (CD):

$$90° - 2\theta = 36.87°$$

$$12'' = \tan 36.87° = 12'' \times 0.75 = 9.00''$$

$$\text{Length AC} = \frac{180''}{\cos \theta} = 201.25'' = 16' - 9\frac{1}{4}$$

$$\text{Length BD} = \frac{201.25''}{2} (\tan \theta) = 50.3125''$$

$$= 4' - 2\frac{5}{16}$$

$$\text{Length AD} = \frac{201.25''}{2\cos\theta} = 112.5 = 9'-4\tfrac{1}{2}$$

$$\text{Length CD} = \text{Length AD}$$

(Note in the value 50.3125″ for the length of BD that 50″ = 4 × 12 + 2, therefore, 4′–2; .3125″ × 16 = 5 sixteenths. Hence, the total length of BD is 4′–2$\tfrac{5}{16}$.)

CAD users can simply enter the coordinates of the ends of a member and use the built-in function in the program to compute the member's length.

■ 22.13 CONCRETE CONSTRUCTION

Concrete is a building material made by mixing sand (fine aggregate) and gravel (coarse aggregate) or other fine and coarse aggregates with *portland cement* and water. The strength of concrete varies with the quality and relative quantities of the materials; with the manner of mixing, placing, and curing; and with the age of the concrete. The compressive strength of concrete depends on the mix design, but concrete has been manufactured to develop an ultimate strength at 28 days as high as 7000 psi. The tensile strength of the material is limited to about one tenth the compressive strength. A new generation of concrete used in today's highrise construction is "high-strength" concrete, with compressive strength up to 17,000 psi. Portland cement is a controlled, manufactured product as compared to natural cements found in some localities. It derives its name from its color, which resembles that of a famous stone found on the island of Portland in southern England.

Since the tensile strength of *plain concrete* is very limited, the usefulness of concrete as a building material can be materially improved by embedding steel reinforcing bars in it in such a way that the steel resists the tension, and the concrete mainly resists the compression. In this way the two materials act together in resisting forces and flexure. Concrete combined with steel in this way is called *reinforced concrete*. When the steel is pretensioned before the application of the superimposed load, thus producing an interior force within the member, the material is called *prestressed concrete*. The steel in prestressed concrete is of a flexible but very strong type.

■ 22.14 REINFORCED CONCRETE DRAWINGS

The design of the reinforcing for a reinforced concrete structure and the preparation of the corresponding drawings are complicated. To simplify this work and to secure uniformity in the many engineering offices, the American Concrete Institute (Detroit, MI) has prepared a *Manual of Standard Practice for Detailing Reinforced Concrete Structures*.

It is recommended in the manual that two sets of drawings be prepared, an *engineering drawing* and a *placing drawing*. The engineering drawing is prepared by the manufacturer who fabricates the reinforcing steel. The engineering drawing is to show the general arrangement of the structure, the sizes and reinforcements of the several members, and such other information as may be necessary for the correct interpretation of the designer's ideas. The drawing is also used for making forms with precise dimensions before placing the reinforcing bars and casting concrete. The placing drawing is to show the sizes and shapes of the several rods, stirrups, hoops, ties, and so forth and to arrange them in tabular forms for ready reference by the building contractor. The method of preparing an engineering drawing for a two-way slab and beam floor of a multistory building is illustrated in Fig. 22.19. For methods of preparing placing drawings, consult the manual referred to earlier.

The design drawing for a reinforced concrete pier, one of the supporting members for a highway bridge, is shown in Fig. 22.20. Note that the steel bars, even though embedded, are shown by full lines and that concrete is always stippled in cross section. Unlike shop drawings for structural steel, concrete drawings are ordinarily made to scale in both directions. Usually, a scale of $\tfrac{1}{4}''$ to the foot is adequate, although when the structure is complicated, scales of $\tfrac{3}{8}''$ or $\tfrac{1}{2}''$ to the foot may be used. An effort should be made to avoid a cluttered appearance, which is usually the result of crowding the drawing with many notes. Cluttering can be avoided largely by using tables and schedules for listing of bar sizes and other necessary data and by covering many important points in a single set of notes, as shown in Fig. 22.20.

■ 22.15 STRUCTURAL CLAY PRODUCTS

Brick and tile, which are manufactured clay products, have been in use for centuries and comprise some of

FIGURE 22.19   Engineering Drawing for a Two-Way Slab and Beam Floor.

the best known forms of building construction. Brick and tile units are made from different types of clay and in many different shapes, forms, and colors. Ordinarily, they are built into masonry forms by the skilled brick or tile mason, who places the units one at a time in a soft mortar. After the mortar hardens, it becomes an integral part of the structure. Typical mortars contain sand, lime, portland cement, and water. Although the compressive and tensile strengths of the clay units themselves are considerable, the overall strength of the structure is limited by the strength of the mortar joints. As with concrete, therefore, the result is a structure of high compressible strength and relatively low tensile strength. Similarly, it is possible to reinforce brick and tile masonry by embedding steel rods within the members, thus adding greatly to their tension resistance and strength. When this is done, the material is called *reinforced brick* (or *tile*) *masonry* (RBM).

Information concerning the manufacture, the weight and strength properties, and the various uses and applications of structural clay products can be obtained from the Brick Institute of America handbooks *Principles of Brick Engineering* and *Principles of Tile Engineering*. These references will be found invaluable to designers and drafters concerned with designs in this material.

Bricks are made of various sizes; the $2\frac{1}{4}'' \times 3\frac{3}{4}'' \times 8''$ building brick is the most common. Thickness of mortar joints usually varies from $\frac{1}{4}''$ to $\frac{3}{4}''$, with $\frac{3}{8}''$ and $\frac{1}{2}''$ most common. Of the several methods of bonding brick (Fig. 22.21), the following are the most common: *running bond*—all face brick are stretchers and are generally bonded to the backing by metal ties; *American bond*—the face brick are laid alternatively, five courses of stretchers and one course of headers; *Flemish bond*—the face brick are laid with

FIGURE 22.20 Reinforced Concrete Pier Deck Girder. *From* Manual of
Standard Practice for Detailing Reinforced Concrete Structures, *ACI 315-80
(American Concrete Institute, Detroit, MI, 48219).*

RUNNING BOND   AMERICAN BOND   FLEMISH BOND   ENGLISH BOND

STRETCHER COURSE   HEADER COURSE   ROWLOCK COURSE   SOLDIER COURSE

STRUCK JOINT   WEATHER JOINT   RAKED JOINT   CONCAVE JOINT   FLUSH JOINT

BRICK & TILE   BRICK & INTER-LOCKING TILE   STONE & BRICK   TERRA-COTTA & BRICK

COURSED ASHLER   RANDOM ASHLER   COURSED RUBBLE   RANDOM RUBBLE

FIGURE 22.21 Methods of Laying and Bonding Brick, Tile, and Stone.

alternate stretchers and headers in every course; and *English bond*—the face brick are laid alternatively, one course of stretchers and one course of headers. In modern work, these standard methods of bonding are frequently modified to produce various artistic effects. Typical brick lintel arches are shown in Fig. 22.22.

In addition to its use as a basic building material, tile is used extensively in fireproofing structural steel members. Most building codes require that the steel members be enclosed in concrete or masonry so that fire will not cause collapse of the structure. Hollow tile units, which are light and relatively inexpensive, are well adapted to this usage.

Brick units-Tapered Sides and Ends

Brick units-Tapered Sides only

FIGURE 22.22   **Typical Lintels.** *From* **Brick and Tile Engineering.** *Courtesy of Structural Clay Products Institute.*

SECTION "C-C"
3/4" = 1'-0"

FIGURE 22.23   **CAD-Generated Structural Steel Detail Drawing.** *Courtesy of Computervision Corporation, a subsidiary of Prime Computer, Inc.*

■ 22.16 STONE CONSTRUCTION

Natural stone, used in masonry construction—most commonly today for ornamental facing—is generally limestone, marble, sandstone, or granite (Fig. 22.21).

Ashlar, or *ashler*, masonry is formed of stones cut accurately to rectangular faces and laid in regular courses or at random with thin mortar joints.

Rubble masonry is formed of stones of irregular shapes and laid in courses or at random with mortar joints of varying thickness.

Manufactured stone is concrete made of fine aggregate for the facing and coarse aggregate for the backing. The fine aggregate consists of screenings of limestone, marble, sandstone, or granite, so that the manufactured stone presents an appearance similar to that of natural stone. Manufactured stone is made of any desired shape, with or without architectural ornament.

Architectural terra cotta is a hard-burned clay product and is used primarily for architectural decoration and for wall facing and wall coping.

Brick, stone, tile, and terra cotta are combined in many different ways in masonry construction. A few examples are shown in Fig. 22.21.

■ 22.17 COMPUTER GRAPHICS

Structural drawings utilize a variety of standard symbols and methods of representation. A number of CAD symbol libraries are available that will allow the user to generate quickly drawings of structural steel shapes (Fig. 22.23), connecting members, and steel erection plans. Once the plans have been created, other programs are available that will automatically calculate areas and perform finite element analysis on the design.

■ KEY WORDS

JOINT

PLAN

STEEL SHAPES

WEB

REINFORCED CONCRETE

GIRDER

PURLIN

TRUSS

ELEVATION

FLANGE

SYMMETRICAL

MATERIAL SCHEDULE

■ CHAPTER SUMMARY

- The structural drawing is one of the most important elements in construction drawings.
- Cost and safety are important considerations when designing a structure that people will use, such as a building or bridge.
- Structural drawings are precise, detailed instructions for general contractors, who must create the structure according to the information in the drawings.
- Steel is commonly used in commercial construction because of its strength and durability. Steel shape and size designations are different from those for other materials, such as wood.
- Structural drawings show both plan and elevation views.

- Details about how structural members are connected and fastened to each other are critical parts of a structural drawing.
- Structural drawings use more notes about size, shape, location, and fastening details than other types of drawings.
- Safety is dependent on correctly following the engineer's design. Careful proofing and checking of every note and detail is an essential part of the engineering process.
- The list of materials, including their size, shape, and detail information, is often included in a material schedule that appears in table form in a corner of the drawing.
- When components are welded together, standard welding symbols and notes must be used.

■ REVIEW QUESTIONS

1. List five structural materials.
2. Draw four different structural steel shapes and label each shape.
3. How is reinforced concrete different from regular concrete?
4. What is shown in the plan view of a structural drawing?
5. What is shown in the elevation view of a structural drawing?

6. Would the spacing for steel roof trusses be shown in a plan view or an elevation view?
7. Would the individual members of a roof truss be shown in a plan view or an elevation view?
8. What are the most common fastening techniques for joining structural steel?

■ STRUCTURAL DRAWING PROBLEMS

The following problems are intended to afford practice in drawing and dimensioning simple structures and in illustrating methods of construction. They may be completed by using either traditional drawing methods or a CAD program.

Prob. 22.1 Calculate point-to-point lengths (the distances between centers of joints) of the web members of the truss of Fig. 22.5. Make a detailed drawing of web member piece No. 4.

Prob. 22.2 Make a complete detail of the top chord member of the truss shown in Fig. 22.5 for a 30° angle of inclination.

Prob. 22.3 Assuming riveted construction, with rivets of $\frac{3}{4}''$ or 20-mm diameter, make a complete shop drawing for a typical filler beam of Fig. 22.7. Detail the same beam for welded construction. Consult the AISC *Manual of Steel Construction*.

Prob. 22.4 Assuming the column size to be W8 × 31, detail the W16 × 36 girder at the center of the drawing of Fig. 22.7.

Prob. 22.5 Referring to Fig. 22.15, make a complete detail for a truss of the same length, but change the height from 10′–0 to 6′–8. Use angle members of the same cross-section sizes as those shown, but of different lengths, as needed.

Prob. 22.6 Referring to Fig. 22.14, make a similar bracing detail, changing the distance between column centers from 20′–0 to 18′–6.

Prob. 22.7 Draw cross sections through panel D of Fig. 22.19, in both directions. Include the supporting beams in each cross section, and show all dimensions, size and spacing of reinforcing steel, and dimensions to locate the ends of bars and the points of bend for the bent bars. Also show and locate the stirrups in these views.

Prob. 22.8 Detail the brickwork surrounding a window frame for an opening 4″–0$\frac{7}{8}$ wide by 6′–9 high. Use the type of curved arch lintel similar to that of Fig. 22.22. Assume standard-size building brick with $\frac{1}{2}''$ mortar joints.

Prob. 22.9 Consult *Principles of Tile Engineering*, and draw a cross-sectional view through a 12″ wall of composite brick and tile construction.

Prob. 22.10 Referring to Fig. 22.24 (a-c), redraw a complete detail of this proposed deck changing the total width of the deck from 12′ to 14′ and the length from 52′ to 54′.

Prob. 22.11 Referring to Fig. 22.24 b, adjust dimension on posts from 4″ × 4″ to 6″ × 6″. Redraw a complete detail of railing view and Section A–A.

PROPOSED   DECK

PLAN VIEW
SCALE 1" = 8'

(a)

FRONT VIEW OF RAILING
SCALE: 1" = 4'

(b)

DECK
SECTION A-A
SCALE: 1" = 4'

(c)

FIGURE 22.24 (a) Deck Floor Plan. (b) Railing front view. (c) Section A–A right side view.

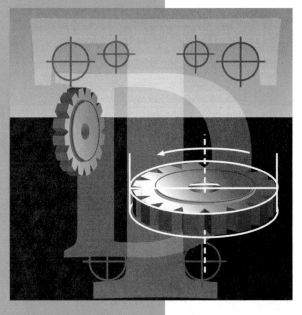

CHAPTER 23

TOPOGRAPHIC DRAWING AND MAPPING

OBJECTIVES

After studying the material in this chapter, you should be able to:

1. Read and draw a plat, topographic contour map, street contour map, and highway plan and profile.

2. Read the elevation of a tract of land using contour lines.

3. Identify the scale and compass orientation of a topographic map.

4. Read and notate property boundaries on a land survey map.

5. Create a profile map from a set of contour lines.

OVERVIEW

Topographic drawing and **mapping** deals with the representation of portions of the Earth's surface—mainly its natural features—to a convenient scale. On such drawings the relative positions of natural features, with respect to certain definitely located points, are shown. Since the shape of the Earth is spherical, any representation on a plane, such as a piece of paper, is necessarily somewhat distorted. In drawing large areas, therefore, some method of projection must be used that results in a minimum of distortion. In such work, the positions of the control or reference points are usually defined by spherical coordinates of latitude and longitude (meridians and parallels), which are shown as reference lines on the drawing. In drawing small areas to a relatively large scale, the distortion due to Earth curvature is so slight that it is unnoticeable and may therefore be entirely neglected. Orthographic projection, as used in technical drawings, in which the line of sight is assumed to be perpendicular to the plane of the map, is the method most commonly used in topographic representation.

The U.S. Coast and Geodetic Survey, the U.S. Department of Interior, and the U.S. Geological Survey all produce contour maps of land boundaries. More detailed maps are created by local communities when subdividing property for residential and commercial construction. Highways and public works, such as dams and bridges, require detailed topographic drawings to define the three-dimensional surface shape of a given geographic area. Topographic drawings use contour lines to define elevation in the plan view. Profile drawings show the sectional elevation of a specified datum plane. Many topographic drawings become legal documents used in resolving disputes over property boundaries.

■ 23.1 DEFINITIONS

The purpose for which a map is to be used determines what features should be represented, what scale should be used, and what detail should be included. Certain commonly used symbols are employed in representing natural features and human-made objects. Also, certain terms and various types of maps are common. Therefore, the following definitions are essential to an understanding of the subject.

A **plat** is a map, usually of a small area, plotted directly from a land survey. It does not ordinarily show relative ground elevations and is drawn for some specific purpose, such as the calculation of areas, the location of property lines, or the location of a building project. Usually it contains a *traverse* (Fig. 23.1).

A **traverse** consists of a series of intersecting straight lines of accurately measured lengths. At the points of intersection, the deflection angles between adjacent lines are measured and recorded. Starting at one point, therefore, we can calculate rectangular coordinates of the other intersection points by trigonometry. A *closed traverse* thus becomes a closed polygon and provides a method for checking the accuracy of work. The land survey plat of Fig. 23.1 illustrates a closed traverse.

Elevations are vertical distances above a common *datum*, or reference plane or point. The elevation of a point on the surface of the ground is usually determined by differential leveling from some other point of known elevation. Commonly, elevations are referenced to mean sea level..

A **profile** is a line contained in a vertical plane, and it depicts the relative elevations of various points along the line. For example, if a vertical section were to be cut into the Earth, the top line of this section would represent the ground profile.

Contours are lines drawn on a map to locate, in the plan view, points of equal ground elevation. On a single contour line, therefore, all points have the same elevation.

Hatchures are short, parallel, or slightly divergent lines drawn in the direction of the slope. They are closely spaced on steep slopes and converge toward the tops of ridges and hills. Hatchures are shade lines to show relief.

Monuments are special installations of stone or concrete to mark the locations of points accurately determined by precise surveying. It is intended that monuments be permanent or nearly so, and they are usually tied in by references to nearby natural features, such as trees and large boulders.

Cartography is the science or art of map making.

Topographic maps depict (1) water, including seas, lakes, ponds, rivers, streams, canals, and swamps; (2) **relief**, or elevations, of mountains, hills, valleys, cliffs, and the like; and (3) **culture**, or human constructions, such

FIGURE 23.1 Land Survey Plat.

as towns, cities, roads, railroads, airfields, and boundaries (Figs. 23.2 and 23.13).

Hydrographic maps convey information concerning bodies of water, such as shoreline locations; relative elevations of points of lake, stream, or ocean beds; and sounding depths.

Cadastral maps are accurately drawn maps of cities and towns, showing property lines and other features that control property ownership.

Military maps contain information of military importance in the area represented.

Nautical maps and charts show navigational features and aids, such as locations of buoys, shoals, lighthouses and beacons, and sounding depths.

(a)

(b)

FIGURE 23.2   **(a) CAD Topographical Mapping.** *Courtesy of Intergraph.*
(b) A Topographic Map.

Aeronautical maps and charts show prominent landmarks, towers, beacons, and elevations for the use of air navigators.

Engineering maps are made for special projects as an aid to locations and construction (See Figs. 23.7 and 23.10–23.12).

Landscape maps are used in planning installations of trees, shrubbery, drives, and other garden features in the artistic design of area improvements (see Fig. 23.7).

■ 23.2 SOURCES OF INFORMATION

The basis of all maps and topographic drawing is the **survey**. Several surveying methods are used to obtain the information necessary for the making of a map.

Short distances are ordinarily measured by steel tape, with stakes being driven to mark the points between field measurements. Distances may also be determined by measuring aerial photographs, when the scale of the photograph is known. An instrumental method, known as the *stadia method*, is also widely used in map making. The *stadia transit* is an optical instrument used in conjunction with a special *stadia rod*. By sighting on the rod and using the necessary conversion factor, the instrument reading can easily be converted to distance.

Recent developments in the art of surveying have revolutionized distance measurement by the use of electronic instruments. To measure to a distant point, the surveyor directs the instrument's aiming head toward the point, where a passive reflector or prism has been set. The instrument generates either a modulated infrared light signal, focused into a narrow beam, or a laser beam, aimed directly at the reflector. When the reflector bounces the beam back to the aiming head, the beam's travel time is electronically measured and directly converted into the distance to the point. A major advantage of the electronic measurement over the distance-taping method is that moving traffic does not have to be stopped while measurements are being taken. Such time-saving instruments are capable of distance measurements up to 4 miles, depending on the quality of the instrument. Accuracy varies from .01 to .03 ft, more than sufficient for topographic surveying.

By use of a **compass**, the bearing of a line, which is the angle between the line and the magnetic north, may be read on the compass. When all bearings of the lines of a traverse have been determined, the angles between the lines are easily computed by addition or subtraction. The correct method of listing bearings requires that they be referenced either to the north or to the south. A bearing, therefore, is either north, and east or west; or it is south, and east or west. In Fig. 23.1, the bearing for traverse line AB is N 44°52′E. Compass readings are not highly accurate because magnetic north and true north are not quite the same; also, local magnetism may affect the position of the compass needle.

When accurate measurement of angles is desired, the **transit** is the instrument usually employed. This optical instrument may be set up directly over a point, then sighted successively on two other points, after which the deflection angle in a horizontal plane can be read on the transit. This instrument is also used for the measurement of vertical angles.

For accurate orientation of lines on a map, the angle of a line with the true north is often desired. For this purpose the transit may again be used for sighting on a star (usually Polaris, the North Star), or on the Sun. From instrument readings, the true angle of a line may then be calculated.

The **level**, also an optical instrument, is equipped with a telescope for sighting long distances. This instrument is commonly used to determine differences in elevation in the field, a process called *differential leveling*. When this accurate instrument is leveled, the line of sight of its telescope is horizontal. A level rod, graduated in feet and decimals of feet, may be held on various points. Instrument readings of the rod then serve to determine the differences in elevations of the points.

Photogrammetry is now widely used for map surveying. This method utilizes actual photographs of the Earth's surface and of manufactured objects on the Earth. Aerial photogrammetry, via aircraft or satellite, is used for such activities as governmental and commercial surveying, explorations, and property valuation. It has the great advantage of being easy to use in difficult terrain having steep slopes, where ground surveying would be difficult or nearly impossible. The utilization of aerial photographs is called *aerial photogrammetry*, whereas that utilizing photographs taken from ground stations with the axis of the camera lens nearly horizontal is known as *terrestrial photogrammetry*. By combining the results of both types of observations, it is possible not only to determine the relative positions of objects in a horizontal plane, but also to determine relative elevations. Thus, the science of photogrammetry can be the basis of contour mapping as well as plan mapping. Generally, aerial photographs are used in matched groups to form a *mosaic*. To form a satisfactory mosaic map, the group photographs must overlap slightly. A distinct advantage of photogrammetry is that a large area can be mapped from a single clear photograph. The method may be used in connection with ground surveying by photographing *control points* already located on the ground by precise surveying.

For large land developments and large construction projects, more modern methods for producing topographic maps have evolved. (See Fig. 23.3.) Some state highway departments and most engineering firms that specialize in surveying and mapping now make use of aerial photography, with computers, terrain digitizers, stereoplotters, geographic information systems (GIS), and various new photolaboratory techniques. Investment in this expensive equipment can be justified when the volume of work is great and sufficient hours can be saved through its use, as is frequently the case (see §23.8 for topographic maps of the United States).

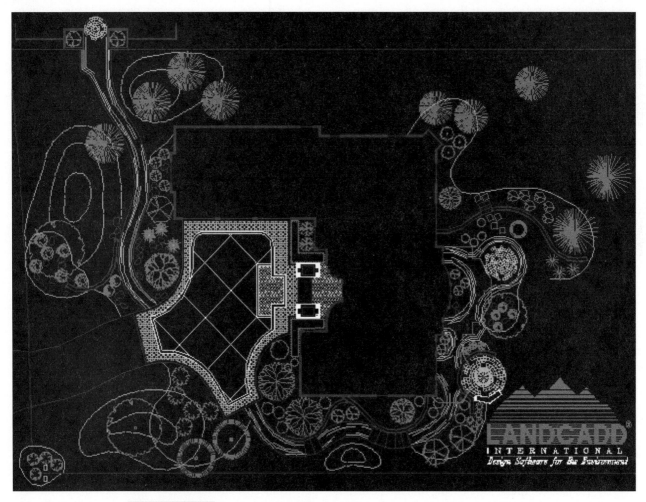

FIGURE 23.3   **Landscape Design using CAD.** *Courtesy of LANDCADD International.*

For additional information, which is beyond the scope of this chapter, the student may refer to other publications, such as the *Manual of Surveying Instructions for the Survey of the Public Lands of the United States*, prepared and published by the Bureau of Land Management (U.S. Government Printing Office, Washington, DC). Many governmental agencies also publicize information about maps and geographic data through the World Wide Web (WWW). Access to the desired files may be obtained using the pertinent agencies' home pages..

■ 23.3 CONTOURS

Although contours have already been defined, their uses and characteristics and the methods of plotting them require further discussion.

A *contour interval* is the vertical distance between horizontal planes passing through successive contours. For example, in Fig. 23.4 the contour interval is 10′. The contour interval should not change on any one map. It is customary to show every fifth contour by a line heavier than those representing intermediate contours.

If extended far enough, every contour line will close. At streams, contours form Vs pointing upstream.

Even spacing between successive contours means that the ground slopes uniformly; uneven spacing between contours means that the slope changes frequently. Widely spaced contours indicate a gentle slope, whereas closely spaced contours indicate steep slopes.

Locations of points on contour lines are determined by *interpolation*. In Fig. 23.4, the locations and elevations of seven control points are determined, and contour lines will be drawn on the assumption that the slope of the surface of the ground is uniform between station A and the six adjacent stations. To draw the contour lines, a contour interval of 10′ was adopted, and the locations of the points of intersection of the contour lines with the straight lines, joining the point A and the six adjacent points, was calculated as follows.

The horizontal distance between stations A and B is 740′. The difference in elevation of those stations is 61′. The difference in elevation of station A and contour 300 is 9′; therefore, contour 300 crosses the line AB at a distance from station A of $\frac{9}{61}$ of 740, or 109.1′. Contour 290 crosses the line AB at a distance from contour 300 of $\frac{10}{61}$ of 740, or 121.3′. This 121.3′ distance between contour lines is constant along the line AB and can be set off without further calculation.

In the same way, points in which the contours cross the other lines of the survey can be interpolated.

FIGURE 23.4 Contours Determined from Control Points.

After this process is completed, the several contour lines can be drawn through points of equal elevation, as shown.

After contours have been plotted, it is easy to construct a profile of the ground line in any direction. In Fig. 23.4, the profile of line KAL is shown in the lower or front view. It is customary, as shown here, to draw the profile to a larger vertical scale than that of the plan, to emphasize the varying slopes.

Contour lines may also be plotted by use of the recorded elevations of points on the ground surface, as in Fig. 23.5a. This figure illustrates a *checkerboard sur-*

vey, in which lines are drawn at right angles to each other, dividing the survey into 100-ft squares, and where elevations have been determined at the corners of the squares. The contour interval is taken as 2′, and the slope of the ground between adjacent stations is assumed to be uniform.

The points where the contour lines cross the survey lines can be located approximately by inspection, accurately by the graphical method shown in Fig. 4.14, or by the numerical method explained for Fig. 23.4.

The points of intersection of contour lines with survey lines may also be found by constructing a pro-

FIGURE 23.5 **Contours Determined from Readings at Regular Intervals.**

file of each line of the survey, as shown for line 1 in Fig. 23.5b. Horizontal lines are drawn at elevations at which it is desired to show contours. The points in which the profile line intersects these horizontal lines indicate the elevations of points in which corresponding contour lines cross the survey line 1 and, therefore, can be projected upward, as shown, to locate these points.

It is obvious that the profile of any line can be constructed from the contour map by the converse of the process just described.

FIGURE 23.6   General Mapping Template.

■ 23.4 SYMBOLS

Various natural and manufactured features are designated by special symbols. A reference list of the most commonly used map symbols is given in Appendix 33. The student should refer to this list for identification of the symbols used in the figures of this chapter.

The use of templates by the drafter, such as that shown in Fig. 23.6, is a convenient timesaver in drawing mapping symbols.

■ 23.5 CITY MAPS

The special use of a map determines what features are to be shown. Maps of city areas may be put to many uses. Figure 23.7, a city plan for location of a new road construction, shows only those features of importance to the location and construction of the road. The transit line starts at the center-line intersection of Park St. and 5th Ave., and it is marked as station 0 + 00. From

FIGURE 23.7   A City Plan for Location of a New Road Project.

CAD-Generated Road Map. *Courtesy of Softdesk, Inc.*

here it extends north over the railroad yard to cross the river. Features near the transit line, such as buildings, are shown and identified by name. Street widths are important and are shown. Contour lines between the railroad yard and the river indicate the steeply sloping terrain.

Maps perform an important function for those who plan the layout of lots and streets. For example, Fig. 23.8a shows an original layout of these features for a new residential area. An examination of the contours will show that this layout is not satisfactory, since the directions of the streets do not fit the natural ground slopes. Streets should be arranged so that the subdivision can be entered from a low point and so that a maximum number of lots will be above street grade. The layout in Fig. 23.8b is a decided improvement, for in it the streets curve to fit the topography and the entrance is located at a low point.

Maps have a definite use in landscape planning. Figure 23.9 is a landscape map showing a proposed layout of lots and trees for beautification of a new subdivision.

■ 23.6 STRUCTURE LOCATION PLANS

When a construction project is contemplated in a particular area, the construction should be located most advantageously to fit the topography of the area. Thus, a location plan on paper is of great advantage. A project location plan for a dam is shown in Fig. 23.10. This map shows the important natural features, contours, a plan view of the structure, and a cross section through Hoover Dam.

Although many drawings (perhaps hundreds) comprise the complete detail drawings for a large bridge, one of the most important early drawings is a general arrangement plan and elevation in the form of a line diagram. For example, Fig. 23.11 shows a plan and elevation of a large bridge structure.

■ 23.7 HIGHWAY PLANS

Before highway construction starts, it is necessary first to plan the location and to arrange both the horizontal and vertical alignment most advantageously. Commonly, both plan and profile are drawn on the same sheet, as in Fig. 23.12. The topographical plan at the top of the figure shows such features as trees, fences, and farmhouses along the right of way. The transit line, locating the center line of the new road, is drawn with stations spotted at 100′ distances apart. Data for laying in the horizontal curves in the field have been calculated and are listed. The point of curve (P.C.) at station 17 + 00 is the point at which the line begins to curve with a 600′ radius, for a curve length of 400′. The central angle is 38°12′, and the degree of curve (angle subtended by a 100′ chord) is shown as 9°33′. The reverse curve of 800′ radius begins at station 21 + 00. Note also the north point and the bearing N73°E of the transit line.

The vertical alignment is shown in profile below the plan. Note the listing of station numbers below the profile. The scale of this view is larger in a vertical than in a horizontal direction to show the elevations clearly. The existing ground profile along the center line of the road is shown, as well as the profile of the

(a)

(b)

proposed vertical alignment. The symbol P.I. denotes the point of intersection of the grade lines, and grade slopes are given in percentages. A 1% grade would rise vertically 1′ in each 100′ of horizontal distance. Station 22 + 00, therefore, is the intersection point of an upgrade of 1.5% and a downgrade of −2.0%.

To provide a smooth transition between these grades, a vertical curve (V.C.) of 1100′ length is used.

Station	Tangent Elevations	Ordinate	Curve Elevations
18	121.50	.19[a]	121.31
19	123.00	.76	122.24
20	124.50	1.72	122.78
21	126.00	3.05	122.95
22	127.50	4.77	122.73
23	125.50	3.31	122.19
24	123.50	2.12	121.38
25	121.50	1.19	120.31
26	119.50	.53	118.97
27	117.50	.13	117.37

[a] $\dfrac{(100)^2\,4.779}{(500)^2} 5\ .199.$

TABLE 23.1   *Calculation of Vertical Curve Elevations*

This curve is parabolic and tangent to grade at stations 17 + 00 and 28 + 00. The straight line joining these points has an elevation 117.96′ directly below the P.I. At this point the parabolic curve must pass through the midpoint of the vertical distance, at a height of 4.77′ below the P.I. Ordinates to parabolas, measured from tangents, are proportional to the squares of the horizontal distances from the points of tangency. Therefore, it is possible to calculate the elevations of points along the curve by first determining the grade elevations and then subtracting the parabolic curve ordinates. The final profile elevations are given in the figure. Calculations are given in Table 23.1.

23.8 UNITED STATES MAPS

Maps of the United States, prepared by the U.S. Coast and Geodetic Survey and the U.S. Geological Survey, are excellent examples of topographic mapping. A small section of a typical U.S. Geological Survey map is shown in Fig. 23.13. Such maps cover large areas, the largest scale used being 1 : 62,500, very nearly one mile to the inch. The contour interval in this example is 20′. To so small a scale, it would be impossible to show clearly any small features—vegetation and fences, for example. Therefore, these maps can show only the main features of the terrain, such as contours, roads, railroads, rivers, lakes, and streams. These maps are very reliable because they are based on precise surveying.

The U.S. Geological Survey has prepared a series of standard topographic maps that cover the United States, Puerto Rico, Guam, American Samoa, and the U.S. Virgin Islands. Each unit of survey (map) is a *quadrangle* bounded by parallels of latitude and meridians of longitude. Quadrangles covering $7\frac{1}{2}$ minutes of latitude and longitude are published at a scale of 1 : 24,000 (1″ = 2000′). Quadrangles covering 15 minutes of latitude and longitude are published at a scale of 1 : 62,500 (1″ = 1 mile, approx.)

Maps (27″ × 41″) showing the status of various phases of mapping and the areas covered by aerial photography in the United States at a scale of 1 : 5,000,000 (1″ = 80 miles, approx.) are available on request from the U.S. Geological Survey, Reston, VA 22092.

23.9 COMPUTER GRAPHICS

Various CAD programs allow the user to create contour maps easily by entering random site data. Point descriptions, contour lines, grid lines, and features such as bodies of water or structures can be depicted, and topographic pictorial drawings are produced (Fig. 23.14). Planners are able to lay out subdivision plots with programs that will also provide the building contractor with earthwork calculations for individual lots or the entire site. Street intersections and features such as cul-de-sacs can be automatically generated (Fig. 23.15).

FIGURE 23.9 **Land Subdivision Showing Use of Cul-de-Sacs (u-shaped streets), Stanford, Connecticut.** *From* **Land Subdivision,** *ASCE Manual No. 16 of Engineering Practice.*

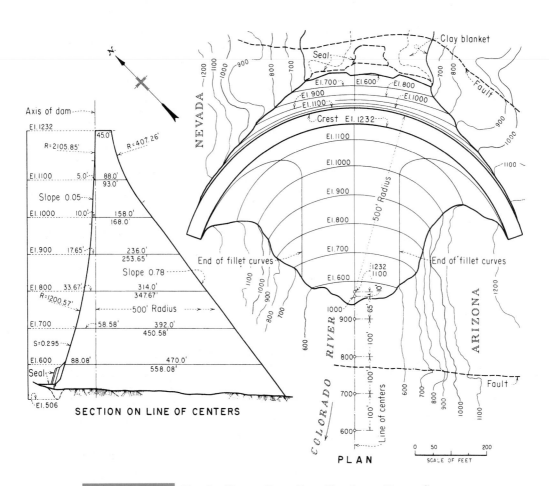

FIGURE 23.10 **Plan for Hoover Dam.** *From* Treatise on Dams. *Courtesy of U.S. Dept. of the Interior, Bureau of Reclamation.*

FIGURE 23.11 **Plan and Elevation of a Bridge Structure.**

FIGURE 23.12 A Highway Plan and Profile.

FIGURE 23.13 A Typical Map prepared by the U.S. Geological Survey.
Courtesy of U.S. Geological Survey.

FIGURE 23.14 Three-Dimensional Digital Terrain Model Created by Computek, Inc., of Taipei, Taiwan, Using CADL (CADKEY Advanced Design Language). *Courtesy of CADKEY, Inc.*

FIGURE 23.15 CAD-Produced Tract Map. *Courtesy of California Computer Products, Inc.*

■ KEY WORDS

TRAVERSE	PLAT
PROFILE	CONTOUR LINES
HATCHURES	MONUMENTS
HYDROGRAPHIC MAPS	TOPOGRAPHIC MAPS
CARTOGRAPHY	CADASTRAL MAPS
NAUTICAL MAPS	TRANSIT
SUBDIVISION	QUADRANGLE
ELEVATION	DATUM
AERONAUTICAL MAPS	LANDSCAPE MAPS
ENGINEERING MAPS	SURVEY
PHOTOGRAMMETRY	STADIA

CHAPTER SUMMARY

- Topographic drawings represent three dimensions on a two-dimensional plan view.
- Land surveys denote the boundaries of tracts of land. Boundaries are defined by bearing and length.
- Contour lines are used to show elevation on a plan drawing. Each contour line represents one elevation level. Closely spaced contour lines indicate a steep slope. Widely spaced contour lines indicate a flatter slope.
- A profile drawing of elevation is created by drawing a cutting-plane datum on the plan view and tranferring distances and elevation from the plan to the profile drawing.

- Profile drawings are often used to determine fill and cut slopes for roadways and railways.
- Land subdivision drawings show roads, property boundaries, and major landscape landmarks like parks, streams, buildings, and large trees.
- Computer graphic workstations can model three-dimensional surfaces from satellite photographs. Computers model surfaces by creating a wire frame structure and then applying solid color contours to the wire frame surface.

REVIEW QUESTIONS

1. What is the purpose of a plat drawing? Is it a plan or an elevation?

2. What is the topographic notation for a plat boundary that runs exactly east and west for 1503.4 feet?

3. What are the lines that indicate elevation on a topographic map?

4. What is the purpose of a profile drawing?

5. If contour lines are very close together, would the slope be steep or gentle?

TOPOGRAPHIC DRAWING PROBLEMS

The following problems are given to afford practice in topographic drawing. They may be completed by using either traditional drawing methods or a CAD program. The drawings are designed for a Size B or A3 sheet. The position and arrangement of the titles should conform approximately to those of Fig. 23.1.

Prob. 23.1   Draw symbols of six of the common natural surface features (streams, lakes, etc.) and six of the common development features (roads, buildings, etc.) shown in Appendix 33.

Prob. 23.2   Draw, to assigned horizontal and vertical scales, profiles of any three of the six lines shown in Fig. 23.4.

Prob. 23.3   Assuming the slope of the ground to be uniform and assuming a horizontal scale of $1'' = 200'$ and a contour interval of $5'$ (see §23.3), plot, by interpolation, the contours of Fig. 23.4.

Prob. 23.4   Using the elevations shown in Fig. 23.5a and a contour interval of $1'$, plot the contours to any convenient

horizontal and vertical scales, and draw profiles of lines 3 and 5 and of any two lines perpendicular to them. Check, graphically, the points in which the contours cross these lines.

Prob. 23.5   Using a contour interval of $1'$ and a horizontal scale of $1'' = 100'$, plot the contours from the elevations given (Fig. 23.16) at $100'$ stations; check, graphically, the points in which the contours cross one of the horizontal lines and one of the vertical lines, using a vertical scale of $1'' = 10'$; sketch, approximately, the drainage channels.

Prob. 23.6   Draw a plat of the survey shown in Fig. 23.1 to as large a scale as practicable. Use an engineers' scale to set off distances and a protractor to set off bearings; if the drawing is accurate, the plat will close.

Prob. 23.7   Draw a topographic map of a country estate similar to that shown in Fig. 23.2.

Prob. 23.8   Calculate profile elevations for a vertical curve $800'$ long to join grades of $+3.00\%$ and -3.00%. Assume grade elevations at points of tangency to be $100.00'$.

144.7	139.2	143.1	144.6	144.3	143.5	142.2
142.5	138.0	139.0	141.3	142.7	139.3	139.1
140.7	137.5	136.1	138.6	138.0	136.1	137.2
138.8	136.5	135.0	136.2	135.7	135.9	136.1
139.1	136.4	134.6	133.5	133.7	134.1	135.8
135.3	134.5	133.0	132.7	132.0	131.9	132.3
135.9	134.0	132.7	131.3	130.8	129.6	131.5

FIGURE 23.16   To Draw Contours (*Prob. 24.5*).

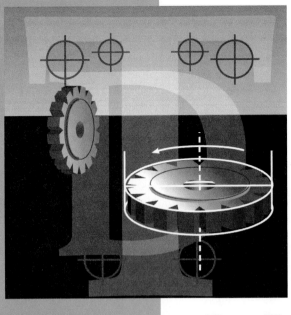

C H A P T E R   2 4

PIPING DRAWING

OBJECTIVES

After studying the material in this chapter, you should be able to:

1. Identify cast iron, brass, and copper pipe and tubing fittings.

2. Draw the common pipe joints and label them using ANSI/ASME standard designations.

3. Draw a multiview piping drawing using standard schematic symbols from a piping pictorial drawing.

4. Draw the schematic symbols for valves and identify flow direction.

OVERVIEW

Pipe is used for transporting liquids and gases and for structural elements such as columns and handrails. The choice of the type of pipe is determined by the purpose for which it is to be used.

Pipe is made of aluminum, brass, clay, concrete (concrete made with ordinary aggregates and in combination with other materials), copper, glass, iron, lead, plastics, rubber, wood, and other materials or combinations of them. Cast-iron, steel, wrought-iron, brass, copper, and plastic pipes are most commonly used for transporting water, steam, oil, or gases.

Building plans for industrial plants, commercial buildings, and residences all use piping diagrams to describe the distribution path of the gases and liquids these buildings require. Special schematic symbols simplify each type of pipe connection. Templates can speed the creation of piping symbols on paper drawings. CAD libraries store piping symbols for instant copying and pasting.

■ 24.1 STEEL AND WROUGHT-IRON PIPE

Steel or wrought-iron pipe is in common use for water, steam, oil, and gas. Until the early 1930s, such pipe was available in only three weights, known as "standard," "extra strong," and "double extra strong." At that time increasing pressures and temperatures, particularly for steam service, made the availability of more diversified wall thicknesses desirable. The American National Standards Institute/American Society of Mechanical Engineers (ANSI/ASME) has developed dimensions for 10 different schedules of pipe (see Appendix 38). The table in Appendix 38 shows that dimensions are established for nominal sizes from $\frac{1}{8}''$ to 24'' and that dimensions have not been established for all schedules. In the different schedules, the outside diameters (O.D.) are maintained for each nominal size to facilitate threading and the uniform use of fittings and valves.

Certain of the schedule dimensions correspond to the dimensions of "standard" and "extra strong" pipe. These are shown in **boldface** type in the appendix. The schedule dimensions so shown for Schedules 30 and 40 correspond to standard pipe, and those for Schedule 80 correspond to extra strong pipe. There are no schedule dimensions corresponding to double extra strong pipe. Pipe corresponding to all the established schedule dimensions is not always commercially

available and should be investigated before specifying pipe on drawings. Generally, Schedules 40, 80, and 160 are readily available; others may or may not be.

Note that the actual outside diameter of pipe in nominal sizes $\frac{1}{8}''$ to 12'' inclusive is larger than the nominal size, whereas the outside diameter of pipe in nominal sizes 14'' and larger corresponds to the nominal size. This pipe in nominal sizes 14'' and larger is commonly referred to as O.D. pipe.

Pipe is available as welded or as seamless pipe. Welded pipe is available in Schedules 40 and 80 in the smaller sizes. Lap-welded pipe is made in sizes up to and including 2''. Butt-welded pipe is available as furnace-welded material, where a formed length is heated in a furnace and then welded, in sizes up to and including 3''. Butt-welded pipe is also available as continuous welded pipe, where the finished pipe is continuously heated, formed, and welded from a roll of strip steel, in sizes up to and including 4''. Seamless pipe is made in both small and large sizes.

Many of today's applications require the use of alloys to withstand the pressure-temperature conditions without having to be excessively thick. Numerous alloys in both ferritic and austenitic material are available. Refer to the various specifications of the American Society for Testing Materials (ASTM) for these alloys and for dimensional tolerances.

Steel pipe can be obtained as *black pipe* or as *galvanized pipe*. Galvanized pipe is used for water distribution, and black pipe for natural gas.

Steel or wrought-iron pipe is available in lengths up to about 40' in the small sizes, the length decreasing with increasing size and wall thickness.

■ 24.2 CAST-IRON PIPE

Cast-iron (C.I.) pipe is used for water or gas service and as soil pipe. For water and gas pipe, it is generally available in sizes from 3'' to 60'' inclusive and in standard lengths of 12'. Various wall thicknesses, to satisfy the internal pressure requirements, can be secured. The dimensions and the pressure ratings of the various classes are shown in Appendix 39.

Generally speaking, water and gas pipes are connected with *bell and spigot joints* (Fig. 24.1a) or *flanged joints* (Fig. 24.1b), although other types of joints (Fig. 24.1c) are also used.

As soil pipe, cast-iron pipe is available in sizes 2'' to 15'' inclusive, in standard lengths of 5', and in *service* and *extra heavy* weights. Soil pipe is generally

(a) BELL & SPIGOT   (b) FLANGED   (c) MECHANICAL

FIGURE 24.1   **Cast-Iron Pipe Joints.**

connected with bell and spigot joints, but soil pipe with threaded ends is available in sizes up to 12″.

In using cast-iron pipe, the designer must consider both the internal pressure and the external loading due to fill and other loadings, such as roads and tracks. Cast-iron pipe is brittle, and settling can cause fracture unless sufficient flexibility is provided in the joints. For this reason, flange joints are not usually employed for buried pipes unless adequately supported.

24.3 SEAMLESS BRASS AND COPPER PIPE

Pipe made of brass and copper, and having approximately the same dimensions as "standard" and "extra strong" steel pipe, is available. Such pipe is suitable for plumbing, including supply, soil, waste drain, and vent lines. It is also particularly suitable for process work in which formation of scale and oxidation of steel pipe are objectionable. Brass pipe and copper pipe are available in straight lengths up to 12′.

Brass pipe is generally known as *red brass pipe*, which is an alloy of approximately 85% copper and 15% zinc. Copper pipe is practically pure copper with less than 0.1% of alloying elements.

Brass pipe and copper pipe should be joined with fittings of copper-base alloy to avoid galvanic action resulting in corrosion. Where screwed joints are used, fittings similar to cast or malleable iron fittings (see Fig. 24.5) are available. Flanged fittings of brass and copper are of different dimensions than those made of ferrous material. Refer to dimensional standards published by the American National Standards Institute

(ANSI/ASME B16.24–1991) for dimensions of such fittings.

24.4 COPPER TUBING

Where nonferrous construction in sizes below 2″ is used, copper tubing is frequently employed. Such tubing is suitable for process work, as mentioned in §24.3, for plumbing (particularly supply lines for hot and cold water), and for heating systems (particularly radiant heating).

Copper tubing is made as *hard temper* and as *soft tubing*. Hard-temper tubing is much stiffer than soft tubing and should be used where rigidity is desired. Soft tubing can be easily bent and, therefore, is generally used where bending during assembly is required. Neither hard- nor soft-temper tubing has the rigidity of iron or steel pipe and, consequently, must be supported at much more frequent intervals than the latter. Where multiple runs of parallel tubes are employed for long distances (20′ or more), it is common practice to use soft tubing and to lay the parallel runs in a trough construction, thus obtaining continuous support.

Copper tubing joints are usually made with *flared joints* (Fig. 24.2a), or with *solder joints* (Fig. 24.2b). There are several types of flared joints, but the basic design of making a metal-to-metal joint is common to all. Fittings, such as tees, elbows, and couplings, are available for flared joints.

Solder joints are also known as *capillary joints* because the annular space between the tube and the fitting is so small that the molten solder is drawn into the

(a) FLARED TUBE FITTING   (b) SOLDER TUBE FITTING

FIGURE 24.2 **Copper Pipe Fittings.**

90° ELBOW   45° ELBOW   TEE   CROSS

COUPLING   CAP   PLUG   RETURN BEND

FIGURE 24.3 **Solder Fittings.**

SOLDER

(a)   (b)

FIGURE 24.4 **Adapters—Copper Tube to Threaded Pipe.**

space by capillary action. The solder may be introduced through a hole in the fitting (Fig. 24.3) or through the outer end of the annular space (Fig. 24.2b), or fittings having a factory-assembled ring of solder in the fitting can be purchased. Solder joints may be made with soft solder (usually 50–50 or 60–40 tin and lead) or with silver solder. This latter material has a higher melting point than soft solder, makes a stronger joint, and is suitable for higher operating temperatures.

Copper pipe or tubing has an upper operating temperature limit of 406°F. If solder fittings are used, the upper temperature limit will be dependent on the softening point of the solder rather than the limit of temperature of the base material.

Copper tubing can be connected to threaded pipe or fittings by means of *adapters*. These adapters are available with either male or female pipe threads and with either flared or solder connections for the tubing. Two types of such adapters are shown in Fig. 24.4.

Copper tubing is available in straight lengths up to 20' or in coils of 60' for soft-temper material. Hard-temper material is available in straight lengths only, since it cannot successfully be coiled. Installation costs for coiled material are lower than for straight material

because fewer joints are needed. Copper tubing is available in both O.D. and nominal sizes.

■ 24.5 SPECIAL PIPES

Pipe and tubing of other materials, such as aluminum and stainless steel, are also available. A wide variety of plastic pipe, both rigid and flexible, is used in modern construction. Plastic pipe is lightweight, corrosion proof, and resistant to many chemicals. It has a smooth inner surface which offers low flow resistance.

PVC (polyvinyl chloride) pipe and fittings are available in Schedule 40 and extra heavy Schedule 80, which is used where higher working pressures are present. Schedule 80 pipe may be threaded; Schedule 40 should not be, and is normally assembled with slip fittings and solvent. The maximum temperature rating for PVC is 140°F (110°C).

CPVC (chlorinated polyvinyl chloride) pipe is similar to PVC and has a higher maximum temperature rating, 180°F (132°C). Both PVC and CPVC pipe are commonly available in sizes ranging from $\frac{1}{2}$-inch to 4-inch inside diameter.

Black polyethylene flexible pipe, approved by the National Sanitation Foundation for use with drinking water, has a rated working pressure of 100 psi when

not exposed to direct sunlight. It is available in sizes from $\frac{1}{2}$-inch to 2-inch I.D. (inside diameter). Black polyethylene pipe should not be used on hot water lines or exposed to temperatures greater than 100°F (88°C). It is often used for underground lawn sprinkler systems.

Service for which these miscellaneous materials are suitable varies widely because of the physical properties and temperature-pressure limitations of the materials. Regardless of the material used in a piping system, the procedure followed in the design of the system and the creation of the necessary drawings remains basically the same.

■ 24.6 PIPE FITTINGS

Pipe fittings are used to join adjacent lengths of pipe and frequently also to provide changes of direction, to provide branch connections at different angles, or to effect a change in size. They are made of cast iron, malleable iron, cast or forged steel, nonferrous alloys, and other materials for special applications. They can be obtained in various weights that should be matched to the pipe with which they are to be used. Ferrous fittings are made for threaded, welded, or flanged joints. Nonferrous fittings are made for threaded, solder, flared, or flanged joints. The common types of fittings for threaded joints are shown in Fig. 24.5, for welded joints in 24.6, for flanged joints in Fig. 24.7, and for solder joints in Fig. 24.3.

FIGURE 24.6 **Butt-Welded Fittings.**

Where both or all ends of a fitting are the same nominal size, the fitting is designated by the nominal size and the description—for example, a 2″ *screwed tee*. Where two or more ends of a fitting are not the same nominal size, the fitting is designated as a *reducing fitting*, the dimensions of the run precede those of the branches, and the dimension of the larger opening precedes that of the smaller opening—for example, a 2″ × $1\frac{1}{2}$″ × 1″ *screwed reducing tee*. See Fig. 24.8 for typical designations.

The threads of screwed fittings conform to the pipe thread with which they are to be used, either male or female as the case may be (see §24.7).

FIGURE 24.5 **Screwed Fittings.**

FIGURE 24.7 **Flanged Fittings.**

FIGURE 24.8   Designating Sizes of Fittings.

Dimensions of 125-lb cast-iron screwed fittings, 250-lb cast-iron screwed fittings, 125-lb cast-iron flanged fittings, and 250-lb cast-iron flanged fittings are shown in Appendixes 40–43 and 45. See §24.7 for reference to steel fittings.

■ 24.7   PIPE JOINTS

The joints between pipes, fittings, and valves may be *screwed, flanged, welded,* or, for nonferrous metallic materials, joints may be *soldered.* Plastic pipes may be screwed together or fastened with slip joints and solvent or with compression fittings.

The American National Standard pipe threads are illustrated in Figs. 13.19–13.21, and tabular dimensions are shown in Appendix 38. The threads of the American Petroleum Institute (API) differ somewhat from the American National Standard pipe threads. Refer to the API Standards for these differences.

Threaded joints can be made up tightly by simply screwing the cleaned threads together. However, it is common practice to use *pipe compound* in making such joints, as this provides lubrication for the threads and enables them to be screwed together more tightly. It also serves to seal irregularities, thus providing a tighter joint. Such material should be applied to the male thread only, to avoid forcing it into the pipe, where contamination or obstruction may result.

Flanged joints are made by bolting two flanges together with a resilient *gasket* between the flange faces. Flanges may be attached to the pipe, fitting, or appliance by means of a screwed joint, by welding, by lapping the pipe, or by being cast integrally with the pipe, fitting, or appliance.

The faces of the flanges between which the gasket is placed have different standard *facings*, such as *flat face*, $\frac{1}{16}''$ *raised face*, $\frac{1}{4}''$ *raised face, male and female, tongue and groove,* and *ring joints*. Flat face and $\frac{1}{16}''$ raised face are standard for cast-iron flanges in the 125-lb and 250-lb classes, respectively. The other types of facing are standard for steel flanges.

The number and size of the bolts joining these flanges vary with the size and the working pressure of the joint. Bolting for Class 125 cast-iron and Class 250 cast-iron flanges is shown in Appendixes 43 and 46, respectively.

For dimensions of the various flange facings and for flange and bolting dimensions of the various sizes and pressure standards of steel flanges, refer to the American National Standard for Steel Pipe Flanges and Flanged Fittings (ANSI/ASME B16.5–1988), which is too voluminous to be included here. Some special types of flanged joints are shown in Fig. 24.9.

Piping construction employing welding joints is in almost universal use today, particularly for higher pressure and temperature conditions. Such joints may either be *socket welded* or *butt welded* (Fig. 24.10).

FIGURE 24.9 Special Types of Flanged Joints.

(a) SCREWED FLANGE WITH RAISED FACE

(b) TONGUE AND GROOVE FLANGES

(c) SLIP-ON WELDED FLANGES

(d) WELDING NECK JOINT

FIGURE 24.10 Welded Joints.

(a) SOCKET WELD

(b) FOR PIPE THICKNESS $\frac{3}{16}$ TO $\frac{3}{4}$ INCL

(c) FOR PIPE THICKNESS OVER $\frac{3}{4}$

Socket-welded joints are limited to use in small sizes. The contours of the butt-welded joints shown in Figs. 24.10b and 24.10c are those shown in ANSI/ASME B16.25–1992.

■24.8 VALVES

Valves are used to stop or regulate the flow of fluids in a pipe line. The more common types are *gate valves*, *globe valves*, and *check valves*. Other types of valves, such as *pressure-reducing valves* and *safety valves*, are special devices used to maintain automatically a desired lower pressure on the downstream side of the valve or to prevent automatically undesirable overpressure, respectively.

■24.9 GLOBE VALVES

Globe valves have approximately spherical bodies with the seating surface at either a right or an acute angle to the center line of the pipe (Fig. 24.11a). In such a valve the flowing fluid must make abrupt turns in the body, thus resulting in considerably higher pressure loss than for a gate valve.

Globe valves are commonly used where close regulation of flow is desired because they lend themselves better to this type of regulation and are less subject to cutting action in throttling service than gate valves.

Valves of the *inside screw* and *outside screw and yoke* (*OS & Y*) types are available (see §24.11). Angle valves and needle valves are special designs of the general class of globe valves (Fig. 24.11c).

■24.10 CHECK VALVES

Check valves are used to limit the flow of fluids to one direction only. The disk may be hinged to swing partially out of the stream (Fig. 24.11b), or it may be guided in such a manner that it can rise vertically from its seat. The two types are called *swing checks* and *lift checks*, respectively.

GRAPHICS SPOTLIGHT

Patents: A Computer Program that Provides Technical Help for Inventors*

Perhaps is was inevitable that someone would one day patent the act of inventing. Certainly the age of computer modeling and powerful, nimble techical software has made it possible for a group of inventors to now own what it calls an "invention that creates new inventions."

The patented software program aims to allow everyday inventors to find out what would happen if they really tried to build a device or carry out a process they have in mind. It takes its inspiration from computer-aided design programs now commonly used by engineers and designers to try out and modify new ideas.

Five inventors, all originally from the former Soviet Union, designed the software, which enables a user to create an engineering model of an invention idea, and then test the model's scientific properties. At each stage, the software offers descriptions and illustrations of the science or engineering concept involved, chooses technical properties that will work in combination, and suggests alternatives to the mechanics or the method.

Theoretically, an inventor should not need a technical background, though the software is laden with physical, geometric and chemical laws, theorems and hypotheses that only an engineer or scientist could love.

The inventors say their software goes beyond computer-assisted design and into what they call in the patent "concept engineering." The purpose, they say, is to help designers and inventors come up with new ideas, evaluate and trouble-shoot them, and consider different engineering approaches for realizing their plans.

"These systems serve to increase the designer's inventive and creative abilities in solving engineering and scientific operational or functional problems and, in the course of such problem solving, induce the designer to invent new structural and functional concepts applicable to his/her design goals," the inventors write in their patent.

The software enables a user to quickly understand the technical results that are being sought, the structure and function of engineering devices, and how such devices might produce those results if two or more are linked together. The inventor can simulate the effect of combining engineering properties, manipulating parts of those properties or adding his own customized properties. The software itself will automatically combine engineering components in an effort to refine the invention or suggest new designs and problem-solving techniques to the inventor.

The program is built around a data base of scientific and engineering concepts and their effects. Using key words, an inventor can search through 6,500 entries and pull up full-motion animation and a text description of each concept.

But first, the inventor must state an objective. The software then suggests engineering concepts that can make that design objective a reality. Each suggestion is accompanied by an explanation and illustration.

An inventor can connect the effects of two or more concepts to see what will happen, or he can simulate the results of changing parameters. He can click on a prompt that leads the software to offer other engineering or scientific facts that will improve the performance of his device or process. The inventor can bookmark his most commonly researched effects, and he can store the system's suggestions in his computer.

The software creates animated versions of the engineering effects, shows 5 to 10 seconds of full-motion video, describes the reactions and gives any examples of similar technologies that already exist.

The patent belongs to the Invention Machine Corporation. The company has already incorporated into its computer-assisted design software, which can be examined at www.invention-machine.com. The inventors, Leonid Batchilo, of Arlington, Mass., Valery Tsourikov of Boston, Vitaly Glazunov of Moscow, and Alexandre Kirkovski and Alexandre Korzoun, from Minsk, Belarus, received patent 5,901,068.

Patents may be viewed on the Web at www.uspto.gov or may be ordered through the mail, by patent number, for $3 from the Patent and Trademark Office, Washington, D.C. 20231.

*Adapted from "Patents—A Computer Program that Provides Technical Help for Inventors without Scientific Training," by Sabra Chartrand, *New York Times*, May 17, 1999.

■24.11 GATE VALVES

Gate valves have full-sized straightway openings that offer small resistance to the flow of fluids. The gate, or disk, may rise on the stem (*inside screw* type) (Fig. 24.11c), or the gate may rise with the stem, which in turn rises out of the body (*rising stem*, or *outside screw and yoke—OS & Y—*type). Inside screw type valves are employed in the smaller sizes and lower pressures.

Seating may be on nonparallel seats, in which case the disk is solid and wedge shaped. There is also a type of gate valve employing parallel seats. In this type, two disks are hung loosely on the stem and are free of the seats until an adjusting wedge reaches a lug at the closed position of the valve, when further movement of the stem causes the wedge to spread the disks and form a tight joint on the parallel seats. Such valves are used only on low-pressure and low-temperature services.

■24.12 AMERICAN NATIONAL STANDARD CODE FOR PRESSURE PIPING

The American National Standards Institute has adopted an American National Standard Code for Pressure Piping (ANSI/ASME B31.1–1995). This compilation of recommended practices and minimum safety standards covers various types of piping, such as power

FIGURE 24.11   Gate, Globe, and Check Valves.

piping, industrial gas and air piping, oil refinery piping, oil transportation piping, refrigerating piping, chemical industry process piping, and gas transmission and distribution piping.

■ 24.13 PIPING DRAWINGS

To simplify the preparation of working drawings of piping systems, the set of symbols shown in Appendix 34 has been developed to represent the various pipe fittings and valves in common use. An application of these symbols in a piping drawing is shown in Fig. 24.12b. The use of templates to draw piping symbols is convenient and timesaving.

Drawings of piping systems may be made as *single-line* drawings (Figs. 24.12b and 24.13–24.15) or as *double-line* drawings (Figs. 24.12a, 24.17, and 24.18). Either type of drawing may be made as multiview projections (Figs. 24.13b, 24.17, and 24.19); as axonometric projec-

tions (Figs. 24.13a and 24.20); or as oblique projections (Figs. 24.15 and 24.16). The oblique projection in Fig. 24.16 is a modified form of oblique projection generally used in representing the piping arrangement for heating systems. In these cases, the pipe mains are shown in plan and the risers in oblique projection in various directions to make the representation as clear as possible.

In most installations, some pipes are vertical and some are horizontal. If the vertical pipes are assumed to be revolved into the horizontal plane or the horizontal pipes revolved into the vertical plane by turning some of the fittings (Fig. 24.13c), the entire installation can be shown in one plane. Such a drawing is a *developed piping drawing*.

In complicated systems, where a large amount of piping of various sizes is run in close proximity and where clearances are important, the use of double-line multiview drawings, made accurately to scale, is

FIGURE 24.12 Piping Symbols.

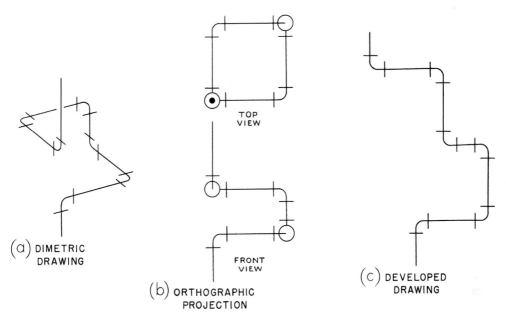

(a) DIMETRIC DRAWING

TOP VIEW

FRONT VIEW

(b) ORTHOGRAPHIC PROJECTION

(c) DEVELOPED DRAWING

FIGURE 24.13 **Representations of Pipe Expansion Joint.**

desirable. The use of such drawings, which show the relative positions of component parts in all views, greatly reduces the probability of interferences when the piping is erected and is almost a necessity where piping components are prefabricated in a shop and sent to the job in finished dimensions. Such a method of fabrication is universal in large systems using large piping; most piping $2\frac{1}{2}''$ and larger is shop fabricated (Figs. 24.17 and 24.18).

■ 24.14 DIMENSIONING

In dimensioning a piping drawing, distances from center to center (c to c), center to end (c to e), or end to end (e to e) of fittings or valves and the lengths of all straight runs of pipe should be given (Fig. 24.18).

Fully dimensioned single-line drawings need not be drawn to scale. Allowances in pipe lengths for make-up in fittings and valves must be made in preparing a bill of materials. All double-line drawings should have center lines if they are to be dimensioned. The size of the pipe for each run is shown by a numeral or by a note at the side of the pipe, with a leader when necessary.

■ 24.15 USING CAD

Computer-aided drafting techniques, as described in Chapter 2, can produce efficiently complicated 2D and 3D single-line and double-line piping diagrams. Figure 24.19 shows a piping drawing produced on a CAD system.

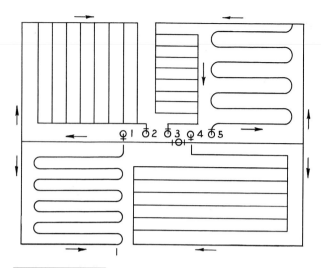

FIGURE 24.14 Pipe Grids and Serpentine Coils for a Panel Radiant Heating System.

FIGURE 24.15 Schematic Drawing of Piping Connecting Boiler to Heating Coils.

FIGURE 24.16 A One-Pipe Steam Heating System.

FIGURE 24.17 A Two-Line Piping Drawing for a Pumping Plant.

FIGURE 24.18 A Dimensioned Piping Drawing—Side View of Steam Piping.

FIGURE 24.19 3D Piping Drawing Produced on a CAD system. *Courtesy of Softdesk, Inc.*

FIGURE 24.20 Piping System Drawing Produced with the VersaCAD Advanced Drafting Software Package. *Courtesy of VersaCAD.*

■ KEY WORDS

STEEL PIPE	CAST-IRON PIPE
COPPER TUBING	THREADED FITTINGS
SOLDER FITTINGS	ELBOW
STREET ELBOW	TEE
REDUCER	Y-BEND
COUPLING	BUSHING
CLOSE NIPPLE	FLANGED FITTINGS
CROSS FITTING	VALVE
COMPRESSION FITTINGS	CPVC
PVC	

CHAPTER SUMMARY

- Steel and wrought-iron pipes are commonly used for water, steam, oil, and gas. Steel provides the strength necessary for the high pressures commonly associated with these substances.
- Cast iron is primarily used for water, gas, and waste. Cast iron is durable for all but the highest pressures. Cast-iron pipe typically uses threaded fittings.
- Copper tubing is typically used for water and compressed air. Copper tubing can be connected with solder joints or with compression fittings.

- Plastic pipe and fittings are lightweight, corrosion resistant, and have a smooth inner surface. They are often used as a substitute for metallic pipe.
- Single-line drawings and simplified symbols are commonly used to represent pipes and fittings on a pipe drawing. Piping drawings are usually not drawn to scale.
- Valves control the flow of material through a pipe.
- A library of computer piping symbols can speed the creation and modification of CAD piping drawings.

REVIEW QUESTIONS

1. What pipe material would be used for the highest pressures?

2. What types of fittings are commonly used with cast-iron pipe? With copper tubing?

3. What fitting would join two pipes at 90° or 45°?

4. What fitting would join two pipes at 180°?

5. What fitting would join four pipes together at one joint?

6. What fitting would connect two pipes of different diameter?

7. What is the purpose of a valve?

8. How is flow direction indicated on a piping drawing?

9. Why is a library of piping symbols important when drawing with CAD?

10. Draw and label five single-line piping symbols.

PIPING DRAWING PROBLEMS

The drawings for Probs. 24.1–24.4 are to be three times as large as the corresponding illustrations in this book.

Prob. 24.1 Make a double-line drawing, similar to Fig. 24.12a, showing the following fittings: a union, a 45° Y-bend, an eccentric reducer, a globe valve, a tee, a stopcock, and a 45° ell. Use $\frac{1}{2}''$ and $1''$ wrought-steel pipe and 125-lb C.I. screwed fittings.

Prob. 24.2 Make a single-line drawing, similar to Fig. 24.12b, showing the following fittings: a 45° ell, a union, a 45° Y-bend, an eccentric reducer, a tee, a reducer, a gate valve, a plug, a cap, and a cross.

Prob. 24.3 Make a single-line drawing of the system of pipe coils and grids in Fig. 24.14; show, by their respective standard symbols, the elbows and tees that must be used to connect pipes meeting at right angles if welding is not used to make the joints.

Prob. 24.4 Make an oblique projection, similar to that in Fig. 24.15, of the one-pipe steam heating system in Fig. 24.16. Show the pipes by single lines, the fittings by their standard symbols, and the boiler and radiators as parallelepipeds.

Prob. 24.5 Make a single-line isometric drawing of the piping layout in Fig. 24.21. Use a scale of $\frac{3}{4}'' = 1'-0$, and a Size C or A2 sheet (this drawing should be similar to the isometric layout shown in Fig. 24.22).

Prob. 24.6 Make a single-line multiview drawing of the piping layout in Fig. 24.22. Use a scale of $1'' = 1'-0$ and a size C or A2 sheet (this drawing should be similar to the piping layout in Fig. 24.21).

Prob. 24.7 Make a double-line multiview drawing of the piping layout in Fig. 24.21 to a scale selected by the student (this drawing should be similar to the two-line piping drawing in Fig. 24.17).

Prob. 24.8 Make a double-line multiview drawing of the piping layout in Fig. 24.22 to a scale selected by the student. Use Schedule 80 wrought-steel pipe throughout, with Class 250 C.I. flanged fittings where pipe is larger than 2″, and Class 250 C.I. screwed fittings where pipe is 2″ and smaller (this drawing should be similar to the two-line piping drawing in Fig. 24.17).

PLAN

0 1 2 3 4 5 6
FEET

1½" PIPE

2" PIPE

SIDE ELEVATION

END ELEVATION

FIGURE 24.21 Pipe Layout for Battery of Air Receivers (Probs. 24.5 and 24.7).

0 1 2 3 4 5
FEET

2"×2"×¾" TEE

2" PIPE

PLUG

¾" PIPE

3"×3"×2" TEE

3"×3"×1" TEE

2"×¾"×2" TEE

3"×3"×4" TEE

BLIND FLANGE

1" PIPE

1" PIPE

2"×1"×1" TEE

4" PIPE

¾" PIPE

90° ELL

X 1'-6 TO FLOOR

TANK 10" FROM FLOOR

2'-0"

3'-0"

X 8"

FIGURE 24.22 Isometric Pipe Layout (Probs. 24.6 and 24.8).

C H A P T E R   2 5

WELDING REPRESENTATION

OBJECTIVES

After studying the material in this chapter, you should be able to:

1. Describe the various welding processes.
2. Draw the common welding symbols.
3. Dimension a welding drawing using standard ANSI welding notations.
4. Identify and draw a fillet weld, groove weld, back weld, spot weld, seam weld, projection weld, and flash weld.
5. Identify typical CAD welding symbols.

OVERVIEW

Welding is often the method of choice for fastening parts together permanently rather than using bolts, screws, rivets, or other fasteners. It is also widely used in fabricating machine parts or other structures that formerly would have been formed by casting or forging, and it is used to a considerable extent in the erection of structural steel frames for buildings, ships, and other structures.

Welding is one of few machine processes that *adds* material to (instead of removes from) a working piece. Welding symbols on a mechanical drawing provide precise instructions for the welder. Weld type and the location of each weld must be clearly defined using standardized symbols. CAD libraries of welding symbols can simplify the drawing process. Welding templates can speed up the drawing process on paper.

■ 25.1 IMPORTANCE OF THE DRAWING

Since welding is used so extensively and for so large a variety of purposes, it is essential to have an accurate method of showing on the working drawings of machines or structures the exact types, sizes, and locations of welds desired by the designer. The old practice of simply lettering a note on the drawing, "To be welded throughout" or "To be completely welded," which actually shifted responsibility for welding control to the welding shop, not only is dangerous but also may be unnecessarily expensive because shops will usually "play it safe" by welding more than necessary.

To provide a means for placing complete welding information on the drawing in a simple manner, a system of welding symbols was developed by the American Welding Society and originally published in 1947 under the title "Standard Welding Symbols." These symbols were adopted by the American National Standards Institute and are currently published as ANSI/AWS A2.4–1993. The text and illustrations of this chapter are based primarily on this standard. Reference may also be made to ANSI/AWS A1.1–1989, "Metric Practice Guide for the Welding Industry," and ANSI/AWS A3.0–1994, "Standard Welding Terms and Definitions."

A typical welding diagram is an assembly drawing in the sense that it is composed of a number of separate pieces fastened together as a unit. The welds themselves are not drawn but are clearly and completely indicated by the welding symbols. The joints are all shown as they would appear before welding. Dimensions are given to show the sizes of the individual pieces to be cut from stock. Each component piece is identified by encircled numbers and by specifications in the parts list.

■ 25.2 WELDING PROCESSES

Three of the principal methods of welding are the oxyacetylene method, generally known as *gas welding*, the electric-arc method, generally known as *arc welding*, and electric-resistance welding, generally called *resistance welding*.

Gas welding was originated in 1895, when the French chemist Le Châtelier discovered that the combustion of acetylene gas with oxygen produced a flame of very high temperature—high enough to melt metals. This discovery was soon followed by the development of practical methods of producing and transporting oxygen and acetylene and by the construction of suitable torches and welding rods.

In arc welding, the heat of an electric arc is used to fuse the metals that are to be welded or cut. The first arc welding was done in 1881 by De Meritens in France, and for a number of years the development of arc welding was very slow. During World War I, the U.S. Navy used welding to a limited extent for repairing machinery. Since that time, as the result of extensive research, basic improvements have been made in the manufacture of electrodes and in the mechanical equipment used for welding, so that now arc and gas welding are important construction processes in industry.

In resistance welding, two pieces of metal are held together under some pressure, and a large amount of electric current is passed through the parts. The resistance of the metals to the passage of the current causes great heating at the junction of the two pieces, resulting in the welding of the metals.

■ 25.3 TYPES OF WELDED JOINTS

There are five basic types of welded joints, classified according to the positions of the parts being joined. A number of different types of welds are applicable to each type of joint, depending on the thickness of metal, the strength of joint required, and other considerations.

FIGURE 25.1   **Sheilded Metal Arc Welding (Stick Welding).** *Courtesy of Hobart Brothers Company.*

FIGURE 25.2   **Welding Gun for Gas Metal Arc Welding.** *Courtesy of Lincoln Electric Co.*

■ 25.4 TYPES OF WELDS

The four types of arc and gas welds are shown in Fig. 25.3: the *back* or *backing* (Fig. 25.3a); the *fillet* (Fig. 25.3b); the *plug* or *slot* (Fig. 25.3c); and *groove.* The groove welds are further classified as square, V, bevel, U, and J, shown in Figs. 25.3d through 25.3h. More than one type of weld may be applied to a single joint. For example, a V weld may be on one side and a back weld

on the other side. Frequently, the same type of weld is used on opposite sides, forming such welds as a double-V, a double-U, or a double-J.

The four basic resistance welds are the *spot weld, projection weld, seam weld,* and *flash* or *upset weld.* Except for the flash or upset weld, the corresponding symbols for these welds and additional basic weld symbols for surfacing, groove, and flange joints are given in Fig. 25.4. See Fig. 25.25d for the use of the square groove weld symbol for the flash or upset resistance weld. Supplementary symbols are represented in Fig. 25.5.

■ 25.5 WELDING SYMBOLS

The basic element of the symbol is the "bent" arrow, as shown in Fig. 25.6a. The arrow points to the joint where the weld is to be made (Fig. 25.6b), and attached to the reference line, or shank, of the arrow is the weld symbol for the desired weld. The symbol would be one of those illustrated in Figs. 25.3 and 25.4. In this case a fillet weld symbol has been used.

The weld symbol is placed below the reference line if the weld is to be on the *arrow side* of the joint, as in Fig. 25.6b, or above the reference line if the weld is to be on the *other side* of the joint, as in Fig. 25.6c. If the weld is to be on *both* the arrow side and the other side of the joint, weld symbols are placed on both sides of the reference line (Fig. 25.6d). This rule for placement of the weld symbol is followed for all the arc or gas weld symbols.

When a joint is represented by a single line on a drawing, as in the top and side views of Fig. 25.7b, the *arrow side* of the joint is regarded as the "near" side to the reader of the drawing, according to the usual conventions of drafting.

For the plug, slot, seam, and projection welding symbols, the arrow points to the outer surface of one of the members at the center line of the weld. In such cases, the arrow side of the joint is the one to which the arrow points, or the "near" side to the reader (see Figs. 25.20 and 25.24).

Note that for all fillet or groove symbols, the *vertical side of the symbol is always drawn on the left* (Fig. 25.6b).

For best results, the welding symbols should be drawn mechanically, but in certain cases where necessary, the symbols may be drawn freehand.

The complete welding symbol, enlarged, is shown in Fig. 25.8. See Appendix 32 for additional welding

GROOVE WELDS

BACK OR BACKING	FILLET	PLUG OR SLOT	SQUARE	"V"	BEVEL	"U"	"J"
(a)	(b)	(c)	(d)	(e)	(f)	(g)	(h)

FIGURE 25.3   Basic Welds and Symbols.

ADDITIONAL BASIC WELD SYMBOLS

SPOT OR PROJECTION	SEAM	SURFACING	GROOVE		FLANGE	
			FLARE	FLARE BEVEL	EDGE	CORNER
Reference line						

FIGURE 25.4   Additional Basic Weld Symbols.

SUPPLEMENTARY SYMBOLS

WELD ALL AROUND	FIELD WELD	MELT-THRU	BACKING OR SPACER MATL	CONTOUR		
				FLUSH	CONVEX	CONCAVE

FIGURE 25.5   Supplementary Symbols.

Vertical side always on left

(a)   (b)   (c)   (d)

FIGURE 25.6   Welding Symbols.

symbol details. In practice, some companies will need to use only a simple symbol composed of the minimum elements, the arrow and the weld symbol; others will make use of additional components.

Reference to a specification, process, or other supplementary information is indicated by any desired symbol in the tail of the arrow (Fig. 25.9a). Otherwise a general note may be placed on the drawing, such as

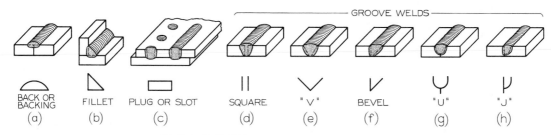

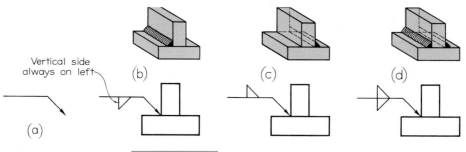

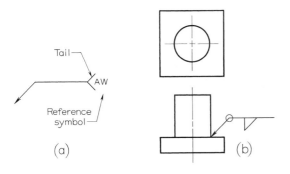

FIGURE 25.7 Arrow Side and Other Side.

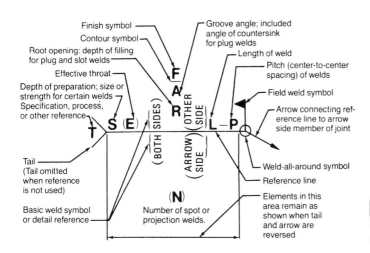

FIGURE 25.8 The Standard Locations of the Elements of the Welding Symbol [ANSI/AWS A2.4–1993].

FIGURE 25.9 Welding Symbols.

UNLESS OTHERWISE INDICATED, MAKE ALL WELDS PER SPECIFICATION NO. XXX

or

ROOT OPENINGS FOR ALL GROOVE WELDS $\frac{3}{16}''$ UNLESS OTHERWISE INDICATED

If no reference is indicated in the symbol, the tail may be omitted.

To avoid repeating the same information on many welding symbols on a drawing, general notes may be used, such as

FILLET WELDS $\frac{5}{16}''$ UNLESS OTHERWISE INDICATED

Welds extending completely around a joint are indicated by an open circle around the elbow of the arrow (Fig. 25.9b). *When the weld-all-around symbol is not used, the welding symbol is understood to apply between abrupt changes in direction of the weld, unless otherwise shown.* A short vertical staff with a solid

FIGURE 25.10 Spot, Seam, and Flash Welding Symbols.

triangular flag at the elbow of the arrow indicates a weld to be made "in the field" (on the site) rather than in the fabrication shop (Fig. 25.9c).

Spot, seam, flash, or upset symbols usually do not have *arrow-side* or *other-side* significance and are simply centered on the reference line of the arrow (Figs. 25.10a through 25.10c). Spot and seam symbols are shown on the drawing as indicated in Fig. 25.10d and 25.10e. Note that the required process must be specified in the tail of the symbol (RSW = resistance spot weld, EBW = electron beam weld).

For bevel- or J-groove welds, the arrow should point with a definite change of direction, or break, *toward the member* that is to be beveled or grooved (Figs. 25.11a and 25.11b). In this case, the upper member is grooved. The break is omitted if the location of the bevel or groove is obvious.

Lettering for the symbols should be placed to read from the bottom or from the right side of the

drawing in accordance with the aligned system (Figs. 25.11c through 25.11e). Dimensions may be indicated on a drawing in the fractional, decimal-inch, or metric system.

When a joint has more than one weld, the combined symbols are used (Figs. 25.11f through 25.11h).

■ 25.6 FILLET WELDS

The usual fillet weld has equal legs (Fig. 25.12a). The size of the weld is the length of one leg, as indicated in Fig. 25.12b by a dimension figure (fraction, decimal-inch, or metric) at the left of the weld symbol. For fillet welds on both sides of a joint, the dimensions may be indicated on one side or both sides of the reference line (Fig. 25.12c). The lengths of the welds and the pitch (center-to-center spacing of welds) are indicated as shown. When the welds on opposite sides are different in size, the sizes are given as shown in Fig. 25.12d.

FIGURE 25.11 Welding Symbols.

FIGURE 25.12 Dimensioning of Fillet Welds.

If a fillet weld has unequal legs, the weld orientation is shown on the drawing, if necessary, and the lengths of the legs are given in parentheses to the left of the weld symbol, as in Fig. 25.12e. If a general note is given on the drawing, such as

ALL FILLET WELDS $\frac{5}{16}''$ UNLESS OTHERWISE
NOTED

the size dimensions are omitted from the symbols.

No length dimension is needed for a weld that extends the full distance between abrupt changes of direction. For each abrupt change in direction, an additional arrow is added to the symbol, except when the weld-all-around symbol is used.

Lengths of fillet welds may be indicated by symbols in conjunction with dimension lines (Fig. 25.13a). The extent of fillet welding may be shown graphically by means of section lining if desired (Fig. 25.13b).

Chain intermittent fillet welding is indicated as shown in Fig. 25.14a. If the welds are staggered, the weld symbols are staggered (Fig. 25.14b).

Unfinished flat-faced fillet welds are indicated by adding the flush symbol (see Fig. 25.5), to the weld symbol (Fig. 25.15a). If fillet welds are to be made flat-faced by mechanical means, the flush-contour symbol and the user's standard finish symbol are added to the weld symbol (Figs. 25.15b through 25.15d). These finish symbols indicate the method of finishing (C = chipping, G = grinding, M = machining, R = rolling, H = hammering) and not the degree of finish. If fillet welds are to be finished to a convex contour, the convex-contour symbol is added, together with the finish symbol (Fig. 25.15e).

■ 25.7 GROOVE WELDS

In Fig. 25.16, various groove welds are shown above and the corresponding symbolic representations below. The sizes of the groove welds (depth of the V, bevel, U, or J) are indicated on the left of the weld symbol. For example, in Fig. 25.16a, the size of the V-weld is $\frac{1}{2}''$, in Fig. 25.16b the sizes are $\frac{1}{4}''$ and $\frac{7}{8}''$, in

FIGURE 25.13   Lengths of Fillet Welds.

FIGURE 25.14   Intermittent Welds.

FIGURE 25.15   Surface Contour of Fillet Welds.

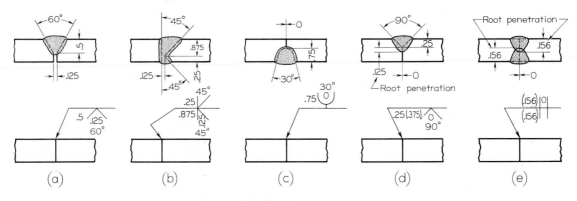

FIGURE 25.16 Groove Welds.

Fig. 25.16c the size is $\frac{3}{4}''$, and in Fig. 25.16d the size is $\frac{1}{4}''$. For the symbol in Fig. 25.16d the size is followed by $\frac{1}{8}''$, which is the additional "root penetration" of the weld. In Fig. 25.16e, the root penetration is $\frac{5}{32}''$ from zero, or from the outside of the members. Note the overlap of the root penetration in this case.

The root opening or space between members, when not covered by a company standard, is shown within the weld symbol. In Figs. 25.16a and 25.16b, the root openings are $\frac{1}{8}''$. In Figs. 25.16c through 25.16e, the openings are zero.

The groove angles, when not covered by a company standard, appear just outside the openings of the weld symbols (Fig. 25.16a and 25.16b).

A general note may be used on the drawing to avoid repeating the symbols, such as

ALL V-GROOVE WELDS TO HAVE 60° GROOVE ANGLE
UNLESS OTHERWISE SHOWN

However, when the dimensions of one or both of two opposite welds differ from the general note, both welds should be completely dimensioned.

When single-groove or symmetrical double-groove welds extend completely through, the size need not be added to the welding symbol. For example, in Fig. 25.16a, if the V-groove extended entirely through the joint, the depth or size would be simply the thick-ness of the stock and would not need to be indicated in the welding symbol.

When groove welds are to be approximately flush without finishing, the flush-contour symbol (see Fig. 25.5) is added to the weld symbols (Figs. 25.17a and 25.17b). If the welds are to be machined, the flush-contour symbol and the user's standard finish symbol are added to the weld symbol (Figs. 25.17c and 25.17d). These finish symbols indicate the method of finishing (C = chipping, G = grinding, M = machining) and not the degree of finish. If a groove weld is to be finished with a convex contour, the convex-contour and finish symbols are added, as in Fig. 25.17e.

■25.8 BACK OR BACKING WELDS

The bead-type welds used as back or backing welds on single-groove welds are indicated by a back or backing symbol opposite the groove weld symbol (Fig. 25.18a). Dimensions of such back or backing welds are not shown on the symbol, but may be shown, if necessary, directly on the drawing.

When back or backing welds are to be approximately flush without machining, the flush-contour symbol is included in the weld symbols (Fig. 25.18b). If they are to be machined, the user's finish symbol is added (Figs. 25.18c and 25.18d). If the welds are to be finished with a convex contour, the convex-contour

FIGURE 25.17 Surface Contour of Groove Welds.

FIGURE 25.18   Back or Backing Weld Symbols.

symbol and the finish symbol are included in the weld symbol, as in Fig. 25.18e.

25.9 SURFACE WELDS

The surface weld symbol used to indicate a surface to be built up by welding, whether by single- or multiple-pass bead-type welds (Fig. 25.19). Since this symbol does not indicate a welded joint, there is no arrow-side or other-side significance; hence, the symbol is always drawn below the reference line. The minimum height of the weld deposit is indicated at the left of the weld symbol, as shown, except where no specific height is required. When a specific area of a surface is to be built up, the dimensions of the area are given directly on the drawing.

FIGURE 25.19   Surface Weld Symbol.

25.10 PLUG AND SLOT WELDS

As shown in Fig. 25.3, the same symbol is used for plug welds and slot welds. A hole or a slot is made in one member to receive the weld (Figs. 25.20a and 25.20d). If the hole or slot is in the arrow-side member, the weld symbol is placed below the reference line (Figs. 25.20b and 25.20c). If in the other-side member, the weld symbol is placed above the line (Figs. 25.20e and 25.20f).

The size of a plug weld, which is the smallest diameter of the hole if countersunk, is placed at the left of the weld symbol (Figs. 25.20b and 20.20c). If the included angle of countersink of plug welds is in accordance with the user's standard, it is omitted from the welding symbol; otherwise, it is indicated adjacent to the weld symbol (Figs. 25.20b and 25.20c).

A plug weld is understood to fill the depth of the hole unless the depth of plug is indicated by a number, in inches or metric units, inside the weld symbol (Fig. 25.21a). The pitch (center-to-center spacing) of plug welds is shown in inches or metric units at the right of the weld symbol (Fig. 25.21b). If the weld is to be approximately flush without finishing, the flush-contour symbol is added (Fig. 25.21c). If the weld is to be made flush by mechanical means, a finish symbol is added (Fig. 25.21d). The flush-contour and finish symbols are

FIGURE 25.20   Plug and Slot Welds.

FIGURE 25.21 **Plug Welds.**

used in the same manner for slot welds and for plug welds.

The depth of filling of slot welds is indicated in the same manner as for plug welds (Fig. 25.21a). The size and location dimensions of slot welds cannot be shown on the welding symbol and must be shown directly on the drawing (Fig. 25.20f) or by a detail with a reference to it on the welding symbol (Fig. 25.21e).

■ 25.11 SPOT WELDS

The spot weld symbol, with the required welding process indicated in the tail, may or may not have arrow-side or other-side significance. Dimensions shall be shown on the same side of the reference line as the symbol, or on either side when the symbol is centered on the reference line and no arrow-side or other-side significance is intended.

The size of a spot weld is its diameter. This value, expressed in customary or metric units, may be shown at the left of the weld symbol on either side of the reference line (Fig. 25.22a). If it is desired to indicate the minimum acceptable shear strength in pounds per spot, instead of the size of the weld, this value is placed at the left of the weld symbol, while pitch (center-to-

center spacing) is indicated in appropriate units at the right of the weld symbol (Fig. 25.22b). In this case the spot welds are 3″ apart. If a joint requires a certain number of spot welds, the number is given in parentheses above or below the symbol, as in Fig. 25.22c. If the exposed surface of one member is to be flush, the flush-contour symbol is added, above the symbol if it is the other-side member, and below if it is the arrow-side member, as in Fig. 25.22d. The use of the welding symbol in conjunction with ordinary dimensions is shown in Fig. 25.22e.

■ 25.12 SEAM WELDS

The seam weld symbol, with the welding process indicated in the tail, may or may not have arrow-side or other-side significance. Dimensions (customary or metric units) are shown on the same side of the reference line as the symbol or on either side when the symbol is centered on the reference line and no arrow-side or other-side significance is intended.

The size of the seam weld is its width. This value, expressed in customary or metric units, may be shown at the left of the weld symbol, on either side of the reference line (Fig. 25.23a). If it is desired to indicate the

FIGURE 25.22 **Spot Welds.**

FIGURE 25.23 **Seam Welds.**

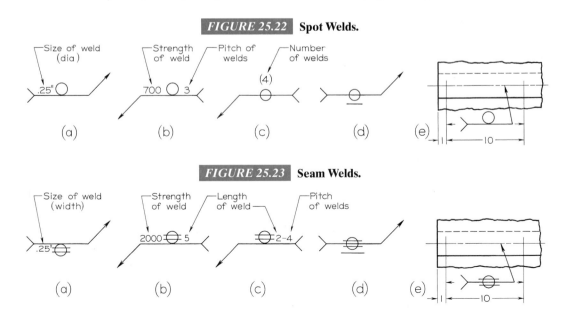

minimum acceptable shear strength in pounds per linear inch, instead of the size of the weld, this value is placed at the left of the weld symbol, and the length of a seam weld may be shown in appropriate units at the right of the weld symbol (Fig. 25.23b). In this case, the seam weld is 5″ long. If the weld extends the full distance between abrupt changes of direction, no length dimension in the symbol is given.

The pitch (center-to-center spacing) of intermittent seam welding is the distance between centers of lengths of welding. The pitch, in customary or metric units, is shown at the right of the length figure (Fig. 25.23c). In this case, the welds are 2″ long and spaced 4″ center to center.

When the exposed surface of one member is to be flush, the flush-contour symbol is added, above the symbol if it is the other-side member and below if it is the arrow-side member (Fig. 25.23d). The use of the welding symbol in conjunction with ordinary dimensions is shown in Fig. 25.23e.

■ 25.13 PROJECTION WELDS

In projection welding, one member is embossed in preparation for the weld (Fig. 25.24a). When welded, the joint appears in section, as in Fig. 25.24b. The weld symbols, in this case, are placed below the reference lines (Fig. 25.24c) to indicate that the arrow-side member is the one that is embossed. The weld symbols would be placed above the lines if the other member were embossed.

Projection welds are dimensioned (customary or metric units) by either size or strength. The size is the diameter of the weld. This value is shown to the left of the weld symbol (Fig. 25.24d). If it is desired to indicate the minimum acceptable shear strength in pounds per weld, the value is placed at the left of the weld symbol (Fig. 25.24e). The pitch (center-to-center spacing) is indicated in appropriate units at the right of the weld symbol (Fig. 25.24e). In this case, the welds are spaced 6″ (152 mm) apart. If the joint requires a definite number of welds, the number is given in parentheses (Fig. 25.24e). If the exposed surface of one member is to be flush, the flush-contour symbol is added (Fig. 25.24f). The use of the welding symbol in conjunction with ordinary dimensions is shown in Fig. 25.24g. The welding process reference is required in the tail of the symbol.

■ 25.14 FLASH AND UPSET WELDS

Flash and upset weld symbols have no arrow-side or other-side significance, but the supplementary symbols do. A flash-welded joint is shown in Fig. 25.25a, and an upset welded joint in Fig. 25.25b. The joint after machining flush is shown in Fig. 25.25c. The complete symbol (Fig. 25.25d) includes the weld symbol together with the flush-contour and machining symbols.

If the joint is ground to smooth contours (Fig. 25.25e), the resulting welding drawing and symbol would be constructed as in Fig. 25.25f, which includes convex-contour and grind symbols. In either Fig. 25.25d or 25.25f, the joint may be finished on only one side, if desired, by indicating the contour and machining symbols on the appropriate side of the reference line. The dimensions of flash and upset welds are not shown on the welding symbol. Note that the process

FIGURE 25.24 Projection Welds.

FIGURE 25.25   Flash and Upset Welds.

reference for flash welding (FW) or upset welding (UW) must be placed in the tail of the symbol.

25.15 WELDING TEMPLATES

To simplify the drawing of welding symbols and to speed up the drafting, welding templates are available. The template shown in Fig. 25.26 has all the forms needed for drawing the arrow, the weld symbols, and the supplementary symbols, as well as an illustration of the complete composite welding symbol for quick reference. The symbols may be drawn in pencil or ink.

FIGURE 25.26   Welding Template. *Courtesy of Berol USA, Div. of Berol Corporation.*

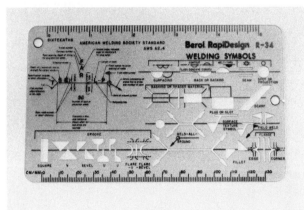

25.16 WELDING APPLICATIONS

A typical example of welding fabrication for machine parts is shown in Fig. 25.1. In many cases, especially when only one or a few identical parts are required, it is cheaper to produce by welding than to make patterns and sand castings and do the necessary machining. Thus, welding is particularly adaptable to custom-built constructions.

Welding is also suitable for large structures that are difficult or impossible to fabricate entirely in the shop, and it is coming into greater use for steel structures, such as building frames, bridges, and ships. A welded beam is shown in Fig. 22.13, and a welded assembly of diagonal bracing between two columns is shown in Fig. 22.14. A welded truss is shown in Fig. 25.27. It is easier to place members in such a welded truss so that their center-of-gravity axes coincide with the working lines of the truss than is the case in a riveted truss. The student should compare this welded truss with the riveted truss of Fig. 22.11.

25.17 COMPUTER GRAPHICS

Welding symbols libraries available to the CAD user (Fig. 25.28) allow for rapid application of accurate, uniform symbols that are in compliance with AWS standards (Fig. 25.29). In addition to standard symbols, many CAD programs permit the operator to create custom symbols as required.

FIGURE 25.27 A Welded Truss.

KEY WORDS

GAS WELDING	ARC WELDING
RESISTANCE WELDING	BUTT JOINT
CORNER JOINT	TEE JOINT
LAP JOINT	EDGE JOINT
V-GROOVE	U-GROOVE
SPOT WELD	FLUSH
CONVEX	CONCAVE
FILLED WELD	GROOVE WELD
SEAM WELD	

BASIC WELDING SYMBOLS AND THEIR LOCATION SIGNIFICANCE

LOCATION SIGNIFICANCE	FLANGE CORNER	GROOVE				
		SQUARE	V	BEVEL	U	J
ARROW SIDE						
OTHER SIDE						
BOTH SIDES	NOT USED					
NO ARROW SIDE OR OTHER SIDE SIGNIFICANCE	NOT USED		NOT USED	NOT USED	NOT USED	NOT USED

LOCATION SIGNIFICANCE	GROOVE		FILLET	PLUG OR SLOT	SPOT OR PROJECTION	SEAM
	FLARE-V	FLARE-BEVEL				
ARROW SIDE						
OTHER SIDE						
BOTH SIDES				NOT USED	NOT USED	NOT USED
NO ARROW SIDE OR OTHER SIDE SIGNIFICANCE	NOT USED	NOT USED	NOT USED	NOT USED		

LOCATION SIGNIFICANCE	BACK OR BACKING	SURFACING	SCARF FOR BRAZED JOINT	FLANGE EDGE	SUPPLEMENTARY SYMBOLS	
ARROW SIDE	GROOVE WELD SYMBOL				ALL AROUND	ALL AROUND
OTHER SIDE	GROOVE WELD SYMBOL	NOT USED			FIELD	FIELD
BOTH SIDES	NOT USED	NOT USED		NOT USED	TAIL	
NO ARROW SIDE OR OTHER SIDE SIGNIFICANCE	NOT USED	NOT USED	NOT USED	NOT USED	TEXT 2-5 / 2-5 / 10	

FIGURE 25.28 **Computervision Production Drafting.**

SECTION "B-B"
.75" = 1'-0"

FIGURE 25.29 **CAD-Generated Welded Structural Detail.**

■ CHAPTER SUMMARY

- The four basic types of arc and gas welds are back, fillet, plug, and groove.
- The four basic types of resistance welds are spot, projection, seam, and flash.
- The welding symbol defines the location of the weld, the type of weld, and the welding process.

- Groove welds are classified as square, V, bevel, U, and J.
- A weld symbol below the leader line indicates that the weld is on the *same* side of the joint as the leader arrow.

■ REVIEW QUESTIONS

1. Which welding process uses oxyacetylene gas combined with oxygen to produce heat?
2. Which welding process uses an electrode?
3. Which welding process passes electricity through the pieces to be welded?

4. List the five types of groove welds.
5. Draw a typical welding symbol and label its parts.
6. What type of weld would join two pieces at 90°?
7. What is a field weld?

■ WELDING DRAWING PROBLEMS

The following problems are given to familiarize the student with some applications of welding symbols to machine construction and to steel structures.

Prob. 25.1 Fig. 5.60. Change to a welded part. Make working drawing, using appropriate welding symbols.

Prob. 25.2 Fig. 5.63. Same instructions as for Prob. 25.1.

Prob. 25.3 Fig. 5.68. Same instructions as for Prob. 25.1.

Prob. 25.4 Fig. 5.79. Same instructions as for Prob. 25.1.

Prob. 25.5 Fig. 5.86. Same instructions as for Prob. 25.1.

Prob. 25.6 Fig. 5.98. Same instructions as for Prob. 25.1.

Prob. 25.7 Fig. 5.107. Same instructions as for Prob. 25.1.

Prob. 25.8 Fig. 5.111. Same instructions as for Prob. 25.1.

Prob. 25.9 Fig. 5.116. Same instructions as for Prob. 25.1.

Prob. 25.10 Make a half-size drawing of the joint at the center of the lower chord of the truss in Fig. 25.27 where the chord is supported by two vertical angles. The chord is a structural tee, cut from an $8 \times 5\frac{1}{4}$, 17-lb, wide-flange shape. Draw the front and side views, and show the working lines, the two angles, the structural tee, and all welding symbols.

Prob. 25.11 Make a half-size front view, showing the welding symbols, of any joint of the truss in Fig. 25.27 in which three or four members meet.

Prob. 25.12 Draw half-size front, top, and left-side views of the end joint of the truss in Fig. 25.27 showing the welding symbols.

APPENDIX

1   Bibliography of American National Standards

American National Standards Institute, 11 West 42nd St., New York, NY. 10036. For complete listing of standards, see ANSI catalog of American National Standards.

Abbreviations

Abbreviations for Use on Drawings and in Text, ANSI/ASME Y1.1–1989

Bolts, Screws, and Nuts

Bolts, Metric Heavy Hex, ANSI B18.2.3.6M–1979 (R1995)

Bolts, Metric Heavy Hex Structural, ANSI B18.2.3.7M–1979 (R1995)

Bolts, Metric Hex, ANSI B18.2.3.5M–1979 (R1995)

Bolts, Metric Round Head Short Square Neck, ANSI/ASME B18.2.2.1M–1981 (R1995)

Bolts, Metric Round Head Square Neck, ANSI/ASME B18.5.2.2M–1982 (R1993)

Hex Jam Nuts, Metric, ANSI B18.2.4.5M–1979 (R1990)

Hex Nuts, Heavy, Metric, ANSI B18.2.4.6M–1979 (R1990)

Hex Nuts, Slotted, Metric, ANSI/ASME B18.2.4.3M–1979 (R1995)

Hex Nuts, Style 1, Metric, ANSI/ASME B18.2.4.1M–1979 (R1995)

Hex Nuts, Style 2, Metric, ANSI/ASME B18.2.4.2M–1979 (R1995)

Hexagon Socket Flat Countersunk Head Cap Screws (Metric Series), ANSI/ASME B18.3.5M–1986 (R1993)

Mechanical Fasteners, Glossary of Terms, ANSI B18.12–1962 (R1995)

Miniature Screws, ANSI B18.11–1961 (R1992)

Nuts, Metric Hex Flange, ANSI B18.2.4.4M–1982 (R1993)

Plow Bolts, ANSI/ASME B18.9–1958 (R1995)

Round Head Bolts, Metric Round Head Short Square Neck, ANSI/ASME B18.5.2.1M–1981 (R1995)

Screws, Hexagon Socket Button Head Cap, Metric Series, ANSI/ASME B18.3.4M–1986 (R1993)

Screws, Hexagon Socket Head Shoulder, Metric Series, ANSI/ASME B18.3.3M–1986 (R1993)

Screws, Hexagon Socket Set, Metric Series, ANSI/ASME B18.3.6M–1986 (R1993)

Screws, Metric Formed Hex, ANSI/ASME B18.2.3.2M–1979 (R1995)

Screws, Metric Heavy Hex, ANSI/ASME B18.2.3.3M–1979 (R1995)

Screws, Metric Hex Cap, ANSI/ASME B18.2.3.1M–1979 (R1995)

Screws, Metric Hex Flange, ANSI/ASME B18.2.3.4M–1984 (R1995)

Screws, Metric Hex Lag, ANSI B18.2.3.8M–1981 (R1991)

Screws, Metric Machine, ANSI/ASME B18.6.7M–1985 (R1993)

Screws, Socket Head Cap, Metric Series, ANSI/ASME B18.3.1M–1986 (R1993)

Screws, Tapping and Metallic Drive, Inch Series, Thread Forming and Cutting, ANSI B18.6.4–1981 (R1991)

Slotted and Recessed Head Machine Screws and Machine Screw Nuts, ANSI B18.6.3–1972 (R1991)

Slotted Head Cap Screws, Square Head Set Screws, and Slotted Headless Set Screws, ANSI/ASME B18.6.2–1995

Socket Cap, Shoulder, and Set Screws (Inch Series) ANSI/ASME B18.3–1986 (R1995)

Square and Hex Bolts and Screws, Inch Series, ANSI B18.2.1–1981 (R1992)

Square and Hex Nuts (Inch Series) ANSI/ASME B18.2.2–1987 (R1993)

Track Bolts and Nuts, ANSI/ASME B18.10–1982 (R1992)

Wood Screws, Inch Series, ANSI B18.6.1–1981 (R1991)

Dimensioning and Surface Finish

General Tolerances for Metric Dimensioned Products, ANSI B4.3–1978 (R1994)

Preferred Limits and Fits for Cylindrical Parts, ANSI B4.1–1967 (R1994)

Preferred Metric Limits and Fits, ANSI B4.2–1978 (R1994)

Surface Texture, ANSI/ASME B46.1–1995

Drafting Manual (Y14)

Casting and Forgings, ANSI/ASME Y14.BM–1989

Decimal Inch, Drawing Sheet Size and Format, ANSI/ASME Y14.1–1995

Dimensioning and Tolerancing, ANSI/ASME Y14.5M–1994

Electrical and Electronics Diagrams, ANSI Y14.15–1966 (R1988)

Electrical and Electronics Diagrams—Supplement, ANSI Y14.15a–1971 (R1988)

Electrical and Electronics Diagrams—Supplement, ANSI Y14.15b–1973 (R1988)

Engineering Drawings, Types, and Applications, ANSI/ASME Y14.24M–1989. Revision of Engineering Drawings, ANSI/ASME Y14.35M–1992

Gear and Spline Drawing Standards—Part 2, Bevel and Hypoid Gears, ANSI Y14.7.2–1978 (R1994)

Gear Drawing Standards—Part 1, for Spur, Helical, Double Helical, and Rack, ANSI/ASME Y14.7.1–1971 (R1993)

Line Conventions and Lettering, ANSI/ASME Y14.2M–1992

Mechanical Spring Representation, ANSI/ASME Y14.13M–1981 (R1992)

Metric Drawing Sheet Size and Format, ANSI/ASME Y14.1M–1995

Multiview and Sectional View Drawings, ANSI/ASME Y14.3M–1994

APPENDIX

1   Bibliography of American National Standards

American National Standards Institute, 11 West 42nd St., New York, NY. 10036. For complete listing of standards, see ANSI catalog of American National Standards.

Abbreviations

Abbreviations for Use on Drawings and in Text, ANSI/ASME Y1.1–1989

Bolts, Screws, and Nuts

Bolts, Metric Heavy Hex, ANSI B18.2.3.6M–1979 (R1995)
Bolts, Metric Heavy Hex Structural, ANSI B18.2.3.7M–1979 (R1995)
Bolts, Metric Hex, ANSI B18.2.3.5M–1979 (R1995)
Bolts, Metric Round Head Short Square Neck, ANSI/ASME B18.2.2.1M–1981 (R1995)
Bolts, Metric Round Head Square Neck, ANSI/ASME B18.5.2.2M–1982 (R1993)
Hex Jam Nuts, Metric, ANSI B18.2.4.5M–1979 (R1990)
Hex Nuts, Heavy, Metric, ANSI B18.2.4.6M–1979 (R1990)
Hex Nuts, Slotted, Metric, ANSI/ASME B18.2.4.3M–1979 (R1995)
Hex Nuts, Style 1, Metric, ANSI/ASME B18.2.4.1M–1979 (R1995)
Hex Nuts, Style 2, Metric, ANSI/ASME B18.2.4.2M–1979 (R1995)
Hexagon Socket Flat Countersunk Head Cap Screws (Metric Series), ANSI/ASME B18.3.5M–1986 (R1993)
Mechanical Fasteners, Glossary of Terms, ANSI B18.12–1962 (R1995)
Miniature Screws, ANSI B18.11–1961 (R1992)
Nuts, Metric Hex Flange, ANSI B18.2.4.4M–1982 (R1993)
Plow Bolts, ANSI/ASME B18.9–1958 (R1995)
Round Head Bolts, Metric Round Head Short Square Neck, ANSI/ASME B18.5.2.1M–1981 (R1995)
Screws, Hexagon Socket Button Head Cap, Metric Series, ANSI/ASME B18.3.4M–1986 (R1993)
Screws, Hexagon Socket Head Shoulder, Metric Series, ANSI/ASME B18.3.3M–1986 (R1993)
Screws, Hexagon Socket Set, Metric Series, ANSI/ASME B18.3.6M–1986 (R1993)
Screws, Metric Formed Hex, ANSI/ASME B18.2.3.2M–1979 (R1995)
Screws, Metric Heavy Hex, ANSI/ASME B18.2.3.3M–1979 (R1995)
Screws, Metric Hex Cap, ANSI/ASME B18.2.3.1M–1979 (R1995)
Screws, Metric Hex Flange, ANSI/ASME B18.2.3.4M–1984 (R1995)
Screws, Metric Hex Lag, ANSI B18.2.3.8M–1981 (R1991)
Screws, Metric Machine, ANSI/ASME B18.6.7M–1985 (R1993)
Screws, Socket Head Cap, Metric Series, ANSI/ASME B18.3.1M–1986 (R1993)
Screws, Tapping and Metallic Drive, Inch Series, Thread Forming and Cutting, ANSI B18.6.4–1981 (R1991)
Slotted and Recessed Head Machine Screws and Machine Screw Nuts, ANSI B18.6.3–1972 (R1991)
Slotted Head Cap Screws, Square Head Set Screws, and Slotted Headless Set Screws, ANSI/ASME B18.6.2–1995
Socket Cap, Shoulder, and Set Screws (Inch Series) ANSI/ASME B18.3–1986 (R1995)
Square and Hex Bolts and Screws, Inch Series, ANSI B18.2.1–1981 (R1992)
Square and Hex Nuts (Inch Series) ANSI/ASME B18.2.2–1987 (R1993)
Track Bolts and Nuts, ANSI/ASME B18.10–1982 (R1992)
Wood Screws, Inch Series, ANSI B18.6.1–1981 (R1991)

Dimensioning and Surface Finish

General Tolerances for Metric Dimensioned Products, ANSI B4.3–1978 (R1994)
Preferred Limits and Fits for Cylindrical Parts, ANSI B4.1–1967 (R1994)
Preferred Metric Limits and Fits, ANSI B4.2–1978 (R1994)
Surface Texture, ANSI/ASME B46.1–1995

Drafting Manual (Y14)

Casting and Forgings, ANSI/ASME Y14.BM–1989
Decimal Inch, Drawing Sheet Size and Format, ANSI/ASME Y14.1–1995
Dimensioning and Tolerancing, ANSI/ASME Y14.5M–1994
Electrical and Electronics Diagrams, ANSI Y14.15–1966 (R1988)
Electrical and Electronics Diagrams—Supplement, ANSI Y14.15a–1971 (R1988)
Electrical and Electronics Diagrams—Supplement, ANSI Y14.15b–1973 (R1988)
Engineering Drawings, Types, and Applications, ANSI/ASME Y14.24M–1989. Revision of Engineering Drawings, ANSI/ASME Y14.35M–1992
Gear and Spline Drawing Standards—Part 2, Bevel and Hypoid Gears, ANSI Y14.7.2–1978 (R1994)
Gear Drawing Standards—Part 1, for Spur, Helical, Double Helical, and Rack, ANSI/ASME Y14.7.1–1971 (R1993)
Line Conventions and Lettering, ANSI/ASME Y14.2M–1992
Mechanical Spring Representation, ANSI/ASME Y14.13M–1981 (R1992)
Metric Drawing Sheet Size and Format, ANSI/ASME Y14.1M–1995
Multiview and Sectional View Drawings, ANSI/ASME Y14.3M–1994

Parts Lists, Data Lists, and Index Lists, ANSI/ASME Y14.34M–1990

Pictorial Drawing, ANSI/ASME Y14.4M–1989 (R1994)

Screw Thread Representation, ANSI/ASME Y14.6–1978 (R1993)

Screw Thread Representation, Metric, ANSI/ASME Y14.6aM–1981 (R1993)

Surface Texture Symbols, ANSI/ASME Y14.36M–1996

Gears

Basic Gear Geometry, ANSI/AGMA 115.01–1989

Gear Nomenclature—Terms, Definitions, Symbols, and Abbreviations, ANSI/AGMA 1012–F90

Nomenclature of Gear-Tooth Failure Modes, ANSI/AGMA 110.04–1980 (R1989)

Design Manual for Bevel Gearing, ANSI/AGMA 2005–B88

Tooth Proportions for Fine-Pitch Spur and Helical Gears, ANSI/AGMA 1003–G93

Graphic Symbols

Public Fire Safety Symbols, ANSI/NFPA 170–1994

Graphic Symbols for Electrical and Electronics Diagrams, ANSI/IEEE 315–1975 (R1994)

Graphic Symbols for Electrical Wiring and Layout Diagrams Used in Architecture and Building Construction, ANSI Y32.9–1972 (R1989)

Graphic Symbols for Fluid Power Diagrams, ANSI/ASME Y32.10–1967 (R1994)

Graphic Symbols for Grid and Mapping Used in Cable Television Systems, ANSI/IEEE 623–1976 (R1989)

Graphic Symbols for Heat-Power Apparatus, ANSI Y32.2.6M–1950 (R1993)

Graphic Symbols for Heating, Ventilating and Air Conditioning, ANSI Y32.2.4–1949 (R1993)

Graphic Symbols for Logic Functions, ANSI/IEEE 91–1984

Graphic Symbols for Pipe Fittings, Valves, and Piping, ANSI/ASME Y32.2.3–1949 (R1994)

Graphic Symbols for Plumbing Fixtures for Diagrams Used in Architecture and Building Construction, ANSI/ASME Y32.4–1977 (R1994)

Graphic Symbols for Process Flow Diagrams in the Petroleum and Chemical Industries, ANSI Y32.11–1961 (R1993)

Graphic Symbols for Railroad Maps and Profiles, ANSI/ASME Y32.7–1972 (R1994)

Instrumentation Symbols and Identification, ANSI/ISA S5.1–1984 (R1992)

Reference Designations for Electrical and Electronics Parts and Equipment, ANSI/IEEE 200–1975 (R1989)

Symbols for Mechanical and Acoustical Elements as Used in Schematic Diagrams, ANSI Y32.18–1972 (R1993)

Symbols for Welding, Brazing, and Nondestructive Examination, ANSI/AWS A2.4–93

Keys and Pins

Clevis Pins and Cotter Pins, ANSI/ASME B18.8.1–1994

Hexagon Keys and Bits (Metric Series), ANSI B18.3.2M–1979 (R1994)

Keys and Keyseats, ANSI B17.1–1967 (R1989)

Pins—Taper Pins, Dowel Pins, Straight Pins, Grooved Pins and Spring Pins (Inch Series), ANSI/ASME B18.8.2–1994

Woodruff Keys and Keyseats, ANSI B17.2–1967 (R1990)

Piping

Cast Bronze Threaded Fittings, Class 125 and 250, ANSI/ASME B16.15–1985 (R1994)

Cast Copper Alloy Pipe Flanges and Flanged Fittings, ANSI/ASME B16.24–1991

Cast Iron Pipe Flanges and Flanged Fittings, Class 25, 125, 250 and 800, ANSI/ASME B16.1–1989

Gray Iron Threaded Fittings, ANSI/ASME B16.4–1992

Ductile Iron Pipe, Centrifugally Cast, ANSI/AWWA C151/A21.51–91

Factory-Made Wrought Steel Buttwelding Fittings, ANSI/ASME B16.9–1993

Ferrous Pipe Plugs, Bushings, and Locknuts with Pipe Threads, ANSI/ASME B16.14–1991

Flanged Ductile-Iron Pipe with Threaded Flanges, ANSI/AWWA C115/A21.15–94

Malleable-Iron Threaded Fittings, ANSI/ASME B16.3–1992

Pipe Flanges and Flanged Fittings, ANSI/ASME B16.5–1988

Stainless Steel Pipe, ANSI/ASME B36.19M–1985 (R1994)

Welded and Seamless Wrought Steel Pipe, ANSI/ASME B36.10M–1995

Rivets

Large Rivets ($\frac{1}{2}$ Inch Nominal Diameter and Larger), ANSI/ASME B18.1.2–1972 (R1995)

Small Solid Rivets ($\frac{7}{16}$ Inch Nominal Diameter and Smaller), ANSI/ASME B18.1.1–1972 (R1995)

Small Solid Rivets, Metric, ANSI/ASME B18.1.3M–1983 (R1995)

Small Tools and Machine Tool Elements

Jig Bushings, ANSI B94.33–1974 (R1994)

Machine Tapers, ANSI/ASME B5.10–1994

Milling Cutters and End Mills, ANSI/ASME B94.19–1985

Reamers, ANSI/ASME B94.2–1995

T-Slots—Their Bolts, Nuts and Tongues, ANSI/ASME B5.1M–1985 (R1992)

Twist Drills, ANSI/ASME B94.11M–1993

Threads

Acme Screw Threads, ANSI/ASME B1.5–1988 (R1994)

Buttress Inch Screw Threads, ANSI B1.9–1973 (R1992)

Class 5 Interference–Fit Thread, ANSI/ASME B1.12–1987 (R1992)

Dryseal Pipe Threads (Inch), ANSI B1.20.3–1976 (R1991)

Hose Coupling Screw Threads, ANSI/ASME B1.20.7–1991

Metric Screw Threads—M Profile, ANSI/ASME B1.13M–1995

Metric Screw Threads—MJ Profile, ANSI/ASME B1.21M–1978

Nomenclature, Definitions and Letter Symbols for Screw Threads, ANSI/ASME B1.7M–1984 (R1992)

Pipe Threads, General Purpose (Inch), ANSI/ASME B1.20.1–1983 (R1992)

Stub Acme Threads, ANSI/ASME B1.8–1988 (R1994)

Unified Screw Threads (UN and UNR Thread Form), ANSI/ASME B1.1–1989

Unified Miniature Screw Threads, ANSI B1.10–1958 (R1988)

Washers

Lock Washers, Inch, ANSI/ASME B18.21.1–1994

Lock Washers, Metric, ANSI/ASME B18.21.2M–1994

Plain Washers, ANSI B18.22.1–1965 (R1981)

Plain Washers, Metric, ANSI B18.22M–1981

Miscellaneous

Knurling, ANSI/ASME B94.6–1984 (R1995)

Preferred Metric Sizes for Flat Metal Products, ANSI/ASME B32.3M–1984 (R1994)

Preferred Metric Equivalents of Inch Sizes for Tubular Metal Products Other Than Pipe, ANSI/ASME B32.6M–1984 (R1994)

Preferred Metric Sizes for Round, Square, Rectangle and Hexagon Metal Products, ANSI B32.4M–1980 (R1994)

Preferred Metric Sizes for Tubular Metal Products Other Than Pipe, ANSI B32.5–1977 (R1994)

Preferred Thickness for Uncoated Thin Flat Metals (Under 0.250 in.), ANSI B32.1–1952 (R1994)

Surface Texture (Surface Roughness, Waviness and Lay), ANSI/ASME B46.1–1995

Technical Drawings, ISO Handbook, 12–1991

2 Technical Terms

"The beginning of wisdom is to call things by their right names."

–CHINESE PROVERB

n *means a* noun; v *means a* verb

acme (*n*) Screw thread form, §§14.3 and 14.13

addendum (*n*) Radial distance from pitch circle to top of gear tooth.

allen screw (*n*) Special set screw or cap screw with hexagon socket in head, §14.31.

allowance (*n*) Minimum clearance between mating parts, §13.12.

alloy (*n*) Two or more metals in combination, usually a fine metal with a baser metal.

aluminum (*n*) A lightweight but relatively strong metal. Often alloyed with copper to increase hardness and strength.

angle iron (*n*) A structural shape whose section is a right angle, §11.20.

anneal (*v*) To heat and cool gradually, to reduce brittleness and increase ductility, §11.22.

arc-weld (*v*) To weld by electric arc. The work is usually the positive terminal.

babbitt (*n*) A soft alloy for bearings, mostly of tin with small amounts of copper and antimony.

bearing (*n*) A supporting member for a rotating shaft.

bevel (*n*) An inclined edge, not at right angle to joining surface.

bolt circle (*n*) A circular center line on a drawing, containing the centers of holes about a common center, §12.25.

bore (*v*) To enlarge a hole with a boring mill, Figs. 11.15b and 11.18b.

boss (*n*) A cylindrical projection on a casting or a forging.

BOSS

brass (*n*) An alloy of copper and zinc.

braze (*v*) To join with hard solder of brass or zinc.

Brinell (*n*) A method of testing hardness of metal.

broach (*n*) A long cutting tool with a series of teeth that gradually increase in size which is forced through a hole or over a surface to produce a desired shape, §11.15.

bronze (*n*) An alloy of eight or nine parts of copper and one part of tin.

buff (*v*) To finish or polish on a buffing wheel composed of fabric with abrasive powders.

burnish (*v*) To finish or polish by pressure upon a smooth rolling or sliding tool.

burr (*n*) A jagged edge on metal resulting from punching or cutting.

bushing (*n*) A replaceable lining or sleeve for a bearing.

calipers (*n*) Instrument (of several types) for measuring diameters, §11.17.

cam (*n*) A rotating member for changing circular motion to reciprocating motion.

carburize (*v*) To heat a low-carbon steel to approximately 2000°F in contact with material which adds carbon to the surface of the steel, and to cool slowly in preparation for heat treatment, §11.22.

caseharden (*v*) To harden the outer surface of a carburized steel by heating and then quenching.

castellate (*v*) To form like a castle, as a castellated shaft or nut.

casting (*n*) A metal object produced by pouring molten metal into a mold, §11.3.

cast iron (*n*) Iron melted and poured into molds, §11.3.

center drill (*n*) A special drill to produce bearing holes in the ends of a workpiece to be mounted between centers. Also called a "combined drill and countersink," §12.35.

COMBINED DRILL & C SINK

chamfer (*n*) A narrow inclined surface along the intersection of two surfaces.

CHAMFER

chase (*v*) To cut threads with an external cutting tool.

cheek (*n*) The middle portion of a three-piece flask used in molding, §11.3.

chill (*v*) To harden the outer surface of cast iron by quick cooling, as in a metal mold.

chip (*v*) To cut away metal with a cold chisel.

chuck (*n*) A mechanism for holding a rotating tool or workpiece.

coin (*v*) To form a part in one stamping operation.

cold-rolled steel (CRS) (*n*) Open hearth or Bessemer steel containing 0.12–0.20% carbon that has been rolled while cold to produce a smooth, quite accurate stock.

collar (*n*) A round flange or ring fitted on a shaft to prevent sliding.

COLLAR

colorharden (*v*) Same as *caseharden*, except that it is done to a shallower depth, usually for appearance only.

cope (*n*) The upper portion of a flask used in molding, §11.3.

core (*v*) To form a hollow portion in a casting by using a dry-sand core or a green-sand core in a mold, §11.3.

coreprint (*n*) A projection on a pattern which forms an opening in the sand to hold the end of a core, §11.3.

cotter pin (*n*) A split pin used as a fastener, usually to prevent a nut from unscrewing, Figs. 14.31g and 14.31h and Appendix 30.

counterbore (*v*) To enlarge an end of a hole cylindrically with a *counterbore*, §11.16.

COUNTERBORE

countersink (*v*) To enlarge an end of a hole conically, usually with a *countersink*, §11.16.

COUNTERSINK

crown (*n*) A raised contour, as on the surface of a pulley.

cyanide (*v*) To surface-harden steel by heating in contact with a cyanide salt, followed by quenching.

dedendum (*n*) Distance from pitch circle to bottom of tooth space.

development (*n*) Drawing of the surface of an object unfolded or rolled out on a plane.

diametral pitch (*n*) Number of gear teeth per inch of pitch diameter.

die (*n*) (1) Hardened metal piece shaped to cut or form a required shape in a sheet of metal by pressing it against a mating die. (2) Also used for cutting small male threads. In a sense is opposite to a tap.

die casting (*n*) Process of forcing molten metal under pressure into metal dies or molds, producing a very accurate and smooth casting.

die stamping (*n*) Process of cutting or forming a piece of sheet metal with a die.

dog (*n*) A small auxiliary clamp for preventing work from rotating in relation to the face plate of a lathe.

dowel (*n*) A cylindrical pin, commonly used to prevent sliding between two contacting flat surfaces.

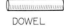

DOWEL

draft (*n*) The tapered shape of the parts of a pattern to permit it to be easily withdrawn from the sand or, on a forging, to permit it to be easily withdrawn from the dies, §§11.3 and 11.21.

PATTERN
DRAFT
DRAFT

drag (*n*)   Lower portion of a flask used in molding, §11.3.

draw (*v*)   To stretch or otherwise to deform metal. Also to temper steel.

drill (*v*)   To cut a cylindrical hole with a drill. A *blind hole* does not go through the piece, §11.16.

drill press (*n*)   A machine for drilling and other hole-forming operations, §11.8.

drop forge (*v*)   To form a piece while hot between dies in a drop hammer or with great pressure, §11.21.

face (*v*)   To finish a surface at right angles, or nearly so, to the center line of rotation on a lathe.

FAO Finish all over, §12.17.

feather key (*n*)   A flat key, which is partly sunk in a shaft and partly in a hub, permitting the hub to slide lengthwise of the shaft, §14.34.

file (*v*)   To finish or smooth with a file.

fillet (*n*)   An interior rounded intersection between two surfaces, §§7.34 and 11.5.

fin (*n*)   A thin extrusion of metal at the intersection of dies or sand molds.

fit (*n*)   Degree of tightness or looseness between two mating parts, as a *loose fit*, a *snug fit*, or a *tight fit*. §§12.9 and 13.1–13.3.

fixture (*n*)   A special device for holding the work in a machine tool, *but not for guiding the cutting tool*.

flange (*n*)   A relatively thin rim around a piece.

FLANGE

flash (*n*)   Same as *fin*.

flask (*n*)   A box made of two or more parts for holding the sand in sand molding, §11.3.

flute (*n*)   Groove, as on twist drills, reamers, and taps.

forge (*v*)   To force metal while it is hot to take on a desired shape by hammering or pressing, §11.21.

galvanize (*v*)   To cover a surface with a thin layer of molten alloy, composed mainly of zinc, to prevent rusting.

gasket (*n*)   A thin piece of rubber, metal, or some other material, placed between surfaces to make a tight joint.

gate (*n*)   The opening in a sand mold at the bottom of the *sprue* through which the molten metal passes to enter the cavity or mold, §11.3.

graduate (*v*)   To set off accurate divisions on a scale or dial.

grind (*v*)   To remove metal by means of an abrasive wheel, often made of carborundum. Use chiefly where accuracy is required, §11.14.

harden (*v*)   To heat steel above a critical temperature and then quench in water or oil, §11.22.

heat-treat (*v*)   To change the properties of metals by heating and then cooling, §11.22.

interchangeable (*adj.*)   Refers to a part made to limit dimensions so that it will fit any mating part similarly manufactured, §13.1.

jig (*n*)   A device *for guiding a tool* in cutting a piece. Usually it holds the work in position.

journal (*n*)   Portion of a rotating shaft supported by a bearing.

kerf (*n*)   Groove or cut made by a saw.

KERF

key (*n*)   A small piece of metal sunk partly into both shaft and hub to prevent rotation, §14.34.

keyseat (*n*)   A slot or recess in a shaft to hold a key, §14.34.

KEYSEAT

keyway (*n*)   A slot in a hub or portion surrounding a shaft to receive a key. §14.34.

KEYWAY

knurl (*v*)   To impress a pattern of dents in a turned surface with a knurling tool to produce a better hand grip, §12.37.

lap (*v*)   To produce a very accurate finish by sliding contact with a *lap*, or piece of wood, leather, or soft metal impregnated with abrasive powder.

lathe (*n*)   A machine used to shape metal or other materials by rotating against a tool, §11.7.

lug (*n*)   An irregular projection of metal, but not round as in the case of a *boss*, usually with a hole in it for a bolt or screw.

malleable casting (*n*)   A casting that has been made less brittle and tougher by annealing.

mill (*v*)   To remove material by means of a rotating cutter on a milling machine, §11.9.

mold (*n*)   The mass of sand or other material that forms the cavity into which molten metal is poured, §11.3.

MS (*n*)   Machinery steel, sometimes called *mild steel* with a small percentage of carbon. Cannot be hardened.

neck (*v*)   To cut a groove called a *neck* around a cylindrical piece.

NECK

normalize (*v*)   To heat steel above its critical temperature and then to cool it in air, §11.22.

pack-harden (*v*)   To *carburize*, then to *caseharden*, §11.22.

pad (*n*)   A slight projection, usually to provide a bearing surface around one or more holes.

PAD

pattern (*n*)   A model, usually of wood, used in forming a mold for a casting. In sheet metal work a pattern is called a *development*.

peen (*v*)   To hammer into shape with a ballpeen hammer.

pickle (*v*)   To clean forgings or castings in dilute sulphuric acid.

pinion (*n*)   The smaller of two mating gears.

pitch circle (*n*)   An imaginary circle corresponding to the circumference of the friction gear from which the spur gear was derived.

plane (*v*)   To remove material by means of the *planer*, §11.11.

planish (*v*)   To impart a planished surface to sheet metal by hammering with a smooth-surfaced hammer.

plate (*v*)   To coat a metal piece with another metal, such as chrome or nickel, by electrochemical methods.

polish (*v*)   To produce a highly finished or polished surface by friction, using a very fine abrasive.

profile (*v*)   To cut any desired outline by moving a small rotating cutter, usually with a master template as a guide.

punch (*v*)   To cut an opening of a desired shape with a rigid tool having the same shape, by pressing the tool through the work.

quench (*v*)   To immerse a heated piece of metal in water or oil to harden it.

rack (*n*)   A flat bar with gear teeth in a straight line to engage with teeth in a gear.

ream (*v*)   To enlarge a finished hole slightly to give it greater accuracy, with a *reamer*, §11.16.

relief (*n*)   An offset of surfaces to provide clearance for machining.

RELIEF

rib (*n*)   A relatively thin flat member acting as a brace or support.

RIB

rivet (*v*)   To connect with rivets or to clench over the end of a pin by hammering, §14.36.

round (*n*)   An exterior rounded intersection of two surfaces, §§7.34 and 11.5.

SAE Society of Automotive Engineers.

sandblast (*v*)   To blow sand at high velocity with compressed air against castings or forgings to clean them.

scleroscope (*n*)   An instrument for measuring hardness of metals.

scrape (*v*)   To remove metal by scraping with a hand scraper, usually to fit a bearing.

shape (*v*)   To remove metal from a piece with a *shaper*, §11.10.

shear (*v*)   To cut metal by means of shearing with two blades in sliding contact.

sherardize (*v*)   To galvanize a piece with a coating of zinc by heating it in a drum with zinc powder, to a temperature of 575–850°F.

shim (*n*)   A thin piece of metal or other material used as a spacer in adjusting two parts.

solder (*v*)   To join with solder, usually composed of lead and tin.

spin (*v*)   To form a rotating piece of sheet metal into a desired shape by pressing it with a smooth tool against a rotating form.

spline (*n*)   A keyway, usually one of a series cut around a shaft or hole.

SPLINED HOLE

spotface (*v*)   To produce a round *spot* or bearing surface around a hole, usually with a *spotfacer*. The spotface may be on top of a boss or it may be sunk into the surface, §§7.33 and 11.16.

SPOTFACE

sprue (*n*)   A hole in the sand leading to the *gate* which leads to the mold, through which the metal enters, §11.3.

steel casting (*n*)   Like cast-iron casting except that in the furnace scrap steel has been added to the casting.

swage (*v*)   To hammer metal into shape while it is held over a *swage,* or die, which fits in a hole in the *swage block,* or anvil.

sweat (*v*)   To fasten metal together by the use of solder between the pieces and by the application of heat and pressure.

tap (*v*)   To cut relatively small internal threads with a *tap.* §11.16.

tape (*n*)   Conical form given to a shaft or a hole. Also refers to the slope of a plane surface, §12.33.

taper pin (*n*)   A small tapered pin for fastening, usually to prevent a collar or hub from rotating on a shaft.

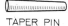
TAPER PIN

taper reamer (*n*)   A tapered reamer for producing accurate tapered holes, as for a taper pin, §§12.33 and 14.35.

temper (*v*)   To reheat hardened steel to bring it to a desired degree of hardness, §11.22.

template or *templet* (*n*)   A guide or pattern used to mark out the work, guide the tool in cutting it, or check the finished product.

tin (*n*)   A silvery metal used in alloys and for coating other metals, such as tin plate.

tolerance (*n*)   Total amount of variation permitted in limit dimension of a part, §13.2.

trepan (*v*)   To cut a circular groove in the flat surface at one end of a hole.

tumble (*v*)   To clean rough castings or forgings in a revolving drum filled with scrap metal.

turn (*v*)   To produce, on a lathe, a cylindrical surface parallel to the center line, §11.7.

twist drill (*n*)   A drill for use in a drill press, §11.16.

undercut (*n*)   A recessed cut or a cut with inwardly sloping sides.

UNDERCUT

upset (*v*)   To form a head or enlarged end on a bar or rod by pressure or by hammering between dies.

web (*n*)   A thin flat part joining larger parts. Also known as a *rib.*

weld (*v*)   Uniting metal pieces by pressure or fusion welding processes, §11.19.

Woodruff key (*n*)   A semicircular flat key, §14.34.

WOODRUFF KEYS

wrought iron (*n*)   Iron of low carbon content useful because of its toughness, ductility, and malleability.

3   CAD/CAM Glossary[*]

access time (or disk access time)   One measure of system response. The time interval between the instant that data is called for from storage and the instant that delivery is completed—i.e., read time. See also *response time.*

alphanumeric (or alphameric)   A term that encompasses letters, digits, and special characters that are machine-processable.

alphanumeric display (or alphameric display)   A work-station device consisting of a CRT on which text can be viewed. An alphanumeric display is capable of showing a fixed set of letters, digits, and special characters. It allows the designer to observe entered commands and to receive messages from the system.

alphanumeric keyboard (or alphameric keyboard)   A work-station device consisting of a typewriter-like keyboard that allows the designer to communicate with the system using an English-like command language.

American Standard Code for Information Interchange (ASCII)   An industry-standard character code widely used for information interchange among data processing systems, communications systems, and associated equipment.

analog   Applied to an electrical or computer system, this denotes the capability to represent data in continuously varying physical quantities.

annotation   Process of inserting text or a special note or identification (such as a flag) on a drawing, map, or diagram constructed on a CAD/CAM system. The text can be generated and positioned on the drawing using the system.

application program (or package)   A computer program or collection of programs to perform a task or tasks specific to a particular user's need or class of needs.

---

[*]Extracted from *The CAD/CAM Glossary,* 1983 edition, published by the Computervision Corporation, Bedford, MA 01730; reproduced with permission of the publisher.

archival storage Refers to memory (on magnetic tape, disks, printouts, or drums) used to store data on completed designs or elements outside of main memory.

array (*v*) To create automatically on a CAD system an arrangement of identical elements or components. The designer defines the element once, then indicates the starting location and spacing for automatic generation of the array. (*n*) An arrangement created in the above manner. A series of elements or sets of elements arranged in a pattern—i.e., matrix.

ASCII See *American National Standard Code for Information Exchange.*

assembler A computer program that converts (i.e., translates) programmer-written symbolic instructions, usually in mnemonic form, into machine-executable (computer or binary-coded) instructions. This conversion is typically one-to-one (one symbolic instruction converts to one machine-executable instruction). A software programming aid.

associative dimensioning A CAD capability that links dimension entities to geometric entities being dimensioned. This allows the value of a dimension to be automatically updated as the geometry changes.

attribute A nongraphic characteristic of a part, component, or entity under design on a CAD system. Examples include: dimension entities associated with geometry, text with text nodes, and nodal lines with connect nodes. Changing one entity in an association can produce automatic changes by the system in the associated entity; e.g., moving one entity can cause moving or stretching of the other entity.

automatic dimensioning A CAD capability that computes the dimensions in a displayed design, or in a designated section, and automatically places dimensions, dimensional lines, and arrowheads where required. In the case of mapping, this capability labels the linear feature with length and azimuth.

auxiliary storage Storage that supplements main memory devices such as disk or drum storage. Contrast with *archival storage.*

benchmark The program(s) used to test, compare, and evaluate in real time the performance of various CAD/CAM systems prior to selection and purchase. A *synthetic* benchmark has preestablished parameters designed to exercise a set of system features and resources. A *live* benchmark is drawn from the prospective user's workload as a model of the entire workload.

bit The smallest unit of information that can be stored and processed by a digital computer. A bit may assume only one of two values: 0 or 1 (i.e., ON/OFF or YES/NO). Bits are organized into larger units called *words* for access by computer instructions.

Computers are often categorized by word size in bits, i.e., the maximum word size that can be processed as a unit during an instruction cycle (e.g., 16-bit computers or 32-bit computers). The number of bits in a word is an indication of the processing power of the system, especially for calculations or for high-precision data.

bit rate The speed at which bits are transmitted, usually expressed in bits per second.

bits per inch (bpi) The number of bits that can be stored per inch of a magnetic tape. A measure of the data storage capacity of a magnetic tape.

blank A CAD command that causes a predefined entity to go temporarily blank on the CRT. The reversing command is *unblank.*

blinking A CAD design aid that makes a predefined graphic entity blink on the CRT to attract the attention of the designer.

boot up Start up (a system).

B-spline A sequence of parametric polynomial curves (typically quadratic or cubic polynomials) forming a smooth fit between a sequence of points in 3D space. The piece-wise defined curve maintains a level of mathematical continuity dependent upon the polynomial degree chosen. It is used extensively in mechanical design applications in the automotive and aerospace industries.

bug A flaw in the design or implementation of a software program or hardware design that causes erroneous results or malfunctions.

bulk memory A memory device for storing a large amount of data, e.g., disk, drum, or magnetic tape. It is not randomly accessible as main memory is.

byte A sequence of adjacent bits, usually eight, representing a character that is operated on as a unit. Usually shorter than a word. A measure of the memory capacity of a system, or of an individual storage unit (as a 300-million-byte disk).

CAD See *computer-aided design.*

CAD/CAM See *computer-aided design/computer-aided manufacturing.*

CADDS® Computervision Corporation's registered trademark for its prerecorded software programs.

CAE See *computer-aided engineering.*

CAM See *computer-aided manufacturing.*

CAMACS™ (CAM Asynchronous Communications Software) Computervision's communications link, which enables users to exchange machine control data with other automation systems and devices, or to interact directly with local or remote manufacturing systems and machines. CAMACS tailors CAD/CAM data automatically for a wide range of machine tools, robots, coordinate measurement systems, and off-line storage devices.

cathode ray tube (CRT) The principal component in a CAD display device. A CRT displays graphic representations of geometric entities and designs and can be of various types: storage tube, raster scan, or refresh. These tubes create images by means of a controllable beam of electrons striking a screen. The term *CRT* is often used to denote the entire display device.

central processing unit (CPU) The computer brain of a CAD/CAM system that controls the retrieval, decoding, and processing of information, as well as the interpretation and execution of operating instructions—the building blocks of application and other computer programs. A CPU comprises arithmetic, control, and logic elements.

character An alphabetical, numerical, or special graphic symbol used as part of the organization, control, or representation of CAD/CAM data.

characters per second (cps) A measure of the speed with which an alphanumeric terminal can process data.

chip See *integrated circuit*.

code A set of specific symbols and rules for representing data (usually instructions) so that the data can be understood and executed by a computer. A code can be in binary (machine) language, assembly language, or a high-level language. Frequently refers to an industry-standard code such as ANSI, ASCII, IPC, or Standard Code for Information Exchange. Many application codes for CAD/CAM are written in FORTRAN.

color display A CAD/CAM display device. Color raster-scan displays offer a variety of user-selectable, contrasting colors to make it easier to discriminate among various groups of design elements on different layers of a large, complex design. Color speeds up the recognition of specific areas and subassemblies, helps the designer interpret complex surfaces, and highlights interference problems. Color displays can be of the penetration type, in which various phosphor layers give off different colors (refresh display) or the TV-type with red, blue, and green electron guns (raster-scan display).

command A control signal or instruction to a CPU or graphics processor, commonly initiated by means of a menu/tablet and electronic pen or by an alphanumeric keyboard.

command language A language for communicating with a CAD/CAM system in order to perform specific functions or tasks.

communication link The physical means, such as a telephone line, for connecting one system module or peripheral to another in a different location in order to transmit and receive data. See also *data link*.

compatibility The ability of a particular hardware module or software program, code, or language to be used in a CAD/CAM system without prior modification or special interfaces. *Upward compatible* denotes the ability of a system to interface with new hardware or software modules or enhancements (i.e., the system vendor provides with each new module a reasonable means of transferring data,

programs, and operator skills from the user's present system to the new enhancements).

compiler A computer program that converts or translates a high-level, user-written language (e.g., PASCAL, COBOL, VARPRO, or FORTRAN) or source, into a language that a computer can understand. The conversion is typically one to many (i.e., one user instruction to many machine-executable instructions). A software programming aid, the compiler allows the designer to write programs in an English-like language with relatively few statements, thus saving program development time.

component A physical entity, or a symbol used in CAD to denote such an entity. Depending on the application, a component might refer to an IC or part of a wiring circuit (e.g., a resistor), or a valve, elbow, or vee in a plant layout, or a substation or cable in a utility map. Also applies to a subassembly or part that goes into higher level assemblies.

computer-aided design (CAD) A process that uses a computer system to assist in the creation, modification, and display of a design.

computer-aided design/computer-aided manufacturing (CAD/CAM) Refers to the integration of computers into the entire design-to-fabrication cycle of a product or plant.

computer-aided engineering (CAE) Analysis of a design for basic error checking, or to optimize manufacturability, performance, and economy (for example, by comparing various possible materials or designs). Information drawn from the CAD/CAM design data base is used to analyze the functional characteristics of a part, product, or system under design and to simulate its performance under various conditions. In electronic design, CAE enables users of the Computervision Designer system to detect and correct potentially costly design flaws. CAE permits the execution of complex circuit loading analyses and simulation during the circuit definition stage. CAE can be used to determine section properties, moments of inertia, shear and bending moments, weight, volume, surface area, and center of gravity. CAE can precisely determine loads, vibration, noise, and service life early in the design cycle so that components can be optimized to meet those criteria. Perhaps the most powerful CAE technique is finite element modeling. See also *kinematics*.

computer-aided manufacturing (CAM) The use of computer and digital technology to generate manufacturing-oriented data. Data drawn from a CAD/ CAM data base can assist in or control a portion or all of a manufacturing process, including numerically controlled machines, computer-assisted parts programming, computer-assisted process planning, robotics, and programmable logic controllers, CAM can involve production programming, manufacturing engineering, industrial engineering, facilities engineering, and reliability engineering (quality control).

CAM techniques can be used to produce process plans for fabricating a complete assembly, to program robots, and to coordinate plant operation.

computer graphics   A general term encompassing any discipline or activity that uses computers to generate, process, and display graphic images. The essential technology of CAD/CAM systems. See also *computer-aided design*.

computer network   An interconnected complex (arrangement or configuration) of two or more systems. See also *network*.

computer program   A specific set of software commands in a form acceptable to a computer and used to achieve a desired result. Often called a *software program* or *package*.

configuration   A particular combination of a computer, software and hardware modules, and peripherals at a single installation and interconnected in such a way as to support certain application(s).

connector   A termination point for a signal entering or leaving a PC board or a cabling system.

convention   Standardized methodology or accepted procedure for executing a computer program. In CAD, the term denotes a standard rule or mode of execution undertaken to provide consistency. For example, a drafting convention might require all dimensions to be in metric units.

core (core memory)   A largely obsolete term for *main storage*.

CPU   See *central processing unit*.

CRT   See *cathode ray tube*.

cursor   A visual tracking symbol, usually an underline or cross hairs, for indicating a location or entity selection on the CRT display. A text cursor indicates the alphanumeric input; a graphics cursor indicates the next geometric input. A cursor is guided by an electronic or light pen, joystick, keyboard, etc., and follows every movement of the input device.

cycle   A preset sequence of events (hardware or software) initiated by a single command.

data base   A comprehensive collection of interrelated information stored on some kind of mass data storage device, usually a disk. Generally consists of information organized into a number of fixed-format record types with logical links between associated records. Typically includes operating systems instructions, standard parts libraries, completed designs and documentation, source code, graphic and application programs, as well as current user tasks in progress.

data communication   The transmission of data (usually digital) from one point (such as a CAD/CAM workstation or CPU) to another point via communication channels such as telephone lines.

data link   The communication line(s), related controls, and interface(s) for the transmission of data between two or more computer systems. Can include modems, telephone lines, or dedicated transmission media such as cable or optical fiber.

data tablet   A CAD/CAM input device that allows the designer to communicate with the system by placing an electronic pen or stylus on the tablet surface. There is a direct correspondence between positions on the tablet and addressable points on the display surface of the CRT. Typically used for indicating positions on the CRT, for digitizing input of drawings, or for menu selection. See also *graphic tablet*.

debug   To detect, locate, and correct any bugs in a system's software or hardware.

dedicated   Designed or intended for a single function or use. For example, a dedicated work station might be used exclusively for engineering calculations or plotting.

default   The predetermined value of a parameter required in a CAD/CAM task or operation. It is automatically supplied by the system whenever that value (e.g., text, height, or grid size) is not specified.

density   (1) A measure of the complexity of an electronic design. For example, IC density can be measured by the number of gates or transistors per unit area or by the number of square inches per component. (2) Magnetic tape storage capacity. High capacity might be 1600 bits/inch; low, 800 bits/inch.

device   A system hardware module external to the CPU and designed to perform a specific function—i.e., a CRT, plotter, printer, hard-copy unit, etc. See also *peripheral*.

diagnostics   Computer programs designed to test the status of a system or its key components and to detect and isolate malfunctions.

dial up   To initiate station-to-station communication with a computer via a dial telephone, usually from a workstation to a computer.

digital   Applied to an electrical or computer system, this denotes the capability to represent data in the form of digits.

digitize   (1) General description: to convert a drawing into digital form (i.e., coordinate locations) so that it can be entered into the data base for later processing. A digitizer, available with many CAD systems, implements the conversion process. This is one of the primary ways of entering existing drawings, crude graphics, lines, and shapes into the system. (2) Computervision usage: to specify a coordinate location or entity using an electronic pen or other device; or a single coordinate value or entity pointer generated by a digitizing operation.

digitizer   A CAD input device consisting of a data tablet on which is mounted the drawing or design to be digitized into the system. The designer moves a puck or electronic pen to selected points on the drawing and enters coordinate data for lines and shapes by simply pressing down the digitize button with the puck or pen.

dimensioning automatic   A CAD capability that will automatically compute and insert the dimensions of a design or drawing, or a designated section of it.

direct access (linkage)   Retrieval or storage of data in the system by reference to its location on a tape, disk, or cartridge, without the need for processing on a CPU.

direct-view storage tube (DVST)   One of the most widely used graphics display devices, DVST generates a long-lasting, flicker-tree image with high resolution and no refreshing. It handles an almost unlimited amount of data. However, display dynamics are limited since DVSTs do not permit selective erase. The image is not as bright as with refresh or raster. Also called *storage tube*.

directory   A named space on the disk or other mass storage device in which are stored the names of files and some summary information about them.

discrete components   Components with a single functional capability per package—for example, transistors and diodes.

disk (storage)   A device on which large amounts of information can be stored in the data base. Synonymous with *magnetic disk storage* or *magnetic disk memory*.

display   A CAD/CAM work station device for rapidly presenting a graphic image so that the designer can react to it, making changes interactively in real time. Usually refers to a CRT.

dot-matrix plotter   A CAD peripheral device for generating graphic plots. Consists of a combination of wire nibs (styli) spaced 100 to 200 styli per inch, which place dots where needed to generate a drawing. Because of its high speed, it is typically used in electronic design applications. Accuracy and resolution are not as great as with pen plotters. Also known as *electrostatic plotter*.

drum plotter   An electromechanical pen plotter that draws an image on paper or film mounted on a rotatable drum. In this CAD peripheral device a combination of plotting-head movement and drum rotation provides the motion.

dynamic (motion)   Simulation of movement using CAD software, so that the designer can see on the CRT screen 3D representations of the parts in a piece of machinery as they interact dynamically. Thus, any collision or interference problems are revealed at a glance.

dynamic menuing   This feature of Computervision's Instaview terminal allows a particular function or command to be initiated by touching an electronic pen to the appropriate key word displayed in the status text area on the screen.

dynamics   The capability of a CAD system to zoom, scroll, and rotate.

edit   To modify, refine, or update an emerging design or text on a CAD system. This can be done on-line interactively.

electrostatic plotter   See *dot-matrix plotter*.

element   The basic design entity in computer-aided design whose logical, positional, electrical, or mechanical function is identifiable.

enhancements   Software or hardware improvements, additions, or updates to a CAD/CAM system.

entity   A geometric primitive—the fundamental building block used in constructing a design or drawing, such as an arc, circle, line, text, point, spline, figure, or nodal line. Or a group of primitives processed as an identifiable unit. Thus, a square may be defined as a discrete entity consisting of four primitives (vectors), although each side of the square could be defined as an entity in its own right. See also *primitive*.

feedback   (1) The ability of a system to respond to an operator command in real time either visually or with a message on the alphanumeric display or CRT. This message registers the command, indicates any possible errors, and simultaneously displays the updated design on the CRT. (2) The signal or data fed back to a commanding unit from a controlled machine or process to denote its response to a command. (3) The signal representing the difference between actual response and desired response and used by the commanding unit to improve performance of the controlled machine or process. See also *prompt*.

figure   A symbol or a part that may contain primitive entities, other figures, nongraphic properties, and associations. A figure can be incorporated into other parts or figures.

file   A collection of related information in the system that may be accessed by a unique name. May be stored on a disk, tape, or other mass storage media.

file protection   A technique for preventing access to or accidental erasure of data within a file on the system.

firmware   Computer programs, instructions, or functions implemented in user-modifiable hardware, i.e., a microprocessor with read-only memory. Such programs or instructions, stored permanently in programmable read-only memories, constitute a fundamental part of system hardware. The advantage is that a frequently used program or routine can be invoked by a single command instead of multiple commands as in a software program.

flatbed plotter   A CAD/CAM peripheral device that draws an image on paper, glass, or film mounted on a flat table. The plotting head provides all the motion.

flat-pattern generation   A CAD/CAM capability for automatically unfolding a 3D design of a sheet metal part into its corresponding flat-pattern design. Calculations for material bending and stretching are performed automatically for any specified material. The reverse flat-pattern generation package automatically folds a flat-pattern design into its 3D version. Flat-pattern generation eliminates major bottlenecks for sheet metal fabricators.

flicker An undesired visual effect on a CRT when the refresh rate is low.

font, line Repetitive pattern used in CAD to give a displayed line appearance characteristics that make it more easily distinguishable, such as a solid, dashed, or dotted line. A line font can be applied to graphic images in order to provide meaning, either graphic (e.g., hidden lines) or functional (roads, tracks, wires, pipes, etc.). It can help a designer to identify and define specific graphic representations of entities that are view-dependent. For example, a line may be solid when drawn in the top view of an object but, when a line font is used, becomes dotted in the side view where it is not normally visible.

font, text Sets of type faces of various styles and sizes. In CAD, fonts are used to create text for drawings, special characters such as Greek letters, and mathematical symbols.

FORTRAN FORmula TRANslation, a high-level programming language used primarily for scientific or engineering applications.

fracturing The division of IC graphics by CAD into simple trapezoidal or rectangular areas for pattern-generation purposes.

function key A specific square on a data tablet, or a key on a function key box, used by the designer to enter a particular command or other input. See also *data tablet*.

function keyboard An input device located at a CAD/CAM workstation and containing a number of function keys.

gap The gap between two entities on a computer-aided design is the length of the shortest line segment that can be drawn from the boundary of one entity to the other without intersecting the boundary of the other. CAD/CAM design-rules checking programs can automatically perform gap checks.

graphic tablet A CAD/CAM input device that enables graphic and location instruments to be entered into the system using an electronic pen on the tablet. See also *data tablet*.

gray scales In CAD systems with a monochromatic display, variations in brightness level (gray scale) are employed to enhance the contrast among various design elements. This feature is very useful in helping the designer discriminate among complex entities on different layers displayed concurrently on the CRT.

grid A network of uniformly spaced points or crosshatch optionally displayed on the CRT and used for exactly locating and digitizing a position, inputting components to assist in the creation of a design layout, or constructing precise angles. For example, the coordinate data supplied by digitizers is automatically calculated by the CPU from the closest grid point. The grid determines the minimum accuracy with which design entities are described or connected. In the mapping environment, a grid is used to describe the distribution network of utility resources.

hard copy A copy on paper of an image displayed on the CRT—for example, a drawing, printed report, plot, listing, or summary. Most CAD/CAM systems can automatically generate hard copy through an on-line printer or plotter.

hardware The physical components, modules, and peripherals comprising a system—computer disk, magnetic tape, CRT terminal(s), plotter(s), etc.

hard-wired link A technique of physically connecting two systems by fixed circuit interconnections using digital signals.

high-level language A problem-oriented programming language using words, symbols, and command statements that closely resemble English-language statements. Each statement typically represents a series of computer instructions. Relatively easy to learn and use, a high-level language permits the execution of a number of subroutines through a simple command. Examples are BASIC, FORTRAN, PL/I, PASCAL, and COBOL.

A high-level language must be translated or compiled into machine language before it can be understood and processed by a computer. See also *assembler: low-level language*.

host computer The primary or controlling computer in a multicomputer network. Large-scale host computers typically are equipped with mass memory and a variety of peripheral devices, including magnetic tape, line printers, card readers, and possibly hard-copy devices. Host computers may be used to support, with their own memory and processing capabilities, not only graphics programs running on a CAD/CAM system but also related engineering analysis.

host-satellite system A CAD/CAM system configuration characterized by a graphic workstation with its own computer (typically holding the display file) that is connected to another, usually larger, computer for more extensive computation or data manipulation. The computer local to the display is a satellite to the larger host computer, and the two comprise a host-satellite system.

IC See *integrated circuit*.

IGES See *Initial Graphics Exchange Specification*.

inches per second (ips) Measure of the speed of a device (i.e., the number of inches of magnetic tape that can be processed per second, or the speed of a pen plotter).

Initial Graphics Exchange Specification (IGES) An interim CAD/CAM data base specification until the American National Standards Institute develops its own specification. IGES attempts to standardize communication of drawing and geometric product information between computer systems.

initialize   To set counters, switches, and addresses on a computer to zero or to other starting values at the beginning of, or at predetermined stages in, a program or routine.

input (data)   (1) The data supplied to a computer program for processing by the system. (2) The process of entering such data into the system.

input devices   A variety of devices (such as data tablets or keyboard devices) that allow the user to communicate with the CAD/CAM system, for example, to pick a function from many presented, to enter text and/or numerical data, to modify the picture shown on the CRT, or to construct the desired design.

input/output (I/O)   A term used to describe a CAD/CAM communications device as well as the process by which communications take place in a CAD/CAM system. An I/O device is one that makes possible communications between a device and a workstation operator or between devices on the system (such as workstations or controllers). By extension, input/output also denotes the process by which communications takes place. Input refers to the data transmitted to the processor for manipulation, and output refers to the data transmitted from the processor to the workstation operator or to another device (i.e., the results). Contrast with the other major parts of a CAD/CAM system: the CPU or central processing unit, which performs arithmetic and logical operations, and data storage devices (such as memories, disks, or tapes).

insert   To create and place entities, figures, or information on a CRT or into an emerging design on the display.

instruction set   (1) All the commands to which a CAD/CAM computer will respond. (2) The repertoire of functions the computer can perform.

integrated circuit (IC)   A tiny complex of electronic components and interconnections comprising a circuit that may vary in functional complexity from a simple logic gate to a microprocessor. An IC is usually packaged in a single substrate such as a slice of silicon. The complexity of most IC designs and the many repetitive elements have made computer-aided design an economic necessity. Also called a *chip*.

integrated system   A CAD/CAM system that integrates the entire product development cycle—analysis, design, and fabrication—so that all processes flow smoothly from concept to production.

intelligent work station/terminal   A workstation in a system that can perform certain data processing functions in a stand-alone mode, independent of another computer. Contains a built-in computer, usually a microprocessor or minicomputer, and dedicated memory.

interactive   Denotes two-way communications between a CAD/CAM system or workstation and its operators. An operator can modify or terminate a program and receive feedback from the system for guidance and verification. See also *feedback*.

interactive graphics system (IGS) or interactive computer graphics (ICG)   A CAD/CAM system in which the workstations are used interactively for computer-aided design and/or drafting, as well as for CAM, all under full operator control, and possibly also for text-processing, generation of charts and graphs, or computer-aided engineering. The designer (operator) can intervene to enter data and direct the course of any program, receiving immediate visual feedback via the CRT. Bilateral communication is provided between the system and the designer(s). Often used synonymously with *CAD*.

interface (*n*)   (1) A hardware and/or software link that enables two systems, or a system and its peripherals, to operate as a single, integrated system. (2) The input devices and visual feedback capabilities that allow bilateral communication between the designer and the system. The interface to a large computer can be a communications link (hardware) or a combination of software and hard-wired connections. An interface might be a portion of storage accessed by two or more programs or a link between two subroutines in a program.

I/O   See *input/output*.

ips   See *inches per second*.

jaggies   A CAD jargon term used to refer to straight or curved lines that appear to be jagged or sawtoothed on the CRT screen.

joystick   A CAD data-entering device employing a hand-controlled lever to manually enter the coordinates of various points on a design being digitized into the system.

key file   A disk file that provides user-defined definitions for a tablet menu. See *menu*.

kinematics   A computer-aided engineering (CAE) process for plotting or animating the motion of parts in a machine or a structure under design on the system. CAE simulation programs allow the motion of mechanisms to be studied for interference, acceleration, and force determinations while still in the design stage.

layering   A method of logically organizing data in a CAD/CAM data base. Functionally different classes of data (e.g., various graphic/geometric entities) are segregated on separate layers, each of which can be displayed individually or in any desired combination. Layering helps the designer distinguish among different kinds of data in creating a complex product such as a multilayered PC board or IC.

layers   User-defined logical subdivisions of data in a CAD/CAM data base that may be viewed on the CRT individually or overlaid and viewed in groups.

learning curve   A concept that projects the expected improvement in operator productivity over a period of time.

Usually applied in the first 1 to $1\frac{1}{2}$ years of a new CAD/CAM facility as part of a cost-justification study, or when new operators are introduced. An accepted tool of management for predicting manpower requirements and evaluating training programs.

library, graphics (or parts library) A collection of standard, often-used symbols, components, shapes, or parts stored in the CAD data base as templates or building blocks to speed up future design work on the system. Generally an organization of files under a common library name.

light pen A hand-held photosensitive CAD input device used on a refreshed CRT screen for identifying display elements, or for designating a location on the screen where an action is to take place.

line font See *font, line*.

line printer A CAD/CAM peripheral device used for rapid printing of data.

line smoothing An automated mapping capability for the interpolation and insertion of additional points along a linear entity yielding a series of shorter linear segments to generate a smooth curved appearance to the original linear component. The additional points or segments are created only for display purposes and are interpolated from a relatively small set of stored representative points. Thus, data storage space is minimized.

low-level language A programming language in which statements translate on a one-for-one basis. See also *machine language*.

machine A computer, CPU, or other processor.

machine instruction An instruction that a machine (computer) can recognize and execute.

machine language The complete set of command instructions understandable to and used directly by a computer when it performs operations.

macro (1) A sequence of computer instructions executable as a single command. A frequently used, multistep operation can be organized into a macro, given a new name, and remain in the system for easy use, thus shortening program development time. (2) In Computer-vision's IC design system, macro refers to macroexpansion of a cell. This system capability enables the designer to replicate the contents of a cell as primitives without the original cell grouping.

magnetic disk A flat circular plate with a magnetic surface on which information can be stored by selective magnetization of portions of the flat surface. Commonly used for temporary working storage during computer-aided design. See also *disk*.

magnetic tape A tape with a magnetic surface on which information can be stored by selective polarization of portions of the surface. Commonly used in CAD/CAM for off-line storage of completed design files and other archival material.

mainframe (computer) A large central computer facility.

main memory/storage The computer's general-purpose storage from which instructions may be executed and data loaded directly into operating registers.

mass storage Auxiliary large-capacity memory for storing large amounts of data readily accessible by the computer. Commonly a disk or magnetic tape.

matrix A 2D or 3D rectangular array (arrangement) of identical geometric or symbolic entities. A matrix can be generated automatically on a CAD system by specifying the building block entity and the desired locations. This process is used extensively in computer-aided electrical/electronic design.

memory Any form of data storage where information can be read and written. Standard memories include RAM, ROM, and PROM. See also *programmable read-only memory; random access memory; read-only memory; storage*.

menu A common CAD/CAM input device consisting of a checkerboard pattern of squares printed on a sheet of paper or plastic placed over a data tablet. These squares have been preprogrammed to represent a part of a command, a command, or a series of commands. Each square, when touched by an electronic pen, initiates the particular function or command indicated on that square. See also *data tablet, dynamic menuing*.

merge To combine two or more sets of related data into one, usually in a specified sequence. This can be done automatically on a CAD/CAM system to generate lists and reports.

microcomputer A smaller, lower-cost equivalent of a full-scale minicomputer. Includes a microprocessor (CPU), memory, and necessary interface circuits. Consists of one or more ICs (chips) comprising a chip set.

microprocessor The central control element of a microcomputer, implemented in a single integrated circuit. It performs instruction sequencing and processing, as well as all required computations. It requires additional circuits to function as a microcomputer. See *microcomputer*.

minicomputer A general-purpose, single processor computer of limited flexibility and memory performance.

mirroring A CAD design aid that automatically creates a mirror image of a graphic entity on the CRT by flipping the entity or drawing on its *x* or *y* axis.

mnemonic symbol An easily remembered symbol that assists the designer in communicating with the system (e.g., an abbreviation such as MPY for *multiply*).

model, geometric A complete, geometrically accurate 3D or 2D representation of a shape, a part, a geographic area, a plant or any part of it, designed on a CAD system and stored in the data base. A mathematical or analytic model of a physical system used to determine the response of that system to a stimulus or load. See *modeling, geometric*.

modeling, geometric   Constructing a mathematical or analytic model of a physical object or system for the purpose of determining the response of that object or system to a stimulus or load. First, the designer describes the shape under design using a geometric model constructed on the system. The computer then converts this pictorial representation on the CRT into a mathematical model later used for other CAD functions such as design optimization.

modeling, solid   A type of 3D modeling in which the solid characteristics of an object under design are built into the data base so that complex internal structures and external shapes can be realistically represented. This makes computer-aided design and analysis of solid objects easier, clearer, and more accurate than with wire-frame graphics.

modem   MOdulator-DEModulator, a device that converts digital signals to analog signals, and vice versa, for long-distance transmission over communications circuits such as telephone lines, dedicated wires, optical fiber, or microwave.

module   A separate and distinct unit of hardware or software that is part of a system.

mouse   A hand-held data-entering device used to position a cursor on a data tablet. See *cursor*.

multiprocessor   A computer whose architecture consists of more than one processing unit. See *central processing unit; microcomputer*.

network   An arrangement of two or more interconnected computer systems to facilitate the exchange of information in order to perform a specific function. For example, a CAD/CAM system might be connected to a mainframe computer to off-load heavy analytic tasks. Also refers to a piping network in computer-aided plant design.

numerical control   (NC) A technique of operating machine tools or similar equipment in which motion is developed in response to numerically coded commands. These commands may be generated by a CAD/CAM system on punched tapes or other communications media. Also, the processes involved in generating the data or tapes necessary to guide a machine tool in the manufacture of a part.

off-line   Refers to peripheral devices not currently connected to and under the direct control of the system's computer.

on-line   Refers to peripheral devices connected to and under the direct control of the system's computer, so that operator-system interaction, feedback, and output are all in real time.

operating system   A structured set of software programs that control the operation of the computer and associated peripheral devices in a CAD/CAM system, as well as the execution of computer programs and data flow to and from peripheral devices. May provide support for activities and programs such as scheduling, debugging, input/output control, accounting, editing, assembly, compilation, storage assignment, data management, and diagnostics. An operating system may assign task priority levels, support a file system, provide drives for I/O devices, support standard system commands or utilities for on-line programming, process commands, and support both networking and diagnostics.

output   The end result of a particular CAD/CAM process or series of processes. The output of a CAD cycle can be artwork and hard-copy lists and reports. The output of a total design-to-manufacturing CAD/CAM system can also include numerical control tapes for manufacturing.

overlay   A segment of code or data to be brought into the memory of a computer to replace existing code or data.

paint   To fill in a bounded graphic figure on a raster display using a combination of repetitive patterns or line fonts to add meaning or clarity. See *font, line*.

paper-tape punch/reader   A peripheral device that can read as well as punch a perforated paper tape generated by a CAD/CAM system. These tapes are the principal means of supplying data to an NC machine.

parallel processing   Executing more than one element of a single process concurrently on multiple processors in a computer system.

password protection   A security feature of certain CAD/CAM systems that prevents access to the system or to files within the system without first entering a password, i.e., a special sequence of characters.

PC board   See *printed circuit board*.

pen plotter   An electromechanical CAD output device that generates hard copy of displayed graphic data by means of a ballpoint pen or liquid ink. Used when a very accurate final drawing is required. Provides exceptional uniformity and density of lines, precise positional accuracy, as well as various user-selectable colors.

peripheral (device)   Any device, distinct from the basic system modules, that provides input to and/or output from the CPU. May include printers, keyboards, plotters, graphics display terminals, paper-tape reader/punches, analog-to-digital converters, disks, and tape drives.

permanent storage   A method or device for storing the results of a completed program outside the CPU—usually in the form of magnetic tape or punched cards.

photo plotter   A CAD output device that generates high-precision artwork masters photographically for PC board design and IC masks.

pixel   The smallest portion of a CRT screen that can be individually referenced. An individual dot on a display image. Typically, pixels are evenly spaced, horizontally and vertically, on the display.

plotter   A CAD peripheral device used to output for external use the image stored in the data base. Generally makes large, accurate drawings substantially better than what is displayed. Plotter types include pen, drum, electrostatic, and flatbed.

postprocessor   A software program or procedure that formats graphic or other data processed on the system for some other purpose. For example, a postprocessor might format cutter centerline data into a form that a machine controller can interpret.

precision   The degree of accuracy. Generally refers to the number of significant digits of information to the right of the decimal point for data represented within a computer system. Thus, the term denotes the degree of discrimination with which a design or design element can be described in the data base.

preplaced line (or bus)   A run (or line) between a set of points on a PC board layout that has been predefined by the designer and must be avoided by a CAD automatic routing program.

preprocessor   A computer program that takes a specific set of instructions from an external source and translates it into the format required by the system.

primitive   A design element at the lowest stage of complexity. A fundamental graphic entity. It can be a vector, a point, or a text string. The smallest definable object in a display processor's instruction set.

printed circuit (PC) board   A baseboard made of insulating materials and an etched copper-foil circuit pattern on which are mounted ICs and other components required to implement one or more electronic functions. PC boards plug into a rack or subassembly of electronic equipment to provide the brains or logic to control the operation of a computer, or a communications system, instrumentation, or other electronic systems. The name derives from the fact that the circuitry is connected not by wires but by copper-foil lines, paths, or traces actually etched onto the board surface. CAD/CAM is used extensively in PC board design, testing, and manufacture.

process simulation   A program utilizing a mathematical model created on the system to try out numerous process design iterations with real-time visual and numerical feedback. Designers can see on the CRT what is taking place at every stage in the manufacturing process. They can therefore optimize a process and correct problems that could affect the actual manufacturing process downstream.

processor   In CAD/CAM system hardware, any device that performs a specific function. Most often used to refer to the CPU. In software, it refers to a complex set of instruc-

tions to perform a general function. See also *central processing unit.*

productivity ratio   A widely accepted means of measuring CAD/CAM productivity (throughput per hour) by comparing the productivity of a design/engineering group before and after installation of the system or relative to some standard norm or potential maximum. The most common way of recording productivity is Actual Manual Hours/Actual CAD Hours, expressed as 4 : 1, 6 : 1, etc.

program   (*n*) A precise sequential set of instructions that direct a computer to perform a particular task or action or to solve a problem. A complete program includes plans for the transcription of data, coding for the computer, and plans for the absorption of the results into the system. (*v*) To develop a program. See also *computer program.*

Programmable Read-Only Memory (PROM)   A memory that, once programmed with permanent data or instructions, becomes a ROM. See *read-only memory.*

PROM   See *programmable read-only memory.*

prompt   A message or symbol generated automatically by the system, and appearing on the CRT, to inform the user of (a) a procedural error or incorrect input to the program being executed or (b) the next expected action, option(s), or input. See also *tutorial.*

puck   A hand-held, manually controlled input device that allows coordinate data to be digitized into the system from a drawing placed on the data tablet or digitizer surface. A puck has a transparent window containing cross hairs.

RAM   See *random access memory.*

random access memory (RAM)   A main memory read/write storage unit that provides the CAD/CAM operator direct access to the stored information. The time required to access any word stored in the memory is the same as for any other word.

raster display   A CAD workstation display in which the entire CRT surface is scanned at a constant refresh rate. The bright, flicker-free image can be selectively written and erased. Also called a digital TV display.

raster scan (video)   Currently, the dominant technology in CAD graphic displays. Similar to conventional television, it involves a line-by-line sweep across the entire CRT surface to generate the image. Raster-scan features include good brightness, accuracy, selective erase, dynamic motion capabilities, and the opportunity for unlimited color. The device can display a large amount of information without flicker, although resolution is not as good as with storage-tube displays.

read-only memory (ROM)   A memory that cannot be modified or reprogrammed. Typically used for control and execute programs. See also *programmable read-only memory.*

real time   Refers to tasks or functions executed so rapidly by a CAD/CAM system that the feedback at various stages in the process can be used to guide the designer in completing the task. Immediate visual feedback through the CRT makes possible real time, interactive operation of a CAD/CAM system.

rectangular array   Insertion of the same entity at multiple locations on a CRT using the system's ability to copy design elements and place them at user-specified intervals to create a rectangular arrangement or matrix. A feature of PC and IC design systems.

refresh (or vector refresh)   A CAD display technology that involves frequent redrawing of an image displayed on the CRT to keep it bright, crisp, and clear. Refresh permits a high degree of movement in the displayed image as well as high resolution. Selective erase or editing is possible at any time without erasing and repainting the entire image. Although substantial amounts of high-speed memory are required, large, complex images may flicker.

refresh rate   The rate at which the graphic image on a CRT is redrawn in a refresh display, i.e., the time needed for one refresh of the displayed image.

registration   The degree of accuracy in the positioning of one layer or overlay in a CAD display or artwork, relative to another layer, as reflected by the clarity and sharpness of the resulting image.

repaint   A CAD feature that automatically redraws a design displayed on the CRT.

resolution   The smallest spacing between two display elements that will allow the elements to be distinguished visually on the CRT. The ability to define very minute detail. For example, the resolution of Computervision's IC design system is one part in 33.5 million. As applied to an electrostatic plotter, resolution means the number of dots per square inch.

response time   The elapsed time from initiation of an operation at a workstation to the receipt of the results at that workstation. Includes transmission of data to the CPU, processing, file access, and transmission of results back to the initiating workstation.

restart   To resume a computer program interrupted by operator intervention.

restore   To bring back to its original state a design currently being worked on in a CAD/CAM system after editing or modification that the designer now wants to cancel or rescind.

resume   A feature of some application programs that allows the designer to suspend the data-processing operation at some logical break point and restart it later from that point.

reticle   The photographic plate used to create an IC mask. See also *photo plotter*.

rotate   To turn a displayed 2D or 3D construction about an axis through a predefined angle relative to the original position.

robotics   The use of computer-controlled manipulators or arms to automate a variety of manufacturing processes such as welding, material handling, painting and assembly.

ROM   See *read-only memory*.

routine   A computer program, or a subroutine in the main program. The smallest separately compilable source code unit. See *computer program: source*.

rubber banding   A CAD capability that allows a component to be tracked (dragged) across the CRT screen, by means of an electronic pen, to a desired location, while simultaneously stretching all related interconnections to maintain signal continuity. During tracking the interconnections associated with the component stretch and bend, providing an excellent visual guide for optimizing the location of a component to best fit into the flow of the PC board, or other entity, minimizing total interconnect length and avoiding areas of congestion.

satellite   A remote system connected to another, usually larger, host system. A satellite differs from a remote intelligent work station in that it contains a full set of processors, memory, and mass storage resources to operate independently of the host. See *host-satellite system*.

scale   (v) To enlarge or diminish the size of a displayed entity without changing its shape, i.e., to bring it into a user-specified ratio to its original dimensions. Scaling can be done automatically by a CAD system. (n) Denotes the coordinate system for representing an object.

scissoring   The automatic erasing of all portions of a design on the CRT that lie outside user-specified boundaries.

scroll   To automatically roll up, as on a spool, a design or text message on a CRT to permit the sequential viewing of a message or drawing too large to be displayed all at once on the screen. New data appear on the CRT at one edge as other data disappear at the opposite edge. Graphics can be scrolled up, down, left, or right.

selective erase   A CAD feature for deleting portions of a display without affecting the remainder or having to repaint the entire CRT display.

shape fill   The automatic painting-in of an area, defined by user-specified boundaries, on an IC or PC board layout, for example, the area to be filled by copper when the PC board is manufactured. Can be done on-line by CAD.

smoothing   Fitting together curves and surfaces so that a smooth, continuous geometry results.

software   The collection of executable computer programs including application programs, operating systems, and languages.

source   A text file written in a high-level language and containing a computer program. It is easily read and understood by people but must be compiled or assembled to generate machine-recognizable instructions. Also known as *source code*. See also *high-level language*.

source language   A symbolic language comprised of statements and formulas used in computer processing. It is translated into object language (object code) by an assembler or compiler for execution by a computer.

spline   A subset of a B-spline where in a sequence of curves is restricted to a plane. An interpolation routine executed on a CAD/CAM system automatically adjusts a curve by design iteration until the curvature is continuous over the length of the curve. See also *B-spline*.

storage   The physical repository of all information relating to products designed on a CAD/CAM system. It is typically in the form of a magnetic tape or disk. Also called *memory*.

storage tube   A common type of CRT that retains an image continuously for a considerable period of time without redrawing (refreshing). The image will not flicker regardless of the amount of information displayed. However, the display tends to be slow relative to raster scan, the image is rather dim, and no single element by itself can be modified or deleted without redrawing. See also *direct view storage tube*.

stretch   A CAD design/editing aid that enables the designer to automatically expand a displayed entity beyond its original dimensions.

string   A linear sequence of entities, such as characters or physical elements, in a computer-aided design.

stylus   A hand-held pen used in conjunction with a data table to enter commands and coordinate input into the system. Also called an *electronic pen*.

subfigure   A part or a design element that may be extracted from a CAD library and inserted intact into another part displayed on the CRT.

surface machining   Automatic generation of NC tool paths to cut 3D shapes. Both the tool paths and the shapes may be constructed using the mechanical design capabilities of a CAD/CAM system.

symbol   Any recognizable sign, mark, shape or pattern used as a building block for designing meaningful structures. A set of primitive graphic entities (line, point, arc, circle, text, etc.) that form a construction that can be expressed as one unit and assigned a meaning. Symbols may be combined or nested to form larger symbols and/or drawings. They can be as complex as an entire PC board or as simple as a single element, such as a pad. Symbols are commonly used to represent physical things. For example, a particular graphic shape may be used to represent a complete device or a certain kind of electrical component in a schematic. To simplify the preparation of drawings of piping systems and flow diagrams, standard symbols are used to represent various types of fittings and components in common use.

Symbols are also basic units in a language. The recognizable sequence of characters END may inform a compiler that the routine it is compiling is completed. In computer-aided mapping, a symbol can be a diagram, design, letter, character, or abbreviation placed on maps and charts, that, by convention or reference to a legend, is understood to stand for or represent a specific characteristic or feature. In a CAD environment, symbol libraries contribute to the quick maintenance, placement, and interpretation of symbols.

syntax   (1) A set of rules describing the structure of statements allowed in a computer language. To make grammatical sense, commands and routines must be written in conformity to these rules. (2) The structure of a computer command language, i.e., the English-sentence structure of a CAD/CAM command language, e.g., verb, noun, modifiers.

system   An arrangement of CAD/CAM data processing, memory, display, and plotting modules—coupled with appropriate software—to achieve specific objectives. The term CAD/CAM system implies both hardware and software. See also *operating system* (a purely software term).

tablet   An input device on which a designer can digitize coordinate data or enter commands into a CAD/CAM system by means of an electronic pen. See also *data tablet*.

task   (1) A specific project that can be executed by a CAD/CAM software program. (2) A specific portion of memory assigned to the user for executing that project.

template   The pattern of a standard, commonly used component or part that serves as a design aid. Once created, it can be subsequently traced instead of redrawn whenever needed. The CAD equivalent of a designer's template might be a standard part in the data-base library that can be retrieved and inserted intact into an emerging drawing on the CRT.

temporary storage   Memory locations for storing immediate and partial results obtained during the execution of a program on the system.

terminal   See *workstation*.

text editor   An operating system program used to create and modify text files on the system.

text file   A file stored in the system in text format that can be printed and edited on-line as required.

throughput   The number of units of work performed by a CAD/CAM system or a work station during a given period of time. A quantitative measure of system productivity.

time-sharing   The use of a common CPU memory and processing capabilities by two or more CAD/CAM terminals to execute different tasks simultaneously.

tool path   Centerline of the tip of an NC cutting tool as it moves over a part produced on a CAD/CAM system. Tool paths can be created and displayed interactively or automatically by a CAD/CAM system, and reformatted into NC tapes, by means of postprocessor, to guide or control machining equipment. See also *surface machining.*

track ball   A CAD graphics input device consisting of a ball recessed into a surface. The designer can rotate it in any direction to control the position of the cursor used for entering coordinate data into the system.

tracking   Moving a predefined (tracking) symbol across the surface of the CRT with a light pen or an electronic pen.

transform   To change an image displayed on the CRT by, for example, scaling, rotating, translating, or mirroring.

transformation   The process of transforming a CAD display image. Also the matrix representation of a geometric space.

translate   (1) To convert CAD/CAM output from one language to another, for example, by means of a postprocessor such as Computervision's IPC-to-Numerics Translator program. (2) Also, by an editing command, to move a CAD display entity a specified distance in a specified direction.

trap   The area that is searched around each digitize to find a hit on a graphics entity to be edited. See also *digitize.*

turnaround time   The elapsed time between the moment a task or project is input into the CAD/CAM system and the moment the required output is obtained.

turnkey   A CAD/CAM system for which the supplier/vendor assumes total responsibility for building, installing, and testing both hardware and software, and the training of user personnel. Also, loosely, a system that comes equipped with all the hardware and software required for a specific application or applications. Usually implies a commitment by the vendor to make the system work and to provide preventive and remedial maintenance of both hardware and software. Sometimes used interchangeably with stand-alone, although stand-alone applies more to system architecture than to terms of purchase.

tutorial   A characteristic of CAD/CAM systems. If the user is not sure how to execute a task, the system will show how. A message is displayed to provide information and guidance.

utilities   Another term for system capabilities and/or features that enable the user to perform certain processes.

vector   A quantity that has magnitude and direction and that, in CAD, is commonly represented by a directed line segment.

verification   (1) A system-generated message to a work station acknowledging that a valid instruction or input has been received. (2) The process of checking the accuracy, viability, and/or manufacturability of an emerging design on the system.

view port   A user-selected, rectangular view of a part, assembly, etc., that presents the contents of a window on the CRT. See also *window.*

window   A temporary, usually rectangular, bounded area on the CRT that is user-specified to include particular entities for modification, editing, or deletion.

wire-frame graphics   A computer-aided design technique for displaying a 3D object on the CRT screen as a series of lines outlining its surface.

wiring diagram   (1) Graphic representation of all circuits and device elements of an electrical system and its associated apparatus or any clearly defined functional portion of that system. A wiring diagram may contain not only wiring system components and wires but also nongraphic information such as wire number, wire size, color, function, component label, and pin number. (2) Illustration of device elements and their interconnectivity as distinguished from their physical arrangement. (3) Drawing that shows how to hook things up.

Wiring diagrams can be constructed, annotated, and documented on a CAD system.

word   A set of bits (typically 16 to 32) that occupies a single storage location and is treated by the computer as a unit. See also *bit.*

working storage   That part of the system's internal storage reserved for intermediate results (i.e., while a computer program is still in progress). Also called *temporary storage.*

workstation   The work area and equipment used for CAD/CAM operations. It is where the designer interacts (communicates) with the computer. Frequently consists of a CRT display and an input device as well as, possibly, a digitizer and a hard-copy device. In a distributed processing system, a work station would have local processing and mass storage capabilities. Also called a *terminal* or *design terminal.*

write   To transfer information from CPU main memory to a peripheral device, such as a mass storage device.

write-protect   A security feature in a CAD/CAM data storage device that prevents new data from being written over existing data.

zero   The origin of all coordinate dimensions defined in an absolute system as the intersection of the baselines of the x, y, and z axes.

zero offset   On an NC unit, this features allows the zero point on an axis to be relocated anywhere within a specified range, thus temporarily redefining the coordinate frame of reference.

zoom   A CAD capability that proportionately enlarges or reduces a figure displayed on a CRT screen.

4 Abbreviations for Use on Drawings and in Text— American National Standard

(Selected from ANSI/ASME Y1.1–1989)

A

absolute	ABS
accelerate	ACCEL
accessory	ACCESS.
account	ACCT
accumulate	ACCUM
actual	ACT.
adapter	ADPT
addendum	ADD.
addition	ADD.
adjust	ADJ
advance	ADV
after	AFT.
aggregate	AGGR
air condition	AIR COND
airplane	APL
allowance	ALLOW
alloy	ALY
alteration	ALT
alternate	ALT
alternating current	AC
altitude	ALT
aluminum	AL
American National Standard	AMER NATL STD
American wire gage	AWG
amount	AMT
ampere	AMP
amplifier	AMPL
anneal	ANL
antenna	ANT.
apartment	APT.
apparatus	APP
appendix	APPX
approved	APPD
approximate	APPROX
arc weld	ARC/W
area	A
armature	ARM.
armor plate	ARM-PL
army navy	AN
arrange	ARR.
artificial	ART.
asbestos	ASB
asphalt	ASPH
assemble	ASSEM
assembly	ASSY
assistant	ASST
associate	ASSOC
association	ASSN
atomic	AT
audible	AUD
audio frequency	AF
authorized	AUTH
automatic	AUTO
auto-transformer	AUTO TR
auxiliary	AUX
avenue	AVE
average	AVG
aviation	AVI
azimuth	AZ

B

Babbitt	BAB
back feed	BF
back pressure	BP
back to back	B to B
backface	BF
balance	BAL
ball bearing	BB
barometer	BAR
base line	BL
base plate	BP
bearing	BRG
bench mark	BM
bending moment	M
bent	BT
bessemer	BESS
between	BET.
between centers	BC
between perpendiculars	BP
bevel	BEV
bill of material	B/M
Birmingham wire gage	BWG
blank	BLK
block	BLK
blueprint	BP
board	BD
boiler	BLR
boiler feed	BF
boiler horsepower	BHP
boiling point	BP
bolt circle	BC
both faces	BF
both sides	BS
both ways	BW
bottom	BOT
bottom chord	BC
bottom face	BF
bracket	BRKT
brake	BK
brake horsepower	BHP
brass	BRS
brazing	BRZG
break	BRK
Brinell hardness	BH
British Standard	BR STD
British thermal unit	BTU
broach	BRO
bronze	BRZ
Brown & Sharpe (wire gage, same as AWG)	B&S
building	BLDG
bulkhead	BHD
burnish	BNH
bushing	BUSH.
button	BUT.

C

cabinet	CAB.
calculate	CALC
calibrate	CAL
cap screw	CAP SCR
capacity	CAP
carburetor	CARB
carburize	CARB
carriage	CRG
case harden	CH
cast iron	CI
cast steel	CS
casting	CSTG
castle nut	CAS NUT
catalogue	CAT.
cement	CEM
center	CTR
center line	CL
center of gravity	CG
center of pressure	CP
center to center	C to C
centering	CTR
chamfer	CHAM

change	CHG
channel	CHAN
check	CHK
check valve	CV
chord	CHD
circle	CIR
circular	CIR
circular pitch	CP
circumference	CIRC
clear	CLR
clearance	CL
clockwise	CW
coated	CTD
cold drawn	CD
cold-drawn steel	CDS
cold finish	CF
cold punched	CP
cold rolled	CR
cold-rolled steel	CRS
combination	COMB.
combustion	COMB
commercial	COML
company	CO
complete	COMPL
compress	COMP
concentric	CONC
concrete	CONC
condition	COND
connect	CONN
constant	CONST
construction	CONST
contact	CONT
continue	CONT
copper	COP.
corner	COR
corporation	CORP
correct	CORR
corrugate	CORR
cotter	COT
counter	CTR
counterbore	CBORE
counter clockwise	CCW
counterdrill	CDRILL
counterpunch	CPUNCH
countersink	CSK
coupling	CPLG
cover	COV
cross section	XSECT
cubic	CU
cubic foot	CU FT
cubic inch	CU IN.
current	CUR
customer	CUST
cyanide	CYN

D

decimal	DEC
dedendum	DED
deflect	DEFL
degree	(°) DEG
density	D
department	DEPT
design	DSGN
detail	DET
develop	DEV
diagonal	DIAG
diagram	DIAG
diameter	DIA
diametral pitch	DP
dimension	DIM.
discharge	DISCH
distance	DIST
division	DIV
double	DBL
dovetail	DVTL
dowel	DWL
down	DN
dozen	DOZ
drafting	DFTG
drawing	DWG
drill or drill rod	DR
drive	DR
drive fit	DF
drop	D
drop forge	DF
duplicate	DUP

E

each	EA
east	E
eccentric	ECC
effective	EFF
elbow	ELL
electric	ELEC
elementary	ELEM
elevate	ELEV
elevation	EL
engine	ENG
engineer	ENGR
engineering	ENGRG
entrance	ENT
equal	EQ
equation	EQ
equipment	EQUIP
equivalent	EQUIV
estimate	EST
exchange	EXCH
exhaust	EXH

existing	EXIST.
exterior	EXT
extra heavy	X HVY
extra strong	X STR
extrude	EXTR

F

fabricate	FAB
face to face	F to F
Fahrenheit	F
far side	FS
federal	FED.
feed	FD
feet	(′) FT
figure	FIG.
fillet	FIL
fillister	FIL
finish	FIN.
finish all over	FAO
flange	FLG
flat	F
flat head	FH
floor	FL
fluid	FL
focus	FOC
foot	(′) FT
force	F
forged steel	FST
forging	FORG
forward	FWD
foundry	FDRY
frequency	FREQ
front	FR
furnish	FURN

G

gage or gauge	GA
gallon	GAL
galvanize	GALV
galvanized iron	GI
galvanized steel	GS
gasket	GSKT
general	GEN
glass	GL
government	GOVT
governor	GOV
grade	GR
graduation	GRAD
graphite	GPH
grind	GRD
groove	GRV
ground	GRD

H

half-round	$\frac{1}{2}$ RD
handle	HDL
hanger	HGR
hard	H
harden	HDN
hardware	HDW
head	HD
headless	HDLS
heat	HT
heat-treat	HT TR
heavy	HVY
hexagon	HEX
high-pressure	HP
high-speed	HS
horizontal	HOR
horsepower	HP
hot rolled	HR
hot-rolled steel	HRS
hour	HR
housing	HSG
hydraulic	HYD

I

illustrate	ILLUS
inboard	INBD
inch	(") IN.
inches per second	IPS
inclosure	INCL
include	INCL
inside diameter	ID
instrument	INST
interior	INT
internal	INT
intersect	INT
iron	I
irregular	IREG

J

joint	JT
joint army-navy	JAN
journal	JNL
junction	JCT

K

key	K
keyseat	KST
Keyway	KWY

L

laboratory	LAB
laminate	LAM
lateral	LAT
left	L
left hand	LH
length	LG
length over all	LOA
letter	LTR
light	LT
line	L
locate	LOC
logarithm	LOG.
long	LG
lubricate	LUB
lumber	LBR

M

machine	MACH
machine steel	MS
maintenance	MAINT
malleable	MALL
malleable iron	MI
manual	MAN.
manufacture	MFR
manufactured	MFD
manufacturing	MFG
material	MATL
maximum	MAX
mechanical	MECH
mechanism	MECH
median	MED
metal	MET.
meter	M
miles	MI
miles per hour	MPH
millimeter	MM
minimum	MIN
minute	(') MIN
miscellaneous	MISC
month	MO
Morse taper	MOR T
motor	MOT
mounted	MTD
mounting	MTG
multiple	MULT
music wire gage	MWG

N

national	NATL
natural	NAT
near face	NF
near side	NS
negative	NEG
neutral	NEUT

nominal	NOM
normal	NOR
north	N
not to scale	NTS
number	NO.

O

obsolete	OBS
octagon	OCT
office	OFF.
on center	OC
opposite	OPP
optical	OPT
original	ORIG
outlet	OUT.
outside diameter	OD
outside face	OF
outside radius	OR
overall	OA

P

pack	PK
packing	PKG
page	P
paragraph	PAR.
part	PT
patent	PAT.
pattern	PATT
permanent	PERM
perpendicular	PERP
piece	PC
piece mark	PC MK
pint	PT
pitch	P
pitch circle	PC
pitch diameter	PD
plastic	PLSTC
plate	PL
plumbing	PLMB
point	PT
point of curve	PC
point of intersection	PI
point of tangent	PT
polish	POL
position	POS
potential	POT.
pound	LB
pounds per square inch	PSI
power	PWR
prefabricated	PREFAB
preferred	PFD
prepare	PREP
pressure	PRESS.

process	PROC	screw	SCR	thread	THD
production	PROD	second	SEC	threads per inch	TPI
profile	PF	section	SECT	through	THRU
propeller	PROP	semi-steel	SS	time	T
publication	PUB	separate	SEP	tolerance	TOL
push button	PB	set screw	SS	tongue & groove	T & G
		shaft	SFT	tool steel	TS
Q		sheet	SH	tooth	T
		shoulder	SHLD	total	TOT
quadrant	QUAD	side	S	transfer	TRANS
quality	QUAL	single	S	typical	TYP
quarter	QTR	sketch	SK		
		sleeve	SLV	**U**	
R		slide	SL		
		slotted	SLOT.	ultimate	ULT
radial	RAD	small	SM	unit	U
radius	R	socket	SOC	universal	UNIV
railroad	RR	space	SP		
ream	RM	special	SPL	**V**	
received	RECD	specific	SP		
record	REC	spot faced	SF	vacuum	VAC
rectangle	RECT	spring	SPG	valve	V
reduce	RED.	square	SQ	variable	VAR
reference line	REF L	standard	STD	versus	VS
reinforce	REINF	station	STA	vertical	VERT
release	REL	stationary	STA	volt	V
relief	REL	steel	STL	volume	VOL
remove	REM	stock	STK		
require	REQ	straight	STR	**W**	
required	REQD	street	ST		
return	RET.	structural	STR	wall	W
reverse	REV	substitute	SUB	washer	WASH.
revolution	REV	summary	SUM.	watt	W
revolutions per minute	RPM	support	SUP.	week	WK
right	R	surface	SUR	weight	WT
right hand	RH	symbol	SYM	west	W
rivet	RIV	system	SYS	width	W
Rockwell hardness	RH			wood	WD
roller bearing	RB			Woodruff	WDF
room	RM	**T**		working point	WP
root diameter	RD			working pressure	WP
root mean square	RMS	tangent	TAN.	wrought	WRT
rough	RGH	taper	TPR	wrought iron	WI
round	RD	technical	TECH		
		template	TEMP		
S		tension	TENS.	**Y**	
		terminal	TERM.		
schedule	SCH	thick	THK	yard	YD
schematic	SCHEM	thousand	M	year	YR
scleroscope hardness	SH				

5 Running and Sliding Fits[a]—American National Standard

RC 1   *Close sliding fits* are intended for the accurate location of parts which must assemble without perceptible play.

RC 2   *Sliding fits* are intended for accurate location, but with greater maximum clearance than class RC 1. Parts made to this fit move and turn easily but are not intended to run freely, and in the larger sizes may seize with small temperature changes.

RC 3   *Precision running fits* are about the closest fits which can be expected to run freely and are intended for precision work at slow speeds and light journal pressures, but they are not suitable where appreciable temperature differences are likely to be encountered.

RC 4   *Close running fits* are intended chiefly for running fits on accurate machinery with moderate surface speeds and journal pressures, where accurate location and minimum play are desired.

Basic hole system. Limits are in thousandths of an inch. See §12.8.
Limits for hole and shaft are applied algebraically to the basic size to obtain the limits of size for the parts.
Data in **boldface** are in accordance with ABC agreements.
Symbols H5, g5, etc., are hole and shaft designations used in ABC System.

Nominal Size Range, inches Over To	Class RC 1			Class RC 2			Class RC 3			Class RC 4		
	Limits of Clearance	Standard Limits		Limits of Clearance	Standard Limits		Limits of Clearance	Standard Limits		Limits of Clearance	Standard Limits	
		Hole H5	Shaft g4		Hole H6	Shaft g5		Hole H7	Shaft f6		Hole H8	Shaft f7
0–0.12	0.1 0.45	+0.2 −0	−0.1 −0.25	0.1 0.55	+0.25 −0	−0.1 −0.3	0.3 0.95	+0.4 −0	−0.3 −0.55	0.3 1.3	+0.6 −0	−0.3 −0.7
0.12–0.24	0.15 0.5	+0.2 −0	−0.15 −0.3	0.15 0.65	+0.3 −0	−0.15 −0.35	0.4 1.12	+0.5 −0	−0.4 −0.7	0.4 1.6	+0.7 −0	−0.4 −0.9
0.24–0.40	0.2 0.6	+0.25 −0	−0.2 −0.35	0.2 0.85	+0.4 −0	−0.2 −0.45	0.5 1.5	+0.6 −0	−0.5 −0.9	0.5 2.0	+0.9 −0	−0.5 −1.1
0.40–0.71	0.25 0.75	+0.3 −0	−0.25 −0.45	0.25 0.95	+0.4 −0	−0.25 −0.55	0.6 1.7	+0.7 −0	−0.6 −1.0	0.6 2.3	+1.0 −0	−0.6 −1.3
0.71–1.19	0.3 0.95	+0.4 −0	−0.3. −0.55	0.3 1.2	+0.5 −0	−0.3 −0.7	0.8 2.1	+0.8 −0	−0.8 −1.3	0.8 2.8	+1.2 −0	−0.8 −1.6
1.19–1.97	0.4 1.1	+0.4 −0	−0.4 −0.7	0.4 1.4	+0.6 −0	−0.4 −0.8	1.0 2.6	+1.0 −0	−1.0 −1.6	1.0 3.6	+1.6 −0	−1.0 −2.0
1.97–3.15	0.4 1.2	+0.5 −0	−0.4 −0.7	0.4 1.6	+0.7 −0	−0.4 −0.9	1.2 3.1	+1.2 −0	−1.2 −1.9	1.2 4.2	+1.8 −0	−1.2 −2.4
3.15–4.73	0.5 1.5	+0.6 −0	−0.5 −0.9	0.5 2.0	+0.9 −0	−0.5 −1.1	1.4 3.7	+1.4 −0	−1.4 −2.3	1.4 5.0	+2.2 −0	−1.4 −2.8
4.73–7.09	0.6 1.8	+0.7 −0	−0.6 −1.1	0.6 2.3	+1.0 −0	−0.6 −1.3	1.6 4.2	+1.6 −0	−1.6 −2.6	1.6 5.7	+2.5 −0	−1.6 −3.2
7.09–9.85	0.6 2.0	+0.8 −0	−0.6 −1.2	0.6 2.6	+1.2 −0	−0.6 −1.4	2.0 5.0	+1.8 −0	−2.0 −3.2	2.0 6.6	+2.8 −0	−2.0 −3.8
9.85–12.41	0.8 2.3	+0.9 −0	−0.8 −1.4	0.8 2.9	+1.2 −0	−0.8 −1.7	2.5 5.7	+2.0 −0	−2.5 −3.7	2.5 7.5	+3.0 −0	−2.5 −4.5
12.41–15.75	1.0 2.7	+1.0 −0	−1.0 −1.7	1.0 3.4	+1.4 −0	−1.0 −2.0	3.0 6.6	+2.2 −0	−3.0 −4.4	3.0 8.7	+3.5 −0	−3.0 −5.2

[a] From ANSI B4.1–1967 (R1994). For larger diameters, see the standard.

5   Running and Sliding Fits^a—American National Standard (continued)

RC 5 ⎫
RC 6 ⎭   *Medium running fits* are intended for higher running speeds, or heavy journal pressures, or both.

RC 7   *Free running fits* are intended for use where accuracy is not essential, or where large temperature variations are likely to be encountered, or under both these conditions.

RC 8 ⎫
RC 9 ⎭   *Loose running fits* are intended for use where wide commercial tolerances may be necessary, together with an allowance, on the external member.

Nominal Size Range, inches Over — To	Class RC 5			Class RC 6			Class RC 7			Class RC 8			Class RC 9		
	Limits of Clearance	Standard Limits		Limits of Clearance	Standard Limits		Limits of Clearance	Standard Limits		Limits of Clearance	Standard Limits		Limits of Clearance	Standard Limits	
		Hole H8	Shaft e7		Hole H9	Shaft e8		Hole H9	Shaft d8		Hole H10	Shaft c9		Hole H11	Shaft
0–0.12	0.6 1.6	+0.6 −0	−0.6 −1.0	0.6 2.2	+1.0 −0	−0.6 −1.2	1.0 2.6	+1.0 −0	−1.0 −1.6	2.5 5.1	+1.6 −0	−2.5 −3.5	4.0 8.1	+2.5 −0	−4.0 −5.6
0.12–0.24	0.8 2.0	+0.7 −0	−0.8 −1.3	0.8 2.7	+1.2 −0	−0.8 −1.5	1.2 3.1	+1.2 −0	−1.2 −1.9	2.8 5.8	+1.8 −0	−2.8 −4.0	4.5 9.0	+3.0 −0	−4.5 −6.0
0.24–0.40	1.0 2.5	+0.9 −0	−1.0 −1.6	1.0 3.3	+1.4 −0	−1.0 −1.9	1.6 3.9	+1.4 −0	−1.6 −2.5	3.0 6.6	+2.2 −0	−3.0 −4.4	5.0 10.7	+3.5 −0	−5.0 −7.2
0.40–0.71	1.2 2.9	+1.0 −0	−1.2 −1.9	1.2 3.8	+1.6 −0	−1.2 −2.2	2.0 4.6	+1.6 −0	−2.0 −3.0	3.5 7.9	+2.8 −0	−3.5 −5.1	6.0 12.8	+4.0 −0	−6.0 −8.8
0.71–1.19	1.6 3.6	+1.2 −0	−1.6 −2.4	1.6 4.8	+2.0 −0	−1.6 −2.8	2.5 5.7	+2.0 −0	−2.5 −3.7	4.5 10.0	+3.5 −0	−4.5 −6.5	7.0 15.5	+5.0 −0	−7.0 −10.5
1.19–1.97	2.0 4.6	+1.6 −0	−2.0 −3.0	2.0 6.1	+2.5 −0	−2.0 −3.6	3.0 7.1	+2.5 −0	−3.0 −4.6	5.0 11.5	+4.0 −0	−5.0 −7.5	8.0 18.0	+6.0 −0	−8.0 −12.0
1.97–3.15	2.5 5.5	+1.8 −0	−2.5 −3.7	2.5 7.3	+3.0 −0	−2.5 −4.3	4.0 8.8	+3.0 −0	−4.0 −5.8	6.0 13.5	+4.5 −0	−6.0 −9.0	9.0 20.5	+7.0 −0	−9.0 −13.5
3.15–4.73	3.0 6.6	+2.2 −0	−3.0 −4.4	3.0 8.7	+3.5 −0	−3.0 −5.2	5.0 10.7	+3.5 −0	−5.0 −7.2	7.0 15.5	+5.0 −0	−7.0 −10.5	10.0 24.0	+9.0 −0	−10.0 −15.0
4.73–7.09	3.5 7.6	+2.5 −0	−3.5 −5.1	3.5 10.0	+4.0 −0	−3.5 −6.0	6.0 12.5	+4.0 −0	−6.0 −8.5	8.0 18.0	+6.0 −0	−8.0 −12.0	12.0 28.0	+10.0 −0	−12.0 −18.0
7.09–9.85	4.0 8.6	+2.8 −0	−4.0 −5.8	4.0 11.3	+4.5 −0	−4.0 −6.8	7.0 14.3	+4.5 −0	−7.0 −9.8	10.0 21.5	+7.0 −0	−10.0 −14.5	15.0 34.0	+12.0 −0	−15.0 −22.0
9.85–12.41	5.0 10.0	+3.0 −0	−5.0 −7.0	5.0 13.0	+5.0 −0	−5.0 −8.0	8.0 16.0	+5.0 −0	−8.0 −11.0	12.0 25.0	+8.0 −0	−12.0 −17.0	18.0 38.0	+12.0 −0	−18.0 −26.0
12.41–15.75	6.0 11.7	+3.5 −0	−6.0 −8.2	6.0 15.5	+6.0 −0	−6.0 −9.5	10.0 19.5	+6.0 −0	−10.0 13.5	14.0 29.0	+9.0 −0	−14.0 −20.0	22.0 45.0	+14.0 −0	−22.0 −31.0

^{a} From ANSI B4.1–1967 (R1994). For larger diameters, see the standard.

6   Clearance Locational Fits[a]—American National Standard

LC   *Locational clearance fits* are intended for parts which are normally stationary but which can be freely assembled or disassembled They run from snug fits for parts requiring accuracy of location, through the medium clearance fits for parts such as spigots, to the looser fastener fits, where freedom of assembly is of prime importance.

Basic hole system. Limits are in thousandths of an inch. See §12.8.
Limits for hole and shaft are applied algebraically to the basic size to obtain the limits of size for the parts.
Data in **boldface** are in accordance with ABC agreements.
Symbols H6, H5, etc., are hole and shaft designations used in ABC System.

Nominal Size Range, inches Over To	Class LC 1 Limits of Clearance	Class LC 1 Standard Limits Hole H6	Class LC 1 Standard Limits Shaft h5	Class LC 2 Limits of Clearance	Class LC 2 Standard Limits Hole H7	Class LC 2 Standard Limits Shaft h6	Class LC 3 Limits of Clearance	Class LC 3 Standard Limits Hole H8	Class LC 3 Standard Limits Shaft h7	Class LC 4 Limits of Clearance	Class LC 4 Standard Limits Hole H10	Class LC 4 Standard Limits Shaft h9	Class LC 5 Limits of Clearance	Class LC 5 Standard Limits Hole H7	Class LC 5 Standard Limits Shaft g6
0–0.12	0 0.45	+0.25 −0	+0 −0.2	0 0.65	+0.4 −0	+0 −0.25	0 1	+0.6 −0	+0 −0.4	0 2.6	+1.6 −0	+0 −1.0	0.1 0.75	+0.4 −0	−0.1 −0.35
0.12–0.24	0 0.5	+0.3 −0	+0 −0.2	0 0.8	+0.5 −0	+0 −0.3	0 1.2	+0.7 −0	+0 −0.5	0 3.0	+1.8 −0	+0 −1.2	0.15 0.95	+0.5 −0	−0.15 −0.45
0.24–0.40	0 0.65	+0.4 −0	+0 −0.25	0 1.0	+0.6 −0	+0 −0.4	0 1.5	+0.9 −0	+0 −0.6	0 3.6	+2.2 −0	+0 −1.4	0.2 1.2	+0.6 −0	−0.2 −0.6
0.40–0.71	0 0.7	+0.4 −0	+0 −0.3	0 1.1	+0.7 −0	+0 −0.4	0 1.7	+1.0 −0	+0 −0.7	0 4.4	+2.8 −0	+0 −1.6	0.25 1.35	+0.7 −0	−0.25 −0.65
0.71–1.19	0 0.9	+0.5 −0	+0 −0.4	0 1.3	+0.8 −0	+0 −0.5	0 2	+1.2 −0	+0 −0.8	0 5.5	+3.5 −0	+0 −2.0	0.3 1.6	+0.8 −0	−0.3 −0.8
1.19–1.97	0 1.0	+0.6 −0	+0 −0.4	0 1.6	+1.0 −0	+0 −0.6	0 2.6	+1.6 −0	+0 −1	0 6.5	+4.0 −0	+0 −2.5	0.4 2.0	+1.0 −0	−0.4 −1.0
1.97–3.15	0 1.2	+0.7 −0	+0 −0.5	0 1.9	+1.2 −0	+0 −0.7	0 3	+1.8 −0	+0 −1.2	0 7.5	+4.5 −0	+0 −3	0.4 2.3	+1.2 −0	−0.4 −1.1
3.15–4.73	0 1.5	+0.9 −0	+0 −0.6	0 2.3	+1.4 −0	+0 −0.9	0 3.6	+2.2 −0	+0 −1.4	0 8.5	+5.0 −0	+0 −3.5	0.5 2.8	+1.4 −0	−0.5 −1.4
4.73–7.09	0 1.7	+1.0 −0	+0 −0.7	0 2.6	+1.6 −0	+0 −1.0	0 4.1	+2.5 −0	+0 −1.6	0 10	+6.0 −0	+0 −4	0.6 3.2	+1.6 −0	−0.6 −1.6
7.09–9.85	0 2.0	+1.2 −0	+0 −0.8	0 3.0	+1.8 −0	+0 −1.2	0 4.6	+2.8 −0	+0 −1.8	0 11.5	+7.0 −0	+0 −4.5	0.6 3.6	+1.8 −0	−0.6 −1.8
9.85–12.41	0 2.1	+1.2 −0	+0 −0.9	0 3.2	+2.0 −0	+0 −1.2	0 5	+3.0 −0	+0 −2.0	0 13	+8.0 −0	+0 −5	0.7 3.9	+2.0 −0	−0.7 −1.9
12.41–15.75	0 2.4	+1.4 −0	+0 −1.0	0 3.6	+2.2 −0	+0 −1.4	0 5.7	+3.5 −0	+0 −2.2	0 15	+9.0 −0	+0 −6	0.7 4.3	+2.2 −0	−0.7 −2.1

[a] From ANSI B4.1–1967 (R1994). For larger diameters, see the standard.

Nominal Size Range, inches Over To	Class LC 6 Limits of Clearance	Class LC 6 Hole H9	Class LC 6 Shaft f8	Class LC 7 Limits of Clearance	Class LC 7 Hole H10	Class LC 7 Shaft e9	Class LC 8 Limits of Clearance	Class LC 8 Hole H10	Class LC 8 Shaft d9	Class LC 9 Limits of Clearance	Class LC 9 Hole H11	Class LC 9 Shaft c10	Class LC 10 Limits of Clearance	Class LC 10 Hole H12	Class LC 10 Shaft	Class LC 11 Limits of Clearance	Class LC 11 Hole H13	Class LC 11 Shaft
0–0.12	0.3 / 1.9	+1.0 / −0	−0.3 / −0.9	0.6 / 3.2	+1.6 / −0	−0.6 / −1.6	1.0 / 3.6	+1.6 / −0	−1.0 / −2.0	2.5 / 6.6	+2.5 / −0	−2.5 / −4.1	4 / 12	+4 / −0	−4 / −8	5 / 17	+6 / −0	−5 / −11
0.12–0.24	0.4 / 2.3	+1.2 / −0	−0.4 / −1.1	0.8 / 3.8	+1.8 / −0	−0.8 / −2.0	1.2 / 4.2	+1.8 / −0	−1.2 / −2.4	2.8 / 7.6	+3.0 / −0	−2.8 / −4.6	4.5 / 14.5	+5 / −0	−4.5 / −9.5	6 / 20	+7 / −0	−6 / −13
0.24–0.40	0.5 / 2.8	+1.4 / −0	−0.5 / −1.4	1.0 / 4.6	+2.2 / −0	−1.0 / −2.4	1.6 / 5.2	+2.2 / −0	−1.6 / −3.0	3.0 / 8.7	+3.5 / −0	−3.0 / −5.2	5 / 17	+6 / −0	−5 / −11	7 / 25	+9 / −0	−7 / −16
0.40–0.71	0.6 / 3.2	+1.6 / −0	−0.6 / −1.6	1.2 / 5.6	+2.8 / −0	−1.2 / −2.8	2.0 / 6.4	+2.8 / −0	−2.0 / −3.6	3.5 / 10.3	+4.0 / −0	−3.5 / −6.3	6 / 20	+7 / −0	−6 / −13	8 / 28	+10 / −0	−8 / −18
071–1.19	0.8 / 4.0	+2.0 / −0	−0.8 / −2.0	1.6 / 7.1	+3.5 / −0	−1.6 / −3.6	2.5 / 8.0	+3.5 / −0	−2.5 / −4.5	4.5 / 13.0	+5.0 / −0	−4.5 / −8.0	7 / 23	+8 / −0	−7 / −15	10 / 34	+12 / −0	−10 / −22
1.19–1.97	1.0 / 5.1	+2.5 / −0	−1.0 / −2.6	2.0 / 8.5	+4.0 / −0	−2.0 / −4.5	3.0 / 9.5	+4.0 / −0	−3.0 / −5.5	5 / 15	+6 / −0	−5 / −9	8 / 28	+10 / −0	−8 / −18	12 / 44	+16 / −0	−12 / −28
1.97–3.15	1.2 / 6.0	+3.0 / −0	−1.2 / −3.0	2.5 / 10.0	+4.5 / −0	−2.5 / −5.5	4.0 / 11.5	+4.5 / −0	−4.0 / −7.0	6 / 17.5	+7 / −0	−6 / −10.5	10 / 34	+12 / −0	−10 / −22	14 / 50	+18 / −0	−14 / −32
3.15–4.73	1.4 / 7.1	+3.5 / −0	−1.4 / −3.6	3.0 / 11.5	+5.0 / −0	−3.0 / −6.5	5.0 / 13.5	+5.0 / −0	−5.0 / −8.5	7 / 21	+9 / −0	−7 / −12	11 / 39	+14 / −0	−11 / −25	16 / 60	+22 / −0	−16 / −38
4.73–7.09	1.6 / 8.1	+4.0 / −0	−1.6 / −4.1	3.5 / 13.5	+6.0 / −0	−3.5 / −7.5	6 / 16	+6 / −0	−6 / −10	8 / 24	+10 / −0	−8 / −14	12 / 44	+16 / −0	−12 / −28	18 / 68	+25 / −0	−18 / −43
7.09–9.85	2.0 / 9.3	+4.5 / −0	−2.0 / −4.8	4.0 / 15.5	+7.0 / −0	−4.0 / −8.5	7 / 18.5	+7 / −0	−7 / −11.5	10 / 29	+12 / −0	−10 / −17	16 / 52	+18 / −0	−16 / −34	22 / 78	+28 / −0	−22 / −50
9.85–12.41	2.2 / 10.2	+5.0 / −0	−2.2 / −5.2	4.5 / 17.5	+8.0 / −0	−4.5 / −9.5	7 / 20	+8 / −0	−7 / −12	12 / 32	+12 / −0	−12 / −20	20 / 60	+20 / −0	−20 / −40	28 / 88	+30 / −0	−28 / −58
12.41–15.75	2.5 / 12.0	+6.0 / −0	−2.5 / −6.0	5.0 / 20.0	+9.0 / −0	−5 / −11	8 / 23	+9 / −0	−8 / −14	14 / 37	+14 / −0	−14 / −23	22 / 66	+22 / −0	−22 / −44	30 / 100	+35 / −0	−30 / −65

[a] From ANSI B4.1–1967 (R1994). For larger diameters, see the standard.

LT   *Transition fits* are a compromise between clearance and interference fits, for application where accuracy of location is important, but either a small amount of clearance or interference is permissible.

Basic hole system. Limits are in thousandths of an inch. See §12.8.
Limits for hole and shaft are applied algebraically to the basic size to obtain the limits of size for the mating parts.
Data in **boldface** are in accordance with ABC agreements.
"Fit" represents the maximum interference (minus values) and the maximum clearance (plus values).
Symbols H7, js6, etc., are hole and shaft designations used in ABC System.

Nominal Size Range, inches Over To	Class LT 1 Fit	Class LT 1 Hole H7	Class LT 1 Shaft js6	Class LT 2 Fit	Class LT 2 Hole H8	Class LT 2 Shaft js7	Class LT 3 Fit	Class LT 3 Hole H7	Class LT 3 Shaft k6	Class LT 4 Fit	Class LT 4 Hole H8	Class LT 4 Shaft k7	Class LT 5 Fit	Class LT 5 Hole H7	Class LT 5 Shaft n6	Class LT 6 Fit	Class LT 6 Hole H7	Class LT 6 Shaft n7
0–0.12	−0.10	+0.4	+0.10	−0.2	+0.6	+0.2							−0.5	+0.4	+0.5	−0.65	+0.4	+0.65
	+0.50	−0	−0.10	+0.8	−0	−0.2							+0.15	−0	+0.25	+0.15	−0	+0.25
0.12–0.24	−0.15	+0.5	+0.15	−0.25	+0.7	+0.25							−0.6	+0.5	+0.6	−0.8	+0.5	+0.8
	+0.65	−0	−0.15	+0.95	−0	−0.25							+0.2	−0	+0.3	+0.2	−0	+0.3
0.24–0.40	−0.2	+0.6	+0.2	−0.3	+0.9	+0.3	−0.5	+0.6	+0.5	−0.7	+0.9	+0.7	−0.8	+0.6	+0.8	−1.0	+0.6	+1.0
	+0.8	−0	−0.2	+1.2	−0	−0.3	+0.5	−0	+0.1	+0.8	−0	+0.1	+0.2	−0	+0.4	+0.2	−0	+0.4
0.40–0.71	−0.2	+0.7	+0.2	−0.35	+1.0	+0.35	−0.5	+0.7	+0.5	−0.8	+1.0	+0.8	−0.9	+0.7	+0.9	−1.2	+0.7	+1.2
	+0.9	−0	−0.2	+1.35	−0	−0.35	+0.6	−0	+0.1	+0.9	−0	+0.1	+0.2	−0	+0.5	+0.2	−0	+0.5
0.71–1.19	−0.25	+0.8	+0.25	−0.4	+1.2	+0.4	−0.6	+0.8	+0.6	−0.9	+1.2	+0.9	−1.1	+0.8	+1.1	−1.4	+0.8	+1.4
	+1.05	−0	−0.25	+1.6	−0	−0.4	+0.7	−0	+0.1	+1.1	−0	+0.1	+0.2	−0	+0.6	+0.2	−0	+0.6
1.19–1.97	−0.3	+1.0	+0.3	−0.5	+1.6	+0.5	−0.7	+1.0	+0.7	−1.1	+1.6	+1.1	−1.3	+1.0	+1.3	−1.7	+1.0	+1.7
	+1.3	−0	−0.3	+2.1	−0	−0.5	+0.9	−0	+0.1	+1.5	−0	+0.1	+0.3	−0	+0.7	+0.3	−0	+0.7
1.97–3.15	−0.3	+1.2	+0.3	−0.6	+1.8	+0.6	−0.8	+1.2	+0.8	−1.3	+1.8	+1.3	−1.5	+1.2	+1.5	−2.0	+1.2	+2.0
	+1.5	−0	−0.3	+2.4	−0	−0.6	+1.1	−0	+0.1	+1.7	−0	+0.1	+0.4	−0	+0.8	+0.4	−0	+0.8
3.15–4.73	−0.4	+1.4	+0.4	−0.7	+2.2	+0.7	−1.0	+1.4	+1.0	−1.5	+2.2	+1.5	−1.9	+1.4	+1.9	−2.4	+1.4	+2.4
	+1.8	−0	−0.4	+2.9	−0	−0.7	+1.3	−0	+0.1	+2.1	−0	+0.1	+0.4	−0	+1.0	+0.4	−0	+1.0
4.73–7.09	−0.5	+1.6	+0.5	−0.8	+2.5	+0.8	−1.1	+1.6	+1.1	−1.7	+2.5	+1.7	−2.2	+1.6	+2.2	−2.8	+1.6	+2.8
	+2.1	−0	−0.5	+3.3	−0	−0.8	+1.5	−0	+0.1	+2.4	−0	+0.1	+0.4	−0	+1.2	+0.4	−0	+1.2
7.09–9.85	−0.6	+1.8	+0.6	−0.9	+2.8	+0.9	−1.4	+1.8	+1.4	−2.0	+2.8	+2.0	−2.6	+1.8	+2.6	−3.2	+1.8	+3.2
	+2.4	−0	−0.6	+3.7	−0	−0.9	+1.6	−0	+0.2	+2.6	−0	+0.2	+0.4	−0	+1.4	+0.4	−0	+1.4
9.85–12.41	−0.6	+2.0	+0.6	−1.0	+3.0	+1.0	−1.4	+2.0	+1.4	−2.2	+3.0	+2.2	−2.6	+2.0	+2.6	−3.4	+2.0	+3.4
	+2.6	−0	−0.6	+4.0	−0	−1.0	+1.8	−0	+0.2	+2.8	−0	+0.2	+0.6	−0	+1.4	+0.6	−0	+1.4
12.41–15.75	−0.7	+2.2	+0.7	−1.0	+3.5	+1.0	−1.6	+2.2	+1.6	−2.4	+3.5	+2.4	−3.0	+2.2	+3.0	−3.8	+2.2	+3.8
	+2.9	−0	−0.7	+4.5	−0	−1.0	+2.0	−0	+0.2	+3.3	−0	+0.2	+0.6	−0	+1.6	+0.6	−0	+1.6

a From ANSI B4.1-1967 (R1994). For larger diameters, see the standard.

8 Interference Locational Fits[a]—American National Standard

LN   *Locational interference fits* are used where accuracy of location is of prime importance and for parts requiring rigidity and alignment with no special requirements for bore pressure. Such fits are not intended for parts designed to transmit frictional loads from one part to another by virtue of the tightness of fit, as these conditions are covered by force fits.

Basic hole system. Limits are in thousandths of an inch. See §12.8.
Limits for hole and shaft are applied algebraically to the basic size to obtain the limits of size for the parts.
Data in **boldface** are in accordance with ABC agreements.
Symbols H7, p6, etc., are hole and shaft designations used in ABC System.

Nominal Size Range, inches Over To	Class LN 1 Limits of Interference	Standard Limits Hole H6	Shaft n5	Class LN 2 Limits of Interference	Standard Limits Hole H7	Shaft p6	Class LN 3 Limits of Interference	Standard Limits Hole H7	Shaft r6
0–0.12	0 / 0.45	+0.25 / −0	+0.45 / +0.25	0 / 0.65	+0.4 / −0	+0.65 / +0.4	0.1 / 0.75	+0.4 / −0	+0.75 / +0.5
0.12–0.24	0 / 0.5	+0.3 / −0	+0.5 / +0.3	0 / 0.8	+0.5 / −0	+0.8 / +0.5	0.1 / 0.9	+0.5 / 0	+0.9 / +0.6
0.24–0.40	0 / 0.65	+0.4 / −0	+0.65 / +0.4	0 / 1.0	+0.6 / −0	+1.0 / +0.6	0.2 / 1.2	+0.6 / −0	+1.2 / +0.8
0.40–0.71	0 / 0.8	+0.4 / −0	+0.8 / +0.4	0 / 1.1	+0.7 / −0	+1.1 / +0.7	0.3 / 1.4	+0.7 / −0	+1.4 / +1.0
0.71–1.19	0 / 1.0	+0.5 / −0	+1.0 / +0.5	0 / 1.3	+0.8 / −0	+1.3 / +0.8	0.4 / 1.7	+0.8 / −0	+1.7 / +1.2
1.19–1.97	0 / 1.1	+0.6 / −0	+1.1 / +0.6	0 / 1.6	+1.0 / −0	+1.6 / +1.0	0.4 / 2.0	+1.0 / −0	+2.0 / +1.4
1.97–3.15	0.1 / 1.3	+0.7 / −0	+1.3 / +0.7	0.2 / 2.1	+1.2 / −0	+2.1 / +1.4	0.4 / 2.3	+1.2 / −0	+2.3 / +1.6
3.15–4.73	0.1 / 1.6	+0.9 / −0	+1.6 / +1.0	0.2 / 2.5	+1.4 / −0	+2.5 / +1.6	0.6 / 2.9	+1.4 / −0	+2.9 / +2.0
4.73–7.09	0.2 / 1.9	+1.0 / −0	+1.9 / +1.2	0.2 / 2.8	+1.6 / −0	+2.8 / +1.8	0.9 / 3.5	+1.6 / −0	+3.5 / +2.5
7.09–9.85	0.2 / 2.2	+1.2 / −0	+2.2 / +1.4	0.2 / 3.2	+1.8 / −0	+3.2 / +2.0	1.2 / 4.2	+1.8 / −0	+4.2 / +3.0
9.85–12.41	0.2 / 2.3	+1.2 / −0	+2.3 / +1.4	0.2 / 3.4	+2.0 / −0	+3.4 / +2.2	1.5 / 4.7	+2.0 / −0	+4.7 / +3.5

[a] From ANSI B4.1–1967 (R1994). For larger diameters, see the standard.

9 Force and Shrink Fits[a]—American National Standard

FN 1 Light drive fits are those requiring light assembly pressures, and produce more or less permanent assemblies. They are suitable for thin sections or long fits, or in cast-iron external members.

FN 2 Medium drive fits are suitable for ordinary steel parts, or for shrink fits on light sections. They are about the tightest fits that can be used with high-grade cast-iron external members.

FN 3 Heavy drive fits are suitable for heavier steel parts or for shrink fits in medium sections.

FN 4 ⎫
FN 5 ⎭ Force fits are suitable for parts which can be highly stressed, or for shrink fits where the heavy pressing forces required are impractical.

Basic hole system. Limits are in thousandths of an inch. See §12.8.
Limits for hole and shaft are applied algebraically to the basic size to obtain the limits of size for the parts.
Data in **boldface** are in accordance with ABC agreements.
Symbols H7, s6, etc., are hole and shaft designations used in ABC System.

Nominal Size Range, inches Over To	Class FN 1 Limits of Interference	Class FN 1 Hole H6	Class FN 1 Shaft	Class FN 2 Limits of Interference	Class FN 2 Hole H7	Class FN 2 Shaft s6	Class FN 3 Limits of Interference	Class FN 3 Hole H7	Class FN 3 Shaft t6	Class FN 4 Limits of Interference	Class FN 4 Hole H7	Class FN 4 Shaft u6	Class FN 5 Limits of Interference	Class FN 5 Hole H8	Class FN 5 Shaft x7
0–0.12	0.05 / 0.5	+0.25 / −0	+0.5 / +0.3	**0.2 / 0.85**	**+0.4 / −0**	**+0.85 / +0.6**				**0.3 / 0.95**	**+0.4 / −0**	**+0.95 / +0.7**	0.3 / 1.3	+0.6 / −0	+1.3 / +0.9
0.12–0.24	0.1 / 0.6	+0.3 / −0	+0.6 / +0.4	**0.2 / 1.0**	**+0.5 / −0**	**+1.0 / +0.7**				**0.4 / 1.2**	**+0.5 / −0**	**+1.2 / +0.9**	0.5 / 1.7	+0.7 / −0	+1.7 / +1.2
0.24–0.40	0.1 / 0.75	+0.4 / −0	+0.75 / +0.5	**0.4 / 1.4**	**+0.6 / −0**	**+1.4 / +1.0**				**0.6 / 1.6**	**+0.6 / −0**	**+1.6 / +1.2**	0.5 / 2.0	+0.9 / −0	+2.0 / +1.4
0.40–0.56	0.1 / 0.8	+0.4 / −0	+0.8 / +0.5	**0.5 / 1.6**	**+0.7 / −0**	**+1.6 / +1.2**				**0.7 / 1.8**	**+0.7 / −0**	**+1.8 / +1.4**	0.6 / 2.3	+1.0 / −0	+2.3 / +1.6
0.56–0.71	0.2 / 0.9	+0.4 / −0	+0.9 / +0.6	**0.5 / 1.6**	**+0.7 / −0**	**+1.6 / +1.2**				**0.7 / 1.8**	**+0.7 / −0**	**+1.8 / +1.4**	0.8 / 2.5	+1.0 / −0	+2.5 / +1.8
0.71–0.95	0.2 / 1.1	+0.5 / −0	+1.1 / +0.7	**0.6 / 1.9**	**+0.8 / −0**	**+1.9 / +1.4**	0.8 / 2.1	+0.8 / −0	+2.1 / +1.6	**0.8 / 2.1**	**+0.8 / −0**	**+2.1 / +1.6**	1.0 / 3.0	+1.2 / −0	+3.0 / +2.2
0.95–1.19	0.3 / 1.2	+0.5 / −0	+1.2 / +0.8	**0.6 / 1.9**	**+0.8 / −0**	**+1.9 / +1.4**	1.0 / 2.6	+1.0 / −0	+2.6 / +2.0	**1.0 / 2.3**	**+0.8 / −0**	**+2.3 / +1.8**	1.3 / 3.3	+1.2 / −0	+3.3 / +2.5
1.19–1.58	0.3 / 1.3	+0.6 / −0	+1.3 / +0.9	**0.8 / 2.4**	**+1.0 / −0**	**+2.4 / +1.8**				**1.5 / 3.1**	**+1.0 / −0**	**+3.1 / +2.5**	1.4 / 4.0	+1.6 / −0	+4.0 / +3.0

[a] ANSI B4.1-1967 (R1994).

Nominal Size Range, inches (Over–To)	Class FN 1			Class FN 2			Class FN 3			Class FN 4			Class FN 5		
	Limits of Interference	Hole H6	Shaft	Limits of Interference	Hole H7	Shaft s6	Limits of Interference	Hole H7	Shaft t6	Limits of Interference	Hole H7	Shaft u6	Limits of Interference	Hole H8	Shaft x7
1.58–1.97	0.4 / 1.4	+0.6 / −0	+1.4 / −1.0	0.8 / 2.4	+1.0 / −0	+2.4 / +1.8	1.2 / 2.8	+1.0 / −0	+2.8 / +2.2	1.8 / 3.4	+1.0 / −0	+3.4 / +2.8	2.4 / 5.0	+1.6 / −0	+5.0 / +4.0
1.97–2.56	0.6 / 1.8	+0.7 / −0	+1.8 / +1.3	0.8 / 2.7	+1.2 / −0	+2.7 / +2.0	1.3 / 3.2	+1.2 / −0	+3.2 / +2.5	2.3 / 4.2	+1.2 / −0	+4.2 / +3.5	3.2 / 6.2	+1.8 / −0	+6.2 / +5.0
2.56–3.15	0.7 / 1.9	+0.7 / −0	+1.9 / +1.4	1.0 / 2.9	+1.2 / −0	+2.9 / +2.2	1.8 / 3.7	+1.2 / −0	+3.7 / +3.0	2.8 / 4.7	+1.2 / −0	+4.7 / +4.0	4.2 / 7.2	+1.8 / −0	+7.2 / +6.0
3.15–3.94	0.9 / 24	+0.9 / −0	+2.4 / +1.8	1.4 / 3.7	+1.4 / −0	+3.7 / +2.8	2.1 / 4.4	+1.4 / −0	+4.4 / +3.5	3.6 / 5.9	+1.4 / −0	+5.9 / +5.0	4.8 / 8.4	+2.2 / −0	+8.4 / +7.0
3.94–4.73	1.1 / 2.6	+0.9 / −0	+2.6 / +2.0	1.6 / 3.9	+1.4 / −0	+3.9 / +3.0	2.6 / 4.9	+1.4 / −0	+4.9 / +4.0	4.6 / 6.9	+1.4 / −0	+6.9 / +6.0	5.8 / 9.4	+2.2 / −0	+9.4 / +8.0
4.73–5.52	1.2 / 2.9	+1.0 / −0	+2.9 / +2.2	1.9 / 4.5	+1.6 / −0	+4.5 / +3.5	3.4 / 6.0	+1.6 / −0	+6.0 / +5.0	5.4 / 8.0	+1.6 / −0	+8.0 / +7.0	7.5 / 11.6	+2.5 / −0	+11.6 / +10.0
5.52–6.30	1.5 / 3.2	+1.0 / −0	+3.2 / +2.5	2.4 / 5.0	+1.6 / −0	+5.0 / +4.0	3.4 / 6.0	+1.6 / −0	+6.0 / +5.0	5.4 / 8.0	+1.6 / −0	+8.0 / +7.0	9.5 / 13.6	+2.5 / −0	+13.6 / +12.0
6.30–7.09	1.8 / 3.5	+1.0 / −0	+3.5 / +2.8	2.9 / 5.5	+1.6 / −0	+5.5 / +4.5	4.4 / 7.0	+1.6 / −0	+7.0 / +6.0	6.4 / 9.0	+1.6 / −0	+9.0 / +8.0	9.5 / 13.6	+2.5 / −0	+13.6 / +12.0
7.09–7.88	1.8 / 3.8	+1.2 / −0	+3.8 / +3.0	3.2 / 6.2	+1.8 / −0	+6.2 / +5.0	5.2 / 8.2	+1.8 / −0	+8.2 / +7.0	7.2 / 10.2	+1.8 / −0	+10.2 / +9.0	11.2 / 15.8	+2.8 / −0	+15.8 / +14.0
7.88–8.86	2.3 / 4.3	+1.2 / −0	+4.3 / +3.5	3.2 / 6.2	+1.8 / −0	+6.2 / +5.0	5.2 / 8.2	+1.8 / −0	+8.2 / +7.0	8.2 / 11.2	+1.8 / −0	+11.2 / +10.0	13.2 / 17.8	+2.8 / −0	+17.8 / +16.0
8.86–9.85	2.3 / 4.3	+1.2 / −0	+4.3 / +3.5	4.2 / 7.2	+1.8 / −0	+7.2 / +6.0	6.2 / 9.2	+1.8 / −0	+9.2 / +8.0	10.2 / 13.2	+1.8 / −0	+13.2 / +12.0	13.2 / 17.8	+2.8 / −0	+17.8 / +16.0
9.85–11.03	2.8 / 4.9	+1.2 / −0	+4.9 / +4.0	4.0 / 7.2	+2.0 / −0	+7.2 / +6.0	7.0 / 10.2	+2.0 / −0	+10.2 / +9.0	10.0 / 13.2	+2.0 / −0	+13.2 / +12.0	15.0 / 20.0	+3.0 / −0	+20.0 / +18.0
11.03–12.41	2.8 / 4.9	+1.2 / −0	+4.9 / +4.0	5.0 / 8.2	+2.0 / −0	+8.2 / +7.0	7.0 / 10.2	+2.0 / −0	+10.2 / +9.0	12.0 / 15.2	+2.0 / −0	+15.2 / +14.0	17.0 / 22.0	+3.0 / −0	+22.0 / +20.0
12.41–13.98	3.1 / 5.5	+1.4 / −0	+5.5 / +4.5	5.8 / 9.4	+2.2 / −0	+9.4 / +8.0	7.8 / 11.4	+2.2 / −0	+11.4 / +10.0	13.8 / 17.4	+2.2 / −0	+17.4 / +16.0	18.5 / 24.2	+3.5 / +0	+24.2 / +22.0

[a] From ANSI B4.1-1967 (R1994). For larger diameters, see the standard.

Dimensions are in millimeters.

Basic sizes		Tolerance grades[b]																	
Over	Up to and Including	IT01	IT0	IT1	IT2	IT3	IT4	IT5	IT6	IT7	IT8	IT9	IT10	IT11	IT12	IT13	IT14	IT15	IT16
0	3	0.0003	0.0005	0.0008	0.0012	0.002	0.003	0.004	0.006	0.010	0.014	0.025	0.040	0.060	0.100	0.140	0.250	0.400	0.600
3	6	0.0004	0.0006	0.001	0.0015	0.0025	0.004	0.005	0.008	0.012	0.018	0.030	0.048	0.075	0.120	0.180	0.300	0.480	0.750
6	10	0.0004	0.0006	0.001	0.0015	0.0025	0.004	0.006	0.009	0.015	0.022	0.036	0.058	0.090	0.150	0.220	0.360	0.580	0.900
10	18	0.0005	0.0008	0.0012	0.002	0.003	0.005	0.008	0.011	0.018	0.027	0.043	0.070	0.110	0.180	0.270	0.430	0.700	1.100
18	30	0.0006	0.001	0.0015	0.0025	0.004	0.006	0.009	0.013	0.021	0.033	0.052	0.084	0.130	0.210	0.330	0.520	0.840	1.300
30	50	0.0006	0.001	0.0015	0.0025	0.004	0.007	0.011	0.016	0.025	0.039	0.062	0.100	0.160	0.250	0.390	0.620	1.000	1.600
50	80	0.0008	0.0012	0.002	0.003	0.005	0.008	0.013	0.019	0.030	0.046	0.074	0.120	0.190	0.300	0.460	0.740	1.200	1.900
80	120	0.001	0.0015	0.0025	0.004	0.006	0.010	0.015	0.022	0.035	0.054	0.087	0.140	0.220	0.350	0.540	0.870	1.400	2.200
120	180	0.0012	0.002	0.0035	0.005	0.008	0.012	0.018	0.025	0.040	0.063	0.100	0.160	0.250	0.400	0.630	1.000	1.600	2.500
180	250	0.002	0.003	0.0045	0.007	0.010	0.014	0.020	0.029	0.046	0.072	0.115	0.185	0.290	0.460	0.720	1.150	1.850	2.900
250	315	0.0025	0.004	0.006	0.008	0.012	0.016	0.023	0.032	0.052	0.081	0.130	0.210	0.320	0.520	0.810	1.300	2.100	3.200
315	400	0.003	0.005	0.007	0.009	0.013	0.018	0.025	0.036	0.057	0.089	0.140	0.230	0.360	0.570	0.890	1.400	2.300	3.600
400	500	0.004	0.006	0.008	0.010	0.015	0.020	0.027	0.040	0.063	0.097	0.155	0.250	0.400	0.630	0.970	1.550	2.500	4.000
500	630	0.0045	0.006	0.009	0.011	0.016	0.022	0.030	0.044	0.070	0.110	0.175	0.280	0.440	0.700	1.100	1.750	2.800	4.400
630	800	0.005	0.007	0.010	0.013	0.018	0.025	0.035	0.050	0.080	0.125	0.200	0.320	0.500	0.800	1.250	2.000	3.200	5.000
800	1000	0.0055	0.008	0.011	0.015	0.021	0.029	0.040	0.056	0.090	0.140	0.230	0.360	0.560	0.900	1.400	2.300	3.600	5.600
1000	1250	0.0065	0.009	0.013	0.018	0.024	0.034	0.046	0.066	0.105	0.165	0.260	0.420	0.660	1.050	1.650	2.600	4.200	6.600
1250	1600	0.008	0.011	0.015	0.021	0.029	0.040	0.054	0.078	0.125	0.195	0.310	0.500	0.780	1.250	1.950	3.100	5.000	7.800
1600	2000	0.009	0.013	0.018	0.025	0.035	0.048	0.065	0.092	0.150	0.230	0.370	0.600	0.920	1.500	2.300	3.700	6.000	9.200
2000	2500	0.011	0.015	0.022	0.030	0.041	0.057	0.077	0.110	0.175	0.280	0.440	0.700	1.100	1.750	2.800	4.400	7.000	11.000
2500	3150	0.013	0.018	0.026	0.036	0.050	0.069	0.093	0.135	0.210	0.330	0.540	0.860	1.350	2.100	3.300	5.400	8.600	13.500

[a] From ANSI B4.2–1978 (R1994).
[b] IT Values for tolerance grades larger than IT16 can be calculated by using the formulas: IT17 = IT × 10, IT18 = IT13 × 10, etc.

Dimensions are in millimeters.

Basic Size		Loose Running			Free Running			Close Running			Sliding			Locational Clearance		
		Hole H11	Shaft c11	Fit	Hole H9	Shaft d9	Fit	Hole H8	f7	Fit	Hole H7	Shaft g6	Fit	Hole H7	Shaft h6	Fit
1	Max	1.060	0.940	0.180	1.025	0.980	0.070	1.014	0.994	0.030	1.010	0.998	0.018	1.010	1.000	0.016
	Min	1.060	0.880	0.060	1.000	0.955	0.020	1.000	0.984	0.006	1.000	0.992	0.002	1.000	0.994	0.000
1.2	Max	1.260	1.140	0.180	1.225	1.180	0.070	1.214	1.194	0.030	1.210	1.198	0.018	1.210	1.200	0.016
	Min	1.200	1.080	0.060	1.200	1.155	0.020	1.200	1.184	0.036	1.200	1.192	0.002	1.200	1.194	0.000
1.6	Max	1.660	1.540	0.180	1.625	1.580	0.070	1.614	1.594	0.030	1.610	1.598	0.018	1.610	1.600	0.016
	Min	1.600	1.480	0.060	1.600	1.555	0.020	1.600	1.584	0.006	1.600	1.592	0.002	1.600	1.594	0.000
2	Max	2.060	1.940	0.180	2.025	1.980	0.070	2.014	1.994	0.030	2.010	1.998	0.018	2.010	2.000	0.016
	Min	2.000	1.880	0.060	2.000	1.955	0.020	2.000	1.984	0.006	2.000	1.992	0.002	2.000	1.994	0.000
2.5	Max	2.560	2.440	0.180	2.525	2.480	0.070	2.514	2.494	0.030	2.510	2.498	0.018	2.510	2.500	0.016
	Min	2.500	2.380	0.060	2.500	2.455	0.020	2.500	2.484	0.006	2.500	2.492	0.002	2.500	2.494	0.000
3	Max	3.060	2.940	0.180	3.025	2.980	0.070	3.014	2.994	0.030	3.010	2.998	0.018	3.010	3.000	0.016
	Min	3.000	2.880	0.060	3.000	2.955	0.020	3.000	2.984	0.006	3.000	2.992	0.002	3.000	2.994	0.000
4	Max	4.075	3.930	0.220	4.030	3.970	0.090	4.018	3.990	0.040	4.012	3.996	0.024	4.012	4.000	0.020
	Min	4.000	3.855	0.070	4.000	3.940	0.030	4.000	3.978	0.010	4.000	3.988	0.004	4.000	3.992	0.000
5	Max	5.075	4.930	0.220	5.030	4.970	0.090	5.018	4.990	0.040	5.012	4.996	0.024	5.012	5.000	0.020
	Min	5.000	4.855	0.070	5.000	4.940	0.030	5.000	4.978	0.010	5.000	4.988	0.004	5.000	4.992	0.000
6	Max	6.075	5.930	0.220	6.030	5.970	0.090	6.018	5.990	0.040	6.012	5.996	0.024	6.012	6.000	0.020
	Min	6.000	5.855	0.070	6.000	5.940	0.030	6.000	5.978	0.010	6.000	5.988	0.004	6.000	5.992	0.000
8	Max	8.090	7.920	0.260	8.036	7.960	0.112	8.022	7.987	0.050	8.015	7.995	0.029	8.015	8.000	0.024
	Min	8.000	7.830	0.080	8.000	7.924	0.040	8.000	7.972	0.013	8.000	7.986	0.005	8.000	7.991	0.000
10	Max	10.090	9.920	0.260	10.036	9.960	0.112	10.022	9.987	0.050	10.015	9.995	0.029	10.015	10.000	0.024
	Min	10.000	9.830	0.080	10.000	9.924	0.040	10.000	9.972	0.013	10.000	9.986	0.005	10.000	9.991	0.000
12	Max	12.110	11.905	0.315	12.043	11.950	0.136	12.027	11.984	0.061	12.018	11.994	0.035	12.018	12.000	0.029
	Min	12.000	11.795	0.095	12.000	11.907	0.050	12.000	11.966	0.016	12.000	11.983	0.006	12.000	11.989	0.000
16	Max	16.110	15.905	0.315	16.043	15.950	0.136	16.027	15.984	0.061	16.018	15.994	0.035	16.018	16.000	0.029
	Min	16.000	15.795	0.095	16.000	15.907	0.050	16.000	15.966	0.016	16.000	15.983	0.006	16.000	15.989	0.000
20	Max	20.130	19.890	0.370	20.052	19.935	0.169	20.033	19.980	0.074	20.021	19.993	0.041	20.021	20.000	0.034
	Min	20.000	19.760	0.110	20.000	19.883	0.065	20.000	19.959	0.020	20.000	19.980	0.007	20.000	19.987	0.000
25	Max	25.130	24.890	0.370	25.052	24.935	0.169	25.033	24.980	0.074	25.021	24.993	0.041	25.021	25.000	0.034
	Min	25.000	24.760	0.110	25.000	24.883	0.065	25.000	24.959	0.020	25.000	24.980	0.007	25.000	24.987	0.000
30	Max	30.130	29.890	0.370	30.052	29.935	0.169	30.033	29.980	0.074	30.021	29.993	0.041	30.021	30.000	0.034
	Min	30.000	29.760	0.110	30.000	29.883	0.065	30.000	29.959	0.020	30.000	29.980	0.007	30.000	29.987	0.000

[a] From ANSI B4.2–1978 (R1994). For description of preferred fits, see Table 12.2.

Dimensions are in millimeters.

Basic Size		Loose Running			Free Running			Close Running			Sliding			Locational Clearance		
		Hole H11	Shaft c11	Fit	Hole H9	Shaft d9	Fit	Hole H8	Shaft f7	Fit	Hole H7	Shaft g6	Fit	Hole H7	Shaft h6	Fit
40	Max	40.160	39.880	0.440	40.062	39.920	0.204	40.039	39.975	0.089	40.025	39.991	0.050	40.025	40.000	0.041
	Min	40.000	39.720	0.120	40.000	39.858	0.080	40.000	39.950	0.025	40.000	39.975	0.009	40.000	39.984	0.000
50	Max	50.160	49.870	0.450	50.062	49.920	0.204	50.039	49.975	0.089	50.025	49.991	0.050	50.025	50.000	0.041
	Min	50.000	49.710	0.130	50.000	49.858	0.080	50.000	49.950	0.025	50.000	49.975	0.009	50.000	49.984	0.000
60	Max	60.190	59.860	0.520	60.074	59.900	0.248	60.046	59.970	0.106	60.030	59.990	0.059	60.030	60.000	0.049
	Min	60.000	59.670	0.140	60.000	59.826	0.100	60.000	59.940	0.030	60.000	59.971	0.010	60.000	59.981	0.000
80	Max	80.190	79.950	0.530	80.074	79.900	0.248	80.046	79.970	0.106	80.030	79.990	0.059	80.030	80.000	0.049
	Min	80.000	79.660	0.150	80.000	79.826	0.100	80.000	79.940	0.030	80.000	79.971	0.010	80.000	79.981	0.000
100	Max	100.220	99.830	0.610	100.087	99.880	0.294	100.054	99.964	0.125	100.035	99.988	0.069	100.035	100.000	0.057
	Min	100.000	99.610	0.170	100.000	99.793	0.120	100.000	99.929	0.036	100.000	99.966	0.012	100.000	99.978	0.000
120	Max	120.220	119.820	0.620	120.087	119.880	0.294	120.054	119.964	0.125	120.035	119.988	0.069	120.035	120.000	0.057
	Min	120.000	119.600	0.180	120.000	119.793	0.120	120.000	119.929	0.036	120.000	119.966	0.012	120.000	119.978	0.000
160	Max	160.250	159.790	0.710	160.100	159.855	0.345	160.063	159.957	0.146	160.040	159.986	0.079	160.040	160.000	0.065
	Min	160.000	159.540	0.210	160.000	159.755	0.145	160.000	159.917	0.043	160.000	159.961	0.014	160.000	159.975	0.000
200	Max	200.290	199.760	0.820	200.115	199.830	0.400	200.072	199.950	0.168	200.046	199.985	0.090	200.046	200.000	0.075
	Min	200.000	199.470	0.240	200.000	199.715	0.170	200.000	199.904	0.050	200.000	199.956	0.015	200.000	199.971	0.000
250	Max	250.290	249.720	0.860	250.115	249.830	0.400	250.072	249.950	0.168	250.046	249.985	0.090	250.046	250.000	0.075
	Min	250.000	249.430	0.280	250.000	249.715	0.170	250.000	249.904	0.050	250.000	249.956	0.015	250.000	249.971	0.000
300	Max	300.320	299.670	0.970	300.130	299.810	0.450	300.081	299.944	0.189	300.052	299.983	0.101	300.052	300.000	0.084
	Min	300.000	299.350	0.330	300.000	299.680	0.190	300.000	299.892	0.056	300.000	299.951	0.017	300.000	299.968	0.000
400	Max	400.360	399.600	1.120	400.140	399.790	0.490	400.089	399.938	0.208	400.057	399.982	0.111	400.057	400.000	0.093
	Min	400.000	399.240	0.400	400.000	399.650	0.210	400.000	399.881	0.062	400.000	399.946	0.018	400.000	399.964	0.000
500	Max	500.400	499.520	1.280	500.155	499.770	0.540	500.097	499.932	0.228	500.063	499.980	0.123	500.063	500.000	0.103
	Min	500.000	499.120	0.480	500.000	499.615	0.230	500.000	499.869	0.068	500.000	499.940	0.020	500.000	499.960	0.000

a From ANSI B4.2–1978 (R1994). For description of preferred fits, see Table 12.2.

12 Preferred Metric Hole Basis Transition and Interference Fits[a]—American National Standard

Dimensions are in millimeters.

Basic Size		Locational Transn. Hole H7	Shaft k6	Fit	Locational Transn. Hole H7	Shaft n6	Fit	Locational Interf. Hole H7	Shaft p6	Fit	Medium Drive Hole H7	Shaft s6	Fit	Force Hole H7	Shaft u6	Fit
1	Max	1.010	1.006	0.010	1.010	1.010	0.006	1.010	1.012	0.004	1.010	1.020	−0.004	1.010	1.024	−0.008
	Min	1.000	1.000	−0.006	1.000	1.004	−0.010	1.000	1.006	−0.012	1.000	1.014	−0.020	1.000	1.018	−0.024
1.2	Max	1.210	1.206	0.010	1.210	1.210	0.006	1.210	1.212	0.004	1.210	1.220	−0.004	1.210	1.224	−0.008
	Min	1.200	1.200	−0.006	1.200	1.204	−0.010	1.200	1.206	−0.012	1.200	1.214	−0.020	1.200	1.218	−0.024
1.6	Max	1.610	1.606	0.010	1.610	1.610	0.006	1.610	1.612	0.004	1.610	1.620	−0.004	1.610	1.624	−0.008
	Min	1.600	1.600	−0.006	1.600	1.604	−0.010	1.600	1.606	−0.012	1.600	1.614	−0.020	1.600	1.618	−0.024
2	Max	2.010	2.006	0.010	2.010	2.010	0.006	2.010	2.012	0.004	2.010	2.020	−0.004	2.010	2.024	−0.008
	Min	2.000	2.000	−0.006	2.000	2.004	−0.010	2.000	2.006	−0.012	2.000	2.014	−0.020	2.000	2.018	−0.024
2.5	Max	2.510	2.506	0.010	2.510	2.510	0.006	2.510	2.512	0.004	2.510	2.520	−0.004	2.510	2.524	−0.008
	Min	2.500	2.500	−0.006	2.500	2.504	−0.010	2.500	2.506	−0.012	2.500	2.514	−0.020	2.500	2.518	−0.024
3	Max	3.010	3.006	0.010	3.010	3.010	0.006	3.010	3.012	0.004	3.010	3.020	−0.004	3.010	3.024	−0.008
	Min	3.000	3.000	−0.006	3.000	3.004	−0.010	3.000	3.006	−0.012	3.000	3.014	−0.020	3.000	3.018	−0.024
4	Max	4.012	4.009	0.011	4.012	4.016	0.004	4.012	4.020	0.000	4.012	4.027	−0.007	4.012	4.031	−0.011
	Min	4.000	4.001	−0.009	4.000	4.008	−0.016	4.000	4.012	−0.020	4.000	4.019	−0.027	4.000	4.023	−0.031
5	Max	5.012	5.009	0.011	5.012	5.016	0.004	5.012	5.020	0.000	5.012	5.027	−0.007	5.012	5.031	−0.011
	Min	5.000	5.001	−0.009	5.000	5.008	−0.016	5.000	5.012	−0.020	5.000	5.019	−0.027	5.000	5.023	−0.031
6	Max	6.012	6.009	0.011	6.012	6.016	0.004	6.012	6.020	0.000	6.012	6.027	−0.007	6.012	6.031	−0.011
	Min	6.000	6.001	−0.009	6.000	6.008	−0.016	6.000	6.012	−0.020	6.000	6.019	−0.027	6.000	6.023	−0.031
8	Max	8.015	8.010	0.014	8.015	8.019	0.005	8.015	8.024	0.000	8.015	8.032	−0.008	8.015	8.037	−0.013
	Min	8.000	8.001	−0.010	8.000	8.010	−0.019	8.000	8.015	−0.024	8.000	8.023	−0.032	8.000	8.028	−0.037
10	Max	10.015	10.010	0.014	10.015	10.019	0.005	10.015	10.024	0.000	10.015	10.032	−0.008	10.015	10.037	−0.013
	Min	10.000	10.001	−0.010	10.000	10.010	−0.019	10.000	10.015	−0.024	10.000	10.023	−0.032	10.000	10.028	−0.037
12	Max	12.018	12.012	0.017	12.018	12.023	0.006	12.018	12.029	0.000	12.018	12.039	−0.010	12.018	12.044	−0.015
	Min	12.000	12.001	−0.012	12.000	12.012	−0.023	12.000	12.018	−0.029	12.000	12.028	−0.039	12.000	12.033	−0.044
16	Max	16.018	16.012	0.017	16.018	16.023	0.006	16.018	16.029	0.000	16.018	16.039	−0.010	16.018	16.044	−0.015
	Min	16.000	16.001	−0.012	16.000	16.012	−0.023	16.000	16.018	−0.029	16.000	16.028	−0.039	16.000	16.033	−0.044
20	Max	20.021	20.015	0.019	20.021	20.028	0.006	20.021	20.035	−0.001	20.021	20.048	−0.014	20.021	20.054	−0.020
	Min	20.000	20.002	−0.015	20.000	20.015	−0.028	20.000	20.022	−0.035	20.000	20.035	−0.048	20.000	20.041	−0.054
25	Max	25.021	25.015	0.019	25.021	25.028	0.006	25.021	25.035	−0.001	25.021	25.048	−0.014	25.021	25.061	−0.027
	Min	25.000	25.002	−0.015	25.000	25.015	−0.028	25.000	25.022	−0.035	25.000	25.035	−0.048	25.000	25.048	−0.061
30	Max	30.021	30.015	0.019	30.021	30.028	0.006	30.021	30.035	−0.001	30.021	30.048	−0.014	30.021	30.061	−0.027
	Min	30.000	30.002	−0.015	30.000	30.015	−0.028	30.000	30.022	−0.035	30.000	30.035	−0.048	30.000	30.048	−0.061

[a] From ANSI B4.2–1978 (R1994).

Dimensions are in millimeters.

Basic Size		Locational Transn.			Locational Transn.			Locational Interf.			Medium Drive			Force		
		Hole H7	Shaft k6	Fit	Hole H7	Shaft n6	Fit	Hole H7	Shaft p6	Fit	Hole H7	Shaft s6	Fit	Hole H7	Shaft u6	Fit
40	Max	40.025	40.018	0.023	40.025	40.033	0.08	40.025	40.042	−0.001	40.025	40.059	−0.018	40.025	40.076	−0.035
	Min	40.000	40.002	−0.018	40.000	40.017	−0.033	40.000	40.026	−0.042	40.000	40.043	−0.059	40.000	40.060	−0.076
50	Max	50.025	50.018	0.023	50.025	50.033	0.008	50.025	50.042	−0.001	50.025	50.059	−0.018	50.025	50.086	−0.045
	Min	50.000	50.002	−0.018	50.000	50.017	−0.033	50.000	50.026	−0.042	50.000	50.043	−0.059	50.000	50.070	−0.086
60	Max	60.030	60.021	0.028	60.030	60.039	0.010	60.030	60.051	−0.002	60.030	60.072	−0.023	60.030	60.106	−0.057
	Min	60.000	60.002	−0.021	60.000	60.020	−0.039	60.000	60.032	−0.051	60.000	60.053	−0.072	60.000	60.087	−0.106
80	Max	80.030	80.021	0.028	80.030	80.039	0.010	80.030	80.051	−0.002	80.030	80.078	−0.029	80.030	80.121	−0.072
	Min	80.000	80.002	−0.021	80.000	80.020	−0.039	80.000	80.032	−0.051	80.000	80.059	−0.078	80.000	80.102	−0.121
100	Max	100.035	100.025	0.032	100.035	100.045	0.012	100.035	100.059	−0.002	100.035	100.093	−0.036	100.035	100.146	−0.089
	Min	100.000	100.003	−0.025	100.000	100.023	−0.045	100.000	100.037	−0.059	100.000	100.071	−0.093	100.000	100.124	−0.146
120	Max	120.035	120.025	0.032	120.035	120.045	0.012	120.035	120.059	−0.002	120.035	120.101	−0.044	120.035	120.166	−0.109
	Min	120.000	120.003	−0.025	120.000	120.023	−0.045	120.000	120.037	−0.059	120.000	120.079	−0.101	120.000	120.144	−0.166
160	Max	160.040	160.028	0.037	160.040	160.052	0.013	160.040	160.068	−0.003	160.040	160.125	−0.060	160.040	160.215	−0.150
	Min	160.000	160.003	−0.028	160.000	160.027	−0.052	160.000	160.043	−0.068	160.000	160.100	−0.125	160.000	160.190	−0.215
200	Max	200.046	200.033	0.042	200.046	200.060	0.015	200.046	200.079	−0.004	200.046	200.151	−0.076	200.046	200.265	−0.190
	Min	200.000	200.004	−0.033	200.000	200.031	−0.060	200.000	200.050	−0.079	200.000	200.122	−0.151	200.000	200.236	−0.265
250	Max	250.046	250.033	0.042	250.046	250.060	0.015	250.046	250.079	−0.004	250.046	250.169	−0.094	250.046	250.313	−0.238
	Min	250.000	250.004	−0.033	250.000	250.031	−0.060	250.000	250.050	−0.079	250.000	250.140	−0.169	250.000	250.284	−0.313
300	Max	300.052	300.036	0.048	300.052	300.066	0.018	300.052	300.088	−0.004	300.052	300.202	−0.118	300.052	300.382	−0.298
	Min	300.000	300.004	−0.036	300.000	300.034	−0.066	300.000	300.056	−0.088	300.000	300.170	−0.202	300.000	300.350	−0.382
400	Max	400.057	400.040	0.053	400.057	400.073	0.020	400.057	400.098	−0.005	400.057	400.244	−0.151	400.057	400.471	−0.378
	Min	400.000	400.004	−0.040	400.000	400.037	−0.073	400.000	400.062	−0.098	400.000	400.208	−0.244	400.000	400.435	−0.471
500	Max	500.063	500.045	0.058	500.063	500.080	0.023	500.063	500.108	−0.005	500.063	500.292	−0.189	500.063	500.580	−0.477
	Min	500.000	500.005	−0.045	500.000	500.040	−0.080	500.000	500.068	−0.108	500.000	500.252	−0.292	500.000	500.540	−0.580

[a] From ANSI B4.2–1978 (R1994).

Dimensions are in millimeters.

Basic Size		Loose Running			Free Running			Close Running			Sliding			Locational Clearance		
		Hole C11	Shaft h11	Fit	Hole D9	Shaft h9	Fit	Hole F8	Shaft h7	Fit	Hole G7	Shaft h6	Fit	Hole H7	Shaft h6	Fit
1	Max	1.120	1.000	0.180	1.045	1.000	0.070	1.020	1.000	0.030	1.012	1.000	0.018	1.010	1.000	0.016
	Min	1.060	0.940	0.060	1.020	0.975	0.020	1.006	0.990	0.006	1.002	0.994	0.002	1.000	0.994	0.000
1.2	Max	1.320	1.200	0.180	1.245	1.200	0.070	1.220	1.200	0.030	1.212	1.200	0.018	1.210	1.200	0.016
	Min	1.260	1.140	0.060	1.220	1.175	0.020	1.206	1.190	0.006	1.202	1.194	0.002	1.200	1.194	0.000
1.6	Max	1.720	1.600	0.180	1.645	1.600	0.070	1.620	1.600	0.030	1.612	1.600	0.018	1.610	1.600	0.016
	Min	1.660	1.540	0.060	1.620	1.575	0.020	1.606	1.590	0.006	1.602	1.594	0.002	1.600	1.594	0.000
2	Max	2.120	2.000	0.180	2.045	2.000	0.070	2.020	2.000	0.030	2.012	2.000	0.018	2.010	2.000	0.016
	Min	2.060	1.940	0.060	2.020	1.975	0.020	2.006	1.990	0.006	2.002	1.994	0.002	2.000	1.994	0.000
2.5	Max	2.620	2.500	0.180	2.545	2.500	0.070	2.520	2.500	0.030	2.512	2.500	0.018	2.510	2.500	0.016
	Min	2.560	2.440	0.060	2.520	2.475	0.020	2.506	2.490	0.006	2.502	2.494	0.002	2.500	2.494	0.000
3	Max	3.120	3.000	0.180	3.045	3.000	0.070	3.020	3.000	0.030	3.012	3.000	0.018	3.010	3.000	0.016
	Min	3.060	2.940	0.060	3.020	2.975	0.020	3.006	2.990	0.006	3.002	2.994	0.002	3.000	2.994	0.000
4	Max	4.145	4.000	0.220	4.060	4.000	0.090	4.028	4.000	0.040	4.016	4.000	0.024	4.012	4.000	0.020
	Min	4.070	3.925	0.070	4.030	3.970	0.030	4.010	3.988	0.010	4.004	3.992	0.004	4.000	3.992	0.000
5	Max	5.145	5.000	0.220	5.060	5.000	0.090	5.028	5.000	0.040	5.016	5.000	0.024	5.012	5.000	0.020
	Min	5.070	4.925	0.070	5.030	4.970	0.030	5.010	4.988	0.010	5.004	4.992	0.004	5.000	4.992	0.000
6	Max	6.145	6.000	0.220	6.060	6.000	0.090	6.028	6.000	0.040	6.016	6.000	0.024	6.012	6.000	0.020
	Min	6.070	5.925	0.070	6.030	5.970	0.030	6.010	5.988	0.010	6.004	5.992	0.004	6.000	5.992	0.000
8	Max	8.170	8.000	0.260	8.076	8.000	0.112	8.035	8.000	0.050	8.020	8.000	0.029	8.015	8.000	0.024
	Min	8.080	7.910	0.080	8.040	7.964	0.040	8.013	7.985	0.013	8.005	7.991	0.005	8.000	7.991	0.000
10	Max	10.170	10.000	0.260	10.076	10.000	0.112	10.035	10.000	0.050	10.020	10.000	0.029	10.015	10.000	0.024
	Min	10.080	9.910	0.080	10.040	9.964	0.040	10.013	9.985	0.013	10.005	9.991	0.005	10.000	9.991	0.000
12	Max	12.205	12.000	0.315	12.093	12.000	0.136	12.043	12.000	0.061	12.024	12.000	0.035	12.018	12.000	0.029
	Min	12.095	11.890	0.095	12.050	11.957	0.050	12.016	11.982	0.016	12.006	11.989	0.006	12.000	11.989	0.000
16	Max	16.205	16.000	0.315	16.093	16.000	0.136	16.043	16.000	0.061	16.024	16.000	0.035	16.018	16.000	0.029
	Min	16.095	15.890	0.095	16.050	15.957	0.050	16.016	15.982	0.016	16.006	15.989	0.006	16.000	15.989	0.000
20	Max	20.240	20.000	0.370	20.117	20.000	0.169	20.053	20.000	0.074	20.028	20.000	0.041	20.021	20.000	0.034
	Min	20.110	19.870	0.110	20.065	19.948	0.065	20.020	19.979	0.020	20.007	19.987	0.007	20.000	19.987	0.000
25	Max	25.240	25.000	0.370	25.117	25.000	0.169	25.053	25.000	0.074	25.028	25.000	0.041	25.021	25.000	0.034
	Min	25.110	24.870	0.110	25.065	24.948	0.065	25.020	24.979	0.020	25.007	24.987	0.007	25.000	24.987	0.000
30	Max	30.240	30.000	0.370	30.117	30.000	0.169	30.053	30.000	0.074	30.028	30.000	0.041	30.021	30.000	0.034
	Min	30.110	29.870	0.110	30.065	29.948	0.065	30.020	29.979	0.020	30.007	29.987	0.007	30.000	29.987	0.000

[a] From ANSI B4.2–1978 (R1994).

Dimensions are in millimeters.

Basic Size		Loose Running			Free Running			Close Running			Sliding			Locational Clearance		
		Hole C11	Shaft h11	Fit	Hole D9	Shaft h9	Fit	Hole F8	Shaft h7	Fit	Hole G7	Shaft h6	Fit	Hole H7	Shaft h6	Fit
40	Max	40.280	40.000	0.440	40.142	40.000	0.204	40.064	40.000	0.089	40.034	40.000	0.050	40.025	40.000	0.041
	Min	40.120	39.840	0.120	40.080	39.938	0.080	40.025	39.975	0.025	40.009	39.984	0.009	40.000	39.984	0.000
50	Max	50.290	50.000	0.450	50.142	50.000	0.204	50.064	50.000	0.089	50.034	50.000	0.050	50.025	50.000	0.041
	Min	50.130	49.840	0.130	50.080	49.938	0.080	50.025	49.975	0.025	50.009	49.984	0.009	50.000	49.984	0.000
60	Max	60.330	60.000	0.520	60.174	60.000	0.248	60.076	60.000	0.106	60.040	60.000	0.059	60.030	60.000	0.049
	Min	60.140	59.810	0.140	60.100	59.926	0.100	60.030	59.970	0.030	60.010	59.981	0.010	60.000	59.981	0.000
80	Max	80.340	80.000	0.530	80.174	80.000	0.248	80.076	80.000	0.106	80.040	80.000	0.059	80.030	80.000	0.049
	Min	80.150	79.810	0.150	80.100	79.926	0.100	80.030	79.970	0.030	80.010	79.981	0.010	80.000	79.981	0.000
100	Max	100.390	100.000	0.610	100.207	100.000	0.294	100.090	100.000	0.125	100.047	100.000	0.069	100.035	100.000	0.057
	Min	100.170	99.780	0.170	100.120	99.913	0.120	100.036	99.965	0.036	100.012	99.978	0.012	100.000	99.978	0.000
120	Max	120.400	120.000	0.620	120.207	120.000	0.294	120.090	120.000	0.125	120.047	120.000	0.069	120.035	120.000	0.057
	Min	120.180	119.780	0.180	120.120	119.913	0.120	120.036	119.965	0.036	120.012	119.978	0.012	120.000	119.978	0.000
160	Max	160.460	160.000	0.710	160.245	160.000	0.345	160.106	160.000	0.146	160.054	160.000	0.079	160.040	160.000	0.065
	Min	160.210	159.750	0.210	160.145	159.900	0.145	160.043	159.960	0.043	160.014	159.975	0.014	160.000	159.975	0.000
200	Max	200.530	200.000	0.820	200.285	200.000	0.400	200.122	200.000	0.168	200.061	200.000	0.090	200.046	200.000	0.075
	Min	200.240	199.710	0.240	200.170	199.885	0.170	200.050	199.954	0.050	200.015	199.971	0.015	200.000	199.971	0.000
250	Max	250.570	250.000	0.860	250.285	250.000	0.400	250.122	250.000	0.168	250.061	250.000	0.090	250.046	250.000	0.075
	Min	250.280	249.710	0.280	250.170	249.885	0.170	250.050	249.954	0.050	250.015	249.971	0.015	250.000	249.971	0.000
300	Max	300.650	300.000	0.970	300.320	300.000	0.450	300.137	300.000	0.189	300.069	300.000	0.101	300.052	300.000	0.084
	Min	300.330	299.680	0.330	300.190	299.870	0.190	300.056	299.948	0.056	300.017	299.968	0.017	300.000	299.968	0.000
400	Max	400.760	400.000	1.120	400.350	400.000	0.490	400.151	400.000	0.208	400.075	400.000	0.111	400.057	400.000	0.093
	Min	400.400	399.640	0.400	400.210	399.860	0.210	400.062	399.943	0.062	400.018	399.964	0.018	400.000	399.964	0.000
500	Max	500.880	500.000	1.280	500.385	500.000	0.540	500.165	500.000	0.228	500.083	500.000	0.123	500.063	500.000	0.103
	Min	500.480	499.600	0.480	500.230	499.845	0.230	500.068	499.937	0.068	500.020	499.960	5.020	500.000	499.960	0.000

[a] From ANSI B4.2–1978 (R1994).

Dimensions are in millimeters.

Basic Size		Locational Transn.			Locational Transn.			Locational Interf.			Medium Drive			Force		
		Hole K7	Shaft h6	Fit	Hole N7	Shaft h6	Fit	Hole P7	Shaft h6	Fit	Hole S7	Shaft h6	Fit	Hole U7	Shaft h6	Fit
1	Max	1.000	1.000	0.006	0.996	1.000	0.002	0.994	1.000	0.000	0.986	1.000	−0.008	0.982	1.000	−0.012
	Min	0.990	0.994	−0.010	0.986	0.994	−0.014	0.984	0.994	−0.016	0.976	0.994	−0.024	0.972	0.994	−0.028
1.2	Max	1.200	1.200	0.006	1.196	1.200	0.002	1.194	1.200	0.000	1.186	1.200	−0.008	1.182	1.200	−0.012
	Min	1.190	1.194	−0.010	1.186	1.194	−0.014	1.184	1.194	−0.016	1.176	1.194	−0.024	1.172	1.194	−0.028
1.6	Max	1.600	1.600	0.006	1.596	1.600	0.002	1.594	1.600	0.000	1.586	1.600	−0.008	1.582	1.600	−0.012
	Min	1.590	1.594	−0.010	1.586	1.594	−0.014	1.584	1.594	−0.016	1.576	1.594	−0.024	1.572	1.594	−0.028
2	Max	2.000	2.000	0.006	1.996	2.000	0.002	1.994	2.000	0.000	1.986	2.000	−0.008	1.982	2.000	−0.012
	Min	1.990	1.994	−0.010	1.986	1.994	−0.014	1.984	1.994	−0.016	1.976	1.994	−0.024	1.972	1.994	−0.028
2.5	Max	2.500	2.500	0.006	2.496	2.500	0.002	2.494	2.500	0.000	2.486	2.500	−0.008	2.482	2.500	−0.012
	Min	2.490	2.494	−0.010	2.486	2.494	−0.014	2.484	2.494	−0.016	2.476	2.494	−0.024	2.472	2.494	−0.028
3	Max	3.000	3.000	0.006	2.996	3.000	0.002	2.994	3.000	0.000	2.986	3.000	−0.008	2.982	3.000	−0.012
	Min	2.990	2.994	−0.010	2.986	2.994	−0.014	2.984	2.994	−0.016	2.976	2.994	−0.024	2.972	2.994	−0.028
4	Max	4.003	4.000	0.011	3.996	4.000	0.004	3.992	4.000	0.000	3.985	4.000	−0.007	3.981	4.000	−0.011
	Min	3.991	3.992	−0.009	3.984	3.992	−0.016	3.980	3.992	−0.020	3.973	3.992	−0.027	3.969	3.992	−0.031
5	Max	5.003	5.000	0.011	4.996	5.000	0.004	4.992	5.000	0.000	4.985	5.000	−0.007	4.981	5.000	−0.011
	Min	4.991	4.992	−0.009	4.984	4.992	−0.016	4.980	4.992	−0.020	4.973	4.992	−0.027	4.969	4.992	−0.031
6	Max	6.003	6.000	0.011	5.996	6.000	0.004	5.992	6.000	0.000	5.985	6.000	−0.007	5.981	6.000	−0.011
	Min	5.991	5.992	−0.009	5.984	5.992	−0.016	5.980	5.992	−0.020	5.973	5.992	−0.027	5.969	5.992	−0.031
8	Max	8.005	8.000	0.014	7.996	8.000	0.005	7.991	8.000	0.000	7.983	8.000	−0.008	7.978	8.000	−0.013
	Min	7.990	7.991	−0.010	7.981	7.991	−0.019	7.976	7.991	−0.024	7.968	7.991	−0.032	7.963	7.991	−0.037
10	Max	10.005	10.000	0.014	9.996	10.000	0.005	9.991	10.000	0.000	9.983	10.000	−0.008	9.978	10.000	−0.013
	Min	9.990	9.991	−0.010	9.981	9.991	−0.019	9.976	9.991	−0.024	9.968	9.991	−0.032	9.963	9.991	−0.037
12	Max	12.006	12.000	0.017	11.995	12.000	0.006	11.989	12.000	0.000	11.979	12.000	−0.010	11.974	12.000	−0.015
	Min	11.988	11.989	−0.012	11.977	11.989	−0.023	11.971	11.989	−0.029	11.961	11.989	−0.039	11.956	11.989	−0.044
16	Max	16.006	16.000	0.017	15.995	16.000	0.006	15.989	16.000	0.000	15.979	16.000	−0.010	15.974	16.000	−0.015
	Min	15.988	15.989	−0.012	15.977	15.989	−0.023	15.971	15.989	−0.029	15.961	15.989	−0.039	15.956	15.989	−0.044
20	Max	20.006	20.000	0.019	19.993	20.000	0.006	19.986	20.000	−0.001	19.973	20.000	−0.014	19.967	20.000	−0.020
	Min	19.985	19.987	−0.015	19.972	19.987	−0.028	19.965	19.987	−0.035	19.952	19.987	−0.048	19.946	19.987	−0.054
25	Max	25.006	25.000	0.019	24.993	25.000	0.006	24.986	25.000	−0.001	24.973	25.000	−0.014	24.960	25.000	−0.027
	Min	24.985	24.987	−0.015	24.972	24.987	−0.028	24.965	24.987	−0.035	24.952	24.987	−0.048	24.939	24.987	−0.061
30	Max	30.006	30.000	0.019	29.993	30.000	0.006	29.986	30.000	−0.001	29.973	30.000	−0.014	29.960	30.000	−0.027
	Min	29.985	29.987	−0.015	29.972	29.987	−0.028	29.965	29.987	−0.035	29.952	29.987	−0.048	29.939	29.987	−0.061

[a] From ANSI B4.2-1978 (R1994). For description of preferred fits, see Table 12.2.

Dimensions are in millimeters.

Basic Size		Locational Transn.			Locational Transn.			Locational Interf.			Medium Drive			Force		
		Hole K7	Shaft h6	Fit	Hole N7	Shaft h6	Fit	Hole P7	Shaft h6	Fit	Hole S7	Shaft h6	Fit	Hole U7	Shaft h6	Fit
40	Max	40.007	40.000	0.023	39.992	40.000	0.008	39.983	40.000	−0.001	39.966	40.000	−0.018	39.949	40.000	−0.035
	Min	39.982	39.984	−0.018	39.967	39.984	−0.033	39.958	39.984	−0.042	39.941	39.984	−0.059	39.924	39.984	−0.076
50	Max	50.007	50.000	0.023	49.992	50.000	0.008	49.983	50.000	−0.001	49.966	50.000	−0.018	49.939	50.000	−0.045
	Min	49.982	49.984	−0.018	49.967	49.984	−0.033	49.958	49.984	−0.042	49.941	49.984	−0.059	49.914	49.984	−0.086
60	Max	60.009	60.000	0.028	59.991	60.000	0.010	59.979	60.000	−0.002	59.958	60.000	−0.023	59.924	60.000	−0.057
	Min	59.979	59.981	−0.021	59.961	59.981	−0.039	59.949	59.981	−0.051	59.928	59.981	−0.072	59.894	59.981	−0.106
80	Max	80.009	80.000	0.028	79.991	80.000	0.010	79.979	80.000	−0.002	79.952	80.000	−0.029	79.909	80.000	−0.072
	Min	79.979	79.981	−0.021	79.961	79.981	−0.039	79.949	79.981	−0.051	79.922	79.981	−0.078	79.879	79.981	−0.121
100	Max	100.010	100.000	0.032	99.990	100.000	0.012	99.976	100.000	−0.002	99.942	100.000	−0.036	99.889	100.000	−0.089
	Min	99.975	99.978	−0.025	99.955	99.978	−0.045	99.941	99.978	−0.059	99.907	99.978	−0.093	99.854	99.978	−0.146
120	Max	120.010	120.000	0.032	119.990	120.000	0.012	119.976	120.000	−0.002	119.934	120.000	−0.044	119.869	120.000	−0.109
	Min	119.975	119.978	−0.025	119.955	119.978	−0.045	119.941	119.978	−0.059	119.899	119.978	−0.101	119.834	119.978	−0.166
160	Max	160.012	160.000	0.037	159.988	160.000	0.013	159.972	160.000	−0.003	159.915	160.000	−0.060	159.825	160.000	−0.150
	Min	159.972	159.975	−0.028	159.948	159.975	−0.052	159.932	159.975	−0.068	159.875	159.975	−0.125	159.785	159.975	−0.215
200	Max	200.013	200.000	0.042	199.986	200.000	0.015	199.967	200.000	−0.004	199.895	200.000	−0.076	199.781	200.000	−0.190
	Min	199.967	199.971	−0.033	199.940	199.971	−0.060	199.921	199.971	−0.079	199.849	199.971	−0.151	199.735	199.971	−0.265
250	Max	250.013	250.000	0.042	249.986	250.000	0.015	249.967	250.000	−0.004	249.877	250.000	−0.094	249.733	250.000	−0.238
	Min	249.967	249.971	−0.033	249.940	249.971	−0.060	249.921	249.971	−0.079	249.831	249.971	−0.169	249.687	249.971	−0.313
300	Max	300.016	300.000	0.048	299.986	300.000	0.018	299.964	300.000	−0.004	299.850	300.000	−0.118	299.670	300.000	−0.298
	Min	299.964	299.968	−0.036	299.934	299.968	−0.066	299.912	299.968	−0.088	299.798	299.968	−0.202	299.618	299.968	−0.382
400	Max	400.017	400.000	0.053	399.984	400.000	0.020	399.959	400.000	−0.005	399.813	400.000	−0.151	399.586	400.000	−0.378
	Min	399.960	399.964	−0.040	399.927	399.964	−0.073	399.902	399.964	−0.098	399.756	399.964	−0.244	399.529	399.964	−0.471
500	Max	500.018	500.000	0.058	499.983	500.000	0.023	499.955	500.000	−0.005	499.771	500.000	−0.189	499.483	500.000	−0.477
	Min	499.955	499.960	−0.045	499.920	499.960	−0.080	499.892	499.960	−0.108	499.708	499.960	−0.292	499.420	499.960	−0.580

[a] From ANSI B4.2–1978 (R1994). For description of preferred fits, see Table 12.2.

15 Screw Threads, American National, Unified, and Metric

AMERICAN NATIONAL STANDARD UNIFIED AND AMERICAN NATIONAL SCREW THREADS[a]

Nominal Diameter	Coarse[b] NC UNC		Fine[b] NF UNF		Extra Fine[c] NEF UNEF		Nominal Diameter	Coarse[b] NC UNC		Fine[b] NF UNF		Extra Fine[c] NEF UNEF	
	Thds. per Inch	Tap Drill[d]	Thds. per Inch	Tap Drill[d]	Thds. per Inch	Tap Drill[d]		Thds. per Inch	Tap Drill[d]	Thds. per Inch	Tap Drill[d]	Thds. per Inch	Tap Drill[d]
0 (.060)			80	$\frac{3}{64}$			1	8	$\frac{7}{8}$	12	$\frac{59}{64}$	20	$\frac{61}{64}$
1 (.073)	64	No. 53	72	No. 53	...	...	$1\frac{1}{16}$	...	...	...	...	18	1
2 (.086)	56	No. 50	64	No. 50	...	...	$1\frac{1}{8}$	7	$\frac{63}{64}$	12	$1\frac{3}{64}$	18	$1\frac{5}{64}$
3 (.099)	48	No. 47	56	No. 45	...	...	$1\frac{3}{16}$	...	...	...	...	18	$1\frac{9}{64}$
4 (.112)	40	No. 43	48	No. 42	...	...	$1\frac{1}{4}$	7	$1\frac{7}{64}$	12	$1\frac{11}{64}$	18	$1\frac{3}{16}$
5 (.125)	40	No. 38	44	No. 37	...	...	$1\frac{5}{16}$	...	...	...	...	18	$1\frac{17}{64}$
6 (.138)	32	No. 36	40	No. 33	...	...	$1\frac{3}{8}$	6	$1\frac{7}{32}$	12	$1\frac{19}{64}$	18	$1\frac{5}{16}$
8 (.164)	32	No. 29	36	No. 29	...	...	$1\frac{7}{16}$	...	...	...	...	18	$1\frac{3}{8}$
10 (.190)	24	No. 25	32	No. 21	...	...	$1\frac{1}{2}$	6	$1\frac{11}{32}$	12	$1\frac{27}{64}$	18	$1\frac{7}{16}$
12 (.216)	24	No. 16	28	No. 14	32	No. 13	$1\frac{9}{16}$	...	...	...	...	18	$1\frac{1}{2}$
$\frac{1}{4}$	20	No. 7	28	No. 3	32	$\frac{7}{32}$	$1\frac{5}{8}$	...	...	...	...	18	$1\frac{9}{16}$
$\frac{5}{16}$	18	F	24	I	32	$\frac{9}{32}$	$1\frac{11}{16}$	...	...	...	...	18	$1\frac{5}{8}$
$\frac{3}{8}$	16	$\frac{5}{16}$	24	Q	32	$\frac{11}{32}$	$1\frac{3}{4}$	5	$1\frac{9}{16}$	...	...	...	...
$\frac{7}{16}$	14	U	20	$\frac{25}{64}$	28	$\frac{13}{32}$	2	$4\frac{1}{2}$	$1\frac{25}{32}$	...	...	...	...
$\frac{1}{2}$	13	$\frac{27}{64}$	20	$\frac{29}{64}$	28	$\frac{15}{32}$	$2\frac{1}{4}$	$4\frac{1}{2}$	$2\frac{1}{32}$	...	...	...	...
$\frac{9}{16}$	12	$\frac{31}{64}$	18	$\frac{33}{64}$	24	$\frac{33}{64}$	$2\frac{1}{2}$	4	$2\frac{1}{4}$	...	...	...	...
$\frac{5}{8}$	11	$\frac{17}{32}$	18	$\frac{37}{64}$	24	$\frac{37}{64}$	$2\frac{3}{4}$	4	$2\frac{1}{2}$	...	...	...	...
$\frac{11}{16}$	...	...	...	...	24	$\frac{41}{64}$	3	4	$2\frac{3}{4}$	...	...	...	...
$\frac{3}{4}$	10	$\frac{21}{32}$	16	$\frac{11}{16}$	20	$\frac{45}{64}$	$3\frac{1}{4}$	4	...	...	...	...	...
$\frac{13}{16}$	...	...	...	...	20	$\frac{49}{64}$	$3\frac{1}{2}$	4	...	...	...	...	...
$\frac{7}{8}$	9	$\frac{49}{64}$	14	$\frac{13}{16}$	20	$\frac{53}{64}$	$3\frac{3}{4}$	4	...	...	...	...	...
$\frac{15}{16}$	...	...	...	...	20	$\frac{57}{64}$	4	4	...	...	...	...	...

[a] ANSI/ASME B1.1–1989. For 8-, 12-, and 16-pitch thread series, see next page.
[b] Classes 1A, 2A, 3A, 1B, 2B, 3B, 2, and 3.
[c] Classes 2A, 2B, 2, and 3.
[d] For approximate 75% full depth of thread. For decimal sizes of numbered and lettered drills, see Appendix 16.

15 Screw Threads, American National, Unified, and Metric (continued)

AMERICAN NATIONAL STANDARD UNIFIED AND AMERICAN NATIONAL SCREW THREADS[a] (continued)

Nominal Diameter	8-Pitch[b] Series 8N and 8UN		12-Pitch[b] Series 12N and 12UN		16-Pitch[b] Series 16N and 16UN		Nominal Diameter	8-Pitch[b] Series 8N and 8UN		12-Pitch[b] Series 12N and 12UN		16-Pitch[c] Series 16N and 16UN	
	Thds. per Inch	Tap Drill[c]	Thds. per Inch	Tap Drill[c]	Thds. per Inch	Tap Drill[c]		Thds. per Inch	Tap Drill[c]	Thds. per Inch	Tap Drill[c]	Thds. per Inch	Tap Drill[c]
$\frac{1}{2}$	...	...	12	$\frac{27}{64}$	...	...	$2\frac{1}{16}$	...	...	...	...	**16**	2
$\frac{9}{16}$	...	...	12[e]	$\frac{31}{64}$	...	...	$2\frac{1}{8}$	...	...	12	$2\frac{3}{64}$	16	$2\frac{1}{16}$
$\frac{5}{8}$	...	...	12	$\frac{35}{64}$	...	...	$2\frac{3}{16}$	...	...	...	...	**16**	$2\frac{1}{8}$
$\frac{11}{16}$	...	...	12	$\frac{39}{64}$	...	...	$2\frac{1}{4}$	8	$2\frac{1}{8}$	12	$2\frac{17}{64}$	16	$2\frac{3}{16}$
$\frac{3}{4}$	...	...	12	$\frac{43}{64}$	16[e]	$\frac{11}{16}$	$2\frac{5}{16}$	...	...	...	...	**16**	$2\frac{1}{4}$
$\frac{13}{16}$	...	...	12	$\frac{47}{64}$	16	$\frac{3}{4}$	$2\frac{3}{8}$	...	...	12	$2\frac{19}{64}$	16	$2\frac{5}{16}$
$\frac{7}{8}$	...	...	12	$\frac{51}{64}$	16	$\frac{13}{16}$	$2\frac{7}{16}$	...	...	...	...	**16**	$2\frac{3}{8}$
$\frac{5}{16}$	...	...	12	$\frac{55}{64}$	16	$\frac{7}{8}$	$2\frac{1}{2}$	8	$2\frac{3}{8}$	12	$2\frac{27}{64}$	16	$2\frac{7}{16}$
1	8[e]	$\frac{7}{8}$	12	$\frac{59}{64}$	16	$\frac{15}{16}$	$2\frac{5}{8}$	...	...	12	$2\frac{35}{64}$	16	$2\frac{9}{16}$
$1\frac{1}{16}$	...	...	12	$\frac{63}{64}$	16	1	$2\frac{3}{4}$	8	$2\frac{5}{8}$	12	$2\frac{43}{64}$	16	$2\frac{11}{16}$
$1\frac{1}{8}$	8	1	12[e]	$1\frac{3}{64}$	16	$1\frac{1}{16}$	$2\frac{7}{8}$	...	...	12	...	16	...
$1\frac{3}{16}$	...	...	12	$1\frac{7}{64}$	16	$1\frac{1}{8}$	3	8	$2\frac{7}{8}$	12	...	16	...
$1\frac{1}{4}$	8	$1\frac{1}{8}$	12	$1\frac{11}{64}$	16	$1\frac{3}{16}$	$3\frac{1}{8}$	...	...	12	...	16	...
$1\frac{5}{16}$	...	...	12	$1\frac{15}{64}$	16	$1\frac{1}{4}$	$3\frac{1}{4}$	8	...	12	...	16	...
$1\frac{3}{8}$	8	$1\frac{1}{4}$	12[e]	$1\frac{19}{64}$	16	$1\frac{5}{16}$	$3\frac{3}{8}$	...	...	12	...	16	...
$1\frac{7}{16}$	...	...	12	$1\frac{23}{64}$	16	$1\frac{3}{8}$	$3\frac{1}{2}$	8	...	12	...	16	...
$1\frac{1}{2}$	8	$1\frac{3}{8}$	12[e]	$1\frac{27}{64}$	16	$1\frac{7}{16}$	$3\frac{5}{8}$	...	...	12	...	16	...
$1\frac{9}{16}$	...	...	...	...	16	$1\frac{1}{2}$	$3\frac{3}{4}$	8	...	12	...	16	...
$1\frac{5}{8}$	8	$1\frac{1}{2}$	12	$1\frac{35}{64}$	16	$1\frac{9}{16}$	$3\frac{7}{8}$	...	...	12	...	16	...
$1\frac{11}{16}$	...	...	...	...	16	$1\frac{5}{8}$	4	8	...	12	...	16	...
$1\frac{3}{4}$	8	$1\frac{5}{8}$	12	$1\frac{43}{64}$	16[e]	$1\frac{11}{16}$	$4\frac{1}{4}$	8	...	12	...	16	...
$1\frac{13}{16}$	...	...	...	...	16	$1\frac{3}{4}$	$4\frac{1}{2}$	8	...	12	...	16	...
$1\frac{7}{8}$	8	$1\frac{3}{4}$	12	$1\frac{51}{64}$	16	$1\frac{13}{16}$	$4\frac{3}{4}$	8	...	12	...	16	...
$1\frac{15}{16}$	...	...	...	...	16	$1\frac{7}{8}$	5	8	...	12	...	16	...
2	8	$1\frac{7}{8}$	12	$1\frac{59}{64}$	16[e]	$1\frac{15}{16}$	$5\frac{1}{4}$	8	...	12	...	16	...

[a] ANSI/ASME B1.1–1989.
[b] Classes 2A, 3A, 2B, 3B, 2, and 3.
[c] For approximate 75% full depth of thread.
[d] Boldface type indicates Amrican National Threads only.
[e] This is a standard size of the Unified or American National threads of the coarse, fine, or extra fine series. See preceding page.

15 Screw Threads, American National, Unified, and Metric (continued)

METRIC SCREW THREADS[a]

Preferred sizes for commercial threads and fasteners are shown in **boldface** type.

Coarse (general purpose)		Fine	
Nominal Size & Thd Pitch	Tap Drill Diameter, mm	Nominal Size & Thd Pitch	Tap Drill Diameter, mm
M1.6 × 0.35	1.25	—	—
M1.8 × 0.35	1.45	—	—
M2 × 0.4	1.6	—	—
M2.2 × 0.45	1.75	—	—
M2.5 × 0.45	2.05	—	—
M3 × 0.5	2.5	—	—
M3.5 × 0.6	2.9	—	—
M4 × 0.7	3.3	—	—
M4.5 × 0.75	3.75	—	—
M5 × 0.8	4.2	—	—
M6 × 1	5.0	—	—
M7 × 1	6.0	—	—
M8 × 1.25	6.8	**M8 × 1**	7.0
M9 × 1.25	7.75	—	—
M10 × 1.5	8.5	**M10 × 1.25**	8.75
M11 × 1.5	9.50	—	—
M12 × 1.75	10.30	**M12 × 1.25**	10.5
M14 × 2	12.00	**M14 × 1.5**	12.5
M16 × 2	14.00	**M16 × 1.5**	14.5
M18 × 2.5	15.50	**M18 × 1.5**	16.5
M20 × 2.5	17.5	**M20 × 1.5**	18.5
M22 × 25[b]	19.5	**M22 × 1.5**	20.5
M24 × 3	21.0	**M24 × 2**	22.0
M27 × 3[b]	24.0	**M27 × 2**	25.0
M30 × 3.5	26.5	**M30 × 2**	28.0
M33 × 3.5	29.5	**M30 × 2**	31.0
M36 × 4	32.0	**M36 × 2**	33.0
M39 × 4	35.0	M39 × 2	36.0
M42 × 4.5	37.5	**M42 × 2**	39.0
M45 × 4.5	40.5	M45 × 1.5	42.0
M48 × 5	43.0	**M48 × 2**	45.0
M52 × 5	47.0	M52 × 2	49.0
M56 × 5.5	50.5	**M56 × 2**	52.0
M60 × 5.5	54.5	M60 × 1.5	56.0
M64 × 6	58.0	**M64 × 2**	60.0
M68 × 6	62.0	M68 × 2	64.0
M72 × 6	66.0	**M72 × 2**	68.0
M80 × 6	74.0	**M80 × 2**	76.0
M90 × 6	84.0	**M90 × 2**	86.0
M100 × 6	94.0	**M100 × 2**	96.0

[a] ANSI/ASME B1.13M–1995.
[b] Only for high strength structural steel fasteners.

16 Twist Drill Sizes—American National Standard and Metric

AMERICAN NATIONAL STANDARD DRILL SIZES[a]

All dimensions are in inches.

Drills designated in common fractions are available in diameters $\frac{1}{64}''$ to $1\frac{3}{4}''$ in $\frac{1}{64}''$ increments, $1\frac{3}{4}''$ to $2\frac{1}{4}''$ in $\frac{1}{32}''$ increments. $2\frac{1}{4}''$ to $3''$ in $\frac{1}{16}''$ increments and $3''$ to $3\frac{1}{2}''$ in $\frac{1}{8}''$ increments. Drills larger than $3\frac{1}{2}''$ are seldom used, and are regarded as special drills.

Size	Drill Diameter	Size	Drill Diameter	Size	Drill Diameter	Size	Drill Diameter	Size	Drill Diameter	Size	Drill Diameter
1	.2280	17	.1730	33	.1130	49	.0730	65	.0350	81	.0130
2	.2210	18	.1695	34	.1110	50	.0700	66	.0330	82	.0125
3	.2130	19	.1660	35	.1100	51	.0670	67	.0320	83	.0120
4	.2090	20	.1610	36	.1065	52	.0635	68	.0310	84	.0115
5	.2055	21	.1590	37	.1040	53	.0595	69	.0292	85	.0110
6	.2040	22	.1570	38	.1015	54	.0550	70	.0280	86	.0105
7	.2010	23	.1540	39	.0995	55	.0520	71	.0260	87	.0100
8	.1990	24	.1520	40	.0980	56	.0465	72	.0250	88	.0095
9	.1960	25	.1495	41	.0960	57	.0430	73	.0240	89	.0091
10	.1935	26	.1470	42	.0935	58	.0420	74	.0225	90	.0087
11	.1910	27	.1440	43	.0890	59	.0410	75	.0210	91	.0083
12	.1890	28	.1405	44	.0860	60	.0400	76	.0200	92	.0079
13	.1850	29	.1360	45	.0820	61	.0390	77	.0180	93	.0075
14	.1820	30	.1285	46	.0810	62	.0380	78	.0160	94	.0071
15	.1800	31	.1200	47	.0785	63	.0370	79	.0145	95	.0067
16	.1770	32	.1160	48	.0760	64	.0360	80	.0135	96	.0063
										97	.0059

LETTER SIZES

A	.234	G	.261	L	.290	Q	.332	V	.377
B	.238	H	.266	M	.295	R	.339	W	.386
C	.242	I	.272	N	.302	S	.348	X	.397
D	.246	J	.277	O	.316	T	.358	Y	.404
E	.250	K	.281	P	.323	U	.368	Z	.413
F	.257								

[a] ANSI/ASME B94.11M–1993.

METRIC DRILL SIZES
Decimal-inch equivalents are for reference only.

Drill Diameter		Drill Diameter		Drill Diameter		Drill Diameter		Drill Diameter		Drill Diameter	
mm	in.	mm	in.	mm	in.	mm	in.	mm	in.	mm	in.
0.40	.0157	1.95	.0768	4.70	.1850	8.00	.3150	13.20	.5197	25.50	1.0039
0.42	.0165	2.00	.0787	4.80	.1890	8.10	.3189	13.50	.5315	26.00	1.0236
0.45	.0177	2.05	.0807	4.90	.1929	8.20	.3228	13.80	.5433	26.50	1.0433
0.48	.0189	2.10	.0827	5.00	.1969	8.30	.3268	14.00	.5512	27.00	1.0630
0.50	.0197	2.15	.0846	5.10	.2008	8.40	.3307	14.25	.5610	27.50	1.0827
0.55	.0217	2.20	.0866	5.20	.2047	8.50	.3346	14.50	.5709	28.00	1.1024
0.60	.0236	2.25	.0886	5.30	.2087	8.60	.3386	14.75	.5807	28.50	1.1220
0.65	.0256	2.30	.0906	5.40	.2126	8.70	.3425	15.00	.5906	29.00	1.1417
0.70	.0276	2.35	.0925	5.50	.2165	8.80	.3465	15.25	.6004	29.50	1.1614
0.75	.0295	2.40	.0945	5.60	.2205	8.90	.3504	15.50	.6102	30.00	1.1811
0.80	.0315	2.45	.0965	5.70	.2244	9.00	.3543	15.75	.6201	30.50	1.2008
0.85	.0335	2.50	.0984	5.80	.2283	9.10	.3583	16.00	.6299	31.00	1.2205
0.90	.0354	2.60	.1024	5.90	.2323	9.20	.3622	16.25	.6398	31.50	1.2402
0.95	.0374	2.70	.1063	6.00	.2362	9.30	.3661	16.50	.6496	32.00	1.2598
1.00	.0394	2.80	.1102	6.10	.2402	9.40	.3701	16.75	.6594	32.50	1.2795
1.05	.0413	2.90	.1142	6.20	.2441	9.50	.3740	17.00	.6693	33.00	1.2992
1.10	.0433	3.00	.1181	6.30	.2480	9.60	.3780	17.25	.6791	33.50	1.3189
1.15	.0453	3.10	.1220	6.40	.2520	9.70	.3819	17.50	.6890	34.00	1.3386
1.20	.0472	3.20	.1260	6.50	.2559	9.80	.3858	18.00	.7087	34.50	1.3583
1.25	.0492	3.30	.1299	6.60	.2598	9.90	.3898	18.50	.7283	35.00	1.3780
1.30	.0512	3.40	.1339	6.70	.2638	10.00	.3937	19.00	.7480	35.50	1.3976
1.35	.0531	3.50	.1378	6.80	.2677	10.20	.4016	19.50	.7677	36.00	1.4173
1.40	.0551	3.60	.1417	6.90	.2717	10.50	.4134	20.00	.7874	36.50	1.4370
1.45	.0571	3.70	.1457	7.00	.2756	10.80	.4252	20.50	.8071	37.00	1.4567
1.50	.0591	3.80	.1496	7.10	.2795	11.00	.4331	21.00	.8268	37.50	1.4764
1.55	.0610	3.90	.1535	7.20	.2835	11.20	.4409	21.50	.8465	38.00	1.4961
1.60	.0630	4.00	.1575	7.30	.2874	11.50	.4528	22.00	.8661	40.00	1.5748
1.65	.0650	4.10	.1614	7.40	.2913	11.80	.4646	22.50	.8858	42.00	1.6535
1.70	.0669	4.20	.1654	7.50	.2953	12.00	.4724	23.00	.9055	44.00	1.7323
1.75	.0689	4.30	.1693	7.60	.2992	12.20	.4803	23.50	.9252	46.00	1.8110
1.80	.0709	4.40	.1732	7.70	.3031	12.50	.4921	24.00	.9449	48.00	1.8898
1.85	.0728	4.50	.1772	7.80	.3071	12.50	.5039	24.50	.9646	50.00	1.9685
1.90	.0748	4.60	.1811	7.90	.3110	13.00	.5118	25.00	.9843		

17 Acme Threads, General Purpose[a]

Size	Threads per Inch	Size	Threads per Inch	Size	Threads per Inch	Size	Threads per Inch
$\frac{1}{4}$	16	$\frac{3}{4}$	6	$1\frac{1}{2}$	4	3	2
$\frac{5}{16}$	14	$\frac{7}{8}$	6	$1\frac{3}{4}$	4	$3\frac{1}{2}$	2
$\frac{3}{8}$	12	1	5	2	4	4	2
$\frac{7}{16}$	12	$1\frac{1}{8}$	5	$2\frac{1}{4}$	3	$4\frac{1}{2}$	2
$\frac{1}{2}$	10	$1\frac{1}{4}$	5	$2\frac{1}{2}$	3	5	2
$\frac{5}{8}$	8	$1\frac{3}{8}$	4	$2\frac{3}{4}$	3	...	...

[a] ANSI/ASME B1.5–1988 (R1994).

18 Bolts, Nuts, and Cap Screws—Square and Hexagon— American National Standard and Metric

AMERICAN NATIONAL STANDARD SQUARE AND HEXAGON BOLTS[a] AND NUTS[b] AND HEXAGON CAP SCREWS[c]

Boldface type indicates product features unified dimensionally with British and Canadian standards.
All dimensions are in inches.
For thread series, minimum thread lengths, and bolt lengths, see §13.25.

Nominal Size D Body Diameter of Bolt		Regular Bolts					Heavy Bolts		
		Width Across Flats W		Height H			Width Across Flats W	Height H	
		Sq.	Hex.	Sq. (Unfin.)	Hex (Unfin.)	Hex Cap Scr.[c] (Fin.)		Hex. (Unfin.)	Hex Screw (Fin.)
$\frac{1}{4}$	**0.2500**	$\frac{3}{8}$	$\frac{7}{16}$	$\frac{11}{64}$	$\frac{11}{64}$	$\frac{5}{32}$	...	...	...
$\frac{5}{16}$	**0.3125**	$\frac{1}{2}$	$\frac{1}{2}$	$\frac{13}{64}$	$\frac{7}{32}$	$\frac{13}{64}$	...	...	...
$\frac{3}{8}$	**0.3750**	$\frac{9}{16}$	$\frac{9}{16}$	$\frac{1}{4}$	$\frac{1}{4}$	$\frac{15}{64}$	...	...	...
$\frac{7}{16}$	**0.4375**	$\frac{5}{8}$	$\frac{5}{8}$	$\frac{19}{64}$	$\frac{19}{64}$	$\frac{9}{32}$	...	...	...
$\frac{1}{2}$	**0.5000**	$\frac{3}{4}$	$\frac{3}{4}$	$\frac{21}{64}$	$\frac{11}{32}$	$\frac{5}{16}$	$\frac{7}{8}$	$\frac{11}{32}$	$\frac{5}{16}$
$\frac{9}{16}$	**0.5625**	...	$\frac{13}{16}$	...	...	$\frac{23}{64}$	...	...	...
$\frac{5}{8}$	**0.6250**	$\frac{15}{16}$	$\frac{15}{16}$	$\frac{27}{64}$	$\frac{27}{64}$	$\frac{25}{64}$	$1\frac{1}{16}$	$\frac{27}{64}$	$\frac{25}{64}$
$\frac{3}{4}$	**0.7500**	$1\frac{1}{8}$	$1\frac{1}{8}$	$\frac{1}{2}$	$\frac{1}{2}$	$\frac{15}{32}$	$1\frac{1}{4}$	$\frac{1}{2}$	$\frac{15}{32}$
$\frac{7}{8}$	**0.8750**	$1\frac{5}{16}$	$1\frac{5}{16}$	$\frac{19}{32}$	$\frac{37}{64}$	$\frac{35}{64}$	$1\frac{7}{16}$	$\frac{37}{64}$	$\frac{35}{64}$
1	**1.000**	$1\frac{1}{2}$	$1\frac{1}{2}$	$\frac{21}{32}$	$\frac{43}{64}$	$\frac{39}{64}$	$1\frac{5}{8}$	$\frac{43}{64}$	$\frac{39}{64}$
$1\frac{1}{8}$	**1.1250**	$1\frac{11}{16}$	$1\frac{11}{16}$	$\frac{3}{4}$	$\frac{3}{4}$	$\frac{11}{16}$	$1\frac{13}{16}$	$\frac{3}{4}$	$\frac{11}{16}$
$1\frac{1}{4}$	**1.2500**	$1\frac{7}{8}$	$1\frac{7}{8}$	$\frac{27}{32}$	$\frac{27}{32}$	$\frac{25}{32}$	2	$\frac{27}{32}$	$\frac{25}{32}$
$1\frac{3}{8}$	**1.3750**	$2\frac{1}{16}$	$2\frac{1}{16}$	$\frac{29}{32}$	$\frac{29}{32}$	$\frac{27}{32}$	$2\frac{3}{16}$	$\frac{29}{32}$	$\frac{27}{32}$
$1\frac{1}{2}$	**1.5000**	$2\frac{1}{4}$	$2\frac{1}{4}$	1	1	$\frac{15}{16}$	$2\frac{3}{8}$	1	$\frac{15}{16}$
$1\frac{3}{4}$	**1.7500**	...	$2\frac{5}{8}$	...	$1\frac{5}{32}$	$1\frac{3}{32}$	$2\frac{3}{4}$	$1\frac{5}{32}$	$1\frac{3}{32}$
2	**2.0000**	...	3	...	$1\frac{11}{32}$	$1\frac{7}{32}$	$3\frac{1}{8}$	$1\frac{11}{32}$	$1\frac{7}{32}$
$2\frac{1}{4}$	2.2500	...	$3\frac{3}{8}$	...	$1\frac{1}{2}$	$1\frac{3}{8}$	$3\frac{1}{2}$	$1\frac{1}{2}$	$1\frac{3}{8}$
$2\frac{1}{2}$	2.5000	...	$3\frac{3}{4}$	...	$1\frac{21}{32}$	$1\frac{17}{32}$	$3\frac{7}{8}$	$1\frac{21}{32}$	$1\frac{17}{32}$
$2\frac{3}{4}$	2.7500	...	$4\frac{1}{8}$	...	$1\frac{13}{16}$	$1\frac{11}{16}$	$4\frac{1}{4}$	$1\frac{13}{16}$	$1\frac{11}{16}$
3	3.0000	...	$4\frac{1}{2}$	...	2	$1\frac{7}{8}$	$4\frac{5}{8}$	2	$1\frac{7}{8}$
$3\frac{1}{4}$	3.2500	...	$4\frac{7}{8}$	...	$2\frac{3}{16}$	...	...	...	...
$3\frac{1}{2}$	3.5000	...	$5\frac{1}{4}$	...	$2\frac{5}{16}$	...	...	...	...
$3\frac{3}{4}$	3.7500	...	$5\frac{5}{8}$	...	$2\frac{1}{2}$	...	...	...	...
4	4.0000	...	6	...	$2\frac{11}{16}$	...	...	...	...

[a] ANSI B18.2.1–1981 (R1992).
[b] ANSI/ASME B18.2.2.–1987 (R1993).
[c] Hexagon cap screws and finished hexagon bolts are combined as a single product.

18 Bolts, Nuts, and Cap Screws—Square and Hexagon— American National Standard and Metric (continued)

AMERICAN NATIONAL STANDARD SQUARE AND HEXAGON BOLTS AND NUTS AND HEXAGON CAP SCREWS (continued)

See ANSI B18.2.2 for jam nuts, slotted nuts, thick nuts, thick slotted nuts, and castle nuts. For methods of drawing bolts and nuts and hexagon-head cap screws, see Figs. 13.29, 13.30, and 13.32.

Nominal Size D Body Diameter of Bolt		Regular Bolts					Heavy Nuts			
		Width Across Flats W		Thickness T			Width Across Flats W	Thickness T		
		Sq.	Hex.	Sq. (Unfin.)	Hex. Flat (Unfin.)	Hex. (Fin.)		Sq. (Unfin.)	Hex. Flat (Unfin.)	Hex. (Fin.)
$\frac{1}{4}$	0.2500	$\frac{7}{16}$	$\frac{7}{16}$	$\frac{7}{32}$	$\frac{7}{32}$	$\frac{7}{32}$	$\frac{1}{2}$	$\frac{1}{4}$	$\frac{15}{64}$	$\frac{15}{64}$
$\frac{5}{16}$	0.3125	$\frac{9}{16}$	$\frac{1}{2}$	$\frac{17}{64}$	$\frac{17}{64}$	$\frac{17}{64}$	$\frac{9}{16}$	$\frac{5}{16}$	$\frac{19}{64}$	$\frac{19}{64}$
$\frac{3}{8}$	0.3750	$\frac{5}{8}$	$\frac{9}{16}$	$\frac{21}{64}$		$\frac{21}{64}$	$\frac{11}{16}$	$\frac{3}{8}$	$\frac{23}{64}$	$\frac{23}{64}$
$\frac{7}{16}$	0.4375	$\frac{3}{4}$	$\frac{11}{16}$	$\frac{3}{8}$	$\frac{3}{8}$	$\frac{3}{8}$	$\frac{3}{4}$	$\frac{7}{16}$	$\frac{27}{64}$	$\frac{27}{64}$
$\frac{1}{2}$	0.5000	$\frac{13}{16}$	$\frac{3}{4}$	$\frac{7}{16}$	$\frac{7}{16}$	$\frac{7}{16}$	$\frac{7}{8}$ a	$\frac{1}{2}$	$\frac{31}{64}$	$\frac{31}{64}$
$\frac{9}{16}$	0.5625	...	$\frac{7}{8}$	...	$\frac{31}{64}$	$\frac{31}{64}$	$\frac{15}{16}$	...	$\frac{35}{64}$	$\frac{35}{64}$
$\frac{5}{8}$	0.6250	1	$\frac{15}{16}$	$\frac{35}{64}$	$\frac{35}{64}$	$\frac{35}{64}$	$1\frac{1}{16}$ a	$\frac{5}{8}$	$\frac{39}{64}$	$\frac{39}{64}$
$\frac{3}{4}$	0.7500	$1\frac{1}{8}$	$1\frac{1}{8}$	$\frac{21}{32}$	$\frac{41}{64}$	$\frac{41}{64}$	$1\frac{1}{4}$ a	$\frac{3}{4}$	$\frac{47}{64}$	$\frac{47}{64}$
$\frac{7}{8}$	0.8750	$1\frac{5}{16}$	$1\frac{5}{16}$	$\frac{49}{64}$	$\frac{3}{4}$	$\frac{3}{4}$	$1\frac{7}{16}$ a	$\frac{7}{8}$	$\frac{55}{64}$	$\frac{55}{64}$
1	1.0000	$1\frac{1}{2}$	$1\frac{1}{2}$	$\frac{7}{8}$	$\frac{55}{64}$	$\frac{55}{64}$	$1\frac{5}{8}$ a	1	$\frac{63}{64}$	$\frac{63}{64}$
$1\frac{1}{8}$	1.1250	$1\frac{11}{16}$	$1\frac{11}{16}$	1	1	$\frac{31}{32}$	$1\frac{13}{16}$ a	$1\frac{1}{8}$	$1\frac{1}{8}$	$1\frac{7}{64}$
$1\frac{1}{4}$	1.2500	$1\frac{7}{8}$	$1\frac{7}{8}$	$1\frac{3}{32}$	$1\frac{3}{32}$	$1\frac{1}{16}$	2 a	$1\frac{1}{4}$	$1\frac{1}{4}$	$1\frac{7}{32}$
$1\frac{3}{8}$	1.3750	$2\frac{1}{16}$	$2\frac{1}{16}$	$1\frac{13}{64}$	$1\frac{13}{64}$	$1\frac{11}{64}$	$2\frac{3}{16}$ a	$1\frac{3}{8}$	$1\frac{3}{8}$	$1\frac{11}{32}$
$1\frac{1}{2}$	1.5000	$2\frac{1}{4}$	$2\frac{1}{4}$	$1\frac{5}{16}$	$1\frac{5}{16}$	$1\frac{9}{32}$	$2\frac{3}{8}$ a	$1\frac{1}{2}$	$1\frac{1}{2}$	$1\frac{15}{32}$
$1\frac{5}{8}$	1.6250	...	...	...	...	...	$2\frac{9}{16}$	...	...	$1\frac{19}{32}$
$1\frac{3}{4}$	1.7500	...	...	...	...	...	$2\frac{3}{4}$	...	$1\frac{3}{4}$	$1\frac{23}{32}$
$1\frac{7}{8}$	1.8750	...	...	...	...	...	$2\frac{15}{16}$	...	...	$1\frac{27}{32}$
2	2.0000	...	...	...	...	...	$3\frac{1}{8}$	...	2	$1\frac{31}{32}$
$2\frac{1}{4}$	2.2500	...	...	...	...	...	$3\frac{1}{2}$	...	$2\frac{1}{4}$	$2\frac{13}{64}$
$2\frac{1}{2}$	2.5000	...	...	...	...	...	$3\frac{7}{8}$	...	$2\frac{1}{2}$	$2\frac{29}{64}$
$2\frac{3}{4}$	2.7500	...	...	...	...	...	$4\frac{1}{4}$	...	$2\frac{3}{4}$	$2\frac{45}{64}$
3	3.0000	...	...	...	...	...	$4\frac{5}{8}$	...	3	$2\frac{61}{64}$
$3\frac{1}{4}$	3.2500	...	...	...	...	...	5	...	$3\frac{1}{4}$	$3\frac{3}{16}$
$3\frac{1}{2}$	3.5000	...	...	...	...	...	$5\frac{3}{8}$	...	$3\frac{1}{2}$	$3\frac{7}{16}$
$3\frac{3}{4}$	3.7500	...	...	...	...	...	$5\frac{3}{4}$	...	$3\frac{3}{4}$	$3\frac{11}{16}$
4	4.0000	...	...	...	...	...	$6\frac{1}{8}$	...	4	$3\frac{15}{16}$

a Product feature not unified for heavy square nut.

18 Bolts, Nuts, and Cap Screws—Square and Hexagon— American National Standard and Metric (continued)

METRIC HEXAGON BOLTS, HEXAGON CAP SCREWS,
HEXAGON STRUCTURAL BOLTS, AND HEXAGON NUTS

Nominal Size D, mm	Width Across Flats W (max)		Thickness T (max)			
Body Dia and Thd Pitch	Bolts,[a] Cap Screws,[b] and Nuts[c]	Heavy Hex & Hex Structural Bolts[a] & Nuts[c]	Bolts (Unfin.)	Cap Screw (Fin.)	Nut (Fin. or Unfin.)	
					Style 1	Style 2
M5 × 0.8	8.0		3.88	3.65	4.7	5.1
M6 × 1	10.0		4.38	4.47	5.2	5.7
M8 × 1.25	13.0		5.68	5.50	6.8	7.5
M10 × 1.5	16.0		6.85	6.63	8.4	9.3
M12 × 1.75	18.0	21.0	7.95	7.76	10.8	12.0
M14 × 2	21.0	24.0	9.25	9.09	12.8	14.1
M16 × 2	24.0	27.0	10.75	10.32	14.8	16.4
M20 × 2.5	30.0	34.0	13.40	12.88	18.0	20.3
M24 × 3	36.0	41.0	15.90	15.44	21.5	23.9
M30 × 3.5	46.0	50.0	19.75	19.48	25.6	28.6
M36 × 4	55.0	60.0	23.55	23.38	31.0	34.7
M42 × 4.5	65.0		27.05	26.97	...	...
M48 × 5	75.0		31.07	31.07	...	...
M56 × 5.5	85.0		36.20	36.20	...	...
M64 × 6	95.0		41.32	41.32	...	...
M72 × 6	105.0		46.45	46.45	...	...
M80 × 6	115.0		51.58	51.58	...	...
M90 × 6	130.0		57.74	57.74	...	...
M100 × 6	145.0		63.90	63.90	...	...

HIGH STRENGTH STRUCTURAL HEXAGON BOLTS[a] (FIN.) AND HEXAGON NUTS[c]

M16 × 2	27.0	...	10.75	...	...	17.1
M20 × 2.5	34.0	...	13.40	...	...	20.7
M22 × 2.5	36.0	...	14.9	...	...	23.6
M24 × 3	41.0	...	15.9	...	...	24.2
M27 × 3	46.0	...	17.9	...	...	27.6
M30 × 3.5	50.0	...	19.75	...	...	31.7
M36 × 4	60.0	...	23.55	...	...	36.6

[a] ANSI/ASME B18.2.3.5M–1979 (R1995), B18.2.3.6M–1979 (R1995), B18.2.3.7M–1979 (R1995).
[b] ANSI/ASME B18.2.3.1M–1979 (R1995).
[c] ANSI/ASME B18.2.4.1M–1979 (R1995), B18.2.4.2M–1979 (R1995).

19 Cap Screws, Slotted[a] and Socket Head[b]— American National Standard and Metric

FLAT HEAD　　ROUND HEAD　　FILLISTER HEAD　　SOCKET HEAD

For methods of drawing cap screws, screw lengths, and thread data, see Fig. 13.32.

Nominal Size D	Flat Head[a]	Round Head[a]		Fillister Head[a]		Socket Head[b]		
	A	B	C	E	F	G	J	S
0 (.060)	...	...	...	...	...	.096	.05	.054
1 (.073)	...	...	...	...	...	.118	$\frac{1}{16}$	.066
2 (.086)	...	...	...	...	...	.140	$\frac{5}{64}$	.077
3 (.099)	...	...	...	...	...	.161	$\frac{5}{64}$	.089
4 (.112)	...	...	...	...	...	.183	$\frac{3}{32}$	.101
5 (.125)	...	...	...	...	...	.205	$\frac{3}{32}$	.112
6 (.138)	...	...	...	...	...	.226	$\frac{7}{64}$	.124
8 (.164)	...	...	...	...	...	.270	$\frac{9}{64}$	.148
10 (.190)	...	...	...	...	...	.312	$\frac{5}{32}$	.171
$\frac{1}{4}$	.500	.437	.191	.375	.172	.375	$\frac{3}{16}$	.225
$\frac{5}{16}$	.625	.562	.245	.437	.203	.469	$\frac{1}{4}$	.281
$\frac{3}{8}$	.750	.675	.273	.562	.250	.562	$\frac{5}{16}$	.337
$\frac{7}{16}$	.812	.750	.328	.625	.297	.656	$\frac{3}{8}$	.394
$\frac{1}{2}$	.875	.812	.354	.750	.328	.750	$\frac{3}{8}$	.450
$\frac{9}{16}$	1.000	.937	.409	.812	.375	...	...	...
$\frac{5}{8}$	1.125	1.000	.437	.875	.422	.938	$\frac{1}{2}$	.562
$\frac{3}{4}$	1.375	1.250	.546	1.000	.500	1.125	$\frac{5}{8}$	.675
$\frac{7}{8}$	1.625	...	...	1.125	.594	1.312	$\frac{3}{4}$	.787
1	1.875	...	...	1.312	.656	1.500	$\frac{3}{4}$	.900
$1\frac{1}{8}$	2.062	...	...	...	...	1.688	$\frac{7}{8}$	1.012
$1\frac{1}{4}$	2.312	...	...	...	...	1.875	$\frac{7}{8}$	1.125
$1\frac{3}{8}$	2.562	...	...	...	...	2.062	1	1.237
$1\frac{1}{2}$	2.812	...	...	...	...	2.250	1	1.350

[a] ANSI/ASME B18.6.2–1995.
[b] ANSI/ASME B18.3–1986 (R1995). For hexagon-head screws, see Appendix 18.

19 Cap Screws, Slotted[a] and Socket Head[b]— American National Standard and Metric (continued)

COUNTERSUNK HEAD   BUTTON HEAD   SOCKET HEAD

For methods of drawing cap screws, screw lengths, and thread data, see Fig. 13.32.

	Metric Socket Head Cap Screws								
	Countersunk Head[a]			Button Head[a]			Socket Head[b]		Hex Socket Size
Nominal Size D	A (max)	H	S	B	S	G	C	S	J
M1.6 × 0.35	...	...	...	...	...	...	3.0	0.16	1.5
M2 × 0.4	...	...	...	...	...	...	3.8	0.2	1.5
M2.5 × 0.45	...	...	...	...	...	...	4.5	0.25	2.0
M3 × 0.5	6.72	1.86	0.25	5.70	0.38	0.2	5.5	0.3	2.5
M4 × 0.7	8.96	2.48	0.45	7.6	0.38	0.3	7.0	0.4	3.0
M5 × 0.8	11.2	3.1	0.66	9.5	0.5	0.38	8.5	0.5	4.0
M6 × 1	13.44	3.72	0.7	10.5	0.8	0.74	10.0	0.6	5.0
M8 × 1.25	17.92	4.96	1.16	14.0	0.8	1.05	13.0	0.8	6.0
M10 × 1.5	22.4	6.2	1.62	17.5	0.8	1.45	16.0	1.0	8.0
M12 × 1.75	26.88	7.44	1.8	21.0	0.8	1.63	18.0	1.2	10.0
M14 × 2	30.24	8.12	2.0	...	...	...	21.0	1.4	12.0
M16 × 2	33.6	8.8	2.2	28.0	1.5	2.25	24.0	1.6	14.0
M20 × 2.5	19.67	10.16	2.2	...	...	...	30.0	2.0	17.0
M24 × 3	...	...	...	...	...	...	36.0	2.4	19.0
M30 × 3.5	...	...	...	...	...	...	45.0	3.0	22.0
M36 × 4	...	...	...	...	...	...	54.0	3.6	27.0
M42 × 4.5	...	...	...	...	...	...	63.0	4.2	32.0
M48 × 5	...	...	...	...	...	...	72.0	4.8	36.0

[a] ANSI/ASME B18.3.4M–1986 (R1993).
[b] ANSI/ASME B18.3.1M–1986 (R1993).

ROUND HEAD | STYLES OF CROSS RECESSES (SIMILAR ON ALL MACH SCREWS EXCEPT HEXAGON) | FLAT HEAD | FILLISTER HEAD | OVAL HEAD

TRUSS HEAD | BINDING HEAD | PAN HEAD | CROWN ON RECESSED PAN HEAD | HEXAGON HEAD | 100° FLAT HEAD

AMERICAN NATIONAL STANDARD MACHINE SCREWS[a]

Length of Thread: On screws 2″ long and shorter, the threads extend to within two threads of the head and closer if practicable; longer screws have minimum thread length of $1\frac{3}{4}$″.

Points: Machine screws are regularly made with plain sheared ends, not chamfered.

Threads: Either Coarse or Fine Thread Series, Class 2 fit.

Recessed Heads: Two styles of cross recesses are available on all screws except hexagon head.

Nominal Size	Max Diameter D	Round Head		Flat Heads & Oval Head		Fillister Head		Truss Head			Slot Width
		A	B	C	E	F	G	K	H	R	J
0	0.060	0.113	0.053	0.119	0.035	0.096	0.045	0.131	0.037	0.087	0.023
1	0.073	0.138	0.061	0.146	0.043	0.118	0.053	0.164	0.045	0.107	0.026
2	0.086	0.162	0.069	0.172	0.051	0.140	0.062	0.194	0.053	0.129	0.031
3	0.099	0.187	0.078	0.199	0.059	0.161	0.070	0.226	0.061	0.151	0.035
4	0.112	0.211	0.086	0.225	0.067	0.183	0.079	0.257	0.069	0.169	0.039
5	0.125	0.236	0.095	0.252	0.075	0.205	0.088	0.289	0.078	0.191	0.043
6	0.138	0.260	0.103	0.279	0.083	0.226	0.096	0.321	0.086	0.211	0.048
8	0.164	0.309	0.120	0.332	0.100	0.270	0.113	0.384	0.102	0.254	0.054
10	0.190	0.359	0.137	0.385	0.116	0.313	0.130	0.448	0.118	0.283	0.060
12	0.216	0.408	0.153	0.438	0.132	0.357	0.148	0.511	0.134	0.336	0.067
$\frac{1}{4}$	0.250	0.472	0.175	0.507	0.153	0.414	0.170	0.573	0.150	0.375	0.075
$\frac{5}{16}$	0.3125	0.590	0.216	0.635	0.191	0.518	0.211	0.698	0.183	0.457	0.084
$\frac{3}{8}$	0.375	0.708	0.256	0.762	0.230	0.622	0.253	0.823	0.215	0.538	0.094
$\frac{7}{16}$	0.4375	0.750	0.328	0.812	0.223	0.625	0.265	0.948	0.248	0.619	0.094
$\frac{1}{2}$	0.500	0.813	0.355	0.875	0.223	0.750	0.297	1.073	0.280	0.701	0.106
$\frac{9}{16}$	0.5625	0.938	0.410	1.000	0.260	0.812	0.336	1.198	0.312	0.783	0.118
$\frac{5}{8}$	0.625	1.000	0.438	1.125	0.298	0.875	0.375	1.323	0.345	0.863	0.133
$\frac{3}{4}$	0.750	1.250	0.547	1.375	0.372	1.000	0.441	1.573	0.410	1.024	0.149

Nominal Size	Max Diameter D	Binding Head			Pan Head			Hexagon Head		100° Flat Head		Slot Width
		M	N	O	P	Q	S	T	U	V	W	J
2	0.086	0.181	0.050	0.018	0.167	0.053	0.062	0.125	0.050	...	...	0.031
3	0.099	0.208	0.059	0.022	0.193	0.060	0.071	0.187	0.055	...	...	0.035
4	0.112	0.235	0.068	0.025	0.219	0.068	0.080	0.187	0.060	0.225	0.049	0.039
5	0.125	0.263	0.078	0.029	0.245	0.075	0.089	0.187	0.070	...	...	0.043
6	0.138	0.290	0.087	0.032	0.270	0.082	0.097	0.250	0.080	0.279	0.060	0.048
8	0.164	0.344	0.105	0.039	0.322	0.096	0.115	0.250	0.110	0.332	0.072	0.054
10	0.190	0.399	0.123	0.045	0.373	0.110	0.133	0.312	0.120	0.385	0.083	0.060
12	0.216	0.454	0.141	0.052	0.425	0.125	0.151	0.312	0.155	...	...	0.067
$\frac{1}{4}$	0.250	0.513	0.165	0.061	0.492	0.144	0.175	0.375	0.190	0.507	0.110	0.075
$\frac{5}{16}$	0.3125	0.641	0.209	0.077	0.615	0.178	0.218	0.500	0.230	0.635	0.138	0.084
$\frac{3}{8}$	0.375	0.769	0.253	0.094	0.740	0.212	0.261	0.562	0.295	0.762	0.165	0.094
$\frac{7}{16}$	.4375	...	...	...	.865	.247	.305	...	...	...	...	.094
$\frac{1}{2}$	.500	...	...	...	.987	.281	.348	...	...	...	...	.106
$\frac{9}{16}$	.5625	...	...	...	1.041	.315	.391	...	...	...	...	.118
$\frac{5}{8}$	.625	...	...	...	1.172	.350	.434	...	...	...	...	.133
$\frac{3}{4}$	.750	...	...	...	1.435	.419	.521	...	...	...	...	.149

20 Machine Screws—American National Standard and Metric (continued)

METRIC MACHINE SCREWS

Length of Thread: On screws 36 mm long or shorter, the threads extend to within one thread of the head: on longer screws the thread extends to within two threads of the head.

Points: Machine screws are regularly made with sheared ends, not chamfered.

Threads: Coarse (genera purpose) threads series are given.

Recessed Heads: Two styles of cross-recesses are available on all screws except hexagon head.

Nominal Size & Thd Pitch	Max. Dia. D. mm	Flat Heads & Oval Head		Pan Heads			Hex Head		Slot Width
		C	E	P	Q	S	T	U	J
M2 × M	2.0	3.5	1.2	4.0	1.3	1.6	3.2	1.6	0.7
M2.5 × 0.45	2.5	4.4	1.5	5.0	1.5	2.1	4.0	2.1	0.8
M3 × 0.5	3.0	5.2	1.7	5.6	1.8	2.4	5.0	2.3	1.0
M3.5 × 0.6	3.5	6.9	2.3	7.0	2.1	2.6	5.5	2.6	1.2
M4 × 0.7	4.0	8.0	2.7	8.0	2.4	3.1	7.0	3.0	1.5
M5 × 0.8	5.0	8.9	2.7	9.5	3.0	3.7	8.0	3.8	1.5
M6 × 1	6.0	10.9	3.3	12.0	3.6	4.6	10.0	4.7	1.9
M8 × 1.25	8.0	15.14	4.6	16.0	4.8	6.0	13.0	6.0	2.3
M10 × 1.5	10.0	17.8	5.0	20.0	6.0	7.5	15.0	7.5	2.8
M12 × 1.75	12.0	…	…	…	…	…	18.0	9.0	…

Nominal Size	Metric Machine Screw Lengths—L																			
	2.5	3	4	5	6	8	10	13	16	20	25	30	35	40	45	50	55	60	65	70	80	90
M2 × 0.4	PH	A	A	A	A	A	A	A	A	A												
M2.5 × 0.45		PH	A	A	A	A	A	A	A	A	A	Min. Thd Length—28 mm										
M3 × 0.5			PH	A	A	A	A	A	A	A	A	A										
M3.5 × 0.6				PH	A	A	A	A	A	A	A	A	A		Min. Thd Length—38 mm							
M4 × 0.7				PH	A	A	A	A	A	A	A	A	A	A								
M5 × 0.8					PH	A	A	A	A	A	A	A	A	A	A	A						
M6 × 1						A	A	A	A	A	A	A	A	A	A	A	A					
M8 × 1.25						A	A	A	A	A	A	A	A	A	A	A	A	A	A	A		
M10 × 1.5							A	A	A	A	A	A	A	A	A	A	A	A	A	A	A	
M12 × 1.75								A	A	A	A	A	A	A	A	A	A	A	A	A	A	A

[a] PH = recommended lengths for only pan and hex head metric screws.

 A = recommended lengths for all metric screw head-styles.

21   Keys—Square, Flat, Plain Taper,[a] and Gib Head

Shaft Diameters	Square Stock Key	Flat Stock Key	Gib Head Taper Stock Key					
			Square			Flat		
			Height	Length	Height to Chamfer	Height	Length	Height to Chamfer
D	W = H	W × H	C	F	E	C	F	E
$\frac{1}{2}$ to $\frac{9}{16}$	$\frac{1}{8}$	$\frac{1}{8} \times \frac{3}{32}$	$\frac{1}{4}$	$\frac{7}{32}$	$\frac{5}{32}$	$\frac{3}{16}$	$\frac{1}{8}$	$\frac{1}{8}$
$\frac{5}{8}$ to $\frac{7}{8}$	$\frac{3}{16}$	$\frac{3}{16} \times \frac{1}{8}$	$\frac{5}{16}$	$\frac{9}{32}$	$\frac{7}{32}$	$\frac{1}{4}$	$\frac{3}{16}$	$\frac{5}{32}$
$\frac{15}{16}$ to $1\frac{1}{4}$	$\frac{1}{4}$	$\frac{1}{4} \times \frac{3}{16}$	$\frac{7}{16}$	$\frac{11}{32}$	$\frac{11}{32}$	$\frac{5}{16}$	$\frac{1}{4}$	$\frac{3}{16}$
$1\frac{5}{16}$ to $1\frac{3}{8}$	$\frac{5}{16}$	$\frac{5}{16} \times \frac{1}{4}$	$\frac{9}{16}$	$\frac{13}{32}$	$\frac{13}{32}$	$\frac{3}{8}$	$\frac{5}{16}$	$\frac{1}{4}$
$1\frac{7}{16}$ to $1\frac{3}{4}$	$\frac{3}{8}$	$\frac{3}{8} \times \frac{1}{4}$	$\frac{11}{16}$	$\frac{15}{32}$	$\frac{15}{32}$	$\frac{7}{16}$	$\frac{3}{8}$	$\frac{5}{16}$
$1\frac{13}{16}$ to $2\frac{1}{4}$	$\frac{1}{2}$	$\frac{1}{2} \times \frac{3}{8}$	$\frac{7}{8}$	$\frac{19}{32}$	$\frac{5}{8}$	$\frac{5}{8}$	$\frac{1}{2}$	$\frac{7}{16}$
$2\frac{5}{16}$ to $2\frac{3}{4}$	$\frac{5}{8}$	$\frac{5}{8} \times \frac{7}{16}$	$1\frac{1}{16}$	$\frac{23}{32}$	$\frac{3}{4}$	$\frac{3}{4}$	$\frac{5}{8}$	$\frac{1}{2}$
$2\frac{7}{8}$ to $3\frac{1}{4}$	$\frac{3}{4}$	$\frac{3}{4} \times \frac{1}{2}$	$1\frac{1}{4}$	$\frac{7}{8}$	$\frac{7}{8}$	$\frac{7}{8}$	$\frac{3}{4}$	$\frac{5}{8}$
$3\frac{3}{8}$ to $3\frac{3}{4}$	$\frac{7}{8}$	$\frac{7}{8} \times \frac{5}{8}$	$1\frac{1}{2}$	1	1	$1\frac{1}{16}$	$\frac{7}{8}$	$\frac{3}{4}$
$3\frac{7}{8}$ to $4\frac{1}{2}$	1	$1 \times \frac{3}{4}$	$1\frac{3}{4}$	$1\frac{3}{16}$	$1\frac{3}{16}$	$1\frac{1}{4}$	1	$\frac{13}{16}$
$4\frac{3}{4}$ to $5\frac{1}{2}$	$1\frac{1}{4}$	$1\frac{1}{4} \times \frac{7}{8}$	2	$1\frac{7}{16}$	$1\frac{7}{16}$	$1\frac{1}{2}$	$1\frac{1}{4}$	1
$5\frac{3}{4}$ to 6	$1\frac{1}{2}$	$1\frac{1}{2} \times 1$	$2\frac{1}{2}$	$1\frac{3}{4}$	$1\frac{3}{4}$	$1\frac{3}{4}$	$1\frac{1}{2}$	1

[a] Plain taper square and flat keys have the same dimensions as the plain parallel stock keys, with the addition of the taper on top. Gib head taper square and flat keys have the same dimensions as the plain taper keys, with the addition of the gib head.

Stock lengths for plain taper and gib head taper keys: The minimum stock length equals 4W, and the maximum equals 16W. The increments of increase of length equal 2W.

22   Screw Threads,[a] Square and Acme

Size	Threads per Inch	Size	Threads per Inch	Size	Threads per Inch	Size	Threads per Inch
$\frac{3}{8}$	12	$\frac{7}{8}$	5	2	$2\frac{1}{2}$	$3\frac{1}{2}$	$1\frac{1}{3}$
$\frac{7}{16}$	10	1	5	$2\frac{1}{4}$	2	$3\frac{3}{4}$	$1\frac{1}{3}$
$\frac{1}{2}$	10	$1\frac{1}{8}$	4	$2\frac{1}{2}$	2	4	$1\frac{1}{3}$
$\frac{9}{16}$	8	$1\frac{1}{4}$	4	$2\frac{3}{4}$	2	$4\frac{1}{4}$	$1\frac{1}{3}$
$\frac{5}{8}$	8	$1\frac{1}{2}$	3	3	$1\frac{1}{2}$	$4\frac{1}{2}$	1
$\frac{3}{4}$	6	$1\frac{3}{4}$	$2\frac{1}{2}$	$3\frac{1}{4}$	$1\frac{1}{2}$	over $4\frac{1}{2}$	1

[a] See Appendix 17 for General-Purpose Acme Threads.

23   Woodruff Keys[a]—American National Standard

Key No.[b]	Nominal Sizes A × B	E	F	G	Maximum Sizes H	D	C	Key No.[b]	Nominal Sizes A × B	E	F	G	Maximum Sizes H	D	C
204	$\frac{1}{16} \times \frac{1}{2}$	$\frac{3}{64}$	$\frac{1}{32}$	$\frac{5}{64}$	.194	.1718	.203	808	$\frac{1}{4} \times 1$	$\frac{1}{16}$	$\frac{1}{8}$	$\frac{3}{16}$	.428	.3130	.438
304	$\frac{3}{32} \times \frac{1}{2}$	$\frac{3}{64}$	$\frac{3}{64}$	$\frac{3}{32}$	.194	.1561	.203	809	$\frac{1}{4} \times 1\frac{1}{8}$	$\frac{5}{64}$	$\frac{1}{8}$	$\frac{13}{64}$	.475	.3590	.484
305	$\frac{3}{32} \times \frac{5}{8}$	$\frac{1}{16}$	$\frac{3}{64}$	$\frac{7}{64}$	.240	.2031	.250	810	$\frac{1}{4} \times 1\frac{1}{4}$	$\frac{5}{64}$	$\frac{1}{8}$	$\frac{13}{64}$	.537	.4220	.547
404	$\frac{1}{8} \times \frac{1}{2}$	$\frac{3}{64}$	$\frac{1}{16}$	$\frac{7}{64}$	.194	.1405	.203	811	$\frac{1}{4} \times 1\frac{3}{8}$	$\frac{3}{32}$	$\frac{1}{8}$	$\frac{7}{32}$	.584	.4690	.594
405	$\frac{1}{8} \times \frac{5}{8}$	$\frac{1}{16}$	$\frac{1}{16}$	$\frac{1}{8}$	.240	.1875	.250	812	$\frac{1}{4} \times 1\frac{1}{2}$	$\frac{7}{64}$	$\frac{1}{8}$	$\frac{15}{64}$	.631	.5160	.641
406	$\frac{1}{8} \times \frac{3}{4}$	$\frac{1}{16}$	$\frac{1}{16}$	$\frac{1}{8}$	.303	.2505	.313	1008	$\frac{5}{16} \times 1$	$\frac{1}{16}$	$\frac{5}{32}$	$\frac{7}{32}$	.428	.2818	.438
505	$\frac{5}{32} \times \frac{5}{8}$	$\frac{1}{16}$	$\frac{5}{64}$	$\frac{9}{64}$	.240	.1719	.250	1009	$\frac{5}{16} \times 1\frac{1}{8}$	$\frac{5}{64}$	$\frac{5}{32}$	$\frac{15}{64}$	.475	.3278	.484
506	$\frac{5}{32} \times \frac{3}{4}$	$\frac{1}{16}$	$\frac{5}{64}$	$\frac{9}{64}$	.303	.2349	.313	1010	$\frac{5}{16} \times 1\frac{1}{4}$	$\frac{5}{64}$	$\frac{5}{32}$	$\frac{15}{64}$	.537	.3908	.547
507	$\frac{5}{32} \times \frac{7}{8}$	$\frac{1}{16}$	$\frac{5}{64}$	$\frac{9}{64}$	.365	.2969	.375	1011	$\frac{5}{16} \times 1\frac{3}{8}$	$\frac{3}{32}$	$\frac{5}{32}$	$\frac{8}{32}$	.584	.4378	.594
606	$\frac{3}{16} \times \frac{3}{4}$	$\frac{1}{16}$	$\frac{3}{32}$	$\frac{5}{32}$	.303	.2193	.313	1012	$\frac{5}{16} \times 1\frac{1}{2}$	$\frac{7}{64}$	$\frac{5}{32}$	$\frac{17}{64}$	.631	.4848	.641
607	$\frac{3}{16} \times \frac{7}{8}$	$\frac{1}{16}$	$\frac{3}{32}$	$\frac{5}{32}$	.365	.2813	.375	1210	$\frac{3}{8} \times 1\frac{1}{4}$	$\frac{5}{64}$	$\frac{3}{16}$	$\frac{17}{64}$	.537	.3595	.547
608	$\frac{3}{16} \times 1$	$\frac{1}{16}$	$\frac{3}{32}$	$\frac{5}{32}$	.428	.3443	.438	1211	$\frac{3}{8} \times 1\frac{3}{8}$	$\frac{3}{32}$	$\frac{3}{16}$	$\frac{9}{32}$	.584	.4065	.594
609	$\frac{3}{16} \times 1\frac{1}{8}$	$\frac{5}{64}$	$\frac{3}{32}$	$\frac{11}{64}$	.475	.3903	.484	1212	$\frac{3}{8} \times 1\frac{1}{2}$	$\frac{7}{64}$	$\frac{3}{16}$	$\frac{19}{64}$	.631	.4535	.641
807	$\frac{1}{4} \times \frac{7}{8}$	$\frac{1}{16}$	$\frac{1}{8}$	$\frac{3}{16}$	.365	.2500	.375	...	....	...	...	...	...	...	...

[a] ANSI B17.2–1967 (R1990).
[b] Key numbers indicate nominal key dimensions. The last two digits give the nominal diameter B in eighths of an inch, and the digits before the last two give the nominal width A in thirty-seconds of an inch.

24   Woodruff Key Sizes for Different Shaft Diameters[a]

Shaft Diameter	$\frac{5}{16}$ to $\frac{3}{8}$	$\frac{7}{16}$ to $\frac{1}{2}$	$\frac{9}{16}$ to $\frac{3}{4}$	$\frac{13}{16}$ to $\frac{15}{16}$	1 to $1\frac{3}{16}$	$1\frac{1}{4}$ to $1\frac{7}{16}$	$1\frac{1}{2}$ to $1\frac{3}{4}$	$1\frac{13}{16}$ to $2\frac{1}{8}$	$2\frac{3}{16}$ to $2\frac{1}{2}$
Key Numbers	204	304 305	404 405 406	505 506 507	606 607 608 609	807 808 809	810 811 812	1011 1012	1211 1212

[a] Suggested sizes; not standard.

25 Pratt and Whitney Round-End Keys

KEYS MADE WITH ROUND
ENDS AND KEYWAYS CUT
IN SPLINE MILLER

Maximum length of slot is 4″ + W. Note that key is sunk two-thirds into shaft in all cases.

Key No.	L[a]	W or D	H	Key No.	L[a]	W or D	H
1	$\frac{1}{2}$	$\frac{1}{16}$	$\frac{3}{32}$	22	$1\frac{3}{8}$	$\frac{1}{4}$	$\frac{3}{8}$
2	$\frac{1}{2}$	$\frac{3}{32}$	$\frac{9}{64}$	23	$1\frac{1}{38}$	$\frac{5}{16}$	$\frac{15}{32}$
3	$\frac{1}{2}$	$\frac{1}{8}$	$\frac{3}{16}$	F	$1\frac{3}{8}$	$\frac{3}{8}$	$\frac{9}{16}$
4	$\frac{5}{8}$	$\frac{3}{32}$	$\frac{9}{64}$	24	$1\frac{1}{2}$	$\frac{1}{4}$	$\frac{3}{8}$
5	$\frac{5}{8}$	$\frac{1}{8}$	$\frac{3}{16}$	25	$1\frac{1}{2}$	$\frac{5}{16}$	$\frac{15}{32}$
6	$\frac{5}{8}$	$\frac{5}{32}$	$\frac{15}{64}$	G	$1\frac{1}{2}$	$\frac{3}{8}$	$\frac{9}{16}$
7	$\frac{3}{4}$	$\frac{1}{8}$	$\frac{3}{16}$	51	$1\frac{3}{4}$	$\frac{1}{4}$	$\frac{3}{8}$
8	$\frac{3}{4}$	$\frac{5}{32}$	$\frac{15}{64}$	52	$1\frac{3}{4}$	$\frac{5}{16}$	$\frac{15}{32}$
9	$\frac{3}{4}$	$\frac{3}{16}$	$\frac{9}{32}$	53	$1\frac{3}{4}$	$\frac{3}{8}$	$\frac{9}{16}$
10	$\frac{7}{8}$	$\frac{5}{32}$	$\frac{15}{64}$	26	2	$\frac{3}{16}$	$\frac{9}{32}$
11	$\frac{7}{8}$	$\frac{3}{16}$	$\frac{9}{32}$	27	2	$\frac{1}{4}$	$\frac{3}{8}$
12	$\frac{7}{8}$	$\frac{7}{32}$	$\frac{21}{64}$	28	2	$\frac{5}{16}$	$\frac{15}{32}$
A	$\frac{7}{8}$	$\frac{1}{4}$	$\frac{3}{8}$	29	2	$\frac{3}{8}$	$\frac{9}{16}$
13	1	$\frac{3}{16}$	$\frac{9}{32}$	54	$2\frac{1}{4}$	$\frac{1}{4}$	$\frac{3}{8}$
14	1	$\frac{7}{32}$	$\frac{21}{64}$	55	$2\frac{1}{4}$	$\frac{5}{16}$	$\frac{15}{32}$
15	1	$\frac{1}{4}$	$\frac{3}{8}$	56	$2\frac{1}{4}$	$\frac{3}{8}$	$\frac{9}{16}$
B	1	$\frac{5}{16}$	$\frac{15}{32}$	57	$2\frac{1}{4}$	$\frac{7}{16}$	$\frac{21}{32}$
16	$1\frac{1}{8}$	$\frac{3}{16}$	$\frac{9}{32}$	58	$2\frac{1}{2}$	$\frac{5}{16}$	$\frac{15}{32}$
17	$1\frac{1}{8}$	$\frac{7}{32}$	$\frac{21}{64}$	59	$2\frac{1}{2}$	$\frac{3}{8}$	$\frac{9}{16}$
18	$1\frac{1}{8}$	$\frac{1}{4}$	$\frac{3}{8}$	60	$2\frac{1}{2}$	$\frac{7}{16}$	$\frac{21}{32}$
C	$1\frac{1}{8}$	$\frac{5}{16}$	$\frac{15}{32}$	61	$2\frac{1}{2}$	$\frac{1}{2}$	$\frac{3}{4}$
19	$1\frac{1}{4}$	$\frac{3}{16}$	$\frac{9}{32}$	30	3	$\frac{3}{8}$	$\frac{9}{16}$
20	$1\frac{1}{4}$	$\frac{7}{32}$	$\frac{21}{64}$	31	3	$\frac{7}{16}$	$\frac{21}{32}$
21	$1\frac{1}{4}$	$\frac{1}{4}$	$\frac{3}{8}$	32	3	$\frac{1}{2}$	$\frac{3}{4}$
D	$1\frac{1}{4}$	$\frac{5}{16}$	$\frac{15}{32}$	33	3	$\frac{9}{16}$	$\frac{27}{32}$
E	$1\frac{1}{4}$	$\frac{3}{8}$	$\frac{9}{16}$	34	3	$\frac{5}{8}$	$\frac{15}{16}$

[a] The length L may vary from the table, but equals at least 2W.

For parts lists, etc., give inside diameter, outside diameter, and the thickness; for example, .344 × .688 × .065 TYPE A PLAIN WASHER.

PREFERRED SIZES OF TYPE A PLAIN WASHERS[b]

Nominal Washer Size[c]			Inside Diameter	Outside Diameter	Nominal Thickness
			A	B	C
...	...		0.078	0.188	0.020
...	...		0.094	0.250	0.020
...	...		0.125	0.312	0.032
No. 6	0.138		0.156	0.375	0.049
No. 8	0.164		0.188	0.438	0.049
No. 10	0.190		0.219	0.500	0.049
$\frac{3}{16}$	0.188		0.250	0.562	0.049
No. 12	0.216		0.250	0.562	0.065
$\frac{1}{4}$	0.250	N	0.281	0.625	0.065
$\frac{1}{4}$	0.250	W	0.312	0.734	0.065
$\frac{5}{16}$	0.312	N	0.344	0.688	0.065
$\frac{5}{16}$	0.312	W	0.375	0.875	0.083
$\frac{3}{8}$	0.375	N	0.406	0.812	0.065
$\frac{3}{8}$	0.375	W	0.438	1.000	0.083
$\frac{7}{16}$	0.438	N	0.469	0.922	0.065
$\frac{7}{16}$	0.438	W	0.500	1.250	0.083
$\frac{1}{2}$	0.500	N	0.531	1.062	0.095
$\frac{1}{2}$	0.500	W	0.562	1.375	0.109
$\frac{9}{16}$	0.562	N	0.594	1.156	0.095
$\frac{9}{16}$	0.562	W	0.625	1.469	0.109
$\frac{5}{8}$	0.625	N	0.656	1.312	0.095
$\frac{5}{8}$	0.625	W	0.688	1.750	0.134
$\frac{3}{4}$	0.750	N	0.812	1.469	0.134
$\frac{3}{4}$	0.750	W	0.812	2.000	0.148
$\frac{7}{8}$	0.875	N	0.938	1.750	0.134
$\frac{7}{8}$	0.875	W	0.938	2.250	0.165
1	1.000	N	1.062	2.000	0.134
1	1.000	W	1.062	2.500	0.165
$1\frac{1}{8}$	1.125	N	1.250	2.250	0.134
$1\frac{1}{8}$	1.125	W	1.250	2.750	0.165
$1\frac{1}{4}$	1.250	N	1.375	2.500	0.165
$1\frac{1}{4}$	1.250	W	1.375	3.000	0.165
$1\frac{3}{8}$	1.375	N	1.500	2.750	0.165
$1\frac{3}{8}$	1.375	W	1.500	3.250	0.180
$1\frac{1}{2}$	1.500	N	1.625	3.000	0.165
$1\frac{1}{2}$	1.500	W	1.625	3.500	0.180
$1\frac{5}{8}$	1.625		1.750	3.750	0.180
$1\frac{3}{4}$	1.750		1.875	4.000	0.180
$1\frac{7}{8}$	1.875		2.000	4.250	0.180
2	2.000		2.125	4.500	0.180
$2\frac{1}{4}$	2.250		2.375	4.750	0.220
$2\frac{1}{2}$	2.500		2.625	5.000	0.238
$2\frac{3}{4}$	2.750		2.875	5.250	0.259
3	3000		3.125	5.500	0.284

[a] From ANSI B18.22.1–1965 (R1981). For complete listings, see the standard.
[b] Preferred sizes are for the most part from series previously designated "Standard Plate" and "SAE." Where common sizes existed in the two series, the SAE size is designated "N" (narrow) and the Standard Plate "W" (wide).
[c] Nominal washer sizes are intended for use with comparable nominal screw or bolt sizes.

27 Washers, [a] Lock—American National Standard

For parts lists, etc., give nominal size and series; for example, $\frac{1}{4}$ REGULAR LOCK WASHER

PREFERRED SERIES

Nominal Washer Size[b]	Inside Diameter, Min.	Regular		Extra Duty		Hi-Collar	
		Outside Diameter, Max.	Thickness, Min.	Outside Diameter, Max.	Thickness, Min.	Outside Diameter, Max.	Thickness, Min.
No. 2 0.086	0.088	0.172	0.020	0.208	0.027	...	...
No. 3 0.099	0.101	0.195	0.025	0.239	0.034	...	...
No. 4 0.112	0.115	0.209	0.025	0.253	0.034	0.173	0.022
No. 5 0.125	0.128	0.236	0.031	0.300	0.045	0.202	0.030
No. 6 0.138	0.141	0.250	0.031	0.314	0.045	0.216	0.030
No. 8 0.164	0.168	0.293	0.040	0.375	0.057	0.267	0.047
No. 10 0.190	0.194	0.334	0.047	0.434	0.068	0.294	0.047
No. 12 0.216	0.221	0.377	0.056	0.497	0.080	...	...
$\frac{1}{4}$ 0.250	0.255	0.489	0.062	0.535	0.084	0.365	0.078
$\frac{5}{16}$ 0.312	0.318	0.586	0.078	0.622	0.108	0.460	0.093
$\frac{3}{8}$ 0.375	0.382	0.683	0.094	0.741	0.123	0.553	0.125
$\frac{7}{16}$ 0.438	0.446	0.779	0.109	0.839	0.143	0.647	0.140
$\frac{1}{2}$ 0.500	0.509	0.873	0.125	0.939	0.162	0.737	0.172
$\frac{9}{16}$ 0.562	0.572	0.971	0.141	1.041	0.182	...	...
$\frac{5}{8}$ 0.625	0.636	1.079	0.156	1.157	0.202	0.923	0.203
$\frac{11}{16}$ 0.688	0.700	1.176	0.172	1.258	0.221	...	...
$\frac{3}{4}$ 0.750	0.763	1.271	0.188	1.361	0.241	1.111	0.218
$\frac{13}{16}$ 0.812	0.826	1.367	0.203	1.463	0.261	...	...
$\frac{7}{8}$ 0.875	0.890	1.464	0.219	1.576	0.285	1.296	0.234
$\frac{15}{16}$ 0.938	0.954	1.560	0.234	1.688	0.308	...	...
1 1.000	1.017	1.661	0.250	1.799	0.330	1.483	0.250
$1\frac{1}{16}$ 1.062	1.080	1.756	0.266	1.910	0.352	...	...
$1\frac{1}{8}$ 1.125	1.144	1.853	0.281	2.019	0.375	1.669	0.313
$1\frac{3}{16}$ 1.188	1.208	1.950	0.297	2.124	0.396	...	...
$1\frac{1}{4}$ 1.250	1.271	2.045	0.312	2.231	0.417	1.799	0.313
$1\frac{5}{16}$ 1.312	1.334	2.141	0.328	2.335	0.438	...	...
$1\frac{3}{8}$ 1.375	1.398	2.239	0.344	2.439	0.458	2.041	0.375
$1\frac{7}{16}$ 1.438	1.462	2.334	0.359	2.540	0.478	...	...
$1\frac{1}{2}$ 1.500	1.525	2.430	0.375	2.638	0.496	2.170	0.375

[a] From ANSI/ASME B18.21.1–1994. For complete listing, see the standard.
[b] Nominal washer sizes are intended for use with comparable nominal screw or bolt sizes.

28 Wire Gage Standards[a]

Dimensions of sizes in decimal parts of an inch.[b]

No. of Wire	American or Brown & Sharpe for Non-ferrous Metals	Birming-ham, or Stubs' Iron Wire[c]	American S. & W. Co.'s (Washburn & Moen) Std. Steel Wire	American S. & W. Co.'s Music Wire	Imperial Wire	Stubs' Steel Wire[c]	Steel Manu facturers' Sheet Gage[b]	No. of Wire
7–0's	.651354	...	.4900	...	.500	...	...	7–0's
6–0's	.580049	...	.4615	.004	.464	...	...	6–0's
5–0's	.516549	.500	.4305	.005	.432	...	...	5–0's
4–0's	.460	.454	.3938	.006	.400	...	...	4–0's
000	.40964	.425	.3625	.007	.372	...	...	000
00	.3648	.380	.3310	.008	.348	...	...	00
0	.32486	.340	.3065	.009	.324	...	...	0
1	.2893	.300	.2830	.010	.300	.227	...	1
2	.25763	.284	.2625	.011	.276	.219	...	2
3	.22942	.259	.2437	.012	.252	.212	.2391	3
4	.20431	.238	.2253	.013	.232	.207	.2242	4
6	.16202	.203	.1920	.016	.192	.201	.1943	6
7	.14428	.180	.1770	.018	.176	.199	.1793	7
8	.12849	.165	.1620	.020	.160	.197	.1644	8
9	.11443	.148	.1483	.022	.144	.194	.1495	9
10	.10189	.134	.1350	.024	.128	.191	.1345	10
11	.090742	.120	.1205	.026	.116	.188	.1196	11
12	.080808	.109	.1055	.029	.104	.185	.1046	12
13	.071961	.095	.0915	.031	.092	.182	.0897	13
14	.064084	.083	.0800	.033	.080	.180	.0747	14
15	.057068	.072	.0720	.035	.072	.178	.0763	15
16	.05082	.065	.0625	.037	.064	.175	.0598	16
17	.045257	.058	.0540	.039	.056	.172	.0538	17
18	.040303	.049	.0475	.041	.048	.168	.0478	18
19	.03589	.042	.0410	.043	.040	.164	.0418	19
20	.031961	.035	.0348	.045	.036	.161	.0359	20
21	.028462	.032	.0317	.047	.032	.157	.0329	21
22	.025347	.028	.0286	.049	.028	.155	.0299	22
23	.022571	.025	.0258	.051	.024	.153	.0269	23
24	.0201	.022	.0230	.055	.022	.151	.0239	24
25	.0179	.020	.0204	.059	.020	.148	.0209	25
26	.01594	.018	.0181	.063	.018	.146	.0179	26
27	.014195	.016	.0173	.067	.0164	.143	.0164	27
28	.012641	.014	.0162	.071	.0149	.139	.0149	28
29	.011257	.013	.0150	.075	.0136	.134	.0135	29
30	.010025	.012	.0140	.080	.0124	.127	.0120	30
31	.008928	.010	.0132	.085	.0116	.120	.0105	31
32	.00795	.009	.0128	.090	.0108	.115	.0097	32
33	.00708	.008	.0118	.095	.0100	.112	.0090	33
34	.006304	.007	.0104	...	.0092	.110	.0082	34
35	.005614	.005	.0095	...	.0084	.108	.0075	35
36	.005	.004	.0090	...	.0076	.106	.0067	36
37	.004453	...	.0085	...	.0068	.103	.0064	37
38	.003965	...	.0080	...	.0060	.101	.0060	38
39	.003531	...	.0075	...	.0052	.099	...	39
40	.003144	...	.0070	...	.0048	.097	...	40

[a] Courtesy Brown & Sharpe Mfg. Co.
[b] Now used by steel manufacturers in place of old U.S. Standard Gage.
[c] The difference between the Stubs' Iron Wire Gage and the Stubs' Steel Wire Gage should be noted, the first being commonly known as the English Standard Wire, or Birmingham Gage, which designates the Stubs' soft wire sizes and the second being used in measuring drawn steel wire or drill rods of Stubs' make.

TAPER .25 PER FT

L (MAX)

D

To find small diameter of pin, multiply the length by .02083 and subtract the result from the larger diameter. All dimensions are given in inches.

Standard reamers are available for pins given above the heavy line.

Number	7/0	6/0	5/0	4/0	3/0	2/0	0	1	2	3	4	5	6	7	8
Size (Large End)	.0625	.0780	.0940	.1090	.1250	.1410	.1560	.1720	.1930	.2190	.2500	.2890	.3410	.4090	.4920
Shaft Diameter (Approx)[b]		$\frac{7}{32}$	$\frac{1}{4}$	$\frac{5}{16}$	$\frac{3}{8}$	$\frac{7}{16}$	$\frac{1}{2}$	$\frac{9}{16}$	$\frac{5}{8}$	$\frac{3}{4}$	$\frac{13}{16}$	$\frac{7}{8}$	1	$1\frac{1}{4}$	$1\frac{1}{2}$
Drill Size (Before Reamer)[b]	.0312	.0312	.0625	.0625	.0781	.0938	.0938	.1094	.1250	.1250	.1562	.1562	.2188	.2344	.3125
Length L															
.250	X	X	X	X	X	X	X								
.375	X	X	X	X	X	X	X								
.500	X	X	X	X	X	X	X								
.625	X	X	X	X	X	X	X	X							
.750	X	X	X	X	X	X	X	X	X						
.875	X	X	X	X	X	X	X	X	X						
1.000	X	X	X	X	X	X	X	X	X						
1.250	:	:	X	X	X	X	X	X	X	X					
1.500	:	:	X	X	X	X	X	X	X	X	X				
1.750	:	:	:	:	X	X	X	X	X	X	X	X			
2.000	:	:	:	:	X	X	X	X	X	X	X	X			
2.250	:	:	:	:	:	:	X	X	X	X	X	X	X		
2.500	:	:	:	:	:	:	X	X	X	X	X	X	X		
2.750	:	:	:	:	:	:	:	X	X	X	X	X	X		
3.000	:	:	:	:	:	:	:	X	X	X	X	X	X		
3.250	:	:	:	:	:	:	:	:	X	X	X	X	X	X	
3.500	:	:	:	:	:	:	:	:	X	X	X	X	X	X	
3.750	:	:	:	:	:	:	:	:	:	X	X	X	X	X	
4.000	:	:	:	:	:	:	:	:	:	X	X	X	X	X	X
4.250	:	:	:	:	:	:	:	:	:	:	:	X	X	X	X
4.500	:	:	:	:	:	:	:	:	:	:	:	X	X	X	X

[a] ANSI/ASME B18.8.2–1994. For Nos. 9 and 10, see the standard. Pins Nos 11 (size .8600), 12 (size 1.032), 13 (size 1.241), and 14 (size 1.523) are special sizes; hence their lengths are special.
[b] Suggested sizes; not American National Standard.

30 Cotter Pins[a]—American National Standard

POINT OF CONTACT WITH HOLE

STANDARD

EXTENDED MITER END PRONG SQUARE CUT HAMMER LOCK CHISEL POINT BEVEL POINT MITER END

PREFERRED POINT TYPES

All dimensions are given in inches.

Nominal Size or Pin Diameter		Diameter A		Outside Eye Diameter B Min.	Extended Prong Length Min.	Hole Sizes Recommended
		Max.	Min.			
$\frac{1}{32}$	.031	.032	.028	.06	.01	.047
$\frac{3}{64}$	.047	.048	.044	.09	.02	.062
$\frac{1}{16}$	.062	.060	.056	.12	.03	.078
$\frac{5}{64}$	.078	.076	.072	.16	.04	.094
$\frac{3}{32}$	.094	.090	.086	.19	.04	.109
$\frac{7}{64}$	.109	.104	.100	.22	.05	.125
$\frac{1}{8}$	.125	.120	.116	.25	.06	.141
$\frac{9}{64}$	.141	.134	.130	.28	.06	.156
$\frac{5}{32}$	.156	.150	.146	.31	.07	.172
$\frac{3}{16}$	.188	.176	.172	.38	.09	.203
$\frac{7}{32}$	.219	.207	.202	.44	.10	.234
$\frac{1}{4}$	.250	.225	.220	.50	.11	.266
$\frac{5}{16}$	.312	.280	.275	.62	.14	.312
$\frac{3}{8}$	.375	.335	.329	.75	.16	.375
$\frac{7}{16}$	.438	.406	.400	.88	.20	.438
$\frac{1}{2}$	.500	.473	.467	1.00	.23	.500
$\frac{5}{8}$	.625	.598	.590	1.25	.30	.625
$\frac{3}{4}$	.750	.723	.715	1.50	.36	.750

[a] ANSI/ASME B18.8.1–1994.

31   Metric Equivalents

Length	
U.S. to Metric	**Metric to U.S.**
1 inch = 2.540 centimeters	1 millimeter = .039 inch
1 foot = .305 meter	1 centimeter = .394 inch
1 yard = .914 meter	1 meter = 3.281 feet or 1.094 yards
1 mile = 1.609 kilometers	1 kilometer = .621 mile
Area	
$1 \text{ inch}^2 = 6.451 \text{ centimeter}^2$	$1 \text{ millimeter}^2 = .00155 \text{ inch}^2$
$1 \text{ foot}^2 = .093 \text{ meter}^2$	$1 \text{ centimeter}^2 = .155 \text{ inch}^2$
$1 \text{ yard}^2 = .836 \text{ meter}^2$	$1 \text{ meter}^2 = 10.764 \text{ foot}^2 \text{ or } 1.196 \text{ yard}^2$
$1 \text{ acre}^2 = 4{,}046.873 \text{ meter}^2$	$1 \text{ kilometer}^2 = .386 \text{ mile}^2 \text{ or } 247.04 \text{ acre}^2$
Volume	
$1 \text{ inch}^3 = 16.387 \text{ centimeter}^3$	$1 \text{ centimeter}^3 = .061 \text{ inch}^3$
$1 \text{ foot}^3 = .028 \text{ meter}^3$	$1 \text{ meter}^3 = 35.314 \text{ foot}^3 \text{ or } 1.308 \text{ yard}^3$
$1 \text{ yard}^3 = .764 \text{ meter}^3$	1 liter = .2642 gallons
1 quart = 0.946 liter	1 liter = 1.057 quarts
$1 \text{ gallon} = .003785 \text{ meter}^3$	$1 \text{ meter}^3 = 264.02 \text{ gallons}$
Weight	
1 ounce = 28.349 grams	1 gram = .035 ounce
1 pound = .454 kilogram	1 kilogram = 2.205 pounds
1 ton = .907 metric ton	1 metric ton = 1.102 tons
Velocity	
1 foot/second = .305 meter/second	1 meter/second = 3.281 feet/second
1 mile/hour = .447 meter/second	1 kilometer/hour = .621 mile/second
Acceleration	
$1 \text{ inch/second}^2 = .0254 \text{ meter/second}^2$	$1 \text{ meter/second}^2 = 3.278 \text{ feet/second}^2$
$1 \text{ foot/second}^2 = .305 \text{ meter/second}^2$	
Force	

N (newton) = basic unit of force, $kg\text{-}m/s^2$. A mass of one kilogram (1 kg) exerts a gravitational force of 9.8 N (theoretically 9.80665 N) at mean sea level.

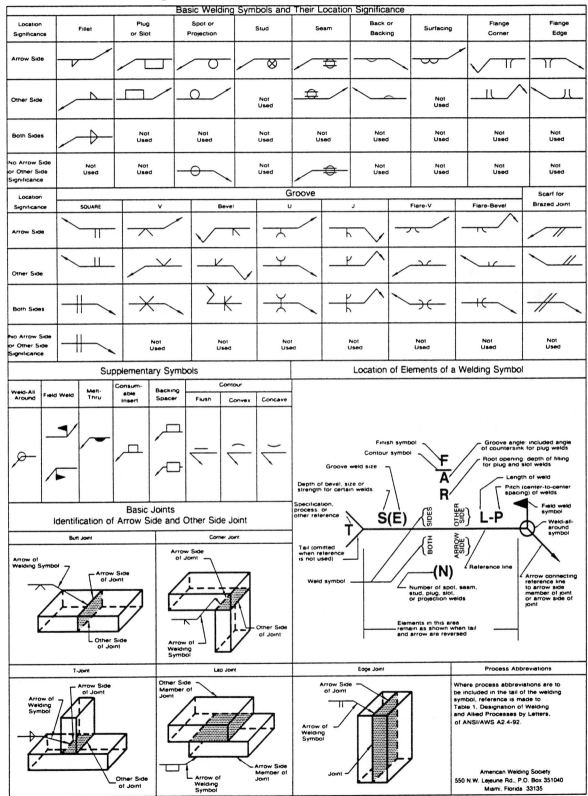

Basic Welding Symbols and Their Location Significance									
Location Significance	Fillet	Plug or Slot	Spot or Projection	Stud	Seam	Back or Backing	Surfacing	Flange Corner	Flange Edge
Arrow Side									
Other Side				Not Used			Not Used		
Both Sides		Not Used	Not Used	Not Used	Not Used	Not Used	Not Used	Not Used	Not Used
No Arrow Side or Other Side Significance	Not Used	Not Used		Not Used		Not Used	Not Used	Not Used	Not Used

Location Significance	Groove							Scarf for Brazed Joint
	SQUARE	V	Bevel	U	J	Flare-V	Flare-Bevel	
Arrow Side								
Other Side								
Both Sides								
No Arrow Side or Other Side Significance		Not Used	Not Used	Not Used	Not Used	Not Used	Not Used	Not Used

Supplementary Symbols

Weld-All Around	Field Weld	Melt-Thru	Consumable Insert	Backing Spacer	Contour		
					Flush	Convex	Concave

Location of Elements of a Welding Symbol

Finish symbol
Contour symbol
Groove weld size
Depth of bevel; size or strength for certain welds
Specification, process, or other reference
Tail (omitted when reference is not used)
Weld symbol

Groove angle: included angle of countersink for plug welds
Root opening: depth of filling for plug and slot welds
Length of weld
Pitch (center-to-center spacing) of welds
Field weld symbol
Weld-all-around symbol
Reference line
Arrow connecting reference line to arrow side member of joint or arrow side of joint

F
A
R
S(E)
T
(N)
L-P

SIDES
OTHER SIDE
BOTH
ARROW SIDE

Number of spot, seam, stud, plug, slot, or projection welds
Elements in this area remain as shown when tail and arrow are reversed

**Basic Joints
Identification of Arrow Side and Other Side Joint**

Butt Joint
Arrow of Welding Symbol
Arrow Side of Joint
Other Side of Joint

Corner Joint
Arrow Side of Joint
Other Side of Joint
Arrow of Welding Symbol

T-Joint
Arrow of Welding Symbol
Arrow Side of Joint
Other Side of Joint

Lap Joint
Other Side Member of Joint
Arrow of Welding Symbol
Arrow Side Member of Joint

Edge Joint
Arrow Side of Joint
Arrow of Welding Symbol
Joint

Process Abbreviations

Where process abbreviations are to be included in the tail of the welding symbol, reference is made to Table 1, Designation of Welding and Allied Processes by Letters, of ANSI/AWS A2.4-92.

American Welding Society
550 N.W. Lejeune Rd., P.O. Box 351040
Miami, Florida 33135

[a] ANSI/AWS A2.4–93.

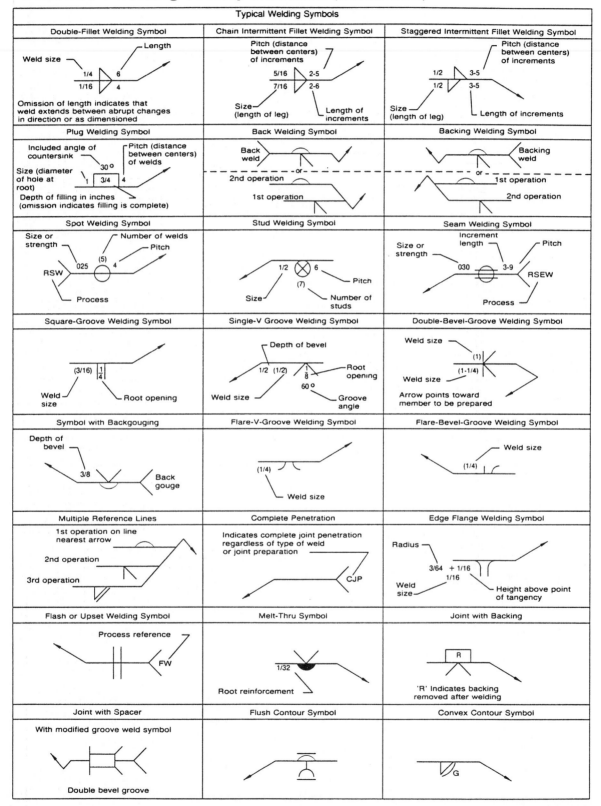

Typical Welding Symbols

Double-Fillet Welding Symbol

Length

Weld size

1/4 6
1/16 4

Omission of length indicates that weld extends between abrupt changes in direction or as dimensioned

Chain Intermittent Fillet Welding Symbol

Pitch (distance between centers) of increments

5/16 2-5
7/16 2-6

Size (length of leg)

Length of increments

Staggered Intermittent Fillet Welding Symbol

Pitch (distance between centers) of increments

1/2 3-5
1/2 3-5

Size (length of leg)

Length of increments

Plug Welding Symbol

Included angle of countersink
Size (diameter of hole at root)
30°
1 3/4 4
Pitch (distance between centers) of welds
Depth of filling in inches (omission indicates filling is complete)

Back Welding Symbol

Back weld
— or —
2nd operation
1st operation

Backing Welding Symbol

Backing weld
— or —
1st operation
2nd operation

Spot Welding Symbol

Size or strength
(5)
025 4
RSW
Number of welds
Pitch
Process

Stud Welding Symbol

1/2 6
(7)
Size
Pitch
Number of studs

Seam Welding Symbol

Increment length
Size or strength
030 3-9
RSEW
Pitch
Process

Square-Groove Welding Symbol

(3/16) 1/4
Weld size
Root opening

Single-V Groove Welding Symbol

Depth of bevel
1/2 (1/2) 1/8
60°
Weld size
Root opening
Groove angle

Double-Bevel-Groove Welding Symbol

Weld size
(1)
(1-1/4)
Weld size
Arrow points toward member to be prepared

Symbol with Backgouging

Depth of bevel
3/8
Back gouge

Flare-V-Groove Welding Symbol

(1/4)
Weld size

Flare-Bevel-Groove Welding Symbol

Weld size
(1/4)

Multiple Reference Lines

1st operation on line nearest arrow
2nd operation
3rd operation

Complete Penetration

Indicates complete joint penetration regardless of type of weld or joint preparation
CJP

Edge Flange Welding Symbol

Radius
3/64 + 1/16
1/16
Weld size
Height above point of tangency

Flash or Upset Welding Symbol

Process reference
FW

Melt-Thru Symbol

1/32
Root reinforcement

Joint with Backing

R
'R' Indicates backing removed after welding

Joint with Spacer

With modified groove weld symbol
Double bevel groove

Flush Contour Symbol

Convex Contour Symbol

G

* It should be understood that these charts are intended only as shop akis. The only complete and official presentation of the standard welding symbols is in A2.4.

32 Welding Symbols and Processes— American Welding Society Standard (continued)

MASTER CHART OF WELDING AND ALLIED PROCESSES

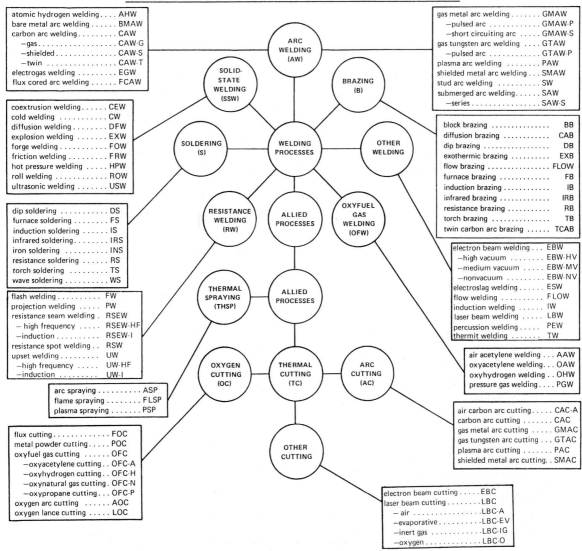

atomic hydrogen welding . . . . AHW
bare metal arc welding . . . . . . BMAW
carbon arc welding . . . . CAW
  —gas . . . . CAW-G
  —shielded . . . . CAW-S
  —twin . . . . CAW-T
electrogas welding . . . . EGW
flux cored arc welding . . . . . . FCAW

coextrusion welding . . . . CEW
cold welding . . . . CW
diffusion welding . . . . DFW
explosion welding . . . . EXW
forge welding . . . . FOW
friction welding . . . . FRW
hot pressure welding . . . . . HPW
roll welding . . . . ROW
ultrasonic welding . . . . USW

dip soldering . . . . DS
furnace soldering . . . . FS
induction soldering . . . . . . IS
infrared soldering . . . . IRS
iron soldering . . . . INS
resistance soldering . . . . . . RS
torch soldering . . . . TS
wave soldering . . . . WS

flash welding . . . . FW
projection welding . . . . . PW
resistance seam welding . RSEW
  — high frequency . . . . . RSEW-HF
  —induction . . . . RSEW-I
resistance spot welding . . RSW
upset welding . . . . UW
  —high frequency . . . . . UW-HF
  —induction . . . . UW-I

arc spraying . . . . ASP
flame spraying . . . . FLSP
plasma spraying . . . . PSP

flux cutting . . . . FOC
metal powder cutting . . . . . POC
oxyfuel gas cutting . . . . . . OFC
  —oxyacetylene cutting . . OFC-A
  —oxyhydrogen cutting . . OFC-H
  —oxynatural gas cutting . OFC-N
  —oxypropane cutting . . . OFC-P
oxygen arc cutting . . . . . . AOC
oxygen lance cutting . . . . . LOC

gas metal arc welding . . . . . . GMAW
  —pulsed arc . . . . GMAW-P
  —short circuiting arc . . . . . GMAW-S
gas tungsten arc welding . . . . GTAW
  —pulsed arc . . . . GTAW-P
plasma arc welding . . . . PAW
shielded metal arc welding . . . SMAW
stud arc welding . . . . SW
submerged arc welding . . . . . SAW
  —series . . . . SAW-S

block brazing . . . . BB
diffusion brazing . . . . CAB
dip brazing . . . . DB
exothermic brazing . . . . EXB
flow brazing . . . . FLOW
furnace brazing . . . . FB
induction brazing . . . . IB
infrared brazing . . . . IRB
resistance brazing . . . . RB
torch brazing . . . . TB
twin carbon arc brazing . . . . . . TCAB

electron beam welding . . . EBW
  —high vacuum . . . . EBW-HV
  —medium vacuum . . . . . EBW-MV
  —nonvacuum . . . . EBW-NV
electroslag welding . . . . . . ESW
flow welding . . . . FLOW
induction welding . . . . . . IW
laser beam welding . . . . . LBW
percussion welding . . . . . PEW
thermit welding . . . . TW

air acetylene welding . . . AAW
oxyacetylene welding . . . OAW
oxyhydrogen welding . . OHW
pressure gas welding . . . . PGW

air carbon arc cutting . . . . . CAC-A
carbon arc cutting . . . . CAC
gas metal arc cutting . . . . . GMAC
gas tungsten arc cutting . . . GTAC
plasma arc cutting . . . . PAC
shielded metal arc cutting. . SMAC

electron beam cutting . . . . . EBC
laser beam cutting . . . . LBC
  — air . . . . LBC-A
  —evaporative . . . . LBC-EV
  —inert gas . . . . LBC-IG
  —oxygen . . . . LBC-O

ᵃ ANSI/AWS A3.0–94.

33 Topographic Symbols

Symbol	Label	Symbol	Label
	Highway		National or State Line
	Railroad		County Line
	Highway Bridge		Township or District Line
	Railroad Bridge		City or Village Line
	Drawbridges		Triangulation Statio
	Suspension Bridge		Bench Mark and Elevation
	Dam		Any Location Station (WITH EXPLANATORY NOTE)
	Telegraph or Telephone Line		Streams in General
	Power-Transmission Line		Lake or Pond
	Buildings in General		Falls and Rapids
	Capital		Contours
	County Seat		Hachures
	Other Towns		Sand and Sand Dunes
	Barbed Wire Fence		Marsh
	Smooth Wire Fence		Woodland of Any Kind
	Hedge		Orchard
	Oil or Gas Wells		Grassland in General
	Windmill		Cultivated Fields
	Tanks		Commercial or Municipal Field
	Canal or Ditch		Airplane Landing Field Marked or Emergency
	Canal Lock		Mooring Mast
	Canal Lock (POINT UPSTREAM)		Airway Light Beacon

34 Piping Symbols—American National Standard

	FLANGED	SCREWED	BELL & SPIGOT	WELDED	SOLDERED
1. Joint					
2. Elbow—90°					
3. Elbow—45°					
4. Elbow—Turned Up					
5. Elbow—Turned Down					
6. Elbow—Long Radius					
7. Reducing Elbow					
8. Tee					
9. Tee—Outlet Up					
10. Tee—Outlet Down					
11. Side Outlet Tee—Outlet Up					
12. Cross					
13. Reducer—Concentric					
14. Reducer—Eccentric					
15. Lateral					
16. Gate Valve—Elev.					
17. Globe Valve—Elev.					
18. Check Valve					
19. Stop Cock					
20. Safety Valve					
21. Expansion Joint					
22. Union					

[a] ANSI/ASME Y32.2.3–1949 (R1994).

35 Heating, Ventilating, and Ductwork Symbols[a]— American National Standard

Symbol	Name	Symbol	Name
	High Pressure Steam		Soil, Waste or Leader (Above Grade)
	Medium Pressure Return		Cold Water
FOF	Fuel Oil Flow		Hot Water
A	Compressed Air		Hot Water Return
RD	Refrigerant Discharge	F — F	Fire Line
RS	Refrigerant Suction	G — G	Gas
B	Brine Supply	S	Sprinklers—Main Supplies

Wall Radiator, Plan

Wall Radiator on Ceiling, Plan

Unit Heater (Propeller), Plan

Unit Heater (Centrifugal Fan), Plan

Thermostatic Trap

Thermostatic Float

Thermometer

Thermostat

Duct Plan (1st Figure, Width; 2nd Depth) — 20X12

Inclined Drop in Respect to Air Flow — D

Supply Duct Section — S — 12 X 20

Exhaust Duct Section — E — 12 X 20

Recirculation Duct Section — R — 12 X 20

Fresh Air Duct Section — A F — 12 X 20

Supply Outlet

Exhaust Inlet

Volume Damper — Plan

Volume Damper — Elev.

Deflecting Damper

Turning Vanes

Automatic Dampers — M

Canvas Connections

Fan and Motor with Belt Guard

Intake Louvres and Screen

[a] ANSI/ASME Y32.2.3–1949 (R1994) and ANSI Y32.2.4–1949 (R1993).

[a] ANSI/ASME Y14.5M–1994.

37 Form and Proportion of Geometric Tolerancing Symbols[a]

[a] ANSI/ASME Y14.5M–1994.

All dimensions are in inches except those in last two columns.

Nominal Pipe Size	D Outside Diameter of Pipe	Threads per Inch	L_1 Normal Engagement by Hand Between External and Internal Threads	L_2 Length of Effective Thread	Nominal Wall Thickness										Length of Pipe, Feet, per Square Foot External Surface[f]	Length of Standard Weight Pipe, Feet, Containing 1 cu. ft.[f]
					Sched. 10	Sched. 20[d]	Sched. 30[d]	Sched. 40[d]	Sched. 60[d]	Sched. 80[d]	Sched. 100	Sched. 120	Sched. 140	Sched. 160		
1/8	.405	27	.1615	.2639	⋮	⋮	⋮	.068	⋮	.095	⋮	⋮	⋮	⋮	9.431	2,533.8
1/4	.540	18	.2278	.4018	⋮	⋮	⋮	.088	⋮	.119	⋮	⋮	⋮	⋮	7.073	1,383.8
3/8	.675	18	.240	.4078	⋮	⋮	⋮	.091	⋮	.126	⋮	⋮	⋮	⋮	5.658	754.36
1/2	.840	14	.320	.5337	⋮	⋮	⋮	.109	⋮	.147	⋮	⋮	⋮	.188	4.547	473.91
3/4	1.050	14	.339	.5457	⋮	⋮	⋮	.113	⋮	.154	⋮	⋮	⋮	.219	3.637	270.03
1	1.315	11.5	.400	.6828	⋮	⋮	⋮	.133	⋮	.179	⋮	⋮	⋮	.250	2.904	166.62
1 1/4	1.660	11.5	.420	.7068	⋮	⋮	⋮	.140	⋮	.191	⋮	⋮	⋮	.250	2.301	96.275
1 1/2	1.900	11.5	.420	.7235	⋮	⋮	⋮	.145	⋮	.200	⋮	⋮	⋮	.281	2.010	70.733
2	2.375	11.5	.436	.7565	⋮	⋮	⋮	.154	⋮	.218	⋮	⋮	⋮	.344	1.608	42.913
2 1/2	2.875	8	.682	1.1375	⋮	⋮	⋮	.203	⋮	.276	⋮	⋮	⋮	.375	1.328	30.077
3	3.500	8	.766	1.2000	⋮	⋮	⋮	.216	⋮	.300	⋮	⋮	⋮	.438	1.091	19.479
3 1/2	4.000	8	.821	1.2500	⋮	⋮	⋮	.226	⋮	.318	⋮	⋮	⋮	⋮	.954	14.565
4	4.500	8	.844	1.3000	⋮	⋮	⋮	.237	⋮	.337	⋮	.438	⋮	.531	.848	11.312
5	5.563	8	.937	1.4063	⋮	⋮	⋮	.258	⋮	.375	⋮	.500	⋮	.625	.686	7.199
6	6.625	8	.958	1.5125	.250	⋮	⋮	.280	⋮	.432	⋮	.562	⋮	.719	.576	4.984
8	8.625	8	1.063	1.7125	.250	.250	.277	.322	.406	.500	.594	.719	.812	.906	.443	2.878
10	10.750	8	1.210	1.9250	.250	.250	.307	.365	.500	.594	.719	.844	1.000	1.125	.355	1.826
12	12.750	8	1.360	2.1250	.250	.250	.330	.406	.562	.688	.844	1.000	1.125	1.312	.299	1.273
14 OD	14.000	8	1.562	2.2500	.250	.312	.375	.438	.594	.750	.938	1.094	1.250	1.406	.273	1.065
16 OD	16.000	8	1.812	2.4500	.250	.312	.375	.500	.656	.844	1.031	1.219	1.438	1.594	.239	.815
18 OD	18.000	8	2.000	2.6500	.250	.312	.438	.562	.750	.938	1.156	1.375	1.562	1.781	.212	.644
20 OD	20.000	8	2.125	2.8500	.250	.375	.500	.594	.812	1.031	1.281	1.500	1.750	1.969	.191	.518
24 OD	24.000	8	2.375	3.2500	.250	.375	.562	.688	.969	1.219	1.531	1.812	2.062	2.344	.159	.358

a ANSI/ASME B36.10M-1995.
b ANSI/ASME B1.20.1–1983 (R1992).
c Refer to §13.22 and Fig. 13.20.
d Boldface figures correspond to "standard" pipe.
e Boldface figures correspond to "extra strong" pipe.
f Calculated values for Schedule 40 pipe.

Size, inches	Thickness, inches	Outside Diameter, inches	16 ft Laying Length — Avg. per Foot[b] Weight (lb)	16 ft Laying Length — Per Length Based on
Class 50: 50 psi Pressure—115 ft Head				
3	.32	3.96	12.4	195
4	.35	4.80	16.5	265
6	.38	6.90	25.9	415
8	.41	9.05	37.0	590
10	.44	11.10	49.1	785
12	.48	13.20	63.7	1,020
14	.48	15.30	74.6	1,195
16	.54	17.40	95.2	1,525
18	.54	19.50	107.6	1,720
20	.57	21.60	125.9	2,015
24	.63	25.80	166.0	2,655
30	.79	32.00	257.6	4,120
36	.87	38.30	340.9	5,455
42	.97	44.50	442.0	7,070
48	1.06	50.80	551.6	8,825
Class 100: 100 psi Pressure—231 ft Head				
3	.32	3.96	12.4	195
4	.35	4.80	16.5	265
6	.38	6.90	25.9	415
8	.41	9.05	37.0	590
10	.44	11.10	49.1	785
12	.48	13.20	63.7	1,020
14	.51	15.30	78.8	1,260
16	.54	17.40	95.2	1,525
18	.58	19.50	114.8	1,835
20	.62	21.60	135.9	2,175
24	.68	25.80	178.1	2,850
30	.79	32.00	257.6	4,120
36	.87	38.30	340.9	5,455
42	.97	44.50	442.0	7,070
48	1.06	50.80	551.6	8,825
Class 150: 150 psi Pressure—346 ft Head				
3	.32	3.96	12.4	195
4	.35	4.80	16.5	265
6	.38	6.90	25.9	415
8	.41	9.05	37.0	590
10	.44	11.10	49.1	785
12	.48	13.20	63.7	1,020
14	.51	15.30	78.8	1,260
16	.54	17.40	95.2	1,525
18	.58	19.50	114.8	1,835
20	.62	21.60	135.9	2,175
24	.73	25.80	190.1	3,040
30	.85	32.00	275.4	4,405
36	.94	38.30	365.9	5,855
42	1.05	44.50	475.3	7,605
48	1.14	50.80	589.6	9,435
Class 200: 200 psi Pressure—462 ft Head				
3	.32	3.96	12.4	195
4	.35	4.80	16.5	265
6	.38	6.90	25.9	415

Size, inches	Thickness, inches	Outside Diameter, inches	16 ft Laying Length — Avg. per Foot[b] Weight (lb)	16 ft Laying Length — Per Length Based on
Class 200: 200 psi Pressure—462 ft Head				
8	.41	9.05	37.0	590
10	.44	11.10	49.1	785
12	.48	13.20	63.7	1,020
14	.55	15.30	84.4	1,350
16	.58	17.40	101.6	1,625
18	.63	19.50	123.7	1,980
20	.67	21.60	145.9	2,335
24	.79	25.80	205.6	3,290
30	.92	32.00	297.8	4,765
36	1.02	38.30	397.1	6,355
42	1.13	44.50	512.3	8,195
48	1.23	50.80	637.2	10,195
Class 250: 250 psi Pressure—577 ft Head				
3	.32	3.96	12.4	195
4	.35	4.80	16.5	265
6	.38	6.90	25.9	415
8	.41	9.05	37.0	590
10	.44	11.10	49.1	785
12	.52	13.20	68.5	1,095
14	.59	15.30	90.6	1,450
16	.63	17.40	110.4	1,765
18	.68	19.50	133.4	2,135
20	.72	21.60	156.7	2,505
24	.79	25.80	205.6	3,290
30	.99	32.00	318.4	5,095
36	1.10	38.30	425.5	6,810
42	1.22	44.50	549.5	8,790
48	1.33	50.80	684.5	10,950
Class 300: 300 psi Pressure—693 ft Head				
3	.32	3.96	12.4	195
4	.35	4.80	16.5	265
6	.38	6.90	25.9	415
8	.41	9.05	37.0	590
10	.48	11.10	53.1	850
12	.52	13.20	68.5	1,095
14	.59	15.30	90.6	1,450
16	.68	17.40	118.2	1,890
18	.73	19.50	142.3	2,275
20	.78	21.60	168.5	2,695
24	.85	25.80	219.8	3,515
Class 350: 350 psi Pressure—808 ft Head				
3	.32	3.96	12.4	195
4	.35	4.80	16.5	265
6	.38	6.90	25.9	415
8	.41	9.05	37.0	590
10	.52	11.10	57.4	920
12	.56	13.20	73.8	1,180
14	.64	15.30	97.5	1,605
16	.68	17.40	118.2	1,945
18	.79	19.50	152.9	2,520
20	.84	21.60	180.2	2,970
24	.92	25.80	236.3	3,895

[a] Average weight per foot based on calculated weight of pipe before rounding.

40 Cast-Iron Pipe Screwed Fittings,ᵃ 125 lb—American National Standard

90° ELBOW   TEE   CROSS   45° ELBOW

DIMENSIONS OF 90° AND 45° ELBOWS, TEES, AND CROSSES (STRAIGHT SIZES)

All dimensions given in inches.

Fittings having right- and left-hand threads shall have four or more ribs or the letter "L" cast on the band at end with left-hand thread.

Nominal Pipe Size	Center to End, Elbows, Tees, and Crosses A	Center to End, 45° Elbows C	Length of Thread, Min. B	Width of Band. Min. E	Inside Diameter of Fitting F		Metal Thick-ness G	Diameter of Band, Min. H
					Max.	Min.		
$\frac{1}{4}$	.81	.73	.32	.38	.58	.54	.11	.93
$\frac{3}{8}$	.95	.80	.36	.44	.72	.67	.12	1.12
$\frac{1}{2}$	1.12	.88	.43	.50	.90	.84	.13	1.34
$\frac{3}{4}$	1.31	.98	.50	.56	1.11	1.05	.15	1.63
1	1.50	1.12	.58	.62	1.38	1.31	.17	1.95
$1\frac{1}{4}$	1.75	1.29	.67	.69	1.73	1.66	.18	2.39
$1\frac{1}{2}$	1.94	1.43	.70	.75	1.97	1.90	.20	2.68
2	2.25	1.68	.75	.84	2.44	2.37	.22	3.28
$2\frac{1}{2}$	2.70	1.95	.92	.94	2.97	2.87	.24	3.86
3	3.08	2.17	.98	1.00	3.60	3.50	.26	4.62
$3\frac{1}{2}$	3.42	2.39	1.03	1.06	4.10	4.00	.28	5.20
4	3.79	2.61	1.08	1.12	4.60	4.50	.31	5.79
5	4.50	3.05	1.18	1.18	5.66	5.56	.38	7.05
6	5.13	3.46	1.28	1.28	6.72	6.62	.43	8.28
8	6.56	4.28	1.47	1.47	8.72	8.62	.55	10.63
10	8.08ᵇ	5.16	1.68	1.68	10.85	10.75	.69	13.12
12	9.50ᵇ	5.97	1.88	1.88	12.85	12.75	.80	15.47

ᵃ From ANSI/ASME B16.4–1992.
ᵇ This applies to elbows and tees only.

41   Cast-Iron Pipe Screwed Fittings,[a] 250 lb—American National Standard

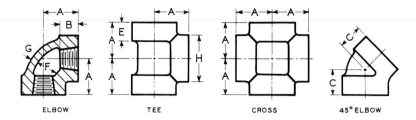

ELBOW   TEE   CROSS   45° ELBOW

DIMENSIONS OF 90° AND 45° ELBOWS, TEES, AND CROSSES (STRAIGHT SIZES)

All dimensions given in inches.

The 250-lb standard for screwed fittings covers only the straight sizes of 90° and 45° elbows, tees, and crosses.

Nominal Pipe Size	Center to End, Elbows, Tees, and Crosses A	Center to End, 45° Elbows C	Length of Thread, Min. B	Width of Band. Min. E	Inside Diameter of Fitting F		Metal Thickness G	Diameter of Band, Min. H
					Max.	Min.		
$\frac{1}{4}$	.94	.81	.43	.49	.58	.54	.18	1.17
$\frac{3}{8}$	1.06	.88	.47	.55	.72	.67	.18	1.36
$\frac{1}{2}$	1.25	1.00	.57	.60	.90	.84	.20	1.59
$\frac{3}{4}$	1.44	1.13	.64	.68	1.11	1.05	.23	1.88
1	1.63	1.31	.75	.76	1.38	1.31	.28	2.24
$1\frac{1}{4}$	1.94	1.50	.84	.88	1.73	1.66	.33	2.73
$1\frac{1}{2}$	2.13	1.69	.87	.97	1.97	1.90	.35	3.07
2	2.50	2.00	1.00	1.12	2.44	2.37	.39	3.74
$2\frac{1}{2}$	2.94	2.25	1.17	1.30	2.97	2.87	.43	4.60
3	3.38	2.50	1.23	1.40	3.60	3.50	.48	5.36
$3\frac{1}{2}$	3.75	2.63	1.28	1.49	4.10	4.00	.52	5.98
4	4.13	2.81	1.33	1.57	4.60	4.50	.56	6.61
5	4.88	3.19	1.43	1.74	5.66	5.56	.66	7.92
6	5.63	3.50	1.53	1.91	6.72	6.62	.74	9.24
8	7.00	4.31	1.72	2.24	8.72	8.62	.90	11.73
10	8.63	5.19	1.93	2.58	10.85	10.75	1.08	14.37
12	10.00	6.00	2.13	2.91	12.85	12.75	1.24	16.84

[a] From ANSI/ASME B16.4–1992.

DIMENSIONS OF ELBOWS, DOUBLE BRANCH ELBOWS, TEES, CROSSES, LATERALS, TRUE Y'S (STRAIGHT SIZES), AND REDUCERS

All dimensions in inches.

Nominal Pipe Size	Inside Diameter of Fittings	Center to Face 90° Elbow, Tees, Crosses True "Y" and Double Branch Elbow A	Center to Face, 90° Long Radius Elbow B	Center to Face 45° Elbow C	Center to Face Lateral D	Short Center to Face True "Y" and Lateral E	Face to Face Reducer F	Diameter of Flange	Thickness of Flange, Min.	Wall Thickness
1	1.00	3.50	5.00	1.75	5.75	1.75	. . .	4.25	.44	.31
1¼	1.25	3.75	5.50	2.00	6.25	1.75	. . .	4.62	.50	.31
1½	1.50	4.00	6.00	2.25	7.00	2.00	. . .	5.00	.56	.31
2	2.00	4.50	6.50	2.50	8.00	2.50	5.0	6.00	.62	.31
2½	2.50	5.00	7.00	3.00	9.50	2.50	5.5	7.00	.69	.31
3	3.00	5.50	7.75	3.00	10.00	3.00	6.0	7.50	.75	.38
3½	3.50	6.00	8.50	3.50	11.50	3.00	6.5	8.50	.81	.44
4	4.00	6.50	9.00	4.00	12.00	3.00	7.0	9.00	.94	.50
5	5.00	7.50	10.25	4.50	13.50	3.50	8.0	10.00	.94	.50
6	6.00	8.00	11.50	5.00	14.50	3.50	9.0	11.00	1.00	.56
8	8.00	9.00	14.00	5.50	17.50	4.50	11.0	13.50	1.12	.62
10	10.00	11.00	16.50	6.50	20.50	5.00	12.0	16.00	1.19	.75
12	12.00	12.00	19.00	7.50	24.50	5.50	14.0	19.00	1.25	.81
14 OD	14.00	14.00	21.50	7.50	27.00	6.00	16.0	21.00	1.38	.88
16 OD	16.00	15.00	24.00	8.00	30.00	6.50	18.0	23.50	1.44	1.00
18 OD	18.00	16.50	26.50	8.50	32.00	7.00	19.0	25.00	1.56	1.06
20 OD	20.00	18.00	29.00	9.50	35.00	8.00	20.0	27.50	1.69	1.12
24 OD	24.00	22.00	34.00	11.00	40.50	9.00	24.0	32.00	1.88	1.25
30 OD	30.00	25.00	41.50	15.00	49.00	10.00	30.0	38.75	2.12	1.44
36 OD	36.00	28.00	49.00	18.00	. . .	. . .	36.0	46.00	2.38	1.62
42 OD	42.00	31.00	56.50	21.00	. . .	. . .	42.0	53.00	2.62	1.81
48 OD	48.00	34.00	64.00	24.00	. . .	. . .	48.0	59.50	2.75	2.00

[a] ANSI/ASME B16.1–1989.

43 Cast-Iron Pipe Flanges, Drilling for Bolts and Their Lengths,[a] 125 lb— American National Standard

Nominal Pipe Size	Diameter of Flange	Thickness of Flange, Min.	Diameter of Bolt Circle	Number of Bolts	Diameter of Bolts	Diameter of Bolt Holes	Length of Bolts
1	4.25	.44	3.12	4	.50	.62	1.75
$1\frac{1}{4}$	4.62	.50	3.50	4	.50	.62	2.00
$1\frac{1}{2}$	5.00	.56	3.88	4	.50	.62	2.00
2	6.00	.62	4.75	4	.62	.75	2.25
$2\frac{1}{2}$	7.00	.69	5.50	4	.62	.75	2.50
3	7.50	.75	6.00	4	.62	.75	2.50
$3\frac{1}{2}$	8.50	.81	7.00	8	.62	.75	2.75
4	9.00	.94	7.50	8	.62	.75	3.00
5	10.00	.94	8.50	8	.75	.88	3.00
6	11.00	1.00	9.50	8	.75	.88	3.25
8	13.50	1.12	11.75	8	.75	.88	3.50
10	16.00	1.19	14.25	12	.88	1.00	3.75
12	19.00	1.25	17.00	12	.88	1.00	3.75
14 OD	21.00	1.38	18.75	12	1.00	1.12	4.25
16 OD	23.50	1.44	21.25	16	1.00	1.12	4.50
18 OD	25.00	1.56	22.75	16	1.12	1.25	4.75
20 OD	27.50	1.69	25.00	20	1.12	1.25	5.00
24 OD	32.00	1.88	29.50	20	1.25	1.38	5.50
30 OD	38.75	2.12	36.00	28	1.25	1.38	6.25
36 OD	46.00	2.38	42.75	32	1.50	1.62	7.00
42 OD	53.00	2.62	49.50	36	1.50	1.62	7.50
48 OD	59.50	2.75	56.00	44	1.50	1.62	7.75

[a] ANSI B16.1–1989.

44 Shaft Center Sizes

Shaft Diameter D	A	B	C	Shaft Diameter D	A	B	C
$\frac{3}{16}$ to $\frac{7}{32}$	$\frac{5}{64}$	$\frac{3}{64}$	$\frac{1}{16}$	$1\frac{1}{8}$ to $1\frac{15}{32}$	$\frac{5}{16}$	$\frac{5}{32}$	$\frac{5}{32}$
$\frac{1}{4}$ to $\frac{11}{32}$	$\frac{3}{32}$	$\frac{3}{64}$	$\frac{1}{16}$	$1\frac{1}{2}$ to $1\frac{31}{32}$	$\frac{3}{8}$	$\frac{5}{32}$	$\frac{5}{32}$
$\frac{3}{8}$ to $\frac{17}{32}$	$\frac{1}{8}$	$\frac{1}{16}$	$\frac{5}{64}$	2 to $2\frac{31}{32}$	$\frac{7}{16}$	$\frac{7}{32}$	$\frac{3}{16}$
$\frac{9}{16}$ to $\frac{25}{32}$	$\frac{3}{16}$	$\frac{5}{64}$	$\frac{3}{32}$	3 to $3\frac{31}{32}$	$\frac{1}{2}$	$\frac{7}{32}$	$\frac{7}{32}$
$\frac{13}{16}$ to $1\frac{3}{32}$	$\frac{1}{4}$	$\frac{3}{32}$	$\frac{3}{32}$	4 and over	$\frac{9}{16}$	$\frac{7}{32}$	$\frac{7}{32}$

45 Cast-Iron Pipe Flanges and Fittings,[a] 250 lb—American National Standard

90 DEG   LONG RADIUS   45 DEG   REDUCING   STRAIGHT TEE   REDUCER

DIMENSIONS OF ELBOWS, TEES, AND REDUCERS
All dimensions are given in inches.

Nominal Pipe Size	Inside Diameter of Fitting, Min.	Wall Thickness of Body	Diameter of Flange	Thickness of Flange Min.	Diameter of Raised Face	Center-to-Face Elbow and Tee A	Center-to-Face Long Radius Elbow B	Center-to-Face 45° Elbow C	Face-to-Face Reducer G
1	1.00	.44	4.88	.69	2.69	4.00	5.00	2.00	...
$1\frac{1}{4}$	1.25	.44	5.25	.75	3.06	4.25	5.50	2.50	...
$1\frac{1}{2}$	1.50	.44	6.12	.81	3.56	4.50	6.00	2.75	...
2	2.00	.44	6.50	.88	4.19	5.00	6.50	3.00	5.00
$2\frac{1}{2}$	2.50	.50	7.50	1.00	4.94	5.50	7.00	3.50	5.50
3	3.00	.56	8.25	1.12	5.69	6.00	7.75	3.50	6.00
$3\frac{1}{2}$	3.50	.56	9.00	1.19	6.31	6.50	8.50	4.00	6.50
4	4.00	.62	10.00	1.25	6.94	7.00	9.00	4.50	7.00
5	5.00	.69	11.00	1.38	8.31	8.00	10.25	5.00	8.00
6	6.00	.75	12.50	1.44	9.69	8.50	11.50	5.50	9.00
8	8.00	.81	15.00	1.62	11.94	10.00	14.00	6.00	11.00
10	10.00	.94	17.50	1.88	14.06	11.50	16.50	7.00	12.00
12	12.00	1.00	20.50	2.00	16.44	13.00	19.00	8.00	14.00
14 OD	13.25	1.12	23.00	2.12	18.94	15.00	21.50	8.50	16.00
16 OD	15.25	1.25	25.50	2.25	21.06	16.50	24.00	9.50	18.00
18 OD	17.00	1.38	28.00	2.38	23.31	18.00	26.50	10.00	19.00
20 OD	19.00	1.50	30.50	2.50	25.56	19.50	29.00	10.50	20.00
24 OD	23.00	1.62	36.00	2.75	30.31	22.50	34.00	12.00	24.00
30 OD	29.00	2.00	43.00	3.00	37.19	27.50	41.50	15.00	30.00

[a] ANSI B16.1–1989.

46 Cast-Iron Pipe Flanges, Drilling for Bolts and Their Lengths,[a] 250 lb—American National Standar

Nominal Pipe Size	Diameter of Flange	Thickness of Flange, Min.	Diameter of Raised Face	Diameter of Bolt Circle	Diameter of Bolt Holes	Number of Bolts	Size of Bolts	Length of Bolts	Length of Bolt Studs with Two Nuts
1	4.88	.69	2.69	3.50	.75	4	.62	2.50	...
$1\frac{1}{4}$	5.25	.75	3.06	3.88	.75	4	.62	2.50	...
$1\frac{1}{2}$	6.12	.81	3.56	4.50	.88	4	.75	2.75	...
2	6.50	.88	4.19	5.00	.75	8	.62	2.75	...
$2\frac{1}{2}$	7.50	1.00	4.94	5.88	.88	8	.75	3.25	...
3	8.25	1.12	6.69	6.62	.88	8	.75	3.50	...
$3\frac{1}{2}$	9.00	1.19	6.31	7.25	.88	8	.75	3.50	...
4	10.00	1.25	6.94	7.88	.88	8	.75	3.75	...
5	11.00	1.38	8.31	9.25	.88	8	.75	4.00	...
6	12.50	1.44	9.69	10.62	.88	12	.75	4.00	...
8	15.00	1.62	11.94	13.00	1.00	12	.88	4.50	...
10	17.50	1.88	14.06	5.25	1.12	16	1.00	5.25	...
12	20.50	2.00	16.44	17.75	1.25	16	1.12	5.50	...
14 OD	23.00	2.12	18.94	20.25	1.25	20	1.12	6.00	...
16 OD	25.50	2.25	21.06	22.50	1.38	20	1.25	6.25	...
18 OD	28.00	2.38	23.31	24.75	1.38	24	1.25	6.50	...
20 OD	30.50	2.50	25.56	27.00	1.38	24	1.25	6.75	...
24 OD	36.00	2.75	30.31	32.00	1.62	24	1.50	7.50	9.50
30 OD	43.00	3.00	37.19	39.25	2.00	28	1.75	8.50	10.50

[a] ANSI B16.1–1989.